学汇中外 语通世界

语言·文学·翻译研究

楚 军 主编

·成都·

图书在版编目（CIP）数据

语言·文学·翻译研究：汉文、英文、日文 / 楚军主编. —成都：电子科技大学出版社，2024.4

ISBN 978-7-5770-0976-6

Ⅰ. ①语… Ⅱ. ①楚… Ⅲ. ①英语－翻译－研究②日语－翻译－研究 Ⅳ. ①H315.9②H365.9

中国国家版本馆 CIP 数据核字（2024）第 061775 号

语言·文学·翻译研究
YUYAN WENXUE FANYI YANJIU
楚　军　主编

策划编辑	龚　煜
责任编辑	龚　煜
助理编辑	蒋　伊
责任校对	赵倩莹
责任印制	梁　硕

出版发行	电子科技大学出版社
	成都市一环路东一段 159 号电子信息产业大厦九楼　邮编　610051
主　页	www.uestcp.com.cn
服务电话	028-83203399
邮购电话	028-83201495
印　刷	四川煤田地质制图印务有限责任公司
成品尺寸	185 mm×260 mm
印　张	20.75
字　数	581 千字
版　次	2024 年 4 月第 1 版
印　次	2024 年 4 月第 1 次印刷
书　号	ISBN 978-7-5770-0976-6
定　价	58.00 元

版权所有　侵权必究

目 录

语言学研究

Emotional Dimensions of Verbal and Visual Metaphor Based on Website Construction for Data Collection ....刘彦池 1

An Analysis of Irony in Gone with the Wind from the Perspective of Speech Act Theory ....文 杰 15

A Comparative Study of Appellations in the Chinese and English Versions of Fortress Besieged from the Perspective of Politeness Principle ....邹 靖 26

历时视角下"have+to+VP"结构的语义—语用界面研究 ....权国庆 37

从合作原则角度分析詹姆斯·乔伊斯《死者》中加布里埃尔的形象 ....王旭蓝 48

「Nスギル」中「スギル」的语义指向研究 ....崔筱玉 53

《白鹿原》中陕西方言行为动词的及物性系统研究 ....刘昭宁 59

及物性系统视角下的诗歌语篇分析——以《未选择的路》为例 ....陆 瑶 66

英译武侠小说与英国奇幻小说语域变异多维分析——以《射雕英雄传》与《指环王》为例 ....向张玉洁 72

维特根斯坦的语言游戏说在二语词汇迁移中的运用 ....钟文欣 81

我国中小学教师压力研究综述——基于CiteSpace的知识图谱分析 ....王小慧 87

基于CiteSpace的国内生态语言学研究热点与前沿分析 ....赵浩雯 97

从面子理论分析《围城》中方鸿渐的形象构建 ....赵美华 108

自由间接引语的语境标识——以曼斯菲尔德的《已故上校的女儿》为例 ....王 宸 114

从构词法角度分析《哈利·波特》系列图书中的咒语名称 ....张怡然 汤朝菊 120

文 学 研 究

Reshape the Past: Identity Construction in Cultural Memory in Relation to The Remains of the Day ....马 嘉 129

The Chronotope in Sweet Tooth: Temporal Indicators of Space ....龙 佳 138

Collective Story-Telling and Individual Life-Experiencing: On the Differences of Chronotope in Epics and Novels ....陆泽懿 150

The Disease Writing and Ethical Pursuit in The Last Gift ....彭 新 160

Embodiment of Spatial Form in The Sound and the Fury ....杨婉儿 169

Confluence and Resonance of Multiple Tones: An Analysis of Dialogicality in Foe ....李怡佳 179

论小说影视化的改编——以《三体》为例 ....朱立源 189

浅析莫迪亚诺《青春咖啡馆》中的创伤书写 ....汪鑫波 195

《最后的礼物》中的家庭创伤书写 ....郭真巧 202

库切的《福》：空白的背后 .... 蒋茜茜 208
《最后的礼物》的创伤书写与身份重构 .... 刘铮儒 212
现实空间与心理空间的叙事比较研究——以《在城崎》为例 .... 张佳琪 218
朦胧诗中的模糊修辞——以舒婷的诗为例 .... 张文俊 224
对话复调：《承诺》中的众声喧哗 .... 张雨婷 235
狄金森自然诗歌中的道家意蕴 .... 尹 慧 240

翻 译 研 究

Analysis of the Translation Methods and Motives of Public Law of Nations from the Perspective of Skopos Theory .... 任佳琦 246
新媒体环境下中国特色词汇的英译技巧探析
　　——以中国日报网"新闻热词"栏目为例 .... 黄晴宇 257
科幻翻译的文学性——以 Philia, Eros, Storge, Agápe, Pragma 的汉译为例 .... 陈 霞 264
林语堂译创《武则天正传》研究 .... 余 琴 273
关联翻译理论下"曰"字英译策略探讨
　　——基于《虬髯客传》四个英译本的分析 .... 李佳怡 汤朝菊 279
女性主义翻译研究视角下《三体》日译本研究 .... 周小萱 287
生态翻译学视域下《雷雨》王佐良英译本赏析 .... 唐 杰 294
《虬髯客传》英译本中的叙事重构——基于蒙娜·贝克叙事理论 .... 谭鑫玥 300
译者主体性视角下《道德经》两个英译本对比研究：以第五章与第四十二章
　　为例 .... 黄雅琪 307
"深化"和"浅化"之论在古文翻译中的运用——以周译《虬髯客传》为例 .... 肖雨杨 314
意象图式下的《早发白帝城》及其英译本研究 .... 张 瑶 321

Emotional Dimensions of Verbal and Visual Metaphor Based on Website Construction for Data Collection

刘彦池

1. Introduction

Metaphor, widely used by writers, is not merely a common rhetorical device in literature. Aristotle referred to metaphor as "the application of an alien name by transference either from genus to species, or from species to genus, or from species to species, or by analogy, that is, proportion" (Aristotle, 1942), which described metaphor as the comparison between two things. Such device had been restricted to the field of literature since then. The notion changed, however, with the publish of *Metaphors We Live By*, in which Lakoff and Johnson proposed the Conceptual Metaphor Theory. They held that metaphors exist not only in poetic language, but also in the structure of our mind (Lakoff & Johnson, 2008). In 2009, Charles Forceville published an article that proposed the idea of multimodal metaphor, which, according to Forceville, refers to those "whose target and source are each represented exclusively or predominantly in different modes" (Forceville, 2009). Forceville suggested that metaphors should be divided into nine modes: spoken language; written language; visuals; music; sound; taste; smell; touch; gestures (Forceville, 2009). The multimodal framework refreshed research on metaphors and left much to discuss within it.

According to Forceville, an image can be labelled as visual metaphors if people can answer that what are the source domain and the target domain, and what properties of the source can be attributed to the target (Forceville, 2009). The target and the source are supposed to be both rendered in visual mode, which indicates that the two domains are usually concrete, which is different from the general phenomena in Conceptual Metaphor Theory. Phillips and McQuarrie proposed a typology in their paper that pictorial metaphors can be categorized into three types: juxtapositions, fusions and replacements (Phillips & McQuarrie, 2004). In juxtapositions, both the target and the source are visible. In fusions, the target and the source are fused together, resulting in a single new entity. In replacements, the target is depicted but the source is merely suggested by the context. They also investigated the complexity and ambiguity of pictorial metaphors in advertisements and found that replacements are the most complex one to understand because they demand more cognitive resources and longer reaction time. Following replacements are fusions, and then juxtapositions.

Pictorial metaphors are hotly discussed in the field of advertising. Based on materials chosen from advertisements, Forceville argued that metaphors can also occur in pictures and provide a framework within which pictorial metaphors can be analyzed (Forceville, 1994). Se-Hoon Jeong tested the persuasive effects of visual metaphors in advertising, finding that visual metaphors may be more persuasive due to both visual argumentation and metaphorical rhetoric (Jeong, 2008). In general, studies like these suggested that the use of pictorial metaphor in advertising resulted in better responses by consumers. Besides advertisement, research also focused on visual metaphors in political cartoons (Refaie, 2003).

Pictorial stimuli vary on different dimensions. Studies suggested that more complex pictures were perceived as more pleasant than less complex pictures, a hypothesis supported by earlier work by Berlyne, Vitz, and Day in the 1960s (Berlyne et al., 1963; Vitz, 1966; Day, 1967). They found that pleasantness and physiological arousal have been found to be higher for more complex abstract shapes. The arousal-complexity bias was further supported in research by C.R. Madan et al (Bayer & Schacht, 2014). Brightness is also a vital perceptual property of visual stimuli. Kübra Eroğlu et al. examined the effect brought by brightness on brain responses and behavior data (Eroğlu et al., 2020). They found that the bright unpleasant images were less arousing than the original ones. Other research evaluating brightness effect showed the similar phenomenon that the brightness of pictures had an impact on emotions, with bright ones activating emotion with positivity and dark ones activating emotion with negativity (Valdez & Mehrabian, 1994). Furthermore, according to Dual Coding Theory (Paivio, 1969), there are two cognitively different subsystems used by human to handle different phenomena, which are imagery system and verbal system. The former one is specialized for processing non-verbal objects while the latter deals with language. Thus, concrete words have two ways to be encoded, but abstract ones have only one way, so that concrete words should have a better chance of being remembered. This hypothesis was tested by many researchers such as Prabu David who used representative pictures of news to improve recall of each news (David, 2008). Pictures have an average higher concreteness than words because they provide existing images for people immediately.

Previous studies suggest that achievements in each field were plentiful but inadequate in the crossover domain. Inspired by them, the present paper aims to investigate the comparison and correlation between verbal metaphors, their corresponding black-and-white photos and line-drawings. Staying in the framework of multimodal metaphors, we focused on written mode and visuals simultaneously, from which verbal metaphors and pictorial ones were chosen respectively as the objects of the present study. To explore the emotional processing of verbal and pictorial metaphor efficiently, the technique of computer science was adopted in data collection. We therefore targeted the following questions: (1) What are the differences among three modes of metaphors, i.e., verbal metaphors, black-and-white photos and line-drawings? (2) Are there any correlations among various dimensions of valence, arousal, familiarity, attractiveness, complexity and brightness? Based on previous studies, four hypotheses were proposed: (1) the ratings of valence of verbal metaphors are higher than line-drawings, and black-and-white photos have the lowest valence rating; (2) the black-and-white photos have higher arousal ratings than line-drawings, and verbal metaphors have the lowest arousal ratings; (3) participants are more familiar to black-and-white photos than line-drawings, and then verbal metaphors; (4) black-and-white photos have higher attractiveness ratings than line-drawings, and verbal metaphors have the lowest attractiveness ratings.

2. Materials and Methods

2.1 Website Construction

Most of the previous behavioral method research was carried out through psychological software such as E-Prime or PsychoPy. However, functions of these software were limited because of the original set codes and the inability of online deployment. Due to the spatial and temporal constraint, offline experiment can be inconvenient sometimes. Additionally, under the background of post-pandemic era, online experiment reduced space costs and time costs, and enabled less contact between participants and the researcher, which provided more safety in times of epidemic. We therefore chose to build an online experiment website to carry out the experiment.

Functions of the website can be categorized into two major parts: the presentation of materials and the storage of data. For the presentation of materials, the website met the requirement of presenting forms of basic information, questionnaires and their introductions and options, instructions of the experiment, stimuli of the experiment, questions of certain dimensions and their options, and an ending page of the whole experiment. For the storage of data, the website required the connection between the front end and the back end. Once participants reacted on the materials, data from the front end should be sent to the back end. To store data and participants' information, MySQL was used to achieve the goal. The procedure of the rating experiment included five major steps, and the functions needed in each step are presented in Figure 1.

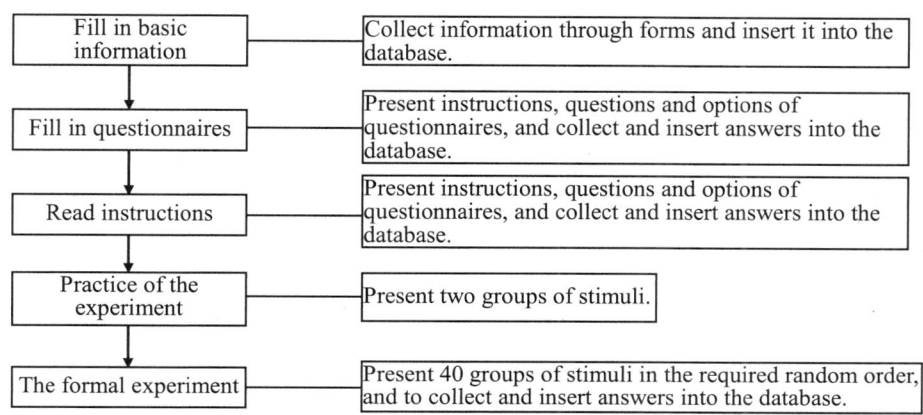

Figure 1 Functions of the website needed in each step of the rating experiment

The operation system used to construct the experiment website was Windows 11 Home edition. The model of CPU was 11th Gen Intel Core i5-11400H, 2.70 GHz, and the development environment was with 16.0 GB RAM. Software used in the development process included PyCharm 2021.1.1, MySQL 8.0 and Python 3.10.2.

In the construction of the website, MySQL played a vital role in the presentation of materials and storage of data. First of all, a database was created to hold all the tables needed in the experiment, including the tables which contained all the questionnaires. Each table contained two lists: the auto increment type integers "id", and the varchar type "text1", "text2" or "text3" that hold all questions in each questionnaire. List "id" was set to be the primary key of the table. In this way, the system only needed to read data in the questionnaire table to go through every question when presenting questionnaires so the code in HTML file can be concise and clear. The structures of these tables are presented in Figure 2.

qtext 1		qtext 2		qtext 3	
PK	gtextid int (11) auto increment	PK	gtextid int (11) auto increment	PK	gtextid int (11) auto increment
	text 1 varchar (512)		text 2 varchar (512)		text 3 varchar (512)

Figure 2   Structures of "qtext1" table, "qtext2" table and "qtext3" table

The storage of data required another two tables. The basic information of participants and their answers to questionnaires were put in the same table, and their reaction to experiment stimuli was put in the other table. Basic information and questionnaires were presented in the same page, additionally, the number of the latter was massive, so one table for each was convenient for not only the storage of data but also the extraction of data. The table for basic information and questionnaires contained five lists. The entity-relationship diagram of these two tables was presented in Figure 3.

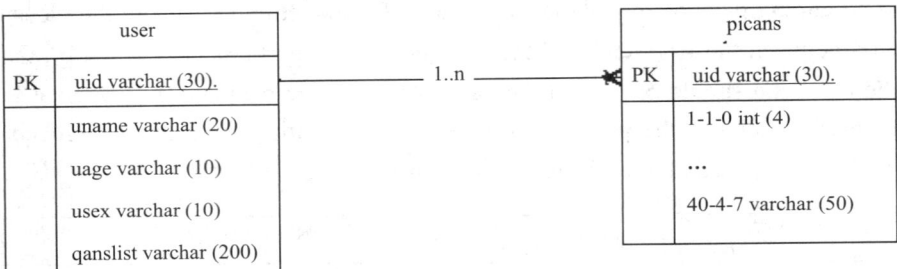

Figure 3   Entity-relationship diagram of "user" table and "picans" table

The front end was the direct presentation to participants so it must be clear and visually friendly. To present questionnaires, instructions, and all the other web interfaces, we created 13 HTML files in PyCharm.

The questionaire.html included forms of basic information of participants, as well as the questionnaires separated by their instructions. The second page was instruction.html, introducing participants to the experiment. HTML files intro1, intro2, intro3, intro4, intro5, intro6 presented explanations for six dimensions, with a vivid ruler with scales from 1 to 5 which was effortlessly understandable. The jumping between these 7 pages was triggered by the submit button. The following page was the practice of the formal experiment: practice.html. We selected two groups of stimuli to be the examples, and stimuli in examples would not appear in the formal experiment to ensure the accuracy of the data. The next page, which was also the most important page, was the experiment part. There were 8 different questions in total, with questions 1 to 5 designed for stimuli A, questions 2 to 7 designed for stimuli B and C, and question 8 for stimuli D.

2.2 Participants

In total, 30 Chinese native speakers (12 males and 18 females) of various dialectal origins participated in the experiment. All the participants were students in University of Electronic Science and Technology of China, who were mentally healthy without any cerebral, optical or cognitive impairment. Before the experiment, questions about their basic information such as name, age and sex, and two questionnaires, which were revised version by Cuiping Tu Kaufman Domains of Creativity Scale (K-DOCS) (Tu & Fan, 2015) and brief version of Chinese Big Five Personality Inventory (CBF-PI-B) (Zhang et al., 2019), as well as several related questions were answered by all the participants (see Table 1). All the participants were informed with the procedure and requirement of the experiment and were checked to be fully aware of all the information.

Table 1 Participants' Personal Demographic Information and Their Scores of Questionnaires

	Male Subjects (N=12)		Female Subjects (N=18)	
	M	SD	M	SD
Age (years)	22.25	1.76	22.11	1.02
Creativity (K-DOCS score)	153.83	4.03	148.11	23.25
Conscientiousness (CBF-PI-B score)	26.08	3.85	21.94	6.73
Agreeableness (CBF-PI-B score)	14.92	5.09	15.39	3.58
Openness (CBF-PI-B score)	30.42	4.17	27.83	6.17
Extraversion (CBF-PI-B score)	13.33	7.72	14.61	7.83
Neuroticism (CBF-PI-B score)	16.08		21.72	1.54

2.3 Stimuli

The source domain and the target domain were concrete nouns in no more than four Chinese characters. For each word, three pictures were chosen from the internet initially and their corresponding line-drawings were drawn by the author. To edit the visual stimuli, Adobe Photoshop 2020 was used to balance the grayscale, brightness, resolution and size. Participants were given 40 groups of three sets of the edited black-and-white photos and line-drawings randomly (different from that of the formal experiment) and were asked to select the most appropriate one to their corresponding Chinese words. The selected ones were chosen to be the final stimuli in the formal experiment.

In each picture presented on the website, no connection was put between the source domain and the target domain because in visual metaphors, the connection "是" (is) was in different mode from written language metaphors. Therefore, in the instruction of the experiment, participants were asked to understand each metaphor by adding a connection word "是" (is) between the source domain and the target domain.

2.4 Procedure

The major part of this experiment was carried out through an experiment website. When a participant entered the website, he or she would be asked to fill in his or her student number, name, sex and age at first, followed by two questionnaires and several information questions. After finishing the above questions, participants would be informed of the instructions of the experiment. Before the formal experiment, a practice one would be given to the participants to get them through the whole procedure. The participants would enter the formal experiment after they became familiar with the requirements and procedure.

The stimuli were presented in random groups and there were 40 groups of them. Each group consisted of four parts, including: A. the verbal metaphor; B. the visual metaphor in black-and-white photos; C. the visual metaphor in black-and-white line-drawings; D. the visual metaphors in both kinds. An example of the metaphor "眼睛是窗户" (The eye is the window) was given in Figure 4. In part A, the target domain of the verbal metaphor was presented on the left side and the source domain was presented on the right side, with space between them. In part B, the edited photo of the target domain was presented on the left side and the photo of the source domain was presented on the right side, with the size, brightness, grayscale and shape of them balanced. In part C, the line-drawing of the target domain was presented on the left side and the line-drawing of the source domain is presented on the right side, with the size, brightness, grayscale and shape of these line-drawings also balanced. Similarly, there was space between pictorial stimuli in part B and C to differentiate two domains. In part D, the matched pairs of balanced photos and line-drawings were presented respectively on the left side and the right side, with label "1" and "2" below each pair.

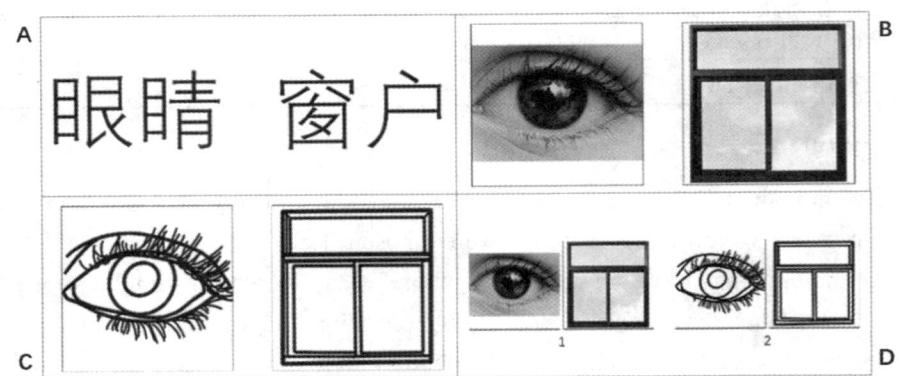

Figure 4   An Example of Stimuli of the Group "眼睛是窗户" (The eye is the window)

Part A, B and C and the sequence of questions were put randomly in each group to balance the order of presentation. For verbal metaphors, participants rated five dimensions (appropriateness, valence, arousal, familiarity and attractiveness) while for visual metaphors of both kinds, participants rated six dimensions (valence, arousal, familiarity, complexity, brightness and attractiveness). For part D, participants chose the more appropriate one in terms of semantic distance to the verbal metaphor and explained why they made such choice. Participants could take a break at any time they wanted to guarantee their consciousness.

2.5   Data Analysis

In the present paper, all the calculations and analysis were done using IBM SPSS version 25.

Before processing data, the average values of the variable appropriateness were calculated as the standard of filtering. Participants were asked to rate appropriateness on a 5-point scale so that groups whose ratings of this dimension were less than 3 were eliminated. In totar four groups have been eliminated for low appropriate values, which are, "塔是利剑" (The towel is the sword): 2.53; "烟斗是手枪" (The pipe is the pistol):2.80; "手是利爪" (The hand is the claw): 2.60; "天鹅是莲花" (The swan is the lotus flower):2.37. The average ratings of appropriateness in all the remaining 36 groups were above 3, with the maximum score being 4.67 and the minimum score being 3.27.

The valid data would be calculated and analyzed in two aspects: (1) between verbal metaphors, black-and-white photos and line-drawings; (2) between black-and-white photos and line-drawings within visual metaphors.

3. Results

3.1 Rating Differences of Multimodal Metaphors

The results of one-way ANOVA showed that there was significant difference among three modes of metaphors in terms of valence ($F = 4.434$, $p = 0.014$), arousal ($F = 23.547$, $p < 0.001$), familiarity ($F = 12.993$, $p < 0.001$), and attractiveness ($F = 22.087$, $p < 0.001$).

Post hoc multi-comparison results further showed that for valence, no significant difference was found between verbal metaphors and black-and-white photos, but ratings of valence of both verbal metaphors and black-and-white photos were higher than that of line-drawings ($M_{verbal} = 3.637$, $SD_{verbal} = 0.566$, $M_{photo} = 3.586$, $SD_{photo} = 0.478$, $M_{line} = 3.305$, $SD_{line} = 0.482$, $p_{verbal-photo} = 1.000$, $p_{verbal-line} = 0.020$, $p_{photo-line} = 0.063$). For arousal ratings, line-drawings received the lowest ratings, while no significant difference was found between the other two modes ($M_{verbal} = 3.439$, $SD_{verbal} = 0.283$, $M_{photo} = 3.576$, $SD_{photo} = 0.276$, $M_{line} = 3.131$, $SD_{line} = 0.286$, $p_{verbal-photo} = 0.124$, $p_{verbal-line} < 0.001$, $p_{photo-line} < 0.001$). In terms of familiarity ratings, both verbal metaphors and black-and-white photos had higher level of familiarity than that of line-drawings ($M_{verbal} = 3.908$, $SD_{verbal} = 0.381$, $M_{photo} = 3.705$, $SD_{photo} = 0.354$, $M_{line} = 3.392$, $SD_{line} = 0.539$, $p_{verbal-photo} = 0.145$, $p_{verbal-line} < 0.001$, $p_{photo-line} = 0.008$). The ratings of attractiveness of verbal metaphors and black-and- white photos were higher than that of line-drawings ($M_{verbal} = 3.517$, $SD_{verbal} = 0.272$, $M_{photo} = 3.517$, $SD_{photo} = 0.272$, $M_{line} = 3.115$, $SD_{line} = 0.340$, $p_{verbal-photo} = 1.000$, $p_{verbal-line} < 0.001$, $p_{photo-line} < 0.001$). Results of post hoc multi-comparison were presented in Table 2.

Table 2 Results of Post Hoc Multi-Comparison

	Verbal		Photo		Line		Verbal vs. photo	Verbal vs. line	Photo vs. line
	Mean	*SD*	*Mean*	*SD*	*Mean*	*SD*	*p*	*p*	*p*
Valence	3.637	0.566	3.586	0.478	3.305	0.482	1.000	0.020	0.063
Arousal	3.439	0.283	3.576	0.276	3.131	0.286	0.124	<0.001	<0.001
Familiarity	3.908	0.381	3.705	0.354	3.392	0.539	0.145	<0.001	0.008
Attractiveness	3.517	0.272	3.517	0.272	3.115	0.340	1.000	<0.001	<0.001

3.2 Correlations of Emotional Dimensions

Between black-and-white photos and line-drawings, two more variables were rated: brightness and complexity. The Pearson Correlation was conducted to study the relation between brightness, complexity and other four dimensions (valence, arousal, familiarity and attractiveness). Results showed that in black-and-white photos, ratings of brightness were in positive correlation with valence, arousal, familiarity and attractiveness ($r_{valence} = 0.674$, $p_{valence} < 0.001$, $r_{arousal} = 0.629$, $p_{arousal} < 0.001$, $r_{familiarity} = 0.487$, $p_{familiarity} = 0.003$, $r_{attractiveness} = 0.556$, $p_{attractiveness} < 0.001$), while ratings of complexity were in positive correlation with arousal levels and ratings of attractiveness ($r_{valence} = -0.020$, $p_{valence} = 0.908$, $r_{arousal} = 0.513$, $p_{arousal} = 0.001$, $r_{familiarity} = -0.234$, $p_{familiarity} = 0.170$, $r_{attractiveness} = 0.474$, $p_{attractiveness} = 0.003$). In line-drawings, ratings of brightness were in positive correlation with valence, arousal, familiarity and attractiveness ($r_{valence} = 0.772$, $p_{valence} < 0.001$, $r_{arousal} = 0.778$, $p_{arousal} < 0.001$, $r_{familiarity} = 0.757$, $p_{familiarity} < 0.001$, $r_{attractiveness} = 0.678$, $p_{attractiveness} < 0.001$), but no significant correlation was found between complexity and other dimensions ($r_{valence} = -0.188$, $p_{valence} = 0.272$, $r_{arousal} = 0.035$, $p_{arousal} = 0.839$, $r_{familiarity} = -0.279$, $p_{familiarity} = 0.079$, $r_{attractiveness} = 0.029$, $p_{attractiveness} = 0.865$). (See Table 3)

Table 3 Results of Pearson Correlation between brightness, complexity and other four dimensions

	Brightness of photo		Complexity of photo		Brightness of line		Complexity of line	
	r	p	r	p	r	p	r	p
Valence	0.674**	<0.001	−0.020	0.908	0.772**	<0.001	−0.188	0.272
Arousal	0.629**	<0.001	0.513**	0.001	0.778**	<0.001	0.035	0.839
Familiarity	0.487**	0.003	−0.234	0.170	0.757**	<0.001	−0.297	0.079
Attractiveness	0.556**	<0.001	0.474**	0.003	0.678**	<0.001	0.029	0.865

** at significance level $p<0.01$.

For part D, significantly more participants chose black-and-white photos to be the more appropriate one in terms of semantic distance to their corresponding verbal metaphors. We calculated the ratio of answers of part D in each group, finding out that the answers of 31 out of 36 groups were black-and-white photos, with ratio of two groups being 50%, which indicated that line-drawings were considered to be more appropriate semantically in only two groups. The results showed an overwhelming preference for black-and-white photos than line-drawings.

4. Discussion

The present paper looks into the comparison and correlation between three cross-domain ways of visual representations by investigating the emotional processing of verbal, their corresponding black-and-white photos and line-drawings. In total, 40 groups of stimuli were presented in random groups and in random parts and reactions of participants were collected and stored in the database through an online experiment website. 30 students from University of Electronic Science and

Technology of China were chosen to be the participants of the experiment.

4.1 Valence Ratings

In the first prediction, it was hypothesized that valence ratings of verbal metaphors are higher than line-drawings, and then black-and-white photos. Results showed that the higher valence ratings of verbal metaphors than line-drawings corresponded to prediction 1, showing that verbal metaphors were more positive than line-drawings in participants' emotional processing. However, no significant difference was found either between verbal metaphors and black-and-white photos, or line-drawings and black-and-white photos. This outcome was not in accordance with prediction 1.

The inconsistency could derive from the fact that all the pictures were edited to be black and white, thus the contrast of colors was inconspicuous. Many studies discovered effects of colors on emotional perceptions. For instance, Patricia Valdez and Albert Mehrabian found that such colors as blue, green, purple and red are the most pleasant hues, whereas yellow and green are the least pleasant hues (Valdez & Mehrabian, 1994). This illustrated that colors played an important role in emotions conveyed by pictures and different colors passed on different emotions. In addition, R. Beau Lotto and Dale Purves investigated the effects of color on brightness, finding that perceptions of luminance were generated according to the empirical frequency of the possible sources of visual stimuli (Lotto & Purves, 1999). This indicated that the perceived brightness was affected by colors of the object. Therefore, without various colors, participants might be less sensitive to the emotional change elicited by black and white, so black-and-white photos and line-drawings differed slightly in valence ratings.

The possible explanation for the insignificant difference between valence ratings of verbal metaphors and black-and-white photos could be similar to the former one that without colors, pictures lost a vital factor to be concrete so there is no privileged access to perception for them. Accompanied with the lack of colors, the sensibility to brightness was affected, so the positivity and negativity conveyed by brightness and darkness became obsolete. Therefore, the only significant difference existed between verbal metaphors and line-drawings.

4.2 Arousal Ratings

In the second prediction, it was hypothesized that the arousal ratings of black-and-white photos would be the highest, with line-drawings second and verbal metaphors third. Results were somewhat inconsistent with the prediction that arousal levels of verbal metaphors and black-and-white photos were higher than line-drawings, but no significant difference was found between verbal metaphors and black-and-white photos.

The higher arousal ratings of black-and-white photos than line-drawings supported research findings by Berlyne that more complex shapes elicited higher arousal level (Berlyne et al., 1963). The lower arousal ratings of line-drawings than verbal metaphors were unexpected. This result was in agreement with Mareike Bayer and Annekathrin Schacht's research that pictures or facial expression did not receive higher arousal ratings than words (Bayer & Schacht, 2014). They explained this disagreement that both words and pictures held the same potential to elicit arousal reactions and arousal ratings for words might reflect different aspects of the arousal concept than in the case of pictorial stimuli. When processing words, participants needed to translate the symbols into meaningful concepts first and then began the comprehension. This processing required more steps than the processing of pictures so presumably words had lower arousal than pictures.

We made a tentative explanation for the inconsistent result that stimuli in the present paper were metaphors in type of juxtaposition in which the image of source domain and target domain were presented separately. To understand the metaphor, participants needed to recognize and connect the two separated images and comprehend the metaphorical ties between them, which added the cognitive difficulty to the task. The processing of metaphorical aspects of stimuli may had an impact on the perception of arousal ratings of verbal metaphors and line-drawings, therefore resulted in the lower arousal ratings of the latter. This effect may also be reflected in the processing of black-and-white photos that made the comprehension of both types of visual metaphors more difficult, and probably explained the insignificant difference between verbal metaphors and black-and-white photos.

4.3 Familiarity Ratings

In the third prediction, black-and-white photos were predicted to receive the highest familiarity ratings and verbal metaphors to receive the lowest familiarity ratings. Consistent to the third prediction, black-and-white photos received higher familiarity ratings than line-drawings, which means that line-drawings were less frequently saw than real pictures.

From the results of data within visual metaphors, complexity ratings of black-and-white photos were significantly higher than line-drawings. This supported research findings by Broduer et al. that more complex pictures had higher level of familiarity (Brodeur et al., 2014). Such result was also in agreement with Dual Coding Theory that more concrete words or pictures have greater chance to be remembered (Paivio, 1969). Black-and-white photos were real pictures only without various colors. They were not merely extreme black and white because the grayscale of each part of the picture was different, indicating its original colors. However, line-drawings consist of purely black lines and white background, and the lack of details, shades, perspective relation and other nature of real objects kept telling participants that they were just abstract representations of the original pictures. Therefore, though line-drawings provided participants already existing images, they were still not concrete enough to be familiar for participants. The explanation was also a possible reason for the lower familiarity ratings of line-drawings than verbal metaphors. Line-drawings had a comparatively lower chance to be exposed to participants especially for metaphors. The abstractness of line-drawings resulted in the loss of metaphorical ties between the source domain and the target domain. For example, in the metaphor "云朵是棉被" (The cloud is the quilt), the metaphorical ties between "云朵" (the cloud) and "棉被" (the quilt) lies in their shapes, colors, and fluffy and soft texture which cannot be depicted adequately in line-drawings without natures of real pictures. The already presented images deprived "云朵" (the cloud) and "棉被" (the quilt) of their texture at the first sight of participants, but for verbal metaphors the situation was different.

We made a tentative hypothesis that in the process of decoding the symbol, participants may imagine the metaphorical ties between the source domain and the target domain to understand the metaphor, which means that what participants actually had in mind are probably images of real objects. This possibility led to the higher concreteness of verbal metaphors than line-drawings, thus to the higher familiarity ratings of verbal metaphors than line-drawings. Nevertheless, familiarity ratings of black-and-white photos and verbal metaphors showed no significant difference. We attributed this result to the black-and-white representation of pictures as well. The lack of colors diminished the concreteness of pictures and shortened the semantic distance between verbal signs and visual representations, offering a possible explanation of the insignificant difference between verbal metaphors and black-and-white photos.

4.4 Attractiveness Ratings

In the fourth prediction, it was assumed that black-and-white photos are more attractive than line-drawings and then verbal metaphors. Results were not completely in agreement with this prediction. Verbal metaphors and black-and-white photos were rated more attractive than line-drawings, while no significant difference was found between verbal metaphors and black-and-white photos.

Interestingly, however, though the results were inconsistent with the fourth prediction, they were in agreement with research findings by the subjective rating norms for The Karolinska Directed Emotional Faces (KDEF) (Garrido & Prada, 2017). Such rating norms showed that the correlation between attractiveness and emotional intensity ratings was positive, which means that the more intense faces received the higher attractiveness ratings. For arousal ratings, verbal metaphors and black-and-white photos were rated higher than line-drawings, which was the same as the results of attractiveness ratings. As explained above, the juxtaposition type of presentation may lead to the insignificant difference between verbal metaphors and black-and-white photos, the vacancy also existed in attractiveness ratings.

4.5 Semantic Distance Between Verbal and Visual Metaphors

Results of the option between black-and-white photos and line-drawings in terms of semantic distance to the corresponding verbal metaphors showed that black-and-white photos were considered to be more appropriate and adequate to convey the semantic meaning of metaphors.

Reasons given by participants were checked and it was found that those reasons can be divided into three kinds. Firstly, black-and-white photos had more details than line-drawings. Participants gave reasons such as "荷叶的叶脉和伞的伞骨有更多的细节，因此二者相似度更高" (The veins of the lotus leaf and the umbrella ribs are more detailed, so they are more similar) in the metaphor "荷叶是雨伞" (The lotus leaf is the umbrella), and "将长城在险峻的山间蜿蜒起伏的形态十分细致地勾勒出来，让人联想到巨龙" (The shape of the Great Wall winding and undulating in the steep mountains is carefully outlined, which reminds me of the loong) in the metaphor "长城是巨龙" (The Great Wall is the loong). Details in black-and-white photos added to the resemblance between the source domain and the target domain and helped participants associate the two domains together to form a metaphor. In the examples given above, details in veins of the leaf and ribs of the umbrella added to the resemblance between these two objects, and the detailed shape of the Great Wall reminded participants of the shape of the loong. Participants comprehended metaphors through the resemblance between two domains and details were where they looked for such resemblance.

Secondly, black-and-white photos had an advantage in colors. Interestingly, participants still sensed colors in grayscale in black-and-white photos. For instance, the reason "明暗对比的变化和色彩的运用能让人清晰地分辨出二者" (Changes in shading and the use of color help people clearly distinguish between the two) was given by participants in the metaphor "书籍是阶梯" (The book is the stairs), and the reason "明暗对比和细节让人联想到二者的相似之处" (Changes in shading and details suggest similarities between the two) was given in the metaphor "塔是利剑" (The tower is the sword). Similar to details, colors were tools to connect or differentiate the source domain and the target domain. In the metaphor "手机是毒药" (The mobile phone is the poison), some participants even associated colors to their metaphorical meaning that black correlates with negativity: "黑色的手机更能体现毒药黑暗的本质" (The black color of the mobile phone better reflects the dark nature of poison). Colors were not merely visual attributes of pictures, but conveyed emotions and information themselves as proved in previous studies, which cannot be neglected in the processing of pictures.

Thirdly, participants gave reasons about concreteness. In the metaphor "塔是利剑" (The tower is the sword), one of the reasons was stated as: "有具体的图片，比较有压迫感" (Specific pictures make people feel a sense of pressure). Similarly was the reason "地球和家具体化更有家的感觉,包括地球家园这样的感觉" (Concretization of the Earth and home makes people feel more at home, including the sense of home planet) in the metaphor "地球是家" (The Earth is the home). Concreteness was a vital attribute in processing verbal metaphors and visual metaphors. Feelings such as touch of the texture cannot be depicted in line-drawings because no line could show the concreteness of the original objects. For example, "a sense of pressure" as stated above could not exist in line-drawings, for line-drawings were abstract shapes in nature which cannot provide any sense of pressure. There was no doubt that black-and-white photos were more concrete than line-drawings, and the concrete attribute shortened the semantic distance between black-and-white photos and real objects. In conclusion, black-and-white photos not only had shorter semantic distance to the verbal metaphors, but were also closer to real life objects.

5. Conclusion

As shown in results and discussions, the ways to present metaphors do have an impact on the processing of emotions. First, levels of valence, arousal, familiarity and attractiveness aroused by verbal metaphors are close to those of black-and-white photos. Second, the arousal, familiarity and attractiveness brought by both verbal metaphors and black-and-white photos were stronger than those of line-drawings. Third, valence aroused by verbal metaphors but not black-and-white photos were stronger than that of line-drawings. Fourth, black-and-white photos with more complex images had higher arousal and attractiveness levels. Both types of visual metaphors with brighter images had higher levels of valence, arousal, familiarity and attractiveness levels.

Due to the temporal and spatial constraints, the present experiment invited 30 participants and used 40 groups of stimuli. The number of participants and stimuli is comparatively small, which can be improved in future studies by enlarging the number of the participants and the groups of stimuli. In addition, the online experiment website has its limitations that participants may be distracted by other websites which could have an impact on the collected data. For future studies using websites to carry out the experiment, the function to prevent participants from switching pages can be designed and added to ensure the validity of data. To further investigate emotional processing of metaphors in different visual representations, future studies could use colored pictures which are closer to objects in the real world instead of black-and-white photos to avoid the insignificant difference brought by the lack of various colors.

Bibliography

[1] ARISTOTLE B, 1942. The Poetics of Aristotle[M]. North Carolina: University of North Carolina Press.

[2] BAYER M, SCHACHT A, 2014. Event-Related Brain Responses to Emotional Words, Pictures, and Faces—A Cross Domain Comparison[J]. Frontiers in Psychology (5): 1106.

[3] BERLYNE D E, CRAW M A, SALAPATEK P, et al., 1963. Novelty, Complexity, Incongruity, Extrinsic Motivation, and the GSR[J]. Journal of Experimental Psychology (66): 560-567.

[4] BRODEUR M B, GUÉRARD K, BOURAS M, 2014. Bank of Standardized Stimuli (BOSS) Phase II: 930 New Normative Photos[J]. PloS One, 9(9): e106953.

[5] DAVID P, 2008. Dual Coding Theory[J]. The International Encyclopedia of Communication, [2008-06-05] http://doi.org/10.1002/9781405186407.wbiecd068.

[6] DAY H, 1967. Evaluations of Subjective Complexity, Pleasingness and Interestingness for a Series of Random Polygons Varying in Complexity[J]. Percept & Psychophysics（2）: 281-286.

[7] EROĞLU K, KAYIKÇIOĞLU T, OSMAN O, et al., 2020. Effect of Brightness of Visual Stimuli on EEG Signals[J]. Behavioural Brain Research（382）: 112486.

[8] FORCEVILLE C, 1994. Pictorial Metaphor in Advertisements[J]. Metaphor and Symbol (9): 1-29.

[9] FORCEVILLE C, 2009. Non-verbal and Multimodal Metaphor in a Cognitivist Framework: Agendas for Research[J]. Multimodal Metaphor（2）: 19-35.

[10] GARRIDO M V, PRADA M, 2017. KDEF-PT: Valence, Emotional Intensity, Familiarity and Attractiveness Ratings of Angry, Neutral, and Happy Faces[J]. Frontiers in Psychology（8）: 2181.

[11] JEONG S H, 2008. Visual Metaphor in Advertising: Is the Persuasive Effect Attributable to Visual Argumentation or Metaphorical Rhetoric?[J]. Journal of Marketing Communications, 14(1): 59-73.

[12] LAKOFF G, JOHNSON M, 2008. Metaphors We Live By[M]. Chicago: University of Chicago Press.

[13] LOTTO R B, PURVES D, 1999. The Effects of Color on Brightness[J]. Nature Neuroscience, 2(11): 1010-1014.

[14] PAIVIO A, 1969. Mental Imagery in Associative Learning and Memory[J]. Psychological Review, 76(3): 241-263.

[15] PHILLIPS B J, MCQUARRIE E F, 2004. Beyond Visual Metaphor: A New Typology of Visual Rhetoric in Advertising[J]. Marketing Theory, 4(12): 113-136.

[16] REFAIE E E, 2003. Understanding Visual Metaphor: The Example of Newspaper Cartoons[J]. Visual Communication, 2(1): 75-95.

[17] TU C P, FAN F M, 2015. Verification and Preliminary Application of Chinese Version of Kaufman Domains of

Creativity Scale[J]. Studies of Psychology and Behavior, 13(6): 811.

[18] VALDEZ P, MEHRABIAN A, 1994. Effects of Color on Emotions[J]. Journal of Experimental Psychology: General, 123(4): 394.

[19] VITZ P C, 1964. Preference for Different Amounts of Visual Complexity[J]. Behavioral Science, 11(2): 105-114.

[20] ZHANG X, WANG M C, HE L, et al., 2019. The Development and Psychometric Evaluation of the Chinese Big Five Personality Inventory-15[J]. PLoS One, 14(8): e0221621.

An Analysis of Irony in *Gone with the Wind* from the Perspective of Speech Act Theory

文 杰

1. Introduction

The famous American writer Margaret Mitchell was born on November 8, 1900 in Atlanta, Georgia. She was involved in a car accident and killed on August 16, 1949. Mitchell did not publish too many works in such a short life, but the only one book *Gone with the Wind* is enough to consolidate her irreplaceable position in the literature world.

Gone with the Wind has aroused wide public concerns since it was published in 1936, becoming the best seller at that time. This book helped Margaret Mitchell not only win the gold medal of the New York Southern Association but also get the Pulitzer Prize in 1937. After the book being adapted into a film of the same name, it has won a world reputation ever since. Throughout the book, though there are more than a million words, the story is lively and attractive enough for readers to read. The reason for this is mainly the author's fantastic writing method, by which there are ingenious character relationship settings and delicate analysis of psychological activities. A lot of research has been done on the above aspects while few scholars pay attention to the irony skills in this book, especially form the perspective of literary pragmatics. Actually, the plot, characters and the conversations in the book and even Margaret Mitchell's own life are full of irony, which characterizes this fiction and therefore is worth analyzing and discussing.

This thesis is based on Margaret Mitchell's novel *Gone with the Wind* and theories that are relevant to speech act are used. By studying the production, effects and response phenomena of irony in the novel, this thesis aims to prove that Speech Act Theory has an interpretive effect on various ironic speech acts in novels and different kinds of literary works.

This thesis will analyze the application of irony skills in *Gone with the Wind* from the perspective of Speech Act Theory. The author of *Gone with the Wind*, Mitchell, used vivid language and ups and downs of the plot to outline the image of a woman in the new era at a historical turning point. At the same time, she also made a mockery of the American upper class at the time. One of the characteristics of the novel is that irony is used from the beginning to the end. Whether in the setting of the plot or in the language of the characters, this irony gives the fiction its unique charm, which makes a deep impression on readers. Therefore, it is far from enough to only understand the plot of the story and analyze the image of the characters. This thesis aims to provide a new perspective for the appreciation and research of such ironic literary works by analyzing the irony in *Gone with the Wind* from the perspective of Speech Act Theory.

This thesis adopts literature research method and qualitative analysis. A literature research method involves studying according to the necessary research purpose or topic and obtain information by investigating the literature, so as fully and correctly understanding a method of mastering the research problem. It provides useful information for the study of irony and speech acts in this article. Qualitative analysis involves qualitatively analyzing the research object and process the obtained materials to understand the essential laws of things. All language materials in this thesis come from *Gone with the Wind*.

2. Literature Review

Judging from the current papers on *Gone with the Wind*, the domestic research on this book can be divided into the following aspects. Some researchers focus on the content, theme, and ideological tendency of the work. In Mitchell's fiction, survival is the theme, showing how a traditional society was disintegrating and how people coped with this arduous process of social change. Professor He Qixin (1992) once pointed out that although the story of this book took place in the time of war, *Gone with the Wind* is not a history book, because being fictitious is one of the characteristics of a novel. Others pay attention to characters' image and personality. The most successfully portrayed character in the work is Scarlett. She is a very complicated southern female and the best representative of personality combination. There are both positive and negative aspects in her. It is precisely because of this complexity and duality that she is deeply rooted in the hearts of the people. Xie Jingzhi (2005) made an in-depth analysis on Scarlett, the heroine of *Gone with the Wind*. She believed that one of the reasons Scarlett's image impresses readers is that she had the courage and independence that women of that era lacked. Besides, there are still other researchers who work on female critical research. The female images in the novel, the living conditions and attitudes towards the life of Ellen, Melanie and Scarlett, show the development trend of feminism during the Civil War. Dong Jinwei's *The Charm, Value and Characteristics of Gone with the Wind* (1999) positively affirmed the significance of the novel to women's liberation, and pointed out that Scarlett's pursuit of independence and freedom implies the awakening of feminist consciousness.

The foreign researchers study *Gone with the Wind* mainly from the following aspects. Some research on the theme and ideological tendency of the work. The famous critic Malcolm once said that *Gone with the Wind* is "an encyclopedia of plantation legends". Others focus on the character image. American scholars represented by John Bishop believed that Scarlett is a morally depraved woman, while other critics believed that her fighting spirit is a portrayal of the American spirit and American cultural character. Also, an intensive study of the content and influence of the work has been made by other researchers. This is because *Gone with the Wind*'s publication has caused a huge response abroad. Who pointed out that *Gone with the Wind* is the first work of an unknown generation, but its sales have exceeded the total number of publications of some masters in the literary world. The secret of its success lies in its readability.

3. Theoretical Foundation

3.1 Irony

Although the term irony appeared long time ago, its definition is constantly changing with the development of society. At previous time of its appearance, that is, in its classical period, irony is generally divided into the following three meanings. First, Socratic irony. It was originated from Socrates' dialogue style, which continuously initiates questioning on the premise of acknowledging the other party's point of view, so that the other party unknowingly reveals flaws under questioning. This kind of irony is therefore named. Second, the Romanesque irony, in which the literal meaning is opposite to the actual meaning. Third, pretending to be ignorant. This type originated from a kind of role in ancient Greek dramas that pretended to be ignorant and said all the stupid words but were finally proved to be reasonable.

As a matter of fact, as a language phenomenon commonly used in human communication, although people in many fields have defined irony with their own understanding, irony has not had an accurate and authoritative concept since its inception. The *Encyclopedia Americana* defines irony as "irony provides a situation where reality and appearance are opposed". Although this definition sounds concise, it does not fully express all the connotation of irony. For the people who first contact with irony, it is difficult to understand. Compared with the *Encyclopedia Americana*, the Soviet Encyclopedia has a more detailed definition: "In literary style, irony is a description that expresses the dual meaning of mockery or cunning. In irony, a word or a tone has acquired a negative, or doubtful meaning that is contrary to the literal meaning according to the context." *The Oxford Dictionary* states that the irony is "the funny or strange aspect of a situation that is very different from what you expect; the use of words that is contrary to what you really mean, often as a joke and with a tone of voice that shows this". In other words, irony is to hide the real intention of the speaker and use opposite words to express meaning.

All in all, from the above-mentioned definitions of irony, the conclusion can be safely drawn that irony is regarded as a form of language expressing meaning, which can reflect the speaker's thoughts and attitudes towards the things under discussion. However, the surface meaning and deep meaning of its language are often opposite. Then the only way for the readers or the listeners to grasp the true connotation of ironic discourse is to understand the words in the context.

Irony is everywhere in modern creation, and its forms are also diverse. Scholars in different fields divide irony according to their own understanding and different standards. Most people have reached an agreement that irony can be divided into the following three categories: verbal irony, situational irony and dramatic irony.

3.2 Ironic Speech Acts

3.2.1 Austin and Searle's Speech Act Theory

The British philosopher Austin (1962) put forward the theory of Speech Act in his speeches and essays in the late 1950s after the publication of his significant work *How to Do things with Words*.

He believed that the basic unit of human communication is not sentences or other means of expression, but to accomplish certain behaviors. Based on this assumption, Austin distinguished three different speech acts, namely locutionary act, illocutionary act and perlocutionary act:

(1) Locutionary act is the act of saying, the literal meaning of the utterance;

(2) Illocutionary act is the extra meaning of the utterance produced on the basis of its literal meaning;

(3) Perlocutionary act is the effect of the utterance on the hearer, depending on specific circumstances.

At that time, most philosophers only paid attention to locutionary act and perlocutionary act, neglecting the existence of illocutionary act. By saying "there are also questions and exclamations, and sentences expressing commands or wishes or concessions", Austin (1962) pointed out that illocutionary act is worthier of research. Then he divided speech acts into the following five categories, namely verdictives, exercitives, commissives, behabitives and expositives. However, due to the fact that the division of speech act is equivalent to the division of verbs, there is no unified standard for classification, and Speech Act Theory does not take the differences in context, communication factors, social factors and culture into account. So this classification is not scientific enough.

After Austin, his student Searle summed up the experience of the predecessors to inherit and develop the Speech Act Theory. He made a more scientific division of illocutionary act as the following five categories, namely, representative/assertive, directive, commissive, expressive and declaration, which have been recognized by most people:

(1) Representative means that the speaker makes a certain degree of statement about something, and at the same time, the speaker is responsible for ensuring the authenticity of the words spoken;

(2) Directive means that the speaker wants the listener to do something, so as to achieve the speaker's purpose;

(3) Commissive refers to a certain promise made by the speaker to the future while speaking, which can also be regarded as a command or request to oneself;

(4) Expressive refers to the speaker's expression of his or her mental state for a certain kind of clarity, and the premise of the implementation of this behavior is to ensure the authenticity of the content of the utterance;

(5) Declaration refers to the agreement between the command expressed by the discourse and the objective reality, that is, the sudden change caused by the speech.

3.2.2 Ironic Speech Acts

On the basis of Searle's theory, the famous linguist Haverkate combined the division of speech act with irony and then divided irony from the perspective of speech act into four categories: assertive irony, directive irony, commissive irony and expressive irony. Searle regards sincerity as a precondition in the execution of every kind of speech act and in his point of view, sincerity is an inherent condition for realizing speech acts, and only when the condition of sincerity is violated can irony be created. And Haverkate also argued that since the objective reality and the content of the speech must be consistent when making a declaration, the speaker cannot say words that are contrary to the facts, so its sincerity cannot be violated, and thus cannot be connected with irony. Therefore, there is no declarative irony.

4. An Analysis of Irony in *Gone with the Wind* from the Perspective of Speech Act Theory

Van Dijk (1976) argued that we can dig into literature with Speech Act Theory from macro and micro aspects. According to his point of view, macro speech act is related to the communication in the novel that takes place between the author and the readers, namely the central idea of the book, while micro speech act happens during conversations. According to Zhu Xiaozhou's enrichment of Van Dijk's classification (Zhu, 2002), macro speech act is about the use of words and the arrangement of the plot; however, micro speech act is reflected in the dialogue between the characters in the novel. Based on such classification, this thesis will analyze the ironic speech acts in *Gone with the Wind* from macro and micro perspectives.

4.1 Macro Ironic Speech Acts in *Gone with the Wind*

In Mitchell's book *Gone with the Wind*, irony is used between the lines. This writing skill can be found not only in the narration but also in the overall structure. So the following part will analyze macro ironic speech acts from literal irony and structural irony.

4.1.1 Literal Irony

Literal irony occurs when the author attempts to use narrative language and plot design to convey to readers something that is inconsistent with the actual situation in the novel.

At the beginning of the novel, Mitchell introduced the heroine Scarlett O'Hara, who was the most beautiful girl in Clayon, but the author described her with the following words.

Example 1:

"Scarlett O'Hara was not beautiful, but men seldom realized it when caught by her charm as the Tarleton twins were." (Mitchell, 2010: 2)

When reading this sentence, readers may be confused. Since Scarlett is not a recognized beauty, why can so many men fall in love with her? This phenomenon is impossible in real life, and it is logically unreasonable. With such doubts, readers will be able to find the answer in the text if they continue reading.

Example 2:

"In her face were too sharply blended the delicate features of her mother, a Coast aristocrat of French descent, and the heavy ones of her florid Irish father. But it was an arresting face, pointed of chin, square of jaw. Her eyes were pale green without a touch of hazel, starred with bristly black lashes and slightly tilted at the ends. Above them, her thick black brows slanted upward, cutting a startling oblique line in her magnolia-white skin—that skin so prized by Southern women and so carefully guarded with bonnets, veils and mittens against hot Georgia suns."(Mitchell, 2010: 2)

From these descriptions, it is not difficult to see that Scarlett's facial features not only conform to the appearance of a typical beauty, but also unique, which is unforgettable. The reason that leads readers to change their thoughts is the irony literary technique used in the opening sentence. Mitchell used a contrasting satirical narrative to let readers experience the implicit meaning. Those descriptions of Scarlett's extraordinary beauty are diametrically opposed to the meaning conveyed by the author at the beginning, leaving a deep impression on the readers and bringing Scarlett's vivid image to the paper.

When Mitchell introduced Tarleton twin brothers, Stuart and Brent, she also used ironic narration as follows.

Example 3:

"And raising good cotton, riding well, shooting straight, dancing lightly, squiring the ladies with elegance and carrying one's liquor like a gentleman were the things that mattered. In these accomplishments the twins excelled, and they were equally outstanding in their notorious inability to learn anything contained between the covers of books." (Mitchell, 2010: 23)

At the beginning the author praised the two brothers for their proficiency in equestrianism, growing cotton and dancing, and for their gentlemanly demeanor, and bold drinking volume. At the end of the second half of the sentence, there is a complimentary words of "equally outstanding". The whole sentence seems to be a compliment, but after careful reading, readers will find that the author used irony to mock the two brothers for their academic failures. This is a typical irony, using praise to express blame or blame to praise. This kind of description will not make readers feel that the author is acrimonious, on the contrary, it makes the novel more lively and interesting.

4.1.2 Structural Irony

Structural irony is the concept that a story is based on an ironic situation. In other words, the characters or even the narrator find themselves in a situation that is the opposite of what they believe is actually happening.

The novel *Gone with the Wind* is based on the love and hatred between the heroine Scarlett and the two men. The reason why this book has endured for so many years and has become a popular work is that it is different from traditional romantic love novels. There is no perfect character image and love at first sight and other classic segments. Instead, Mitchell placed the story in the American Civil War, such a cruel environment, using realistic brushstrokes to describe love stories that are most likely to be encountered in reality.

There are many structural ironies interspersed in the complicated relationship between Scarlett and Rhett. Firstly, Scarlett firmly believed that Ashley loved her under any circumstances, and even simply thought that confessing to Ashley can stop this marriage. She even naively thought that her beauty could be favored by everyone, but it turned out not to be the case. Secondly, although Scarlett was married to Rhett at last, she still kept Ashley in her mind. She offered Ashley a lumber yard to make a living and sleep separately with Rhett. Her behaviors always remind her of her love for Ashley, but the truth is that, she had already regarded Rhett as an important person in her life. Lastly, when Scarlett woke up and found that the person she loved deeply was Rhett, Rhett was heartbroken because he hadn't received Scarlett's love for a long time, and decided to leave. Scarlett did not come to realize many things until the breakup of her marriage. And what she expected and thought was usually contrast to the reality. The author used this kind of ironic plot setting to deepen the theme: when the true love finally comes, the person has gone with the wind.

4.2 Micro Ironic Speech Acts in *Gone with the Wind*

As mentioned before, macro ironic speech acts are reflected in the dialogue between the characters in the novel. In *Gone with the Wind*, the author used a lot of brushstrokes to depict the lives of people in Atlanta. In this kind of daily life, dialogue and communication are happening anytime and anywhere, which provides a lot of material for the analysis of micro irony speech acts in this fiction.

4.2.1 Assertive Irony

Assertive irony means that the speaker still utters the words without believing in the truth of the proposition.

When Stuart and Brent's mother saw the two children pursuing Scarlett, whom she didn't really like, she said the following words.

Example 4:

" It will serve you right if that sly piece does accept one of you, or maybe she'll accept both of you, and then you'll have to move to Utah, if the Mormons'll have you—which I doubt…All that bothers me is that some one of these days you're both going to get licked up and jealous of each other about that two-faced, little, green-eyed baggage, and you'll shoot each other. But that might not be a bad idea either." (Mitchell, 2010: 62)

Scarlett was a well-known beauty in the local area, and naturally attracted the attention of young men. But as a well-experienced southern woman, Mrs.Tarleton believed that Scarlett will not be a good wife who could help her son in the future. Therefore, she imagined the worst situation that two sons would have to fight for the same woman. Nothing in the world can be more cruel to a mother than seeing her children killing each other, and no mother wants to see such a scene. But Mrs. Tarleton said "that might not be a bad idea either". Obviously, an assertive irony is applied here.

Another example is that, in the book *Gone with the Wind*, Scarlett was enamored with Ashley from the beginning, and even before he announced his engagement, she desperately showed her love to him, hoping that he could change his mind. However, during the lunch break, Scarlett's confession was rejected, which made her irritated, and angrily agreed to Charles Hamilton's marriage proposal. Scarlett herself also regretted marrying someone she didn't love and becoming the sister-in-law of the one she admired. Anyone who knows the truth will think Scarlett's decision is absurd. The following funny conversation happened the second time when Rhett saw Scarlett.

Example 5:

"I am sure that is a great gain to two charming ladies." (Mitchell, 2010: 234)

By saying "I am sure that is a great gain to two charming ladies", on the surface, Rhett was admiring two beauties and their perfect marriage. Nevertheless, he used assertive irony to laugh at Scarlett's unilateral infatuation with Ashley and impulsive marriage.

On the way Rhett crossed the fire to send Scarlett back to Tara Manor. They saw a collapsed South all the way. This result might have been known to Rhett before the war, but knowing and witnessing were still two different things. The South was his home, even if he did not want to admit. In the scenes before him, he had doubts about his long-standing attitude. He thought maybe he can do something for the South, even if it could not change the defeat. So Rhett decided to join the army at the last moment. When Scarlett persuaded Rhett, Rhett responded as follows.

Example 6:

" I'm not joking, my dear. And I am hurt, Scarlett, that you do not take my gallant sacrifice with better spirit. Where is your patriotism, your love for Our Glorious Cause? Now is your chance to tell me to return with my shield or on it. But, talk fast, for I want time to make a brave speech before departing for the wars."(Mitchell, 2010: 385)

He knew Scarlett was exactly an egoist, let alone talked about patriotism in front of her. So these sentences show his different opinion against Scarlett and are representative instances of assertive irony.

4.2.2 Directive Irony

Directive irony refers to the fact that the speaker instructs someone to do something literally, but actually wants him to do the opposite of the words. This behavior includes requests or suggestions, orders, etc. When the listener judges that the speaker's command is unreasonable based on the context, he or she will understand it from the opposite side of the utterance, then the effect of directive irony is achieved.

After the death of Scarlett's first husband, in order to test Scarlett's heart, Rhett specially ordered a top hat for her from Paris. After Scarlett got the hat, she asked Rhett if he wanted to marry her. Obviously Rhett had no intention in this regard. He clearly understood that Scarlett's heart was still on Ashley, and flirting with him was just for material enjoyment. In order to get her to accept the gift, Rhett said the following words.

Example 7:

"If you really felt that way, you'd stamp on the bonnet. My, what a passion you are in and it's quite becoming, as you probably know. Come, Scarlett, stamp on the bonnet to show me what you think of me and my presents." (Mitchell, 2010: 233)

Obviously, Scarlett loved this hat very much, as a vain woman she would not stamp on such a beautiful hat no matter how Rhett annoyed her. And Rhett bringing her a beautiful hat during the war was to please her instead of letting her trample on the gift.

What is more, after Rhett's confession, Scarlett realized that Rhett had already thought of marrying her. But still the same as before, Rhett talked about the principle of not getting married, which made Scarlett, who had fascinated countless men, burst into anger. Scarlett slammed the door and left after cursing Rhett, but could not pull the hook on the door. At this time, Rhett, who should have been angry because of being scolded, showed a gentlemanly demeanor by saying "May I help you? " (Mitchell, 2010: 432), mocking at Scarlett's rude behavior.

4.2.3 Commissive Irony

Commissive speech act refers to the speaker's promise to the listener to do or not to do something. In the promised discourse, the speaker also assumes a certain responsibility while uttering the words. If this kind of responsibility is completely impossible to achieve, then this kind of promise is commissive irony.

For example, after the death of her first husband, Scarlett put on a black dress in accordance with local customs. She knew that if she didn't do this, the discussion that was already among people would become a storm in the city. But Rhett pointed out that Scarlett looked ten years older after putting on the dress, and Scarlett immediately went to the front of the mirror to look at it. And he said the following words.

Example 8:

"I should think you'd have more pride than to try to look like Mrs. Merriwether, and better taste than to wear that veil to advertise a grief I'm sure you never felt. I'll lay a wager with you. I'll have that bonnet and veil off your head and a Paris creation on it within two months." (Mitchell, 2010: 315)

Rhett knew that Scarlett was never a conservative person, and she took her appearance too importantly. Within two months, Scarlett would take off her black clothes and put on colorful ones. There was no need for Rhett to bring "a Paris creation" for her.

Moreover, when Scarlett went to Rhett, who was in the Yankee Military Prison, to borrow money to pay off the taxes on Tara Manor, the following situation happened.

Example 9:

" 'Cheer up,' he said, as she tied the bonnet strings. 'You can come to my hanging and it will make you feel lots better. It'll even up all your old scores with me—even this one. And I'll mention you in my will.' "(Mitchell, 2010: 755)

In fact, there are two reasons for the commissive irony here. First, during the American Civil War, Rhett would not be hanged according to law. Second, Rhett had a large amount of wealth. The Yankees would give Rhett a chance before finding out where the wealth was hidden, and the shrewd Rhett would use his wealth to deal with them. Therefore, Rhett did not need to write a will at all, let alone mention Scarlett's name in the will. He knew Scarlett desperately needed money now, so this way of using commissive irony is to joke with her and mock her use of deception for money.

4.2.4 Expressive Irony

Expressive speech act is used to express the speaker's attitude or mental state towards a certain event. Its performative verbs mainly include thanks, congratulations, apologies, welcome, condolences, etc. If the speaker's true emotion is inconsistent with the content of the proposition, then the utterance is expressive irony.

At the bazaar held by the Hospital Nursing Association, Captain Rhett asked about Scarlett's deceased husband, and the following dialogue occurred.

Example 10:

" 'Your husband has been dead long?' 'Oh, yes, a long time. Almost a year.' 'An aeon, I'm sure.' 'Had you been married long? Forgive my questions but I have been away from this section for so long.' 'Two months,' said Scarlett, unwillingly, 'tragedy, no less, his easy voice continued.'" (Mitchell, 2010: 237)

Rhett clearly knew that Scarlett married Charles only out of revenge and self-esteem. In the meanwhile, Scarlett's acceptance of the bazaar invitation indicated her strong desire for dancing. So he deliberately said that one year of death is "an aeon". He also described Charles's death as "a tragedy", which Scarlett did not think so. He used expressive irony to satirize Scarlett's indifference.

At the donation bazaar, Scarlett donated all the wedding rings with Charles. Everyone thought she was kind and generous. In fact, it was because Scarlett hated Charles, so she felt disgusted with the things Charles touched or gave her. So she took this opportunity to throw it away and created a good image for herself by the way. Of course Rhett knew this, so he said the following words.

Example 11:

"What a beautiful gesture. It is such sacrifices as yours that hearten our brave lads in gray." (Mitchell, 2010: 243)

He knew the reason why Scarlett donated these wedding rings without hesitation, so his praise here actually was expressive irony and ridiculed Scarlett's hypocrisy.

Not long ago, Tara Manor faced a heavy tax burden. Scarlett went to jail to seek help from Rhett but failed, so she married Frank for a sum of money. Of course, Rhett, who knew the truth, also knew that Scarlett did not love this man, so her marriage was not happy at all. Rhett's words "I didn't come to gloat over your poverty" may be true, but "happiness in your marriage"(Mitchell, 2010: 814) is obvious an expressive irony to satirize Scarlett's ridiculous marriage.

Finally when Rhett escaped from jail, he came to lend Scarlett money but with only one condition, that was not to give money to Ashley.

Example 12:

"Ashley is too sublime for my earthy comprehension." (Mitchell, 2010: 825)

Both Ashley and Rhett are wise, intelligent and talented, but Ashley lacks Rhett's courage to face reality. It was indeed an embarrassment for him to stay with his family in Tara Manor. And in the face of Scarlett's pursuit, he did not refuse it simply and neatly. And he had been using Scarlett all the time. Rhett's hostility to Ashley was not only out of man's jealousy, but also criticizing Ashley's spinelessness and irresponsibility.

5. Conclusion

Gone with the Wind is the only work left by Mitchell when she was alive. The love story of the protagonists Scarlett and Rhett in the context of the American Civil War and reconstruction has become an enduring love classic. In this novel, Mitchell used a lot of irony to deepen the theme of the novel and highlight the characters. Based on the Speech Act Theory and combined with the scholars' classification of ironic speech acts, this thesis conducts an in-depth discussion on irony in *Gone with the Wind* from macro and micro perspectives. Macro ironic speech acts focus on literal irony and structural irony, highlighting the theme of the novel. Micro ironic speech acts are analyzed from four aspects, assertive irony, directive irony, commissive irony and expressive irony, making the characters in the novel show their own distinctive attitude. After the above efforts, this paper further confirms the feasibility of analyzing literary works from the perspective of linguistics, demonstrates the charm of pragmatics, and shows the vivid characters in *Gone with the Wind* to a varying degree.

Bibliography

[1] AUSTIN J L, 1962. How to Do Things with Words[M]. New York: Bantam Dell Publishing Group.
[2] ITO H, 2015. The Analytical Outline for Ironic Speech Acts: Short Version[J]. Acta Theologica: 484-485.
[3] MITCHELL M, 2010. Gone with the Wind[M]. New York: Simon & Schuster.
[4] 戴林红，2007. 言语行为理论综述[J].成都纺织高等专科学校学报(3)：61-63.
[5] 胡露，2016. 《了不起的盖茨比》原著与汉译著中反讽语言的对比研究[D]. 广西：广西师范大学.
[6] 黄晴晶，2015. 言语行为理论视角下《飘》的反讽研究[D]. 成都：成都理工大学.
[7] 荆兴梅，2008. 论《飘》中的反讽[J]. 湖南工程学院学报（社会科学版）(3)：45-48.
[8] 田现辉，2016. 探究小说《飘》中的反讽言语行为的运用[J]. 语文建设(6)：59-60.
[9] 覃乃川，2016. 言语行为理论视角下《钻石项链》的反讽探究[J]. 英语广场(5)：12-14.
[10] 邱志华，张艳，朱小玉，2013. 小说《飘》中的反讽言语行为探析[J]. 赤峰学院学报（哲学社会科学版）(1)：199-202.
[11] 涂靖，2000. Irony 言语行为研究[J]. 四川外语学院学报(4)：50-53.
[12] 王欣欣，2016. 言语行为理论视域中《傲慢与偏见》（中译本）的反讽研究[D]. 哈尔滨：黑龙江大学.
[13] 王振庆，2015. 认知语用学视角下的反讽话语理解[D]. 昆明：云南师范大学.
[14] 张阿慧，2016. 从言语行为理论角度分析《双城记》中的反讽[D]. 沈阳：辽宁大学.
[15] 张立群，2015. 语用学视角下《唐顿庄园》的反讽言语行为研究[D]. 南昌：南昌大学.
[16] 韦晓保，2006. 言语交际中的反语理解语用认知研究[D]. 上海：上海外国语大学.
[17] 周骞，2011. 《飘》中言语反讽的言语行为理论研究[D]. 合肥：安徽大学.
[18] 周思齐，2014. 言语行为理论视角下《傲慢与偏见》中的反讽研究[D]. 长春：吉林大学.
[19] 朱小舟，2002. 反讽的语用研究[J]. 湖南师范大学学报(社会科学版)(3)：99-101.

A Comparative Study of Appellations in the Chinese and English Versions of *Fortress Besieged* from the Perspective of Politeness Principle

邹 靖

1. Introduction

Appellations, or forms of address, are of great significance in interpersonal communication as they not only reflect cultural values and social norms but also influence power dynamics. In the context of cross-cultural communication, understanding the variations in appellations across different languages and cultures is essential for fostering effective communication and mutual understanding. Therefore, this comparative analysis aims to investigate the divergences in appellations between Chinese and English, with a specific focus on the novel *Fortress Besieged* by Qian Zhongshu.

Fortress Besieged is chosen as a case study due to its cultural significance and intricate portrayal of social interactions. Written originally in Chinese and subsequently translated into English by Jeanne Kelly and Mao Guoquan, the novel presents an excellent opportunity to examine the translation and adaptation of appellations across languages. Furthermore, the theme of politeness in *Fortress Besieged* offers a rich context for comprehending the cultural nuances and linguistic strategies employed in both languages. As such, the source text and Jeanne Kelly and Mao Guoquan's translated version of *Fortress Besieged* will be analyzed.

This comparative analysis will employ a multidisciplinary approach, integrating theories from sociolinguistics, pragmatics, and translation studies. By adopting a pragmatic perspective, the paper investigates how politeness theories, Leech's politeness maxims, can shed light on the choice and use of appellations in both Chinese and English. Additionally, translation theories, such as equivalence and adaptation, will guide our examination of the challenges and strategies involved in translating appellations between the two languages.

Through this comparative analysis, this paper anticipates contributing to the fields of sociolinguistics, pragmatics, and translation studies by providing insights into the role of appellations in reflecting cultural norms and politeness strategies. Moreover, this study aims to enhance cross-cultural understanding and promote effective communication between Chinese and English speakers.

2. Leech's Politeness Principle

Grice put forward the Cooperative Principle of conversation in 1967, pointing out that in order to make the communication go smoothly, both parties in speech communication will follow the Cooperative Principle in communication. If the speaker deliberately violates the Cooperative Principle, the listener should infer the speaker's implied meaning according to the context at that time, that is, the conversational implication. Although the Cooperative Principle explains the relationship between the literal meaning of a discourse and its actual meaning, and explains how conversational implicatures are produced and understood, it does not explain why people violate conversational maxims to express themselves implicitly and indirectly.

To this end, the famous British scholar Leech supplemented, enriched and developed Grice's Cooperation Principle, and proposed a systematic Politeness Principle. He believes that the principle of politeness can rescue the principle of cooperation and make up for its deficiency. The principle of politeness mainly includes six maxims with two sub-rules as follows (Leech, 1983):

(1) Tact Maxim (in impositives and commissives)
① Minimize cost to other
② Maximize benefit to other
(2) Generosity Maxim (in impositives and commissives)
① Minimize benefit to self
② Maximize cost to self
(3) Approbation Maxim (in expressives and assertives)
① Minimize dispraise of other
② Maximize praise of other
(4) Modesty Maxim (in expressives and assertives)
① Minimize praise of self
② Maximize dispraise of self
(5) Agreement Maxim (in assertives)
① Minimize disagreement between self and other
② Maximize agreement between self and other
(6) Sympathy Maxim (in assertives)
① Minimize antipathy between self and other
② Maximize sympathy between self and other

According to Leech's Politeness Principle, following the principle of politeness is an important aspect of cooperative conversation and determines the success of normal interaction between individuals. In communication, the parties involved always try to provide convenience or benefit to others, while minimizing their own gain or advantage. In this way, both parties receive respect and develop a favorable impression of each other. Polite behavior can be seen as asymmetric because being polite to the listener or a third party implies impoliteness towards the speaker. At the same time, polite behavior is also symmetric because people strive to maintain a balance between verbal behavior and psychological state.

Certain speech acts, such as thanking and apologizing, are used to restore the symmetry in the relationship or uphold the asymmetry between the parties involved. In terms of the hierarchy of benefit and cost, language that benefits the listener at the expense of the speaker is considered more damaging to the speaker. The degree and level of politeness increase accordingly. In communication, the speaker always seeks inappropriate language to increase their own cost while maximizing the listener's benefit. In terms of expression, the more indirect the speech that causes harm to the listener is, the more choices the listener has, and thus the more polite the speech is. Even when the speech benefits the listener, it can still be considered as polite, even if it is direct (Wang, 2009).

3. Appellations

In the context of this research, appellations play a significant role in interpersonal communication. As for the definition, appellations refer to the names used by individuals to address each other based on kinships, relationships, identities, occupations, and other factors. Appellations are not only linguistic forms but also social and cultural phenomena.

Appellation can be mainly divided into three categories: kinship appellations, social appellations, and honorific and humble forms. These three classifications classify the main appellations in modern Chinese, reflecting different levels, social hierarchies, values, and social consciousness of individuals. As an important aspect of interpersonal communication, appellations reflect attitudes, emotions, preferences, social hierarchies, and identities between individuals. Through the study of appellations, we can gain a deeper understanding of the underlying relationships between individuals, as well as the social structures and political contexts that influence their usage.

4. Analysis of Appellation in *Fortress Besieged*

4.1 Kinship Appellations

The so-called kinship appellations refer to those words that represent kinship to people directly, such as mother, father, uncle, aunt, grandfather, grandmother and so on. But in daily life, people often use the following names (nicknames): mom/mommy, mum/mummy, dad/daddy, auntie/aunty, grandma, grandpa and so on. Different families may have different names for their parents. In kinship appellations, some names also contain the function of social appellations, such as uncle, aunt, grandpa, grandma, etc. In addition to expressing kinship, they also have the general meaning of the words "uncle" "aunt" "grandfather" "grandmother" and so on. In addition, uncle, auntie, grandma, grandpa and other appellations can sometimes be used in conjunction with names, such as "Uncle David" "Aunt Polly" "Auntie Jane" "Grandma Peterson".

Kinship appellations are governed by at least four pragmatic principles: proximity, age, status and politeness. Kinship appellations express the social relationship and emotional feeling between characters. In the novel *Fortress Besieged*, there is a relatively high frequency of kinship appellations being used. For example, the protagonist Fang Hung-chien refers to the parents of his deceased fiancée as "丈人" (father-in-law) and "丈母" (mother-in-law), and refers to his own parents as "父亲" (father) and "母亲" (mother). These translations of kinship appellations align with the source text as they accurately depict ordinary forms of address without invoking the principles of politeness. Conversely, translating kinship appellations with considerations of politeness proves to be more challenging in conveying the original meaning vividly.

Example 1: 丈人说:"我知道你不会有。你<u>老太爷</u>家教好,你做人规矩,不会闹什么自由恋爱,自由恋爱没有一个好结果的。"(《围城》——钱钟书)

Translation: His father-in-law said, "I knew you wouldn't. Your **father** gave you a good upbringing. You're a gentleman and not the type to get mixed up with any free courtship. Free courtship never comes to a good end." (*Fortress Besieged* — translated by Jeanne Kelly and Mao Guoquan)

In this section, the protagonist Fang Hung-chien's father-in-law inquires about whether he has a girlfriend and, upon receiving a negative answer, expresses great admiration. Therefore, he says this phrase, which not only praises Fang Hung-chien's adherence to etiquette but also commends the upbringing of the protagonist's father. Fang Hung-chien's father-in-law doesn't directly say "你父亲" but instead uses the term "你老太爷", which further demonstrates his respect for Fang Hung-chien's father and reflects the commendation criterion of the politeness principle. It is precisely this authentic appellation that gives the passage a distinctive traditional Chinese flavor. After all, modern young people would never use such appellation, which also highlights the author's delicate and vivid writing style. However, in Jeanne Kelly's translation version, this phrase is directly translated as "your father", which, although conveying the basic meaning and enabling readers to grasp the overall idea of the sentence, fails to convey the praise and respect of the original text and does not reflect the use of the politeness principle in this context.

Example 2: 苏小姐怕她讲出昨天打三次电话的事来,忙勾了她腰,抚慰她道:"瞧你<u>这孩子</u>,讲句笑话,就要认真。"(《围城》——钱钟书)

Translation: Afraid that Miss T'ang might say something about her three telephone calls the day before, Miss Su quickly put her arm around Miss T'ang's waist and said placatingly, "Look at **you**. I was joking and you take it so seriously." (*Fortress Besieged* — translated by Jeanne Kelly and Mao Guoquan)

In the given dialogue, the phrase "这孩子" refers to Miss Su's cousin, T'ang Hsiao-fu. This term reflects both the age and generational difference between the speaker and the person being addressed. T'ang Hsiao-fu is Miss Su's younger female cousin, implying that Miss Su is older and of a different generation. Furthermore, it also reflects Miss Su's affection for her cousin, playfully referring to her as "孩子" ("child"). In this sentence, when addressing someone who is younger or a junior, the choice of address also plays a decisive role in the politeness principle. However, in the translation version provided ("look at you"), it fails to convey the age and generational difference between Miss Su and her cousin, T'ang Hsiao-fu. It also doesn't capture the affection between the two individuals, thus neglecting the role of the politeness principle in this context.

Example 3: 辛楣道:"去瞻仰瞻仰汪太太也无所谓。也许老汪有<u>侄女、外甥女或者内姨</u>之类——汪太太听说很美——要做给你。"(《围城》——钱钟书)

Translation: Hsin-mei said, "I don't mind going to get a look at Mrs. Wang. Maybe Old Wang has a **niece on his or his wife's side** —Wang is supposed to be quite a beauty — whom he wants to give to you. (*Fortress Besieged* — translated by Jeanne Kelly and Mao Guoquan)

In this dialogue, there are many kinship terms used, including "侄女""外甥女" and "内姨". These terms reflect the intricate and strict nature of traditional Chinese kinship terminology. On the one hand, "侄女" refers to the daughter of one's paternal siblings, indicating a paternal kinship relationship. On the other hand, "外甥女" refers to the daughter of one's spouse's siblings, indicating a maternal kinship relationship. And "内姨" generally refers to the sister of one's mother or father, indicating both generational and kinship relationships and indicating that the aunt and one's parents are of the same generation.

Traditional Chinese kinship relationships can be discerned based on the specific kinship terms, reflecting both generational differences and degrees of closeness. In the provided translation, the term "niece" is used to represent all these kinship terms, which blurs the distinctiveness of the blood relationships that carry strong Chinese cultural characteristics. Qian Zhongshu's precise and masterful use of language, including the choice of kinship terms, is a notable feature of *Fortress Besieged*, reflecting traditional Chinese culture. It is unfortunate that the translation fails to capture this particular characteristic.

It is known that the Chinese kinship terminology system is intricate and diverse. It strictly differentiates between direct and collateral relatives, blood relatives and in-laws, elder and younger generations, males and females, close relatives and distant relatives, and so on. In modern Chinese, most kinship terms clearly indicate the person's identity, such as generation (父辈: 伯, 舅; 同辈: 哥, 妹, 堂弟), paternal or maternal lineage (姑, 姨), direct or collateral relationship (孙, 侄孙), age (叔, 伯, 哥, 弟), and blood relatives or in-laws (哥, 嫂子, 姐, 姐夫). In contrast, English kinship terms are relatively impoverished and have broader and more ambiguous referents. Apart from distinguishing generations, the distinctions of closeness, such as insider/outsider and seniority/juniority can be overlooked. For example, the word "sister" encompasses both older sister and younger sister without indicating age; "grandmother" can refer to both maternal grandmother and paternal grandmother without distinguishing the lineage; "uncle" can refer to uncle, elder uncle, younger uncle, or aunt's husband without considering age or lineage. The English term "cousin" is even more versatile, as it does not differentiate by age, lineage, or gender, encompassing a range of Chinese kinship terms, such as "堂兄, 堂弟, 堂姐, 堂妹, 表哥, 表弟, 表姐, 表妹". Thus the different cultures of kinship produce the challenge to vividly translate the source texts, especially when the texts carry the underlying emotion such as affection, respect and likes.

4.2 Social Appellations

Social appellations, in the context of Chinese culture, encompass the terms and customs used to address individuals in social interactions, excluding kinship-based appellations. They play a significant role in reflecting and maintaining social relationships and etiquette in various social settings. Social appellations can be further divided into non-kinship terms and contextual terms. Non-kinship terms refer to the appellations used to address individuals in interpersonal relationships, apart from the kinship appellations that denote family relationships. These terms are based on the fundamental identity of being a person and have certain norms and traditional customs in social interactions. Contextual terms are appellations that vary depending on specific contexts or situations.

They take into account factors such as age, occupation, social status, and the nature of the relationship between individuals.

Example 4: 鸿渐说："**老伯**可以见见么?"(《围城》——钱钟书)

Translation: "May I meet **your father**?" he asked. (*Fortress Besieged* — translated by Jeanne Kelly and Mao Guoquan)

In the given example, the male protagonist Fang Hung-chien is asking if he can meet Miss T'ang's father, but he refers to him as "老伯" instead of "你的父亲". The term "老伯" carries cultural significance within Chinese society, emphasizing the tradition of respecting and honoring the elderly. The character "老" denotes wisdom and resourcefulness acquired through experience.

The term "老" is commonly used in addressing others, such as "老人家" (the elderly), "张老" (Zhāng Lǎo or Mr. Zhang), "老李" (Lǎo Lǐ or Old Lee), and even foreigners are called "老外" (lǎo wài). In this specific context, Fang Hung-chien's use of "老伯" to address an older person reflects the politeness maxim of showing respect. It expresses reverence for the elder without employing a more formal honorific term like "令尊", implying a sense of closeness and familiarity and indirectly reflecting the emotional connection between Fang Hung-chien and Miss T'ang.

Translating the term "老伯" directly into English poses challenges as the concept of "老" carries different connotations in western cultures. In western societies, the term "old" can be associated with negative notions such as being "old and useless" and it may connote advanced age, physical decline, conservatism, and a loss of vitality and creativity. Westerners typically prefer to be addressed by their names, finding it natural and comfortable. Being referred to as "old grandma" would be considered offensive and could provoke irritation. Western culture does not emphasize the veneration of age but rather values youth, vitality, power and capability. Thus, finding an appropriate translation for "老伯" that conveys both respect and intimacy in the English version can be challenging.

Example 5: 回旅馆不多一会,伙计在梯子下口里含着饭嚷"**侯营长**来了!"大家赶下来。(《围城》——钱钟书)

Translation: Shortly after they returned to the inn, the waiter yelled from the foot of the ladder with his mouth full of food, "**Major Hou** is here!" and they all hurried downstairs. (*Fortress Besieged* — translated by Jeanne Kelly and Mao Guoquan)

In Chinese culture, it is common to use the structure of "surname + title" to address someone. The term "侯营长" is the most common form of address in interpersonal relationships. This form of address reflects the social role and status of the person being referred to, as well as the relationship between the communicators. In Chinese social etiquette, as long as someone has a title, it can be used to address the person. For example, "石班长" (Sergeant Shi), "张助理" (Assistant Zhang), "吴科长" (Director Wu), "陈会计" (Accountant Chen), and so on. Any positions (minister, governor, etc.), military ranks (brigadier, major, etc.), professional titles (engineer, professor, etc.), academic degrees (doctor, etc.), and occupations (doctor, nurse, teacher, etc.) can be used with the surname to address others. This practice is considered polite in Chinese culture, as directly calling someone by their name is seen as impolite. Therefore, the "surname + title" form of social address, based on the principle of politeness, is the most common.

The English translation of "侯营长" is "Major Hou", which has different word order from the original Chinese term, using "title + surname" to address someone. However, according to the *Collins Dictionary*, a major is an officer who holds a rank above captain in the British army or the United States army, air force or navies. Considering the differences in military rank systems between China and the West, it may be uncertain whether foreign readers can fully grasp the meaning of the term "营长" without additional context. Furthermore, the form of using western structure "professional titles + surname/given name" is commonly used to address members of the royal family, high-ranking government officials, religious figures, legal professionals, and military personnel in the western context. For example, "President Clinton" "Prince Charles" "Pope John" "Judge Jackson". The most common form of address using the structure "professional titles/ occupations + surname" is "Doctor" and "Professor". For example, "Dr. White" or "Prof. White". Overall, the form of "professional titles + surname/given name" is a concentrated reflection of the principle of politeness in both Chinese and Western cultures. However, it is evident that this usage is more widespread in China, possibly due to the Chinese tradition of emphasizing politeness as a core aspect of its etiquette-oriented society.

4.3 Honorifics and Humble Forms

Honorifics and humble forms reflect power relationships based on aspects such as age, social status, wealth, or social position. Common power relationships include parent-child relationships, hierarchical relationships, teacher-student relationships, employer-employee relationships, and other relationships. Generally, when the addressee holds power, the speaker tends to use honorifics to address them or humble forms of address to refer to himself/herself. The use of honorifics or humble forms of address acknowledges the disparity in status between the speaker and the addressee while expressing respect and maintaining a certain distance. The rhetorical authority carried by honorifics or humble forms of address can exert a degree of influence over the addressee, compelling them to respond in a similar linguistic manner.

In traditional Chinese culture, the use of honorifics and humble forms of address is expected as a way to show respect, politeness and humility when interacting with others. This aspect is vividly portrayed in the use of honorifics and self-deprecating language in social interactions by the protagonist in *Fortress Besieged*. On the one hand, honorifics refer to linguistic expressions used to address others, elevating their status and position through appropriate titles. On the other hand, humble forms of address are used to refer to oneself, lowering one's own status and position as a sign of politeness.

Generally, honorifics embody a traditional moral authority because, according to traditional morals, the party in a power relationship that is disadvantageous in terms of age, social status, wealth or social position should show respect to others.

Example 6: 李妈反说:"姑爷,晒衣服是娘儿们的事,**您**不用管。小姐大清早就出去办事了,**您**为什么不出去?这时候出去,晚上早点回来,不好么?"(《围城》——钱钟书)

Translation: Mama Li then said, "Master, sunning clothes is woman's business. **You** needn't worry about it. Young Lady left early this morning to go to work. Why don't **you** go out? Wouldn't it be nice if you left now and came back a little earlier this evening?" (*Fortress Besieged* — translated by Jeanne Kelly and Mao Guoquan)

Given the master-servant relationship between Fang Hung-chien and Mama Li, the use of "您" in this context signifies the speaker's (Mama Li's) respect for the addressee (Fang Hung-chien) and permeates the traditional moral authority associated with the addressee. The invisible pressure exerted by this authority compels Mama Li to use the pronoun "您" as a communicative stance that aligns with her social power status and facilitates smooth communication. If Mama Li were to disregard Fang Hung-chien's moral authority and use the pronoun "你", it would lead to a disruption in communication or a lack of smooth rhetorical activity. This aligns with the principle of politeness to elevate others as much as possible, showcasing the guidelines of politeness embedded in Chinese humble and honorific language.

However, the direct translation of "您" as "you" in English overlooks the master-servant relationship and the principle of politeness in the original text. The traditional cultural heritage of the Chinese nation requires people to use honorific and humble forms of address in their interactions, striving to humble oneself and elevate others to demonstrate humility, respect, and politeness. Chinese language is rich in honorifics and humble forms of address, while English lacks equivalent terms and phrases, resulting in a significant semantic gap. It is challenging to achieve an equivalent translation that fully captures the underlying principles of politeness and traditional authority inherent in Chinese honorifics and humble forms of address.

Example 7: 斜川客观地批判说："<u>内人</u>长得相当漂亮，画也颇有家法。"(《围城》——钱钟书)

Translation: Hsieh-ch'uan observed objectively, "**<u>My wife</u>** is rather pretty, and her painting is quite professional in style." (*Fortress Besieged* — translated by Jeanne Kelly and Mao Guoquan)

In the provided sentence, Tung Hsieh-ch'uan refers to his wife as "内人", which is a way of belittling his own family and humbling himself, aiming to foster harmonious dialogue between both parties. This usage aligns with the concept of humble forms of address mentioned earlier. However, English lacks equivalent terms or structures to convey the unique usage of Chinese honorifics and humble forms of address. Therefore, it can only be translated directly as "my wife".

While English does have some honorifics and forms of respect, such as "Your Majesty" for a king or queen, "Your Highness" for a prince, "Your Honor" for a judge, and "Your Excellency" for a cardinal, their usage is highly specific and limited. English lacks a broader range of honorifics and humble forms of address similar to those found in Chinese language and culture. As a result, there is still a significant gap in translating the nuanced aspects of honorifics and humble forms of address between Chinese and English.

5. Discussion

The previous chapters took *Fortress Besieged* as an example to compare the Chinese-English translations of three appellations—kinship appellations, social appellations, and honorifics and humble forms—analyzing their different characteristics and use from the perspective of Politeness Principles. In fact, the influence of Politeness Principles on these three types of appellations varies.

5.1　Kinship Appellations

In Chinese, kinship appellations emphasize a clear distinction between "inner" and "outer", as well as a hierarchical order between elders and juniors. This not only follows the principles of politeness but also reflects the traditional family and kinship culture of the Chinese ethnic group. Based on patrilineal blood relationships, one's identity within the family or clan is determined around the patriarch. Feudal ethics deeply rooted in society and strict social etiquette naturally result in a rich variety of appellations. In contrast, western culture emphasizes legal systems and lacks intricate social etiquette and a strong sense of hierarchical distinctions. Western societies value equality, individual dignity and freedom, considering those politeness rules as mere decorations and adornments of the upper class. These different ways of life are shaped by different socio-economic backgrounds.

In China, where self-sufficiency prevailed for a long time, people mostly lived with their extended families and shared economic, educational, political, and self-defense functions within clans and lineages. Therefore, terms like "亲亲" "尊尊" "父父" and "子子" strictly denote hierarchical kinship relationships within clans. In the West, people tend to prefer nuclear family structures, and children become independent as they reach adulthood. The more flexible modes of production and lifestyle in western societies lead to less emphasis on ancestral surnames and clan identity. Therefore, Western culture emphasizes personal equality, and individuals of any age can be addressed by their given names to express familiarity. As a result, English has fewer kinship appellations compared to Chinese, and they are less frequently used.

5.2　Social Appellations

Rooted in the hierarchical feudal society of the past, Chinese language frequently uses honorifics and titles to show respect and politeness towards others. As long as someone has a title, it can generally be used as an appellation. In English, the common forms of address for respect are "Mr." "Ms." "Mrs." "Miss" "Sir" "Madam", etc., with the first four typically used with surnames or full names. However, the usage of honorifics and titles is limited in English, such as "professor" and "doctor". Additionally, there is a notable difference in the use of the honorific "老" in Chinese social appellations. Chinese society has a long tradition of respecting and honoring the elderly, while western culture is quite the opposite.

Furthermore, modern Chinese has generalized kinship terms in social use. In Chinese, as a polite gesture, we often use "爷爷" (grandpa) and "奶奶" (grandma) to address older individuals that we don't know, or "叔叔" (uncle) and "阿姨" (aunt) to address our parents' friends or strangers of the same generation. This form of address is warm and endearing, effectively reducing the distance between interlocutors. However, if applied in English, the effect would be counterproductive. For example, if someone's car is behind an elderly person's car and urging the elderly person by saying "Move it, grandpa!" would be very disrespectful. Similarly, if a middle-aged woman who has become a grandmother is called "granny" by a stranger, she might feel offended and displeased.

5.3 Honorifics and Humble Forms

The greatest difference between Chinese and English appellations lies in the use of humble forms of address. Chinese culture places great emphasis on humility and politeness, resulting in a rich variety of humble forms of address. Humility is a prominent adherence to and the embodiment of Politeness Principles in Chinese culture, leading to frequent usage of humble forms of address. In contrast, English lacks humble forms of address and has only a small number of honorifics and forms of respect. This distinction may be related to the emphasis on freedom, dignity, equality and independence in western social and cultural contexts.

6. Conclusion

Indeed, Chinese culture is extensive and profound, and appellations hold a significant role in cultural dissemination and social interaction. Analyzing the appellations in the novel *Fortress Besieged* and their translation through the lens of Politeness Principles sheds light on the characteristics and comparative differences between Chinese and English appellations. However, it is important to note that the translation of Chinese appellations still faces challenges due to the need to convey their literal meaning as well as their profound connotations and pragmatic value. This requires further efforts in the fields of pragmatics and literature.

Moreover, some appellations cannot be fully explained solely based on the principle of politeness, suggesting the necessity for additional research and exploration in the domains of pragmatics and literature. These appellations may carry cultural and historical implications that go beyond politeness considerations, and a comprehensive understanding of their significance requires delving into the broader context of Chinese language, culture and social dynamics.

Overall, the analysis of appellations in *Fortress Besieged* highlights the importance of considering cultural and pragmatic aspects in translation, and it underscores the ongoing need for scholarly investigation to bridge the gaps and complexities that arise in translating appellations across different languages and cultures.

Bibliography

[1] CHEN C, 2019. A Comparative Study on English and Chinese Kinship Terms and Their Translation Strategies[J]. Theory and Practice in Language Studies(9): 1237-1242.

[2] LU J, THROSSEL P, 2015. The Innovative Trend of Using Address Terms in China[J]. The International Journal of Interdisciplinary Cultural Studies(4): 1-11.

[3] LEECH G N, 1983. Principles of Pragmatics[M]. London: Longman.

[4] MANNING H P, 2001. On Social Deixis[J]. Anthropological Linguistics(3): 55-100.

[5] MOUSAVI H, 2020. Terms of Address and Fictive Kinship Politeness in Lori[J]. Journal of Politeness Research(2): 217-247.

[6] KYOUNG Y, 2019. A Study on the Type and Characteristics of Address Terms in Chinese[J]. Journal of Chinese Literature: 291-310.

[7] 曹军，2002. 社会指示语的英汉互译[J]. 外语研究(6)：56-58.

[8] 曹炜，2005. 现代汉语中的称谓语和称呼语[J]. 江苏大学学报（社会科学版）(2)：62-69.
[9] 何兆熊，2000. 新编语用学概要[M]. 上海：上海外语教育出版社.
[10] 何自然，1988. 语用学概论[M]. 长沙：湖南教育出版社.
[11] 李克，李淑康，2010. 修辞权威视域下的社会指示语研究[J]. 上海外国语大学学报(5)：49-58.
[12] 刘宏丽，2011. 敬谦语视野下传统敬谦文化的特点[J]. 中国海洋大学学报（社会科学版）(5)：94-97.
[13] 刘宏丽，2010. 中国传统礼文化与敬谦语传播关系研究[J]. 河南大学学报（社会科学版），50(5)：127-132.
[14] 钱钟书，2003. 围城（中英文对照）[M]. 珍妮·凯利，茅国权，译. 北京：人民文学出版社.
[15] 宋娇，2010. 中英称谓语的对比及运用[J]. 经济研究导刊(19)：222-223.
[16] 孙云梅，夏钲鹃，2021. 合作及礼貌语言视角下的中国女性语言特征探究——以《围城》为例[J]. 外语教育(1)：49-59.

历时视角下"have+to+VP"结构的语义-语用界面研究

权国庆

1. 引言

　　一直以来,"have+to+VP（verb phrase,动词短语）"结构作为一种饱受争议的构式,其能否拥有情态功能受到国内外众多语言学家的关注。由于受到英语语法发展历史的影响,当前大多数学者仅从教学语法、语义学等单一视角对其进行研究,却忽略了语用因素。近年来,随着语用学理论的迅速发展,对英语将来时助动词的研究也逐渐趋向于从多角度出发对其意义进行解释。因此,本论文试图将语用机制与传统意义融合,从语言动态发展的视角出发,同时运用默认语义学模式对"have+to+VP"结构的语义-语用界面意义作出合理的解释。分析该结构在古英语、中古英语、现当代英语这几个历史时期内,其语义意义、语用情态意义的演变。同时,运用默认语义学模式为"have+to+VP"结构语法化过程的不同阶段内的意义分别提供了统一的解释。

2. 默认语义学模式在语义-语用界面问题上的理论优势

　　目前,国外语言学家对"have+to+VP"结构的研究还有不少缺陷。首先,许多学者对"have+to+VP"结构的研究仍然停留在单一视角,仅从语义学、语用学或语法化的角度对其进行单方面的意义研究（林忠、刘存伟,2015）。实际上,这种研究方法本身就存在一定的片面性。从单一视角对"have+to+VP"结构的研究使学者们的研究停留在静态意义领域,而忽视了语言结构的动态意义演变。其次,纵观各类研究成果,学者们都尝试从不同角度对此结构作出一个合理的解释,而研究发现对"have+to+VP"结构多维度意义的研究仍然缺乏一个整体的意义解释模式。同时,运用默认语义学理论解释"have+to+VP"结构的并合表征意义的学者仍屈指可数。

　　雅兹科特（Jazcott）提出默认语义学理论,认为"既然语言意义不能准确地表达命题内容,就应该找寻一个完整的语用机制代表最优化语言解释程序"。在默认语义学中,最优化的实现主要通过四种信息资源,即词汇意义与句子结构、有意识的语用推论、认知默认、社会文化默认,这些因素共同构成意义的"并合表征"（merger representation）模式。雅兹科特认为意义表征是由不同种类资源组成的并合信息集合,这些资源都处于同等的地位。在该模式下不存在对语法输出的优先性,也不存在任何衍生而来的内容对逻辑形式的语用入侵。雅兹科特的看法与主流的观点有很大不同,主流的意义观认为逻辑形式是基础,通过语用推论以及对默认意义扩展才能进一步推论说话人的真实意图。然而,在默认语义学中,语义学与语用学融合在一起表达意义,因此并和表征中不仅同时包含语义和语用成分,还组成有意识的推论（需要结合环境因素推导）和无意识的默认（根据话语内部即可推导）。默认语义学理论的并合表征意义模式中涉及的真值条件内容与经典格莱斯理论中的所言不同,前者的所言融合了有意识的语用推论、认知默认与社会文化默认。

纵观整个后格莱斯语用学意义解释模式，相比较而言，雅兹科特构建的默认语义学模式的优势主要体现在以下几个方面。

首先，相对于卡斯顿的关联理论，默认语义学承认在真值条件内容中存在假定的、凸显的、默认的意义解释，但这些因素与有意识的语用推论处于平等的地位。卡斯顿的理论将显性含义（explicature）和隐性含义（implicature）区分开来。卡斯顿认为"语义表征是典型的不完整命题，对句子的真值不起决定性作用，却构成一系列完整的概念表征并为命题形式的语用构建提供图示功能"（Sperber、Wilson，1986）。关联理论者定义的"所言"过于激进，过多地强调意义不充分性与语用推论的作用，将"所言"粗略地划分为两部分：语义表征与显性含义。毫无例外，"所言"的内容是欠明确的，必须经过有意识的语用推论才能产生显性含义，同样一个完整的话语意义，不仅涉及显性含义与隐性含义，还必须涉及有意识的语用推论过程。

其次，与利卡纳提观点在一定程度上对立的是温和语境论观点，默认语义学认为信息资源在语用加工过程中不依赖语法，即逻辑形式的填充不需要任何"语法槽"（slots）。语用输入在某种意义上仅仅追求的是句法信息的平衡，任何信息在某些语境下都可以颠覆对其他信息的输出。利卡纳提认为从句子意义到交际内容的过程主要涉及两个语用过程，最初的主要语用过程是一种潜意识的、自动的过程。利卡纳提这样评论道："所言发生在潜意识的层面，就像是直接看到的内容一样。"那么，主要语用过程本质上到底属于语义范畴，还是语用范畴呢？在默认语义学中，雅兹科特给出了更好的解释："将认知默认与社会文化默认看作人们潜意识的自主的意义解释，而对真值条件内容的语用推论意义是有意识的。默认意义与语用推论意义所起的作用是同时的，彼此不存在优先性。因此，默认语义学解决了语用上的意识性困难。"利卡纳提将默认和推理的语用加工看作自由的、由上到下的扩充过程。

最后，对于以巴赫为代表的试图解决经典格莱斯理论缺陷的学者而言，默认语义学模式有着经济性。巴赫提出意义解释的三分法，即所言、隐形意义、所含。他的意义解释模式并没有解决经典格莱斯理论中的缺陷，而是在所言和所含中间假定存在另一层表征意义。这使意义划分模式更为复杂。然而，在默认语义学中雅兹科特提倡意义层面的"经济原则"，即除非在必要情况下，意义层面不做过多的划分。也就是说，同时作用于同一意义层面上的语义不完整性与语用欠明确彼此之间互不干涉。此外，巴赫在语义学与语用学之间也划定了清晰的界限，与格莱斯理论的不同之处在于，他认为所言或逻辑形式本身属于语义学研究范畴，而将隐形意义与所含归为语用学研究范畴。然而，雅兹科特的理论中将语义学和语用学融合在一起，形成一个统一的并合表征意义的解释模式。

纵观后格莱斯意义解释模式，雅兹科特构建的默认语义学理论为当今语用学的发展提供了全新的意义解释模式，该模式具有更强的意义解释力，解决了争论已久的语义-语用层面的问题。作为一个全新的意义解释模式，默认语义学解释了近年来许多有争议的意义现象，例如限定摹状词、命题态度词、将来时情态动词、预设、句子连接词以及数词现象等。本文利用该理论试图解决"have+to+VP"结构的意义和功能纷争，亦是对该理论适用性的测试。

3. "have+to+VP"意义中的动态性——语法化与情态因素

语言作为世界的一部分，其也处在不断变化的进程之中。下面本文就分别从语法化、情态因素两方面阐述语言结构共时与历时的意义演变。

3.1 "be going to"结构的语法化过程及意义变化

英语中的"have+to+VP"通常被认为是一种半情态动词或者半助动词结构。不论是所谓的半情态动词或者半助动词结构，这些称谓都是"have+to+VP"在句法上的一些显著特征的直接结果。然而，该结构最初是以"have +NP+to+VP"的形式被使用的。这几个独立的成分不断融合发展，核心词 have 由最初表示词汇意义的实义动词演变为表示义务性的"have+to+VP"结构。在整个语法化的过程中，谢应光（2008）等认为"have+to+VP"结构的意义发展与动词的跨语言研究相一致。意义的发展是基于"事件是物体"的隐喻，从而投射出"拥有某事等同于不得不做某事"的概念，这样在语法化的进程中被语法化的结构变得越来越抽象。

以 Quirk（1973）等传统教学语法学家为代表的一众人最先通过比较 must 与"have+to+VP"在表示义务性含义用法上的区别，指出"have+to+VP"结构通常用于说话人强调其当前意图的语境下，而 must 常用于条件句中。

Brinton（1991）在国际第十届历史语言学大会上首次从构式语法的观点出发，分析"have+to+VP"结构义务性的产生。Brinton 认为"have+to+VP"表现出的"义务性"并不单纯来自 have 这个词，而是"have + NP（noun phrase，名词短语）+ to-infinitive"这样的组合结构。其情态功能（义务性）的产生涉及这整个结构如何发生变化的问题，也就是说从"所有"到"义务"的语法化以及语义扩展的过程。Brinton 用以下四个阶段概括了此过程。

（1）全动词结构（full verb structure）。have 只表示所有（possession），后接动词不定式表示主体针对该所有物即将施加的行为，举例如下。

I have a dollar to pay.

这里有两点：首先，以上例句暗含一种"义务"的表达，即"我有必要去花掉这张钱"；其次，这里的"a dollar"同时是 have 和 pay 两个动词的目标。

（2）语义转换（semantic shift）。have 从具象的"持有物品"淡化为抽象的"持有状态"：

I have a dollar to earn.

注意此时的变化：首先，一张还没有赚到手的钞票，是不可能在物理上被一个人"持有"的；其次，在这样的句子里，"所有"的意义淡化，"义务"的意义渐渐占据主导。

（3）述语结构（predicative structure）。"所有"的意义继续消失，句子里的 NP 不再是 have 的对象。于是原本在 have 后面的 NP 就通过移位到了不定式结构的后面，举例如下。

I have to earn a dollar.

这种构式形成于中古英语时期，其涵义和功能已经接近大众所熟悉的"have+to+VP"了。

（4）固定结构（periphrastic structure）。"have+to+VP"这个结构里已经不再有"所有"的意义，于是可以共现的词汇也没有那么多限制了。之前还存在 NP，现在可以舍弃了，举例如下。

I have to struggle.

许多表示所有、存在等意义的词，语法化之后都会具备情态用法，这是一个普遍的语言现象。在"义务"和"所有"的表达方式之间的联系可以被称为 Obligation-Possession Link，简称"OP 联系"，这样的联系在印欧语系语言中普遍存在。Benveniste、Freeze、Kayne 等人提出了 have-be 联系假说（Bhatt，1998）。例如：

A. John has a book.
B. Be-existential[(a book)(to John)]
C. There is a book on the table.
D. Be-existential[(a book)(on the table)]

A 对应的是汉语中的"所属-有"，而 C 则对应汉语中的"存现-有"。这两者在语义上都可以用存现谓词 be（此处 be 为元语言）来统一。"have+to+VP"和上述结构其实有着密切的关系。have 也可以用存现谓词 be 来解释。用 Benveniste 等人的观点来看，其暗含的语用情形是"义务"。例如：

A. You have to answer my question.
B. Be-existential[(to answer my question)(for you)]

此处的"义务"情态是暗含的。动词不定式结构 to answer my question 不直接表达情态，并且 have 作为普通的存现谓词，也不直接表达情态，但 have 和 to 的语义组合则包含了情态，这个情态被认为是隐含意义的。Kayne 首次提出了要从语用的层面上分析这种情态性质的产生。

总结以上前人的研究，可以得出 have 相关结构的历时演变过程：核心词"have+NP"最初作为实义动词，表示"持有""拥有"某种事物的含义。随后出现了"have+NP+to"结构，表示"持有某物的目的""有意愿利用某物进行某项活动"等含义，这样介词 to 基本上稳定下来组成该结构。同时，伴随着语言的动态发展，"have+to+VP"结构以名词短语的形式出现在一些文学作品当中，逐渐被看作一个不可分割的固定短语，也出现了表示"义务性"的含义。此时表示"义务性"的含义主要指非抽象"义务"，一般认为标准的语法化理论会不断演变，其中一些典型的语言结构会变得愈发抽象。

3.2 "have+to+VP"结构意义中的情态因素

评价说话人意向性的一个重要标准就是情态因素，在运用默认语义学模式详细介绍"have+to+VP"结构的各类意义之前，我们先从方法论和本体论出发探究情态的本质。

从"意义"参数视角，可以划分出四个意义等级：潜在性、倾向性、可能性、必然性。Palmer（1979）则根据"来源"参数，将情态分为认识情态与非认识情态，又将非认识情态进一步分为道义情态和动力情态。认识情态意义与责任、义务或允许有关，受外在因素的影响；非认识情态意义依赖于内部因素，与个体的能力、意愿有关。动力情态主要考虑的是句子主语所具有的能力或意志，与其他情态类型不同的是它不具有主观性。雅兹科特在默认语义学框架中将"意义"参数与"来源"参数融合在一起，并对将来时助动词作出全面的意义解释。运用情态领域的几个专业术语，例如"认识必然和倾向必然"，来区分不同含义的情态，同时借助"逻辑和道义情态"引入"情态算子"。

按照"意义"参数角度对情态划分的方式，通过情态可以衡量说话人的确定性等级以及命题内容真值的可能性与必然性。当说话人说出一个命题时，该命题的确定性等级是由说话人本身的意向性决定的。雅兹科特同时运用心理状态中的意向性特征、语用学中涉及的交际与信息特征，以及交际过程中的指称意图，来表明造成不同类型情态解释的结果是由不同的意图等级造成的。因此，雅兹科特提出："最强有力的指向事件的意图会产生对交际事件最强有力的许可，而同时也会产生最弱的情态等级。"同时，雅兹科特认为通过意向性等级可以衡量情态，情态等级与意向性的关系成反比。当人们使用较高的情态等级时，表明说话人对事件的确定性程度把握较低或说服力度相对较低；而当使用较低的情态等级时，却表明说话人对所表达的内容非常有把握。

不同种类的情态具有不同的情态等级。认识情态所表示的是说话人对某一命题真值的确定性等级，主要分为认识必然性和认识可能性。而道义情态与态度范畴相关，它所表示的是说话人所承诺事物外在道义原则的等级，Nuyts（2001）等指出，"道义情态一般指说话者在话语中所表达的事物状态的道义方面的合意性等级。按照所蕴含的'等级'概念，就可以产生这样渐变的等级：绝对道义必然性、处于中间阶段的合意性、可接受性、不合意性、绝对道义不可接受性。"动力情态表示说话人的意愿等级，如意志、意图、能力、潜能等，从中间层次等级到实现内部需要的等级。

情态的发展普遍被看作一个语法化过程。Hansen（2017）认为"情态处于语法化的链条上，从实义词充分发展为情态助动词。情态形成小核心范畴并产生过渡带的模糊外围范畴"。长期以来，情态的语法化过程是由动力或者道义情态意义向认识情态意义转变的一个过程。

通过对情态等级以及连续性的介绍，以证明此对"have+to+VP"结构意义解释过程中情态所起的至关重要的作用。情态的连续性就如一根没有节点的绳子，是一个连续统一体，不可分割。同时，在情态系统内对该结构意义进行解释，可以有效地避免语义模糊。下文将从历时的角度详细解释"have+to+VP"结构的不同情态意义之间的关系，进一步表明不同的情态意义的表征意义解释模式是由不同的情态等级主导的。

4. 历时下运用默认语义学模式对"have+to+VP"结构的语义－语用界面的分析

以上文字介绍了后格莱斯时期语用学中有关语义-语用界面研究的几种意义解释模式，并重点阐明了默认语义学意义解释模式的优势。本节则以"have+to+VP"结构为例，运用默认语义学理论来验证其在语法化过程的不同阶段中，在前人研究的基础上扩充和完善其自身的语义-语用意义的发展及演变规律，并且试图为不同历史时期的该结构分别构建一个完整的意义并合表征模式。

4.1 古英语时期的语义-语用界面分析

古英语时期，动词 have 主要以 hæbban 形式表达，其公认的词源是早期日耳曼语 habejanan，意为"拥有、占有、是……的主人、经历"。由此看出 have 一词早就呈现出了占有性。另外，"have+to+VP"结构的核心词 have 在这一阶段并没有出现表示义务性的含义，仅仅作为一个实义动词表达存现状态，例如：

A. Ic hæbbe anweald mine sawle to alætanne & ic hæbbe anweald hig eft to nimanne.
   I have power to release my soul and I have power to take it back again.

B. Ic hæbbe þone mete to etene þe ge nyton.
   I have the food to eat which you do not need.

C. Nu ic longe spell hæbbe to secgenne.
   Now I have a long story to tell.

上述例句表明在古英语时期"have+to+VP"结构并没有出现"强迫性"的情态涵义。尽管在该时期"have+to"类型结构的表达中,"have+NP+to+VP"的形式占了绝大部分(NP 此时还未被省略),但可以看出该时期"have+NP+to+VP"结构的用法已经出现分化。(1)A、B 例句中的客体在 to+VP 表示的事件发生之前就已存在;(2)C 例句中客体需要在 to+VP 表示的事件发生之后才能存在。其中,第二种用法被语法学家标记为"未完成类"事件,该用法已经逐步衍生出动力情态语用意义。

雅兹科特指出"并不存在语义-语用界面意义,意义的表达主要体现在语义和语用的并合作用。"因此,雅兹科特所构建的"并合表征模式"中既包含语义成分,又包含语用成分;既包含有意识的推论意义,又包含无意识的默认意义。运用默认语义学模式对上例 C 中"have+NP+to+VP"的语义-语用界面意义作出合理的意义解释,可以看出在上例 C 中 hæbbe 字面意义为"拥有",表示说话人"将会拥有一个故事"的倾向,而经过听话人的语用推论,hæbbe 在这句话中还暗含了实施者表示在未来的某一天必定会讲述一个故事,来让说话人完成"持有一个故事"的意愿。

基于默认语义学理论,运用格莱斯提出的"可接受性算子"作为"情态算子"来表达"have+NP+to+VP"结构在古英语时期表达动力情态意义的可接受性,记为 $ACC\triangle^n e/s$。其中,n 表示说话人的情态等级,△表示情态函数。表达式 $ACC\triangle^n e/s$ 的含义为:对于说话人来说,事件 e 或状态 s 的情态等级 n 所对应的情态意义是可接受的。那么,借鉴雅兹科特对将来时助动词 will 构建的一般表征模式,对古英语时期"have+NP+to+VP"结构的道义情态意义构建完整统一的并合表征模式,如下所示。

$$
\begin{array}{l}
x\ t\ e \\
[ic]_{CD}(x) \\
Now\ (\ t\ ) \\
[ACC\triangle^{de}\ s]_{WS,\ CPI} \\
s : [Nu\ x\ longe\ spell\ hæbbe\ to\ secgenne]_{WS}
\end{array}
$$

图 1　古英语中"have"的并合表征模式

如上图所示,古英语时期核心词 have 除了作为实义动词还具有动力情态意义,并不能表现出一种义务性。上例 C 中 I 为默认的主语,表示为 $[ic]_{CD}$;与该时期核心词 have 的实义动词意义相比,其动力情态意义为有意识的语用推论意义,即 $[ACC\triangle^{de}\ s]_{WS,\ CPI}$。同时例中所表达的说话人意向性特征可以用自上而下、由高到低的矢量来表示,如下所示。

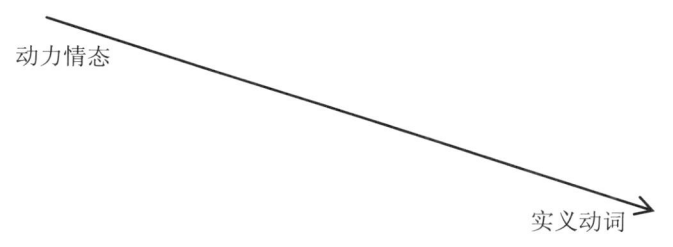

图 2　说话人意向性特征矢量变化

4.2　中古英语时期的语义-语用界面分析

中古英语时期，大量的 VP+PP（preposition phrase，介词短语）结构迎来了语法化，并在早期现代英语阶段完成了句法和语义上的固定。"have+NP+to+VP"结构也不例外，最明显的特征就是对于组成成分的泛化：一方面，不定式 to 后面可以选择不及物性的动词接续；另一方面，have 所支配的客体也由实体名词衍生为抽象名词，在后期出现了非名词作为 have 支配的客体，甚至非名词作为 have 的主体支配人。这样的变化衍生出的"have+（NP）+to+VP"结构开始逐渐表现出了一种义务性，例如：

D. To yow hath I to speke of o matere.
　　To you have I to speak of one matter.

E. for þe sculleð habben to drinken.
　　for you shall have (something) to drink.

F. He, that hath a longe jorney to do.
　　He, who has a long journey to do.

G. for I have had inowghe to do.
　　for I have had enough to do.

H. a trewe man…hath nat to parten with a theves dede.
　　a true man does have not to participate in a thief's deeds.

Lehmann（2015）把这样的现象定义为语言减缩（condensation），即某一时期的固定表达出现成分脱落或者纵向选择关系上的泛化。他认为这样的泛化是造成情态性由自我动因向外部动因过渡的原因。在上例 D 中，说话人将抽象的外力条件隐喻为支配自己的主体（这一点由受到 to yow 产生形态变化产生的 hath 体现），但同时说话人自身又是"speak"这一行为的主体，因此达到了一种支配与被支配的平衡。而在上例 H 中，说话人将抽象的否定条件隐喻为自己所支配的客体，这样的客体不仅被主体所支配（一个真男人不会参与偷盗的行为），也一定程度上支配主语进行活动（道义上的条件限制真男人去偷盗）。值得一提的是，上例 D 中的表达习惯在现代英语中发展为了倒装而表示强调的用法，而上例 H 中的 have 则逐渐演变为助动词用来修饰谓语动词。

由此看来，"have+NP+to+VP"结构由古英语过渡到中古英语时期的过程中，不仅其语义意义有了新的含义，同时其语用意义也有了进一步的发展。在这一阶段，"have+to+VP"结构的分化用法虽然十分复杂，但都首次出现了表示"义务、强迫"的语用意义，而又在一定程度上保持了古英语中主动性较强的语用意义，因此在这一阶段其可被归纳为道义情态意义。

在这一部分中本文试图运用雅兹科特的默认语义学理论为中古英语时期"have+（NP）+to+VP"结构的语义-语用层面意义构建并合表征的意义解释模式，以上例 D 为例，可以得出：

```
                    x t e
[To yow]_CD(x)
⌀ ( t )
[ACC△^de s]_WS, CPI
s : [x hath I to speke of o matere]_WS
```

图 3　说话人义务性

显然，在该时期"have+（NP）+to+VP"结构已表现出说话人的义务性，因此遵循该结构的语法化轨迹并结合其在语法化过程中所体现的情态意义，说话人对事件的意向性等级可以用下图表示。

图 4　说话人意向性等级

从上图的虚线部分可以看出虽然在中古英语时期的语料中"have+（NP）+to+VP"结构一定程度上继承并体现了动力情态意义，但其小于道义情态意义，实线部分则表示的是"have+（NP）+to+VP"结构在中古英语时期产生的经过新发展和继承的平衡之后形成的道义情态意义。根据默认语义学理论，人们头脑中信息加工和指称的意向性与意义的情态等级成反比，我们可以推断出中古英语时期该结构具有较高的情态等级，该结构所产生的道义情态意义属于语用推论意义。

4.3　现当代英语时期的语义-语用界面分析

现当代英语时期（20 世纪初以来），"have+to+VP"结构已经完全被视为不可拆分的固定结构，是英语中最重要的表达义务性的一种方式。纵观"have+（NP）+to+VP"结构的意义发展过程，实际上其发展最初起源于 NP 位置上的选择。Hopper、Traugott（2003）提出语义改变的语法化过程所依据的是把转喻看作意义改变的方式。把表示"have+to+VP"结构看成语法化的范式，可以假定其意义的发展经历了这几个阶段：NP 代表实体名词、NP 可以代表抽象名词、NP 可以消失、NP 消失后的结构形成新的固定结构。

同时，Hopper、Traugott 认为特定结构经历的典型语法化过程只可能出现在局部语境下，也就是表示目的方向性的非限定性补语中，如下例 I。并且，他们认为语法化不会出现在带有处所或目的副词的方向性语境中，如下例 J。

I. I have to eat lunch.

J. I have lunch to eat.

在此选取 BNC 语料库（英国国家语料库）的实例具体分析"have+to+VP"结构或"have+NP+to+VP"结构在当代英语中的多维度情态意义，从而证明该结构可以被视为一个语用变体并得以构建统一的意义解释模式。

（1）动力情态意义（只是主体内在固有的本质，它与主体的能力、意志或意愿有关，只能通过"have+NP+to+VP"结构表达），例如：

K. Now I have a girl to bang.

L. She has good news to share.

（2）道义情态意义（属于道义用途，表达主观性的允许、责任以及委任等概念，同时还与社会或机构法律所规约的责任、义务有关，可以通过"have+NP+to+VP"结构或"have+to+VP"表达），例如：

M. I have something to tell you.

N. Children have a lot of things to learn.

O. My other sister and I have to do all the housework.

P. Children have to learn a lot of things.

（3）认识情态意义（认识情态意义主要表达说话人对命题真值条件的确定性，只能通过"have+to+VP"结构表达，可与 must 替换），例如：

Q. This has to be the biggest ant-hill ever seen.

R. It has to be the same boulder that he sat upon so often.

基于以上对于当代英语中"have+（NP）+to+VP"结构的分析，可以选取雅兹科特提出的默认语义学作为分析框架，为现当代英语时期 NP_1+have+（NP_2）+to+VP 句式中的该结构的不同用法提供一个统一的、公式化的并合表征意义解释模式，如下图所示。

$$
\begin{array}{l}
\text{x t e} \\
[NP_1]_{CD}(x) \\
\varnothing\ (\ t\ ) \\
[ACC\triangle^n\ e/s]_{WS,\ CPI} \\
e/s : [x\ have\ NP_2\ to\ VP]_{WS}
\end{array}
$$

图 5　并合表征意义解释模式

根据事件或状态的具体特征，如说话人的推测、假设、允许、责任、委托、能力以及意志等不同的情态力量将 dy（dynamic）、de（deontic）、ep（epistemic）选择性带入公式中的 n。"have+（NP）+to+VP"结构的意向性特征和情态等级也可以用矢量来表示：

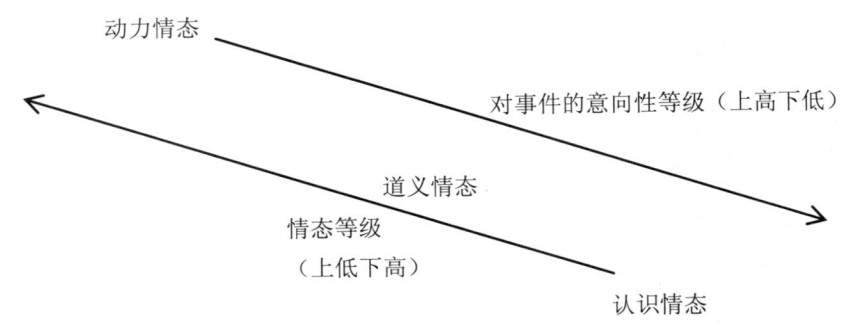

图 6　意向性特征和情态等级矢量

5. 总结

本文运用默认语义学意义解释模式，从历史语言学角度出发，对"have+（NP）+to+VP"结构在古英语时期、中古英语时期、现当代英语时期的语义意义、语用情态意义以及语义-语用意义进行系统的研究，揭示了语法结构的意义产生不能只从单一的语义或语用层面进行解释，而是要在默认语义学中并合表征模式下的语义-语用融合意义。通过搜集各个时期的文学作品以及 BNC 语料库中该结构的典型例句，分析该结构在整个语法化过程中的语义演变以及情态意义的发展。本文运用默认语义学理论验证了不同历史时期中该结构的语义意义（即默认意义）与语用意义（即动力情态意义、道义情态意义、认识情态意义），两种意义在"一般并合表征"模式下彼此融合，其定义应为毫无模糊性的并合表征。

类似这样的语法结构的意义研究也避开了学术界一直以来"语义或语用谁为主导"的争论。在并合表征模式下对不同阶段的"have+（NP）+to+VP"结构意义进行解释，可以看到语法结构的意义是由词汇意义、句子结构、语用推论、认知默认和社会文化默认五个因素共同作用的并合表征意义，是语义-语用融合意义。同时，该结构在语法化过程中的语义意义演变及语用情态意义的变化发展也为今后共时语言现象的研究提供了强有力的证据

以往学界对特定争议性结构的研究多从语料库、语法化及教学语法角度展开，研究其意义构成及演变。实际上，以往的意义解释模式不够科学，也不够严谨，结论并不具有很强的说服力。本文通过运用默认语义学理论，构建统一的并合表征意义解释模式，分别为古英语

时期、中古英语时期、现当代英语时期"have+(NP)+to+VP"结构的语义-语用层面动态意义提供强有力的解释模式，从而增强了研究的说服力与实用性。

参考文献

[1] BHATT R, 1998. Obligation and possession [J]. Papers from the UPenn/MIT roundtable on argument structure and aspect, MITWPL, 32: 21-40.

[2] BRINTON L J, 1991. The origin and development of quasimodal *have to* in English[R]. Workshop on the origin and development of verbal periphrases, Amsterdam:10th International Conference on Historical Linguistics (ICHL 10).

[3] FISCHER O, 1994. The development of quasi-auxiliaries in English and changes in word order[J]. Neophilologus, 78(1): 137.

[4] GRABEN P B, 2006. Pragmatic information in dynamic semantics[J]. Mind and matter, 4(2): 169-193.

[5] HANSEN B, 2017. What happens after grammaticalization? Post-grammaticalization processes in the area of modality [J]. Aspects of grammaticalization: (inter) subjectification and directionality, 257-280.

[6] HOPPER P J, TRAUGOTT E C, 2003. Grammaticalization[M]. Cambridge: Cambridge University Press.

[7] JACOBSSON B, 1994. Recessive and emergent uses of modal auxiliaries in English[J].English studies, 2:166-182.

[8] JANKOWSKI B, 2004. A transatlantic perspective of variation and change in English deontic modality[R]. Toronto: Working Papers in Linguistics.

[9] JAZCOLT K M, JAZCOLT K, 2005. Default semantics: foundations of a compositional theory of acts of communication[M]. Oxford:Oxford University Press.

[10] JAZCOLT K M, 2006. Futurity in default semantics[J]. Current research in the semantics/pragmatics Interface, 16: 471-492.

[11] JAZCOLT K M, 2006. Meaning merger: pragmatic inference, defaults, and compositionality[J].Intercultural pragmatics, 3(2): 195-212.

[12] LEHMANN C, 2015. Thoughts on grammaticalization[M]. Berlin: Language Science Press.

[13] LEVINSON S C, LEVINSON S, 1983. Pragmatics[M]. Cambridge: Cambridge University Press.

[14] NUYTS J, 2001. Subjectivity as an evidential dimension in epistemic modal expressions[J]. Journal of pragmatics, 33(3): 383-400.

[15] PALMER F R, 1979. Modality and the English modals[M]. New York: Longman.

[16] QUIRK R , GREENBAUM S, 1973. A concise grammar of contemporary English[M]. Boston: Houghton Mifflin Harcourt School.

[17] SPERBER D, WILSON D, 1986. Relevance: Communication and cognition[M]. New Jersey: Wiley and Blackwell.

[18] 林忠, 刘存伟, 2015. "X have Y"的功能解释: 认知参照点与主观化视角[J].外国语文, 31(4)：47-53.

[19] 冉永平, 2011. 当代语用学研究的跨学科多维视野[J]. 外语教学与研究, 43(5)：763-771，801.

[20] 谢应光, 2008. 英语现在完成体的认知阐释[J]. 天津外国语学院学报（6）：22-27.

[21] 赵学德, 王晴, 2009. 国外语法化理论探究——语法化的过程、本质特征和机制[J].西安外国语大学学报，17(3)：1-5.

[22] 张权, 李娟, 2006. 默认语义学对语义学、语用学界面的研究及其评价[J].上海外国语大学学报（1）：69-73.

从合作原则角度分析詹姆斯·乔伊斯《死者》中加布里埃尔的形象

王旭蓝

1. 《死者》的研究背景

詹姆斯·乔伊斯,爱尔兰作家,出生于1882年2月2日,20世纪最伟大的作家之一。《都柏林人》是詹姆斯·乔伊斯的代表作。《死者》作为其短篇小说集《都柏林人》的最后一篇,将整本书的情节推向高潮,詹姆斯·乔伊斯用复杂的语言形式以及大量的象征手法加深了读者理解文本的难度,充分体现了詹姆斯·乔伊斯的独创性与写作功底。学者对此篇给予了大量关注,研究范围包括写作技巧、叙事策略、死亡、功能文体分析、象征意义、精神顿悟和解构主义。

尽管已经有学者从语言学的角度对《死者》的文本进行了分析,但他们是以系统功能语法理论为基础,从及物性、语气和主谓结构来分析《死者》。此外,大多数学者认为詹姆斯·乔伊斯塑造加布里埃尔这个角色批判了以其为代表的都柏林人的麻木,认为他"回避关于社会政治、民族事业等意识形态的问题"(李依宸,2016),而本文则认为加布里埃尔是全文中唯一痛苦而清醒之人,他爱爱尔兰这个国家,这是他的祖国。同时,爱尔兰弥漫的死亡又麻木的气息又让他想要逃离这个国家。清醒地、痛苦地逃离并不是麻木的体现。加布里埃尔既想拥抱祖国,抚慰这个麻木又可怜的国家,又对现状暂时无法改变而感到痛苦,所以选择远远注视。其实,加布里埃尔是处于想要靠近与逃离祖国的状态之间,文中可见他的矛盾性。《死者》的内容呈现大多数是通过对人物的对话,辅之以动作、神态描写,表达出许多隐含意义,所以本文试图结合格莱斯的合作原则及会话含义理论,分析文中人物对话,并分析加布里埃尔对国家命运深刻关心但又主动选择远离的痛苦又清醒的知识分子形象。

在语用学理论中,1967年美国哲学家格莱斯在哈佛的演讲中首次提出著名的合作原则及会话含义理论。后来格莱斯发表《逻辑与会话》,再次提出合作原则。在日常对话中,说话双方为了使话语符合当前谈话目的,似乎遵循着某些不成文的原则,以使谈话顺利进行。合作原则包含四个范畴:数量原则、质量原则、关系原则和方式原则。

合作原则是使你所说的话语,在其所发生的阶段,符合你参与的谈话所公认的目标或方向(格莱斯,1975)。而在某些特定场合,说话者并不会完全遵守合作原则,交际也不会沿着当前谈话方向进行,而因为对合作原则的违反产生的隐含意义,被叫作"会话含义"。本文选取了《死者》中的人物对话并运用语用学中的合作原则对其进行分析,旨在揭示小说主人公加布里埃尔的内心活动以及情感变化,帮助读者更好理解其形象。

2. 违反《死者》中对话的合作原则

迫于宗教压力与英国殖民统治,20世纪的第二个十年和三十年代的爱尔兰社会一团混乱,毫无生气，下层民众麻木浑噩。都柏林作为爱尔兰的中心，中下层的社会氛围更是死气沉沉。詹姆斯·乔伊斯受父亲的影响，对爱尔兰有着强烈的民族情绪，面对死气沉沉的社会、麻木的爱尔兰人民，他想要表达自己的不满，试图唤醒爱尔兰民众。

在《死者》中，主人公加布里埃尔出生于爱尔兰，接受的是欧洲大陆先进文化的熏陶，这在某种程度上加强了加布里埃尔对割裂现实的认识。原本出生于爱尔兰的他，接受了来自殖民地的先进教育，他深刻地认识到爱尔兰处于水深火热之中，感受到城市的麻木与瘫痪，在某种程度上，这是加布里埃尔想要逃离的原因之一。加布里埃尔接受先进教育，作为大学讲师、《每日邮报》的撰写者，是名副其实的知识分子。面对瘫痪的爱尔兰社会，加布里埃尔本该背负解放爱尔兰社会的责任。可是面对精神瘫痪的民众，他清醒地知道这是多么地难。所以在关怀爱尔兰的同时，他又企图逃离爱尔兰，远离失望，远离民众的冷漠麻木与社会的生气全无。

《死者》一共有三处场景，宴会前与莉莉的寒暄、宴会中客人之间的交谈和宴会后与格丽塔的交谈。先前提到加布里埃尔接受过欧洲先进文化教育，这在某种程度上会影响加布里埃尔对欧洲的感知，同时也会让他对爱尔兰的瘫痪现状的感知更加深刻，让其产生逃离爱尔兰的决心。他对爱尔兰的关怀体现在对待仆人莉莉的态度上。他询问莉莉是否还在读书、婚期是否已定。麻木已久的莉莉似乎接受不了这样的关心，暗讽他。在宴会上，他积极地修改自己的演讲稿，害怕讲稿内容超出听众的认知水平，从此举来看，加布里埃尔在为唤醒民众作出努力。当宴会进行时，他与同为知识分子的爱尔兰民族拥护人士艾弗斯交谈，却暴露自己内心脆弱的一面，那就是他内心是亲近，身体上却选择逃离祖国爱尔兰。当艾弗斯询问他是否去高尔韦旅行时，加布里埃尔回答只会去法国、比利时，而不会选择回祖国爱尔兰看望。加布里埃尔的特殊身份使他的性格复杂多变。面对瘫痪的爱尔兰社会，他内心深处滋生出焦虑与不安，渴望为爱尔兰民族与社会作出奉献，他逃避现实、避重就轻、紧张。文中加布里埃尔清醒而痛苦，想要为爱尔兰社会的觉醒奉献力量，却一边又要防止自己堕落、变得麻木，于是想要逃离爱尔兰。本文运用语用学的合作原则，对《死者》中人物对话进行分析，通过剖析语言来分析加布里埃尔内心活动与情感变化，理解他清醒并非麻木，关怀爱尔兰但又选择身体上的逃离，剖析其内心矛盾，体会詹姆斯·乔伊斯的写作艺术。

3. 加布里埃尔的清醒与逃离

3.1 加布里埃尔对爱尔兰的关怀

例1

"O, Mr.Conroy," said Lily to Gabriel when she opened the door for him, "Miss Kate and Miss Julia thought you were never coming. Good-night, Mrs.Conroy."

"I'll engage they did,"said Gabriel, "but they forget that my wife here takes three mortal hours to dress herself."(James Joyce, 1914）

合作原则中的数量原则：一是提供当前谈话所需要的信息量，二是所提供的信息不得多于当前谈话所需要的信息。这里违反了合作原则的数量原则的第二条准则：所提供的信息不得多于当前谈话所需要的信息。宴会即将开始，加布里埃尔夫妇迟迟未来。女佣莉莉看见加布里埃尔夫妇终于来到宴会，向加布里埃尔寒暄问候并且提到姨母以为他不会来了，加布里埃尔本作为客人，本寒暄回应即可，不必向莉莉说明迟到的理由，但是他向莉莉解释了迟到理由。从这一例子可以看出加布里埃尔非常有礼貌，平易近人。通过对莉莉的态度，可以观察他对爱尔兰人民的态度，他企图以一种最平常的口气询问莉莉的近况。

例 2

"O, Lily," he said, thrusting it into her hands, "it's Christmas, isn't it? Just...here's a little..."

…

"O no, sir!"cried the girl, following him. "Really, sir, I wouldn't take it."(James Joyce, 1914）

加布里埃尔原本是出于对莉莉的关心，才询问莉莉的私事，但是莉莉对他冷嘲热讽。他为了防止莉莉的自尊心受到伤害，借口说是因为圣诞节的到来想给莉莉小费。此时，加布里埃尔想要给莉莉小费来弥补自己的话带来的伤害。但加布里埃尔原本是出于关心问候，却被莉莉暗讽一番。他不仅没有解释，也没有生气，甚至还感到不安，反思自己的所作所为。加布里埃尔在待人接物方面的敏感与不安，正说明了其内心柔软与对他人深切的关怀。合作原则中的质量原则：一是不能提供自知是虚假的信息，二是不能提供缺乏证据的信息。这里加布里埃尔违反了质量原则的第一条准则：不能提供自知是虚假的信息。加布里埃尔给莉莉小费是出于同情莉莉，但是他编了一个自知的谎言让莉莉接受了小费。

例 3

"Quite right, Gabriel, quite right," she said. "You can't be too careful."

"But as for Gretta there," said Gabriel, "She'd walk home in the snow if she were let." （James Joyce, 1914）

当姨母夸赞加布里埃尔细心时，加布里埃尔并没有回应姨母的夸奖，而是将话题带到格丽塔身上：如果允许的话，格丽塔会在大雪里走回家。合作原则中的关系原则：不能说与话题无关的话。这里加布里埃尔违反了关系原则。他本该回应姨母的赞美，但是他提到格丽塔，将自己与格丽塔进行对比。在加布里埃尔的话语中，格丽塔是会在雪中行走之人，这样的行为让人无法理解。格丽塔的灵魂仿佛与外面的漫天大雪融为一体，冰冷麻木，所以在雪中行走也不觉冰冷难耐。格丽塔算是众多精神已经麻木的爱尔兰人中的一员。说出这句话时，加布里埃尔语气有些平静，对于麻木的妻子，他在关怀中加入了一份体谅与包容。

3.2　加布里埃尔对爱尔兰的逃离

例 1

"She's from Connacht, isn't she?"

"Her people are," said Gabriel shortly.（James Joyce, 1914)

合作原则中的方式准则：一是避免晦涩难懂，二是避免歧义，三是简洁，四是有条理。在宴会上，加布里埃尔与艾弗斯跳舞。艾弗斯是爱尔兰的狂热拥护者。她提出邀请格丽塔暑假去奥兰群岛玩耍，并向加布里埃尔询问格丽塔是否来自康纳特时，加布里埃尔本该直接回答是或者不是，但是他回答了一句极为模糊的话"她的家乡在那边"。这里加布里埃尔违反了合作原则中的方式准则的第二条准则：避免歧义。他并没有直接回答是或者不是，而是模糊地回答，并没给出确切答案。由此可见，加布里埃尔内心深处是逃避谈论爱尔兰的。面对瘫痪的爱尔兰社会，他无法改变，于是对问题避重就轻地回答。而他之前对于莉莉的行为，体现了他对于爱尔兰民众的关怀与爱，但是当艾弗斯提到爱尔兰这片土地时，加布里埃尔是回避的。面对艾弗斯的诘难，加布里埃尔非常羞愧，但是也并不能改变他想远离爱尔兰的想法。

例 2

"And haven't you your own language to keep in touch with—Irish?" asked Miss Ivors.

"Well," said Gabriel, "if it comes to that, you know, Irish is not any my language."(James Joyce, 1914)

在宴会上，艾弗斯质问布里埃尔难道没有自己的语言，加布里埃尔回答自己不说爱尔兰语——这明显违背了合作原则中的质量原则：不能提供自知是虚假的信息。加布里埃尔出生于爱尔兰，却不承认爱尔兰语是自己的母语。其实，加布里埃尔是面对瘫痪麻木的爱尔兰社会，尽管自己学识渊博，但也束手无策只能看着爱尔兰瘫痪，只能逃避这一现实，极力撇清自己与祖国爱尔兰的关系。这样看来，加布里埃尔仿佛是爱尔兰的"叛徒"，毫无疑问，加布里埃尔的内心非常煎熬。"远离国土"这个动作显得他不近人情，但是这个行为也是他心怀爱尔兰的证明，因为不忍看见破碎的国家，也为了自己不身陷囹圄，他选择回避谈论爱尔兰，也不去探访这片国土。

例 3

"Of course I was. Didn't you see me? What row had you with Molly Ivors?"

"No row. Why? Did she say so?" (James Joyce, 1914)

艾弗斯羞辱加布里埃尔为"西不列颠人"之后，格丽塔问起加布里埃尔是否和艾弗斯吵架。加布里埃尔回答说没有，但是他又追问"她说的吗？"这里加布里埃尔违反了合作原则中的数量原则：所提供的信息不得多于当前谈话所需要的信息。加布里埃尔被称作"西不列颠人"，并因此非常难堪与屈辱。在艾弗斯看来，加布里埃尔是一个反叛者，背叛了自己的祖国。加布里埃尔被人误会，但无法为自己的行为言说，因为一切的证据似乎都指明他是爱尔兰的背叛者。当格丽塔询问加布里埃尔是否与艾弗斯产生争论时，加布里埃尔回复说没有。这里加布里埃尔为了维护自己的尊严，说了明知是谎言的话，违反了合作原则中的质量原则：不能提供自知是虚假的信息。从这里可以看出布里埃尔确实是想逃离祖国的，但是这不是麻木，而是清醒。因为过于清醒，他选择离开可能会带给他失望的、破碎的、死亡的爱尔兰。作为一个知识分子，他应该将唤醒社会作为自己的使命，这点他也非常清楚。但或许正是因为责任的重大，或是为了使自己不牵连其中，他选择逃离爱尔兰。

4. 结束语

本文从语用学的角度，利用合作原则及会话含义理论分析詹姆斯·乔伊斯的《死者》中的人物对话，旨在探索主人公加布里埃尔的内心活动以及情感变化，揭示其心理和性格特征，把握其形象。通过对作品中人物对话的分析，小说主人公加布里埃尔是一个清醒而痛苦的知识分子。他关怀着瘫痪的爱尔兰社会，爱这里的民众，但他承受不了拯救爱尔兰失败或者看着爱尔兰继续堕落的后果，所以他选择逃离爱尔兰。

参考文献

[1] GRICE H P, 1975. Logic and conversation[M]. Oxford: Oxford University Press.

[2] 胡向华, 2008. 从乔伊斯的《都柏林人》论抒情式短篇小说的艺术形式特色[J]. 天津外国语学院学报, 2: 58-63.

[3] 胡壮麟, 姜望琪, 2002. 语言学高级教程[M]. 北京：北京大学出版社.

[4]李依宸，2016. 知识分子的失声、狭隘和流亡——论乔伊斯《死者》中知识分子的抉择[J]. 名作欣赏（24）：127-129.

[5]刘鲁蓉，朱宾忠，2018. 顿悟的徒劳——论乔伊斯《死者》中男主人公的杂交身份[J]. 合肥工业大学学报(社会科学版)，32(1)：71-74.

[6]吕云，2008. 都柏林人精神状态的形象描述——析乔伊斯《死者》中的精神瘫痪及其象征手法[J]. 理论学刊（7）：121-123.

[7]姜望琪，2003. 当代语用学[M]. 北京：北京大学出版社.

[8]王健平，2016. 论合作原则及其准则[J]. 华南师范大学学报（社会科学版）（1）：182-188，192.

[9]徐晓莹，2009. 对《傲慢与偏见》会话含义的语用学分析[J]. 学术交流（11）：147-149.

「Nスギル」中「スギル」的语义指向研究

崔筱玉

1. 引言

日语中「～スギル」常常接在形容词、形容动词和动词后表示某种性质的过剩（影山太郎，1993），例如「暑すぎる」「綺麗すぎる」「食べすぎる」。除此之外，我们还经常可以看到「～スギル」接在名词后面的现象，「～スギル」的这种名词接续属于一种边缘的用法（中村嗣郎，2005），但近年来在口语或网络用语中经常出现。本文将「～スギル」的名词接续表示为「Nスギル」。

「Nスギル」强调前方名词的某些性质的过剩，但名词的语义通常具有多个层面，「スギル」所指向的并非名词语义的所有层面，而是根据前面接续的名词的不同有选择的指向特定语义，比如：

例1　a.りんごすぎる　　b.神すぎる　　c.タイプすぎる

以上三句中「スギル」都强调前方的名词的某些性质的过剩，但所指的语义皆不同：a. 句中的「スギル」指向名词"苹果"的比喻意义，表示很像苹果的形状；b. 句中「スギル」指向名词"神"的情感意义，表示非常厉害，含有褒义；c. 中「スギル」指向名词「タイプ」的联想意义，表示非常符合自己的喜好，这里根据听话人的理解和认知，联想出的语义各不相同。

可见，名词不同，「Nスギル」中「スギル」的语义指向也不同，因此有必要对具体的语义指向进行解释。本文以「Nスギル」为研究对象，分析「スギル」的语义指向。本文首先介绍了一些相关的先行研究；其次，以英国语义学家利奇的语义七分法等相关研究为理论基础，提出了在「Nスギル」研究中名词的语义类型的再分类；最后，结合语料库中的例子分析了「Nスギル」的五种语义指向。

2. 先行研究

「～スギル」相关的先行研究有很多，但多数研究都着眼于动词、形容词、形容动词接续的基本用法，「Nスギル」作为其边缘用法，相关的先行研究较少。佐藤らな（2019）对于「Nスギル」句法的意思进行了论述。佐藤主张「Nスギル」句法的意思是把从"名词"的百科知识中推导出的特定性质作为焦点，表示其过剩。

例2　天使すぎる（佐藤，2019）

比如例2中，佐藤表示该句焦点集中在天使的百科知识中的"可爱"，表示该性质过剩。且迄今为止，一直有学者主张将日语的名词看成是名词和形容动词的连续体（加藤重広，2015），「Nスギル」句法就是其中之一。佐藤（2020）对「Nスギル」的句法进行了进一步的分析，提出名词此时带有程度的性质，主张名词通过焦点移动来表示其性质。

佐藤阐述了「Nスギル」句法成立的原理是通过焦点移动，但名词具有多种性质，该文章中没有指明「Nスギル」中「スギル」可以指向哪些具体的性质。比如例2中，在没有上下文的前提下，日本人通常会将「天使すぎる」理解为"非常可爱"，但是很少有人会将它理解为"非常像天使"，具有"+头顶有光环，+有翅膀，+可以飞"的外延意义。因此有必要进一步说明「Nスギル」的语义指向。

中村嗣郎（2005）对于「スギル」句法的书面语实例进行了细致分析，其中关于「Nスギル」，中村提出，相较于「スギル」直接连接名词，名词短语的接续更多，接续名词短语时，「スギル」修饰的并不是名词，而是修饰的名词的要素。

例3　いい人すぎる（中村嗣郎，2005）

例3中，中村提出「すぎる」修饰的成分是「いい」，并不能说「*人すぎる」。

吴伟丽（2018）提出，「Nすぎる」是语义兼容性的体现，名词作为「すぎる」前项时，表示「Nのような性状」的"形状量"的过剩。同时，吴伟丽对其中的N进行了限制，提出不具有性状性且无法表达说话主体主观性评价的名词，则无法成为「すぎる」的前项。

首先，中村（2005）没有对「Nスギル」句法直接进行分析，认为其占比很小，但语料库中仍然存在「Nスギル」的接续。根据中纳言的BCCWJ检索，「Nスギル」共有1740例，且根据历时研究，「Nスギル」的接续现象至少在80年代就已出现，且比例有所增加，因此应该对名词接续的现象给予重视。其次，吴伟丽将「Nスギル」的语义解释为「Nのような性状」，也没有解释「Nスギル」中「スギル」的具体指向问题。

因此，本文将在佐藤らな的基础上，结合语料库中的使用实例，解释「Nスギル」中「スギル」的几种具体的语义指向。

3. 语义类型

研究的角度不同，对语义类型的分类也不同，对「Nスギル」的语义解释，本文主张：首先需要在现有的理论基础之上，对「Nスギル」研究中的名词的语义进行再分类；其次根据名词的语义种类和语境综合判断「スギル」的具体的语义指向。

词汇的语义分类方式按照不同的标准有不同的分类方式。利奇（1974）在《语义学》中将语义分为7种，除主题意义之外，可以分为两大类：理性意义和联想意义。其中联想意义可以细分为内涵意义、社会意义、情感意义、反映意义和搭配意义。其中理性意义也称概念意义，是指关于逻辑、认知和外延内容的意义（胡壮麟，2021），理性意义是静态的，是词汇相对稳定的部分，可以说是一个词的核心意思。比如"秋天"这个词是相对于春天、夏天、冬天这些其他的季节而获得的理性意义。联想意义和理性意义相比，具有不确定性以及可变化性，一个词语的联想意义会因语言使用者的不同背景及语境的变化而变化。联想意义中最重要的是内涵意义，内涵意义是通过语言所指所传达的意义（胡壮麟，2021）。比如「秋すぎる」这句中，「秋」指的是有秋天特色的。不同国家的人所联想的内涵意义也不同。

关于语义的分类，除利奇的词汇七分法外，以传统逻辑为基础，词项的意义还可以分为两大类：外延意义和内涵意义。其中外延意义指一种语言基本的概念性的意义，而内涵意义是与外延意义相关的情感意义的总和，与文化、情感、态度有关。现代汉语中将词义分为概念义和色彩义，其中概念义表示与概念有关的意义部分，色彩义包括感情色彩、语体色彩、形象色彩、搭配义和文化义。另外，由本义还可以派生出比喻义。

对于词汇的分类，不同的学者主张不同的分类方式，本文在国内外有代表性的研究的基础上，在「Nスギル」语义研究方面，对其中名词的词汇意义进行了重新划分，以传统逻辑分类为基础，分为两大类：理性意义和内涵意义。理性意义分为外延意义和由外延意义派生出的比喻意义，内涵意义分为联想意义、属性意义和情感意义。此种分类方式并非基于逻辑关系，所以各意义之间可以有重叠的部分。

4. 语义指向

根据以上所述的语义分类，在「Nスギル」组合中，「スギル」指向的主要是前方接续名词的外延意义、联想意义、属性意义和情感意义和比喻意义。

4.1 语义指向外延意义

外延意义是指一种语言基本的概念意义，是字典释义中包含的意义，具有高度的概括意义。在「Nスギル」中所指向的是具有代表性的义素，具体采用哪种义素由语境决定。这类名词的语义中往往包含形容词类语素，「スギル」的指向焦点是其中的形容词类语素，表示其性质过剩。因为形容词类语素本身具有程度性特征，所以语义上可以和具有程度性修饰的「スギル」进行搭配。这类名词主要分为两类：一是形态素上表现出形容词性语素和名词性语素的普通名词，比如「大物、美人、気分屋、低額、正義」等，以及同时具有形容动词性质的名词，比如「豪華、高尚、無謀、贅沢、高級」等；二是形态素上没有表现，但是语义中具有形容词性质的名词，比如「草、イケメン、くそ、幸せ」等。其中「草」在网络用语中已经失去原义"草"，义为"有趣"，因此义素中含有「面白い」的形容词性质，由「スギル」强调其外延意义，义为"非常有趣"。

例 4　江川とはあまり話をしたことがなかったなあ。なにしろあいつは大物すぎて—。（BCCWJ 阿部牧郎『悲しまぬおれたち』）

例 5　ねえ、先生。あなたは紳士すぎますわ。確かにお花はきれいですけど、まったく必要ありませんのよ。（BCCWJ マーガレット・P・ブリッジズ（著）/春野丈伸（訳）『わが愛しのワトスン』）

例 6　美人か、女として魅力があるといいけど。彼女は、良妻賢母すぎて、面白くないですよ。まあ、家事とか育児をまかすのならいいんでしょうが。（BCCWJ 山村美紗『宮崎旅行の殺人』）

例 4 中的「スギル」焦点在于「大物」的「大」，例 5、例 6 中的「スギル」焦点在于「紳士」的「紳」和「賢母」的「賢」。

4.2 语义指向联想意义

这类名词以普通名词为主，此类名词本身具有鲜明的特征，并且被多数人或群体所熟知，当这类名词接续「スギル」时，「スギル」的指向焦点不在于词汇的外延意义，而指向听话人对词汇的联想意义。因此，指向联想意义的「Nスギル」取决于听话人对该名词的认知，个体不同、群体不同，所指向的语义也不同。比如指人的「俺、タイプ、マイペース、先生、日本人」等，其中「俺、タイプ、マイペース」是关于个人的认知，「先生、日本人」是群体的认知。再比如指地点的「東京、日本、中国」等，指物或者时间的「春、夏、秋、冬、朝、

太陽」等，其中中文"太秋天了"和日语「秋すぎる」在各自语境下听话人会分别联想到和本国文化相关的意向，而联想到的意向并不完全相同。

这里需要特殊说明的是，「Nスギル」还有一个语义是"过了……（时间/地点）"，而不是表示前方名词性质的过剩。这种语义是基于「スギル」单词的原义，"过了……（时间/地点）"的语义用法不在本文的研究范围之内。

例 7　治安はいいと思いますが、私には田舎すぎて合いません。お金を貯めて早く引っ越したいと思っています。

例 8　老けて見えるってゆうか、高校生らしくないんです……大人すぎてしまうんです。

例7中「田舎すぎて」义为"太乡下了"，在日本人的联想中，这往往是指治安好、安静且每个人的经济水平都是正常水准的情况；若是放在中文语境下的"太乡下了"，往往给人的印象就是简陋的平房，且指大多数人的经济水平比较低下的情况。因此，由于文化不同，即使是相同的词汇，指向的联想意义也不同。例8中「大人すぎる」在中日语境下的联想意义中都有稳重的感觉，除此之外，日语的语境中还会多出一种西装革履、会看氛围的联想意义。

4.3　语义指向属性意义

语义指向属性意义的名词的内涵意义中通常存在有代表性的属性意义。当与「スギル」搭配时，其指向焦点在于该名词中内涵意义中的属性，而并非指向其内涵意义，比如「迷子、病気、名探偵、沼、インドア」等。以「迷子すぎる」为例，「迷子」的原义是"走失的孩子""迷路""下落不明"等，当与「スギル」搭配时，其语义指向的焦点在于主语拥有了迷路的属性，义为「すごく迷子になっている」，表示说话人最近具有"经常迷路"的属性，而不指代说话人找不到家等具体含义。

例 9　……名探偵すぎるって。

例 10　ニコ本当に沼すぎる。

例9中，「名探偵すぎる」中的「名探偵」的内涵意义中具有解决问题快、能够发现细节、解决难题的能力高等属性，当与「スギル」搭配时，语义指向其内涵意义中的这些属性，而不是指外延意义中的有名的解决案件的侦探。例10中的「沼すぎる」作为网络用语被大量使用。其中的名词「沼」原义为"沼泽""池塘"，其内涵意义中有容易深陷其中的属性，日语口语中源于其内涵义的属性，产生了「沼にハマる」这个短语，表示"非常沉迷……"。在「沼すぎる」搭配中，语义指向的也是「沼」内涵义中的容易深陷其中的属性，义为「すごくハマって抜け出せない」。

4.4　语义指向情感意义

利奇的词汇意义七分法中，情感意义是关于讲话人或者文章写作者的个人感情，包括他对听他说话的人和他所谈论的事物的态度的意义（胡壮麟，2021）。情感意义可以分为褒义、贬义和中性。在「Nスギル」中，语义指向情感意义时，接续的名词的性质如果是中性，常常转为褒义或贬义，从而拥有形容词性意义，可以和「スギル」进行语义上的搭配。比如「王子すぎる」「神すぎる」，「王子、神」本是中性词，和「スギル」搭配时，由中性词转变为褒义，表示褒义性质的过剩，分别义为「王子のようにかっこいい、本当にすごすぎる」。而中性词后接「スギル」也可以转为消极或贬义含义，如：

例 11　あるけど、この辺のは末端すぎるなあ。やっぱり食道街のセンター・ビルからエレベーターに乗った方が早いよ。（BCCWJ 筒井康隆『最後の伝令』）

例 12　私は注意深く黙っていた。私にとっては話題がヘビーすぎてどう言ったらいいか分からなかったのだ。（BCCWJ 山本文緒『紙婚式』）

例 11 和例 12 中，中性名词「末端、ヘビー」后加上「すぎる」后都转换为了贬义词，起到了消极描述的效果。例 11 中「末端すぎる」有「便利ではない」含义。例 12 中名词「ヘビー」原义为"重，大"，而「ヘビーすぎる」义为"太沉重了"，所以后句表明"不知道说什么才好"，具有消极含义。

4.5　语义指向比喻意义

名词相比于形容词和形容动词，具有更高的描述性。在语用学的角度上，形容词和形容动词的描述性都是抽象的，而名词的所指的对象是具象的，且一个名词具有多种性质，在表达上可以起到语义补偿的作用。「N スギル」中「スギル」指向比喻意义时，前面接续的名词往往是所指物的具体名词，而不是具有形容动词词性的名词，这类情况常常在口语表达或者网络用语中出现。且这类名词通常具有特征性，如外形、气味、个性等。在和「スギル」组合时，前方的名词充当喻体，指向其比喻义。比如「リンゴ、イチゴ、犬、猫」，其中「りんごすぎる」通常修饰像苹果性状一样的其他物品，义为「りんごの形が似ている」，「イチゴすぎる」常用于修饰某物很像草莓的形状，或者是味道很像草莓，本体都是草莓之外的物品。具体指向哪种比喻意义需要结合语境，通过语境激发其相对应的比喻意义。指向比喻意义和指向联想意义的不同在于，指向比喻意义的名词一定是被群体所认知的，并且同一群体对它的认知基本相同，而指向联想意义的名词往往会因个体、群体的不同而有不同的语义。

例 13　思っていた以上に、と言うか完全にイチゴすぎてコーラどこ行った感がやべえ。

例 14　差し色がイチゴすぎんだよな。

例 13 中，「イチゴすぎて」通过语境激发出"草莓的味道"这一比喻意义，义为"这个可乐非常像草莓的味道"。例 14 中，通过前面的「差し色」的主语，将特征定为颜色，义为"很像草莓的颜色"。

例 15　撫でられる前メテユヒョンのこと見つめてるのに撫でられた瞬間に目閉じるの犬すぎるし可愛すぎる。

例 16　このおはるちゃん、猫すぎる。

例 15 中是描述被摸头时闭眼的动作非常像「犬」，通过比喻意义表达后半句的「可愛すぎる」。例 16 中，描述的是女生的样子和动作和猫很像，日语用「猫すぎる」来表达比喻意义。

5. 结语

本文聚焦于「N スギル」句法，结合语料库中的实例，分析了「スギル」的名词语义指向，得出以下结论：「N スギル」中「スギル」指向的是前方名词的性质过剩，前方接续的名词不同，语义指向亦不同。「N スギル」中「スギル」的语义指向主要可分为五类。第一，「スギル」指向名词的外延意义，这类语义指向最为常用。搭配的名词中常常包含形容词类语素，语义指向的焦点是其中的形容词类语素。第二「スギル」指向名词的联想意义，这类名词被多数人或者群体熟知，群体不同，联想的意义也有所不同。第三，语义指名词的属性意义，这类名词的内涵含义中具有代表性的属性，「スギル」的语义指向焦点是该名词内涵意义中的属性，

表示主语带有其属性。第四，语义指向情感意义，此类名词的褒义或贬义需要结合语境进行判断，若名词是中性的，常常会转为褒义或贬义。第五，语义指向比喻意义，这类名词通常具有特征性的属性，如外形、气味、个性等，因此占比较低，在和「スギル」组合时，前方的名词充当喻体，语义指向其比喻义。此种语义指向更常在口语和网络用语中出现，相较于形容词和形容动词在表达上可以起到语义补偿的作用。

参考文献

[1] 加藤重広, 2015. 形容動詞から見る品詞体系（特集品詞論の現代的意義）[J]. 日本語文法, 158（2）: 48-64.

[2] 影山太郎, 1993. 文法と語形成[M]. 東京：ひつじ書房.

[3] 中村嗣郎, 2005.「すぎる」構文：書き言葉における実例の分析[J]. コミュニケーション科学, 3(22): 139-177.

[4] 佐藤らな, 2019. 天使すぎるアイドルは何が過剰なのか：N すぎる構文の意味[J]. 東京大学言語学論集（41）: 279-293.

[5] 佐藤らな, 2020. X すぎる構文の考察：天使すぎるはなぜ言えるのか[C]//日本認知言語学会. 日本認知言語学会論文集. 東京：日本認知言語学会（20）: 67-78.

[6] 胡壮麟, 2021. 语言学教程[M]. 北京：北京大学出版社.

[7] 利奇, 1987. 语义学[M]. 李瑞华, 译. 上海：上海外语教育出版社.

[8] 吴伟丽, 2018.「～スギル」的语义范畴及其语义指向类型[J]. 日语学习与研究（4）: 17-25.

《白鹿原》中陕西方言行为动词的及物性系统研究

刘昭宁

1. 引言

  《白鹿原》是陈忠实历时六年创作出的长篇小说，全书约 50 万字，一经出版，这部沉甸甸的小说就席卷大江南北。这部小说以白嘉轩的一生为线索讲述了白、鹿两大家族祖孙三代的爱恨纠葛。故事缘起于我国陕西关中地区白鹿原的白鹿村，故事发展时间横跨清朝末年至20 世纪七八十年代。陈忠实于《白鹿原》扉页引用了巴尔扎克的一句话："小说是一个民族的秘史。"以寻根主题为宗旨，《白鹿原》尽其所能地描绘了陕西关中平原上的风土人情，这不仅归功于其紧凑生动的故事情节，其中地道贴切的陕西方言更是发挥了不可小觑的作用。本文聚焦米利娟、许巧枝老师于国家级大学生创新创业训练项目"《白鹿原》中的陕西方言词汇研究"中总结的最具关中地区方言特色、关中人在生活中使用频率较高的 29 个行为动词（米利娟、许巧枝，2022），以韩礼德的系统功能语言学中的及物性系统理论为框架，探讨其中方言动词的使用意义，从而帮助我们进一步理解陈忠实的写作技巧与语言使用风格。

2. 理论基础

  系统功能语法是英国语言学家韩礼德于 20 世纪 60 年代提出的一种语法模型，该理论认为语言研究应该以语言的用途和语境为研究重点。语言的基本功能是使我们的经验有意义，并表现出我们的社会关系。据此，韩礼德提出了语言具有的三种元功能：概念功能，人际功能以及语篇功能，这三大功能构成了一个统一体，缺一不可。其中，概念功能就是由及物性系统实现的。韩礼德（Halliday，1994）将及物性系统定义为"能够将经验世界建构为可操控的过程类型集的系统"。及物性系统又进一步被划分为六个子系统：物质过程、行为过程、心智过程、言语过程、关系过程以及存在过程。韩礼德指出：动作过程、心理过程和关系过程是及物性系统中最基本的过程。一个过程可能由三部分组成：过程本身，过程中的参与者以及与过程有关的环境成分。物质过程主要指动作过程，牵涉到动作者（actor）和目标（goal）；心智过程主要指心理活动过程，牵涉到感觉者（senser）和现象（phenomenon）；关系过程是表明各个实体之间的关系的过程，是有关实体的性质、状况的过程，牵涉到识别（identifying）和归属（attributive）。在这三大过程之间，还有三个过程，即行为过程（behavioral process）、言语过程（verbal process）和存在过程（existential process）。行为过程是有关生命体生理行为的过程，如呼吸、咳嗽、微笑等；言语过程是说的过程，包括所有有意义的符号交换；存在过程是有关事物的存在或发生的过程。及物性分析始于过程小句识别，"小句是（潜在地）以一个动词词组为中心的语言的延伸"（Halliday，1994）。本文将从及物系统的六个子系统出发，从各个子系统的参与者以及环境成分角度进行例证分析。

3. 研究过程

3.1 语料整理

《白鹿原》作为一部记录了半个多世纪历史的长篇叙事小说，讲述了各色人物的不同人生以及他们之间错综复杂的关系，没有深厚的文学功底是难以做到的（刘春藤、马东峰，2022）。因此，我们极有必要对其书写话语进行深入分析。本文选取了人民文学出版社于2012年出版的《白鹿原》20周年荣誉纪念版作为研究对象，这个版本较为完整地还原了1993年初版的《白鹿原》内容，用词更加贴近陈忠实先生的初始风格。笔者自建小型语料库，总形符数为463687个，从及物性系统分析其中的陕西方言行为动词。

3.2 研究问题

通过检索前人文献，笔者发现，《白鹿原》中的陕西关中方言是该书的一大研究热点，但大多数从文学角度探析写作语言对于叙事建构的作用，从语言学角度研究方言写作的却少之又少。因此，本文希望借助韩礼德的系统功能语法，主要回答以下两个问题：（1）《白鹿原》中的29个代表性方言动词的出现频率以及分布情况如何？（2）这些方言动词从及物性系统的角度来看表达了何种意义？

3.3 研究步骤

本文主要采用 Antconc（Version 4.2.0）语料库分析软件，首先通过词表检索功能，确定29个特色行为动词的出现频率；然后参考关键词的搭配、索引等检索功能，确定这些关键词的发生语境，进行人工识别并标注该行为动词所体现的及物性过程，统计各类及物性过程的出现频率以及分布情况，并选取其中具有代表性的作为叙述例证。

4.《白鹿原》中的代表性陕西方言行为动词的及物性系统研究

4.1《白鹿原》中的代表性陕西方言行为动词出现频率及分布情况

《白鹿原》作为叙事长篇，动词的出现频率极高。根据米利娟、许巧枝老师的《〈白鹿原〉中的陕西方言词汇研究》，共有29个行为动词最具关中地区方言特色（米利娟、许巧枝，2022），分别是："哐""谝""弹嫌""熬活""圪蹴""浪""捋码""擩草""拾掇""跫摸""撒滑""绞水""跋拉""箍""呷""料就""捐""悦意""整饬""苦""撂""蹾""抻""剋""足来""挨挫""掼""操""惜耐"。使用 Antconc（Version 4.2.0）的关键词检索功能分别检索这29个代表性行为动词的出现频率，可以得出如下统计结果，如表1所示。

表1 29个代表性行为动词的出现频率

词语	出现频率	词语	出现频率
撂	51	跫摸	5
箍	30	呷	5
蹾	28	苦	5

（续表）

词语	出现频率	词语	出现频率
熬活	24	掼	4
拾掇	22	操	4
哐	21	跛拉	3
谝	14	整饬	3
悦意	14	圪蹴	2
掮	13	擩草	2
弹嫌	10	撇滑	1
抻	10	剋	1
浪	7	趸来	1
绞水	7	挨挫	1
料就	6	惜耐	1
捋码	5		

通过对表 1 中的 29 个动词进行归类，笔者发现：属于物质过程的共有 9 个，分别为擩、熬活、捋码、擩草、绞水、跛拉、蹴、趸来、挨挫；属于行为过程的共有 13 个，分别为哐、圪蹴、浪、拾掇、趸摸、撇滑、箍、呷、掮、整饬、抻、掼、操；表现心智过程的有 4 个，分别为：弹嫌、料就、悦意、惜耐；谝和剋两个动词表现了言语过程；苦体现的是存在过程；这组动词中没有表现关系过程的表达，如图 1 所示。

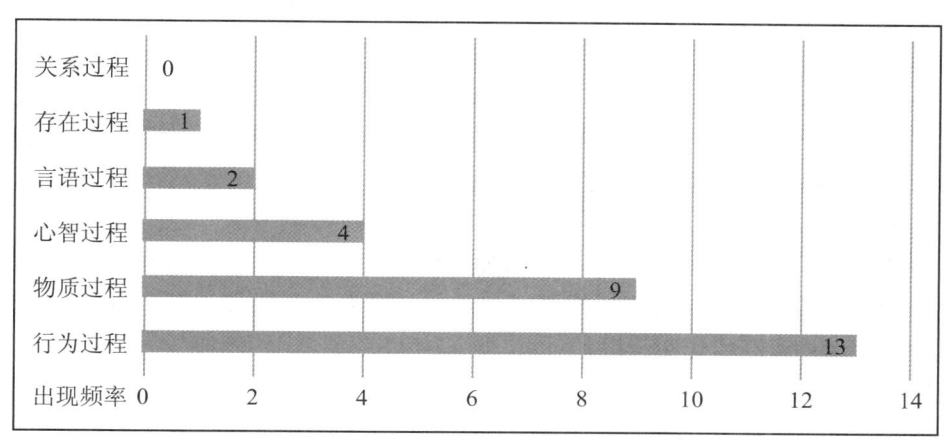

图 1 《白鹿原》中代表性陕西方言动词分布情况

通过第一组统计数据可以看出，表示行动的单字出现频率较高，统计结果中的前三位甚至都是单字的行为动词，这体现了百姓日用的关中方言简洁有力，这是千百年来百姓智慧的结晶，生动形象，意蕴无穷。柱状图显示，表示行为过程的动词在这 29 个方言动词中占比最高，真实再现了当时关中百姓的生活状态，体现了当时的广大农民群众仍以体力劳动为主，而这组词中没有体现关系过程的词语，说明叙事文学中的关中方言使用更多表示日常起居的行为词语以推进剧情发展、描绘人物形象，文中对于关系属性大多仍沿用普通话的表述。

4.2 从及物性系统的角度看方言动词的内在意义

（1）行为过程分析

韩礼德（Halliday，1994）认为行为过程是身体内部机能的外在表现，是意识和生理状况行为化的结果。语义配置结构包括行为者+过程、行为者+过程+范围、施事+过程+［行为者+过程（+范围）］（张建东，2023）。29个代表性动词中，属于行为过程的有13个：咥、圪蹴、浪、拾掇、趸摸、撒滑、箍、呷、掮、整饬、抻、掼、操，其中单字表意的就有8个，这体现了关中方言极强的生动性。

"咥"，《辞海》中解释为"至、咬"。在普通话中表示"吃"的意思。黄土高原地区的人民豪爽洒脱，蹲在路边、端着一碗面大快朵颐的汉子在这里随处可见，"咥"这个字就生动再现了这一场景。"咥"与普通话的"吃"略有不同，"咥"带有更加浓厚的情感意义，体现的是酣畅淋漓的吃饭场景。"俩人饥肠辘辘走进灶房咥两个烤得焦黄酥软的蒸馍，然后再跨进轧花房踩踏轧花机。"第二十六章描绘了兔娃和孝义干完农活回家吃饭的场景。正如陕西八大怪的顺口溜中传唱的那样："面条宽得像裤带，锅盔大得赛锅盖，油泼辣子一道菜"。吃饭时发出吸溜的声音在秦人眼中并非不礼貌的表现，反而是"咥"的标准表现，是对厨师技艺的高度赞赏，"咥"这个字从食物的角度体现了当地的风土人情。

"圪蹴"即为蹲下，主要为内蒙古乌盟地区、河北张家口地区、山西大同地区、陕西关中地区、河南中北部的方言，是对身体状态的描述。"黑娃吃惊地盯着白嘉轩，已经没有不丢开她的任何托词和借口了。他突然蹲下去，圪蹴在马号的脚地上。"第十章中的这一句话，用"圪蹴"这一动作表现了黑娃对田小娥的不舍和对宗族守旧传统的无奈。

"箍""呷""掮""抻""掼""操"这六个单字都是对人体上肢部分动作的描述。"箍"指的是"系紧"，但也有"强迫某人做事"的引申义。如"鹿子霖原以为白嘉轩抓着了满仓的什么把柄儿寻隙闹事，完全料想不及白嘉轩这一番话，悻悻地笑笑说：'孝文实在箍得我没……'白嘉轩打断他的话：'孝文箍住你踢地卖房我知道……我叫满仓甭走，是他给你把事没办完哩！'""呷"与"咥"相对应，是普通话中"喝"的意思，但多了小口细品的内涵。掮、抻、掼、操分别指将东西扛到肩上、拉长、扔以及抓住的意义，这些都体现了关中地区的庄稼人们以苦力劳作为主，体现了下层人民的悲苦生活。

"浪"指闲逛或四处游玩，义通"浪子回头金不换""浪荡子"等普通话短语中的"浪"。大拇指芒儿说："我当土匪当腻了，也累了，我想一个人浪逛四方。"这句话体现了土匪对自由的向往，是关中人无拘无束天性的体现。

"拾掇"原义为拾取或收拾、整理，亦可引申为修理或惩治之义，最早可以追溯到晋代葛洪的《抱朴子·审举》："而有党有力者，纷然鳞萃，人乏官旷，致者又美，亦安得不拾掇而用之乎！""我把他们一个一个慢慢地处置掉，最后才拾掇你的老子；你的老子先前给打断了腰杆子，这回我再把他的腰杆子抻直拉平，你们白家就从原上雪消化水了。"这一段中的"拾掇"就采用了"惩治"的引申之意，大拇指郑芒通过描绘残暴图景要挟白孝文营救自己的好兄弟黑娃。"整饬"义类似"拾掇"，也指"整理，整顿"。

"趸摸""撒滑"两个词语是对动态动作的描述。《集韵》："趸，旋倒也。"有"盘旋、旋转、折回、横"等意思。小说大多表示的是难为情，小心翼翼地走来走去（米利娟、许巧枝，2022）。例如第十二章中对鹿子霖的描写："白鹿仓的庆典宴席结束后，父亲鹿子霖不大好意思地踅磨到他跟前，暗示他回家去一趟，他有话说。"鹿子霖作为白鹿原上与白嘉轩几乎平起平坐的人，在面对自己的儿子鹿北鹏这个共产党员时却不免局促，体现了当时老百姓对共产党等政治概念的陌生。"撒滑"即为"离开、溜走"，文中仅在第三十章出现了一次："白孝武连连应承着：'对对对，这样好。那我明天一早就撒滑了，免得节外生枝。'"

（2）物质过程分析

物质过程用于描述做某件事的过程或者某件事发生的过程，分为物质动作过程和社会动作过程，涉及许多参与者角色，包括施事（agent）、受事（affected）、创造物（created）、范围（range）、方式（manner）、程度（degree）、方向（direction）及其他复合参与者角色（何伟、张瑞杰、谈晓红等，2017）。代表性动词中属于物质过程的共有9个：撂、熬活、捋码、擩草、绞水、趿拉、墩、戽来、挨挫。

"熬活""挨挫""擩草""绞水"这四个词语已经包含了动作的受事者。"熬活"即为劳作、当苦力以谋求生计。"渭北人生地不熟。咱们给人熬活不管门楼高低，不管财东大小，要紧的是寻到一个仁义的主儿。"鹿三的这句话一方面体现了他对主家态度的重视，另一方面也体现了旧时代长工到处找营生的艰辛生活，这是对广大底层民众吃苦耐劳、勤恳老实无声的赞歌。"挨挫"指受惩戒、受打压，"挨"即承受，"挫"指打压，是该动词的目标。"挨挫"一词出现在第十五章中："鹿子霖慷慨地说：'放心亲蛋蛋，你放心！你不看大咋着心疼你哩！你有啥难处就给大说。谁敢哈你一口大气大就叫他挨挫！'鹿子霖弹了烟灰坐起来穿衣服。"这句话中，鹿子霖自大轻浮的形象一览无余。"擩草"与"绞水"是对关中百姓田间劳作的最好描述。"擩草"指铡草时一人将双手所揽持之草塞入铡口以内（米利娟、许巧枝，2022）。"绞水"描绘的是百姓们用吊桶置于井中，转动把手将水提上来的情景。这两个词语都贴切地展现了关中人民靠山吃山、靠水吃水的生活风貌。

"撂"和"墩"意义相近，都表示将物品向下放。例如，"白灵却冷淡地说：'你该不是从月亮上刚下来吧？城里的枯井几乎天天都有活人被撂进去，你却在这儿抒情。'"这句话体现了白灵作为一名共产党员对救百姓于水火的急迫心情。

"捋码"指整理、梳理，这个方言词语用两个形象的动词"捋"和"码"结合在一起，却表现了抽象的意义。例如在第三章中："把白鹿村挨家挨户捋码一遍，有力量一次买走这二亩水地的除非鹿子霖再数不出第二家来。"这句话从侧面反映了白、鹿这两个大姓家族的实力不可小觑。

"趿拉"是拖着、随便穿着的意思，一般后面的目标受事者为鞋。《白鹿原》中三次使用了这个词语，两次都用来形容白孝文："孝文趿拉上棉窝窝（即棉鞋）走到院子，就看见漆黑的院庭里站着父亲的佝偻的形体"以及"孝文从火炕上溜下来趿拉上鞋，刚跨出窑洞一步……"这样的用词足以看出陈忠实先生深厚的用词功底，用地道的方言将白孝文浪荡虚伪、自以为是的形象淋漓尽致地表现了出来，也不断暗示了白孝文最终堕落的结局。

"戽来"的出现只有一次，在第十一章中，黑娃对鹿兆鹏说道："你从哪儿戽来这些吓人的说词？""戽"本身就有表示整数的意义，这里"戽来"表现了黑娃对鹿兆鹏关于自由恋爱的进步言论的惊讶，冲击着他落后的婚姻思想和与田小娥的辛酸往事。

（3）心智过程分析

心智过程描述人们心理活动发生、发展的过程，是脑对现实的反映，主要涉及两个参与者角色，一个为参与心理体验的人或者人格化的物，另一个参与者是"现象"（张建东，2023）。

心智过程下属的三个子过程为：感知过程、认知过程和感受过程。弹嫌、料就、悦意、惜耐四个词体现的就是及物性过程中的心智过程。

"弹嫌"体现的是感受过程，指的是对某人或某事的厌恶、嫌弃。例如在第三章中："吴长贵有二子五女，个个女子都长得细皮嫩肉，秀眉重眼，无可弹嫌。"这里的无可弹嫌即类似于普通话中的"无可挑剔"一词，体现了关中自古多美女，表现的是陈忠实对这片土地深沉的爱。"悦意"和"惜耐"意义相通，都表示对一个事物的喜爱珍重，也是感受过程的体现。"悦意"另一方面也可以作形容词，构成了一个动宾组合词，表示心情愉快。

"料就"表示预判、猜测，并且要得出一个确定的结果，体现了心智过程中的认知过程。"白赵氏冷冷地说：'还是一个短命的。'其实在孩子刚刚发生尖锐的啼哭时，她就料就了这种结局。"这句话体现了白赵氏在生育之事上经验十足，塑造了白赵氏这一聪明贤惠但也固执守旧的形象，体现了旧社会中女性的地位低下，打理家务和传宗接代是当时女性一生中最重要的主题。

（4）言语过程分析

言语过程是关于言说的过程，是信息交互的过程。这个过程包括任何意义象征的交换。《白鹿原》的代表性方言动词中，"剋"和"谝"两个动词表现了言语过程。

《白鹿原》中对"剋"字的使用仅在岳维山对鹿子霖的一句话中："你不要想不开。省上剋我姑息养奸。你还要什么脾气，使什么性子？"联系这句话的前后文背景可知，"剋"指轻度的批评。这里岳维山想要表达的是自己处境艰难，体现了这一人物不关心百姓真正需求，满眼只有自己的"政治需求"。

"谝"即聊闲天。《说文解字·卷四·言部》中对"谝"字的解释为"谝，便巧言也。从言扁声。"《周书》曰："戳戳善谝言。"《论语》曰："友谝佞。"在关中方言中，"谝"字基本脱离了贬义的"巧言"之义，只表示中性的"聊天、交谈"之义。第十六章写道："太阳冒红时，白鹿原的官道小路上，庄稼汉男女穿着浆捶得平展硬峥的家织布白衫青裤，臂弯里挎着装有用新麦子面蒸成的各色花馍的竹提盒笼儿，乐颠颠地去走亲访友，吃了喝了谝了，于日落时散散悠悠回家去。"一系列的动词生动地展现了关中地区庄稼人农闲时的自得生活。《白鹿原》作为一篇时间跨度极大的恢宏巨著，陈忠实巧妙结合人物之间的"谝"，展现了这一时间段内陕西关中地区政治、经济、思想、社会生活。

（5）存在过程分析

存在过程是一个非动态的过程，表示某人或某物的存在情况。韩礼德（Halliday，1994）认为，存在小句有一个参与者，即存在物，因为它直接参与存在过程，而为存在物定位的方位成分只是可有可无的环境成分。在代表性方言动词中，只有"苫"一个字体现的是存在过程。当"苫"作名词时，指的是茅草所做的覆盖物本身；当词性为动词时，最初指编茅盖屋，后泛指用席、布等遮盖东西。例如在第二十三章中对田地的描写："所有土地被秋庄稼苫着，农人们无法踏进田地就在村巷树荫下乘凉。"

5. 结语

研究表明，依据米利娟与许巧枝老师的研究，陈忠实在《白鹿原》中使用的 29 个代表性方言动词基本上涉及了韩礼德系统功能语法中及物性系统的各个方面。这些动词一方面帮助作者塑造了白鹿原上栩栩如生的人物形象，生动刻画了当时陕西关中地区淳朴、豪爽的底层老百姓形象；另一方面，这些动词推动了故事情节的发展，展现了三秦大地浓厚而又独特的风土人情，为我们了解当时的百姓风貌提供了文学依据。

参考文献

[1] HALLIDAY M A K, 1994. An introduction to functional grammar[M]. London: Hodder Education Publisher.
[2] 何伟，张瑞杰，淡晓红，等，2017. 汉语功能语义分析[M]. 北京：外语教学与研究出版社.
[3] 刘春藤，马东峰，2022.《白鹿原》的叙事话语分析[J]. 文学教育（上）（10）：22-24.
[4] 米利娟，许巧枝，2022.《白鹿原》中的陕西方言行为动词研究[J]. 文化创新比较研究，6(33)：33-37.
[5] 张建东，2023. 基于汉语及物性系统的语篇特征对比分析[J]. 西安外国语大学学报，31(1)：25-29.

及物性系统视角下的诗歌语篇分析
——以《未选择的路》为例

陆 瑶

1. 引言

系统功能语言学，作为一个不断发展、完善的语言理论，受到了很多人的关注与使用。目前，有许多人尝试用该理论进行文本分析。及物性系统是系统功能语言学的重要理论之一，该理论被运用于许多文本分析之中，比如小说、影视作品台词，但运用于诗歌分析中的做法还尚未十分普遍。本文将对及物性系统进行详细阐释，对于将进行细致分析的诗歌《未选择的路》会作简短的概要叙述。

1.1 系统功能语言学之及物性系统概述

在吸收、融入了布拉格学派相关理论以及其他许多的前人先辈的语言学研究理论成果之后，语言学家韩礼德便于 20 世纪 60 年代创立了系统功能语言学，此后逐渐完善。韩礼德认为语言与社会有着千丝万缕的联系，它就是社会中语言符号的一种，充当着人们在社会中相互交流思想观念的工具（胡壮麟、朱永生、张德禄等，2005）。根据韩礼德的系统功能语言学理论，语言有三大功能，即概念功能、人际功能以及谋篇功能。概念功能的实现离不开及物性系统。实现人际功能则必须依赖语气系统，主述位结构则是用以谋篇功能的实现。由于本文是对诗歌进行及物性视角的分析，因此接下来着重介绍及物性系统的相关概念。

根据韩礼德的系统功能语言学理论，及物性系统包括六种不同类别的过程：物质过程、心理过程、关系过程、行为过程、言语过程以及存在过程。前三种过程为主要的过程，后三种则为次要过程。每种过程基本包含过程本身、过程中的参与者、与过程有关的环境成分。

六种类型的及物性过程内涵如下。物质过程是表现动作"做"的过程。此过程包含的成分通过举例来说明，比如在句子"I kick the ball."中，动词"kick"是表示此过程的动词，标记为"过程"。句中的"I"是动作者成分，"ball"是目标成分，在此类过程中，动作者是必须存在的，而目标不是。心理过程就是指感觉、意识的过程，分为三类：感受、认知和感知过程。心理过程除了表示过程本身的感受动词之外，如"see""like""think"，还包含两种参与者，即感觉者和现象。关系过程表示事物之间的关系，分为三类：集约、环境、领属。每种类型分两种方式：属性和身份方式。在属性方式中，两个参与者分别为属性和载体，在身份方式中，两个参与者分别为被鉴别者和鉴别者。行为过程与生理和心理行为相关。行为过程中的参与者大多数情况下为一个，称之为行为者。言语过程则与说话这个动作相关，因此该过程表示过程本身的动词就有"say""tell"等，参与者根据引用话语的类型，分为引语与报告语。存在过程表示事物的存在或者发生（楚军、文旭，2013）。常用表该过程类型的句型为

there be 句型。表存在过程的动词后接的名词性词群被称作存在物。关于及物性过程中的环境成分，可大致分为四类：时间类、空间类、方式类以及伴随类。

1.2 诗歌背景简括

《未选择的路》的作者弗罗斯特是美国当之无愧的诗坛巨匠。《未选择的路》是他流传度最广、最为脍炙人口的诗歌。该诗发表于1915年，收录在他的著名诗集《山间》中。诗歌描述了一个旅人遇到需要作出选择的分岔路口时，内心不断煎熬、纠结，最终作出选择。迄今为止，该诗歌受到人们的广泛青睐，关于此诗歌的研究层出不穷。一些学者致力于探究诗歌丰富的内涵（Hason, 2015）；一些学者对该诗歌进行隐喻方面的解析，例如对文中树的隐喻内涵探析（杨海英，2020）；也有一些学者对诗歌进行哲学层面的探究（张建慧，2016）；也有学者对该诗歌进行宗教层面的解读（夏党华，2012）；还有一些学者对这首诗歌的写作手法很感兴趣（关长平、文倩，2012）；一些学者也进行了关于这首诗歌翻译方向的研究（佘艺玲，2007）。但目前，还鲜有人从系统功能语言学视角对这首诗歌进行分析解读。

综上所述，系统功能语言学的及物性系统可以用来实现语言的概念功能，表达人们所想所思。鉴于目前对于诗歌《未选择的路》在此角度的解读鲜少有人涉及，因此笔者意欲运用系统功能语言学中的及物性理论对此首诗歌进行语篇分析，从一个新的角度挖掘该诗歌的语篇意义和作者意图传达之意。

2. 诗歌的及物性过程详析

本节将诗歌分为四节，诗的每一节中都会先简述本节诗歌的大致内容，接着列出及物性过程类型，每种类型的数量。然后，根据每种过程的参与者、过程、环境成分，按照过程类型的顺序进行每一个过程的系统、综合、细致的分析，探索作者的内涵之意。

2.1 第一节诗歌的及物性过程分析

Two roads diverged in a yellow wood,
And sorry I could not travel both
And be one traveler, long I stood
And looked down one as far as I could
To where it bent in the undergrowth.

诗歌的第一节描述了主人公置身于一片黄色树林之中，他的面前有两条路可供其选择，但无法同时踏上两条路。因此主人公必须做出选择，于是他先观察了其中的一条路。经过仔细的及物过程分析，本首诗歌的第一节中，有2个物质过程，2个行为过程，1个心理过程以及1个关系过程。接下来的部分将会对这4种类型的及物性过程进行具体而详细的分析。

首先，对这一节诗歌的物质过程进行分析。在本节诗歌第一句蕴含的第一个物质过程中，所用的动词是"diverged"，参与者为"two roads"，该词也是此物质过程的动作者，"in a yellow wood"则是属于这个物质过程中的环境成分。本节诗歌的第一句构成一个物质过程，描绘了一幅美丽又寂寥的画面：在一片黄色树林之中，形单影只的主人公的面前出现了两条路，这两条路形成了一个分叉口，主人公若想继续走下去则需要选择接下来该走哪一条路。通过"黄色树林"这个环境成分，我们可以知道，这首诗歌的背景设定在秋冬时节。而秋冬时节是树叶飘落，万物开始凋零的季节，这就给整首诗歌定下了忧郁、惆怅的基调。

在本节诗歌第五句蕴含的第二个物质过程中，所使用的动词为"bent"，参与者为"it"，"in the undergrowth"是环境成分，第五句中的物质过程描述了主人公对于两条路中的其中一条的观察程度。物质过程中的"it"和动词"bent"表现出了小路的蜿蜒曲折，也反映出了主人公内心面对选择的犹豫、煎熬。

其次，对这一节诗歌的行为过程进行分析。在本节诗歌的第三句蕴含的第一个行为过程中，所使用的动词为"stood"，参与者即行为者是"I"，"long"为环境成分。"stood"为一个静态动词，表示一种持续一段时间的状态，与环境成分"long"相配合，描述了主人公久久驻足在两条路前的场景，体现出作者面对选择的纠结心情。这一心情延续到了第四句。第四句中所蕴含的行为过程中所使用的动词词组为"looked down"，参与者即行为者是"I"和"one"，句子剩余部分都为环境成分，该过程通过描述主人公远眺着其中一条路，体现了他置身选择困境的状态。

再次，对这一节诗歌的心理过程进行分析。这一节诗歌的心理过程寓于第二句中，真正表示心理过程的动词"felt"未能在语篇中出现，它与"sorry"构成心理过程的本身，"I could not travel both"是现象，"I"为这一过程的参与者即感觉者。其余部分为环境成分。这一心理过程充分体现了主人公面对两条路的选择时，感到遗憾的心情，遗憾自己不能够同时涉足两条道路。这句诗句，以感受者"I"为视角描述了主人公的纠结心情，用词朴素无华，但由于"I"的视角选择能够让人可以即时地感受到主人公遗憾的心情。

最后，对这一节诗歌的关系过程进行分析。本节诗歌的关系过程主要体现在第三句中，属于集约性的关系过程，更具体来说，是具有属性性质的集约性关系过程。"be"是关系过程的标识，"one traveler"是属性，"I"是载体。这个关系过程体现了主人公的身份属性，即一个旅人，给予了主人公漂泊、孤寂的身份特征，增添诗歌的寂寥氛围，引起读者共鸣。

诗歌的第一节为整首诗歌奠定了忧愁、惆怅的基调，直截了当地指出了诗歌的主题与"选择"的关联，引发读者的思考。

2.2 第二节诗歌的及物性过程分析

Then took the other, as just as fair,
And having perhaps the better claim,
Because it was grassy and wanted wear;
Though as for that the passing there
Had worn them really about the same.

此首诗歌的第二节的大意为主人公最后选择了另一条少有人迹的路，并给出了他的理由。经过笔者的及物过程分析，本首诗歌的第二节中，包含3个物质过程，1个心理过程以及1个关系过程。接下来的部分将会对这3种类型的及物过程进行具体、详细的分析。

首先，对物质过程进行分析，在本节诗歌第一句蕴含的第一个物质过程中，所用的动词是"took"，"the other"是目标，动作者为该诗句中未出现的"I"，其余部分"as just as fair"为环境成分。这一过程简单陈述了主人公面对着两条道路，最后做出了选择，选择了另一条路，并且认为这条路并不比第一节中所观察的那条路差。第二个物质过程是在本节诗歌的第二句中，体现物质过程的动词为"having"，动作者为未出现的"I"，"the better claim"是目标。这一物质过程所表达的含义承接第一句的内容，在第一句提出了主人公作出了选择，第二句则进一步说明主人公的这一选择出于他认为选择第二条路有着比第一条路更好的解释。第三个物质过程体现在本节诗歌的第四句和第五句中，动作者为第四句中"the passing"，体现物质过程的动词为"had worn"，目标为"them"，"about the same"为环境成分。这一物质过程表示了主人公虽然作出了他的选择，但其实内心还留有一丝犹豫的复杂内心情感。

其次，对心理过程进行分析。这节诗歌的心理过程体现在第三句中，感受者为"it"，指代第二条路，"wanted"为表示心理过程的动词，"wear"为现象。这个心理过程表面上是写这第二条路渴望人的踏足，但由于使用了"wanted"，这个表达人内心感情偏向的动词，就表达出了其实是主人公自己想要涉足这第二条路的内心想法。

最后，对关系过程进行分析。这节诗歌的唯一的关系过程出现在第三句中，属于具有属性性质的集约性关系过程。指代第二条路的"it"是此过程的载体。"was"是关系过程的象征性词汇，"grassy"是属性。这个关系过程体现了主人公选择的第二条路的其中一个特质——被茂密的草覆盖，即较少有人涉足，而这个特质恰是主人公内心所偏爱的。

第二节诗歌呈现了主人公的最终选择并且给出了理由——另一条路芳草萋萋、鲜有人至，因此他意欲踏上这条道路，继续他的旅途。本节诗歌表现出了主人公不走寻常路的特点，放弃了被更多人选择涉足的路，但他又在最后对两条路进行了比较，内心仍然存着些许犹豫。

2.3 第三节诗歌的及物性过程分析

And both that morning equally lay,
In leaves no step had trodden black.
Oh, I kept the first for another day!
Yet knowing how way leads on to way,
I doubted if I should ever come back.

此诗歌的第三节主要通过种种描述表达了主人公作出选择之后的犹豫心情。经过及物性过程分析，本首诗歌的第三节中，包含 5 个物质过程和 2 个心理过程。接下来的部分将会对这 2 种类型的及物过程进行具体、详细的分析。

第一个物质过程寓于第一句和第二句中，"both"是动作者，"lay in"是代表物质过程的动词词组，"leaves"是目标，"that morning"则是环境成分。这个物质过程所表达的主要含义是两条路上都有着树叶。第二个物质过程寓于第二句中，动作者为"no step"，"had trodden"为表示物质过程的动词，"leaves"是目标，"black"是环境成分。在这一物质过程中，目标"leaves"放在了靠前的位置，突出了叶子被人踩踏的特点，即两条路都还未被人踩踏。读者应结合第二个物质过程与第一个物质过程才能更好地理解本节诗歌第一句和第二句的意义，即两条道路上都有着落叶，落叶上还未曾有被人踩踏的痕迹。从这两个物质过程可以看出，主人公的内心此时还是有些犹豫，不能够确定自己的选择是否正确。

第三个物质过程存在于第三句诗句中，"I"为动作者，"kept"为表示物质过程的动词，"the first"是目标，"for another day"是环境成分。这个物质过程体现出了主人公还是选择了走第二条路，但内心又割舍不下对于踏足另一条路的想法，又一次体现了主人公矛盾的心情。第四和第五个物质过程分别由动词词组"leads on"和"come back"所引导，动作者分别是"way"和"I"，第四个物质过程的环境成分为"to way"，第五个物质过程则没有环境成分。第四个物质过程陈述了一个事实即一条路会通向另一条陌生的路。第五个物质过程陈述了主人公对未来的猜测，即他可能会回到此处的岔路口，也有不回来的情况。由于这两个物质过程的含义需要结合本节诗歌的两个心理过程才能完全被阐释，因此具体的解读就在下一段对两个心理过程的分析之中。

第一个心理过程寓于第四句之中，"knowing"是表示心理过程的标识，感受者为"I"，"how way leads on to way"是现象。这个心理过程所要体现的是主人公关于前面所说的要将第一条路留给另外的日子再走这个问题，进行了思考。通过这个心理过程，体现出了主人公知道自己作出选择之后的内心的惆怅。第二个心理过程寓于本节诗歌的第五句中，"doubted"为这个心理过程的标志，"I"为感受者，"if I should ever come back"为现象。这个心理过程揭示了主人公内心对于自己以后是否还能回到这个分岔路口的怀疑。尽管作出了选择，但他对于未来抱有着不确定的心情。

本节诗歌描绘了主人公犹豫的内心，即使做出了选择但还是不由得对两个选择进行了对比，心里充满了对选择一条路便无法回头的惆怅之意。

2.4 第四节诗歌的及物性过程分析

I shall be telling this with a sigh,
Somewhere ages and ages hence:
Two roads diverged in a wood, and I,
I took the one less traveled by,
And that has made all the difference.

此首诗歌的第四节主要描述了主人公对于未来自己作出选择后再提起此事的预想。经过及物性过程分析，本首诗歌的第四节中，包含 3 个物质过程以及 1 个言语过程。接下来的部分将会对这 2 种类型的及物过程进行具体详细的分析。

首先，对这节诗歌唯一的言语过程进行分析。这节诗歌的言语过程就在第一句诗句中，由动词"telling"来体现。"I"是说话者，"this"是报告语，"with a sigh"是环境成分。这个言语过程展现了主人公构想的自己未来进行选择之后的心情、境遇，他将会叹着气说着他之前经历的选择。"with a sigh"这个环境成分体现出了主人公对于未来自己作出选择之后而产生的心情预测是消极的，这体现出他的内心对于放弃走第一条路是不舍的、遗憾的，但是由于做出选择之后再也没有回头路了，于是他也只能沿着自己选的路走下去，在未来提起这段往事。

其次，对本节诗歌中的物质过程进行分析。第一个物质过程寓于第三句诗句中，"two roads"是动作者，"diverged"是表示物质过程的动词，"in a wood"是环境成分。这个物质过程陈述了主人公对未来自己的构想，构想自己以后提起了他曾经面前摆着两条路，面临着选择的困境。第二个物质过程是在第四句中，"I"是动作者，"took"是表示物质过程的动词，"the one less traveled by"是目标。这个物质过程陈述了主人公的选择，他最后选择了第二条道路，那条人烟更为稀少的路，体现出了主人公具有不走寻常路、有胆识的特点。第三个物质过程寓于第五句诗句中，"that"是动作者，"has made"是表示物质过程的动词，"all the difference"是目标，这个物质过程所传达的便是，在未来由于主人公做出的选择，导致了完全不同的结果。这个结果不知好坏，主人公做出的选择可能会给他的未来带来好的结果，但也有可能带来坏的影响。这就留给了读者无限的想象与思考。

本节诗歌体现出了主人公矛盾、复杂的心理，虽然选择了第二条路，但是遗憾未能选择第一条路，而正由于他的选择，导致了完全不同的结果。此外，本节诗歌生动形象地描绘出了我们日常生活所不可避免的选择后心理，引起读者的共鸣与在生活中做选择的思考。

3. 结论

本文以系统功能语言学的及物性视角对诗歌《未选择的路》进行了详细的分析。根据及物性系统的分析结果，本首诗歌以物质过程和心理过程为两种主要的及物性过程类型，表明了这首诗歌以叙事和描写心理活动为主。本首诗歌以陈述性的叙事手法描述了主人公面对岔路口要走哪条路时，作出了自己的选择，以及呈现了在做出了选择之后，内心不断犹豫、思考、踌躇、纠结的思想情态。诗人弗罗斯特意欲通过这首诗歌告诉读者一个深刻的人生哲理，即在人的一生中，会如同这首诗歌中的主人公一样，遇到很多的岔路口。面前会出现两个选择，而人们在做出选择之后便会纠结、犹豫，思考是否自己当初做了另一个选择会得到更好的结果。这首诗歌启示了读者既然做出了选择之后就无法回头，那么就应该义无反顾地坚持自己当初的选择，继续自己的人生旅程。

通过本文的及物性过程分析，可以得出结论，即系统功能语言学视域下的及物性系统理论可用于诗歌的语篇分析，能够使读者用一种全新的角度来理解一首诗歌，体会其中诗人意欲传递的道理。

参考文献

[1] HALLIDAY M A K, 1994. An introduction to functional grammar[M]. London: Hodder Education Publisher.
[2] HASAN R, 2015. Frost: The Road Not Taken[M]. Sheffield: Equinox Publishing.
[3] 楚军，文旭，2013. 句法学[M]. 成都：电子科技大学出版社.
[4] 关长平，文倩，2012. A review of Robert Frost's poem: The Road Not Taken[J]. 海外英语（12）：200-201.
[5] 胡壮麟，朱永生，张德禄，等，2005. 系统功能语言学概论[M]. 北京：北京大学出版社.
[6] 佘艺玲，2007. "歧路"的意象内涵与译文的信度——谈弗罗斯特的诗歌"The Road Not Taken"[J].哈尔滨学院学报（6）：97-99.
[7] 夏党华，2012.《未选择的路》的宗教意识解读[J]. 时代文学（下半月）（2）：151-152.
[8] 杨海英，2020. 罗伯特·弗罗斯特诗歌中的"树林"隐喻探析[J]. 兰州教育学院学报，36(5)：22-23，26.
[9] 张建慧，2016. 弗罗斯特诗歌中的多维空间构建及其哲学内涵[J]. 名作欣赏（36）：128-129

英译武侠小说与英国奇幻小说语域变异多维分析
——以《射雕英雄传》与《指环王》为例

向张玉洁

1. 引言

Irwin（1961）将幻想文学定义为"在违反常识的基础上构建变形的社会或个人，通常是对历史或文学范式的戏仿和改编，伴随着有意的或非正统的天真无邪气质，超自然力量通常在叙事中占主导地位"。带有"幻"这一色彩的东方或西方幻想文学均发生在"架空"世界，都带有虚幻的风格。虽同为幻想文学，不同国家的文学土壤又滋养了富有独特民族风格的幻想文学，例如诞生于 19 世纪的西方科幻小说、第二次世界大战后的西方奇幻文学、中国近代的新武侠小说和发展迅猛的中国当代的网络玄幻仙侠小说。

对中国幻想文学的研究主要集中在幻想文学的起源（张玉，2015），幻想文学在新时代的发展（黄悦，2021；韩云波，2005），幻想文学特点和流派（孟秀坤，2007；陈晓明、彭超，2017；孙金燕，2022），幻想文学的对外传播（Mok，2001；吴玥璠、刘军平，2019；张泪、王志伟，2020）。此外，也有众多学者将中国幻想文学同西方幻想文学进行比较。有学者尝试研究两者之间的关系，例如，夏春梅与陈曦（2015）发现《西游记》与《指环王》在自然观和善恶观方面有极大相似之处；也有研究认为英国现代奇幻文学直接促进了中国当代幻想文学的诞生和勃兴（高红梅，2015）；也有学者以西方奇幻小说为参照，认为中国当代的幻想文学沿袭了西方奇幻小说传统，虽然在一方面汲取了本国传统文化的养分（赵臻，2019），但是本土特色和人文传统仍显不足（姜淑芹，2021；高红梅，2015）。

上述研究发现，目前学界对中西幻想文学的认识已有相当数量的学术成果，但不难发现这些研究在研究方法和研究视角上存在一定局限：研究视角聚焦于母语原创文本之间的差异性，但鲜有研究将目标语翻译文本纳入研究范围；有学者收集原创文本作为语料库，但大多基于主观判断来挑选和分析部分语料，缺少客观、系统的语料数据的支撑，对语言数据的考查仍有不足。鉴于此，本研究采用 Biber（1984）的多维分析模型，借助语料库工具，并选取典型例证，尝试以更客观的视角考察二者在多个维度上的潜在异同。

2. 数据来源及研究方法

2.1 多维分析方法

多维分析是本研究使用的主要方法。多维分析"使用多元统计的方法来考察一种语言中的语域变异"（Biber，2004），已应用于各种体裁的研究，包括世界英语（Xiao，2009）、口语体和书面写作（Biber，2009）、小说、散文和信件（Biber、Edward，1989）。多维分析模型包含 6 个维度，包含 67 个语言特征。语言特征的共现模式决定维度特征，维度特征再通过数据的正负值和绝对值高低（下文描述为分值）反映出来。

笔者首先使用 Nini 开发的 MAT（分析工具）软件进行文本标记和文本分析。该工具具有自动生成文本标注、语言特征（词汇和句法）提取、功能维度归类和数据统计等功能，此软件还内嵌斯坦福词性赋码器，能有效地对两种语料进行自动词性赋码识别并给予优化。SPSS 统计分析软件可以对两组数据进行初步的描述统计，并确认数据间是否存在显著区别（$p<.05$）。鉴于数据呈非正态分布，所以本研究对 MAT 所报告的维度分值进行曼-惠特尼 U 检验，找出有显著区别的维度，接下来采取同样的方法分析各维度下的语言特征分值，以更详细地展示和解释两组文本之间的语域差异。

2.2 研究语料

本研究采用自建语料库，选取的语料是《射雕英雄传》英译本和《指环王》英文原本。西方幻想文学的杰出代表是托尔金的作品——《指环王》，讲述的是中土人民反抗魔王索伦的探险故事。中国幻想文学杰作以武侠巨匠金庸的小说《射雕英雄传》为首，描绘了主角郭靖和一众人物在女真入侵南宋的背景下的冒险经历。2018 年，由瑞典译者郝玉青（Anna Holmwood）翻译的《射雕英雄传》英译本首卷在海外出版，一经推出就广受好评，有海外媒体将其比作中国的《指环王》；而现代奇幻文学之父托尔金的作品《指环王》凭借其奇幻的人物设定和瑰丽宏大的背景，被翻译为 60 多种语言，备受全球读者的喜爱。

本研究首先将《射雕英雄传》英译本和《指环王》原著的电子文本存为文本文档格式，再进行人工清洗，最后获得两个子语料库，两个子语料库的文本分别被划分为 40 个文件，总库共计 80 个文件。语料库具体信息如表 1 所示。

表 1 语料库构成

文本	型符	类符	标准化类符型符比/%
Legends of Condor Hero（《射雕英雄传》）	627 428	16 551	44.45
The Lord of Ring（《指环王》）	557 649	14 528	39.79

2.3 研究问题

本研究主要尝试回答以下问题：《射雕英雄传》和《指环王》在语域风格上分别具有什么特征？如果二者在语域风格层面表现出差异，那么差异的原因是什么？这对我国武侠小说的外译有何启示？

3. 数据结果与分析

在 MAT 对语料库文本进行标注和分析后，利用统计工具 SPSS 对语料进行描述统计获得表 2，并根据表 2 生成维度差异趋向图，如图 2 所示。

表 2 《射雕英雄传》英译本与《指环王》原本描述统计

	《射雕英雄传》n=40	《指环王》n=40
维度 1	−9.05	0.37
维度 2	4.86	4.84

（续表）

	《射雕英雄传》n=40	《指环王》n=40
维度 3	−0.58	−1.90
维度 4	−0.58	−0.52
维度 5	−0.76	0.21
维度 6	−1.74	−0.94

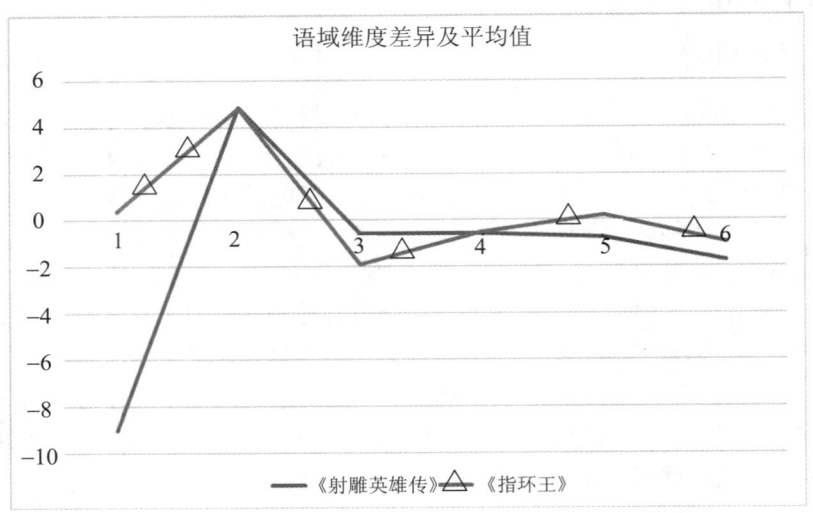

图 2　维度差异趋向图

在得出语料基本特征后，研究对维度分值进行 2 个独立样本曼-惠特尼 U 检验。如表 3 所示，两部作品在维度 1、3、5、6 上呈现显著性差异（$p<.05$），在维度 2、4 上则未见显著差异（$p>.05$）。

表 3　各维度 p 值

维度	维度 1	维度 2	维度 3	维度 4	维度 5	维度 6
p 值	0.000	0.191	0.000	0.973	0.000	0.000

3.1　六个维度曼-惠特尼 U 检验结果

维度 1 区分交互性与信息性文本，正值代表交互性特征，分值越高，文本交互特征越明显；负值代表信息性特征，分值越高，文本信息密度越高。表 2 显示《射雕英雄传》在维度 1 上维度值为负，《指环王》维度值为正，这说明两作品在维度 1 上有相反的语域风格，《射雕英雄传》属于信息密度高的信息型文本，而《指环王》交互性更加显著，文本风格更自由，符合口语体文本特征。

维度 2 为叙事性和非叙事性维度，正值代表叙述性语域，分值越高，叙述性越强；负值表示非叙述性语域，分值越高，非叙述性越强。两部作品的维度值均为正，且分值在 6 个维度中最小，几乎重合，这说明在该维度两者风格趋同，均带有明显的叙事性特征。

维度 3 的两极分别代表语境独立指称和语境依赖指称，正值说明指称独立化，分值越高的指称越明晰、准确；负值说明指称依赖语境，分值越高代表对情境依赖程度越大。两部作品维度值均为负说明指称与文本语境联系紧密，属于语境依赖型文本，但《射雕英雄传》的维度值高于《指环王》，这说明虽然前者的指称依赖语境，但较后者而言更为明晰和准确。

维度 4 上是显性劝诱性程度维度，正值说明分值越高，文本显性劝诱程度越强；负值说明两者维度值为负且差异较小，说明两者均不属于显性劝说型表述。两部小说主题为主人公的冒险故事，一般注重读者的感官刺激，劝诫教化功能属性较弱。

维度 5 为信息抽象程度维度，正值说明分值越高，信息越抽象；负值说明我们可以发现，维度值为负的《射雕英雄传》呈现出语言表达更具体的语言特征，而维度值为正的《指环王》的文字则倾向于抽象风格。

维度 6 与即兴信息组织细致度相关，正值说明分值越高，即席话语特征越明显；负值说明分值越高，即兴表达风格越不明显。两部作品在维度 6 上均为负值，这说明两部作品即席话语风格不明显，语言表达精细度较高；但《射雕英雄传》维度得分低于《指环王》说明前者的信息安排更正式有序，而后者则更为松散自由。

此外，MAT 产出的文本类型结果表示，《指环王》符合虚拟性叙事性文本特征，而《射雕英雄传》属于一般叙事阐明型文本。一般叙事阐明型文本是最常见的英文文本类型，带有大量信息，并呈现明显叙事风格。该文本类型的典型文体有新闻报道、自传和小说等，在划分叙事和非叙事风格的维度 2 上，与"虚拟叙事"同有较为明显的叙事特征。本研究发现两文本在维度 2 的得分基本重合也证明了这一观点。

综上，两文本在维度 1、3、5、6 的语域风格呈现显著差异，尤其是在维度 1 和维度 5 上表现出相反的语域风格。本研究将基于这四个维度对具体的文本语言特征进行进一步的探讨。

3.2 维度特征对比分析

如表 4 所示，维度 1 呈现的是交互性特征和信息性特征的对比，携带正值的语言特征具有明显的交互或情感目的，携带负值的语言特征则与信息表达密切相关。MAT 产出的结果显示，《指环王》在维度 1 的得分明显高于《射雕英雄传》，此外，与前者语域风格最相近的是通俗小说，与后者语域风格最相近的是广播，这进一步佐证了两者分别偏向交互和信息的语域差异。《射雕英雄传》关注信息输出，该语域特征体现在拥有五个高负值的语言特征（高于 0.45），包括名词、介词短语、形容词、平均词长、类符型符比，"这些特性的高频率代表文本关注信息密度和信息细致程度"（Biber，1989）。名词承担指称意义的功能，介词短语有整合信息的作用，形容词的修饰功能为文本增添更多细节信息；此外，平均词长卡说明用词考究复杂，类符型符比高表明文本词汇丰富，表达多样。以上语言特征表现出高分值均可以说明《射雕英雄传》语域特征偏向信息性，注重信息输出，文本信息密度大。

表 4 维度 1 语言特征值

语言特征	《射雕英雄传》		《指环王》		p
	平均秩	秩总和	平均秩	秩总和	
私动词（PRIV）	27.53	1101.00	53.48	2139.00	$p<.00$
THAT 删除（THATD）	33.56	1342.50	47.44	1897.50	$p<.01$

(续表)

语言特征	《射雕英雄传》		《指环王》		p
	平均秩	秩总和	平均秩	秩总和	
动词（VB）	21.64	865.50	59.36	2374.50	p<.00
代动词 Do（PROD）	52.10	2084.00	28.90	1156.00	p<.00
分析型否定（XX0）	32.34	1293.50	48.66	1946.50	p<.01
指示代词（DEMO）	29.13	1165.00	51.88	2075.00	p<.00
强调语气（EMPH）	51.48	2059.00	29.53	1181.00	p<.00
第一人称代词（FPP1）	29.89	1195.50	51.11	2044.50	p<.00
代词（PIT）	23.08	923.00	57.93	2317.00	p<.00
BE 作主要动词(BEMA)	35.66	1426.50	45.34	1813.50	p<.05
小品词（DPAR）	26.03	1041.00	54.98	2199.00	p<.00
委婉词（HDG）	24.39	975.50	56.61	2264.50	p<.00
加强语（AMP）	31.58	1263.00	49.43	1977.00	p<.01
WH 问句（WHQU）	50.46	2018.50	30.54	1221.50	p<.00
滞留介词（STPR）	50.44	2017.50	30.56	1222.50	p<.00
副词（RB）	24.03	961.00	56.98	2279.00	p<.00
条件状语从属词(COND)	26.03	1041.00	54.98	2199.00	p<.00
名词（NN）	59.36	2374.50	21.64	865.50	p<.00
平均词长（AWL）	57.25	2290.00	23.75	950.00	p<.00
介词（PIN）	21.99	879.50	59.01	2360.50	p<.00
类型符比（TTR）	53.45	2138.00	27.55	1102.00	p<.00
形容词（JJ）	31.66	1266.50	49.34	1973.50	p<.01
地点状语（PLACE）	26.39	1055.50	54.61	2184.50	p<.00
过去分词省略助动词（WZPAST）	49.00	1960.00	32.00	1280.00	p<.01
现在分词省略助动词（WZPRES）	50.71	2028.50	30.29	1211.50	p<.00

如表 5 所示，维度 3 区分指称明晰型和语境依赖型文本。两文本在维度 3 上的维度值均为负值，表明两部作品的指称均依赖语境，但《射雕英雄传》的均值高于《指环王》，说明相较之下《射雕英雄传》的指称更为明晰和准确。《射雕英雄传》指称明晰的语域特征主要

表现为名物化因子出现频率较高,当名物化出现频率高说明文本信息较为独立,读者无须依赖上下文语境即可判断指称。此外,WH 在关系从句中作宾语这一语言特征在《射雕英雄传》的特征值也高于《指环王》,WH 关系从句以明确和详细的方式指定文本中的指称对象,以便受话人对发话人的指称不产生歧义(Biber,1989)。

表 5 维度 3 语言特征值

语言特征	《射雕英雄传》		《指环王》		p
	平均秩	秩总和	平均秩	秩总和	
WH 在关系从句作宾语(WHOBJ)	52.09	2083.50	28.91	1156.50	p<.00
短语并列(PHC)	22.99	919.50	58.01	2320.50	p<.00
名物化(NOMZ)	57.88	2315.00	23.13	925.00	p<.00
WH 在关系从句作主语(WHSUB)	29.00	1160.00	52.00	2080.00	p<.00

维度 5 呈现的是信息在抽象和具体上的语域差异,维度值越高则文本信息抽象度越高。如表 6 所示,《指环王》与《射雕英雄传》相比在维度 5 有较高的维度值,说明《指环王》的语言表达更加抽象,例如,包括无主被动与 by 引导的被动在内的语言特征削弱对主位的强调,将主位降级到宾语位置或完全省略主位;而用来突出动词的述位,即宾语,通常是抽象概念,而不是具体的指称"(Biber,1989);与此同时,维度 5 不存在负载荷语言特征。

表 6 维度 5 语言特征值

语言特征	《射雕英雄传》		《指环王》		p
	平均秩	秩总和	平均秩	秩总和	
BY 引导被动(BYPA)	23.28	931.00	57.73	2309.00	p<.00
过去分词小句(PASTP)	52.73	2109.00	28.28	1131.00	p<.00
过去分词省略助动词(WZPAST)	49.00	1960.00	32.00	1280.00	p<.01
其他状语从句(OSUB)	22.54	901.50	58.46	2338.50	p<.00
类型符比(TTR)	53.45	2138.00	27.55	1102.00	p<.00

维度 6 为即席信息组织精细度,分值越高,即席话语特征越明显,两部作品在该维度上均为负值,语言精细度较高。如表 7 所示,"THAT 从句作动词补语"和"指示代词"均为维度 6 的高权重正值语言特征,两者往往共现于非正式话语文本中,通常被认为代表未经计划的碎片化话语模式。《指环王》文本在这两个语言特征上有较高的分值,可以进一步佐证《射雕英雄传》语言表达更加正式,《指环王》的话语信息稍随性松散。

表 7　维度 6 语言特征值

语言特征	《射雕英雄传》		《指环王》		p
	平均秩	秩总和	平均秩	秩总和	
THAT 从句作动词补语（THVC）	23.94	957.50	57.06	2282.50	*p*<.00
THAT 从句作形容词补语（THAC）	41.94	1677.50	39.06	1562.50	*p*<.00
指示代词（DEMO）	29.13	1165.00	51.88	2075.00	*p*<.01
WH 作宾语从句（WHOBJ）	52.09	2083.50	28.91	1156.50	*p*<.00
滞留介词（STPR）	50.44	2017.50	30.56	1222.50	*p*<.00
短语并列（PHC）	22.99	919.50	58.01	2320.50	*p*<.00

4. 讨论

经上述分析，《射雕英雄传》英译本和《指环王》原本在叙事性维度和显性劝诱性程度维度趋同，都有较强的叙事性，显性劝说特点均不明显；两者的不同点在于《射雕英雄传》属于一般叙事阐明型文本，信息性强，语言表达具体，指称较独立于语境，语言精细度更高；《指环王》则被归类为虚拟性叙事性文本，交互性更强，指称更依赖语境，表达较抽象，且语言风格稍松散自由。

《射雕英雄传》作为文化内涵深厚的文学作品，基于真实的历史背景，有丰富的人物形象和曲折的故事情节，其间也传递出作者有关家国大义的价值观，且最初刊载于报纸，发行方对于文本的信息密度有较高要求，作者注重有效的信息输出，作品因此具有典型的信息型文本的语域特征；而《指环王》则是托尔金早年创作的儿童幻想小说《霍比特人》的续篇，低龄的受众更容易被人物互动明显的作品所吸引。例如，文中出现频率明显高于《射雕英雄传》的第一人称更能让读者有身临其境的感受，仿佛同故事主人公一起经历惊险刺激的冒险，因此文本交互性更加明显。

此外，两者在指称方面的不同是《射雕英雄传》的译者考虑目标语读者体验的结果。如上文提到，《射雕英雄传》人物形象丰满，故事情节跌宕起伏，时常出现多人物并行的叙事场景，独立于语境的指称能够将故事线索明晰化，让读者有流畅的阅读体验，能够最大程度地沉浸体验情节。

最后，《射雕英雄传》作为 20 世纪创作的含有大量文化负载词的作品，对于西方读者来说理解难度较高。考虑到海外传播的因素，译者需要在翻译过程中克服文化差异的障碍，消解抽象文化概念（如"江湖"和"道义"等），降低阅读难度，因此不难解释为何《射雕英雄传》英译本的语言表达更为具体；与此同时，文化负载词翻译难度较高，译者需要基于源语的文化背景进行更为精细的分析、处理再传递给目标语读者。因此《射雕英雄传》英译本作为技术性较强的话语明显不会带有即席话语的特征。

从两部作品的创作背景和《射雕英雄传》的译者动机可以得出两者在 4 个语域特征表现出鲜明差异的原因，与此同时，不同的语域特征也可以为武侠小说的外译提供参考，幻想文学对于读者的感官刺激是作品吸引受众的重要因素，通过研究不难发现《指环王》交互特征明显是其坐拥广大读者的原因之一。鉴于此，在今后包括武侠小说在内的幻想文学的外译过程中，译者可以更加注重故事中人物的交流互动，为读者创造一个身临其境的阅读环境。

5. 结语

本研究采用中西幻想文学代表作——《射雕英雄传》英译本和《指环王》原本作为语料，在 MAT 多维分析软件和 SPSS 数据统计与分析工具的辅助下，进一步揭示了英译武侠小说和英国奇幻小说在语域风格上的差别，为中国武侠小说的外译和传播提供了新的观察视角，助力中国文学和中国文化走出去。但本研究也有其局限，例如语料规模较小，只选取了两部作品建立语料库。针对这一点，在未来可以扩大语料库规模，通过引入一位作者的更多作品或多位作者的作品，以此让研究结果推而广之，更具普适性。

参考文献

[1] BIBER D, EDWARD F, 1989. Drift and the evolution of English style: a history of three genres[J]. Language, 65(3): 487-517.

[2] BIBER D, 1989. Variation across speech and writing[M]. Cambridge: Cambridge University Press.

[3] BIBER D, 2004. Historical patterns for the grammatical marking of stance: a cross-register comparison[J]. Journal of historical pragmatics, 5(1):107-136.

[4] BIBER D, 2009. A corpus-driven approach to formulaic language in English: multi-word patterns in speech and writing[J]. International journal of corpus linguistics, 14(3):275-311.

[5] IRWIN W R, 1961. There and back again: the romances of Williams, Lewis, and Tolkien[J]. The sewanee review, 69(4):566-578.

[6] MOK O, 2001. Translational migration of martial arts fiction East and West[J]. International journal of translation studies, 13(1):81-102.

[7] XIAO R, 2009. Multidimensional analysis and the study of world Englishes[J]. World Englishes, 28(4):421-450.

[8] 陈晓明，彭超，2017. 想象的变异与解放——奇幻、玄幻与魔幻之辨[J]. 探索与争鸣（3）：29-36.

[9] 高红梅，2015. 英国现代奇幻文学在中国大众文化语境中的接受与影响[J]. 社会科学战线（4）：170-174.

[10] 韩云波，2005. 大陆新武侠和东方奇幻中的"新神话主义"[J]. 西南师范大学学报（人文社会科学版）(5)：65-68.

[11] 胡富茂，宋江文，2022. 中国博物馆翻译文本的语域变异多维分析[J]. 外语电化教学（5）：31-36，109.

[12] 黄悦，2021. 中国神话的网络裂变与传播规律初探[J]. 文化遗产（2）：118-125.

[13] 姜淑芹，2021. 奇幻小说文类探源与中国玄幻武侠小说定位问题[J]. 西南大学学报(社会科学版)，47(4)：198-208，230.

[14] 孟秀坤，2007. 论现代幻想文学[J]. 电影文学（22）：84-85.

[15] 孙金燕，2022. 中国当代奇幻小说叙事风格及其青年文化症候——以"九州"系列小说为讨论对象[J]. 当代文坛（5）：179-184.

[16] 夏春梅，陈曦，2015. 奇幻文学中的善恶归宗与天人合一——从《西游记》《魔戒》看中西文化异同[J]. 中华文化论坛（9）：185-188.

[17] 吴玥璠，刘军平，2019. 小议《射雕英雄传》英译本的海外热销[J]. 出版广角（14）：88-90.

[18] 赵臻，2019. 中国当代奇幻影视文学对中国传统文化的"挪用"与"改写"[J]. 江苏大学学报(社会科学版)，21(3)：23-29.

[19] 张汨，王志伟，2020. 金庸《射雕英雄传》在英语世界的接受与评价——基于Goodreads网站读者评论的考察[J]. 东方翻译（5）：18-25.

[20] 张玉，2015. 当代奇幻文学的神话学解析[J]. 兰州学刊（9）：37-41.

维特根斯坦的语言游戏说在二语词汇迁移中的运用

钟文欣

1. 引言

作为 20 世纪最伟大的数理学家、哲学家之一，维特根斯坦凭借其出色的思辨能力和哲学巧思，创作了《逻辑哲学论》和《哲学研究》等鸿篇巨作。最引人瞩目的是《哲学研究》一书，这本书标志着维特根斯坦的思想在后期开始转变，从原先的意义原子论转向了意义即用法，标志其对日常语言的进一步关注。其中，最重要的一个概念就是语言游戏说（韩林合，1996）。

维特根斯坦在其著作《哲学研究》的第七章表明"我把语言和活动交织到一起而组成的整体称为'语言游戏'"（维特根斯坦，1953）。这个观点抛开了原有传统的语法的禁锢，将游戏这一概念带入语言哲学范畴。维特根斯坦这里所说的"语言游戏"是用于指称由语言活动和非语言活动的复杂交际单位的术语。他强调的重点是按照规则的这一系列使用活动（苏鹏，2011）。他将数千万的语言游戏放入这种规则中萌芽，在规则中不断变化，一直处于一种动态的变化中，可以说是具有多样性和变动性的集合体。并且，他本人其实也指出"游戏"形成一个家族。

家族相似性对于维特根斯坦的语言游戏说是至关重要的，因为家族相似性这个概念其实是在说明事物与现象之间不存在本质的东西，共同拥有的只是通过"家族相似性"联系起来的，并且这种共享特征越多的成员越容易居于一个范畴的中心，也可以称作原型成员（胡荣，2006）。可以说，家族相似性是原型理论的一个基础，而这其实为二语词汇学习提供了一个全新的观点认知。

不仅如此，后期的维特根斯坦还对语言哲学的基础和核心"意义论"进行了阐释，认为只有"语言游戏"才有独立的意义，只有在语言游戏中才能确定语句的意义。换句话说，他认为语言游戏根植于日常语言，来源于生活形式，只有当语言作为生活形式中的一部分时才能理解语言，因此词句的意义发生于语言的使用，语义是模糊性、不确定性、开放性和动态性的集合（张国、左青青，2013）。这种"意义即用法观"能体现在母语学习中，对于二语学习者其实也有很大的用处。

根据吴亚敏对我国 2009 年到 2018 年的二语词汇习得研究，中国二语学习者对于词汇本身的内部因素联系不够，也就是对于词汇的广度、词汇的深度和词汇本身词义的联系还存在许多不足，这其实也导致了词汇和语篇理解的脱节（吴亚敏，2020）。在二语学习中，只有我们想要去高水平地学习。要对于词汇和句法有一个深度的学习认识，我们就要从多维度、从语境中学习，将实际运用放在二语学习中一个至关重要的位置。我们只有在理解日常语言情境的情况下，才能增加认知经验和记忆强度，更好地把握语言，更好地运用语言。

那么，维特根斯坦的语言游戏观中的家族相似性、意义即用法可以实际运用于中国二语学习者中。不论是从二语词汇习得角度，还是从语句习得角度，我们可以通过家族相似性原理将语义具有开放性、模糊性的词汇范畴放入同一部分进行学习，并且通过意义即用法的哲学思想将词汇和句法学习放入真实语境进行吸收，在日常语言中不断发展我们的二语能力。

2. 二语习得中的词汇迁移现象

Ellis 指出任何一个二语习得理论，如果没有描写母语迁移，都是不完整的（Ellis，1994），这其实是在向我们说明语言迁移的必要性和必然性。学习者在学习第二语言时，不可避免地会将第二语言与之前的语言经验进行对比分类，激活母语中的概念意义范畴，在这种基础上建立起来的二语结构类别势必会受到母语的影响，出现正迁移和负迁移两种情况。这种迁移，也受到认知神经科学的关注并得到了佐证，Kroll 等人的实验证明了高水平的双语者在加工二语时，母语仍然在发挥效用（Kroll、Ma，2002）。除此以外，Wu 等人的论文也指出了母语的潜意识和无意识激活在二语图像识别中的应用（Wu、Cristino、Leek, et al., 2013）。

因此在二语习得中，语言负迁移所造成的生造词现象，如中式英语现象也就显得不足为奇了。例如，"小心地滑"被翻译成"carefully slide"就是因为对 carefully、slide 两个单词并未通过语境进行学习，仅仅通过单字意义的衍生和组装将两个单词放在一起进行意义的拼凑。所以，要想把握住意义的重要性，我们就要体会语境，把握最重要的语境。回到这句话，"小心地滑"是作为一条警示语来使用，用来提醒人们注意地面当心滑倒，因此应该翻译成"beware of slippery"。这样类似的双语负迁移现象层出不穷，这其实是要求我们要用二语去思考，在二语的环境和世界观里去学习词汇、运用句法，跳出原有的母语负迁移影响。

而回到维特根斯坦的语言游戏说中去，家族相似性不仅指同一语言系统中的不同语言游戏，还指的是不同语言系统中的语言游戏存在相似性，这也就是语言迁移现象的理论基础（国防、陈秀英，2017）。并且在二语学习时，这样的相似性虽然能够帮助汉语的"规则"向英语的语法转化，但是同样也存在着因为所处环境的变化、规则的调整而产生负迁移的现象，两种语言的相似性反而起到了反作用。

这种静态系统状态下的语言学习存在着上述那样负迁移的影响，而通过语言游戏说，我们能把语言学习转换成一个动态的过程，在语言运用中培养语言能力，将语言游戏作为一种学习方式。归根结底，二语能力也是以交际为目的能力的培养，这其实与语言游戏的主张不谋而合，所以语言游戏对于二语习得有着重要且深刻的影响。

3. 家族相似性指导下的词汇习得

维特根斯坦对于词的定义是这样解释的："词的意义由词在语言游戏中的功能决定或者词的意义存在于它的用法中，一个词的含义是它在语言中的用法。"（维特根斯坦，1953）词汇学习的重要性是不言而喻的，没有词汇，我们无法搭建句法框架，更没有办法遣词造句，更谈不上语言交际能力。因此对于词汇的学习，我们在传统的教学活动中把规则性放在了首位，简单来说，就是先记住意思是什么。但是，从家族相似性的观点来说，母语词汇和二语词汇具有相似性，也具有差异性。学习二语时应该从母语到目的语进行正迁移，但是两种语言的对比也是十分必要的，发现两种语言的差异性就是防止负迁移的有效手段。

在中国学生的二语习得词汇中，我们能发现许多由于对汉语词汇的不深刻理解而对英语词汇表达发生错误的情况。以英语单词的曲折变化为例，我们在初期学习二语时候常常会造出如"two apple""many banana"等这样的错误小句。这是因为中文的量词几乎不带单位变换，属于孤立性语言。而英语通过派生、转换、合成并按照一定的语法规则来生成语义相同且词类符合上下文要求的词语（郭红霞，2011）。因此对于中文母语者而言，在不改变词性的情况下，许多词可以在不同语境中具有不同词类功能，即许多汉语词类的转换往往不涉及词形改变，就这两个句子而言，英语中可数名词进行量化时受到本族语言负迁移的影响，出现不带"s"这种情况。不仅如此，过去时态"ed"、完成时态"have done"的变换，也是容易产生负迁移的地方，这些汉语规则对于英语规则的影响，就是我们需要注意的狭义语法。因此，从语言游戏说的语言哲学观点出发，二语学习者在学习英语时可以从家族相似性出发，先进行两种语言相似性的对比。

除此以外，家族相似性的动态观点要求我们把语言和日常活动联系在一起，强调日常语言与真实世界的交互关系（国防、陈秀英，2017）。这种开放性和变化性的原则，在单词教学中也能够解决一些问题。以蔬菜的单词教学为例，引入单词的时候可以进行一个类别的划分，让同学们发现一些蔬菜与别的蔬菜之间有什么关系，构建出一个浅显的原型特征。然后，这样一种原型特征构建出一个"家庭树"，再把要学的单词 carrot、tomato、potato 等进行填充。不仅如此，家族相似性的多样性观点还要求我们进一步联系日常世界，标记蔬菜的使用方法。这时候肯定会拓展到做菜的方法，那么教师就能自然而然地讲解如何制作菜肴，以及在餐桌上的礼仪规范。如此，通过语言游戏的指导不仅可以扩大词汇量，还教会二语习得者们如何在具体的语言环境中使用恰当的语言。

上述初级的单词学习方法是对于初级的二语学习者而言的。而对于更高级的二语学习者而言，在不同语言游戏下对词类进行转换，具体到单词上就十分困难了。例如，一段句子中出现形容词当名词，名词当形容词，动词当名词等的这些种情况，一定要进行动态的语境把握。从语类的使用度来看，英语属于静态语言，名词的作用很大，而汉语属于动态的语言，动词串联起整个句子，以下面的中英互译为例。

例 1 The old man had no suggestion to our plan. 那个老人没有给我们的计划提建议。

例 2 The youths always dream fondly of their future. 年轻人对前途总是怀有美好的想象。

具体分析来看，这些句子之所以让我们觉得符合英语特点、灵活流畅，是因为这些句子的翻译在单字翻译中并没有字对字翻译，而是在某一语境中对于词类形式进行了充分的变换。在例 1 中，我们发现"提建议"这个动词的词组放入英语句子中反而变成了名词"suggestion"，例 2 中名词"想象"却又作为了动词"dream"的主体部分。可见，各个词的义项假如是集中地存在于二语学习者的头脑中，在理解造句时，就能通过语言环境进行灵活的推导。这样的话，二语知识能够随语境进行变换时，母语词汇将减少二语应用负迁移。

通过语言游戏说中的家族相似性，我们在单词学习和词汇转换翻译上都能得到启迪。但最重要的是词义的这种模糊性、不确定性、开放性，要求我们不能简单地用逻辑命题和事实的简单对应来解释，我们必须要把握中英语言游戏有一个"相似性"的认识，但是也要学会去对比。要想真正地掌握二语词汇，就更应该掌握其特定的使用语境，这样才能在合适的情况下说出符合交际目标的话语。这样的话，即使我们无法逐一阐述场景的多样性，通过"家族相似性"强调学生的实践与感悟，通过逐步增加新的形式，我们也可以从多种原始形式构建诸多复杂的形式。

4. 在语言使用中习得词汇

西方语言哲学几乎都涉及意义问题，指称论、行为论、真值条件论都是对于句子进行的思考。而对于维特根斯坦而言，"一个词在语言中的使用就是它的意义。"（维特根斯坦，1953）使用论的观点其实标志着意义理论从静态研究转向了动态研究（刘龙根，2004）。

具体到词的研究方面，这种"意义即使用"的观点要求我们用一种动态规则的观点来进行语言游戏，也就意味着语言用法依赖于遵守规则，而遵守规则依赖于生活形式。这种"规则"从狭义上说是语法，从广义上说是语言本地化的一种无形形式（杨佑文，2011）。让我们用"意义即使用"的方法来分析以下几个词组，"白酒——white wine""眼红——red-eyed""爱屋及乌——love me, love my raven"，这些词组就是对同一种事物有认知上的偏差而出现的命名错误。我们可以看到受到母语迁移的影响把"white wine"翻译成白酒，因为对于我们来说白酒才是更为常见的，而实际上外国人把"白葡萄酒"称作"white wine"。除此以外，"眼红"的翻译不能按照中国的文化背景进行字对字翻译，在英语国家地区"green"才是代表嫉妒的意思，因此"green-eyed"才是我们真正想表达的意思。而对于最后一句"爱屋及乌"的翻译，英语国家更是翻译为"love me, love my dog"而不是"love my raven"。因为在英语国家中，乌鸦是邪恶的代表，这从爱伦坡的《乌鸦》中就能看出。由此可见，我们的生活形式导致了不同的认知方式，从而也就形成了不同的习惯性语言表达，而这种一以贯之的思维模式也就是导致负迁移的原因之一。

简单说来，当学习二语词汇时，我们要以意义为核心进行整合，上述的例子也在启示我们，一个词并非简单的所指关系或一个词对一个词的对应关系，而是涉及感知、范畴化、概念化的复杂的认知心理过程（张国、左青青，2013）。二语词汇的习得与对二语词汇意义的理解有着密切的关系，而词义的理解在于对词汇的使用，在这一过程中，我们不能一味追求词类关系的对等，而是要去真正关注词的实际运用，掌握词的真正使用方法。

而涉及文化方面的语言游戏，我们只有更多地接触、理解目标语国家的习俗文化看法，增加认知经验，才能适应这种"规则"和"生活形式"，从而更好地运用语言。并且简单地讲授规则并不能让人理解运用，当二语学习者明白这个句子的具体含义时，并且能够由输入者转变成输出者时，他才能够完全掌握这个词的真正意义。那么，我们在平时就要进行输出训练，可以通过利用所学的单词进行情境表演、小组讨论、辩论等多种形式。并且，随着科技的发展，ChatGPT也可以对我们的输出内容进行有效的纠正，对我们的输出内容进行错误改正和更加优化的修改。

5. 词汇学习的情境性运用

通过具体的示例和分析，我们从语言游戏说的观点分析了二语习得中的一些问题，揭示了语言学习的动态过程，语言游戏既是目的，又是媒介。对于我们而言，无论在教学中还是日常学习中，都应该把握目标语国家的"生活形式"，才能成为真正的"语言游戏者"。不论是作为二语学习者还是教学者，我们都不能孤立地运用词汇，而是要依据"词不离句，句不离文"的原则，将词汇融入语境中实现其交际功能并掌握其意义，这样才能够"身临其境"，准确把握词汇的意义（李增眼，2013）。

具体而言，针对家族相似性的研究，我们可以合理运用英语本族学习者语料库（LOCNESS）和非本族语英语作文语料库（CLEC）这两个语料库。从语言游戏说的"家族相似性"观点，我们可以把这两个语料库进行一个对比式的迁移学习（孙丽丽，2015）。例如，在家族相似性的指导下，想要知道"提高"这个词对应的英语单词，那么就可以运用语料库，用简明的方式找出"enhance""enrich""upgrade"等，找出相似性，找出某种语境下的"语言规则"。简单说来，即找出义项相关的词类，然后挖掘实际语言情况下的规则运用。调动主观能动性，不拘泥于词典上的条条框框，才能先行后知，在行中知。在这样的规则引导下，才能从简单的语言游戏过渡到复杂的语言游戏，不断在原有的知识上进行积累，进行创新学习。

除此以外，挖掘词汇的文化因素也是理解整体文化的一种重要方式。作为语言载体的一部分，词汇中常常带有特定的文化信息，它在典故、习惯性用语中的表现经常和书面、字典中展现不尽相同。要想全面深刻地掌握二语词汇，我们就必须对跨文化知识有一定的了解，通过学习中西文化的差异，加强对词汇的理解与掌握。

6. 结论

对于课堂教学而言，"儿童学说话主要是通过生活和游戏，向家里人学习，向游戏的同伴学习，在很大程度上是不自觉的，可是收效之快是惊人的。"（吕叔湘，1992）这提示学习语言的时候应该全面发展，不拘泥于课本结构，要全方位、立体地创造语言环境。具体而言，在低年级的二语习得者课堂上，在注重写的能力时，还应该注重口语能力，倡导情景式的教学，为学生学习设定相应的任务和问题，让学生可以在真实情境中习得语言。除此以外，语言游戏说对生活形式的注重要求采用日常语言，脱离原有的传统教学，挣脱生搬硬套的句型束缚，更加注重语言过程中的语用学意义（孙自挥，2008）。

在"意义即使用"的观点指导下，在习得时既要注重输入，又要注重输出。在输入时，要从全面动态的观点了解每一种语言游戏的特点，不仅是确定的规则，还有文化背景背后的规则。引导二语习得者从目标语群体的角度去思考，对这种语言游戏情境下的规则进行把握，在提高知识水平的同时，对文化认知又有了一个全面的理解。针对二语学习者而言，在词汇学习上和词汇教学上都可以采用语言游戏说的观点进行思考，用词库翻译手段来了解相关义项，用情景式教学来激活语境记忆，用角色扮演的方式来思考文化背景，如此的强化方法目的都是充分运用"语言游戏"，这样才能提高二语词汇的习得效果。

可以说，"家族相似性"和"意义即运用"的语言哲学方法对二语习得有所启示，从更全面、广泛的观点吸取优质的教学资源，打下坚实的理论依据。并且，在新课标要求下的课堂中，不应只简单地把维特根斯坦的"语言游戏说"作为一种方法和手段，而是应该把这种"游戏说"作为一种意识，一种全方位贯通语言运用中的意识，跳出课堂教学，尽量用有限的规则指导开辟无限的创意空间，穿梭于语法之间。

参考文献

[1] ELLIS R, 1994. The study of second language acquisition[M]. Oxford: Oxford University Press, 1994.
[2] KROLL J F, MA F Y DIJKSTRA T, 2017. The bilingual lexicon[J]. The Handbook of Psycholinguistics, 294-319.
[3] WITTGENSTEIN L, 1953. Philosophical investigations[M]. New York: The Macmillan Company.

[4] WU Y J, CRISTINO F, LEEK C, et al, 2013. Non-selective lexical access in bilinguals is spontaneous and independent of input monitoring: evidence from eye tracking[J]. Cognition, 129(2): 418-425.

[5] 国防，陈秀英，2017. 从语言游戏论看二语词汇习得过程中的语言迁移现象[J]. 北京科技大学学报(社会科学版)，33(4)：26-31.

[6] 郭红霞，2011. 二语词汇习得中跨语言迁移的语言类型分析[J]. 外语学刊（2）：114-117.

[7] 韩林合，1996. 维特根斯坦论"语言游戏"和"生活形式"们[J]. 北京大学学报（哲学社会科学版）（1）：25-33.

[8] 胡荣，2006. 语言输入与原型理论——关于情状体假设的解释[J]. 外语教学（1）：26-29.

[9] 李增垠，2013. "语言游戏"理论与词汇教学的语境化策略研究[J]. 西南科技大学学报(哲学社会科学版)，30(2)：46-50.

[10] 刘龙根，2004. 维特根斯坦"语言游戏说"探析[J]. 广西社会科学（7）：34-36.

[11] 苏鹏，2011. 维特根斯坦的语境观及其影响[J]. 外语学刊（2）：25-27.

[12] 孙丽丽，2015. "语言游戏说"指引下的二语词汇习得[J]. 鄂州大学学报，22(12)：46-48.

[13] 孙自挥，2008. 维特根斯坦遵从规则说及其对外语教学的启示[J]. 中国外语（4）：23-26.

[14] 维特根斯坦，2009. 哲学研究[M]. 李步楼，译. 北京：商务印书馆.

[15] 吴亚敏，2020. 近十年国内二语词汇习得分析研究综述——基于四种国内外语类核心期刊[J]. 现代交际（3）：202-203.

[16] 杨佑文，2011. 维特根斯坦"语言游戏说"与二语习得[J]. 外语学刊（2）：20-24.

[17] 张国，左青青，2013. 二语词汇语义及语用习得障碍之认知初探——后期维特根斯坦语言哲学观[J]. 中国海洋大学学报（社会科学版）（1）：110-113.

我国中小学教师压力研究综述
——基于CiteSpace的知识图谱分析

王小慧

1. 引言

2021年7月,中共中央办公厅和国务院办公厅印发了《关于进一步减轻义务教育阶段学生作业负担和校外培训负担的意见》(以下简称"双减"),该意见旨在减轻学生学习负担。2022年3月2日,北京师范大学中国教育与社会发展研究院教育国情调查中心发布了《全国"双减"成效调查报告》(以下简称《报告》)。《报告》一方面肯定了"双减"政策卓有成效,另一方面指出"双减"改革面临的痛点,其中包括教师的工作压力和负担加重。过重的压力和负担不仅对教师身心造成影响,还会进一步影响学生的学业表现和身心健康。Oberle 和 Schonert-Reichl(2016)的研究发现小学教师因压力引起的职业倦怠越严重,学生表现出的压力程度就越大。同时,Herman 等人(2018)的研究也证实处于高压、表现出职业倦怠且具有低应对水平的教师所教的学生更有可能有破坏性行为以及较差的学习表现。

出于以下研究问题:(1)国内学界对教师压力的研究始于多少年,每年发文量如何?(2)该领域内奠基性的人物有哪些?学者间的合作情况如何?(3)国内学者们的研究关注哪些方面?(4)未来可能的研究方向是什么?本文在CNKI(中国知网)上以关键词"中小学教师+压力""中小学教师+负担"搜索文献,剔除会议文献后,获得初始文献706篇(截至2022年9月)。后将数据导入CiteSpace 6.1.R3中进行除重,去除118篇相似文献以及248篇学位论文后,得到338篇期刊文献作为样本用于分析。在处理文献时,时间跨度(timespan)选择为2000—2022年,处理时间单位(slice length)为1,处理对象选择标准为默认值(g-index:知识单元提取方式,其中k=25;Top n=50,意思是选择每个时间切片中出现频率前n的节点;Top n%=10%,意思是选择每个时间切片中出现频率排名前10%的节点)。为使效果图更为清晰明了,图片裁剪方式选择寻径网络(pathfinder)和裁剪选择网络(pruning sliced networks)。

2. 近20年研究概况

2.1 发文量统计

2000—2022,我国关于教师压力的研究发文总量为338篇,具体发文情况见图1。由图1可见,总体发文趋势可大致分为三个阶段。第一阶段为2000—2002,为研究准备期,前两年没有教师压力的相关文章发表,2002年发文量破零并达到了14篇。2003—2011为研究发展阶段,其间的发文量大幅上涨,总体呈现上升趋势。第三阶段为2012—2022,对教师压力的研究热度回落并逐步稳定到每年发文10余篇。

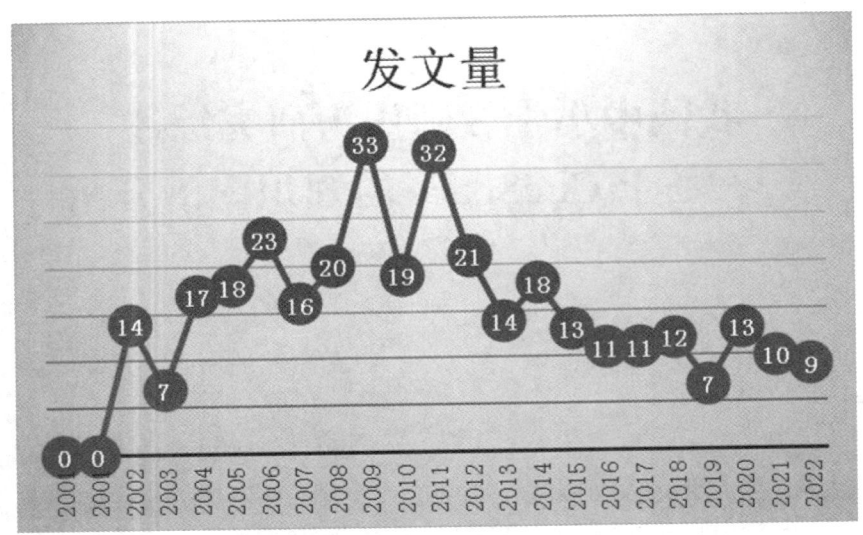

图 1 教师压力研究发文趋势

2.2 作者分析

在 CiteSpace 中选择作者（author）作为节点分析，阈值（threshold）设置为 2，让图谱显示发文量为 2 篇及以上的作者的名字，其他参数保持不变，调整画面布局后，得到的结果如图 2 所示。图中节点 n=447，表示共计有 447 名学者；学者之间的线段表示彼此之间有合作，图中连线共计 312 条（部分发文频率少于 2 的作者未在图中显示）。作者发文量越多，其名字对应的节点越大；发文时间越近，节点的灰度越重。

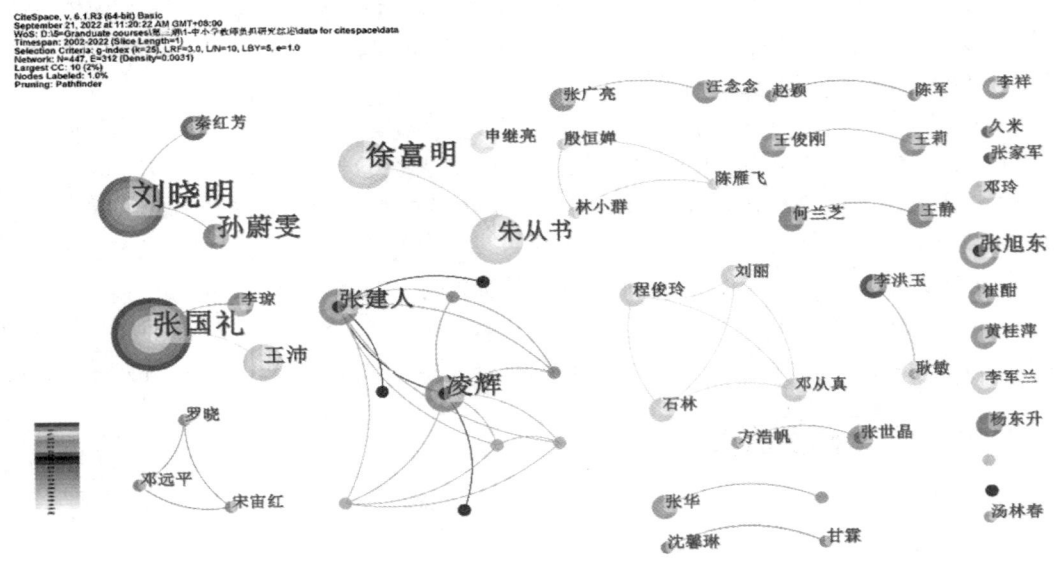

图 2 作者图谱

根据图 2，对教师压力研究贡献最大的几位学者包括刘晓明、徐富明、张国礼、凌辉、张建人、朱丛书、张旭东、王沛、孙蔚雯等。从学者间的合作来看，凌辉和张建人两位学者与其他学者合作最为紧密，分别与 8 人合作发文，且 8 人之间又有相互合作。其次，还有刘晓明与秦红芳、孙蔚雯等三位学者，张国礼与李琼、王沛等学者，以及邓从真与刘丽、石林、程俊玲等学者之间的合作发文较多。从节点颜色看，近几年发文的作者有李宏玉、张旭东、张家军、黄桂萍、李祥等学者。

发文量最多的学者刘晓明主要关注农村中小学教师群体，从心理学角度研究这类教师的压力源、应对压力方式以及职业压力与职业倦怠作用机制。在他的最近一篇文章中，他用人格交互理论（PSI理论）解释行动控制在工作压力与工作倦怠方面的作用机制，研究发现行动控制风格和策略能调节中小学教师的工作压力和工作倦怠，建议采用PSI理论指导干预训练以预防和缓解教师工作倦怠情况（秦红芳、刘晓明，2015）。张国礼除了关注中小学教师的压力源及现状，还重点关注中小学教师职业承诺对工作压力和职业枯竭的调节关系、工作压力与教师主观幸福感的关系等。他表示教学理念能直接或间接地对教师工作压力和主观幸福感产生影响，因此先进的教学理念能帮助教师降低压力感，保持较健康的心理状态，并获得高水平的主观幸福感（张国礼、边玉芳、董奇，2012）。凌辉的研究焦点是工作压力与不同心理因素如倦怠感、职业幸福感、工作价值观等方面以及社会支持之间的关系，研究对象主要为中学教师。他指出这类教师的工作压力与工作投入呈负相关，并且当这些教师关注外部工作价值如薪酬、福利等时，工作压力对工作投入的负面影响更为深刻（李光程、王怀南、张建人，等，2018）。

近几年发文较多的学者张旭东着眼于珠三角地区，研究该片区中小学教师工作压力对心理生活质量的影响。他的研究表明中小学教师工作压力、心理弹性、自尊和生活质量呈现出两两相关性，心理压力不仅能直接影响生活质量，还能通过心理弹性和自尊间接影响生活质量（李清、李瑜、张旭东，2021）。李洪玉的研究与张旭东的有相似之处，他主要从心理学维度探究工作压力如何对中小学教师职业倦怠产生影响。他指出中小学教师工作压力能直接影响或间接通过情绪劳动和工作满意度影响职业倦怠程度，并建议学校可从情绪劳动和工作满意度角度提出改进措施（李鹏、张志超、杨洋，等，2022）。李祥等人与上述学者不同，没有从心理学角度研究问题，而是关注国家下发的减轻中小学教师负担的政策，分析这一系列政策的有效性、合法性，并提出改进建议。他们的研究指出减负政策有效性不足，缺乏对教师负担问题的回应，忽视了心理负担和职业发展负担，只关注了非教学的额外负担和教学的形式负担。他们从国家、学校和教师个体角度提出建议，包括教育局应明确教育责任范围，增强学校自主办学权力，明确主体地位，提升教师权力等（迟明阳、李祥，2020）（李祥、周芳、蔡孝露，2021）。

3. 研究热点

3.1 关键词共现分析

文章的关键词在一定程度上能体现出研究的焦点，对关键词进行研究可对文章主题进行窥探。不同的关键词在同一篇文章中出现的次数越多，表明各主题之间的联系越加紧密。一篇文章的多个关键词之间存在的联系可用共现频率表示。在CiteSpace中设置关键词为节点，将阈值（threshold）设置为10，其余参数保持不变，得到结果如下。表1和表2所列分别为出现频率前10以及中心性前10的关键词。

表 1　出现频率前 10 的关键词表

序号	频率	关键词
1	99	职业压力
2	61	工作压力
3	41	教师
4	40	职业倦怠
5	26	压力源
6	24	心理压力
7	21	压力
8	21	心理健康
9	19	中小学
10	17	对策

表 2　中心性前 10 的关键词表

序号	中心性	关键词
1	0.6	职业压力
2	0.44	工作压力
3	0.23	中小学
4	0.17	初中教师
5	0.16	教师
6	0.15	压力源
7	0.15	压力
8	0.1	职业倦怠
9	0.1	教师负担
10	0.09	对策

由上述两表可见，2000—2022，我国学者对中小学教师压力的研究以职业压力为中心，以压力来源、应对策略以及压力与心理学等其他维度的关系为主要切入点展开，呈现出跨学科、多维度的特点。在表 1 中，关键词出现的频率越高，说明它得到了越多学者的关注。出现频率前四位的关键词为"职业压力"（99）、"工作压力"（61）、"教师"（41）、"职业倦怠"的频率（40）远远高于其他关键词，但它们在表 2 中的排位有所不同。所谓中心性（centrality），也叫中介中心性（betweenness centrality），是对某节点在网络中位置重要性的量化，可反映具有潜力的研究以及方向（Chen, Ibekwe-SanJuan, Hou, 2010）。中心性大于 0.1 的关键词在共现网络中起到了关键节点的作用。如"中小学""初中教师""教师负担"等出现的频率不高，但在共现网络中都是关键节点，在中小学教师压力研究中起到了重要作用。

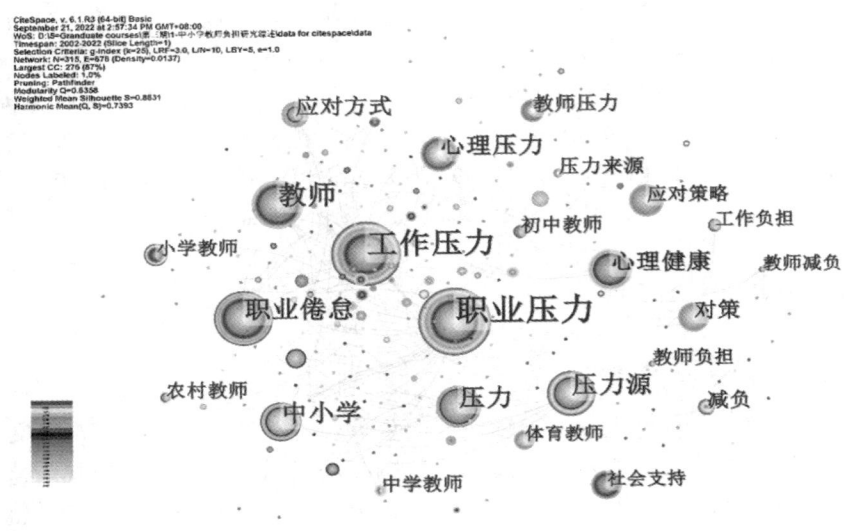

图 4　关键词共现图谱

图 4 更为清晰明了地展示了各个关键词在网络中的相互关系。图中关键词节点的圆圈越大，表示其出现频率越高；圆圈灰度不同的环对照时间图谱表示关键词出现的时间段。"工作压

力""职业压力""职业倦怠"等关键词在保持高频率出现的同时,也是近几年发文的核心词汇;此外,"减负""小学教师""教师负担""压力源""工作负担"等关键词在近几年的文章中逐渐出现,虽然频率不高,却是今后研究较为热门的方向,这样的趋势也是对教师减负政策的回应。

3.2 关键词聚类分析

CiteSpace 采用谱聚类,聚类标签选择从关键词(keyword)中提取,算法采用 LLR(log-likelihood ratio),最终得到 10 个聚类,且模块值(modularity Q)=0.6358,平均轮廓值(silhouette)=0.8831,当 Q 值大于 0.3 时,说明分类结构是显著的;当 S 值大于 0.7 时,说明结果是令人信服的(陈悦、陈超美、刘则渊,等,2015)。由图 5 可见,根据各个聚类的颜色,在共计 11 个聚类中,有关"工作压力""初任教师"和"教师负担"的三类主题是近几年研究的重点。表 3 显示了各个聚类包含的子类信息。

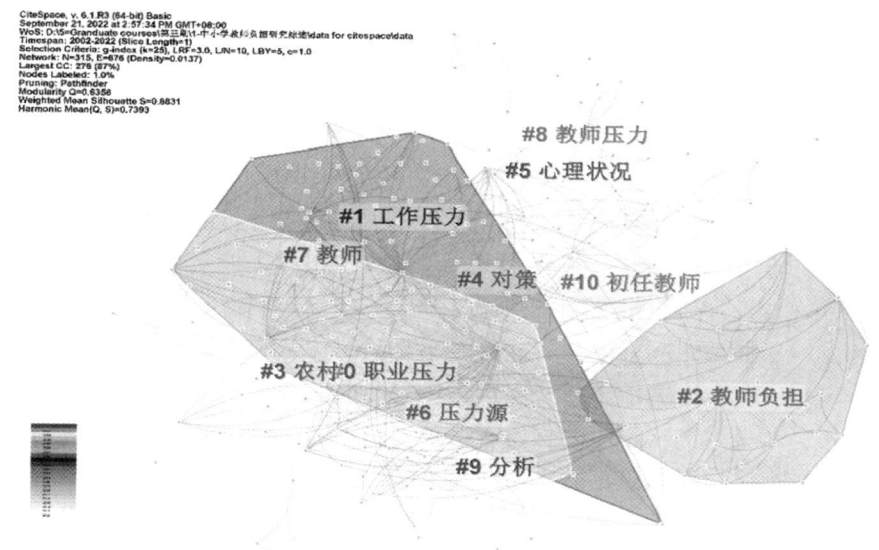

图 5 关键词聚类

表 3 聚类详情表

Cluster ID	size	silhouette	mean year	Top Terms (log-likelihood ratio, P-level)
0	44	0.869	2011	职业压力(36.99, 1.0E-4);中学教师(12.14, 0.001);教师(9.19, 0.005);西藏(9.09, 0.005);心理资本(9.09, 0.005)
1	40	0.925	2010	工作压力(38.9, 1.0E-4);职业倦怠(34.74, 1.0E-4);社会支持(9.67, 0.005);小学教师(9.67, 0.005);中介作用(9.67, 0.005)
2	30	0.953	2019	教师负担(13.21, 0.001);教师减负(13.21, 0.001);减负(13.21, 0.001);教师权利(6.56, 0.05);教育政策(6.56, 0.05)
3	29	0.916	2009	农村(19.75, 1.0E-4);压力(16.75, 1.0E-4);应对方式(14.75, 0.001);社会学(9.79, 0.005);职业(9.79, 0.005)

(续表)

Cluster ID	size	silhouette	mean year	Top Terms (log-likelihood ratio, P-level)
4	27	0.796	2008	对策（35.46, 1.0E-4）；心理压力（23.23, 1.0E-4）；心理健康（15.63, 1.0E-4）；成因（13.07, 0.001）；自我调查（8.69, 0.005）
5	26	0.938	2007	心理状况（10.97, 0.001）；教师心理压力（10.97, 0.001）；初中教师（10.97, 0.001）；压力来源（7.29, 0.01）；显著差异（5.46, 0.05）
6	25	0.857	2008	压力源（29.77, 1.0E-4）；中小学（16.33, 1.0E-7）；访谈研究（9.63, 0.005）；信息技术（4.79, 0.005）；总工作时间（4.79, 0.05）
7	25	0.715	2008	教师（25.45, 1.0E-4）；策略（9.47, 0.005）；课改（9.47, 0.005）；小学（9.47, 0.005）；教案（4.71, 0.005）
8	16	0.909	2007	教师压力（39.05, 1.0E-4）；应对策略（12.65, 0.001）；影响因素（6.28, 0.05）；重庆市黔江区（6.28, 0.05）；预测变量（6.25, 0.05）
9	8	0.975	2012	分析（21.35, 1.0E-4）；工作负荷（14.11, 0.001）；体育教师（10.35, 0.005）；减负策略（6.99, 0.01）；义务制教育（6.99, 0.01）
10	6	0.984	2016	初任教师（10.78, 0.005）；抗逆力（10.78, 0.005）；压力管理（10.78, 0.005）；中小学教师（0.54, 0.5）；职业压力（0.46, 0.5）

3.2.1 工作压力

"工作压力"聚类包括"职业倦怠""社会支持""小学教师"和"中介作用"等子类。这方面的文章主要聚焦中小学教师，尤其是小学教师，探寻工作压力和职业倦怠以及其他因素的相互影响关系。研究发现中小学教师工作压力与职业倦怠的各个次维度有高度相关性，而不同来源的压力对倦怠的次维度的作用有所不同。教师工作特征、学生学业压力、社会因素、专业发展要求、学校组织氛围等因素能显著预测倦怠程度。工作负荷和学校组织氛围对教师情绪衰竭有明显预测作用，工作特征和学生学业压力对身体衰竭维度的解释力最大，社会因素和专业发展压力能显著预测职业倦怠的非人性化维度，而学生问题带来的压力则与教师的成就感呈正相关（徐富民、安连义、牛芳，2004）（李琼、王松丽、张艳，2009）（刘晓明、王丽荣、金宏章，等，2008）。其他因素如教师职业承诺、教学效能感、社会支持、核心自我评价、情绪劳动和工作满意度等在工作压力和职业倦怠之间起到中介作用，通过对这些因素进行调节，可适当减轻教师压力，减弱倦怠程度（刘晓明，2004）（甘霖、沈馨琳，2011）（李鹏、张志超、杨洋，2022）（吕邹沁、凌辉，2014）（张国礼、边玉芳、董奇，2013）（杨玲、巫文胜，2013）。

3.2.2 教师负担

2 号聚类"教师负担"着眼于教师权力、国家政策等方面，探讨教师减负这一议题。学者多从理论角度分析教师工作负担过重的表现、成因以及解决方案。研究发现中小学教师过重的工作负担主要来源于三个方面：首先，繁杂的非教学任务，尤其是行政任务占据了教师的大量工作时间，同时教师的自主权力不足，自我分配工作乏力；其次，应试教育压力束缚教师自我提升以及科研活动的开展；最后，部门管理不当，未形成学校、教师、社会减负合力。建议创建多元支持体系，在保障并进一步提升教师权利、福利的同时，明确教师工作内容，提升部门管理能力，优化评价体系，将工作压力转换为内驱力，并建立基于大数据的检测系统，以实现精准减负等（张家军、闫君子，2022）（张家军、陈苗，2022）（任娇旸、王颖，2013）（迟明阳、李祥，2020）（付睿，2019）。

3.2.3 初任教师

"初任教师"这一聚类研究的对象为任职时间在5年内的新教师，以访谈、开放式问卷的方式探究新教师的压力来源。这类教师的主要压力源包括工作特征、学生因素、学校管理、职业发展、社会压力等（吴文春、余洁玲，2014），与程俊玲等人（2004）以及丁凤琴（2006）针对中小学全体教师做的研究结果一致，说明教师入职时间对教师感受到的压力源并没有显著影响。也有学者对不同学校类型的新教师的压力情况进行调查分析，探寻教师压力水平与学校类型以及教师心理水平之间的关系。研究发现不同类型学校的新教师在情绪状态、成就感以及抑郁水平上差异显著，名校分校教师在职业与心理状态上表现更好，但这类教师在职业发展和社会问题上的压力水平相较而言更高；学校类型和压力水平与抑郁有交互作用，在高压力和中压力教师组中，这种作用在重点学校的新教师身上更为显著（郭华、汪婷，2019）。

3.3 小结

CiteSpace 可用变异检测算法提取出现频率高以及出现变异的词汇，以此来反映某一领域的研究方向。在 CiteSpace 中选择关键词作为突现（burstness）检测词汇，系统默认伽马值为1，但得出的突现词只有2个，因此修改伽马值为0.5，得到如图6所示的18个突现词。

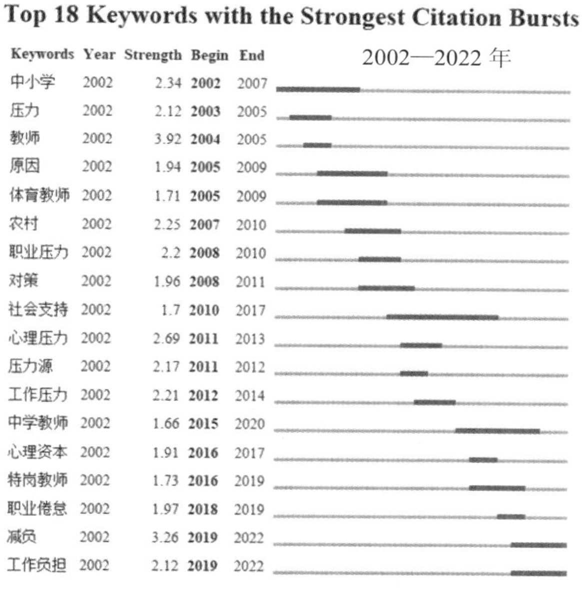

Top 18 Keywords with the Strongest Citation Bursts
2002—2022 年

Keywords	Year	Strength	Begin	End
中小学	2002	2.34	2002	2007
压力	2002	2.12	2003	2005
教师	2002	3.92	2004	2005
原因	2002	1.94	2005	2009
体育教师	2002	1.71	2005	2009
农村	2002	2.25	2007	2010
职业压力	2002	2.2	2008	2010
对策	2002	1.96	2008	2011
社会支持	2002	1.7	2010	2017
心理压力	2002	2.69	2011	2013
压力源	2002	2.17	2011	2012
工作压力	2002	2.21	2012	2014
中学教师	2002	1.66	2015	2020
心理资本	2002	1.91	2016	2017
特岗教师	2002	1.73	2016	2019
职业倦怠	2002	1.97	2018	2019
减负	2002	3.26	2019	2022
工作负担	2002	2.12	2019	2022

图 6 关键词突现图

图中年份（year）为检测文献的最早发文时间，强度（strength）为关键词的突现强度，开始（begin）为关键词突现时间点，结束（end）为关键词结束时间点，每个关键词后的红色线条表示该关键词出现的时间跨度。

2000年以来，学校教育走上了改革之路，加上国外研究的影响，我国学者逐渐开始关注中小学教师，研究这个群体面临的压力情况。这股研究的势头猛烈，关键词"教师"的突变强度高达 3.92，在此期间，国内学者将中小学教师这个群体的压力研究进一步细化为：（1）具体某个学科，如体育（杨剑、陈开梅，2006）、英语（王群锋、石婕妤、颜健生，2012）等；（2）某个地域范围，如农村地区（张劲松，2005）、贫困地区（王官诚，2008）；（3）不同民族（杨翠娥、黄祥祥，2008）；（4）不同职位，如特岗教师（吴日晖、高敏、刘伟方，2018）、校长（彭勇，2004）；（5）不同压力类型，如心理压力（慕彦瑾，2011）、经济压力（刘敏，2006）；（6）压力应对方式以及如何减轻压力负担（申艳娥，2004）（杨蕊、王琦林，2021）（张家军、闫君子，2022）。

随着生活水平的提高，人们对优质教育的需求逐年上涨，这进一步加重了教师的压力。自 2009 年后，关键词"体育教师"在期刊发文中出现频率逐年降低，更多的学者以教师和社会为切入点研究教师压力与社会支持的相互关系。如高萍和张宁（2009）研究教师压力与社会支持和教学效能感的关系。2018 年，在全国两会上出现了"把时间还给老师"的呼声，习近平总书记在同年的全国教育大会上强调"办学有规律，学校有主业"。2018 年后出现研究转向，以"减负""减轻工作负担"等为主题的文章符合现实特征，其数量以强劲的势头增长，从 2019 年至 2022 年都保持了高度的活力。自 2021 年 7 月"双减"政策下达后，国家加大了对体育这门课程的关注，也调整体育在中小学总课程中的占比。今后的研究可关注"双减"政策下中小学体育教师的压力源有何变化以及应对、缓解压力的方法。

此外，笔者在文献梳理的过程中，发现多名学者就不同维度的教师压力感的结果差异较大。就学校类型而言，程俊玲等人（2004）认为在家庭因素和社会因素方面，普通学校的教师压力显著高于重点学校教师。而该结果与邵光华和顾泠沅（2002）的研究结果不一致。学者对不同教学阶段教师在总体压力感方面也没有得到一致的结果。程俊玲等人（2004）经过调查发现高中教师的总体压力最大，初中教师次之，小学教师压力最小。这与不同阶段教师面临学生考试压力有关。而丁凤琴（2006）则认为小学和中学教师在考试、学生因素等方面的压力并无显著差异。后续研究可着眼于导致这些不同结果的因素，并研究在新的时代背景和环境下的教师压力源以及成因。

4. 结论

为了解我国学者对中小学教师压力的研究情况以及今后的研究趋势，本文使用文献分析软件 CiteSpace 对 CNKI 上收录的相关期刊文献进行了发文统计、核心学者分析、关键词共现和聚类分析，并根据关键词突现展望今后的研究。本文发现：（1）我国对中小学教师压力的研究约始于 2000 年，2009—2012 年出现了一股研究热潮，此后发文量趋于平稳，每年发文保持在 10 篇左右。（2）学者徐富明、张国礼、刘晓明、朱丛书等较早开始研究中小学教师压力情况，他们的文章在领域内有奠基性的地位。凌辉、张建人、邓从真等学者与其他学者间的合作较多，其他学者间鲜有合作。发文机构大多为高校，身处教学前线的中小学教师和中小学校则很少发文。（3）"工作压力""职业压力""职业倦怠""教师""压力源"等关键词是核心词汇，在发文中出现频率较其他词汇高，但"减负""教师负担""中小学""职业压力""工作压力"等关键词是近几年学者关注的重点。研究内容方面近几年发文聚焦于工作压力、教师负担和初任教师。（4）根据关键词突现，"教师减负"这一议题保持着强劲的势头，是今后研究的重点。同时根据国家政策和实际情况，中小学体育教师的压力情况以及新时代背景下中小学教师的压力情况也是值得关注的方面。

参考文献

[1] CHEN C M, IBEKWE-SANJUAN F, HOU J, 2010. The structure and dynamics of co-citation clusters: a multiple-perspective co-citation analysis[J]. Journal of the American society for information science and technology, 61(7): 1386-1409.

[2] HERMAN K C, HICKMON-ROSA J, REINKE W M, 2018. Empirically derived profiles of teacher stress, burnout, self-efficacy, and coping and associated student outcomes[J]. Journal of positive behavior interventions, 20: 90-100.

[3] OBERLE E, SCHONERT-REICHL K A, 2016. Stress contagion in the classroom? The link between classroom teacher burnout and morning cortisol in elementary school students[J]. Social science & medicine, 159: 30-37.

[4] 陈悦，陈超美，刘则渊，等，2015. CiteSpace知识图谱的方法论功能[J]. 科学学研究，33(2)：242-253.

[5] 程俊玲，邓从真，石林，等，2004. 中小学教师工作压力状况及相关因素调查研究[J]. 教育理论与实践（6）：27-30.

[6] 迟明阳，李祥，2020. 中小学教师减负问题的形成与破解路径[J]. 教学与管理（3）：27-31.

[7] 丁凤琴，2006. 基础教育课程改革中的教师心态探析——中小学教师职业压力与心理健康的问卷调查[J]. 教育探索（12）：113-115.

[8] 丁凤琴，2006. 中小学教师与工作相关的压力源研究[J]. 教育理论与实践（20）：27-30.

[9] 付睿，2019. 论中小学教师减负[J]. 河北师范大学学报(教育科学版)，21(2)：13-16.

[10] 高萍，张宁，2009. 中小学教师职业压力、社会支持与教学效能感的关系研究[J]. 中国健康心理学杂志，17(6)：680-682.

[11] 甘霖，沈馨琳，2011. 中小学教师核心自我评价、工作压力与职业倦怠关系的实证研究[J]. 教育学术月刊（7）：42-45.

[12] 郭华，汪婷，2019. 新入职中小学教师的工作压力分析——名校分校与重点学校、普通学校的差别[J]. 中国教师（10）：68-72.

[13] 李光程，王怀南，张建人，等，2018. 新生代中学教师工作压力、工作价值观与工作投入的关系[J]. 中国临床心理学杂志，26(4)：792-795.

[14] 李鹏，张志超，杨洋，等，2022. 工作压力对中小学教师职业倦怠的影响：情绪劳动和工作满意度的链式中介作用[J]. 心理与行为研究，20(3)：412-418.

[15] 李清，李瑜，张旭东，2021. 中小学教师工作压力对心理生活质量的影响：心理弹性、自尊的中介作用[J]. 中国健康心理学杂志，29(2)：217-230.

[16] 李琼，王松丽，张艳，2009. 教师工作压力对职业倦怠的影响：一个路径分析[J]. 教育学报，5(5)：78-82.

[17] 李祥，周芳，蔡孝露，2021. 中小学教师减负政策的价值分析：权利保障的视角[J]. 现代教育管理（7）：62-69.

[18] 刘晓明，2004. 职业压力、教学效能感与中小学教师职业倦怠的关系[J]. 心理发展与教育（2）：56-61.

[19] 刘晓明，王丽荣，金宏章，等，2008. 职业压力影响中小学教师职业倦怠的作用机制研究[J]. 中国临床心理学杂志（5）：537-539.

[20] 吕邹沁，凌辉，2014. 中小学教师工作压力、社会支持与职业倦怠的关系[J]. 中国健康心理学杂志，22(9)：1344-1348.

[21] 彭勇，2004. 中小学校长职业压力及其减轻方法初探[J]. 教学与管理（7）：18-20.

[22] 秦红芳，刘晓明，2015. 行动控制在农村教师工作压力与工作倦怠中的作用：PSI理论的分析视角[J]. 心

理发展与教育, 31(5): 633-640.

[23] 邵光华, 顾泠沅, 2002. 关于我国青年教师压力情况的初步研究[J]. 教育研究 (9): 20-24.

[24] 申艳娥, 2004. 正、负性压力情境下教师应对方式的比较研究[J]. 心理发展与教育 (4): 66-69.

[25] 王官诚, 2008. 贫困地区中小学教师职业压力与职业倦怠研究——以四川省雅安市芦山县为例[J]. 教学与管理 (18): 38-40.

[26] 王沛, 张国礼, 2005. 中小学教师职业压力现状调查及其启示[J]. 教育探索 (10): 116-117.

[27] 王群锋, 石婕妤, 颜健生, 2012. 瑶族中学英语教师工作压力与职业倦怠的相关性研究[J]. 湖北函授大学学报, 25(10): 21-22.

[28] 王毓珣, 王颖, 2013. 关于中小学教师减负的理性思索[J]. 湖南师范大学教育科学学报, 12(4): 56-62.

[29] 吴文春, 余洁玲, 2014. 新任教师压力源研究[J]. 教学与管理 (33): 80-83.

[30] 吴日晖, 高敏, 刘伟方, 2018. 特岗教师职业倦怠与工作压力、人格特征状况及其关系研究[J]. 海南广播电视大学学报, 19(2): 145-151.

[31] 徐富明, 安连义, 牛芳, 2004. 中小学教师职业倦怠与职业压力应对策略研究[J]. 中国学校卫生 (5): 569-570.

[32] 杨翠娥, 黄祥祥, 2008. 民族地区中小学教师职业压力及原因探析[J]. 湖南师范大学学报教育科学版 (1): 111-114.

[33] 杨剑, 陈开梅, 2006. 江苏省中小学体育教师职业压力源研究与分析[J]. 山东体育学院学报 (3): 56-60.

[34] 杨玲, 巫文胜, 2013. 小学教师心理韧性、核心自我评价与工作压力的关系[J]. 湖南师范大学学报教育科学版, 12(1): 99-103.

[35] 杨蕊, 王琪林, 何佩, 等, 2021. 中小学教师压力知觉和抑郁、焦虑的关系: 应对方式的中介作用[J]. 中国健康心理学杂志, 29(12): 1842-1848.

[36] 张国礼, 边玉芳, 董奇, 2012. 中小学教师教学素养、工作压力、主观幸福感的关系[J]. 中国特殊教育 (4): 89-92.

[37] 张国礼, 边玉芳, 董奇, 2013. 教师工作压力与职业枯竭的关系: 职业承诺的调节效应[J]. 心理与行为研究, 11(1): 110-114.

[38] 张家军, 陈苗, 2022. 中小学教师减负的系统分析与行动路径[J]. 南京社会科学 (4): 143-152.

[39] 张家军, 闫君子, 2022. 中小学教师负担: 减与增的辩证法[J]. 教育研究, 43(5): 149-159.

[40] 张劲松, 2005. 农村中小学教师压力困境及其疏导[J]. 现代中小学教育 (7): 61-63.

基于CiteSpace的国内生态语言学研究热点与前沿分析

赵浩雯

1. 引言

"生态学"（Ökologie）一词由德国生物学家恩斯特·海克尔于1866年首次提出，主要"研究生物在其生活过程中与环境的关系"（林祥磊，2013）。生态系统（ecosystem）概念的提出使得生态学研究开始从系统论的角度思考自然和人类社会的功能，解决人类社会生存发展问题，同时推动了自然科学与人文科学的学科交叉（于贵瑞等，2021）。随着研究的深入，生态学的概念从"研究生物生存状态及其与环境关系"拓展到了"生物圈—人类社会—自然资源环境的相互作用关系"；生态和环境的概念也从生物和环境范畴拓展到语言、人口、社会和政治等范畴。

生态语言学（eco-linguistics/ecological linguistics）作为生态学和语言学的新型交叉学科，主要涉及"从生态的视角探讨环境对语言的影响以及从生态的视角揭示语言对环境的影响"（何伟，2018）。目前生态语言学研究有两个范式：豪根（Haugen）模式和韩礼德模式。豪根模式又被称作"语言（的）生态学（ecology of language）"和"隐喻模式"（Fill，2001；范俊军，2005；韩军，2013），研究"任何特定的语言与其环境的相互作用"（Haugen，1972），例如语言多样性、语言进化和濒危语言的保护等。20世纪90年代，生态环境的恶化使得研究者开始关注语言对生态环境造成的影响。韩礼德认为"语言主动建构现实"（Halliday，2001），他强调语言与增长主义、物种歧视、环境污染、性别歧视等之间的密切关系（Halliday，1990），凸显语言学家的社会责任。所以，韩礼德模式又被称为"非隐喻模式"和"环境（的）语言学"，关注话语和行为的生态特征和非生态特征。这两个模式为研究语言和生态问题提供不同视角和研究路径，它们是互补而非互斥的（Fill，2001）。

自豪根1970年提出"语言生态"以来，该交叉学科仅发展了50余年，体系尚未完全建立，中国学界的研究也才刚刚起步。为了促进国内生态语言学研究的发展，有必要对生态语言学的研究现状及热点进行可视化分析和梳理。对于"生态语言学"和"语言生态学"术语，欧美及国内很多学者倾向于将其等同起来（Fill、Mühlhäusle，2001；范俊军，2005；韩军，2013；黄国文等，2016），也有学者认为应将其视作两个独立的分支学科（刘丽芬，2018），但它们的核心都是探究语言与生态关系问题，因此本研究采用"生态语言学"研究主题词。

纵观国内对于生态语言学的研究成果，本文借助科学计量学的可视化分析工具CiteSpace，采用定性、定量相结合的方法，绘制生态语言学学科知识图谱，对国内生态语言学的研究概况、研究热点、研究前沿及趋势进行可视化分析。

2. 数据来源及研究方法

本研究的中文文献数据下载于CNKI（中国知网）数据库，检索日期为2023年6月19日。

本研究首先以"生态语言学"为主题词进行检索，检索字段之间关系为"OR"，文献检索时间范围选择"不限"，来源类别为"全部期刊"，检索得到学术期刊文章 834 篇；随后通过人工排查方式，剔除与本领域不相关或关联较弱的论文，共得到有效文献 790 篇，将作者、摘要、关键词、期刊等数据信息以 Refworks 格式导出。

本研究采用 CiteSpace 6.2 R4 对文献进行分析。通过该软件能得到可视化的知识图谱，呈现研究领域的知识结构、发展规律和分布情况，以探索分析该领域的研究热点、知识前沿和发展趋势等（陈悦、陈超美、胡志刚，2014）。对于文献热点和趋势分析，首先，本文对发文量和学科分布进行统计，分析生态语言学研究的整体发展情况；使用 CiteSpace 的"Data-Import/Export-CNKI"功能将 790 篇有效文献进行格式转换并导入，设置时间区间为 2004—2023 年，时间分区（year per slice）为 1 年；利用关键词共现和聚类归纳梳理研究核心，并采用 LLR（对数似然率）算法寻找具体研究热点；通过关键词时区图谱和突现词探究研究前沿及趋势。

3. 结果与讨论

3.1 生态语言学整体发展情况

基于 CNKI 数据库中所得文献数据，对生态语言学相关研究发文量进行统计（见图 1）。从图 1 可得从 1990 年开始至今，生态语言学研究整体呈现上升趋势。在 1990—2013 年，国内生态语言学得到初步发展；2013—2016 年持续稳步发展研究；2016 年开始呈直线上升状态，在 2018 年到达顶峰；2020 年发文量缓慢下降，但仍保持在 80 篇以上。由此可以看出，随着生态学和语言学的发展以及人们生态意识的不断提高，语言与生态环境的关系得到国内学界持续关注。

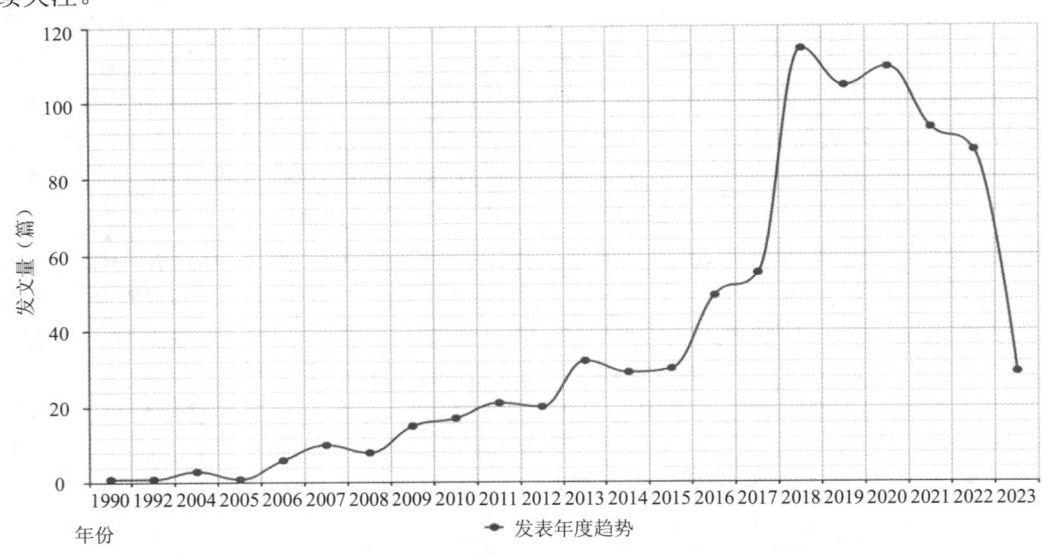

图 1　生态语言学研究发文量随年份变化折线统计图

从 CNKI 数据库的学科分布图（图 2）可见，在"生态语言学"方向的研究中，中国语言文字学科发文量最多，占比 33%；其次是外国语言文字，占比 52%；随后是教育理论与教育管理、计算机软件与计算机运用、世界文学以及新闻与媒体，分别占 4%、3%、2% 和 2%。由此可得，对生态语言学的研究集中于中国、外国语言学领域，研究倾向于对语言文本进行生态解读或探究语言演变；跨学科性较低，虽然有其他学科参与，但总体占比不到 15%，且参与学科主要为文科领域，例如世界文学和教育理论与管理。未来生态语言学的研究可以朝着文理交叉的新方向发展，例如结合心理学、生态学相关理论以及语料库分析等。

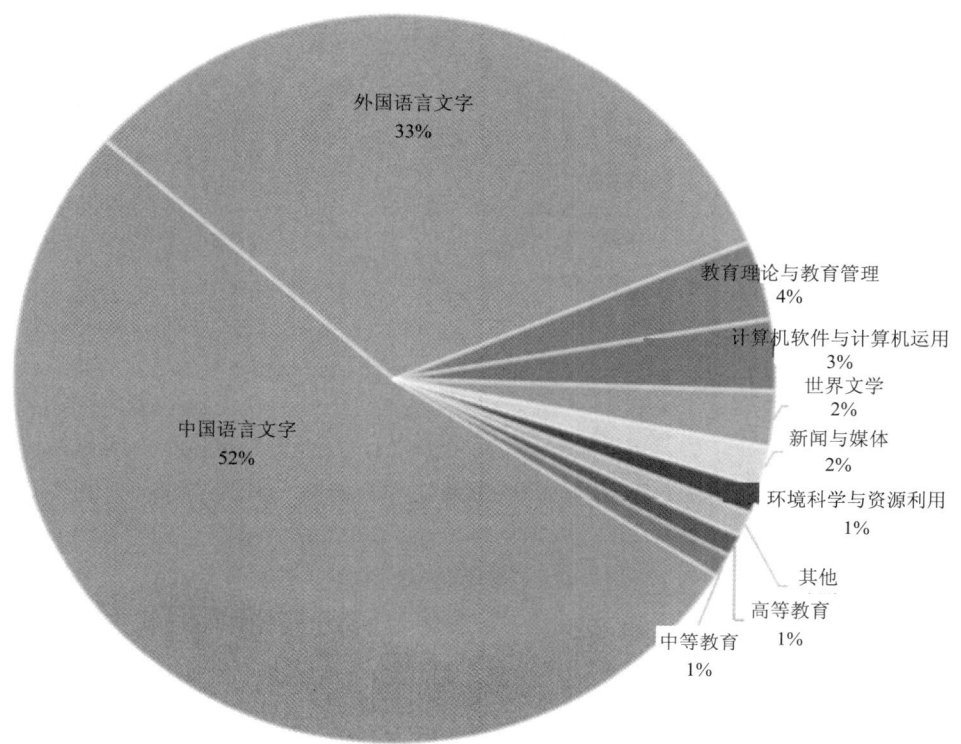

图 2　生态语言学研究学科类别分布图

3.2　研究热点

关键词是对论文内容的高度概括，能反映某学术领域的研究议题。通过对关键词的共词和聚类分析，能够掌握该研究领域的热点内容、主体分布和学科结构等（李杰、陈超美，2016：103）。

（1）关键词研究热点共现分析

运用 CiteSpace 6.2. R4 生成生态语言学研究的关键词共现图谱（图 3），图谱中节点（node）越大表示关键词出现的频率越高，节点之间的连线表明关键词之间在同篇文献中存在共现关系，连线的粗细和数量与节点间的紧密程度成正比。从图 3 可以看出，"生态语言学"的节点最大，并向四周广泛辐射；其次是"生态话语分析""语言生态""系统功能语言学"等。

根据图 3 以及 CiteSpace 数据绘制高频关键词统计表（表 1）和中心度统计表（表 2）。高频关键词反映该学术领域的研究热点，而中心性反映出该热点的重要性，通常认为中心性超过 0.1 的节点为关键节点。一个关键词的中心性越高，控制的关键词之间的信息流越多（Small，1986）。

图 3　生态语言学研究关键词共现图谱

表 1　生态语言学研究的高频词统计表（2004—2018 年）

序号	关键词	频率	中心度	平均年份
1	生态语言学	547	1.47	2004
2	生态话语分析	70	0.06	2016
3	语言生态	39	0.09	2009
4	系统功能语言学	34	0.04	2017
5	大学英语	26	0.00	2012
6	语言生态学	21	0.10	2009
7	网络流行语	18	0.00	2015
8	生态哲学观	17	0.01	2018
9	和谐话语分析	16	0.00	2017
10	生态课堂	11	0.00	2018

表 2　生态语言学研究中关键词的中心度统计表

序号	关键词	中心度	序号	关键词	中心度
1	生态语言学	1.47	9	语言变异	0.02
2	语言生态学	0.10	10	翻译	0.02
3	语言生态	0.09	11	话语分析	0.02
4	生态话语分析	0.06	12	生态批评	0.02
5	认知	0.05	13	生态哲学	0.02
6	生态环境	0.04	14	生态学	0.02
7	系统功能语言学	0.04	15	国际生态话语	0.01
8	多样性	0.03	16	及物性系统	0.01

高频词和中心度统计表显示，出现超过 20 次的高频词有 6 个，为"生态语言学""生态话语分析""语言生态""系统功能语言学""大学英语"和"语言生态学"。从中心性角度来看，有 16 个关键词的中心性超过了 0.1，说明生态语言学研究呈现良好态势，研究重点较多，话题多方向拓展；有些关键词频率和中心性都很高，如"生态语言学"（频率 547，中心度 1.47）、"语言生态学"（频率 21，中心度 0.10）、"语言生态"（频率 39，中心度 0.09）、"生态话语分析"（频率 70，中心度 0.06）、"系统功能语言学"（频率 34，中心度 0.04），这表明运用生态概念和话语分析框架等探讨话语的生态/非生态特征以及语言现象是国内学界的研究重点和热点。而"生态课堂"和"大学英语"尽管中心度不高，但其对教育生态研究的构架和思路起到很大影响，也是该领域讨论的热点话题。

国内"生态语言学"的初期发展研究和国际上其他的研究相似，都围绕学科本身的概念确定和理论体系的完善。从数据中可以看出在国内学界，"生态语言学"和"语言生态学"有区别但关联密切，这是由于语言生态环境的界限十分模糊，不同学者对语言生态环境有不同解释，例如语言存在与社会环境、语言存在于自然环境等（Steffensen、Fill，2014），但它们的研究目的一致——揭示语言与环境的相互作用，追求语言与生态环境的和谐发展。另外，数据显示当前的生态语言学有两个研究路径，为"生态话语分析"和"语言生态"。"系统功能语言学"为"生态话语分析"提供主要理论支撑，其中"及物性系统"被重点用来分析语言系统和语篇的生态/非生态特征；"语言生态"路径重点考察"语言变异"与"多样性"，即语言的可持续性和生态现象。还需要提及的是，"生态哲学观"和"生态哲学"体现出国内学者开始在宏观层面意识到：应当构建一套本土化的生态哲学观念体系，为学者生态理念与生态话语、行为研究提供普遍性指导。

（2）关键词聚类分析

CiteSpace 可以对所选文献的关键词进行聚类分析并产生聚类标识，每个聚类代表一个联系相对紧密的独立研究领域。为进一步探究生态语言学的热点研究领域，本文运用 CiteSpace 关键词聚类分析生成关键词聚类分析，通过 LLR（对数似然率）算法得出生态话语分析研究热点的代表性关键词。详细见生态语言学关键词聚类图谱（图 4）和关键词聚类信息表（表 3）。

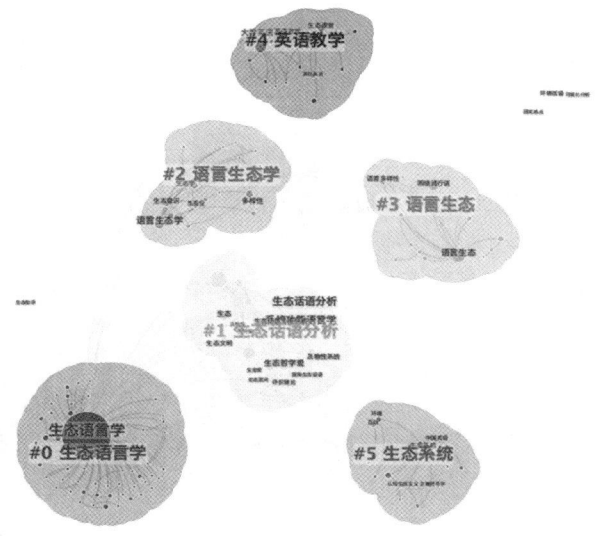

图 4　生态语言学关键词聚类图谱

表 3　关键词聚类信息表

聚类名称	同质度	大小	LLR（对数似然率）
聚类0 生态语言学	1	58	生态语言学（32.1，1.0E-4）；生态话语分析（25.84，1.0E-4）；语言生态（23.19，1.0E-4）；系统功能语言学（15.59，1.0E-4）；英美文学（8.78，0.005）
聚类1 生态话语分析	0.868	35	生态话语分析（72.58，1.0E-4）；系统功能语言学（34.76，1.0E-4）；生态哲学观（18.8，1.0E-4）；及物性系统（17.41，1.0E-4）；和谐话语分析（15.67，1.0E-4）
聚类2 语言生态学	0.932	18	语言生态学（29.47，1.0E-4）；生态学（17，1.0E-4）；生态位（10.87，0.001）；交叉学科（10.87，0.001）；多样性（9.89，0.005）
聚类3 语言生态	0.887	17	语言生态（78.42，1.0E-4）；语言多样性（13.74，0.001）；语言变异（10.11，0.005）；语言系统（10.11，0.005）；危机（10.11，0.005）
聚类4 英语教学	0.915	16	英语教学（17.26，1.0E-4）；大学英语（15.26，1.0E-4）；生态课堂（14.75，0.001）；高校英语（14.75，0.001）；大班教学（11，0.001）
聚类5 生态系统	0.909	13	生态系统（14.16，0.001）；认知生成主义（13.78，0.001）；环境（13.78，0.001）；生物符号学（13.78，0.001）；中国英语（10.02，0.005）
聚类6 话语分析	0.935	8	话语分析（22.13，1.0E-4）；研究热点（17.68，1.0E-4）；可视化分析（17.68，1.0E-4）；主题演变（7.29，0.01）；批评话语分析（7.29，0.01）
聚类7 认知	0.997	4	认知（10.69，0.005）；习俗（10.69，0.005）；地域（10.69，0.00）；同义词（10.69，0.005）；生态（5.32，0.05）
聚类8 生态批评	0.994	4	生态批评（10.69，0.005）；沃尔夫假说（10.69，0.005）；世界图景（10.69，0.005）；几点思考（10.69，0.005）；生态话语分析（0.28，1.0）
聚类9 景观	0.997	2	景观（11.19，0.001）；语类（11.19，0.001）；翻译（11.19，0.001）；话语（11.19，0.001）；生态语言学（1.81，0.5）

同质值是聚类内部相似度指标平均轮廓值（Silhouette），若S>0.5则聚类合理。表3中的数据表明聚类内节点联系紧密，聚类内节点的主题关联性强，具有参考价值（S>0.85且大部分聚类S>0.9）。

根据图4和表3，聚类0"生态语言学"的代表性关键词有生态语言学；生态话语分析；语言生态；系统功能语言学和英美文学。聚类1"生态话语分析"主要从"系统功能语言学"（尤其是"及物性系统"）、"和谐话语分析""生态哲学观"的视角进行话语分析；聚类2"语言生态学"重视"交叉学科"，尤其是语言学与"生态学"的融合发展，探究"多样性"以及语言中的"生态位"概念。聚类3主要分析语言（如少数民族语言、濒危语言）的生态现象："语言多样性""语言变异""语言危机"，并企图结合生态系统概念建立"语言系统"理论体系。聚类4"英语教学"属于外语教学生态研究，探究"大学英语""高校英语"，研究微观"生态课堂"；聚类5"生态系统"研究主要结合"认知生成主义""生态符号学"研究话语与"环境",如"中国英语"。聚类6"话语分析"主要是指文献综述和批评话语分析,文献综述包括"可视化分析",探究"研究热点"和"主题演变"。聚类7体现出认知语言学和生态语言学的结合,考究"同义词""习俗""地域"和"生态",由此可以看出生态语言学与认知语言学之间存在可相互借鉴之处——认知语言学能够为生态语言学提供理论分析工具,生态语言学也在一定程度上丰富了认知语言学的意义构建研究(王馥芳,2017)。聚类8"生态批评"代表性关键词是"沃尔夫假说""世界图景""几点思考""生态话语分析"。聚类9"景观"主要探讨语言景观,关键词有"语类""话语"和"翻译",是生态语言学和"社会语言学"的结合发展;生态翻译学也是学界关注的一个重要领域。对于聚类的整合,本文倾向于将聚类1和聚类6中的"批评话语分析"整合为"生态话语分析"。

鉴于"生态语言学"与"生态话语分析"的子成员数量众多(分别为58和35)且代表性强(S分别为1和0.868),下文将对以上两个聚类主题进行讨论。

(1)生态语言学

国内学者从不同角度对生态语言学开展研究,整体上可以分为理论研究和应用研究两个方面。

在理论层面上,首次将"生态语言学"理论引入国内的是李国正(李国正,1987)。他将语言置于自然生态系统中进行考察研究,运用生态学原理研究汉语问题,同时引入生态系统的基本原则,继而提出"生态语言系统"概念;范俊军(2005)就当代生态语言学的产生与发展、原理、研究领域和课题作了评述;冯广艺(2013)出版了我国第一本题为"语言生态学"的专著;孔江平等人(2016)就生态语言学研究目标、研究方法等方面展开论述。何伟、高然(2019)对生态语言学缘起和发展历程进行回顾,指出应当在统一生态哲学观的指导下,逐步确立适合生态语言学研究的统一框架、系统的研究方法以及清晰的研究范围,并致力于各种语言生态问题的解决。

除了对理论进行综述,不少学者开始关注生态语言学理论本土化问题。潘世松(2013)在生态学、伦理学、生态伦理学等学科的基础上提出了语言生态伦理概念,并详细描述理论依据与实践性。黄国文(2017)认为是分析者的生态观决定话语和行为分析标准,他基于儒家传统,提出"以人为本"和以良知、亲知、制约原则来指导生态话语和行为分析。何伟、魏榕(2018)论证了生态语言学的超学科本质属性,并随后提出生态话语分析的价值取向与生态哲学观。

在理论应用层面,对语言生态系统以及语言和环境的相互作用的研究,体现在话语分析、教学、翻译、语言保护等层面。例如,曹晓玲(2015)将生态语言学理论创造性地运用于高校英美文学教育研究领域,将教师、学生、文学及环境作为英美文学教育的生态因子纳入英美文学教育生态系统中进行辩证思考;汤红娟(2017)提出了在生态语言学视角下外语能力及儿童外语能力的构建、属性及其应用价值;冯广艺、冯念(2015)从我国少数民族语言生态研究的意义、机遇和路径等方面论述了我国少数民族语言生态研究的相关问题。

(2)生态话语分析

生态环境的恶化进一步推动了语言与生态的研究,语言学家开始尝试通过话语分析探究解决生态环境问题。当前生态话语分析分为两大类,即生态批评话语分析与生态积极话语分析或和谐话语分析。

生态批评话语分析侧重于具体语言的使用,通过批判话语或文本中的词法、句法和语用,揭示话语背后所隐含的意识形态,这种意识形态在生态语言学中就表现为生态意识(何伟、高然，2019）。戴桂玉、仇娟（2012）从及物性过程和态度资源两方面对生态酒店英文简介的语言特征进行分类、数据统计和分析，阐释语言、环境和社会之间的联系与互动。汪少华、纪燕（2019）从生态批评架构的视角分析，提出基于"生命共同体"的生态思想创建新架构。

和谐话语分析主要关注文本中对生态系统有益的话语和行为，探讨如何使语言更适于和谐生态系统的构建，从而引导人们推广有益性话语，促进人与人、自然和社会之间的和谐共存。黄国文的许多文章都提到中国语境下的和谐话语分析问题（黄国文、陈旸，2016；黄国文，2016），认为和谐话语分析本身就是生态的，它综合了生态系统中各个要素的动态发展，广泛适用于不同发展阶段、不同国情下的生态话语分析（黄国文、赵蕊华，2017），并随后建构了和谐话语分析的研究框架（黄国文、赵蕊华，2021）。闫娜（2018）以系统功能语言学为理论指导，通过分析语句的及物性系统，试图去完善和谐话语分析的模式，并唤起人类社会的生态意识。曾蕾、黄芳（2022）基于和谐话语分析的研究方法，构建了历史语境视角下自然文学的和谐话语分析框架，探讨了自然文学经典之作的语言特点。

从上可以看出生态话语分析的对象既可以是环境文本，又可以是任何能进行生态取向分析的话语，如社会热点话题、诗歌话语、政治话语和广告语等。

目前国内生态语言学研究主要依据"韩礼德范式"，研究内容多为及物性视角下的生态话语分析。虽然相关研究中也有结合了其他理论（如视觉语法、多模态、语料库语言学），但相关关键词的词频很低，说明运用这些方法开展的生态话语分析在研究方法上仍是以及物性分析为主，在方法论上还未形成百花齐放的局面。以"非隐喻模式"为基础，国内学者将自己的学科成果和生态语言学进行融合，构建相关的理论框架。例如，国际生态话语及物性分析模式（何伟、魏榕，2017）、生态语言学视角下的人际意义系统（张瑞杰、何伟，2018）、生态语言学视角下的评价系统（何伟、马子杰，2020）、生态语言学视角下的逻辑关系系统（何伟、程铭，2021），这些都为生态语言学的应用研究提供了坚实的理论基础。

3.3 研究前沿与趋势

基于收集到的国内生态语言学论文数据，本文通过 CiteSpace 6.2. R4 生成危机话语相关主题词时间线（timeline view）知识图谱（图6），并利用突发检测（burst detection），按照突现词出现时间的由远至近，将主题词形成突现词图（图5），通过词频及其变动趋势来确定生态语言学研究领域的前沿领域和发展趋势。

根据突现词统计图可以看出，主题词突变率最高的生态话语分析，突变率达到了7.99%，是2016年开始至今的研究热点。除生态话语分析外，主题词突变率从高到低的分别是语言生态、大学英语、生态哲学观和英美文学。"语言生态"爆发点主要集中在2009—2013年，突变率达5.77%；"生态哲学观"研究热点开始于2018年，何伟、魏榕（2018）促进了生态哲学观的发展。

可视化时间线图谱能更直观地展现各聚类关键词按时间发展的情况和聚类间的关系紧密程度。从图6可知，这5组聚类的关键词彼此之间形成了明显的线条连接，说明各组聚类的研究热度存在一定的延续性。从各聚类的时间横跨线来看，聚类0和聚类5最早的关键词均出现于2004年，属于聚类时间点出现较早的研究热点，但各聚类的发展速度和结束时间存在差异，演变路径也不尽相同。其中，聚类0的演变路径最为丰富，除了自身研究热度不减以外，还向聚类1、聚类2、聚类3、聚类4、聚类5横向演变，奠定了语言生态、英语教学及生态话语分析等之间的网络关系。聚类2、聚类3、出现在2006—2008年之间；聚类1和聚类 4 出现时间较迟，均在 2010 年以后出现首个热点关键词，但这两个聚类发展速度很快，逐步成为近年研究热点和主要发展趋势。

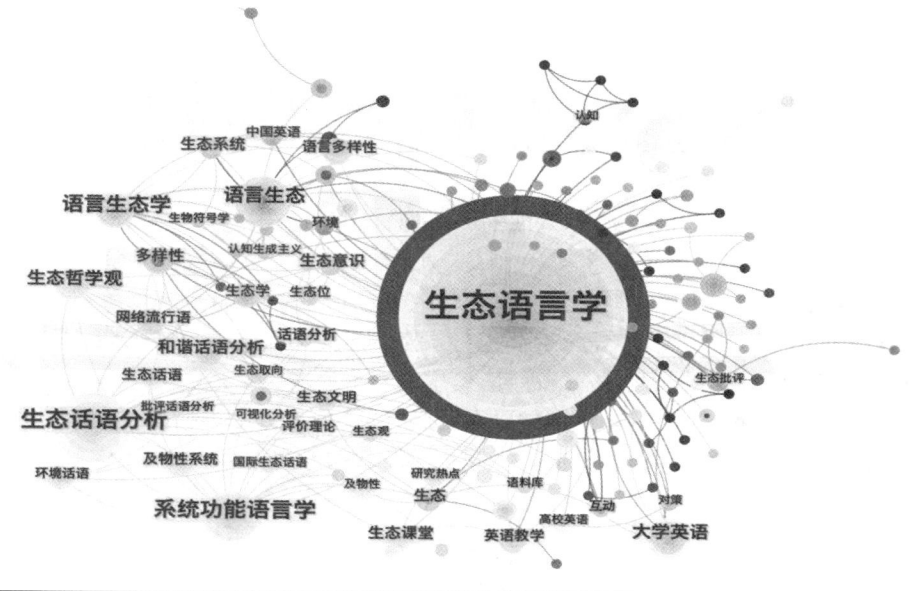

图 5　生态语言学研究主题词时间线知识图谱

Keywords	Year	Strength	Begin	End	2004—2023
语言生态	2009	5.77	2009	2013	
大学英语	2012	4.74	2013	2016	
英美文学	2015	3.77	2015	2017	
生态哲学观	2018	4.29	2020	2021	
生态话语分析	2016	7.99	2021	2023	

图 6　生态语言学研究突现词统计图

从聚类 0 "语言生态学"的研究关键词和时间横跨线可以看出，国内生态语言学研究逐渐开始尝试跨学科跨领域，如结合认知语言学（王馥芳，2017）、语料库和生态学相关理论；同时，生态语言学的理论框架和哲学观的构建也在如火如荼地进行。虽然聚类 1 "生态话语分析"起步时间较晚，但从 2015 年起至今发展迅猛，涌现大量研究主题，如"和谐话语分析""评价理论""及物性分析""语料库"等，发展潜力巨大，是生态语言学领域研究的重要前沿；聚类 4 "英语教学"研究发展态势良好，这方面的研究涉及生态课堂建构、大学英语教学、写作教学等内容。可以看出，生态语言学与外语教学的触及面较为广泛，有着一定的系统性，但该聚类研究主要引用生态学术语或概念，几乎没有系统地构建外语生态教学模式的理论研究。

4. 讨论与总结

本文通过可视化计量工具 CiteSpace 对 CNKI 收录的生态语言学的文献梳理和分析，以知识图谱和统计表的方式展现研究热点与前沿趋势，得出三点结论：（1）近 20 年生态语言学研究呈现显著增长趋势，研究热度持续攀升，学科领域呈现多样化；（2）当前生态语言学研究热点有生态话语分析、系统功能语言学、外语生态教学、语言生态以及理论本土化研究。（3）当前研究前沿趋势是生态语言学理论框架构建、生态话语分析、生态哲学观和外语生态教学。

生态语言学理论框架的构建主要是基于"非隐喻模式"，在系统功能语言学的基础上，结合生态学进行扩展和补充。生态话语分析主要以生态话语批评分析与和谐话语分析为主，批评话语大多基于及物性系统开展话语分析，国内和谐话语分析框架从2016年开始不断建立和完善；文本来源和话语内容多样化，分析范围从人与自然发展到人与社会。生态哲学观本土化发展是目前国内的热点和趋势，当前形成了"多元和谐，交互共生""和谐"等生态观，但学界仍未形成统一认可、具有普遍意义的生态哲学观。

国内研究的学科分类虽然也出现较多分支，但多集中于语言学领域，属于传统的人文学科范畴。生态语言学在本质上具有超学科性和强大的应用功能，与科学发展趋势息息相关。因此，（1）未来国内生态语言学研究应当在完善生态语言学理论体系的基础上，注意破除"韩礼德范式"带来的约束，发展多方法、多理论视角的研究，大胆尝试将非语言学领域的理论应用于生态语言学研究中，加强与其他学科的融合发展，例如生态学、环境学、心理学等。（2）重视"豪根范式"的研究，将理论构建和实证研究结合，为少数民族语言以及方言的保护和规划提供理据和应用。（3）重视生态语言学的应用性，为教学、翻译、环保与国际关系等提供新思路和路径探索。此外，"生态语言学"与"语言生态学"术语的规定和应用并未实现统一，有碍学科的深入研究和学术的顺畅交流，未来可以进一步统一术语或具体使用语境。

参考文献

[1] FILL A, 1998. Ecolinguistics: state of the art 1998[J].Arbeiten aus Anglistik und Amerikanistik, 23(1):3-16

[2] FILL A, MUHLHAUSLER P, 2001. The ecolinguistics reader: language, ecology, and environment[M]. London: Continuum.

[3] HALLIDAY M A K, 2001. New ways of meaning: the challenge to applied linguistics[M]//FILL A, MUHLHAUSLER P. The ecolinguistics reader: language, ecology, and environment. London: Continuum, 175-202.

[4] HAUGEN E, 2001. The ecology of language[M]// FILL A, MUHLHAUSLER P.The ecolinguistics reader: language, ecology, and environment. London: Continuum, 55-66.

[5] SMALL H,1986. The synthesis of specialty narratives from cocitation clusters[J]. Journal of the American society for information science, 37(3): 97-110.

[6] STEFFENSEN S V, FILL A, 2014. Ecolinguistics: the state of the art and future horizons[J]. Language sciences, 41: 6-25.

[7] 曹晓玲，2015. 生态语言学视域下英美文学教育研究[J]. 教育理论与实践，35(24): 56-57.

[8] 陈悦，陈超美，胡志刚，等，2014. 引文空间分析原理与应用：CiteSpace 实用指南[M]. 北京：科学出版社.

[9] 戴桂玉，仇娟，2012. 语言、环境、社会——生态酒店英文简介之生态批评性话语分析[J]. 外语与外语教学（1）：48-52.

[10] 范俊军，2005. 生态语言学研究述评[J]. 外语教学与研究（2）：110-115.

[11] 冯广艺，2013. 语言生态学引论[M]. 北京：人民出版社.

[12] 冯广艺,冯念，2015. 新常态下我国少数民族语言生态研究[J]. 湖南师范大学社会科学学报,44(5)：20-24.

[13] 韩军，2013. 中国生态语言学研究综述[J]. 语言教学与研究（4）：107-112.

[14] 何伟，2018. 关于生态语言学作为一门学科的几个重要问题[J]. 中国外语，15(4)：1，11-17.

[15] 何伟，程铭，2021. 生态语言学视角下的逻辑关系系统[J]. 解放军外国语学院学报，44(3)：51-59，160.
[16] 何伟，高然，2019. 生态语言学研究综观[J]. 浙江外国语学院学报（1）：1-12.
[17] 何伟，马子杰，2020. 生态语言学视角下的评价系统[J]. 外国语(上海外国语大学学报)，43(1)：48-58.
[18] 何伟，魏榕，2017. 国际生态话语之及物性分析模式构建[J]. 现代外语，40(5)：597-607，729.
[19] 何伟，魏榕，2018. 生态语言学：发展历程与学科属性[J]. 国外社会科学（4）：113-123.
[20] 黄国文，2016. 生态语言学的兴起与发展[J]. 中国外语，13(1)：1，9-12.
[21] 黄国文，陈旸，2016. 生态哲学与话语的生态分析[J]. 外国语文，32(6)：55-61.
[22] 黄国文，赵蕊华，2017. 生态话语分析的缘起、目标、原则与方法[J]. 现代外语，40(5)：585-596，729.
[23] 孔江平，王茂林，黄国文，等，2016. 语言生态研究的意义、现状及方法[J]. 暨南学报(哲学社会科学版)，38(6)：2-28，129，140.
[24] 李国正，1987. 生态语言系统说略[J]. 语文导报（10）：54-58.
[25] 李杰，陈超美，2016. CiteSpace：科技文本挖掘及可视化[M]. 北京：首都经济贸易大学出版社.
[26] 林祥磊，2013. 梭罗、海克尔与"生态学"一词的提出[J]. 科学文化评论，10(2)：18-28.
[27] 刘丽芬，2018. 论语言学与生态学融合的确指性研究[J]. 中国外语，15(5)：51-61.
[28] 潘世松，2013. 语言生态伦理概念提出的理论依据及实践可能[J]. 南昌大学学报(人文社会科学版)，44(1)：144-149.
[29] 汤红娟，2017. 论生态语言学视角下的儿童外语能力及其应用——兼与戴曼纯教授商榷[J]. 中国外语，14(5)：72-80.
[30] 汪少华，纪燕，2019. 生态话语的批评架构分析——以《变革我们的世界：2030年可持续发展议程》为例[J]. 中国外语，16(5)：59-67.
[31] 王馥芳，2017. 生态语言学和认知语言学的相互借鉴[J]. 中国外语，14(5)：47-55.
[32] 闫娜，2018. 系统功能视角下的和谐话语分析——生态文明概念的解读[J]. 牡丹江大学学报，27(7)：79-82.
[33] 于贵瑞，王秋凤，杨萌，等，2021. 生态学的科学概念及其演变与当代生态学学科体系之商榷[J]. 应用生态学报，32(1)：1-15.
[34] 张瑞杰，何伟，2018. 生态语言学视角下的人际意义系统[J]. 外语与外语教学（2）：99-108，150.
[35] 赵蕊华，黄国文，2021. 和谐话语分析框架及其应用[J]. 外语教学与研究，53(1)：42-53，159-160.

从面子理论分析《围城》中方鸿渐的形象构建

赵美华

1. 引言

钱锺书先生所著的《围城》是中国现代文学史上一部独特的讽刺小说，有"新儒林外史"的称誉（柯灵，1990）。《围城》中蕴含着大量中国独有的文化色彩和历史背景赋予的特征，"面子文化"便是其中所蕴含的文化内涵之一。

中国人的面子观与中华民族的传统文化和社会特点密不可分。在人际交往中，人们都自觉地遵循面子理论中的规范，注重对自己和他人面子的维护。在抗战初期的背景下，我们亦能从《围城》中人物的交往，感受到知识分子的生活百态和中国面子文化的影响。

关于《围城》这部小说，学界已从多个方面展开研究，涵盖翻译学、比较文学和语料库等。钱锺书的《围城》是汉语言幽默的典范，有关《围城》的翻译研究多集中在其英译本的幽默语言翻译中。研究发现，英译本基本上保持了原文的幽默效果，在跨国界的传播当中没有使幽默感遗失，但是也出现了一些不足，失去了修辞的色彩（张扬，2016；鲁平平，2016；焦飏，2016；沈淋，2016）。因此，在对文学作品进行翻译时要掌握适当的翻译方法，尽量使目的语读者能够获得源语发出者的幽默信息。除此之外，也有学者对《围城》中的文学修辞语言进行解析，解析钱锺书独特的审美内蕴，雅俗共赏、纯真且独具一格、辛辣嘲讽、极富哲理的审美效果（梁造禄，2015；樊佳，2016）。

《围城》作为一部极具影响力的现当代小说，难免有学者将其与其他类型相似的文学作品进行比较。刘青（2007）将《寒夜》和《围城》这两部同为描写抗战时期知识分子的酸甜苦辣人生的现代小说进行比较，认为《寒夜》在情感上比《围城》更能打动人心，而《围城》在艺术价值上更胜一筹。也有学者对比分析《围城》与《城堡》这两部东西方现代文学作品，感叹《围城》语言的形象生动和风格的淋漓畅快，赞扬《城堡》独树一帜的小说形式（郑秀芬，2013；Zeng，2022）。《围城》中人物性格刻画十分精细，因此，也有许多文章聚焦于其中的人物形象塑造，尤其是小说中给读者留下深刻印象的女性形象（杨新生，2009；余红梅，黄勇，2015）。她们兼修中西文化，融通古今，在新思想的感召下为了追求理想生活和人生价值，然而迫于现实沦为父权宗法制度牺牲品的命运，在尚有浓厚封建残留的社会里率先尝到了其中的苦涩与辛辣。

对于《围城》中的人物刻画，除了女性角色外，还有男主人公方鸿渐，但是有关方鸿渐的性格剖析多聚焦于其男女关系或与青年钱锺书的性格对比（夏伟，2021；郜元宝，2019），很少有文章由语言学理论切入。因此，本文将通过语言学中的面子理论研究《围城》中方鸿渐的形象建构。

2. 面子理论

中国人类学家胡先缙（2006）提出中国人的面子包括"脸"和"面"，"脸"是群体对有着良好道德品质和较高社会地位的个人的尊重，"面子"是通过一个人的成功而获得的声望。Goffman（1967）从社会学的角度提出，面子是个体在特定的社会交往过程中极力主张的正向社会价值，也是其他人认为该个体所具备的社会价值。

语言学家和心理学家 Brown 和 Levinson（1978）对 Goffman 的面子理论进行了拓展，力图将面子作为一种普遍的语言现象加以研究，他们认为面子就是个体要求他人认可的公众自我形象，是一种个人的愿望和目的，并进一步把面子分为积极面子（positive face）和消极面子（negative face）。积极面子是指在人际交往的过程中，人们希望自己的言行、取得的成就等得到别人的认可和赞同。说话人自己的道歉、接受恭维、自我否定、忏悔、情绪失控等都是对说话人积极面子的损害，而对听话人的不同意、不关心、批评、抱怨、责备、质疑等都是对听话人积极面子的损害。消极面子是指人们希望自身的言行和行动自由不要受到他人的干涉和妨碍。说话人的抱歉、感谢、辩解、接受批评等都是损害说话人的消极面子。说话人对听话人的命令、请求、建议、提醒、威胁、警告等都是对听话人消极面子的损害。

积极面子和消极面子是相悖而又同时存在的两个层面。在社会交际中，人们既要维护自己的面子权利，又要尊重他人的面子权利；既要尊重对方的积极面子，又要照顾到对方的消极面子。

3. 从面子理论分析《围城》中方鸿渐的形象

3.1 从积极面子分析方鸿渐的形象

例 1 苏小姐胜利地微笑，低声说："Embrasse-moi！"说着一脸害羞，奇怪自己竟有做傻子的勇气，可是她只敢躲在外国话里命令鸿渐吻自己。鸿渐没法推避，回脸吻她。这吻的分量很轻，范围很小……鸿渐不敢动，好一会儿，苏小姐梦醒似的坐直了，笑着说："月亮这怪东西，真教我们都变了傻子了。""并且引诱我犯了不可饶恕的罪！我不能再待了。"鸿渐这时候只怕苏小姐会提起订婚结婚，跟自己讨论将来的计划。他不知道女人在恋爱胜利快乐的时候，全想不到那些事的，要有了疑惧，才会要求男人赶快订婚结婚，爱情好有保障（钱锺书，2013）。

例 2 鸿渐摇头叹气，急得说抽去了脊骨的法文道："苏小姐，咱们讲法文。我——我爱一个人，——爱一个女人另外，懂？原谅，我求你一千个原谅。"（钱锺书，2013）

方鸿渐对苏文纨从未有过喜欢，可因为"现成的女朋友太缺少了"，也不想让苏小姐没面子，所以鬼使神差地迎合苏小姐。后来方鸿渐对唐晓芙一见钟情，遂想和苏小姐划清界限，但碍于自身的胆怯与懦弱，他反复纠结却也只敢用法语委婉地表达自己真实的想法，祈求苏小姐的原谅。

例 3 "方先生人聪明，一切逢场作戏，可是我们这种笨蛋，把你开的玩笑都得认真——"唐小姐听方鸿渐嗓子哽了，心软下来，可是她这时候愈心疼，愈心恨，愈要责罚他个痛快——"方先生的过去太丰富了！我爱的人，我要能够占领他整个生命，他在碰见我以前，没有过去，留着空白等待我——"鸿渐还低头不响——"我只希望方先生前途无量。"

鸿渐身心仿佛通电似的发麻……

唐小姐鼻子忽然酸了。"你说得对。我是个骗子，我不敢再辩，以后决不来讨厌了。"站起来就走。

唐小姐恨不能说："你为什么不辩护呢？我会相信你。"可是只说："那么再会。"（钱锺书，2013）

唐晓芙表面上假意恭维方鸿渐聪明、经验丰富，维护了他的积极面子，实则表达了自己的愤怒。面对唐晓芙的指责，方鸿渐没有勇气为自己辩护，而是轻易地放弃对唐小姐的追求，把本存希望的爱情草草结束，也足以看出他本性怯懦、软弱和自卑。

例 4　李梅亭脸色白了一白，看风便转道："你最喜欢说笑话。别扯淡，讲正经话，你们什么时候请我们吃喜酒啦？"

鸿渐道："到时候不会漏掉你。"

孙小姐迟疑地说："那么咱们告诉李先生？"

……

鸿渐如在云里，失掉自主，尽他们拉手拍肩，随口答应了请客，两人才肯走。孙小姐等他们去远了，道歉说："我看见他们两个人，心里就慌了，不知怎样才好。请方先生原谅，刚才说的话，不当真的。"

鸿渐忽觉身心疲倦，没精神对付，搀着她手说："我可句句当真，也许正是我所要求的。"（钱锺书，2013）

在痛失至爱唐晓芙后，方鸿渐不再相信爱情，也没有心思追求他人。孙柔嘉策划的假书信事件，促使方鸿渐担当起"护花使者"，在同事面前维护孙柔嘉的积极面子，半推半就地与孙订婚。他对现实妥协，把自己困在了婚姻的"围城"里。在方鸿渐与四位女士的感情纠葛里，无处不体现出他胆小、软弱、没有主见。

例 5　苏小姐忙道："不要管字的好坏，你看诗怎样？"

鸿渐道："王尔恺那样热衷做官的人还会做好诗吗？我又不向他谋差使，没有恭维歪诗的义务。"他没注意唐小姐向自己皱眉摇头。

苏小姐怒道："你这人最讨厌，全是偏见，根本不配讲诗。"便把扇子收起来。

鸿渐道："好，好，让我平心静气再看一遍。"苏小姐虽然撅嘴说："不要你看了。"仍旧让鸿渐把扇子拿去。鸿渐忽然指着扇子上的诗大叫道："不得了！这首诗是偷来的。"

例 6　方鸿渐见董斜川像尊人物，又听赵辛楣说他是名父之子，不胜倾倒，说："老太爷沂孙先生的诗，海内闻名。董先生不愧家学渊源，更难得是文武全才。"他自以为这算得恭维周到了。

例 7　鸿渐经不起辛楣苦劝，勉强喝了两口，说："辛楣兄，我只在哲学系混了一年，看了几本指定参考书。在褚先生前面只能虚心领教做学生。"（钱锺书，2013）

对于和自己无关，自己也不会向他谋差使的人，方鸿渐会直接不顾情面地批判他所做诗的真实水平，损害其积极面子。但对于身份地位高于他的董斜川和褚慎明，虽不是真心，方鸿渐也会殷勤地对其表达赞美之情，维护他们的积极面子。从中可以看出方鸿渐在人情交往中为人虚伪、趋炎附势、攀高结贵的性格特征。

例 8　分别时还是好好的，为什么重见面变得这样生分？这时候他的心里，仿佛临考抱佛脚的学生睡了一晚，发现自以为温熟的功课，还是生的，只好撒谎说，到上海不多几天，特来拜访。苏小姐礼貌周到地谢他"光临"，问他"在什么地方得意"。方鸿渐有点生气，想不理他不可能,"点金银行"又叫不响,便含糊地说:"暂时在一家小银行里做事。"

例 9 周经理软弱地摆出尊严道:"鸿渐,我告诉你别误会!你不久就远行,当然要忙着自己的事,没工夫兼顾行里,好在行里也没有什么事,我让你自由,你可以不必每天到行。至于薪水呢,你还是照支。""谢谢你,这钱我可不能领。""你听我说,我教会计科一起送你四个月的薪水,你旅行的费用,不必向你老太爷去筹。""我不要钱,我有钱。"鸿渐说话时的神气,就仿佛国立四大银行全在他随身口袋里,没等周经理说完,高视阔步出经理室去了。(钱锺书,2013)

例 10 辛楣笑说:"孙小姐,是你在前面领着他?还是他在后面照顾你?"鸿渐恍然明白,人家未必看出自己的懦怯无用,跟在孙小姐后面可以有两种解释,忙抢说:"是孙小姐领我过桥的。"这对孙小姐是老实话,不好辩驳,而旁人听来,只觉得鸿渐在客气。鸿渐的虚荣心支使他把真话来掩饰事实;孙小姐似乎看穿他的用心,只笑笑,不说什么。(钱锺书,2013)

在这三处例子中,方鸿渐均通过语言维护了自己的积极面子。面对苏小姐的冷淡,碍于面子,他不敢说出自己真实的工作单位;他即使身上的钱所剩无几,还是拒绝了周经理的钱,为自己保留了最后的面子;为了满足自己的虚荣心,不使别人看出自己的胆小,便抢先一步回答说是孙小姐带他过桥。方鸿渐最大的性格特征就是"爱面子",这也是他在回国前买了假"克莱登大学"学士学位的原因。而"爱面子"的性格也使方鸿渐在之后的工作和生活中陷入虚伪说谎的人格中。

例 11 赵辛楣鉴赏着口里吐出来的烟圈道:"大材小用,可惜可惜!方先生在外国学的是什么呀?"鸿渐没好气道:"没学什么。"苏小姐道:"鸿渐,你学过哲学,是不是?"赵辛楣喉咙里干笑道:"从我们干实际工作的人的眼光看来,学哲学跟什么都不学全没两样。"

"那么得赶快找个眼科医生,把眼光验一下;会这样看东西的眼睛,一定有毛病。"方鸿渐为掩饰斗口的痕迹,有意哈哈大笑。(钱锺书,2013)

此时赵辛楣还错误地将方鸿渐视作情敌,所以免不了对其挖苦。面对赵辛楣对他的专业——哲学——的嘲笑时,方鸿渐立马假装幽默地斗嘴,在损害赵辛楣积极面子的同时保全了自己的积极面子。

例 12 辛楣顽皮道:"要讲贵人,咱们孙小姐也是贵人,没有她——"李梅亭不等他说完,就敬孙小姐酒。鸿渐道:"我最惭愧了,这次我什么事都没有做,真是饭桶。"李梅亭道:"是呀!小方是真正的贵人,坐在旅馆里动也不动,我们替他跑腿。"(钱锺书,2013)

例 13 "别胡闹。我问你,你经过这次旅行,对我的感想怎么样?觉得我讨厌不讨厌?"
"你不讨厌,可是全无用处。"

鸿渐想不到辛楣会这样干脆地回答,气得只好苦笑。兴致扫尽,静默地走了几步,向辛楣一挥手说:"我坐轿子去了。"上了轿子,闷闷不乐,不懂为什么说话坦白算是美德(钱锺书,2013)。

方鸿渐本想得到李梅亭和赵辛楣对自己的认同和肯定,却等到他们直白的批评,直接地损害了方鸿渐的积极面子。

例 14 鸿渐跳起来大喝道:"谁要她替我找事?我讨饭也不要向她讨!她养了Bobby跟你孙柔嘉两条走狗还不够么?你对她说,方鸿渐'本领虽没有,脾气很大',资本家走狗的走狗是不做的。"两人对站着。柔嘉怒得眼睛异常明亮,说:"她那句话一个字儿没有错。人家倒可怜你,你不要饭碗,饭碗不会发霉。好罢,你父亲会替你'找出路'。不过,靠老头子不稀

奇，有本领自己找出路。"（钱锺书，2013）

方鸿渐和孙柔嘉的婚后生活并非顺风顺水、举案齐眉，困于生活中的琐事，他们的婚姻也摇摇欲坠。在争吵中，他们两人借着"气话"说出"实话"，从孙柔嘉对方鸿渐的积极面子毫不留情面地损害中，也侧面表达出了方鸿渐确实是只能靠着父亲、前岳父和朋友找出路的"草包"。方鸿渐在朋友、同事和妻子眼中都是一个毫无用处的人。

3.2 从消极面子分析方鸿渐的形象

例15 "我不知道为什么。高松年信上明说要她去，可是汇款只给我们四个人分。也许助教的职位太小了，学校觉得不配津贴旅费，反正这种人才有的是。"

"这太岂有此理了。我们已经在赚钱，倒可以不贴旅费，孙小姐第一次出来做事，哪里可以叫她赔本？你到了学校，一定要为她向当局去争。"

"我也这样想，补领总不成问题。"（钱锺书，2013）

例16 辛楣把这事问明白，好言抚慰了半天，鸿渐和着他。辛楣发狠道："这种学生非严办不可，我今天晚上就跟校长去说，你报告刘先生没有？"

鸿渐道："这倒不是惩戒学生的问题。孙小姐这一班决不能教了。你该请校长找人代她的课，并且声明这事是学校对不住孙小姐。"

孙小姐道："我死也不肯教他们了。我真想回家！"声音又哽咽着。（钱锺书，2013）

孙柔嘉初入职场时受到了来自学校的不公平待遇和学生的故意捣乱，方鸿渐在听说后为她打抱不平，要赵辛楣一定要帮孙小姐和领导争取公正。方鸿渐虽然胆小，不敢与领导正面抗争，但在有着错综复杂的人际关系的三闾大学里，不愿意与高松年、李梅亭之流同流合污，这便体现出他骨子里的正直和善良。

此处方鸿渐对赵辛楣使用了直接使役的表达方式，看似损害了赵辛楣的消极面子，但此时他们已经是很亲密的朋友了，所以西方文化中以行动自由为核心和以非强加为特征的消极面子观念在汉文化中并不总是适用。因为汉文化亲属关系之间甚至是熟识关系之间浓厚的亲情意识和义务感，中国人能够自然地使用和接受直接使役方式，干涉他人的言行和行动。中国人的面子感受侧重于体面或情面的损益，是一种对尊严与尊重的要求，妨碍行动自由不是构成消极面子危害的决定性因素（李军、宋燕妮，2004）。

4. 结论

本文从Brown和Levinson的面子理论中的积极面子和消极面子观念入手，通过分析《围城》中的人物对话，剖析了男主人公方鸿渐的性格特点。但由于中西方文化的差异，消极面子的观念在汉文化中不总是适用。本文认为，方鸿渐本人不学无术、爱慕虚荣、胆小怯懦、趋炎附势，但他同时具有正直、善良的优点。他的自身性格特点是在中西方文化共同影响下形成的，作为一个中国人，他深受中国传统儒、道思想和社会取向的影响，虽出国留学却未领略到西方文化的核心和精髓，两种文化之间有着不可调和的冲突。方鸿渐不断在理想和现实之间做斗争，走进了学业、事业和婚姻的"围城"。

参考文献

[1] BROWN P, LEVINSON S, 1978. Universals in language usage: politeness phenomena[M]//Goody E N.

Questions and politeness: strategies in social interaction. Cambridge: Cambridge University Press, 56-311.

[2] BROWN P, LEVINSON S, 1987. Politeness: some universals in language usage[M]. Cambridge: Cambridge University Press.

[3] GOFFMAN E, 1967. Interaction ritual: essays on face-to-face behavior[M]. New York: Pantheon.

[4] ZENG Y B, 2022. Into "Fortress Besieged" and out of "The Castle": a comparative analysis of Qian Zhongshu's Fortress Besieged and Kafka's The Castle[J]. Franz Kafka and Chinese culture, 2022.

[5] 郜元宝，2019. 方鸿渐的男女关系——兼谈"教授小说"的两重标准[J]. 小说评论（4）：21-25.

[6] 胡先晋，欧阳晓明，2006. 中国人的脸面观[J]. 中国社会心理学评论（1）：1-17.

[7] 焦飓，2016. 以《围城》为例探讨汉语言语幽默的翻译[J]. 语文建设（27）：97-98.

[8] 柯灵，1990. 喜《围城》上荧幕[J]. 文汇月刊（6）：23.

[9] 李军，宋燕妮，2004. 面子理论在汉文化中的考察[J]. 修辞学习（2）：29-32.

[10] 刘青，2007. 抗战时期知识分子写作的话语指向——解读钱钟书《围城》与巴金《寒夜》[J].名作欣赏（16）：48-52.

[11] 鲁平平，2016.《围城》中的幽默辞格翻译策略[J]. 语文建设（30）：71-72.

[12] 钱钟书，2013. 围城[M]. 北京：人民文学出版社.

[13] 沈淋，2016.《围城》英译本中幽默翻译研究[J]. 语文建设（15）：63-64.

[14] 夏伟，2021. 方鸿渐性格与青年钱锺书——对《围城》主题作另种细读[J]. 南方文坛（6）：115-121.

[15] 夏志清，2005. 中国现代小说史[M]. 刘绍铭等，译. 上海：复旦大学出版社.

[16] 杨新生，2009.《围城》中知识女性的现代思想意识及其悲剧根源[J]. 河南师范大学学报(哲学社会科学版)，36(5)：166-168.

[17] 余红梅，黄勇，2015.《围城》中大龄知识女性的心理解读[J]. 中华文化论坛（1）：78-81.

[18] 张扬，2016. 浅析《围城》英译本中的幽默翻译[J]. 语文建设（36）：78-79.

[19] 郑秀芬，2013.《围城》和《城堡》比较研究[J]. 小说评论（5）：188-192.

自由间接引语的语境标识
——以曼斯菲尔德的《已故上校的女儿》为例

王 宸

1. 引言

《已故上校的女儿》中的自由间接引语（free indirect discourse，以下简称"FID"）一直是该短篇小说研究的关键焦点。在国内，学者们从叙述学和文体学的角度或将两者结合，分析了该小说的内外聚焦和用词细节。而在国外，对自由间接引语的研究主要侧重于其句法形式特征。关于如何准确识别自由间接引语，学者们存在分歧。埃尔利希是第一个在 FID 研究中引入话语分析方法的学者，他指出，仅依赖句法特征无法完全判断句子是否属于自由间接引语，更遑论在没有句法特征的情况下。他认为，FID 研究应该超越句子层面，扩展到跨句层次，语境在正确识别和理解 FID 的过程中扮演着关键角色。换句话说，即使一组句子没有明显的 FID 句法形式特征，在特定语境下有时也可以被视为 FID。在语用学领域，言语主体是构成语境的重要因素，也是句子中不可或缺的成分。因此，从语用学的角度看，如果能在语境中发现标识，表明叙述者的意识主体不同于小说中的人物，则可以有效识别自由间接引语（余素青，2013）。余素青教授创造性地提出了 8 种语境标识：心理动词、感觉动词、限定性名词词组、回指的限定性名词、确指的非限定性名词和代词、特殊的句子形式、表示价值判断的词汇以及方言成分。这些标识与《已故上校的女儿》中自由间接引语的出现位置高度吻合，因此可被应用于该小说的研究。本文旨在叙述运用余素青教授提出的这 8 种标识，识别《已故上校的女儿》中的自由间接引语，以更深入地理解该小说的叙事艺术。

2. FID 的句法特征

自由间接引语（FID）被视为直接引语和间接引语的混合形式。它采用了类似于间接引语的时态和人称代词形式，将叙述者的时态作为基准，保留了间接引语中后移的时态，并使用第三人称代词。然而，它通常省略了间接引语中常见的转述结构，例如"他认为"或"她说"。与此同时，FID 中的一些成分，如"here""now""this""yesterday"，表现得更像直接引语，而不是间接引语中常见的"there""then""that""the day before"（余素青，2013）。

具有明显句法特征的 FID 相对容易辨认，但问题在于缺乏句法特征的 FID 可能导致语用模糊，即一个句子在形式上既可以是叙述者的话语，又可以是人物 FID。这实质上是由于话语的言语主体或意识主体（意识的主体）的模糊。任何句子都必然隐含一个言语主体（余素青，2013）。因此，为了消除这种语用模糊，必须明确话语的言语主体。FID 本身并不明确其言语主体，只能依赖语境来判断。因此，要确定话语材料是否为 FID，关键在于是否能在其语境中发现与叙述者不同的言语或意识主体（即小说中的人物）的存在。如果能够找到这样的存在，就表明该话语可能是 FID；否则，该话语属于叙述者的默认主体，即叙述者本人。我们将叙述者话语中能够指示小说人物言语或意识主体存在的语言材料称为 FID 语境标识。

当在小说话语中出现 FID 语境标识时，读者可以根据这些标识来判断随后的话语是否由叙述者的话语转变为人物 FID，也可以重新确认之前的话语是否为 FID。根据经验，绝大部分的 FID 语境中都存在这种标识，但也不排除例外的情况。通过关注这些语境标识，我们能够更准确地识别 FID，进而深入理解小说的叙事结构和语言运用。

3. 《已故上校的女儿》中的 FID 语境标识

3.1 心理动词

从逻辑上看，tell oneself、think、wonder、realize、remember 等描述思维活动的动词,隐含了一个不同于叙事者的意识主体，意味着随后话语可能是 FID（余素青，2013）。如：

例 1　Josephine thought of her dark-red slippers, which matched her dressing-gown, and of Constantia's favorite indefinite green ones which went with hers. Black! Two black dressing gowns and two pairs of black woolly slippers, creeping off to the bathroom like black cats. (Mansfield, 2006)

例 2　But the idea of a little Communion terrified them. What! In the drawing-room by themselves—with no—no altar or anything! The piano would be much too high, thought Constantia, and Mr. Farolles could not possibly lean over it with the chalice. And Kate would be sure to come bursting in and interrupt them, thought Josephine. And supposing the bell rang in the middle? It might be somebody important about their mourning. Would they get up reverently and go out, or would they have to wait…in torture?　(Mansfield, 2006)

例 3　Then they remembered. It didn't matter. They would never have to stop the organ-grinder again. Never again would she and Constantia be told to make that monkey take his noise somewhere else. Never would sound that loud, strange bellow when father thought they were pot hurrying enough. The organ-grinder might play there all day and the stick would not thump.　(Mansfield, 2006)

在例 1 中，第二句因其言语行为无疑是 FID，该句的感叹句式提供额外的 FID 标识。第一句比较模糊，但根据第一句中的"Josephine thought"，可以判断第一句是"Josephine"的脑海中想象的二人穿着黑色睡袍、黑色拖鞋，如同两只黑猫的滑稽画面，应为 FID。同样，例 2 第一句中的"terrified"一词表明第二句、第三句应是 Josephine 和 Constantia 被男访客的"热心"吓到而产生的心理活动，第三句、第四句中的两个"thought"则进一步证实了之前的话语是 FID。例 3 中的"remember"提示读者紧随其后的段落是人物自身的醒悟，是 Josephine 意识到她们已经不用再活在父亲的控制之下了，为后文的顿悟做了铺垫。

另外，表示心理状态的形容词（如 delighted、happy、frightened 等）也具有心理动词的作用。如：

例 4 Was the door just behind them? They were too frightened to look. (Mansfield，2006)

3.2 感觉动词

表示听觉、视觉、触觉及嗅觉的感觉动词（如 see、hear、smell，feel 等），意味着一个感知中心的存在，随后的话语往往是其感知的内容，因此，对人物的感官行为的描写往往是 FID 出现的先兆（余素青，2013）。如：

例 5 ...both Constantia and Josephine felt privately she had rather overdone the not leaving him at the very last. For when they had gone in to say good-bye Nurse Andrews had sat beside his bed the whole time, holding his wrist and pretending to look at her watch. It couldn't have been necessary. It was so tactless, too. Supposing father had wanted to say something—something private to them. Not that he had. Oh, far from it! ...Oh, what a difference it would have made, what a difference to their memory of him, how much easier to tell people about it, if he had only opened both! But no— one eye only. (Mansfield, 2006)

例 6 Really they couldn't help feeling that about butter, at least, she took advantage of their kindness. (Mansfield, 2006)

在例 5、例 6 中，由于第一句主句包含了两位小说人物的一个感觉行为（"felt""feeling"），因此可以认为该句从句是人物因所感而作出的评价（"overdone""It couldn't have been necessary. It was so tactless，too.""She took advantage of their kindness."）应为其 FID，而非叙述者话语。但这种情况存在例外，余素青教授在文章中以 look 和 see 为例，"He looked into her eyes. She seemed angry." 并阐明"在例⑤中，由于第一句包含了小说人物的一个视觉行为（"looked"），可以认为第二句是该人物因所见而作出的判断（"seemed angry"），应为其 FID，而非叙述者话语"（余素奇，2013）。在《已故上校的女儿》中有一个与该例句极其相似的句子："Constantia looked up; she seemed surprised." 而这句话应被认定为叙述者话语。原因在于以上两个句子有两点不同：一为前者感觉动词存在感知对象而后者不存在；二为前者句子主语不同而后者则相同。前者"look"的感知对象为"eyes"，从中"he"可以猜测"she"的情绪，而后者"looked"并无感知对象且前后主语一致，因此并不存在不同于叙述者的言语或意识主体。由此可知，尽管感觉动词可以作为 FID 的语境标识，但在具体语境中是否符合还需将感知对象考虑在内。

3.3 名词和代词

余素青教授强调了小说中的名词和代词的重要性，这些词汇包括限定性名词短语、回指的限定名词、确指的非限定名词和代词。这些词汇能够反映小说中人物独特的知识或认知状态，与叙述者或读者的认知状态有所不同。因此，当在小说的文本片段中发现这些名词或代词反映了非叙述者特有的认知状态时，可以将这些文本片段归属为该人物的 FID，即人物视角。

在支持这一观点的过程中，余素青教授引用了小说中的例句，为他的观点提供了有力的解释和论证。与此同时，在《已故上校的女儿》这部小说中，虽然并没有出现与前述标识完全对应的情况，但可以观察到一些特定的亲属关系称呼，这些称呼表明了句子中存在与这些词所指对象有关的特定亲属关系的主体。因此，包含这种特定亲属关系称呼的句子也可以被认定为 FID。

总的来说，在文学作品中，特定的名词和代词选择不仅仅是语言表达的形式，还是人物视角和叙事者意图的体现。通过对这些词汇的分析，我们可以更好地理解人物的内心世界和情感体验，进一步深入挖掘小说的叙事深度。

例 7　Josephine had had a moment of absolute terror at the cemetery, while the coffin was lowered, to think that she and Constantia had done this thing without asking his permission. What would father say when he found out? For he was bound to find out sooner or later. He always did. "Buried. You two girls had me buried!" (Mansfield, 2006)

例 8　Father would never forgive them... (Mansfield, 2006)

以上选段和选句位于小说哥特式氛围非常浓厚的位置。从 Josephine 与 Cyril 对话的这句直接引语，即 "'And now, Cyril, you must come and see father,' said Josephine"中，我们可以得知"father"是 Josephine 和 Constantia 对她们父亲的称呼，因此包含"father"这一亲属称呼语的句子并非叙事者话语而是 Josephine 的 FID。通过对这一亲属称呼语的巧妙设定，曼斯菲尔德将第三人称全知视角与第三人称有限视角自然地融合在了一起，从而达到了渲染父亲死后其余威仍然笼罩着两姐妹的哥特式恐怖效果。另外例 5 中的代词"she"也证明了这段小说语言是 Josephine 的 FID。"she"实际上是 Josephine 自身，符合叙述学上的代词无指性，由此从叙述学上我们判定姐姐 Josephine 是内部聚焦者（王敏琴、杨璐，2007）。

3.4　情感成分

特殊的句子形式，如感叹句、问句、句子片段等一般蕴含着小说人物强烈的情感。表达价值判断的评价性形容词及由其修饰的名词词组，具有表达小说人物对所指人或物的评价的功能。一些连系动词或情态动词一般表达涉及义务、可能性或必要性等方面的判断，如"had better""ought to""should""be supposed to""might"等。这些带有情感成分的词汇、词组或句子都指向潜在的主体，在《已故上校的女儿》中也多有运用。如：

例 9　Strange! She couldn't have put it on—but twenty-three times. Even now, though, when she said over to herself sadly "We miss our dear father so much," she could have cried if she'd wanted to.　(Mansfield, 2006)

上句表达了 Josephine 对自己难以抑制的悲伤之情的强烈困惑。同样的情况也发生在以上除例 3、例 6、例 8 外的所有选段中，可见频率之高。

例 10　A spasm of pity squeezed her heart. Poor little thing! She wished she'd left a tiny piece of biscuit on the dressing-table.　(Mansfield, 2006)

例 11　If it hadn't been for this idiotic woman she and con would, of course, have eaten their blancmange without. (Mansfield, 2006)

这两个例句中的"poor"和"idiotic"都属于带有情感的评价性形容词。例 9 这句由 Constantia 听到老鼠响动而出现的 FID 表现了人物对老鼠的同情。而例 10 则传递了 Josephine 对"woman"的鄙视和不耐烦。同时，"con"这一亲密称呼语也表明了这句话是 Josephine 的 FID。

例 12　Not, of course, that she felt in the least like giggling. It must have been habit. Years ago, when they had stayed awake at night talking, their beds had simply heaved. And now the porter's head, disappearing, popped out, like a candle, under father's hat... (Mansfield, 2006)

"must have been"承接前文主体 Josephine，是她对自己情难自禁的笑声作出的可能性判断，且"must"表明可能性很大，她极力抗拒将这一行为定义为笑，而认为是一种习惯，反映了 Josephine 不成熟的性格特征。

除以上余素青教授提到的三种情况，笔者认为还有一种情况也可归属于此类，即反映不属于叙事者的某种认知状态的隐喻用法，这一情况在该小说中可找到例证。如：

例 13　And proud young Kate, the enchanted princess, came in to see what the old tabbies wanted now. (Mansfield, 2006)

该句包含两个隐喻"princess"和"old tabbies"。前者的源域是 princess，目标域是 Kate，而后者的源域是 old tabbies，目标域是 two sisters，一个呈褒义，另一个呈贬义。根据这两个句子前后包含的两个目标域，可知其对应的两个源域应分属不同的人物，即前者是两姐妹对 Kate 的认知，后者是 Kate 对两姐妹的认知。在两姐妹眼中 Kate 年轻又高傲，像是公主一般，而在 Kate 看来这两姐妹又老又无知，就像老斑猫，由此表现了两姐妹对 Kate 的羡慕和敬畏以及 Kate 对两姐妹的鄙视。在这短短的一句话中，曼斯菲尔德不着痕迹地完成了视角的转换，而对两个隐喻的分析则可以对这一转变进行有效的识别。

综上所述，以余素青教授的 8 种 FID 语境标识为参照，《已故上校的女儿》中的 FID 语境标识以心理动词、感觉动词、情感成分三类为主，指代名词和代词较少，常出现几种标识共用的情况。同时，本文分别在名词和代词及情感成分类别里增加了亲属称呼语和隐喻两种新的标识。而且，这些标识指示的大多是姐姐 Josephine 的 FID，符合国内学者对 Josephine 是内部聚焦者的论断。

4. 时态后移和 FID 标识

在 FID 研究中，时态后移通常被认为是 FID 的典型句法特征。以过去完成时为例，在 FID 中，一般过去时常经过后移变成过去完成时（Banfield, 2015）。问题在于，是否小说话语中的过去完成时就必然是一般过去时后移的结果，从而能够独立指示 FID 呢？其实不然，如：

例 14　If the huge wardrobe had lurched forward, had crashed down on Constantia, Josephine wouldn't have been surprised. On the contrary, she would have thought it the only suitable thing to happen. But nothing happened. (Mansfield, 2006)

例 14 因为不知道其中的过去完成时是否由一般过去时后移而来，所以难以判断是叙事者话语还是 FID。如果假设该句为 FID，那么这是谁的 FID 呢？由于难以在语境中找到作为 FID 的意识主体或中心的成分（例 14 中句子的主语为无生命主语），我们判断该句应该是叙事者的客观描述，是叙述者对柜子未倒下这一既成事实（一般过去时）作出的反向假设。显然，要判断一个过去完成时的句子为 FID，必须能够在语境中为该句找到一个意识主体或中心，然后建立起该句和意识主体的联系，从而证明该句为此意识主体的 FID，而不能仅凭时态后移就妄下定论。但这并不是说明时态后移这一 FID 语境标识的失效，而是说明其应符合某个条件，即如果提供时间基准的是以某个小说人物为主语的转述，则这些过去完成时的句子有很大的可能被解读为该小说人物的 FID。

5. FID 标识的强度及补充说明

在前述探讨中，心理和感觉动词及其所派生的形容词和名词，被认为是最为显著的 FID 语境标识。这些词汇通常能够直接指向 FID 语境，因为它们直接联系到某个意识主体。因此，在这些词汇后面通常会出现描述小说人物心理状态的 FID 句子。需要强调的是，包含心理和感觉动词的句子本身并不构成 FID，而是通过指向一个非叙述者的言语主体来构建 FID 语境，将读者的认知焦点从叙述者的话语引导至人物的话语。由此可见，心理和感觉动词构建的 FID 语境对于 FID 的辨识，尤其是那些缺乏明显表面句法特征的 FID，具有至关重要的意义。值得注意的是，这类语境也可能出现在 FID 之后的句子或句子片段中，这就需要读者回顾前文，确认之前的句子是否为人物的 FID。

一般认为，即使在句子中没有心理和感觉动词，或者相应的形容词和名词，情感成分也能独立地表明小说人物作为情感或价值判断的意识主体在语境中的存在。这些元素在小说叙述中扮演了重要的角色，不仅丰富了文本内涵，还引导着读者对人物内在情感世界的深入思考。

6. 总结

综上所述，曼斯菲尔德的《已故上校的女儿》这部短篇小说包含了大量的 FID，且基本能够运用余素青教授提出的 8 种语境标识进行有效识别，本文仅选取了归属于各类的典型例句，实际上小说中的 FID 数量不只本文所列举出来的这些。对于在小说中没有找到的对应的语境标识，本文仅概括了余素青教授对其的说明,而对于余素青教授未提及的类型进行了一定的补充。

其中，在感觉动词一类中，应该注意是否存在与感觉动词搭配使用的感知对象，以及动作主体与被感知对象是否一致的问题。若存在且不一致，则可能属于 FID，反之则为叙述者视角。在名词与代词类别中增加的亲属称呼语可以归为代词一类，其使用能够证明与这些词所指对象具有特定亲属关系的言语主体的存在，进而可以对该主体的 FID 进行识别。最后在情感成分类中补充了使用隐喻的情况，目标域具有的内在特征和表达的情感褒贬可以对应不同的言语主体，因而可以识别 FID 主体的转变。

余素青教授提出的 FID 语境标识为小说言语的解读和视角转换分析提供了一个可供参考的范式，在此范式之下，读者和研究者可以对小说中隐含的 FID 进行有效的识别。读者通常会将叙事者话语默认为背景话语，一旦在阅读时发现小说中某个句子包含有 FID 标识，便会判定该句属于小说人物的 FID，将该句的视角转换为人物的视角，并回头观察之前的句子是否也可以理解为小说人物的 FID，从而确定 FID 语境的开端。然后，读者依据惯势原理对随后的句子进行判断，如果随后的句子依然包含 FID 标识，或同前面的 FID 句子存在某种指称上、语义上或时序上的关联，则继续扩展其 FID 语境，直至语言材料不支持为止。因此，FID 可以说是读者对文本成分在特定语境中进行语用解读的结果，特别是在没有明显语境标识的情况下。这就需要读者对于识别 FID 语境有一定的经验，本文结合了余素青教授的 FID 语境识别标识，对读者识别 FID 能力的提高具有一定的参考价值。但是也不排除小说文本的个体差异影响，这提示读者在分析的过程中还要具体语境具体分析。小说中叙事话语和人物话语的界限也是存在模糊性的，而 FID 的最大特点也许就是这一模糊性，也是阅读乐趣的来源之一。

参考文献

[1] BANFIELD A, 2015. Unspeakable sentences: narration and representation in the language of fiction [M]. NewYork: Routledge.

[2] EHRLICH S, 1990. Point of view: a linguistic analysis of literary style[M]. London and New York: Routledge.

[3] MANSFIELD K, 2006. The collected stories of Katherine Mansfield[M]. Hertfordshire: Wordsworth Editions Limited.

[4] 王敏琴，杨璐，2007. "已故上校的女儿"的叙述学和文体学分析[J].外国文学研究（1）：146-153.

[5] 余素青，2013. 自由间接引语的语用分析[J]. 外国语(上海外国语大学学报),36(2)：58-65.

从构词法角度分析《哈利·波特》系列图书中的咒语名称

张怡然　汤朝菊

1. 引言

1.1 研究背景

学界对于语言学中形态学的研究已有很长的历史，形态学是语言学的一个分支，它主要研究词的内在结构。语言学家安德鲁·麦卡锡在《英语形态学导论：单词及其结构》（*An Introduction to English Morphology: Words and Their Structure*）中对于形态学的研究就包括了对词、词的分类、词的组成部分的研究，包括：词根、词缀、词基、词干等，以及曲折词与派生词等。当然，构词法的研究也是形态学研究的一个重要组成部分。比如现今一些高校使用的《语言学高级教程》中就包括了对构词法的讲解。再比如剑桥大学出版社出版的《英语构词法》（*Word-Formation in English*）一书中，其作者英戈·普拉格对英语构词法进行了详细、全面、完整的介绍（Plag，2003）。

在中国知网搜索栏中输入关键词"language morphology（语言学形态学）"之后，共得到508个结果，而对于构词法的研究，目前国内主要集中在两个部分。一是二语教学研究，比如魏恒健（2007）在《新课程理念下的高中英语词汇教学》一文中提出了英语词汇教学的新方式。二是对某语言发展历史的研究，比如汪榕培（1997）在《英语词汇的最新发展》一文中向读者展示的第二次世界大战以来英语词汇的一些发展原因，作者还从构词法的角度分析了其发展途径。

对于《哈利·波特》系列图书的研究，在中国知网搜索栏中输入该关键词后，可以得到一万多条结果，但筛选了"北大核心"与"CSSCI"来源之后的核心期刊来源的论文只有154篇，且大多集中于文学研究以及对《哈利·波特》系列电影的研究。黄娟（2018）在《〈哈利·波特〉系列中的西方文化元素》中重点分析了这一文学作品中的西方文化元素。沈国荣（2013）在《论〈哈利·波特〉电影字幕翻译》中，以该文学作品的改编电影为研究对象，分析了归化和异化的翻译手法在电影字幕翻译中的具体应用。

总之，国内外对构词法的研究很少以人造语言为研究对象，对于《哈利·波特》系列图书的研究也就也很少集中在其中的人为创造的咒语上。对于《哈利·波特》中咒语的来源分析也大多来源于网络，现有不多的关于其作者（J.K. Rowling）罗琳创造的这一虚拟魔法世界的研究的书籍中也没有系统地对咒语的来源进行全面的分析。《哈利·波特的魔法世界——神话传说和那些有趣的事实》（*The Magical Worlds of Harry Potter—A Treasure of Myths Legends and Fascinating Facts*）一书的作者（Colbert，2008）甚至曾提出，《哈利·波特》系列图书中大部分的咒语都是来自作者的想象。

1.2 研究目的与研究意义

本文从构词法的角度出发，旨在对《哈利·波特》系列图书中作者罗琳创造的80余个咒语名字进行全面、系统的分析。人工语言也必定存在其有规律可循之处，本文旨在寻找这种潜在的规律，为阅读《哈利·波特》系列图书经典文学作品的读者提供更多的辅助理解材料，也为今后的文学创作提供一些灵感来源。

1.3 研究方法与研究问题

本文收集了《哈利·波特》系列图书中共八十余条咒语。基于作者罗琳是英国人的背景，将这些咒语先与相似的英语单词进行对比，然后在《拉丁语和其他斜体语言词源词典》《牛津英语词源词典》《牛津拉丁语词典》《牛津新希腊语词典》中进行查询，寻找其词源。最后，根据词源对《哈利·波特》系列图书中咒语的取名进行归类，并对每一类别中的个别咒语进行详细分析。

本文旨在解决《哈利·波特》系列图书中咒语名的创造是否只是简单的灵机一现、是否具有规律性的问题。

2. 理论背景

2.1 构词法

构词法大致可分为两类：一类为派生构词，一类为曲折构词。除此之外，还有截取构词法、首字母构词法、借用构词法等几种构词方法（Booij, 2007: 19, 20）。埃约尔·豪根（Einar Haugen, 1950）曾在《语言借用分析》（"The Analysis of Linguistic Borrowing"）一文中对"借用"这一概念下了定义，他认为借用是重新在一种语言中创造本属于另一种语言的模式。根据借用与源语言之间的相似性，豪根又把借用分为了三类，并给出了三个术语，借用语（loanwords）、混合语（hybrid）、仿造语（loan translation）[或语义借用词（semantic loan）]。

借用语可以用来指所有由借用产生的词，但在这个分类下特指形式和意义都是借用另一种语言的词汇，有时新词的语音结构或形态结构会有细微的变化。比如英语单词"厨师"（chef）便是由法语而来，其意义和形式完全相同。混合语指一个词的一部分，或是词素，或是音素是由其他语言引进而来，以英语中的"椰子"（coconut）一词为例，其前半部分"coco"是来自西班牙语，后半部分"nut"则来自英语。语义借用词指被借用语言中的词汇，直接被翻译成为目标语言中的词，也就是说，目标语言中没有出现新的词的形式，只是出现了新的意义，比如拉丁语中的"omnipotens"一词，意为全能的，这一意义后来为英语中的"almighty"所借用。

2.2 咒语

咒语指那些带有魔法效果的字符串。《哈利·波特》系列图书中的咒语在本文中大致可分为以下几类。第一类为只有咒语，且咒语为非英文字符串，上下文中也没有给出咒语名的魔咒，这类魔咒一般都是以非英语字符串的形式出现，只能靠读者从语境中提取其功能，比如现形咒语"Aparecium"，防水防湿咒语"Impervius"，以及摄魂咒语"Legilimens"。与第一类相同，第二类也有只有咒语，但咒语一般为简体英文构成的一句话或者一个单词，简单明了，比如"Point Me"可以让自己的魔杖如指南针一样为自己指明方向。第三类为有咒语，且有咒语名，且咒语名为英文的魔咒，这类魔咒能让读者从其名字中更好地理解其功能，比如护身咒"Expecto Patronum"，在上下文中，罗琳为其命名为"Patronus Charm"，再比如夺命咒"Avada Kedavra"，在上下文中也以"Killing Curse"的形式出现。第四类咒语同样具有咒语名，但其咒语名也为非英文字符串，也只能通过上下文来推断其使用效果。比如释放清水的咒语"Aguamenti"，作者给出的咒语名是"Aguamenti Charm"，迷惑对手的咒语"Confundo"的咒语名为"Confundus Charm"，以及使对手粉身碎骨的咒语"Reducto"，被命名为"Reductor Curse"。

而对于第二类，本文不做细究，重点分析其余三类，即咒语或咒语名中含有非英文字符串的咒语，本文将从形态学角度来分析其成分。

3. 从构词法的角度分析《哈利·波特》系列图书中的咒语

3.1 以其中八个咒语为例，全面分析其词源与构词法

本部分将依据总结部分中的分类，选取《哈利·波特》系列图书中八个具有代表性的咒语，从构词法的角度，追溯其词源，分析其发展变化。

（1）飞来咒 Accio（Summoning Charm）

"韦斯莱夫人用魔杖指着乔治的口袋，念道：'飞来飞去！'"（Accio）

"一些花花绿绿的小玩意儿从乔治口袋里跳了出来。乔治伸手去抓，没有抓住，它们径直跳进了韦斯莱夫人伸出的手掌中。"（罗琳，2018：302）

"这真是令人难受的一幕。那对孪生兄弟显然想把大量的太妃糖从家里走私出去，韦斯莱夫人用上了她的飞来咒（Summoning Charm），才把那些糖果找了出来。"（罗琳，2018：303）

从文中我们可以看出，这一魔咒的作用是把某一物品从某处召集到施咒人的手里。而"Accio"一词取自拉丁语"acciō"，"acciō"在《牛津希腊语拉丁语词典》（2012：23）中的释义有：召集、发送、拿取、邀请、使某物被拿取、被发送等。如此看来，是和文中的用法完全符合的。而罗琳本人也称此咒语为"飞来咒"（Summoning Charm）。因此这一咒语的创作属于构词法中的借用，而飞来咒的名字便是完全来自拉丁语，属于豪根所提到的借用词，咒语中的形式和意义都是借用的拉丁词汇，只有读音上发生了细小的差别。

（2）飞鸟群群 Avis

"'没错……鹅耳枥木，含有龙的心脏腱索，对吗？'他扫了克鲁姆一眼——克鲁姆点了点头，'比人们通常见到的粗得多……非常刚硬……十又四分之一英寸……飞鸟群群（Avis）！'鹅耳枥木的魔杖发出砰的一声巨响，像手枪开火一般，一群小鸟扑扇着翅膀从魔杖头上飞出来，从敞开的窗口飞进了淡淡的阳光中。"（罗琳，2018：379）

从文中可以推断，"Avis"这一咒语用于召唤成群的飞鸟，而根据《拉丁语与其他意大利语言词源词》（*Etymological Dictionary of Latin and the Other Italic Languages*）（De Vaan，2008：65），"avis"一词的意思是飞鸟、鸟儿。许多现代英语词汇中都有这一词缀的身影，根据词源词典"航空"（aviation）一词便是由"avis"和"ation"（Onions、Friedrichsen、Burchfield，1966：65）这两个词素组成，而"鸟类饲养场"（aviary）中的词缀"avi"也是源自拉丁词语"avis"一词。此处罗琳发明的这一咒语属于借用词，借用希腊词语来创造自己的咒语，并且

没有对原词汇的形式进行任何的改动。

但原词在词形上属于传统语法中的名词，罗琳在此将其作为动词，意为"召唤飞鸟"，属于派生构词法中的一种：零位派生。安德鲁·麦卡锡在《英语形态学导论：单词及其结构》（*An Introduction to English Morphology: Words and Their Structure*，2018：48）一书中曾提到一些语言学家更愿意说转换也是派生形态学的一种，在这个过程中，一个本属于一个词性的词可以直接转换为另一个词性的词，但是词的形态不会发生任何变化。"avis"一词便由原来的名词，直接转化为了动词，形态没有发生任何变化。

因此在整个咒语的创造过程中，借用和派生这两个构词过程参与了进来。

（3）安咳消 Anapneo

"不幸的是，马科斯刚吃了一大口鹌鹑，他急于回答斯拉格·霍恩的问题，咽得太快，脸一下子转成了猪肝色，呛得说不出话来。

"'安咳消'（Anapneo）"。斯拉格·霍恩用魔杖指着贝尔比，平静地说，贝尔比的气管似乎一下子就通畅了。"（罗琳，2018：818）

文中斯拉格·霍恩使用了这一魔咒之后，贝尔比的呼吸立马通畅了。而"anapeno"一词对应的希腊单词为"αναπνέω"，根据《牛津希腊语拉丁语词典》，该词是呼吸的意思。与原文中的意思完全对应，而且其形态没有发生变化，希腊字母中的形式与文中罗琳用的英文字母形式是一一对应的。

（4）清水如泉 Aguamenti（Aguamenti Charm）

"'清水如泉'（Aguamenti）！他用魔杖指着酒杯大喊了一声。杯里立刻出现了满满的清水。"（罗琳，2018：950）

"'今天上午有魁地奇选拔赛呢！'罗恩说，'而且还要练习弗立维布置的清水如泉咒（Aguamenti Charm）！再说了，有什么可解释的？我们总不能跟他说我们讨厌他那门愚蠢的课程吧！'"（罗琳，2018：841）

从文中不难看出，主人公哈利在使用了"Aguamenti"这一咒语之后，高脚杯里装满了水。根据《牛津希腊语拉丁语词典》，拉丁语中与之相近的"aqua"一词有水、雨水、海水之意，现代英语中使用这一词素的词包括水族馆（aquarium）、水生的（aquatic）和水产养殖（aquaculture）等。虽然"aqua"和"agua"有一字之差，但在构词法中，一字母或者两字母之差较为常见。例如，由"television"一词演变为"telly"，但前者的发音为[tɛlə vɪʒən]（美），后者的发音为['teli]（英），这一演变可由其发音上的相似性来解释。"aqua"读音为[ækwə]（美），"[ægwə]"，根据胡壮麟《高级语言学教程》一书中的辅音发音方式和发音位置表格来看（2015：62），/k/和/g/两个辅音发音方式和发音位置都是相同的，唯一的区别在于一个是浊辅音，一个是清辅音，由"aqua"演变为罗琳笔下的"aqua"也可以由二者发音上的相似性来解释。

而"meti"这一词素则来自拉丁语中的"mentiō"（《牛津希腊语拉丁语词典》，2012：1210）一词，该词的其中一个意思为"提到、指某个事物、事件"。在英语中/i/和/o/是两个元音，而英语中的双元音有八个，分别是/aɪ/、/eɪ/、/aʊ/、/əʊ/、/ɔɪ/、/ɪə/、/eə/、/ʊə/，很显然/i/和/o/的组合并不是其中一个，因此将二者连起来的读音并不符合英语的发音习惯，由此推断作者罗琳直接将"mentiō"中的最后一个字母删去变为了"menti"。

（5）阿拉霍洞开 Alohomora

"她夺过哈利·波特的魔杖，敲了敲门锁，低声说道：'阿拉霍洞开！（Alohomora）'锁

咔嗒一响，门突然开了——他们一拥而入，赶紧把门关上，将耳朵贴在上面听着。"（罗琳，2018：42）

我们可以从文中推断，主人公之一赫敏在使用了"Alohomora"这个咒语之后，锁着的门便被打开了，这是一个开门咒。

与"aloho"一词相近的语言来自夏威夷语"aloha"，一般是打招呼或告别时使用，读音为/əˈləʊhə/。"mora"一词源自拉丁语，有"一段时间""做某事需要花费的时间""时间的流逝""推迟、延迟""一个障碍物、阻挡物"等意思。（《牛津希腊语拉丁语词典》，2012：1279-1280）在文中，摆在哈利一行三人面前的便是一个障碍，"mora"一词在此处的意思为"障碍物"的说法较为中肯。结合"aloha"一词的第二个意思，即告别用语，二者组合起来的意思就是"拜拜，障碍物。"这与文中的情景也非常相符。

（6）阿瓦达索命 Avada Kedavra（Killing Curse）

"'阿瓦达索命！'（Avada Kedavra）"

"一片强烈的绿光刺透哈利的眼皮，他听见什么东西在他身旁沉重地倒下。伤疤疼到了极点，他恶心得想吐。然后疼痛减轻了，他恐惧地慢慢睁开刺痛的双眼。

"塞德里克四肢伸开躺在地上，他死了。"（罗琳，2018：479）

文中，墓地里一个人影走出来，念出这句咒语之后，塞德里克就去世了，从语境可以推断出，这个咒语的作用是索取人命。

而这一明显非英语的字符串组合，其来源十分古老。与其有联系的词语，可追溯到一种叫作阿拉姆语的古老中东语言中的短语——Abhadda Kedhabhra（Colbert，2008：29）其意思是"像这个词一样消失"。古代巫师用它来使疾病消失。然而，没有证据表明它曾被用来杀死任何人。

公元2世纪的罗马医生昆图斯·塞雷努斯·萨莫尼库斯（Quintus Serenus Sammonicus）在他的著作《药书》（Liber Medicinalis）中曾提到一种治疗疟疾的方法。首先，病人要在纸上写"Abracadabra"这个词，然后在下一行重复这个词的同时，删掉最后一个字母（Colbert，2008：30）。

词源词典中也收录了这一词语。其对"Abracadabra"的解释为"巴西理得诺斯底教派的一个咒语"。但这一词语在语义和形态方面都与"阿瓦达索命"（Avada Kedavra）区别很大，二者之间的联系并不多。"Abhadda Kedhabhra"这一更原始的形态与现如今的索命咒较为相似，其使某物消失的意义也与索命咒相似。

（7）摄神取念 Legilimens

"他笑道，'然而，会摄神取念（Legilimens）的人可以在某些情况下研究别人的头脑，并作出正确的解释。比如说，黑魔头几乎总能看出别人对他说谎。只有擅长大脑封闭术人才能封住与谎话矛盾的感觉和记忆，在他面前说谎而不被发现。'"（罗琳，2018：669）

原文中，斯内普教授在告诉哈利，习得"摄神取念"这一咒语的人会有怎样的技能。从文中不难看出，这一咒语的作用是读取他人的想法。

而英语中义为"有阅读能力的"的词为"legible"，与文中作者给出的咒语形态和语义上都较为接近。但"legible"一词源自拉丁语"legibilis"（《牛津希腊语拉丁语词典》，2012：1115），这一拉丁语单词又由"legō"一词变形而来，"legō"大致有十几种语义，包括"把东西一起放进嘴里""穿过""移除"，但也有"阅读、精读"的意思。"Legilimens"的后半部分则来自拉丁词语"mens"，意为"进行智力活动的器官、大脑"。

由于"legible"一词本身的特殊性，与上文提到的"Accio"这一咒语不同，英文中没有"accio"这一单词，其唯一可能来源便是拉丁语。但"legible"这一英语词汇本身也是来自拉丁语，所以至于作者罗琳在创造这一词语时，到底是参照拉丁语"legibilis"还是英语"legible"，我们不得而知。

（8）无声无息 Sliencio

"赫敏抓过罗恩的乌鸦换掉了她那只肥青蛙。'无声无息！'（Sliencio）乌鸦的尖嘴还在一张一合，但没有了声音。'很好，格兰杰小姐！'弗立维教授用尖细的嗓门说。"（罗琳，2018：626）

与这个词的形态和语义都比较相近的词是英语词汇"silence"。但拉丁语中也有疑似的来源"silentium"一词，有"没有声音""安静的""静谧的"的意思，其也有自己的变体"silentiōsus"（《牛津希腊语拉丁语词典》，2012：1974），而"silentiōsus"毫无疑问在形态上与作者罗琳所使用的咒语更加相似。

与上文提到的"Legilimens"的词源相同，作者罗琳在创作时，具体是参考了英文中本身就已经经过借用形成的"silence"一词，还是拉丁语原语"silentium"一词，还是与之更为接近的其变体形式"silentiōsus"，我们无从得知，但其词源也不外乎是拉丁语或英语。虽然没有定论，但可大致推测出其范围。

3.2 小结

在对所有的咒语进行上述分析之后，笔者得到了表 3-1 至表 3-5 的内容。

表 3-1　"Accio""Avis"和"Anapneo"类

咒语名	词源	语种来源
Accio	acciō	Latin
Avis	avis	Latin
Bombardo	bombard	French
Confringo	confringō	Latin
Confumdo	confumdō	Latin
Crucio	cruciō	Latin
Defodio	dēfodiō	Latin
Deprimo	dēprimō	Latin
Descendo	descendō	Latin
Diffindo	diffindō	Latin
Duro	dūrō	Latin
Episkey	επισκευ	Greek
Ferula	ferula	Latin
Nox	nox	Latin
Oppugno	oppugnō	Latin
Portus	portus	Latin
Quietus	quiētus	Latin

（续表）

咒语名	词源	语种来源
Reparo	reparō	Latin
Anapneo	αναπνέω	Greek
Apparate	apparātē	Latin
Densaugeo	Dens, augeō	Latin

表 3-2 "Aguamenti" "Alohomora" 类

咒语名	词源	语种来源
Aguamenti	aqua, mentiō	Latin
Alohomora	aloha, mora	Latin
Aparecium	aperio	Latin
Cave Inomicum	caveō, inimīcus	Latin
Colloportus	collocō, porta	Latin
Deletrius	dēleō	Latin
Dissendium	discēdō	Latin
Engorgio	engorge	Latin
Erecto	ērectus	Latin
Expecto Patronum	expect, patrōnus	English, Latin
Expelliarmus	Expellō, arma	Latin
Expulso	evanescō	Greek
Finite Incantatem	finīt, incantō	Latin
Flagrate	flagriō	Latin
Funnunculus	fūrunculus	Latin
Glisseo	glisser	French
Geminio	geminō	Latin
Homenum Revelio	homō, revelō	Latin
Tergeo	tergō	Latin
Inpedimenta	inpedīmentum	Latin
Imperio	imperiōsus	Latin
Impervius	imperuius	Latin
Incarcerous	incarcerate	English
Incendio	incendō	Latin
Langlock	language, lock	English
Levicorpus	levis, corpus	Latin

（续表）

咒语名	词源	语种来源
Liberacorpus	liberātiō, corpus	Latin
Locomotor Mortis	Locō, mōtō, mortuus	Latin
Loocomotor Trumk	locō, mōtō, trunk	Latin, Latin, English
Lumos	lumino	Latin
Meteolojinx Recanto	Μετεωρολογία, jinx, recanto	Greek, English, Latin
Mobiliarbus	mōbilitō, arbōs	Latin
Morsmordre	mos, mordre	Latin, French
Muffliato	muffle	English
Orchideous	orchid	English
Petrificus Totalus	pétrifer, totus	French, Latin
Peskipiksi Pestemomi	peskey, pixie, pester, me	English
Protegon Totalum	prōtegō, totus	Latin
Reducio	reducō	Latin
Reducto	reductiō	Latin
Relashio	relaxō	Latin
Renneverate	re-, neruus	English, Latin
Rictusempra	rictus, semper	Latin
Salvio Hexia	saluus, hex	Latin, English
Sectumsempra	sectūra, simper	Latin
Serpensortia	Serpens, sortior	Latin
Scourgify	scour	English
Sonorus	sonor	Latin
Specialis Revelio	speciālis, revelō	Latin
Stupefy	stupefaciō	Latin
Tarantallegra	tarantella, allergo	English, Latin
Wingardium Leviosa	wing, arduus, levis	English

表 3-3　"Legilimens"类

咒语名	可能词源 1	语种来源	可能词源 2	语种来源
Fidelius Charm	fides	Latin	Fideliry	English
Legilimens	legibilis, mens	Latin	Legible, mens	English, Latin
Obliviate	obliviō	Latin	oblivion	English
Obscuro	obscur	Latin	obscure	English
Riddikulus	rīdiculus	Latin	ridiculus	English
Sliencio	silentum	Latin	silence	English

表 3-4　"Avada Kedavra"类

咒语名	可能词源	语种来源	可能词源 2	语种来源
Avada Kedavra	Abhadda Kedhabhra	Aramaic	Abracadabra	Latin

表 3-5　"Repello Muggletum"类

咒语名	可能词源	语种来源
Repello Muggletum	repellō, muggle	Latin, constructed word

如上面的表格所示，从构词法的角度来分析《哈利·波特》系列图书中咒语名的创作过程，大致可将咒语分为五类。第一类中包括前面所分析的"Accio""Avis"和"Anapneo"。这一类的构词方式属于完完全全的借用，其形态结构完全从拉丁语中，或是希腊语、法语中借用而来。第二类包括上一部分所分析的"Aguamenti"以及"Alohamora"，其形式多由拉丁语、英语或希腊语演变而来，但其形态与源语言相比并非没有差别。作者在采用源语言时，或是因为语音结构，或是由于作者个人的一些原因，对几个字母做出了改变，但依其大体形态，仍不难推断出其词源。前面所分析的"Sliencio"与"Legilimens"则属于第三类，英语与拉丁语中都能找到其词源。至于作者罗琳在写作的过程中到底采用哪种语言中的哪种形式，或是采取了二者结合的形式，我们无从得知。除了这比较普遍的三大类构词法以外，还有另外两个比较特殊的类别。第四类是包括了"Avada Kedavra"在内的咒语，其形式及意义都与其能联系到的词源相差较大，其具体词源尚不可知。最后一类是"Repello Muggletum"这一咒语，其前半部分取自拉丁语，后半部分则取自罗琳在作品中自己创造的另外一个词，不属于任意一种语言。

总的来说，第一类较多，有 21 个；第二类最多，有 52 个；剩下三类分别有 6 个、1 个、1 个。由此可见，罗琳在进行咒语创作时并不是一时兴起，几乎每一个咒语都与拉丁语词源有联系，并且她或许完全采用，或许部分地采用了源语言的形式。她的创作是有章可循的。

4. 总结

构词法的研究是形态学研究中的一个重要组成部分。但我国大部分学者都把构词法运用在对英语二语词汇教学的改善，以及对某一种语言发展历史的研究上。同样，对于《哈利·波特》系列图书的研究也很少集中在其咒语名字上，虽然有学者研究其翻译策略，但少有学者对其名字的构成进行研究。

本文从构词法的角度，运用权威词典，对《哈利·波特》系列图书中作者创造的咒语名字进行了系统的词源分析，并将其分为了五类，其中包括三类作者常用的、两类较为特殊的。这证明，罗琳的咒语创作是有章可循的，循着这个规律，也许可以创作出更多类似的咒语。

索绪尔曾说过，语言是系统的。虽然罗琳创造的这种特殊的字符串不能被称为语言，但其研究价值依然存在。

参考文献

[1] BOOIJ G, 2007. The gramma of words: an introduction to linguistic morphology[M]. Oxford: Oxford University Press.

[2] CARSTAIRS-MCCARTHY A, 2018. An introduction to English morphology: words and their structure[M]. Edinburgh: Edinburgh University Press.

[3] COLBERT D, 2008. The magical worlds of Harry Potter: a treasure of myths legends and fascinating facts[M]. London: Penguin Publishing Group.

[4] DE VAAN M, 2008. Etymological dictionary of Latin and the other Italic languages[M]. Brill NV: Leiden.

[5] HAUGEN E, 1950. The analysis of linguistic borrowing[J]. Language, 26(2): 210-231.

[6] ONIONS C T, FRIEDRICHSEN G W S, BURCHFIELD R W, 1966. The Oxford dictionary of English etymology[M]. Oxford: Oxford University Press.

[7] OXFORD LANGUAGE, 2012. Oxford Latin dictionary[M]. Oxford: Oxford University Press.

[8] PATRICK J J, 2008. The Oxford new Greek dictionary[M]. Oxford: Oxford University Press.

[9] PLAG I, 2003. Word-formation in English[M]. Cambridge: Cambridge University Press.

[10] 胡壮麟，姜望琪，2002. 语言学高级教程[M]. 北京：北京大学出版社.

[11] 黄娟，2018. 《哈利·波特》系列中的西方文化元素[J]. 电影文学（1）：146-148.

[12] 罗琳，2018. 《哈利·波特全集》[M]. 马爱农，马爱新，译. 北京：人民文学出版社.

[13] 沈国荣，2013. 论《哈利·波特》电影字幕翻译[J]. 电影文学（18）：30-31.

[14] 汪榕培，1997. 英语词汇的最新发展[J]. 外语教学与研究（3）：36-42.

[15] 王瑛，2021. 哈利波特小说中咒语翻译策略研究[J]. 作家天地（11）：7-8.

Reshape the Past: Identity Construction in Cultural Memory in Relation to *The Remains of the Day*

马 嘉

1. Introduction

Kazuo Ishiguro is a Japanese-born British novelist, whose works of fiction have earned him honors around the world, including the Nobel Prize in literature. *The Remains of the Day* is one of his most famous works, which made him win the Booker Prize and one of the best-known European novelists. *The Remains of the Day*, a first-person narrative, records Stevens' six-day trip to the west of England, interweaving with his reminiscence of three decades of service at Darlington Hall. As a typical English butler, Stevens always wears a prim mask of formality in front of others, which has shut him off from understanding and intimacy. In this novel, identity construction and memory are the main themes. Under the influence of historical contexts and selective memory, Stevens reshapes the past and reconstructs his individual identity at the same time. Through the analysis of the relation between memory and identity construction, it can be more explicit to understand how the social-cultural memory changes Stevens' identity recognition and also to get a glimpse of his spiritual world and the underlying social changes in Britain after World War II.

There are abundant studies about *The Remains of the Day*. Some foreign scholars analyzed it from the perspective of politics with postcolonial theory. Ryan S. Trimm (2006) believed Darlington Hall and its servants can only be fully understood in a colonial or globalized context, one that provides hidden support and a rebranded identity. Sonali Thakkar (2017) discussed how the repression of the imperial crisis in Stevens' narrative is entangled with his memories of fascist appeasement and complicity. Besides, others also explore it from the aspect of identity construction and narration. Kathleen Wall (1994) claimed that the novel challenges our usual definition of an unreliable narrator as one whose "norms and values" differ from those of the implied author, and questions the concept of an ironic distance between the dishonest narrator and the implied author. For domestic scholars, the transformation of physical time and space and unreliable narration are the major research directions. The novel portrays a nostalgic landscape and reveals the hero's bewilderment and reflection on nostalgic complex and imperialness with the aid of an illusive special environment, reminding pastoral moment, and self-reflective characters. (Bao & Zhang, 2009). According to Deng Yingling (2016), Stevens' narration of past events reflects the characteristics of unreliability, fragmentization, and selectivity of remembering narration. In addition, Stevens finally wakes up from the lonely soul who lost his "self" and realizes the disintegration of the "old self" and the reconstruction of the "new self" because of the transformation of physical time and space (Huo & Li, 2023).

The scholars above discussed the memory, politics, historical contexts, and identity construction. However, they did not conclude the relation among these four factors. In other words, while exploring Stevens' identity construction, they just chose one aspect instead of combining individual and public reasons. However, Jan Assmann's theory of cultural memory (2015) provided a new perspective to understand this novel, which combines all the factors above. Therefore, this essay applies Jan Assmann's theory of cultural memory to analyze the process of Stevens' identity construction, trying to reveal how cultural memory could affect individual identity construction. Starting from signs and symbols that are full of Englishness, this novel metaphorically expresses original identity construction. Then comes the second step in the process of shaping identity: communication with "others". It discusses how Stevens deals with the relationship between "others" and himself, which also includes historical contexts and hierarchy at that time. Finally, it focuses on selective memory and interpretation to analyze its decisive role in identity construction.

2. Signs and Symbols: Metaphorical Expression in Identity Construction

According to Assmann (2015), cultural memory consists of texts, pictures, rituals, etc., which are essential and used repeatedly by a society over a given period of time. At its core is the traditions of political identity shared by all members, through which the related groups define themselves and establish a self-image, based on which the members of the group are aware of their common attributes and differences. Through various media, cultural memory is able to serve its function.

There are plenty of signs and symbols in *The Remains of the Day*, and Darlington Hall comes first. As a hall serving the most powerful English aristocracy and a meeting place for Senior dignitaries from developed countries, it represents the glory of the British Empire. In the eyes of Stevens, Darlington Hall is a veritable, luxurious, and historic English-style mansion, with a serious owner and a loyal and dedicated butler. It is not only the workplace for Stevens but also home for him. He is so proud of the hall and the profession. However, with the bankruptcy of Mr. Darlington and the sale of Darlington Hall, its glory and dazzling light gradually fade away. For the new lord Mr. Farraday, the genuine grand old English house and the genuine old-fashioned English butler are just comedies to show off. The old power has disappeared, and new rules are established. The dramatic decline of the conditions of Darlington Hall also epitomizes the decline of the empire. If the hall is a museum, then Stevens seems to be the living fossil.

Then comes the idyllic scenery. Leaving the hall, where he has stayed for almost three decades, and facing unfamiliar places, Stevens is a little bit anxious but is attracted by the typical English-style idyllic scenery. When standing on the high ledge and viewing the land, he has a rare feeling—the feeling that one is in the presence of greatness. As he says: "We call this land of ours

Great Britain, and there may be those who believe this an immodest practice. Yet I would venture that the landscape of our country alone would justify the use of this lofty adjective." (Ishiguro, 1990, p.26) The calmness of that beauty and its sense of restraint make Britain distinctive and sacred. Besides, with the invasion of Capitalism in Britain, the countryside may be the last place that keeps previous living habits. When Stevens goes into the Moscombe village, Mr. Taylor tells him that they do not miss electricity, instead, oil gives a warmer light. In this sense, the countryside is the last place to retain old Englishness. Also, Stevens states in this novel that he does not like changes. Thus, it is natural to get the conclusion: Stevens is trying to insist on and maintain Englishness and is reluctant to adapt to the present new conditions.

In addition to the architecture and idyllic scenery, clothing is another significant sign in this novel, playing a significant role in shaping Stevens' identity. In the prologue, Stevens ponders his outfit for the trip, from the size to the occasion. Because he believes that "it is important that one be attired at such times in a manner worthy of one's position" (Ishiguro,1990, p.12), he pays too much attention to clothing. When discussing about the definition of "great butler", Stevens points out that "The great butlers are great by virtue of their ability to inhabit their profession role and inhabit it to the utmost. They wear their professionalism as a decent gentleman will wear his suit: he will not let ruffians or circumstance tear it off him in the public gaze." (Ishiguro, 1990, p.39) Clothing is essential because it is closely associated with professional dignity. Once losing it, the butler must lose his dignity and cannot be praised as great. Stevens criticizes butlers in other European countries: "They are not real butlers. They are like a man who will, at the slightest provocation, tear off his suit and his shirt and run about screaming." (Ishiguro, 1990, p.39) From this dimension, Stevens can be seen as a decent English butler with great dignity.

Language, an invisible sign, is an essential carrier of culture and the impact of culture upon a given language is something intrinsic and indispensable. In *The Remains of the Day*, Englishness is presented by the mode of expression. As a typical English aristocratic butler, Stevens pays much attention to his oral expression. The words he uses are so tactless and unpleasurable that it may lead to a sense of suffocation when reading this novel, especially when he talks with his father, an old butler who has been in poor physical condition: "I hope Father is feeling better now" "I'm glad Father is feeling so much better" "I'm so glad you're feeling better now" (Ishiguro, 1990, p.88). By repeating such words three times, readers are easily able to sense the estrangement between father and son, and the concern repressed by the son at the same time. Out of the English butler's professionalism, Stevens cannot freely express his concern and love for his father. The only thing he can do is employing such boring words but in fact being self-restrained to show respect for his father.

In addition, Stevens seems to be at a loss every time when facing banters. After Mr. Darlington's bankruptcy, Mr. Farraday, a humorous American gentleman, becomes the new owner of Darlington Hall. Totally different from Lord Darlington, Mr. Farraday always banters with Stevens, expecting him to be more funny and less prim. Under such conditions, Stevens is awkward and anxious. As he says in the novel: "It is quite possible, then, that my employer fully expects me to respond to his bantering in a like manner, and considers my failure to do so a form of negligence. This is, as I say, a matter which has given me much concern." (Ishiguro, 1990, p.16) Mr. Farraday is far more informal and far less interested in keeping up a certain social distance, one based on the inevitable difference of class and status, between himself and his butler. Instead, he jokes and seems at ease with Stevens, who responds with confusion rather than relief. Stevens is uncomfortable in this new post-war world, one that has increasingly little place for rigid class hierarchies and the kind of formal service. Old English traditions have been deeply rooted in him, making him reluctant to adapt to the new rules and regulations built in Britain. However, during his trip to the west of England, he tries to change himself little by little after chatting with various people. He also tries to banter with villagers when informed that the couple upstairs could be very noisy at night. Besides, at the end of the story, Stevens finds that banter is a useful and popular means to narrow the distance between people. Also, it is the banter that makes him find the meaning to continue to serve the new lord. From this point, it is obvious that Stevens is a conscientious and diligent butler. He tries his best to dedicate himself to his work, whether to silence or banter.

In a word, all these signs and symbols consolidate Stevens' self-recognition. Englishness is fully embodied in him. He is a representative of an English aristocratic butler and an epitome of the society at that time.

3. Communication with the Past and Others: Gradual Changes in Identity Construction

From the perspective of cultural memory, recalling and reviewing history is not simply reproducing the past, but reshaping the past for the present. In other words, in cultural memory, the past is not represented as a chronological sequence of one event followed by another, but serving for the present, a process of giving new meaning to the past by the needs of the present (Jin, 2017). It is the same for Stevens, during the process of the journey, he recollects the past three decades. He recalls his career as a butler, rethinking his relationship with his father and Miss Kenton. At the end of this book, Stevens persuades himself that "I should cease looking back so much, that I should adopt a more positive outlook and try to make the best of what remains of my day." (Ishiguro, 1990, p.216) He realizes the deconstruction of the "old self" and the reconstruction of the "new self". From this point, it becomes understandable why the record of the present journey is always interwoven with the past. He tries to throw away his old traditional identity as a typical English butler and find a new individual identity to adapt himself to the post-war world.

However, recalling and reviewing history is not just a personal act. It is not only about individual memory but also closely associated with the community's memory. Jan Assmann's theory of cultural memory is based on Halbwachs' theory of collective memory. According to Halbwachs, individual memory has, or requires a social framework, which is conditioned and facilitated by the social context. He argues that memory is central to the perception of identity, which is formed and changes within a specific collective or social framework. Assmann develops his theory and divides collective memory into communicative memory and cultural memory. Through cultural memory, members belonging to the same community establish and consolidate their identity, which also means the appearance of "others".

In *The Remains of the Day*, Stevens classifies people he meets including himself into separate groups. In "Day One Evening: Salisbury", Stevens mentions evenings he spent with other butlers and the most debated question: What is a great butler? Here, he puts himself into the butler category with other butlers. They all serve in the distinguished household and are the senior servants, knowing all the ins and outs of the profession. Those ignorant valets who lacked any fundamental understanding of it are the "others". They are depicted by Stevens as "the worst offenders, aspiring as they usually do to the position of butler with some urgency (Ishiguro, 1990, p.28)". Besides, he also distinguishes himself from his father, an old traditional butler. Although inspired by his father and taking him as a role model, Stevens still believes they belong to separate groups. There is a fundamental difference between the values of Stevens' generation and those of the previous generation. The former is much more idealistic, because they tend to concern themselves much more with the moral status of an employer while the elders might have been more concerned with employers' descent. Also, they hold different world ideologies. The older generation sees the world as a ladder, while the younger sees it as a wheel. The elder strictly complies with the hierarchy, taking descent as the only standard, while the younger, after witnessing the WW II, begins to doubt the previous rules and value morality far more than descent. Under such conditions, Stevens realizes his original identity, which is different from the ordinary servants and old English aristocratic butler as well.

In addition, the apparent hierarchy makes it difficult for Stevens to ignore the social class divide. In "Day Three Evening", after running out of oil in his car, Stevens goes to a village and stays at Mr. Taylor's home. He is grateful for Taylor's kindness and generosity, but he is also tired of the hospitality of other villagers who specially come to visit him. This feeling reaches its peak when Mr. Harry, a villager, rambles on about his political ideals and his understanding of "dignity". Stevens, as a butler serving the most powerful gentlemen of Europe, comes close to the great hub of things and definitely disagrees with Harry's statements. He even comments "his statements are far too idealistic, far too theoretical, to deserve respect" (Ishiguro, 1990, p.173). The huge gap between the upper class and lower class completely separates them and puts them into two groups. However, there is still a change in Stevens himself. At the beginning, he is reluctant to talk too much with others. Thanks to his experience as an aristocratic butler for more than three decades, it has been his professional habit to be discreet. As he meets more and more people, he gradually talks more than before. In the end, he communicates with a stranger about his career, his new lord, and inner confusion. Stevens is no more a butler restricted in the hall, but a man with his trouble and various emotions. He is free from the invisible fetter and finds a solution so that he can adapt himself to the new community and society.

What's more, different nationality also consolidates Stevens' identity—an English butler. He claims that only English butlers are the true butlers with self-constraint and great dignity. Meanwhile, Stevens realizes great differences between him and his new lord, Mr. Farraday, a humorous American gentleman. He is too prim and proper to respond to Farraday's banter. Also, at the end of the story, while talking with a man, Stevens admits that Americans are the only ones who can afford

Darlington Hall, and he himself is also a part of the package. The Great Britain was falling and America was rising, which is in line with the historical context at that time. The specific historical position of the frame narrative, July 1956, is rather salient. Anglo-American relations were suffering traumas throughout the early 1950s: Suez was the final straw. Stevens takes his trip through the west of England, anxious about such change. He reflects on the past and wants to find a solution to adapting to the new conditions. In conclusion, through communication with the past and others, Stevens begins to doubt his original identity and rethink the distinction between "others" and himself. He tries to change himself little by little and pursues a comfortable state to adapt to the post-war world.

4. Selective Memory and Interpretation: Final Confirmation in Identity Construction

Cultural memory often takes two diametrically opposed approaches to deal with the past, which Assmann calls "cold memory" and "hot memory" (Assmann, 2015). Cold memory is the process of viewing people and events of the past as cyclical, thus excluding or denying any social changes. In contrast, hot memory means that someone draws useful experience and motivation from the past and uses it to clarify direction and boost confidence (Assmann, 2015). In other words, one is able to see the distance and difference between the past and the present through hot memory. In *The Remains of the Day*, Stevens keeps recalling the past all the way. He reflects on his service for Mr. Darlington, his relationship with his father and Miss Kenton. By doing so, he finds a way to free himself from emotional fetters and express his inner mind, which is still ambivalent and even contradictory. Therefore, the process of recalling belongs to hot memory. History is not only a tool to measure the depth of time, but a mirror to reflect the present. The past turns out to be meaningful because of various changes.

According to Assmann (2015), the way of retrieving and expressing the past is determined by the system of meaning associations in which the relevant individuals and collectives are respectively situated, and by what meanings need to be derived from the past. It provides the theoretical basis to explain why Stevens selectively recalls and interprets in records. At the very beginning, when it comes to Mr. Darlington, Stevens shows great respect for him. When hearing a great deal of nonsense and reports about Mr. Darlington from outside, he defends him. As he says in the story: "I can declare that he was a truly good man at heart, a gentleman through and through, and one I am today proud to have given my best years of service to." (Ishiguro, 1990, p.54) Here, he shows the complete loyalty to Mr. Darlington without any doubts. It is the same when firing two Jewish housemaids and when facing the question from Mr. Cardinal. He fully trusts in Mr. Darlington and every decision he makes. He tries to persuade Miss Kenton: "The fact is, the world of today is a very complicated and treacherous place…Whereas his lordship, I might venture, is somewhat better placed to judge what is for the best." (Ishiguro, 1990, p.131) However, when asked about Mr. Darlington by an American lady who is visiting Darlington Hall, Stevens denies his service for him: "Oh no, I am employed by Mr. John Farraday, the American gentleman who bought the house from the Darlington family." (Ishiguro, 1990, p.108) Also, when asked about Mr. Darlington by folks during his trip, he still denies it. It can be learned that in this period, Stevens is reluctant to admit he is Lord Darlington's butler. In fact, he starts to suspect the value and meaning of his service to Mr. Darlington. In the end, he talks about him with a stranger: "You see, I trusted. I trusted in his lordship's wisdom. All those years I served him, I trusted I was doing something worthwhile. I can't even say I made my own mistakes. Really—one has to ask oneself—what dignity is there in that?" (Ishiguro, 1990, p.215) Stevens overturns his previous belief and permits that there is little dignity in the three decades due to blind and unconditional trust.

Stevens' inner mind is also contradictory when rethinking his relationship with his father and Miss Kenton. In the beginning, he adores and respects his father very much. In his eyes, his father "not only knew all there was to know about how to run a house, he did in his prime come to acquire that 'dignity in keeping with his position', as the Hayes Society puts it" (Ishiguro, 1990, p.32). The old Stevens is a role model to Stevens. Therefore, Stevens enforces others to respect his father as well. He requires Miss Kenton to call his father "Mr. Stevens" or "Mr. Stevens senior". Moreover, he deliberately ignores the fact that his father is getting older and older and is not capable of doing the present work. While Miss Kenton notices mistakes made by his father and tries to remind him, Stevens is annoyed: "At first, I found it hard to credit such an error to my father. But I soon reminded myself that such trivial slips are liable to befall anyone from time to time, and my irritation soon turned to Miss Kenton for attempting to create such unwarranted fuss over the incident." (Ishiguro, 1990, p.49) He is unwilling to admit that his father is too old to finish his present work perfectly. Instead, he believes that his father is still "a person of considerable dependability" (Ishiguro, 1990, p.55). However, because of extreme pursuit of being a great butler, he constantly represses emotions and always wears an invisible mask in front of others. He is alienated from his father. For several years, his father and he have tended to converse less and less, and even the brief exchanges necessary to communicate information relating to work take place in an atmosphere of mutual embarrassment. Even when his father dies, he misses the chance to have a last glance. It seems that Stevens is too indifferent to his father. According to his interpretation, he should keep professionalism as his father expects and is proud of passing the test. However, his state and behavior show that what he explains is not completely true. His facial expression and state expose everything. And Lord Darlington perceives it, as he talks to Stevens: "You look as though you're crying." (Ishiguro, 1990, p.96)

Stevens does the same with Miss Kenton. He hides his real feelings under the prim mask. He tries to avoid responding to Miss Kenton's confession. When she asks him "Are you not in the least interested in what took place tonight between my acquaintance and I, Mr. Stevens?" (Ishiguro, 1990, p.194), Stevens changes the subject naturally. Especially when hearing the news that Miss Kenton will marry another man, he just offers his congratulations to her. However, although he constantly represses affection for her, he always chats with her by the name of work. When learning about the death of her aunt, he intends to comfort her. But his words finally turn into accusations of inadequacies of her work. Although he pretends to be calm, his shaking hands expose his unusual state. During his trip, he finally permits his affection for Miss Kenton and builds up courage to ask about her marriage. At the beginning of his narration, Stevens is sure that she will return to Darlington Hall. He also spends a large amount of time recalling his past with her. After hearing her real feelings, he does not cover up anymore. He eventually admits: "Indeed—why should I not admit it?—at that moment, my heart was breaking." (Ishiguro, 1990, p.212) He takes off his mask and faces to real emotions in his heart. During this process, Stevens' selective memory and interpretation plays a decisive role in shaping his individual identity. He continuously tries to persuade and doubt himself, oscillating between self-affirmation and self-denial. Finally, he succeeds in facing his real feelings, getting rid of the emotional fetters, and going to the future. Through selective memories and interpretation, he reaches the bottom of his heart and builds up a new ego.

5. Conclusion

To sum up, cultural memory greatly influences individual identity construction. From signs and symbols to collective memories of community and historical contexts to selective memory and interpretation, Steven shapes his identity step by step. The employment of signs and symbols full of Englishness is a metaphorical way to shape individual identity. They lay the deep foundation for identity construction. In this step, Stevens is still a typical English aristocratic butler. Then comes the second step: a journey to the west of England. After communicating with "others", he gradually doubts previous rules and beliefs that he strictly complied with before. Also, with the influence of changing social contexts and hierarchy, Stevens begins to rethink the value and meaning of his past service in Darlington Hall. At last, selective memory and interpretation play a decisive role in identity construction. It makes it possible for him to finally face his repressed emotions and feelings. In other words, he becomes a real man instead of a butler with a prim mask all the time. In fact, Stevens' trip to the west of England is not so much a parallel process of seeking a solution to a professional dilemma and enjoying the beauty of nature, but rather a journey of a "prisoner" who was originally "locked up" in his "self", trying to get out of the dilemma, face the future, free himself, and seek the soul.

Bibliography

[1] ISHIGURO K, 1990. The Remains of the Day[M]. New York: Vintage.

[2] TRIMM R S, 2005. Inside Job: Professionalism and Postimperial Communities in *The Remains of the Day*[J]. Literature Interpretation Theory, 16(2): 135-161.

[3] THAKKAR, SONALI, 2017. Resurfacing Symptomatic Reading: Contrapuntal Memory and Postcolonial Method in *The Remains of the Day*[J]. The Cambridge Journal of Postcolonial Literary Inquiry, 4(1): 89-108.

[4] WALL K, 1994. *The Remains of the Day* and Its Challenges to Theories of Unreliable Narration[J]. The Journal of Narrative Technique, 24(1): 18-42.

[5] WESTERMAN M, 2004. Is the Butler Home? Narrative and the Split Subject in *The Remains of the Day*[J]. Mosaic: A Journal for the Interdisciplinary Study of Literature, 37(3): 157-170.

[6] 阿斯曼，2015. 文化记忆：早期高级文化中的文字、回忆和政治身份[M]. 金寿福，译. 北京：北京大学出

版社.

[7] 鲍秀文, 张鑫, 2009. 论石黑一雄《长日留痕》中的象征[J]. 外国文学研究, 31(3): 75-81.

[8] 邓颖玲, 2016. 论石黑一雄《长日留痕》的回忆叙述策略[J]. 外国文学研究, 38(4): 67-72.

[9] 霍士富, 李汶珈, 2023. "旧我"解体与"新我"重构: 论石黑一雄《长日将尽》[J]. 西安外国语大学学报, 31(1): 124-128.

[10] 金寿福, 2017. 扬·阿斯曼的文化记忆理论[J]. 外国语文, 33(2): 36-40.

[11] 王卫新, 2010. 试论《长日留痕》中的服饰政治[J]. 外国文学评论(1): 216-223.

The Chronotope in *Sweet Tooth*: Temporal Indicators of Space

龙 佳

1. Introduction

1.1 McEwan and *Sweet Tooth*

Ian Russell McEwan is one of the most influential writers in British literature. Born on 21 June in 1948 in Aldershot, Hampshire, England, he was awarded the Shakespear Prize by the Alfred Toepfer Foundation, Hamburg, in 1999. His books were shortlisted several times for the Booker Prize for Fiction. His book, *The Child in Time* (1987) and *Atonement* (2001) won the Whitbread Novel Award. The novel *Solar*, focusing on climate change, won the 2010 Bollinger Everyman Wodehouse Prize. McEwan's early pieces were criticized for their dark themes and horrific and grotesque styles. He is a great hand at depicting the psychological states, such as the uneasiness and fear of modern people, and he explores the issues of violence, murder, pedophilia, and incest and so on (Groes, 2013). *Atonement* is a turning point of the writing style of McEwan, which marks the change from the "horror Ian" to the "national writer". And *Sweet Tooth* is the second book of his new style. *Sweet Tooth* is a story about love and spy. Serena, the protagonist, is an innocent and lovely girl who grows up in a conservative church family. She is recruited by the MI5 because of the recommendation of Canning, who is a middle-aged professor and the lover of Serena. Serena is appointed with the "Sweet Tooth Operation", which aims to intrude into the writing of writers, subtly guiding the writers to an anti-communist trend. Gradually, Serena falls in love with the writer, Tom, and has to cheat him involuntarily. In the end, Tom writes a book, fighting against the capitalism and the lie of Serena is exposed. The turn in *Sweet Tooth* is arranged to make the readers rectify and change their understanding of what they have been reading (Cojocaru, 2015). One of the pleasures of reading *Sweet Tooth* is waiting for the end to strike literature, spy and writer, reader and author, deception and love—to be given a new meaning.

1.2 Literature Review

Since *Sweet Tooth* was published in 2012, academia from the home and abroad have focused on the topic of spy story, ethical issues, freedom, narrative strategies and readers' experiences. The literature review on this novel will be presented from to two aspects of research, abroad and at home, as well as the theory of chronotope.

1.2.1 Previous Studies of *Sweet Tooth* Abroad

The book is normally concerned with spy, history, romance, deceive, ethics and so on. However, when it comes to McEwan's *Sweet Tooth*, the focus of people in Western countries is usually put on the delicate arrangement at the beginning and ending of the novel without too much attention on its plots or characters. Therefore, inevitably, the attention of researchers and critics abroad is mostly focused on the narrative strategies, rather than its intriguing stories about Serena's experience at MI5 and love stories. For example, from the aspect of the advantage of narrative technique for novel writing, Petr Chalupský points out that *Sweet Tooth* not only combines the characteristics of McEwan's novel, multi-theme and one protagonist, more importantly, it also contains a notable degree of intertextual and factors of a quality narrative (Chalupský, 2015). And Alaa Alghamdi, from metafiction, metanarrative, poststructuralism, explores the relationship between author, subject, and reader, and concludes that metanarrative techniques in *Sweet Tooth* challenge the traditional concept of literature by creating and destroying the illusions of reality and offering an alternative dissolution to the subject, allowing the survival and emergence of the author (Alghamdi, 2015). Laura Savu Walker from the narrative strategy and the text itself, provides that McEwan uses covert authorship in *Sweet Tooth* to achieve a balance of power between male and female, reader and author (Walker, 2015). Charles Cornelius Pastoor answers the question in *Atonement*: "How can a novelist achieve Atonement when, with her absolute power of deciding outcomes, she is also God?" (McEwan, 2001) and thinks that the relation between readers and author in *Sweet Tooth* is the best answer because they are in collaboration (Pastoor, 2019). Although these researchers have grasped the most prominent features of *Sweet Tooth*, narrative strategies, and conveyed very deep ideas, it is still far from realizing a good novel's value from just one perspective.

1.2.2 Previous Studies of *Sweet Tooth* at Home

Compared with the foreign studies on McEwan's *Sweet Tooth*, the domestic research started later. Although the domestic research on *Sweet Tooth* started late and the number of studies is small, there are a variety of research angles. Domestic analysis focuses on individual freedom, narrative strategies, feminism, and ethical issues. About freedom, Shi Yafang uses Foucault's "aesthetic theory of survival" to analyze Tom's paradoxes of political discipline and freedom of writing, and to explore people's thinking about breaking free from the shackles of disciplined subjects and realizing the possibility of aesthetic survival (Shi, 2021). Zhong Ying and Song Yanfang use Bakhtin's theory of chronotope to analyze the author's breaking the boundary between reality and fiction and the individual's pursuit of freedom (Zhong & Song, 2019). The ethical discussion of McEwan's works has also been hot for critics in China. Shang Biwu believes that ethics and emotions are the important themes of McEwan in this work, and while studying the ethical identities of Serena, Canning and Tom, the article focuses on their state of mind and reasons for emotional and ethical choices, and excavates the emotions and ethics of the novel's forgiveness theme on this basis (Shang, 2013). Wu Ling points out that McEwan used the surface of espionage warfare to reflect the irrational and weak discourse of women in the male hegemonic culture (Wu, 2020). The deceitful reconnaissance and anti-reconnaissance behavior of the characters in the novel correspond precisely to the dynamic relationship between men using hegemony to gaze at women and women staring at them after awakening.

Based on the literature at home and abroad, it can be seen that since the publication of *Sweet Tooth*, the number of relevant studies has increased. There are also some studies about the space in *Sweet Tooth*, but it is shown that critics at home and abroad have paid less attention to the integration between time and space. The chronotope is a supplement for the studies of this book.

1.2.3 Chronotope

Chronotope is a great theoretical achievement in the field of literature and art since the 20th century, and the Russian expression of this concept is a combination of "хроооп", derived from the Greek word chronos (время) and topos (место), equivalent to "Zeit-Raum" in German and "space-time" in English, belonging to most ontological research objects in the natural sciences and humanities and social sciences (Zhang, 2018). The chronotope is not a word without proof, and it derives from the intense discussion of time and space in the natural sciences. The theory of chronotope has been successfully introduced into the field of humanities and social sciences, especially in the field of literature and art, and immediately caused great repercussions in the academic circles. The degree of discussion has become deeper and deeper, the scope has become wider and wider, and the research enthusiasm has continued today.

Most researchers believe that the term, chronotope, used to denote the concept of a space-time unity, should have first appeared in the research papers of the Russian theorist, Bakhtin. Bakhtin did not systematically elaborate the concept of chronotope, and the essay *Forms of Time and of the Chronotope in the Novel* is the main sources for his chronotope thinking. In the essay, he explained that "We will give the name chronotope (literally, "time space") to intrinsic connectedness of temporal and spatial relationships that are artistically expressed in literature" (Bakhtin, 1982). With regard to the term, Bakhtin thinks that time and space are interconnected and inseparable and he describes the literary chronotope as a "concrete whole", mentioning that "time as it were, thickens, takes on flesh, become artistically visible; likewise, space becomes charged and responsive to the movements of time, plot and history." (Bakhtin, 1982) Bakhtin put forward the chronotope and applied it to literary research. This is conducive to expanding the scope of literary theory research, and makes up for the space-only or time-only theory when people study literary works. As Bakhtin mentioned in his article, "it expresses the inseparability of space and time, time as the fourth dimension of space." (Bakhtin, 1982) Bakhtin proposed that the core of the chronotope is the intersection of space and time, but did not point out the specific types of chronotope, which is precisely the potential of using chronotope to analyze literary works.

From abstract to concrete, from macroscopic to microscopic, Xue Genghua divides the meaning of chronotope into three levels: at the abstract level, the connotation of chronotope is presented as a holistic world view, and sees the flow of time in the world, which is mainly reflected in the author, and is embodied in the different ways different writers deal with time and space; the second dimension is related to the episodic organization function of the chronotope, which visualizes events and is also responsible for literary significance; at the third level, the chronotope is embodied as a specific artistic image, of which places and fields are the most numerous (Xue, 2018). The meaning of chronotope on three levels were also divided from abstraction to figuration into three types of chronotope. Among them, the most is also the third type of chronotope, such as the chronotope of gate, the chronotope of city, the pastoral chronotope, the chronotope of family, and so on. However, in different texts, the above chronotopes may also fall into the second category. Therefore, the three types of chronotope are interconnected and can also be transformed into each other in certain cases. Most of the chronotope used in this article belong to the third category, but they also incorporate the characteristics of the second category.

In "The Forms of Time and Chronotope in the Novel", Bakhtin (1982) proposes a variety of chronotopes from the perspective of the fusion of time and space, but there is a rupture in his exposition before and after the main text. The construction of the chronotope system has incompleteness and discontinuity in many aspects such as concept, scope, application, classification, etc., which is prominently manifested in classification. Although there are some problems indeed in the chronotope theory, this paper refers to the concrete types of chronotopes that have been proposed by other analyzers and lays the emphasis on the relationship between time and space with the carriers—the chronotope of family, the chronotope of body and the chronotope of city—which differs from other study orientations of chronotope, such as the exploration of the characters or the themes of the literary works. For example, the authors of the paper "The Theme of Freedom Reflected by Multidimensional Chronotopes in *Sweet Tooth*" (Zhong & Song, 2019), which also studies the chronotope of body, mention that the state of Canning is different in different time and space, but they do not put forward the relationship between time and space, instead they stress the body confined as a whole to study the freedom of individual. What's more important is that this paper takes the body itself as the space and explores the relationship between time and space in the body itself as chronotope.

Analyzing novels from the perspective of choronotope can allow traditionally separated novel elements such as plot, characters, realization themes, artistic techniques, etc., to be treated as a whole (Pan, 2005). Therefore, when the chronotope is used to analyze the relationship between time and space, the plot, characters and themes may be involved.

2. Temporal Indicators of Chronotope of Family

"In the literary artistic chronotope, spatial and temporal indicators are fused into one carefully thought-out, concrete whole." (Bakhtin, 1982) Therefore, the indicators of time are to be displayed in space, and space is to be understood and measured by time.

2.1 The Stagnation of Time in Queen Anne House

The first space appearing in *Sweet Tooth* is the house of Serena's parents where she grew up. Through the times in which Queen Anne House was constructed, the look of it, the activities in the house and the stagnation of time can be found. The Queen Anne house is a specific Victorian house, equipped with turrets, wraparound porches, intricate trim, and steeply pitched roofs. The Queen Anne House experienced a peak of popularity from the 1880s to the 1910s. However, the Fromes live in the 1970s, in which the architectural style tended to be more simple, modern and economical because of the industrialization and the consequence of World War Ⅱ. From the perspective of the specific time of the house, it did not match with the trend of the time and it stayed in the past.

The style of the house reflects people's aesthetic and ideological concepts to a certain extent. One of the characteristics of the Anne Queen House is the steeply pitched roof of unusual and irregular shape, normally with a dominant front-facing gable. Another feature of this style is the ingenious decorative patterns of "scallops, curves, diamonds or triangles" (McAlester & McAlester,1985). These two features illustrate that the house is noticeable and attracting, which reflects the importance that Serena's parents placed on dignity and external evaluations. A final characteristic is the wraparound porch which contains the front door area and then extends to the right or left of the house. The whole house is walled and closed. To some degrees, the closeness of space shows the stagnation of the flowing of time. What's important, this kind of architecture reveals more of a conservative and old style, lacking vitality, and actually making people feel depressed.

The activities in the space are also a reflection of the features of the space itself. The house is gorgeous and imposing, but when the reader looks into the house, the family is diametrically opposed to its enviable luxurious beauty. The parents of Serena are Anglican Bishop and the Bishop's wife. The Bishop was silent and lacked concern for his family. Their daily routine was to go to church and go home, and there seemed to be no flow of time in the life of the bishop. Serena's mother was a housewife, and the most important thing in her eyes was the non-departure of her husband and the integrity of the family. When Serena's mother talked about Serena's college major choices, she said, "This was the only time she expressed or implied dissatisfaction with her lot." (McEwan, 2012)

From the above characteristics of the house, as well as the daily life of the characters in the space, the cycle and stagnation of time are reflected. Time is read out of space, and time can be reflected by the characteristics of space.

2.2 The Closeness of Time in the Isolated Cottage with Canning

The closeness of time is shown by the isolation of space. Serena and Canning lived in an isolated cottage in the weekend. The time is limited and the place is remote. Turning from the narrow alleys to the dim paths, the fence of the cottage appeared in view after passing through the fields and hawthorn forests, and from the fence to the cottage there was a winding cobblestone road (McEwan, 2012). The narrow alley and dim path implied that few people knew this place and come here. The cottage was cut off from the outside by the field and forest, which made it impossible to discover the cottage easily. The fence was built and itself represents the isolation and closeness. Between the fence and the cottage, there was a winding cobble stone. The cottage that are put in a confined space embodies the closure of time.

Canning and Serena's affair is cut off the outside world, forming two parallel worlds, the former belonging to a squeezed enclosed space. The cottage was the only place they could meet, and as long as Serena was there, Canning wouldn't invite any friends here. After Canning's death, an obituary described his life simply and hastily, and there was no Serena's name there, as if she had never appeared in Canning's life (McEwan, 2012). The closure of the outer space shows the closure of the time they spent together. As a formally essential category, the chronotope, to a significant degree, determines the image of man in literature. The image of man is always intrinsically chronotopic (Bakhtin, 1982).

From the external space to the characters, the closeness is revealed. There were several visitors coming to the cottage and Canning just asked Serena to have a longish walk and didn't explain anything after. A white four-inch scar was on the right of Tom's chest reaching towards his neck (McEwan, 2012), the history of which he would never explain. Canning seemed like a house walled by the iron, just like the isolated cottage. Although Serena lived with him, she never knew what he had experienced, what he was thinking and what would he do next. The summer they spent together is not related to the past, neither the future, so it is just a period of time closed. The disillusion of the happy life is doomed at the beginning because of the closure of space, time and themselves.

2.3 The Duality of Time in the Flat with Tom

The story of Serena and Tom happens in two spaces, which is in accordance with two explicit timelines at the same time. With the transit of place of characters, the two explicit timelines entangled with each other to form two implicit timelines in one space. The lodgings at No.70 St. Augustine's Road, London North West One, is the place where Serena lived working as the lowest staff and was paid by less than one thousand a year. The room with little furniture was darkened by a horse chestnut tree and everything there was damp. The bed occupied about half the size of the room and it was unstable with a musty yellow bedcover (McEwan, 2012). The time in airs of dimness and coldness of the room is long and slow, which implies the life of Serena is depressed, boring and lonely. The timeline is considered with the life of Serena as an agent. After the encounter with Tom, Serena became more intolerable with this place. She felt sad at the prospect of returning to her lonely room, of using the old and worn single-bar electric fire, of dressing up for work (McEwan, 2012).

Another space is the flat at the Clifton Street in the Britain. As is described in the novel, "I was trying to forget Volt and my heart belonged to Sweet Tooth, my private portion of it" (McEwan, 2012), this place is the shelter where she found the meaning of her job, her value in this masculine society and her happy life. In her eyes, the air is fresh and clean, the furniture is modern, and this is a place that totally belongs to her: "Within weeks I came to think of this place as home." (McEwan, 2012) The life in this two-room flat is warm, cozy and lovely. The timeline of this space goes on with the identification of Serena as a lover.

With cheating and being cheated of the characters, in the flat of Tom, there are two implicit timelines in Tom and Serena respectively. In the novel, "Like Sebastian Morel in 'Pawnography', I was tumbling through dimensionless space, even as I sat smiling demurely in a Brighton fish restaurant. But always, at the furthest edges of thought, was that tiny stain." (McEwan, 2012) Serena lived with Tom with the inseparable timeline from MI5 and the room in the St. Augustine's Road, London North West One. After the discovery of Tom on Serena's secret and cheating, he didn't confront Serena, instead, the opportunity was spotted by him and he just regarded Serena as the real model for his novel: "Now I knew what you knew, what you had to conceal, I tried to imagine being you, being in two places at once, loving and…reporting back." (McEwan, 2012) At that time, Tom was in one place but experienced two timelines: one is the lover, another is the writer.

There are two spaces and two timelines of Serena and Tom, which is not isolated but entangled mutually. And they had their own private world and cheated each other, which is the biggest crack of their happy life. However, a letter by Tom brought the remedy to them. The letter was placed in the room where they cheated and capitalized on each other, which indicates the repursuit and reconstruction of their "domestic bliss" (Zhong, 2019). Tom cleaned out the junk and swept the floor, which, in fact, is the eraser of time and memories for a new start.

The pursuit of Serena for "domestic bliss" involves three stages and in every stage there is undergone construction and disillusion of happy life. The characteristics of different space reveals the temporal indicators and these indicators attribute to the discovery of the theme—pursuit of domestic bliss: construction, disillusion and finally repursuit.

3. Temporal Indicators of Chronotope of Body

Time enters people's interior and the character image itself, which has greatly changed the fate of the characters and the significance of all factors in life (Bakhtin, 1982). Body is also a space and the time get into it, making the body entails the quality of chronotope. Poetic images are regarded as an image of temporal art, which represents perceptible phenomena of space in their movement and development (Bakhtin, 1982). The time reflected by the space in the chronotope of body is embodied in the specific time of actions, events of poetic images. That is to say, the time is investigated from the perspective of the characters themselves.

3.1 The Control of Time of Canning

The experiences, acts of Canning show his control of time. Canning used to be in the Guards, participated in the action in the Western Desert, Special Operations Executive, Security Service and had a good connection with MI5. Most of time in his life was spent in the war and after the war. These experiences in his life melt into his body and gave him the ability to control the time well. The encounter with Serena is carefully planned by Canning: "Suddenly, from out of an alley, there appeared before us under the inadequate street lighting Jeremy's history tutor, Tony Canning." (McEwan, 2012) Here, "suddenly" means Canning appeared in a short time and unexpectedly, which indicates that Canning was waiting in the alley intently. And the time when they encounters was also chosen deliberately. Canning knew well about how to read time in people and utilize the time. Though he did not get along with Serena, Canning knew perfectly the personality and weak points, so during the conversation, he gave enough attention to Serena and always showed his support for her innocent ideas, which made Serena develop a sneaky fondness for him.

The most powerful proof to Canning's control of time is the arrangement of abandoning Serena for a faked excuse. From the outset, Canning had already got the cancer and he knew it, but he still contacted with Serena and he had already planned all these things, from encounter, abandonment to Serena's employment in the MI5. When Canning decided to abandon Serena, he used every moment to practice it, as described in the novel: "He interrupted himself and without drawing breath said quickly, 'Just drop it in there with mine. We'll be back soon.' Just that, a mundane domestic instruction, and then he continued with his line of thought." (McEwan, 2012) All of these display the control of time of Canning. The time Canning spent in the Guards and MI5 shaped the way he treated time. In his eyes, time should be well-planned and everything should be under the control of himself. The time in his body reflects the characteristics of Canning in return.

3.2 The Destructiveness of Time in Canning

The time leaves track on Canning's body, which reveals the destructiveness of it. The body of Canning was in a morbid state. When Serena saw the body of Canning for the first time, the naked foot was like a worn-out old shoes and folds of flesh were in improbable place, even under his arm. There was over-eating, scars from knee and appendicitis operation, a dog bite, a rocking-climbing accident in the body of Canning. When it is really hot, Canning would suffer from nosebleed and he got tired easily. The weak body symbolizes the mental and spiritual sickness. Canning was in a state of self-isolation for what he experienced in the past. He couldn't believe others and was not willing to express anything about his plan or thinking. His wife and he were not in a close relationship, proved by the affair between Serena and Canning and their different attitude towards the cottage.

However, there are different states in Canning, and sometimes he was well-dressed. "Well-dressed body" pays attention to life—eat on the polished pine table and know how and what to eat and drink. Therefore, Zhong and Song (2019) think that "two kinds of states exist in the same person, and this dual nature appears alternately with the change of time and space". As Serena said, "and there was something I've since noticed over the years—the mountain range that separates the naked from the clothed man. Two men on one passport." (McEwan, 2012) The well-dressed body displays the Canning's fight against the time, as "he liked talking to me about his childhood" (McEwan, 2012). On the isolated island of Kumlinge, his parents bought a stone cottage and they lived there happily. In Canning's eyes, his childhood was spent in paradise and he missed it every much and wanted to return that time. In certain degrees, the summer in the cottage spent with Serena is a kind of re-appearing and recalling of the childhood. However, this kind of re-appearing and recalling is disillusioned and fragile because of the closure and calculation of Canning. There was no real happy life. The time had destroyed Canning's appearance and it also prevented him from the happy life.

4. Temporal Indicators of Chronotope of City

Social public events and private events, personal struggles and political and economic competitions, state secrets and private secrets, historical series and daily series are intertwined in chronotope of city, forming the indicators of the times, and all spatial elements—buildings, living rooms, streets, rural scenes, etc., —have become the display of the times (Zheng & Xu, 2021). The space of city can be divided into politics, economy, culture, and they are classified into different degrees from the abstract to the specific, at the same time, entangling with each other.

4.1 The Turbulence of Politics

The space of city includes the physical appearance and inner operation of the main politics department, and the public events and even the news media are also an important role in it, which shows the politics in the time.

MI5 was the representative of Cold War and its activities happened in a building in Great Marlborough Street, on the western edge of Soho where the building was depressed, closed, dirty and suffused strange smell. It seemed that people who worked there did not care the environment at all and were absorbed in their duties, what they did in this building was just about sending and receiving files, like the slaves of pyramids. The whole building was just like a factory of lifeless machine and there were also some "elites" who controlled and managed it. The building of MI5 was a microcosm of Cold War. The political elites decided to implement for the so-called maintenance of democracy, freedom to dominate the world, while the obedient just followed the order without thinking.

The calculation, disguise, exploitation and penetration into the lives of ordinary people and Canning's unfortunate life are strong evidence. People argued with indignation in the newspapers, adding to the political friction. When there was a huge ignition point, various sparks would appear around it, igniting the surroundings. The lecture organized by the MI5 told some information about IRA Terrorism. Provisional RIA split into small groups, scattered inland, planted bombs in various places and created riots. Children, shopkeepers and ordinary workers, were all targets. In the same time, the government itself was very unstable. The national labor unions went on strike, but the government appeared extremely cowardly. In short, Cold War, RIA terrorism, and strike, all of which shows the turbulence of politics in the 1970s.

4.2 Depression of Economy

The streets in the city and the bars reflects the depression of economy. The street was filthy, littered with garbage, discarded snacks, ketchup coated hamburgers and hot dogs. The stores on the street were almost the sex shops, in the show windows of which the sex products were listed at will. When the economy was steady and prosperous, the stores should sell products of all kinds, and the customers came and went all the time, rather than a rotten atmosphere. The Tube tunnel and Green Park were also the public facilities which could be classified into the same category of street, "where the litter and grit and stinking subterranean gales that we took as our due slapped our faces and restyled our hair" (McEwan, 2012).

The look of a city represents the quality and civilization of residents, and the management ability of the government, more importantly, and the level of economy. The filthy street conceals that after the Second World War, industry began to decline and the once vibrant cities gradually declined. Bars could be found everywhere in the city. In the bars, people indulged in the paralysis of alcohol and the noise of the environment. Loud music, the anesthesia of alcohol, and the indulgence of desire were all manifestations of people's unfulfilled reality. The stagnant waters of life and dissatisfaction at work prompted people to find a way to vent. This reflects the emptiness of people's psychology from the side, as well as the unsatisfactory life. And the unsatisfactory life is often brought about by the lack of material conditions, especially for ordinary people who often come and go to bars. At the same time, in the bars, most of people were normal workers. It is because the factories did not have so much business for them, they tended to stay at the bars overnight and even fight and quarrel, not caring about the consequences. The description of the city proves the economic depression of the 1970s.

4.3 Abuse of Culture

The economic part of the city space, the cultural part itself of the city, and the entanglement of different aspects of the city space illustrate the characteristics of culture in the times. The abuse of culture in the city mainly illustrate in the economic space—bars, the cultural nihilism of the "free spirit" and the entanglement of culture and politics. The space that people often visit represents their state of life and mind. The places where people chose to spent the time most were bars. There are several descriptions of the bars and other places are seldom mentioned. The cathedrals, the parliament, the paintings, the court of law, the libraries and labs are thrown behind, as "In the early seventies, the best bands played in pubs, often cavernous Victorian establishments" (McEwan, 2012). In the past, the Victorian establishments represented the wealth, dignity and nobility. But in the 1970s, people regarded them as a place for fun. The stronger the contrast between the past and present is, the more excited and free people feel.

As is mentioned in the novel, "Lucy had told me more than once that the past is a burden, that it was time to bear everything down" (McEwan, 2012), the belief of Lucy is on behalf of the hippie culture. The hippie culture in essence was a kind of idealism to boycott the war and then gradually turned into anti-culture and anti-mainstream. In the 1970s, the hippie culture was declined but still had a great impact on the society. Unable to be satisfied with music, literature and painting, some hippie youth began to look for new representative cultures and resources of stimulation, so they began to be exposed to alcohol and drugs. In addition to taking drugs, most of the gradually degenerated people developed the habit of promiscuity, and interpret the representative costume culture of hippies as sloppy and messy. The so-called "free spirit" is a kind of self-indulgence and cultural nihilism.

Another distinct manifestation of the abuse of culture is that the politics tries to interpose and utilize the culture. Social press is an important space to show the situation of culture of a city. After the Second World War, the "fast media" pursuing timeless was no longer the only need and the society began to build a new sustainable relationship. Books translation and films became an important part of the "slow media" focusing on communication effect (Hu, 2020). Developed countries began to make impacts through the ideological propaganda of "winning without war". Therefore, the West used the intellectual community as an agent to promote its value with a pen. The so-called "Sweet Tooth Operation" is the code name of a spy operation launched by MI5, the purpose of which was to fund potential young writers and help them publish works in line with the Cold War. Therefore, Serena contacted Tom as a staff member of "freedom international" and proposed a funding plan to him. With hesitation and doubt, Tom finally accepted the "kindness" (Shang, 2013).

In *Sweet Tooth*, it is pointed out clearly that the operation "Sweet Tooth" was affected by the global promotion of George Orwell's *1984* and *Animal Farm* by the Intelligence Department of the British Foreign Office and the CIA's funding for Dr. Zhigwa and Encounter. So, the "Sweet Tooth" reflects the reality of culture in the 1970s. At the same time, McEwan also clarifies that "woe to the nation whose literature is disturbed by the intervention of power" (McEwan, 2012).

The *Sweet Tooth* is a book that connected with the times closely. The description of the city displays the features of that time. in the 1970s, no matter politics, economy, or culture, all of them were in disorder and chaos.

5. Conclusion

The chronotope explores the artistic relationship between time and space, which provides a new prospective to study the works. The number of the chronotope in a novel is more than one and these chronotope differs in the status in the novel, the degree of abstraction and the themes reflected. This paper applies the chronotope proposed by Bakhtin to analyze the temporal indicators in different chronnotopes in the *Sweet Tooth* for the relationship between time and space. The chronotope of family reflects the pursuit of domestic bliss. The different spatial and temporal characteristics in different houses illustrate the stagnation, closeness and duality of time. The chronotope of body reveals the huge impact of time on human and the view about time of the character himself. The chronotope of city reflects the characteristics of the times, which is in line with the writing style of McEwan—the novel is connected with the era closely.

In conclusion, the chronotope makes it possible for the readers to constantly discover the new theme of a novel. What's more, it sets an example for exploring the complex relationship between time and space.

Bibliography

[1] ALGHAMDI A, 2013. The Survival of the Author in Ian McEwan's *Sweet Tooth*[J]. Arab World English Journal: 89-101.

[2] BAKHTIN M M, 1982. The Dialogic Imagination: Four Essays[M]. Texas: University of Texas Press.

[3] CHALUPSKÝ P, 2015. Playfulness as Apologia for a Strong Story in Ian McEwan's *Sweet Tooth*[J]. Brno Studies in English:101-115.

[4] COJOCARU M, 2015. Metafictional Twist Endings in Ian McEwan's *Atonement* and *Sweet Tooth*[J]. East-West Cultural Passage: 7-19.

[5] GROES S, 2013. Ian McEwan: Contemporary Critical Perspectives[M]. London: A & C Black.

[6] MCEWAN I R, 2012. Sweet Tooth[M]. London: Jonathan Cape.

[7] MCALESTER V S, MCALESTER L, 1985. A Field Guide to American Houses[M]. New York: Alfred A. Knopf.

[8] MCEWAN I R, 2001. Atonement[M]. London: Jonathan Cape.

[9] PASTOOR C C, 2019. Authorial Atonement in Iran McEwan's *Atonement and Sweet Tooth*[J]. The Christianity

& Literature, 68(2):297-310.

[10] WALK L S, 2015. "A Balance of Power": The Covert Authorship of Ian McEwan's Double Agents in *Sweet Tooth*[J]. Modem Fiction Studies:494.

[11] 胡慧勇，2020. 伦理困境中的"马基雅维利"：《甜牙》的历史书写[J]. 文学教育：40-41.

[12] 潘月琴，2005. 巴赫金时空体理论初探[J]. 俄罗斯文艺(3)：60-64.

[13] 尚必武，2013.《甜牙》——"原谅"的伦理和情感[J]. 当代外国文学：64-72.

[14] 史雅芳，2021. 论《甜牙》中汤姆的生存美学[J]. 中南财经政法大学研究生论丛：110-116.

[15] 吴玲，2020.《甜牙》中的凝视与反凝视分析[J]. 湖南科技大学学报(社会科学版)，23(4)：52-58.

[16] 薛亘华，2018. 巴赫金时空体理论的内涵[J]. 俄罗斯文艺：36-41.

[17] 郑晔，许宏，2021. 19 世纪俄罗斯文学中的舞会——以巴赫金时空体理论为视角[J]. 俄罗斯文艺：139-148.

[18] 钟瑛，2019.《时间中的孩子》和《甜牙》中主体对家宅幸福时空的寻觅[J]. 外国文学动态：62-70.

[19] 钟瑛，2019，宋艳芳.《甜牙》中的多元时空体所折射的自由主题[J]. 外语研究，36(3)：101-105.

[20] 章小凤，2018. 时空体[J]. 外国文学：87-96.

Collective Story-Telling and Individual Life-Experiencing: On the Differences of Chronotope in Epics and Novels

陆泽懿

1. Introduction

In the literary theory academia of the 20th century, the novel, as a narrative type, has been studied by many theorists, such as Bakhtin, Watt, Lukacs and Benjamin. What is more, in the second half of the 20th century, narratology came into being as a subject developed on the basis of novel studying. Standing on the shoulders of these giants of literary theory, no matter what kind of narrative cannot be separated from the time process and space transformation, but in many narrative types, especially in the ancient ones, the "Chronotope", or spacial-temporal structure, does not constitute a complete or mature form. Take epic as an example, it only has the embryonic form of a complete time form at most and the fixedness of space. In the ancient Greek legends, its time is built up by fantasy and imagination, with strong abstractness, and its plot is driven by occasionality, which makes the unreal space changeable in the dream-like narrative. While the form of Chronotope in the novel is different, because it is not transcendental, empty, completed and bygone. The novel, which emerged after the Renaissance and was popular in the capitalist period, has a complete form of time, which is centered on the present. On the one hand, it connects the past and eliminates the "absolute past" in the epic; on the other hand, it continues to rush into the future because the present will never be possible to be in the end. The space of the novel tends to be tense and instant, and it must be involved in the movement of time, plot and history. The sign of time in the novel is to be displayed in space, and space is to be understood and measured through time. With the pen in his hand as the paddle, the novelist is free and unconstrained to let the characters and plots move forward and backward in the flowing timeline, and makes time sometimes stuck in a certain point and sometimes gallop away, and eventually, the novelist will eventually let the characters and the plots reach to "a must be" place through logical relationship of cause and effect, while none of this can happen in "a long epic which is definitely about the past when it is sung at the first time" (Bakhtin, 1998).

Epic is a romantic imitation of the objective world, it shows the ancient people's desire and pursuit of "wholeness", people at that time expected to integrate the relationship between men and themselves, with others and nature as a harmonious whole. Just as Benjamin advocates for general whole perfect rules of art, the ancient ancestors passed on their expectations of wholeness from one tribe to another through story-telling. In contrast, the novels emerging in the capitalist period show more individualistic spirit as opposed to "wholeness", as the novel is a literary form in the capitalist society, and the act motives of the characters in the novel are mainly secularized, which is consistent with the views of Lukacs, Bakhtin and Watt. Hence, they agree that novels embody unique individual experience rather than inherited collective experience. The individual, personal and present time is emphasized in the novel, which shows a completely different concept of time and space from the epic.

2. The Absolute Past: Time and Space in the Epic

In Ancient Greek, the word "epic" means "speaking" or "telling a story", and this definition appropriately sums up one of the characteristics of epic poetry, which is dominated by "oral narration" and ultimately shaped by oral transmission from generation to generation. Therefore, strictly speaking, the hero of the epic is not a single individual, but a person representing a nation or a clan, and the hero carries the original spirit of the entire nation, which can be passed down orally from generation to generation by their descendants. Epic is different from other genres because it recounts the legendary story of the nation and imprints the original spirit of the whole nation. The troubadours who sing and recreate the epic must also be very familiar with the details of the epic subject matter, from the outside world to the inner mind of each character, and have close or even common spiritual beliefs with those heroic stories. Hence, for Bakhtin, "in the epic, the authorial intention (the intention of the narrator), which is the essential element of the epic, is really the intention of the speaker to narrate a past age beyond his reach, a pious intention of future generations" (Bakhtin, 1998). This pious intention leads the narrator to believe, "In this past, all things were good, and the absolute past of the epic is the only source and foundation of all good things" (ibid.), which is beyond the comprehension and reach of the contemporary reader, or narratee. According to the epic narrator, the world is characterized by "wholeness". Therefore, in the epic, the concept of time can be hardly found. Even if the ancient people could feel the passage of time and the change of seasons, these feelings about the time flowing still cannot shake the epic as the foundation of the absolute past.

Eternal time and a unified culture permeate the epic, and the world is a unity infused with the recognized national spirit. Therefore, it is said that "the world of epics contains the heroic past of nations, the boundary formed by the 'foundation' and 'peaks' of national history, the world of Fathers and ancestors, the world of 'pioneers' and 'elites'" (ibid.). Thus, around the world presented by the stories in the epics, it establishes an impenetrable boundary in time between the "absolute past" and the "ongoing present". Within the boundary is the world where the glory of the nation is written, where the sublime and the memory of the nation are held; beyond the boundary lies the age of the writer and the listener, and lies the passage of time and "the consideration of the future". The context in the epic tends to be unified, while the context outside the epic is toward chaos, so the context inside and outside the epic is opposite, which makes a kind of mindset of "history inversion" internalized in the epic, that is, the purpose, ideal, justice, perfection, and the harmonious state of man and society that cannot be realized now are placed in the past time. In the epic, "time itself has no significant meaning or historical color" (ibid.). Hence, the characters are stagnant, unchanged from beginning to end. The epic only involves the embryonic historical time, so the space presented in the world is still broken, the character is also fixed and unchanged, and "in the whole process, people are still unchanged, the novel events constitute not the growth of people, but the fate of people" (ibid.). Epics should portray the personal experiences of heroes, so they inevitably involve irreversible time, but because epics focus on the integrity, wholeness and unity of the heroes' character rather than their growth and change, the development sequence of the characters themselves is often ignored and disorganized, and their external manifestations are interchangeable in time and space, rather than linear logic.

As the "absolute past", time in the epic is obviously closed. Within this closed timeframe, the story has already taken on its complete form, and there are no factors within it that drive the overall development towards the future. That is to say, it is in a state of absolute completion. Moreover, in such a closed time, there is no time flow and change between the time of the beginning and the end of the epic, and the space is therefore fragmented, and the connection between time and space is not organically integrated, but mutual conditional that "the time series can be changed, and the space can also be changed" (ibid.). Therefore, instead of exerting effort to reimagine and rethinking the setting, the narrators of the epic could begin and end at any part of the story as they pleased, because it was already well known at that time, just as Homer does with the storytelling of *The Iliad*. Even if it is only one part of the story of the Trojan War, it is enough to reflect the overall shape of the heroic age. Besides, the protagonists also show a perfect form, either in their eyes of themselves or in the eyes of others, and they are completely overlapping with no internal and external differences. The characters' actions in epics only ebb and flow with the fate of the arrangement rather than their own autonomy, so their personalities cannot be changed. Although the above features "give the human image a special beauty, completeness, extreme clarity and artistic perfection, they also give man limitations and a certain lack of vitality under the new conditions of human existence" (Bakhtin, 1998), while novels based on personal experience break this limitation of epics.

The world of the epic is only to be remembered, not to be experienced. The existence of boundaries not only brings about the partition of time, but also brings about the partition of evaluation. Epics, which gather various folk legends, lack a specific origin and author. They rely solely on oral tradition to reinforce themselves. Within them, a fixed interpretation of the same story has already been formed, so it is difficult for contemporary readers to challenge the established "collective identity" with their own "personal experiences". Therefore, people are trapped in the epic form, unable to escape. The epics are too sacred and inviolable for individuals to enter the world depicted in epics, so people are completely prostrate beneath the epic, unable to participate in it and impossible to experience it. Any attempt to close the distance between the epic characters is not only blasphemous to the national spirit, but also contains a challenge to the epic form.

Therefore, in Bakhtin's view, to truly break the distance in the epic, the image of man must be transferred from the distant level to the field connected with the unfinished events in the present, which leads to a fundamental change in the image of man. Man is not only noble, but also delicate and selfish; man is no longer the hero of the nation; man can also be the hero of the individual, or himself. This is similar to the point made by Ian Watt in *The Rise of the Novel*.

3. The Ongoing Present: Time and Space in the Novel

As for the connotation of "novel", since the maturity of this art form, many scholars have given their own understandings from various angles. Lukacs, for example, sees the novel as a product of the development of modern capitalism, an "epic of a world abandoned by God" (Lukacs, 2019). Milan Kundera (2012) believes that the novel is a product of the modern world, a kind of "discovery" and "inquiry", and in his opinion, "to discover what only the novel can discover" is the only reason for the existence of the novel. Bakhtin determines that the novel, as a genre, is always related to the form of time. The novel is rooted in the present-centered consciousness of time, and the particular and even unique modern time form of the novel makes the unfinished present and the changing modern life interact (Fan, 2020). As for Watt (1957), he redefines the distinction between "novel" and "fiction". He uses the two different English words to make a preliminary distinction between the meaning of novelty and authenticity contained in novel and the central feature of fiction, which is fictionality, and then proposes the concept of "formal realism" to further summarize the characteristics of the genre, novel.

According to Watt, the use of unconventional plots in the novel is very different from the previous fictional stories. The materials are no longer limited to myths, history, legends or the literary works of previous great writers, but highlight the importance of personal experience and evolve from special characters in special circumstances. The naming of characters in the novel is also more proper because it is based on the way people name special individuals in daily life, which increases their personal particularity and authenticity. The characters presented are no longer typical characters, and the characterization focuses on describing special individuals rather than outlining typical characters. In the expression of time and space, it is no longer like the story without time expressed in the previous literary forms, but the story and character creation are placed in the process of time, so that it develops in a form of causality.

3.1 The Relationship between Space and Time in the Novel

In Bakhtin's view, the time and space in the novel are connected with real time and real life. Novelists write the jokes and insults between living people, describe things in real life, satirize and simulate the sublime genre, and pull the gods and heroes who are unreachable in both time and evaluation level back to contemporary life from the "absolute past", obtain a close view, and complete the process of disenchantment. Ian Watt in *The Rise of the Novel* also puts forward a similar point of view; in his view, the rapid development of the capitalist economy has transformed the social structure unified in religion into a loose secular society, mainly characterized by philosophical realism and individualism cultural trends. Therefore, under such a philosophical and social context, the novel, as a literary genre, contrary to the previous literary forms, adopts the narrative method of formal realism. The story development of the novel is no longer a reflection of the unchanged moral truth without time, but a causal logic in accordance with the time line in a special environment.

Bakhtin also emphasizes that during the Renaissance, the form of time in novels has undergone a new change of modern meaning: God is dead, and the concept of eternal time is deteriorating. Contemporary life changes the past, and the seeds of the future will be revealed. Therefore, the method of observing and describing time in this period is also presented in the novel. Ian Watt's discussion of *Robinson Crusoe* nicely supports Bakhtin's view: Defoe is "the first writer to construct an entire narrative in accordance with the actual physical environment"; his "vivid details…It allows us to relate Robinson Crusoe and Moll Flanders to their environment in a way that is far more comprehensive than the previous literary figures' connection to their environment" (Watt, 1957). The novel uses concrete space to represent the time it intends to present, rather than "the concept of place is almost as vague and obscure as the concept of time in the traditional tragedy, comedy and legend stories" (ibid.). Take Hamlet as a reference, this figure's actions and all the actions that arise around him can be placed either in Denmark around the 12th century or in England in the 17th century. The specific era, time, and space in which the story takes place are almost negligible. However, novels are different, as their narrative about time reflects the characteristics of formal realism.

Under the dominance of formal realism, novelists directly imitate personal life experiences in their temporal time, describing the uniqueness of time and space to provide readers with an authentic experience. Daniel Defoe, through the diary format, enhances the credibility of time in *Robinson Crusoe*. Samuel Richardson meticulously accounts for every second of Clarissa's activities. Henry Fielding accurately portrays the travel time for each journey of Tom Jones. All of this naturally enhances the authenticity of novel characters in the dimension of time. The emphasis on time in novels is actually to satisfy readers' desire for strict coherence between life and art. When the "wholeness" expressed in epics is disrupted, novels attempt to utilize their unique capability for mimicking time and space to construct a new quality of unity between the individual and society in literature.

3.2 The Relationship Between Characters and Time in the Novel

Regarding novel characters, Bakhtin believes that with the changing configuration of time in novels and the shift from depicting the "absolute past" of epics to depicting the unfinished present, there is a fundamental change in the temporal coordinates of novel characters, leading to important and profound transformations in their characterizations. The characters in novels undergo a fundamental transformation, and therefore, new character images emerge. As mentioned earlier, in sublime and distant genres like epics, characters represent the absolute past of a bygone era. These character images are complete and finished entities, with no distinction between their essence and appearance, and lack any active spirit of thought or concept. However, when the distance of epic is broken and the portrayal of characters transitions from the distant past to an unfinished contemporary state, novelists rely on their personal experiences to create characters in the present moment. As a result, characters are inevitably connected to the ongoing reality, and they undergo necessary changes within the complete time framework of the novel. This perspective aligns with Watt's statement that "the primary criterion of the novel is its fidelity to personal experience—personal experience is always unique and therefore fresh" (Watt, 1957).

Due to the widespread influence of economic individualism, literary works have also shifted their focus to individual characters and begun to pay attention to the daily lives of ordinary individuals. By referencing specific personal life experiences, this trend has promoted the novel as a literary form that concerns individual experiences in real life. The world portrayed in the novel can be understood, sympathized and experienced. Readers can enter the fictitious world based on their own experiences and imaginatively experience the lives depicted in the work alongside the protagonist. Firstly, the names of the protagonists in novels are sufficiently authentic and correspond to the temporal and spatial backgrounds of the stories. According to Watt, in many literary genres prior to the novel, although characters generally had names, "from the variety of names actually used, it can be seen that earlier authors did not try to establish characters as fully individualized entities" (ibid.). Furthermore, characters in previous literary genres often had surnames but no given names, or vice versa. All these phenomena "exclude any association with real-life or contemporary life" (ibid.). However, in the novel, most characters have complete and realistic names, such as Robinson Crusoe, Tom Jones, etc. These names convey to the readers that the protagonists in the novel are unique and tangible individuals, unlike the lifeless, abstract, stereotyped and intangible characters in epics.

Moreover, in novels, the characters' actions are closely related to the time period. For example, Don Quixote must also live during the Renaissance period when chivalric tales have long declined. Only then can his path of adventurous imagination, influenced by knightly literature, be incomprehensible and serve the purpose of irony; Robinson Crusoe must live in an era when the bourgeoisie is just emerging, so that his impulse and desire for venturing out to sea, as well as his primitive accumulation on the island like a capitalist, can be understood; Jane Eyre could only be born in an era when women were not valued under the patriarchal system, and it is her journey of self-reliance and empowerment, as well as her pursuit of gender equality, that shocks the society of that time.

In a nutshell, the novel introduces a new relationship between space and time, which makes the characters in the novel more distinct and imbued with individualistic spirit. It also allows for greater variability in the portrayal of novel characters, ultimately infusing them with vitality and dynamism.

4. Between Ruins and Redemption: The Unity of Chronotope in Epics and Novels

In the view of western Marxist literary theorists, epics achieve the unity of literary essence and life, and the harmony contained in epics can save sentient beings. However, with the birth and continuous development of capitalism, the present world is built on the fissured and ruined modern culture, which is the real situation behind the illusory prosperity of western modern capitalist material civilization. Then, the novel, as a literary genre closely related to capitalism, in its text world, can only mimic and depict the real world in a fissured and ruined way. So, how to reconstruct the integrality, wholeness and unity in the epic through the novel has become an urgent problem to be discussed.

4.1 A New Epic under Temporal Chronotope: Lukacs' View on Novels

Lukacs, in his work, *The Theory of the Novel*, extensively examines the connection between novels and epics through a historicist approach. He believes that literary forms should be closely related to the historical and social development, as well as the existential conditions of human society. Epics, on the one hand, followed by tragedies, depict a contrast with life. On the other hand, modern novels have always been exploring narrative forms that unite essence and life. Therefore, the novel can be called as "the epic of the world abandoned by God".

Lukacs believes that after ancient Greek epics, writers often view heroes with nostalgia, as a lament for the lost ideal world, which also leads to the rise of tragedy after epics. In literary forms that emerged after epics, such as ancient Greek tragedies, characters are often separated from their living environments. Thus, from his perspective, Lukacs considers that epics are a part of life, an inseparable whole, while tragedy itself is an independent conceptual entity. There is a difficult-to-cross boundary between life and the text world existing in tragedies. However, what inherits from epics in terms of literary forms? According to Lukacs, it is not tragedy that truly inherits from epics, but the novel. Although the novel and the epic exist in different eras and have different characteristics, the novel portrays the entirety of social life. However, this wholeness is hidden and obscured, no longer directly connected to reality like the epic, and cannot be obtained directly. Instead, readers need to discover and search for it through their own life experiences. From a formal perspective, Lukacs believes that the form of the novel is relatively fixed, unlike the free form of the epic, but their missions are the same.

The difference between novels and epics lies in the environments they exist in. The living environment of epics is primordial, while novels belong to the modern era. On the one hand, epics depict the world of heroes and their lives, presenting the unity and wholeness of human actions and meanings. On the other hand, novels portray the contradictory relationship between individuals and the world. The protagonist of an epic is a collective entity, while the protagonist of a novel is an individual who is detached from the external world. In essence, the novel is a product of modern social alienation, an artistic form where individuals transform their own experiences or hearsay into experiences for the readers. Novels evoke a longing for a complete world among people living in a fissured and fragmented world. In the chaotic world, novels not only shoulder the responsibility of social history but also bear the duty of seeking social totality, as well as rectifying and shaping social wholeness.

Regarding characters, Lukacs believes that unlike epics, the world shaped and reconstructed by novels is different from the primordial and transcendental world of epics. After all, the objective world in which novels exist is chaotic and fragmented. In ancient Greek epics, there is a correspondence between the epic and objective reality, where subjectivity and objectivity are unified. However, in the world of novels, there is a greater emphasis on individual subjective experiences, which represents a distorted reconstruction. In novels, the protagonist's personality is fragmented. Therefore, although Lukacs categorizes novel characters into two types based on their characteristics, one being "abstract idealism" and the other being "disillusioned romanticism", both types of characters exist within the same temporal and spatial framework. The gap between the textual world and the idealized world still remains. Therefore, Lukacs believes that these two types should be properly combined to provide a more comprehensive revelation of the alienation and ideals of the world. Besides, Lukacs believes that "the biggest difference between concept and reality is time" (Lukacs, 2019), and only novels can reveal the meaning of time for human survival, which can transcend the homelessness of the mind and place a meaningful space for the value of individual life, which is hope and memory.

In summary, the epic of ancient Greece is an artistic form that aligned with a society characterized by unity and wholeness. During that era, everything was not merely assimilated into society but appeared with a shared essence, where external forms and the spiritual world were identical. Lukacs explores the unity between the epic and the spiritual world of the ancient Greeks through an analysis of the narrative form of the epic and the portrayal of its main characters. He believes that the novel is the successor of the epic, carrying forward its legacy.

4.2 Passing-down or Fissure: The Continuation of Epics and Novels

Based on his assessment of modernity, Walter Benjamin questions the art form of the novel because he believed that it was the rupture between experience and tradition that led to the emergence of the novel. In his work *The Storyteller*, Benjamin (2008) affirms the ability of storytellers to inherit experiences. Firstly, storytellers embed their narratives deeply within the historical traditions because "orally transmitted experiences" serve as the source of their stories. Travelers bring back what they have seen and heard from distant lands, blending it with the long-standing collective memories of the local residents. Eventually, these experiences merge into a river of memory and future, flowing endlessly without knowing where it will halt, without the need to worry about the final destination. Even death, the ultimate endpoint of natural life, does not become a hindrance or detrimental sign to life itself, as both death and the redemption of the soul are encompassed within a "mysterious grand process". Moreover, the inherent "fairy tale spirit" of stories imparts the best advice to people, because the fairy tale tends to have a happy ending, and it can tell the readers that the protagonists in the story live happily together. Therefore, fairy tales put the benign rules of harmonious coexistence between man and nature and the victory of good over evil in people's hearts, turning them into a burning flame that lights up the wick of life.

According to Walter Benjamin's admiration for the art of storytelling, he believes that it is the solitary individual that helps novel come into being and then rise, because people are unable to communicate their experiences to others in these fleeting moments of shock. The works produced under the condition of experiential poverty cannot convey profound wisdom but only present the surface richness of life. In other words, they are unable to provide enlightenment to the existential confusion people faced. The spatiotemporal consciousness of the novel is ruptured, and the dialogic nature between characters cannot bridge the gap between the storyteller and the listener. However, "the epic, as a broad scale, encompasses elements of both story and novel" (Benjamin, 2008).

Benjamin, starting from the perspective of "memory", analyzes the issues of "absorbing space-time" and "inheriting memory" in relation to the epic and the novel. In Benjamin's view, the prominent feature of the epic is its ability to absorb the process of events, thereby confronting death with memory after the passing of time and space in which the events occurred (Benjamin, 2008). The novel, inherited from the epic, also possesses the characteristic of inheriting memory. During the process of creating a novel, the novelist engages in long-term recording and depiction of the surrounding space-time and devotes themselves to presenting the protagonist's growth process within the textual world. Consequently, the growth of the protagonist becomes closely connected to the space-time in which the novelist creates the novel. However, the novel is a literary genre that has emerged from the ruins of modern industrial society. Even though it has the function of "inheriting memory", the memories presented in the novel are fragmented, personal, and disjointed. Therefore, the novel cannot serve as a channel for modern people to grasp the wholeness. Above the ruins of culture and civilization, Benjamin, unlike Bakhtin, Watt, and Lukacs, advocates a return to a past fable-like era rather than the current the new novelistic-epic era.

5. Conclusion

Through the exploration of the arrangement and configuration of Chronotope in epics and novels, it can be observed that the transition from epics to novels represents not only a shift from oral to written narratives, from verse to prose, and from mythical heroic stories to realistic life stories, but also a reflection of philosophical ideas and social trends. Since the Renaissance, individual experiences have gradually replaced collective traditions as the most authoritative judge of reality. It is this change that, to some extent, gives the temporal form in novels a sense of being worldly and unfinished, rather than the completely past and unattainable temporal form found in epics.

By reviewing the viewpoints of Bakhtin, Watt, Lukacs, and Benjamin regarding the relationship between the novel and the epic, it can be observed that Bakhtin and Watt, starting from the era in which they lived, affirm the reconstructive power of the novel in foreseeing the future and reconceptualizing reality. On the other hand, Lukacs, with a retrospective perspective, regards the novel as the epic of the sinful era of capitalist society. Benjamin, however, takes a different stance. Standing amidst the ruins of modernity, he watches as the angel of history flies forward without ever looking back. Therefore, he laments the loss of the mythical fable era, and believes that the novel, inheriting the muse consciousness from the epic, is inadequate to fulfill the task of unifying the world. Those trapped within modernity can no longer grasp the whole.

As for the author, whether immersed in the utopian consciousness of lamenting and retracing the epic era or placing oneself within the personal fortress constructed by the novel that imitates reality, it is undeniable that the novel form born in the dawn of the new world indeed takes root on the soil where the old era perished, bringing humanity the dawn of a new day.

The novel itself presents an unfinished and ongoing form of time. The novel is the only one genre born in modern times, and compared to epics, novels are closely connected to the era. Their incompleteness is reflected in various aspects, including genre form, characters, and narrative content, all of which are vivid and yet to be fully shaped. Based on unique and innovative life experiences, novels use unfinished time as one of their forms, striving to emulate the world in a detailed and authentic manner. Through narrative forms that encompass the overall form of life, novels ultimately reveal and construct vibrant narrative structures.

Bibliography

[1] WATT I., 1957 The Rise of the Novel: Studies in Defoe, Richardson and Feilding[M]. London: Chatto and Windus.
[2] 巴赫金,1998. 小说理论[M]. 白春仁,晓河,译. 石家庄：河北教育出版社.
[3] 本雅明,2008. 启迪:本雅明文集[M].张旭东,王斑,译. 北京：生活·读书·新知三联书店.
[4] 范能维,2020. 巴赫金小说理论视阈下现代性"时间形式"的展开[J]. 俄罗斯文艺(2)：131-138.
[5] 卢卡奇,2019. 小说理论[M]. 燕宏远,李怀涛,译. 北京：商务印书馆.
[6] 昆德拉,2012. 小说的艺术[M]. 董强,译. 上海：上海译文出版社.

The Disease Writing and Ethical Pursuit in *The Last Gift*

彭 新

1. Introduction

Abdulrazak Gurnah, a Tanzanian-British writer born in Zanzibar in 1948, has been engaged in the literary field for more than thirty years and published ten novels and several short stories, winning the Nobel Prize for Literature in 2021 and attracting widespread attention. Gurnah's work is often devoted to exposing the present plight of the African diaspora and their traumatic memories of the past. As he slowly uncovers the scars of the past, he addresses the inescapable issues of race and colonization, as well as the identity predicament caused by the struggle among "memory" "reality" "homeland" and "foreign land", which are shown in his works such as *By the Sea*, *Admiring Silence* and *The Last Gift*. Or, as in *Paradise* and *The Afterlives*, he writes stories about the struggles, splits and suffering of people growing up in Africa, highlighting the miseries caused by imperial colonization and the mutual victimization among the underclass.

The Last Gift makes readers shuttle between memory and reality, presenting both the current situation of the African diaspora and their "buried" traumatic past, "exploring the path of their lives and spiritual redemption, and making an optimistic attempt to reconstruct cultural identity" (Zhu & You, 2022). *The Sunday Times* claims that "musings on identity and immigration are central to this story of one man's physical and emotional unravelling"[①], while *Publishing Weekly* applauds it "with powerful musings on mortality, the weight of memory, and the struggle to establish a postcolonial identity"[②]. The story centers on family and features Abbas, the male protagonist from Zanzibar, East Africa. Abbas leaves his pregnant wife, his home, and his friends at the age of 19, and embarks on a wandering sailing career. Fifteen years later, in Exeter he meets Maryam, a seventeen-year-old black girl whose parentage is obscure. They fall in love and elope, giving birth to Hanna and Jamal. However, Abbas remains silent about Zanzibar, and the entire family is shrouded in gloomy mystery. The third stroke makes his ultimate awakening, and thus he records the story of his past as "the last gift" to his family. Gurnah forgoes the authority of narrative in his character portrayals and "does not override his characters as an arbiter or a pitier", but rather disguises himself within them, capturing "the whisper of fate" (Jiang, 2023).

Compared with Gurnah's other works, *The Last Gift* has received relatively less attention from

---

① CUMMINS A. *The Last Gift* by Abdulrazak Gurnah[J]. The Sunday Times, 2011, www.thetimes.co.uk/article/the-last-gift-by-abdulrazak-gurnah-h2dch0h5sh2/ Accessed 1 August 2023.

② ROGERS D. *The Last Gift* by Abdulrazak Gurnah[J]. Publishing Weekly, 2013, www.publishersweekly.com/9781620403280/ Accessed 1 August 2023.

academics so far. Many of them have concentrated on the identity of African immigrants in the novel, highlighting Gurnah's narrative as "surfacing from 'family' to the entire postcolonial diasporic cultural community, explaining the universal identity dilemma of the cultural group and the common way-out" (Zhu & You, 2022), while other scholars have examined the portrayal of African-British Muslims in the text to explore the construction of the cultural group. In addition, Sun Luyao (2023), writing from a cosmopolitan perspective, examines the cognitive mapping on the spatial relationship between the character and the world in the novel and asserts that Gurnah provides an ideal identity of "glocality" with both local spirit and global vision. Several scholars have discussed *The Last Gift*'s narrative strategy, which employs "silence" to generate African immigrant subjectivity (Kaigai, 2013), reflecting the complexity of the indescribable immigrant experience and difficulties tied to "silence" (Yuan, 2022). These studies have brought depth to the work's investigation of identity concerns, but they have mostly ignored the characters' intersubjectivity and the community they are a part of, instead focusing on family members or the outside world. Disease is a recurring theme in the novel, serving as a connecting thread between individuals, the setting for the plot's development, and creating psychological and physical influence on characters. What do metaphors and implications underlie about diseases? What ethical pursuit does Gurnah hope to convey by modeling on Victorian novels in setting the scene of confession on a sickbed (Jiang, 2023)?

In *Illness as Metaphor* (1978), Susan Sontag points out that "illnesses have always been used as metaphors to enliven charges that a society was corrupt or unjust". In literature, writing about diseases is a common theme that performs remarkable metaphorical and critical functions and is frequently given novel interpretations to convey the intentions of the writer. Writing about this specific life experience allows writers to explore mental illness in people, expose social injustices, and subtly transmit moral critique and ethical pursuit. Therefore, the goal of this essay is to expose the trauma and predicament of the characters' "past" and "present", and to explore Gurnah's critique of the unjust power discourse, his concern for "healing" the African diaspora, as well as his ethical pursuit for the reconstruction of the social value system. To achieve this, this essay is going to focus on the diagnosis, treatment, and hospice care of Abbas' diseases, analyze the metaphors behind the diseases, and interpret the delicate relationship between Abbas' family members and the doctors in this crisis.

2. Diseases as a Metaphor for the Plight and Pain of the African Diaspora

"Everyone who is born holds dual citizenship, in the kingdom of the well and in the kingdom of the sick. Although we all prefer to use only the good passport, sooner or later each of us is obliged, at least for a spell, to identify ourselves as citizens of that other place." (Sontag, 1978) The life clock switches to a countdown as Abbas enters the "kingdom of the sick" at the start of *The Last Gift*. Following come diabetic crisis, stroke and aphasia, which catch Abbas and his family unpreparedly. The patient's and his family's repressed memories and unrelieved traumas are revealed by the particular life experience of diseases.

The body, as Foucault implies, is "the most important mediating field in which the individual relates to society, to nature, to the world, the necessary link between the individual self and society as a whole, and the key chain that connects the individual to intellectual discourse power and to social morality" (Gao, 2005). The body as an entity is a continuum between the past and the present, and regardless of geographic displacement or cultural betrayal, physical traits such as appearance, skin color and familial-hereditary disease cannot be altered, avoided or concealed, and they mark the identity of an individual. The largely genetic nature of diabetes raises directly to the question of identity as "where I come from". When a patient is diagnosed with diabetes, it is customary for doctors to inquire about the patient's family medical history: "Was there diabetes in his family? His parents, his uncles or aunts?" (Gurnah, 2014: 9), and the apparently simple inquiry opens the door to Abbas' memories, which he has been holding onto for more than thirty years. Abbas has been using the "I-don't-know" response for years to avoid answering the question about where he come from. However, as a result of his diabetes diagnosis and deteriorating health, Abbas is compelled to reflect on his life, dream about his own country, and starts to consider his identity. Gurnah eventually gives Abbas access to his history from the diagnosis of diabetes.

"The diaspora, carrying cultural elements such as experiences, customs, language, and ideas acquired in their homeland to a country with very different historical traditions, cultural backgrounds, and social development, is bound to face the dilemma of self-identity" (Zhu & Yuan, 2019). Abbas' origin and cultural roots are hinted at by the familial nature of diabetes, which also suggests that Abbas is currently in a dislocated cultural space and deals with an unfamiliar language. He is caught between Zanzibar and England due to his early experiences, his time in college, and his links to his family. He is in a condition of "being suspended" where he cannot "return" and refuses to "force a landing". He lives neither a Christian nor a Muslim life, denying his children all Christian activities at school, while giving Hanna and Jamal Muslim names but denying them any real knowledge of Muslims, leaving them know "not a service, nor a christening, nor a church wedding, nor any of those things" (Gurnah, 2014: 102). In this aspect, "he kept them in ignorance about everything" (ibid.: 104). Abbas' desire to escape his identity and his inability to do so completely is as much a part of him as the family's hereditary diabetes, displaying a screwed-up state that his daughter Hanna describes as "still a stranger after all these years, coping with that strangeness all his life" (ibid.: 108). Abbas himself is well aware that in fleeing his homeland and avoiding his identity, he has "lost my place in the world" (ibid.: 220) and is in a permanent state of identity suspended.

As an outsider, Abbas always dresses "light so he could throw the coat off quickly when the time came to move on" (ibid.: 6), but the cold winds of England, the unexpected diabetes attack and the doctor's questioning make him realize that he is travelling light, but carrying a heavy mental burden and being trapped in identity crisis. Digby can infer from Hanna's looks that her father is from the sea and, like his appearance, Abbas' diabetes not only hints at his origins, but also means that "now the children must have blood tests at least once a year" because, according to the family doctor, "these conditions are passed on in families" (ibid.: 15). Abbas might choose to be silent about his family and hide his Muslim background, but when he receives a diabetes diagnosis, he must come out of hiding and reveal his identity dilemma. "Exile…is restlessness, movement, constantly being unsettled, and unsettling others. You cannot go back to some earlier and perhaps more stable condition of being at home; and, alas, you can never fully arrive, be at one with your new home or situation." (Said, 1996) Diabetes reminds Abbas of his origin and cultural identity, expressing the anxiety and confusion of the African diaspora over the issue of identity being "suspended". As a consuming disease, it symbolizes Abbas' delay in resolving his identity dilemma and his ongoing internal battle.

Compared with diabetes, the sudden, fatal and severely incapacitating nature of the stroke leaves Abbas in a paralyzed state, he "could not speak or laugh or feed himself, or clean himself properly after using the toilet" (Gurnah, 2014: 98). This state of helplessness and powerlessness mirrors the situation in which, at the age of nineteen, he was unable to resolve his marital problem and had to flee, falling into a condition of mental paralysis.

It was only after his second stroke that Abbas really began to tell the story of his past. More than thirty years of silence and an increasingly fractured physical condition have given rise to a growing urge to speak about it. As soon as he was able to speak, he took the initiative to tell Maryam about his past for the first time. At first, he only mentions his hometown Zanzibar, his school, and his wonderful university life (ibid.: 132). But if the memories are so happy, why has Abbas been silent for over thirty years? For years he has avoided personal topics and covered up mistakes by selectively recounting the past and unconsciously embellishing memories. When Hanna and Jamal were children, Abbas told them stories and referred to Africa only in terms of fairy tales and festive celebrations (ibid.: 33), full of beauty and innocence. Before reaching the real reason for his departure, it seems that he "was circling away from what lay ahead" (ibid.: 133). It is not until many days later that he mentions "the girl on the terrace" and "the woman he married and abandoned when she was pregnant" (ibid.: 134). Gurnah's narrative is consistent with the psychology of the character since Abbas's departure and long period of silence were caused by exactly what he is most reluctant and ashamed to disclose, which renders him mentally incapacitated like a fatal stroke.

"Ethical knots are a concentration of contradictions and conflicts in the structure of literary works...ethical knots constitute an ethical dilemma." (Nie, 2014) Nineteen-year-old Abbas, young, shy, lacking in self-confidence and living on family financial help, accidentally marries the daughter of a wealthy businessman who has emigrated from Yemen, Sharifa. However, not long after the marriage, Sharifa's delivery date draws near and Abbas begins to worry that the baby is not his and "that there was some trick, some plot, that they had trapped him to save her from dishonor" (Gurnah, 2014: 128). His heart was full of doubt, fearing that he would spend the rest of his life in ridicule, being "skinny cuckold" (ibid.: 129), and the disrespect and contempt shown to him by the Sharifa's family, filling his heart with anguish and discomfort. So, in early December 1959, at the age of nineteen, he fled his country and everything. The choice to abandon his pregnant wife and family left Abbas in a deep ethical dilemma, making him suffer alone for years and cover his shame with silence. Whenever Maryam asks Abbas about his past, the thought of this burdened and shameful past makes him reluctant to recount it, demonstrating the depth of pain and shame this experience has brought him.

The stroke leaves Abbas paralyzed in bed, and late at night he still weeps "like a baby after all that time" (ibid.: 129) when he thinks of his past life. Years later he is still unable to untie the knot. He thought "I would keep quiet about all that for as long as I could" (ibid.: 215), but after suffering his second stroke, he lost self-autonomy. Before his third stroke he already feels death approaching and has to give an account of his past to Maryam and his children. This personal shameful past for Abbas, like the stroke, haunts him suddenly and unexpectedly, striking him hard and leaving him helpless as he describes "I was nothing but a little shit, a frightened little shit and I cut the heart out of my own life with what I did" (ibid.: 220). It could be said that stroke rendered him physically paralyzed, implying that the ethical knot of his past caused him to become mentally paralyzed, making it challenging for him to help himself.

And in contrast to diabetes and stroke, aphasia is a metaphor for the plight of the immigrants' collective loss of voice. When Abbas was hospitalized for diabetic emergency, Dr. Kenyon predicted that he would lose some of his speech, stating that "he would lose some function. Paralyzed. But some of it might come back" (ibid.: 51). After his second stroke, Abbas lost his speech totally and was unable to speak. The disease deprived Abbas of his ability to speak, and the aphasia that left him unable to speak actually alludes to Abbas' years of silence. "Silence becomes a way of evading the pain that remembering forces upon Abbas", and through silence Gurnah points to the complexity of narrating the lives of marginalized groups (Kaigai, 2013). Whether it is "being made silent" or a voluntary choice of being silent as an expression of resistance, defiance and escape, it reflects the fact that Abbas is in an ailing society that is unable to tolerate differences and implicitly racist. It does not allow marginalized groups to utter their voice, while at the same time representing them. Therefore, aphasia presents the predicament of being silent of the African diaspora.

In *The Last Gift*, Gurnah writes about "a literature of collective crisis rather than a literature about individual crisis", where "I is capitalized 'I', which does not point to an individual, but to a community, a nation, a culture" (Jiang, 2016). Abbas' aphasia is a metaphor for the universal problem of the "loss of voice" of the African diaspora. Months after Jamal moved, he did not once greet his next-door black neighbor, knowing that the young men were making fun of Harun, but never helping him or at least expressing sympathy. His being silent towards racist behavior is due to the unconscious insecurity of being in a society that is indifferent to marginalized groups. He fears of "being browbeaten and mocked by loud voices, of being made to look foolish by cruel laughter" (Gurnah, 2014: 140). When he hears the sounds of the young men causing mischief to Harun, the only thing he can think of doing is that he should have a latch installed on his door in the future. At the family dinner in celebration of Easter, Nick's family constantly exudes a sense of superiority, talking condescendingly and extending pity to Hanna's family. Hanna is unable to refute Digby when she is questioned about her ancestry, so she withdraws to the toilet and sobs in private.

Karl Marx once said in *The Eighteenth Brumaire of Louis Bonaparte*, "they cannot represent themselves; they must be represented." The silence of Abbas, Jamal and Hanna is a choice made to maintain the current peace in the racially prejudiced society they are in. What is projected behind the inability to speak out is discrimination, prejudice and arrogance.

Through the metaphors of diabetes, stroke and aphasia, Gurnah presents the struggles, dilemmas and traumas faced by African diasporas on the margins of society. The personal ties of the past cause them deep mental anguish, while the situation of being the "other" in a foreign country makes them "voiceless" and imprisoned in the dilemma of identity. Therefore, disease is the externalization of the characters' psychological struggles.

3. Treatment Process as a Mirror of the Current "Sick" Society

If diseases are an externalization of the mental pain and struggle that the African diaspora has endured for years, then the treatment of Abbas' diseases reflects the current situation of African migrants in a foreign country. In *Illness as Metaphor* (1978), Sontag points out that "the calamity of disease can clear the way for insight into lifelong self-deceptions and failures of character". Gurnah enables readers to see the ills of the time via the perspective of the sufferer by writing about Abbas' struggle to take his ailing body home, Maryam's initial response to Abbas' coma, and the repressive treatment of the doctors.

Abbas' crumbling physical state and his frantic attempts to examine and control his body are described at the beginning of the novel. Gurnah gives readers a close-up view of Abbas through stream-of-consciousness. The pain and weakness he experiences on the trip home overwhelm, suffocate, and swallow him like a ferocious beast. Abbas experiences an even stronger sense of powerlessness and pain after stepping off the bus, along with a chilling feeling as he "watched himself beside himself, a little panicked by the sly, irresistible dissolution of his rib cage and his hip joints and his spine, as if body and mind were separating themselves from each other" (Gurnah, 2014: 5). He warns himself not to fall down, "What are you doing? Having a seizure?" (ibid.: 6). Even though he travels this road every day, he still has an outsider attitude, and his surroundings remain to him like a "wilderness" devoid of any sense of security. He manages to get home before he lets the dizziness overwhelm him. According to Foucault, "it is always the body that is at issue…the body is also directly involved in a political field; power relations have an immediate hold upon it; they invest it, mark it, train it, torture it, force it to carry out tasks, to perform ceremonies, to emit signs." (ibid.: 25) Abbas has lived in Britain for a long time, yet he still doesn't feel the slightest sense of security or belonging. Quite the contrary, alienation has taken over. He tries so hard to control the progression of his illness and prevent fainting outside because he can visualize the scene like Harun fainting and no one coming to his aid. The familiarity of living here is nothing more than the sense of strangeness and oppression that British society has given him for so long. The author alludes to the invisible repression that an indifferent society imposes on African immigrants. Abbas' self-regulation of his body is in fact repression of his subjectivity beneath the weight of external power, turning him into an internalized "other".

Abbas is in excruciating pain and need immediate medical treatment, but Maryam decides to take care of him first by taking off his clothes and wiping him in order to preserve his decency until the clinic doctor shows up. In fact, "she did not think why it was necessary to undress him and clean him first before covering him…a superfluous courtesy she had not reflected upon" (ibid.: 8), that is, the habit of choosing to maintain the dignity and decency of the body over the instincts of life in the face of the outside world, confirms that she, like Abbas, is a marginalized "other" whose subjectivity has been dissolved.

The doctors' treatment of Abbas has complex ethical connotations. The clinic doctor appears with professional courtesy and politeness, and her formulaic enquiries and examinations appear to treat Abbas as if she is "dealing with a broken radio" (ibid.: 9). Abbas' body is objectified under the doctor's treatment, and the "broken radio" implies that he is the object of indoctrination and discipline. Moreover, the couple is placed in a dichotomous relationship with Dr. Mendez. Her orders must be fully complied with, and her diagnoses are often reproachful, and Maryam is always confronted with a sense of fear and self-recrimination. In the case of this diabetic crisis, Mendez took the high ground, accusing Abbas of negligence in monitoring his health, stressing the hereditary nature of diabetes, and demanding that Abbas' children have an annual blood test. Whereas normally Mendez is dismissive of Maryam's gastrointestinal problems: "She could not really take the difficulties her mother was having with her bowels seriously and she listened out of politeness." (ibid.: 87), and this time Mendez accuses Abbas that "older men are too vain to go to the doctor until something terrible happens to them and then they are a nuisance to everyone" (15). Maryam's condition is unimportant in Dr. Mendez's thoughts, and Abbas is an uncooperative and dishonest patient. Therefore, Dr. Mendez holds the power to interpret Abbas's illness, and as the embodiment of intellectual authority, her accusation and indoctrination of Abbas negates him as a sensual being, objectifies him, and weakens and disintegrates his subjectivity.

"Health care professionals (have) profound duties to acknowledge the inviolability of the patient's body as a locus of the person's self. While doctors and nurses might breach the body's unity, we do our best to maintain the 'wholeness' of the patient." (Charon, 2006) Clearly, what Dr. Mendez did in the treatment of Abbas was to devalue and disdain the patient's ego. As a family doctor for many years, she neglects to consider the situation of Abbas' family and allows them to be confined by the perception of the "other". The unequal ethical relationship between doctor and patient projects an ethical order that upholds the stance of the "colonizer".

African immigrants are marginalized and objectified under oppressive social and ethical structures, as is seen in Abbas' medical treatment. They become the targets of discipline and suppression, of scrutiny and transformation. Gurnah uses the examples given above to show how African immigrants' subjectivity is being subtly indoctrinated and oppressed, eroded and dismantled in the present society.

4. Hospice Care: The Search for Intergrowth of Subjectivity and Intersubjectivity

The medical treatment of Abbas' diseases does not save his life, and after suffering his third stroke, he passes away quietly. In fact, Abbas begins receiving hospice care from the novel's commencement. Maryam tends to him by his bedside, the children keep looking back and reflecting on their lives, and all the narrative revolves around the patient and the hospital. The entire process is filled with stress, suffering and misunderstanding, but in Abbas' final confession, everyone finds peace and rebirth, making the third stroke "happy" (Gurnah, 2014: 211).

"Without the narrative acts of telling and being heard, the patient cannot convey to anyone else—or to self—what he or she is going through." (Charon, 2006) When Abbas realizes that "one day soon it (his rotting body) would collapse into the melting rot inside him" (Gurnah, 2014: 114), he relives the past in his mind. As he progressively gains the ability to talk, he is eager to express his "pitiful cowardice" and explain why he has been silent for so long. The encouragement and support of Maryam are essential for Abbas to open up completely. Throughout the process, Maryam takes notes, goes into the library to do research, and makes Abbas receive speech rehabilitation therapy every week. When Abbas loses control of his emotions, for example, "he became angry, fidgeting and gesticulating at her when she wrote something down, accusing her of plotting against him, speaking in a language she did not understand" (ibid.: 133), she would allow him to calm down and continue his story. She becomes a quiet listener to Abbas, and lest he loses his nerve, she does not "ask him anything that might seem like a challenge, in case he lost courage and stopped" (ibid.: 134). The narrative act of confiding and listening not only eases Abbas' inner pain, but more importantly, places them in a unity of each other, leading to their mutual redemption and reconciliation.

"Meaning is intersubjective, moving from one subject to another and in this way forming a world of meaning." (Guo, 2001) The tape recorder, which records the stories of Abbas' past, becomes a vehicle for the transmission of meaning. By reviving the African oral tradition, Gurnah gives Abbas' self-repentance the power of redemption and love, forming intersubjectivity within the family, helping them to affirm the intergrowth of subjectivity and intersubjectivity at the same time as they affirm their subjectivity. The companion, listening and understanding provided at the end of life both heals the individuals' wounds and brings the family out of the gloom of its identity crisis. Thus, it can be said that "Abbas was like Jesus who suffered for the immigrants" (Jiang, 2023), and his confession allow the entire family to start anew.

5. Conclusion

The 2021 Nobel Prize for Literature is awarded to Gurnah for his uncompromising and compassionate penetration of the effects of colonialism and the fate of the refugee in the gulf between cultures and continents. In *The Last Gift*, he depicts the everyday struggles of immigrants via his disease writing, shedding light on societal ills and the aspirations of the African diaspora for spiritual healing. He presents the particular life experiences of the patient and his family through the artistic vision of disease narrative, reveals the struggles and crises of African diasporas caught between different cultures, and employs the metaphor of diseases to attack the ingrained prejudice and discrimination in the sick society. Gurnah employs death as a source of authority for storytelling, and the dying Abbas' confession serves as the last gift that inspires reconciliation and redemption. "The very rise of ethnic literature represents an appeal to ethical reconfiguration, in essence an ethical composition." (Nie, 2014) There is no moral preaching or grievance in the novel. The story is told unhurriedly, urging the intergrowth of subjectivity and intersubjectivity so as to get out of the identity predicament, and also expressing the ethical pursuit for healing the ailing society and reconstructing social order.

Bibliography

[1] CHARON R, 2006. Narrative Medicine: Honoring the Stories of Illness[M]. Oxford: Oxford University Press.

[2] FOUCAULT M, 1995. Discipline and Punish[M]. New York: Penguin Random House.

[3] GURNAH A, 2014. The Last Gift[M]. New York: Bloomsbury USA.

[4] KAIGAI K, 2013. At the Margins: Silences in Abdulrazak Gurnah's *Admiring Silence* and *The Last Gift*[J]. English Studies in Africa, 56(1): 128-140.

[5] MANQOUSH R A, SAKKAF A A, AI-HAWTALI A M, 2021. Minority Identity in African-British Muslim Diaspora: A Critical Analysis of Abdulrazak Gurnah's *The Last Gift*[J]. Scientific Journal of Seiyun University, 2(1): 12-23.

[6] SONTAG S, 1978. Illness as Metaphor[M]. New York: Farrar, Straus and Giroux.

[7] SAID W E, 1996. Representations of the Intellectual[M]. New York: Penguin Random House.

[8] 高宣扬，2005. 当代法国思想五十年（上册）[M]. 北京：中国人民大学出版社.

[9] 郭湛，2001. 论主体间性或交互主体性[J]. 中国人民大学学报(3)：32-38.

[10] 何卫华，聂珍钊，2020. 文学伦理学批评与族裔文学：聂珍钊教授访谈录[J]. 外国语文研究，6(1)：1-12.

[11] 蒋晖，2016. 论非洲现代文学是天然的左翼文学[J]. 文艺理论与批评(2)：20-26.

[12] 蒋晖，2023. 无名时代的节日：古尔纳小说中的移民[J]. 读书(4)：43-50.

[13] 聂珍钊，2014. 文学伦理学批评导论[M]. 北京：北京大学出版社.

[14] 孙鲁瑶，2023. 在地全球性：古尔纳《最后的礼物》中的文学绘图与身份政治[J]. 外国文学研究，45(2)：137-147.

[15] 袁俊卿，2022. "最后的礼物"：阿卜杜勒拉扎克·古尔纳的沉默叙事[J]. 当代外国文学，43(2)：102-109.

[16] 朱振武，游铭悦，2022. 身份认同与共同体意识——最新诺奖作家古尔纳《最后的礼物》的创作旨归[J]. 山东外语教学，43(2)：71-82.

[17] 朱振武，袁俊卿，2019. 流散文学的时代表征及其世界意义——以非洲英语文学为例[J]. 中国社会科学(7)：135-158.

Embodiment of Spatial Form in *The Sound and the Fury*

杨婉儿

1. Introduction

1.1 Literature Review

The Sound and the Fury is a classic modernist novel written by William Faulkner. It has attracted the attention of major literary and art criticism movements in the past 70 years, especially in the late 1940s and early 1950s. This novel takes its title from the famous line of *Macbeth* in Act 5 of Shakespeare's: "Life is a fool's tale, full of sound and fury, and meaningless." The novel is divided into four parts and each part tells the same story four times from four different perspectives, which distinguishes itself from the traditional novel that "proceeds in linear or chronological time and derives its unity from narrative plot" (Alldredge, 1978). The first three chapters are narrated in the first person by the sons of the Compson family, Benjy, the eldest son Quentin and the second son, Jason. The fourth part is narrated by Dilsey from the third person's objective point of view. In the first chapter, "I" Benjy is an idiot, who can't use words to express what the heart feels but only cry to express his sense of love and evil. Quentin's suicide was the victim of the collision between the traditional society and the modern society, and he was a representative of the traditional social class. Jason is indifferent and callous in family, which is a typical mercenary figure in modern society. The fourth part, from the third person perspective of Dilsey, narrates various social conflicts at that time.

In the late 20th century, the field of "spatial narrative" began to attract the attention of critics. It should be noted that the "space" in "spatial form" is not the space in the geographical sense, but the perceptual space in the abstract sense presented in the text. *The Sound and the Fury* has been studied by many domestic critics and scholars from a variety of important perspectives. Some scholars at home have analyzed various themes in the novel, such as Faulkner's *Theme of Southern Tradition and Time* written by Zhang Liyuan. Some scholars narrate the opening part from the perspective of Benjy, the fool, especially the analysis of the stream of consciousness method adopted in it, such as Li Minghui's *Mad Narrative Research under the Identity of an Idiot*. But they all focus on the narrative techniques and time frames to understand fiction. The separation of time and the stream of consciousness monologues have made it difficult to analyze the novel, and many scholars have begun to explore new ways of interpreting *The Sound and the Fury*. It breaks away from the traditional sense of cause and effect, presenting a state of nature. The plot is weakened because of fragmentation and dispersion, which leads to the diluted and hazy plot and even fragmented. However, from the aesthetic perspective of modern novels, it can better grasp the essence of feeling experience in modern life, so as to reveal the essence of man and communicate the essence of the world (Guan, 2003).

In *On the Spatial Form of Faulkner's Novels*, Liu Daoquan (2007) points out that "the complex form and profound ideological content of Faulkner's novels are perfectly integrated, and his novels have obvious characteristics of spatial form novels". In *Time and Space in Faulkner's Narrative Art*, Guan Jianming (2003) discusses Faulkner's creative use of stream of consciousness techniques and time dictation in *The Sound and the Fury*, as well as the spatial form formed by juxtaposition of multiple narrative perspectives and plot clues.

In abroad, in *Spatial Form and Plot*, Eric S. Curtis believes that the juxtaposition structure in Faulkner's *The Sound and the Fury* provides new ideas for readers to construct a new value system. This powerful juxtaposition greatly serves the content. Lawrence Bowling mentions in his *Technique of The Sound and the Fury* that "the disorder, disintegration, and absence of perspective in the lives of the Compsons is intended to be symbolic and representative of a whole social order, or perhaps it would be better to say a whole social disorder" (1948). He views the disorder and disintegration as an integration to present the entirety picture of the southern world.

Vickery, in *The Sound and the Fury: A Research Perspective*, states that Faulkner's novels have no plot or character development, and that the four chapters are arranged for their own specific reasons, as "everything in the novel is fixed because the consciousness of the character becomes the actual force that illuminates and is illuminated by the central scene" (Vickery, 1958). In 2001, Robert Jelliffe applied Frank's spatial form theory to analyze Faulkner's major works. In *The Innumerable Elements of Namelessness*, he analyzes Faulkner's major works from the perspective of language and narrative. So far, few critics have approached the novel from a theoretical point of view. It can be seen from the above research that domestic scholars have made a lot of contributions to the field of the spatial form of Faulkner's works, but the research in this aspect is still not sufficient. Most scholars still focus on the narrative angle and techniques to analyze the theme and meaning of Faulkner's novels, but do not comprehensively and deeply interpret the spatial form of his novels as an entirety.

1.2 Spatial Form

According to Frank, "spatial form" is the literary complement to the developments that occur in the plastic arts, trying to overcome the temporal element contained in their structure (Frank, 1977). Initially, the theory of spatial morphology was developed by Joseph Frank in an insightful essay entitled *Spatial Morphology in Modern Literature*, published in 1945. In Frank's view, modern literature, represented by writers such as T.S. Eliot, Pound, Marcel Proust and James Joyce, is moving towards spatial form, which means "abandoning syntactic order in favor of structures that depend on the perception of the relationship between the two".

To build a bridge for connecting critic theories and literary works in the 20th century, spatial form was put forward by Joseph Frank in 1945 with the aim of tracing "the evolution of form in poetry, and more particularly, in novel" (Frank, 1977). However, some scholars question spatial form and regard it just a "merely metaphor which has been given misplaced concreteness and that it denies the essentially temporal nature of literature" (Mitchell, 1980). Inspired by art theory, Frank pointed out that the spatial form in modern literature can now clearly realize that the in the field of literature, like the plastic art in the field of art, has a characteristic of overcoming the factor of time. In conclusion, the development of spatial form has gone through three periods.

In the initial stage, inspired by art theory, Frank holds the idea that spatial form is a generalization and summary of the spatialization phenomenon in modern novels and poetry and whose conceptual connotation is closely related to the three words "reflective reference", "reading with unity" and "juxtaposition" (Frank, 1977). The second stage is a period of argumentation. Scholars understand it as an application of literature, novels, or narrative skills, and Giovanini and Walter Sutton first questioned Frank's concept of spatial form. Giovanni's idea that "method in the study of literature in its relation to the other fine arts" analyzed the problem of applying Frank's spatial form to the field of art, and questioned Frank's theoretical logic of it. He believes that no matter how the structure is broken, the stable meaning of the text depends on the current order. Frank responded to him during the debate in the 1970s and claimed that spatial form is not the reproduction of a simple fragment, but that different feelings and ideas at the same time are presented in the space as a complex and unified whole. In the debate period, the spatial form at this stage can be briefly summarized as "the spatial form of modern avant-garde narrative". Frank realizes the connection between spatial form and narration. The expression of "spatial form" has also triggered different understandings among scholars in the debate, which also makes the concept of spatial form pluralistic. The third stage is maturity. The presentation of "the idea of spatial form" in 1991 marks the maturity of the concept of spatial form.

Now, scholars' understanding of spatial form is mainly reflected in the following aspects. First, scholars understand spatial form as an application of skills, which is related to narrative skills represented by Giovanni, Eric, etc. Second, they refine the local content of the spatial form, such as the language, structure, plot and so on. This kind of inquiry is represented by scholars such as David Michelson and Daghistany.

2. Presentation of Space: Orange Structure and Image

Frank have borrowed the word "juxtaposition" from Imagism to explain the narrative technique in novels. As Frank's spatial form has influenced by the art, juxtaposition refers to the process of generating an organic unity by reflective reference and cross-reference through juxtaposing the images, groups of words and relations that out of the narrative process. Orange structure is one of the space forms proposed by Gottfried Benn, who compared the structure of the novel to that of an orange, which is made up of several adjacent orange lobes running parallel with each other. The spatial form of orange structure, namely the so-called juxtaposition (the juxtaposition of several time clues), is an important structural mode of modern novels. This kind of structure has played an important role in breaking the linear causal logic of traditional novels (Long, 2005). Futhermore, Mickelsen (1978) also makes an explanation of it that orange structure or orange-structured form that it is a metaphor which refers to that "an absence of development; a number of similar episodes and chapter are arranged spherically". It connected with the structure built by the narrative process that the four different narratives have construct a space for Caddy. Therefore, the juxtaposition in *The*

Sound and the Fury can be found in the following two aspects. First, it abandons the traditional omniscient narrative and reconstructs Caddy's image by using multiple characters Benjy, Quentin, and Jason to tell her story which shows a juxtaposition of the orange structure from a macro point of view. Second, through the description, images are formed by the repetition of meaning unites such waters and shadow.

2.1 The Construction of Orange Structure

If we think of a text as the core of a fruit or of a species, preferably the fruit as an onion, then the onion has no core, no secret and nothing but its apparent unity (Mcneil, 1980). In a word, the story is not organized in chronological order or the traditional way of narration through one perspective, but all chapters are designed relate to a central focus, that is the image of Caddy, who is the central figure but does not appear as a narrator, forming the so-called "linguistic absence". In *The Sound and the Fury*, the author gives the power of speech to Benjy, Quentin and Jason, the multi-voice of narrators for four times makes the image of Caddy appear. Therefore, the narrations of the three narrators are like the orange petals and Caddy is the hollow inside it. In a novel that is orange-structured: "Temporal change, though present, has no functional role in the action, and it is simply a convenient thread to connect episodes." (Mickelsen, 1978) That's to say, each narrator is equal, and their information is different and then generates the juxtaposition of plot. At the same time, each part is an independent one but the content is related to the other parts. Owning to the non-chronological order of narration, each part is independent. To step further, they are related to each other for each section had combined a central plot that makes it possible for the readers to comprehend the whole story, which shows an inner relation. To conclude, orange structure is reflected in subverting the natural logic of traditional novel narrative, disrupting the linear logic of novel development and eliminating time dimension.

During the process of writing, Faulkner points out that "I had already begun to tell it through the eyes of an idiot since I felt that it would be more effective as told by someone capable of knowing what happened, but not why" (Howe, 1975). However, Faulkner doesn't satisfy with the work after finishing the part of Benjy. He thinks the story is still incomplete. Therefore, Quentin becomes the second narrator. After a period of thinking, he thinks the story can be more perfect if there are more than two narrators, so he adds Jason and Dilsey as the last two narrators. Faulkner's violent gluing together of the parts of a broken world brings disparate stories together to tell a common theme, creating a truly integrated experience (Kartiganer, 1970). Finally, the story comes out after unremitting revision and the center of narration still is Caddy.

Caddy only remains in the memory of her family members as a symbol, so "her meaning does not exist in herself, but in other people's understanding of her and her relationship with others" (Hu, 2009). Taking Benjy's comments for example, he thinks "Caddy smelled like trees and like when she says we were asleep" (Faulkner, 1946). This time we can conclude that Caddy is still a symbol of love and warm for Benjy. While Quentin holds a different view, he thinks that "Caddy is a woman to remember. She must do things for woman's reasons too" (Faulkner, 1946). And the last petal is composed by the narration of Jason. In the third chapter, Jason shows his indifferent and cold attitude towards Caddy that he called Caddy by "she" in the whole chapter and treat her apathetically. From the parallel narrative perspective of Benjy, Quentin and Jason, we can find the symbolic nature of Caddy. Unlike traditional novels, Caddy's image is not directly formed by her own continuous words and actions, but by the juxtaposition of the Compson's three brothers. The character Caddy appears in four parts at the same time. Only by juxtaposing the different parts presented from these four perspectives can we form a complete understanding of Caddy's character. Quentin, the egoist Jason, and Benjy, the great idiot, are the descendants of the Compsons in *The Sound and the Fury*, while Caddy, the lost innocent, is created in the narration of the first three characters. And the theme of "family decline" is complete in the repeated writing of the three parallel parts. Therefore, both the shaping of characters and the presentation of themes are completed in the juxtaposition of multiple perspectives. Only in the reading of Benjy, Quentin and Jason from different perspectives, can readers combine their different feelings and narration of Caddy together, so as to complete the shaping of the character of Caddy. This juxtaposition creates the image of Caddy, presenting a spatial form just like orange petals. That's the orange structure or orange-structured form.

2.2 The Shaping of Image

Image is the most important notion of the Imagism. Images formed by meaning units such as words and sentences also show "spatiality" in the novel. The representative of Imagist Ezra Pound shows his ideas of writing poetry through the juxtaposition of images. For example, Pounds thinks that poetry emphasizes "the juxtaposition of things" rather than the logic of language which can be seen in his masterpiece *In a Station of the Metro*: "Petals on a wet, black bough." He thinks an image with instantaneous presentation can provide an emotional complex which gives "that sense of sudden liberation; that sense of freedom from time limits and space limits; that sense of sudden growth, which we experience in the presence of the greatest works of art" (Frank, 1977). After making a further study of image, Frank applies the juxtaposition of images into novels. But in order to maintain the totality of meaning, we can only break the time-flow of narrative, which means, images can be distributed freely in a novel without breaking its coherent sequence. The following parts will analyze some images in this novel so as to show the spatiality.

In *The Sound and the Fury*, the author gives symbolic meanings to objects such as shadows and water. Through the processing of developing the plot, environment setting, character shaping and so on, they become images with religious connotation. These images do not appear just once, but repeatedly, each time in a different atmosphere. Only when these single images appear frequently and repeatedly can they be juxtaposed into a whole, and the whole meaning can be organically arranged and spliced. Each image is repeated in different atmospheres and scenes, and they remain juxtaposed with each other over time. Together, they explain the archetypal meaning of religious mythology.

Water is an ominous image in the novel, which is manifested as rain, wine and river. Water could purify things, and it also represents rebirth and redemption. Although Benjy is a fool, his senses, especially his sense of smell, are very keen. Whenever he discovered that Caddy had done something wrong, he would urge her to take a bath in order to wash away her sins. After losing her virginity, Caddy jumped into the river to wash herself, praying that the current would wash away her shame. According to Benjy, "She put her arms around me again, but I went away" (Faulkner, 1946). At the same time, Benjy could smell the rain on his father and brother, the very smell that foretold misfortune and death: "Father took me up. He smelled like rain." (Faulkner, 1946); because Benjy's father drank himself to death and his older brother Quentin committed suicide by jumping into a river, hoping the river will free him from the shame of his family, "We could hear the roof. Quentin smelled like rain, too." (Faulkner, 1946)

The word "shadow" appears many times in this novel especially in Quentin's section. The juxtaposition of shadow has profound meaning after being stressed by Quentin in different conditions especially said by Quentin's words of treading his shadow: "I walked upon belly of my shadow." (Faulkner, 1946) In western culture, stepping on one's own shadow is regarded as an omen of one's imminent death. At first the author writes the shadow of the window frame. Moreover, Quentin deliberately turned his back on the shadow of the window frame in order to avoid it. Later, when Quentin saw the shadows of the railings, the bridge, and his own on the river, he even wonders what must be done in order to drown them: "The shadow of the bridge, the tiers of railing, my shadow leaning flat upon the water, so easily had trickled it that would not quit me." (Faulkner, 1946) In addition, Quentin has heard that the shadow of the drowned man has been waiting for him in the water all along. He often spoke of stepping the shadow into the mud and standing on the belly of the shadow. These juxtaposed details foretell Quentin's eventual suicide by drowning. The image of the shadow is formed by the juxtaposition of how Quentin deals with the individual shadow.

From the above juxtaposition of images, repeated images, words, symbols and other references become an important means to understand the novel. These images are related to each other and echo each other, connecting isolated or messy information into a coherent and logical entirety.

3. Relations between Spatial Form and Time in *The Sound and the Fury*

In *The Sound and the Fury*, "time" associated with space has a special meaning. First of all, when time is the theme, the narrative technique of spatial form adopted in the novel reflects Faulkner's philosophy of time to some extent. Second, space is associated with the usage of the technique of time montage. Benjy's memory is triggered by the present senses, the present objects, scenes appear in his mind synchronously with the similar objects and scenes in his memory. The use of time montage makes the novel no longer narrate steadily along the traditional time sequence, but constantly shuttling back and forth between the past and the present, presenting a complex network structure centered on the character consciousness which brings readers extraordinary experience.

3.1 Time as Theme

"Spatial form" is not a form in the physical sense, but rather an abstract or perceptual space. It requires the reader to understand the overall structure and the original disorganized time clues of the target novel, and then can present a clear logic of the story. This spatial form exists only in the mind of the reader. In other words, time is the key element of the spatial morphological organization of the novel. In *The Sound and the Fury*, the development of the novel is absent and the characters are static owing to the orange-structured form and the juxtaposition between the past and present. The time of *The Sound and the Fury* is the eternal "present" without the dimension of future. The narrative time of the novel stagnates, presenting detailed fragments synchronously in the present space. Sartre (1960) believes that "the novelist's aesthetic always sends us back to his meta-physic… and it is obvious that Faulkner's is a meta-physic of time". To conclude, this arrangement is a reflection of Faulkner's philosophy of time.

The theme of this novel is the inescapable decline of the southern tradition which is presented through the confrontation between the past and present reflected by the juxtaposition to form the picture of the decline of the Compsons. The Compsons are aristocrats, who were born with dignity and glory. However, after the baptism of the Civil War and the impact of industrialization, the backward traditional culture of the south could no longer be adapted to the development of modern civilization. Therefore, the southern people could not be able to recover from the past glory, but wallowed themselves in the past honor and escaped the reality of the present. As is described, "Instead of days filled with new experiences arousing new reactions, they relive the lives of their ancestors; instead of gathering memories for their own old age, devote themselves to remembering and so preserving legends of a past they have seen"(Vickery, 1958).

The Compsons, like the most southerners, are tragically incapable of dealing with the past and the present. For example, "Benjy was saved by someone outside of time; Quentin is destroyed by his excessive consciousness" (Vickery, 1958). First, idiot Benjy, confuses past and present memories and believes that Caddy doesn't leave and that nothing has changed. Quentin, as the eldest son, has the sole responsibility to restore the family's glory. However, time passes and nothing changes. Quentin even breaks his watch in an attempt to lose track of time. Unlike Benjy and Quentin, Jason is greedy and shrewd. He's more interested in money than family glory or Caddy's tragedy. He even yearns to break away from the Compsons and their traditions. For example, he abandoned his youngest child and chose to live alone because offspring meant future and hope. Dilsey is the only lovable character in the book, and she has a strong belief in God. "…lifted into the driving day with an expression at once fatalistic and of a child's astonished disappointment" (Faulkner, 1946), she not only witnessed the prosperity of the Compsons, but also foresaw their doom. She knows how cold and scattered the Compsons are because they never tried to get through a difficult time together and express love for each other in the family. Instead, they indulge themselves in self-paralysis. If men give up changing, they will die. Since man cannot overcome the decay of the body and the perils of the inevitable, consciousness alone can transcend the bonds of time and space (Messerli, 1974). Thus, we can see that Faulkner wants to tell people the importance of living in the present.

Southerners attach great importance to the role of history, believing that history records people's courage and cowardice, generosity and greed, nobility and meanness. They think that human beings cannot get rid of the influence of history, and the mistakes and achievements of the past cannot be erased by people in the present world (Hu, 2009). Faulkner holds the view that people should change over time to adapt to the present, the reality, because man is the product of time. If people stop changing, they will suffer misfortune. In *The Sound and the Fury*, the loss of tradition and the decline of economic made aristocrats lose sight of the meaning of real life, so they escape from reality and focus on the past, which also leads to the demise of southern aristocrats. This phenomenon can "destroy the continuity of time and paralyze the mobility not only of individuals, but of entire societies" (Vickery, 1958). Thus, through the different characters' perspectives on the present and past and their final endings, Faulkner uses time as a reminder of the theme, hoping that southerners will forget the past, live in the present, cherish the present and finally look forward to the future.

3.2 Synchronic Space under Time Montage

There are many ways to form spatial forms, such as ellipsis, repetition, reference, contrast, multiple perspectives, fracture, collage, multi-plot, montage, etc. (Chen, 2009). Montage was originally an architectural term that is borrowed into film production. Editing, combination or overlay of shots are often used in filming. David Dykes points out that there are two expressive techniques in the novel: "time montage" and "space montage". Faulkner's *The Sound and the Fury* mainly use the technique of "time montage" in the narration of Benjy's stream of consciousness. It refers to the fact that the characters remain static at the spatial level, while the consciousness of the characters jumps and flows over time, and the story develops with the consciousness of the characters. Synchronic space under time montage refers to the spatial form formed by the existence of synchronic past and present.

The Sound and the Fury is narrated by Benjy in the first part. Benjy is incapable of rational thought and he has to follow his senses. Benjy's idiotic identity is easier to cater to the description of the stream of consciousness, and it is easier to shape the inner hustle and bustle of the characters. Benjy's consciousness often returns to the past especially in childhood. People can't help recalling warm memories, so as to Benjy. The love and care Caddy gave him in his childhood left a deep mark in his subconscious. Benjy's flow of consciousness is largely triggered by the senses of the present. These senses can be hearing, sight, touch, smell, and so on. The scenes related to the topographic level become the place, the scenes related to the spatial-temporal level become the field of action, and the scenes related to the text level become the field of view (Cheng, 2007).

When Benjy heard golfers calling for Caddie, he was reminded the same pronunciation of his sister's name, Caddy, and began to hum. Because he can't smell the trees from Caddy, Benjy remembers Caddy losing her scent when she first put on perfume and dressed up as an adult when she was 14. "Here, Caddie." (Faulkner, 1946), the calling of Caddie reminded Benjy of his sister Caddy. "Caddy uncaught me and we crawled through." (Faulkner, 1946), when he saw the scene of little Quentin swinging, Benjy recalled the scene of Caddy swinging and Caddy's care for him. "Caddy smelled like trees. They sat up in the swing, quick." (Faulkner, 1946) But now while he is recalling, the little Quentin unjustifiably calls him "crazy loon". The most frequent part is when the current situation triggers Benjy to see the same thing as he remembers. Benjy sees the old carriage in the garage, and his mind goes back to the family wagon ride; the barn brings his mind back to the Christmas Eve trip with Cathy to the vicinity of the barn, and how he and the boy have lain drunk in the barn when Cathy gets married; the sight of the hut reminds him of the scene where he lives in the servants' room. When these memories are repeated or scenes are transferred, Benjy's memories usually trigger a "past" memory from the "present", but sometimes recall multiple "past" memories from the "present", resulting in multiple things similar to the present and scenes synchronously filling his mind. In this way, linear textual narration and dramatic plot changes are combined with time, and the consciousness of the narrator and the association formed in the reader's mind create a four-dimensional space in which characters live. Only masters of narrative skills like Faulkner can create character Benjy carrying exclusive distinctions to form the spatial form (Lu, 2011).

Therefore, the spatial form of synchronic existence of the past and present expounds that Benjy's thoughts are stimulated by the present senses. Similar things and scenes in the past and present emerge in his mind at the same time, which shows a series of co-occurring pictures.

4. Conclusion

The discreteness of spatial novels poses a strong challenge to readers. Readers need to juxtapose and recombine the intentions scattered throughout the article due to different personal narrative angles, and regard nonlinear time as a tool to understand the theme, so as to form a picture from the discrete fragments of the text. Readers need to read repeatedly in order to connect the various intentions, symbols and interrupted narratives to restructure according to their own understanding and grasp the main body of the novel.

The Sound and the Fury perfectly embodies the unity of content and form. Faulkner, with the help of his own constructed southern world Yoknapatawpha County, brought his thoughts by describing the impact of the decline of aristocrats on tradition and modernity. He wants to show that the plight of the people of the south is in fact the plight of the whole human race, which serves as a reminder to enlighten or warn the readers to grasp the present. The plot of *The Sound and the Fury* is not presented in a coherent way, but rather distributed like handfuls of candy to children, and maximized by reactive references. This relatively novel form of modernism novel divides a large number of meaning units into small meaning groups, and elucidates new meanings through superposition, blending and comparison of relevant parts of meaning, so that readers can understand modernism novel from an overall perspective when reading and understanding.

This thesis analyzes *The sound and the Fury* from the perspective of spatial form, and the main findings are as follows: First, the novel is divided into four chapters, and each chapter is narrated by a specific character. They are independent of each other in form, but their meanings are related to each other, presenting a juxtaposition structure like orange petals. At the same time, the structure also presents a state of juxtaposition. Each chapter of the novel takes a certain day in the past as the background, showing the characters' different conflicts between tradition and modernity. Second, the juxtaposition of intention, meaning units such as water and shadows appear repeatedly in different backgrounds, forming the juxtaposition of image. Third, time in the novel also has a special connection with space. The theme of the novel is the decline of southern tradition under the impact of modern times. The author reveals the importance of time through the different reactions of the four characters to the impact and the final outcome, which embodies Faulkner's philosophy of time that people should forget the past, live in the present and look into the future. Finally, the memory flashback formed by the time montage is the comparison between the past scene and the present scene. Therefore, by analyzing the relationship between spatial form and time in the novel, it can be found that Faulkner believes that time is organized and represented through spatial form. And the use of spatial forms also reflects Faulkner's philosophy of time. By studying the spatial form of *The Sound and the Fury*, on the one hand, this thesis gives sparkling inspirations to modern novels, exploring new forms of presenting and combining ideas; on the other hand, this thesis allows people to emerge in a splendid and magic world enriched by space and sublimates their understanding of it.

Bibliography:

[1] ALLDREDGE B, 1978. Spatial Form in Faulkner's *As I Lay Dying*[J]. The Southern Literary Journal:3-19.

[2] BOWLING L E, 1948. Faulkner: Technique of *The Sound and the Fury*[J]. The Kenyon Review, 10(4): 552-566.

[3] FAULKNER W, 1946. The Sound and the Fury[M]. New York: The Viking Press.

[4] FRANK J, 1977. Spatial Form: an Answer to Critics[J]. Critical Inquiry, 4(2): 231-252.

[5] HOWE I, 1975. William Faulkner: A Critical Study[M]. Chicago: The University of Chicago Press.

[6] KARTIGANER D, 1970. *The Sound and the Fury* and Faulkner's quest for form[J]. English Literature History, 37(4): 613-639.

[7] HOFFMAN F J, VICKERY O W, FAULKNER W, 1960. Three Decades of Criticism[M]. East Lansing: Michigan State University Press.

[8] MCNEIL L D, 1980. Toward a Rhetoric of Spatial Form: Some Implications of Frank's Theory[J]. Comparative Literature Studies, 14(6): 355-367.

[9] MICKELSEN D, 1978. A Rebours: Spatial Form[J]. French Fourum, 12(8): 48-55.

[10] MESSERLI D, 1974. The Problem of Time in *The Sound and the Fury*: A Critical Reassessment and Reinterpretation[J]. The Southern Literary Journal, 6(2): 19-41.

[11] MITCHELL W J T, 1980. Spatial Form in Literature: Toward a General Theory[J]. Critical Inquiry, 6(3): 539-567.

[12] SARTRE J P, 1960. Time in Faulkner: *The Sound and the Fury*[J]. William Faulkner: Three Decades of Criticism: 225-232.

[13] VICKERY O W, 1958. Faulkner and the Contours of Time[J]. The Georgia Review, 12(2): 192-201.

[14] 陈德志，2009. 隐喻与悖论：空间、空间形式与空间叙事学[J]. 江西社会科学(9)：63-67.

[15] 程锡麟，2007. 叙事理论的空间转向——叙事空间理论概述[J]. 江西社会科学(11)：25-35.

[16] 管建明，2003. 福克纳叙事艺术中的时间和空间形式[J]. 外语教学(4)：72-76.

[17] 胡晓萍，2009. 论《喧哗与骚动》中的时间叙事艺术[D]. 南昌大学.

[18] 龙迪勇，2005. 空间形式：现代小说的叙事结构[J]. 思想战线, 6(31)：102-109.

[19] 汉弗莱，1987. 现代小说中的意识流[M]. 长沙：湖南文艺出版社.

[20] 刘道全，2007. 论福克纳小说的空间形式[J]. 国外文学(2)：71-77.

[21] 陆春香，2011. 福克纳作品中的视阈空间——以《喧哗与骚动》中班吉的叙述为例[J]. 学习与探索(4)：226-228.

[22] 肖明翰，1997. 威廉•福克纳研究[M]. 北京：外语教学与研究出版社.

Confluence and Resonance of Multiple Tones: An Analysis of Dialogicality in *Foe*

李怡佳

1. Introduction

"Is conversation not simply a species of music in which first the one takes up the refrain and then the other? Does it matter what the refrain of our conversation is any more than it matters what tune it is we play?" (Coetzee, 1987) In J.M. Coetzee's novel *Foe*, Susan Barton's use of music as an analogy illuminates the communicative and melodic essence of dialogue. As Bakhtin (2013) aptly notes, "Dialogic interaction is indeed the authentic sphere where language lives. The entire life of language, in any area of its use (in everyday life, in business, scholarship, art, and so forth), is permeated with dialogic relationships". This highlights the significance dialogue holds as a vital conduit, connecting and facilitating the complex network of social relations within human society. Bakhtin's philosophy revolves around the formation of human subjects. By focusing on the process through which individuals construct their identities via self-awareness and interaction with others, he argues that subjectivity can only be fully realized through dialogue. Coetzee also recognizes the importance of dialogue and draws parallels between writing and conversation. In his portfolio, he asserts that writing transcends mere free expression, embodying a dialogic essence that entails awakening the counter-voices within oneself and engaging in speech with them (Coetzee, 1992). Consequently, a solid foundation exists for examining Coetzee's novels from a dialogical perspective. The "dialogicality" of *Foe* finds its primary expression in the confrontations between characters and their innermost thoughts, as well as in the intricate interplay of communication that transpires between the author and the characters. Indeed, the very essence of "dialogue" permeates the novel, giving rise to the convergence and interplay of diverse ideas that contribute to the work's pervasive sense of uncertainty and unfinalizability.

J. M. Coetzee, the Nobel Prize laureate in Literature and a prominent African literary scholar, was born and raised in South Africa. Growing up as a South African of Dutch heritage, Coetzee faced rejection from both the white Anglo and white Dutch communities during his upbringing, which contributed to the development of a complex cultural identity that plagued him for many years. Coetzee's writing delves into the intersection of politics, history and individual lives, exploring historical narratives while examining humanity's position. Through his writing, Coetzee aims to shed light on the isolation and alienation of marginalized groups, often identified as "the other", throughout history. By subverting traditional binary modes of thinking, Coetzee challenges the ethical framework enforced by authority, concentrating on portraying marginalized populations rather than heroic characters and employing free-flowing dialogue between characters in his fictional texts, serving as a means to contemplate individual values, the significance of human existence, and history itself. These thematic elements of Coetzee's writing align harmoniously with the foundational principles of Bakhtin's dialogue theory. It is through Coetzee's rejection of authoritative writing that his characters develop their subjectivity, embodying a complex interplay of identities and perspectives.

According to Christopher Peterson, Coetzee's novel *Foe* centers around an alleged absence (Peterson, 2017). This absence is primarily associated with the character Friday's severed tongue. In Defoe's *Robinson Crusoe*, Friday is portrayed as a "civilized" individual possessing manners, shame and obedience. However, Coetzee's adaptation takes a contrasting approach, subjecting Friday to the cruel removal of his tongue, rendering him forever speechless. This physical "incommunicability" of Friday not only forms a strong intertextuality with the Western literary classic but also contributes paradoxically to the work's most significant aspect of dialogue—the internal communication within Susan Barton. Simultaneously, Coetzee's modification of the original text facilitates the emergence of the "absent" female voice and unfolds the novel's dialogic nature. Within the narrative, the perspective shifts from Cruso to Barton, a woman stranded on the deserted island with Cruso and Friday after a shipwreck. Over time, Barton yearns for civilization and is eventually rescued by a passing merchant ship to England. Seeking to transform her experiences on the desert island into a memoir for her livelihood, she seeks the assistance of a writer named Foe. However, Foe disregards Barton's intentions and instead summarizing her story with his own twist. This sparks a series of debates between them, centering on the authenticity of the writing and the question of whether the tale of the silent Friday can be told, which forms the foundation of the characters' interactions within the novel. As the story progresses, various types of dialogues are presented, engaging with propositions in the realm of human spirituality and life, imbuing the work with a sense of openness and dynamic incompleteness. This study primarily examines the different levels of dialogue present in the novel, employing Bakhtin's dialogue theory to analyze how Coetzee makes use of writing as a form of dialogue and communicates with the characters in his narrative. Through this approach, Coetzee allows the marginalized "other" to assert their existence.

2. The Contradictory Dialogue Between the Characters

Bakhtin posits that dialogue extends beyond mere linguistic communication, permeating every aspect of human existence. He emphasizes the significance of the interaction between the "self" and the "other" as crucial for self-expression. Bakhtin asserts that dialogue is essential to existence, stating, "…dialogue is the end. A single voice ends nothing and resolves nothing. Two voices is the minimum for life, the minimum for existence" (Bakhtin, 2013). Through the medium of dialogue, the inner workings of the human mind are revealed in novels, contributing to a comprehensive understanding of the human condition. This concept of dialogue encompasses both a broad and narrow interpretation. In its narrower sense, dialogue refers to direct verbal exchanges between individuals, involving a range of relationships such as agreement, disagreement, affirmation, complementation, question and answer, and other relationships. However, dialogue extends beyond mere communication through linguistic symbols. In its broader sense, dialogue includes any form of verbal communication. Here, Bakhtin introduces the notion of dialogicality, which describes how dialogue permeates both monologue and non-dialogical forms of communication, representing "a special form of interaction among autonomous and equally signifying consciousnesses" (Bakhtin, 2013). Scholar Dong Xiaoying further elucidates that dialogicality goes beyond the components that dialogue contains (such as interlocutors, dialogue content and dialogue mode) and is more complex in nature. It includes interactions not only between characters within the text but also between the author and characters, the author and the reader, and the characters and the reader. Additionally, the content of dialogue extends beyond the words enclosed in quotation marks, incorporating external voices and textual gaps, hence offers greater flexibility (Dong, 1994). The dialogical nature of discourse, derived from real-life language usage, according to Bakhtin, adds depth to the narrative and enhances the richness of speech, as exemplified in the works of Coetzee.

In *Foe*, Coetzee skillfully explores the protagonist's struggle with contradictions and challenges, thereby highlighting the underlying themes and promoting introspection. Through the exploration of dichotomies such as silence vs. voice, fantasy vs. reality, and freedom vs. resistance, the author artfully creates a chorus of voices. Moreover, Coetzee effectively juxtaposes multiple voices within the characters, allowing them to navigate their internal conflicts and reveal their inherent dialogical nature. The dialogicality at the core of *Foe* finds its primary manifestation in the ambivalent attitude exhibited by the main female character, Susan Barton, towards herself and others. She embodies the state of being an "exile", perpetually caught between foreign territories and desolate islands, assuming the role of a troubled narrator whose identity lacks a genuine sense of belonging and substance. Susan Barton transcends the confines of a conventional character; she embodies a "multifaceted collection of ideas", and gives expression to interconnected psychological states within her limited personal consciousness. Her continuous engagement in "potential conversations", as illuminated by Dong Xiaoying (1994), breathes vitality into her character. This amalgamation of external consciousness with her own engenders a dialogue between two voices—the discourse of the other and the discourse of the self. This internal dialogue mirrors the protagonist's encounter with their objectified self, akin to standing before a mirror and engaging in an introspective exchange.

2.1 Barton towards Friday: Evasion, Self-reflection and Struggle

One notable aspect lies in Barton's attitude towards Friday, which is marked by a multitude of contradictions. Upon discovering the truth about Friday's mutilated tongue, she experiences a profound unease towards his body. Simultaneously, she confronts a deep sense of shame for her repugnant conduct, candidly admitting,

"I could not help myself—with the horror we reserve for the mutilated. It was no comfort that his mutilation was secret, closed behind his lips, that outwardly he was like any black people. Indeed, it was the very secretness of his loss that caused me to shrink from him…I was ashamed to behave thus, but for a time was not mistress of my own actions." (Coetzee, 1987: 24)

Barton regrets her decision to prompt Cruso to recount Friday's story, recognizing the disgrace associated with her withdrawal from Friday's disability. However, she grapples with the management of her emotions, unable to suppress this visceral response. Consequently, she deliberately avoids contemplating Friday in her mind, refusing to envision his past experiences. Her evasion and fear towards trauma and disability, intertwined with the dominant constructs of white consciousness, cause her subconscious to perceive him as an inferior being unworthy of attention, someone devoid of "soul". Nevertheless, her attitude towards him still oscillates between fear and maternal affection, as conflicting voices clash and meld within her, contributing to the complexity of her emotional state. Following Cruso's death from illness, Barton naturally assumes the role of Friday's guardian. However, unconsciously, a sense of wariness lingers within her, associating Friday with the image of a cannibal who consumes corpses, and retaining suspicions that he may still keep feral instincts. This perception is further heightened by her observation of Friday's lips, leading her to ponder: "Is it not only a matter of time before the new Friday whom Cruso created is sloughed off and the old Friday of the cannibal forests returns?" (Coetzee, 1987: 95) She entertains the doubt that Friday might have resorted to consuming the abandoned baby out of sheer hunger, or worse, pose a threat to her own safety. This deep fear compels her to lie beside Friday, too anxious to allow herself to succumb to sleep until daybreak.

Barton's anxieties largely stem from Cruso's retelling of Friday's unsearchable past, a tale lacking substantiation yet one she cannot help but entertain. Friday, rendered incapable of vocalizing his own experiences, exists in a realm where his narrative can only be constructed. Hence, Barton's attitude towards Friday at this juncture becomes a complex blend of neglect, unease and fear. However, despite these concerns, Barton nurtures a motherly sense of duty and affection towards Friday. She personally drafts a deed to secure Friday's freedom and endeavors to assist him in returning to his homeland (even though she remains unaware of his true origins). When the Indian captain attempts to deceive her, with the intention of selling Friday as a slave elsewhere, Barton firmly rejects his offer and ultimately keeps Friday by her side.

To some extent, Barton assumes multiple roles, including that of a mother, a bearer of responsibility, and even a teacher. Reflecting upon her connection with Friday, she states, "A woman may bear a child she does not want, and rear it without loving it, yet be ready to defend it with her life. Thus it has become, in a manner of speaking, between Friday and myself. I do not love him, but he is mine" (Coetzee, 1987: 111). Her one-sided affection for Friday possesses an aspect of compassion and maternal instinct, yet it fails to encompass a true understanding of the complicated relationship between individuals of differing racial backgrounds.

Throughout her endeavors to teach Friday English, Barton's sentiments towards him remain a blend of mixed and conflicting emotions. In her correspondence with Foe, she acknowledges:

"I tell myself I talk to Friday to educate him out of darkness and silence. But is that the truth? There are times when benevolence deserts me and I use words only as the shortest way to subject him to my will…I understand, that is to say, why a man will choose to be a slaveowner. Do you think less of me for this confession?" (Coetzee, 1987: 60-61)

Barton's primary objective is to empower Friday to articulate his own story by imparting him language skills. However, she wrestles with the idea that this endeavor may inadvertently resemble a form of slave ownership, driven by her self-centered desire to shape Friday according to her own wishes, all the while haunted by the fear of judgment from Mr. Foe. Barton's contemplations concerning Friday exemplify a tangible tension that mirrors the uneasy dynamics prevailing between contrasting races within a historical context of long-standing segregation. Her uncertain stance is influenced by the perceptions of those around her and a primal consciousness deeply ingrained, thus creating a contradictory image fraught with bipolar tensions. This introspection reflects the psyche of white individuals in the post-colonial era within a broader historical and social framework. Ultimately, Barton's relationship with Friday proves to be both awkward and complex, as encapsulated in her own words, "He is not free, but he is not in subjection" (Coetzee, 1987: 147), a sentiment equally applicable to her association with Cruso.

2.2 Barton with Cruso: Resistance, Obedience and Companionship

Throughout her time on the desert island with Cruso, Barton displayed a deliberate manifestation of her female consciousness, which was evident in her intentional defiance of Cruso's warning, her self-sufficiency in cobbling shoes for herself, and her solitary exploration of the island, and those actions frequently incited his anger. However, more often than not, Barton deemed it imperative to conform to the regulations of the desert island realm and willfully adopt a submissive role as a "subject." This is exemplified by her compassionate disposition, readily offering solace to the gravely ill Cruso and exerting her utmost endeavors to restore his health.

Furthermore, she did not reject his desire for sexual intimacy, despite possessing the physical strength to resist him, stating "No doubt I might have freed myself, for I was stronger than he. But I thought, He has not known a woman for fifteen years, why should he not have his desire?" (Coetzee, 1987: 27) The outcome mentioned above emanates from Barton's decision to engage in introspection and heed her inner voice, as well as the subsequent choices she made following her interaction with Cruso. While this conduct may be perceived as a submissive and accommodating gesture, it also signifies her mastery over her own corporeal domain through introspective dialogue, exemplifying the comforting power of women. At this juncture, Barton ceases to be merely Cruso's servant, assuming a position more akin to that of a close companion. Subsequently, Barton embarks on a deeper contemplation of the events that transpired between them:

"Chance had cast me on his island, chance had thrown me in his arms. In a world of chance, is there a better and a worse? We yield to a stranger's embrace or give ourselves to the waves; for the blink of an eyelid our vigilance relaxes; we are asleep; and when we awake, we have lost the direction of our lives. What are these blinks of an eyelid, against which the only defence is an eternal and inhuman wakefulness? Might they not be the cracks…through which another voice, other voices, speak in our lives? By what right do we close our ears to them? The questions echoed in my head without answer" (Coetzee, 1987: 27).

Through this monologue, we are prompted to question whether it is Barton herself who articulates these thoughts or if they emanate from the voice of Coetzee. Their ruminations intertwine, forming the groundwork for a dialogue—a process wherein comprehension and truth within an indifferent world can only be unraveled through active listening. Language, serving as the conduit for communication, carries its own profound significance. In this instance, Barton's internal reflections encapsulate not only the exchange between the author and the character but also the interaction between the character and the reader. This emphasis on dialogue is not merely an isolated occurrence but "rather part of a lifetime inquiry into profound questions about the entire enterprise of thinking about what human life means" (Booth, 1984).

2.3 Barton to Foe: Trust, Doubt and Debate

As Barton undertakes the task of narrating her experiences on the deserted island, she confronts a profound desire to assume authorship of her own narrative, while simultaneously doubting her creative abilities. Initially, she acknowledges her role as a mere provider of material to Mr. Foe, relying on him to reproduce her story. However, the bulk of the text in the novel is, in fact, articulated in Barton's own narrative voice, encompassing not only her letters to Foe but also the ensuing debates they engage in. She later challenges fixed gender roles, learns to express herself through writing, and gradually realizes that gaining recognition from the dominant discourse is crucial in establishing her identity. Her storytelling is characterized by clarity and intuition, yet the passive position assigned to women in the realm of writing perpetually undermines her confidence, even leading her to be swayed by Foe's arguments. This internal conflict, arising from the tension between her desire to share her experiences and the societal expectations surrounding women's writing, engulfs her in a state of authorial anxiety.

Moreover, Mr. Foe's denial, scrutiny, and the challenges of articulation deepen her self-doubt and uncertainty. As a self-proclaimed "professional writer", Foe insists that Susan's desert island story requires fortuitous events, opportunities and dramatic moments to enhance its engagement, disregarding the intrinsic value of her story itself. Pressured by dominant male writers, Barton confesses, "…now I am full of doubt. Nothing is left to me but doubt. I am doubt itself. Who is speaking me?…To what order do I belong?" (Coetzee, 1987: 133) Furthermore, the invasion of the space in which she sleeps by Foe, whether due to the unfamiliar surroundings or their physical proximity in the narrow bed, impedes her ability to find rest. This intrusion also appears to imply a concession to Foe's narrative dominance. Barton's pursuit of authorship reflects her longing for self-expression and rebellion against the pervasive influence of patriarchal discourse in contemporary society. However, this rebellion is overshadowed by a deepening lack of self-assurance and incessant questioning, engendering an ongoing internal dialogue within Barton's mind. These uncertainties contribute to her multifaceted character, embodying both subjectivity and otherness.

In sum, Barton's inner world is characterized by a chorus of voices, each advocating self-justification or self-condemnation, resulting in a dialogical nature that encapsulates an ongoing ideological struggle and coordination, with each voice presenting its possibilities. Consequently, Barton frequently adopts ambiguous attitudes in her discourse, exposing her complicated self. Through the process of dialogue with Foe and Cruso, she endeavors to influence them while simultaneously undergoing her own transformation. This highlights the profound impact of human consciousness on the ebb and flow of dialogue, embodying the essence of its meaning.

3. The Communication between the Author and the Characters

When considering the relationship between authors and protagonists in literary creation, Bakhtin challenges the inclination in traditional monologues to diminish the protagonist to a mere conduit for the author's thoughts. He rather emphasizes the concept of "interactive subjectivity" present in Dostoevsky's works, highlighting the importance of meaningful communication and dialogue between the author and the protagonist. Bakhtin argues that authors should refrain from imposing their characters' perspectives or stifling their freedom of expression. As Wayne Booth states, "When novelists imagine characters, they imagine worlds that characters inhabit, worlds that are laden with values" (Booth, 1984). When a single value dominates the author's voice, it becomes artificial. To achieve a "full acknowledgment of and participation in a Great Dialogue" (ibid.), characters must engage in equitable and meaningful interaction with the author, transcending their role as mere extensions of the author's consciousness. The purpose of authors creating characters is to delve into their own thoughts and illuminate them, thereby establishing their distinct subjectivity. Given that the author's consciousness is in a perpetual state of evolution and incompleteness, and this inherent sense of unfinalizability is inherited by the characters. Consequently, the author must engage in an equal dialogue with the protagonist's self-awareness to attain a comprehensive understanding of themselves. Fundamentally, the creation of the "other" is necessary for the completion of the "self". In his Nobel Prize acceptance speech, Coetzee reflects upon the author-character relationship using the example of Cruso and Friday:

"How are they to be figured, this man and he? As master and slave? As brothers, twin brothers? As comrades in arms? Or as enemies, foes?... If he must settle on a likeness for the pair of them, his man and he, he would write that they are like two ships sailing in contrary directions, west, the other east. Or better, that they are deckhands toiling in the rigging, the one on a ship sailing west, the other on a ship sailing east...they pass each other by, too busy even to wave." (Coetzee, 2004)

In the realm of the author's imagination, characters emerge as autonomous entities, possessing their own unique identities and existing in a parallel temporal and spatial dimension, intricately connected to the author. This relationship can be metaphorically likened to "sailors heading in different directions", delineating the boundaries between reality and fiction.

Fundamentally, profoundly influenced by Coetzee's writing position, *Foe* is thematically suggestive of an open and unrestricted relationship between the author and the character. This narrative prompts critical inquiries into the authority of writing and sheds light on marginalized voices that have been overlooked within historical narratives. Coetzee seeks to convey the absence of an absolute historical truth, underscoring the tendency of "realist" and historical writing to disregard these silenced voices. As articulated by Hayden White (1973): "The historian should try to be 'scientific' in his investigation of the documents and in his efforts to determine 'what actually happened' in the past, and that he ought to represent the past 'artistically' to his readers." Coetzee subverts and reinterprets the plots and characters of realist writers, such as Defoe, as a means to confront and expose the power dynamics prevalent in historical accounts. Thus, *Foe* serves as a manifestation of Coetzee's rejection of exclusive storytelling, which deprives a part of the object of its inherent "substance" and reduces the character's narrative to a mere arbitrary construct of the writer. Similar to Barton's yearning for reciprocation in her interactions with others: "How can I make you understand the cravings felt by those of us who live in a world of speech to have our questions answered! It is like our desire, when we kiss someone, to feel the lips we kiss respond to us." (Coetzee, 1987: 76), one-sided storytelling becomes a frigid shell that inevitably masks the existence of other living "souls". Consequently, the characters in the novel possess distinct voices, identities, and reasoning that are independent of the author's perspective. Furthermore, as the characters freely express their opinions, the author silently engages in a dialogue with them, thereby gaining a deeper comprehension of the issues at hand.

Secondly, the characters depicted in the novel exhibit a profound sense of selfhood and independence, aligning seamlessly with Coetzee's perspective on creation. They undergo a logical and autonomous development, asserting themselves even in the absence of direct authorial control. As Bakhtin (2013) emphasized: "Self-consciousness, as the artistic dominant in the construction of the hero's image, is by itself sufficient to break down the monologic unity of an artistic world." Through ongoing communication, the characters continuously evolve and establish their individuality. These diverse perspectives converge within the narrative, with characters interpreting truth in their own unique manner. The novel directly presents their self-awareness, granting them opportunities to reflect, express themselves and take action, thereby enhancing their subjectivity.

A striking illustration of this aspect can be observed in Cruso's resolute obstinacy, which is shaped during his time on the desert island and poignantly portrayed in the narrative. His labor culminates in terraces that serve as mere reminders of human existence rather than actual creative outputs. Cruso demonstrates a reluctance to document his life, dismissing Susan Barton's suggestion that "Nothing is forgotten...Nothing I have forgotten is worth the remembering." (Coetzee, 1987: 17) However, he is even unable to provide a definitive account of his own story. In stark contrast to the diligent and practical Crusoe from *Robinson Crusoe*, he spends his days as the solitary ruler of a deserted island, showing minimal desire to return to civilization. In *Foe*, Cruso advocates for the futility of history and memory, embodying a nihilistic belief. Although the novel does not offer a direct depiction of his inner thoughts, he serves as the central figure of intertextuality with Western classics. The world, the nation and the cultural traditions represented by Coetzee engage in communication with the ideals of the old West, and the latter is completely subverted in the work.

The character of Friday in the novel emerges as a complex and somewhat self-aware individual. While he acts as a slave without complaint, he consistently rejects learning the language and script of the Empire, adamantly preserving his distinct identity. Despite Barton's efforts to trigger his memory and educate him, Friday responds with vacant stares, indifference and deliberate silence. Similar to Abbas in *The Last Gift*, who maintains reticence regarding the past, Friday possesses an inherent individuality. He engages in solitary activities, such as playing the reed flute and performing the ritual of scattering flower petals into the sea. Additionally, he adorns himself with a wig and robe, twirling and dancing ceaselessly under the sun, seemingly indulging in a vibrant world of personal imagination. He refused to show Barton what he had drawn while writing, and it was only then that Barton became bitterly aware that "it might not be mere dullness that kept him shut up in himself, nor the accident of the loss of his tongue, nor even an incapacity to distinguish speech from babbling, but a disdain for intercourse with me" (Coetzee, 1987: 98). This profound passivity and negative disposition serve as an effective self-protective mechanism. In summary, characters in *Foe* exhibit autonomy and agency, existing independently from the author. As Barton confronts Cruso and Foe and endeavors to communicate with Friday, Coetzee similarly explores themes related to the role of the writer and the presentation of history through the medium of his characters.

Lastly, the novel culminates with an indeterminate ending, strategically crafted by the author to prevent the characters from being objectified and to emphasize the unfinished nature of the narrative. The main plot concludes with a conversation between Barton and Mr. Foe, wherein they discuss teaching Friday the alphabet. Departing from conventional stereotypes, the characters' thoughts and potential for growth are left unresolved, mirroring the complexities of real individuals. Will Susan Barton write her own story, or will Foe assimilate it into his consciousness to create a totally different account? Does Friday ultimately return to his homeland or just follow Barton's guidance? Coetzee deliberately abstains from providing a clear answer, intertwining his consciousness with the progression of the novel. Towards the end of the novel, a mysterious first-person narrator "I" emerges, causing a shift in viewpoint. This narrator immerses within Barton's world, closely examining the departed Friday and other deceased characters. At this point, the illusory nature of the narrative dissipates, and the depicted world is no longer solely controlled by words; instead, the body itself conveys meaning. This unexpected and enigmatic ending highlights that concluding a literary work definitely only brings a partial resolution to the story. The author's deeper intentions concealed beneath the level remain open-ended, defying incontestable conclusions amidst deconstruction and construction. Due to the novel's inherent uncertainty and openness, readers are unable to arrive at a conclusive interpretation but are instead presented with boundless possibilities for understanding. This openness facilitates a dialogue between the author and readers, allowing for subjectivity and adding a lasting charm to the work.

4. Conclusion

Coetzee's multicultural background exerts a profound influence on his worldview, emphasizing the value of diversity and instigating a critical examination of authority. He envisions a liberated existence where individuals can freely express their unique identities and perspectives, fostering peaceful coexistence among people of different ethnicities and races through dialogue. In his novel, Coetzee rebels against traditional historical narratives, replacing them with the concept of "dialogue" and according due reverence to the subjectivity of "the others". In Conclusion, Coetzee skillfully creates meaningful character interactions through dialogue. These exchanges allow individuals in his works to convey their distinct ideas while gaining valuable insights from others, ultimately leading to personal growth and transformations. This peculiarity aligns harmoniously with Bakhtin's dialogical theory, emphasizing the coexistence of diverse subjects and the embrace of heterogeneous perspectives. Coetzee's novel *Foe* prominently exemplifies this concept through a polyphony of potential conversations, most notably manifested in the vibrant conversations among the main character, Susan Barton, herself, and other characters who engage in interaction with the author. In the face of Friday, she is an awkward, painful escapist as well as a responsible guardian. In her interactions with Cruso, she displays a rebellious temperament while also providing him with companionship and humane care. During her communication with Foe, she emerges as a staunch advocate for her own subjectivity and a rebel against authority but simultaneously exhibits a susceptibility to assimilation and persuasion. In the dialogue with diverse characters, a contradictory image is portrayed and continues to reflect the characteristics of uncertainty and openness. This latter form of dialogue is connected to the novel's themes, the characters' self-awareness, and the openness of its ending. Consequently, readers are unequivocally invited to engage in an enlightening dialogue with the author, immersing themselves in a complex realm of "heteroglossia" that allows for the ultimate exploration of literary creation.

Bibliography

[1] BAKHTIN M, 2013. Problems of Dostoevsky's Poetics[M]. Minneapolis: University of Minnesota Press.

[2] BOOTH W C, 1984. Introduction: Problems of Dostoevsky's Poetics[M]//. Mikhail Bakhtin. Problems of Dostoevsky's Poetics. Minneapolis: University of Minnesota Press.

[3] COETZEE J M, 2004. He and His Man[J]. PMLA, 119(3): 547-552.

[4] COETZEE J M, 1987. Foe[M]. London: Penguin Books.

[5] COETZEE J M, 1992. Doubling the Point: Essays and Interviews[M]. Cambridge: Harvard University Press.

[6] HAYDEN W, 1973. Metahistory: The Historical Imagination in Nineteenth Century Europe[M]. Baltimore: The Johns Hopkins University Press.

[7] PETERSON C, 2017. Monkey Trouble: The Scandal of Posthumanism[M]. New York: Fordham University Press.

[8] 董小英, 1994. 再登巴比伦塔：巴赫金与对话理论[M]. 上海：生活·读书·新知三联书店.

论小说影视化的改编——以《三体》为例

朱立源

1. 引言

影视剧是一门综合艺术，集结了小说、音乐、美术、戏剧等多种形式，而小说是与其联系最为紧密的。要讲述故事情节，影视剧就需要有剧本，而剧本的来源除了编剧原创，大多数是由小说改编而来。小说的影视化是一种历久弥新的形式。影视剧一方面可以集声乐、视听、特效等众多元素于一体，另一方面在相同时间内也比文字传递的信息更为丰富、广泛。自电影诞生以来，已有成千上万部电影改编自小说，有的改编反响不错，当然也有禁不起推敲的改编。

《三体》自 2006 年在《科幻世界》杂志连载以来，受到了众多读者的青睐，也为中国的科幻文学立下一座里程碑。随后，刘慈欣又整合出版了三本独立的书籍。2015 年 8 月 23 日，《三体》摘下堪称"科幻界的诺贝尔奖"——雨果奖的桂冠之后，它的文学地位又提升了一个层次，这对中国科幻乃至世界科幻文学的影响也是史无前例的。因此，众多科幻爱好者对于《三体》的影视化十分期待。2023 年 1 月 15 日，《三体》电视剧被首次搬上荧幕，一经播出就立刻产生了热烈的反响，各大平台关于《三体》的讨论进入白热化阶段。而该剧对于原著的还原度之高，为其赢得了受众与口碑。

对于小说影视化的改编，一般是从故事情节、人物形象、表达的情感与营造的氛围入手。除了对小说改编的方式，作品播出后的效益也是制作方需要考虑的一个因素，而且也是主要目的。改编的质量是收益的保障，这就需要影视工作者秉持创作的热情，将原作品与影视技术相结合，进行合理的改编并形成良好的剧本；反过来作家要切忌为了迎合作品的影视化而创作，因为这将在一定程度上使作品本身的文学内涵丧失。当改编的质量取得优秀的效果时，就会迎来观众的赞赏，因此，影视剧既要把受众脑海中的想象转化为具体的形象，也创造经济效益；而当观众看到影视剧把小说中的形象呈现得符合自己的期待时，其精神上也会受到鼓舞和感染。

2. 小说与影视剧的特质及其在作品中的表现

2.1 小说：善于情感的表达

小说作为一种文学形式，理所当然具有一些文学的功能特质：叙事、抒情、反映现实。同时，它也是一种文字信息的表达与传递的载体：通过情节的跌宕起伏，展现故事的发展脉络。

与影视剧呈现在眼前的画面相比，文字可以更好地抒发人物的情感，表现人物的内心世界。例如，在意识流小说中，人物的思绪流动与遐想没有太多的规律可循，要把这种场景通过镜头呈现在观众面前，并非那样容易。在弗吉尼亚·伍尔芙的《达洛维夫人》(*Mrs. Dalloway*)

中，女主人公的无限思绪和打破时空的思维跳跃，在字里行间仍表达的是同一个人物的所思所想与情感的流露；而根据该小说改编的电影《时时刻刻》(*The Hours*)则分别采用三个场景，把女主人公不同时空的思绪分开阐述，虽然这种处理方式比较巧妙，也便于观众理解和接受，但也同时割裂了人物作为个体的完整性。

小说通过文字的形式，也可以更清晰地表达人物的心理状态，记录心理活动的轨迹。在《三体》原著中，当倒计时在汪淼的视网膜上出现时，他的内心犹如巨浪起伏：恐惧和好奇在他的心里交替出现着，他一方面急于知道倒计时的尽头是什么，另一方面又想尽办法让它在眼前消失。当发现所做的一切都是徒劳后，字里行间描述的都是他的恐惧和无助。

"倒计时的尽头是什么？"汪淼无力地问。

"不知道。"说了这简短的三个字后，电话挂断了。

是什么？也许是自己的死亡，像杨冬那样；也许是一场像前几年印度洋海啸那样的大灾难，谁也不会将其与自己的纳米研究项目相联系（由此联想到，以前的每一次大灾难，包括两次世界大战，是否都是一次次幽灵倒计时的尽头？都有一个谁都想不到的像自己这样的人要负的最终责任）；也许是全世界的彻底毁灭，在这个变态的宇宙中，那倒对谁都是一种解脱……有一点可以肯定，不管幽灵倒计时的尽头是什么，在这剩下的千余个小时中，对尽头的猜测将像恶魔那样残酷地折磨他，最后在精神上彻底摧毁他（刘慈欣，2008：92-93）。

通常影视剧表现人物的精神状态与心理感受是比较间接的，观众需要通过对话、台词或者神情来推测。在小说中，作者可以把人物的思绪跃然纸上，包括说话与行动的情绪，以及内心的悸动，读者都可以较为准确地把控，捕捉人物的心理状态。

2.2 影视剧：视觉与技术的呈现

自影视剧诞生以来，其技术获得了显著的飞跃，如今甚至可以为观众提供沉浸式的观影体验。与小说相比，影视剧的优势则明显得多。

首先，影视剧的视觉冲击是小说无可企及的。小说的情节脉络需要读者自己进行梳理，而且人物的形象性格全靠脑海中的想象。而影视剧可以将抽象的人物形象具体化，通过进度条来把握故事发展的进度。此外，一些科幻电影中呈现的 3D（三维）和 VR（虚拟现实）效果，是科幻小说所远远无法达到的。对于像《三体》这样的一部科幻小说，读者对书中很多画面只能停留在脑海里，无法将其具象化，但影视技术可以比较容易做到这一点，当特效在屏幕前播放时，画面就会瞬间印刻在观众脑海中了。

其次，影视剧的剪辑可以让观众更好地掌握时间线与信息。影视剧的蒙太奇手法能够把不同的场景连接在一起，实现镜头的无缝拼接，进行多个故事线的平行组合。采用不一样的拍摄手法和角度则可以用不同形式讲述同一个故事，使得呈现的方式更加多样化。良好的拼接手段会让观众有沉浸式的体验，适当的剪辑处理可以制造悬念，吸引观众的注意力。

另外，影视剧可以采用多样化的形式，如电影、电视剧、动漫、纪录片、综艺等，能够最大限度呈现最为合适的场景。倘若宫崎骏的电影采用真人演绎，可能精彩度会大打折扣；如果长剧本限定在两个小时的时长内，那讲述的故事很可能会让人大失所望。当然，有些影视剧蓝本可以采用多种形式呈现，而小说只能通过文字这种单一的形式呈现。

最后，影视剧也是集音乐、美术、摄影等多种形式于一体的一种综合艺术（黄文泉，2003：67）。影视剧需要配乐来展现剧情的起承转合，需要美术的指导表现不同的视觉效果以达到大众的审美标准，需要拍摄的取景方式与角度调整来表达演绎的惊艳。

2.3 双向互动

即使影视剧和小说各有特点与优势，但也不乏一些共通性。二者都是叙述故事的形式，因而具有较强的叙事性。相比小说的叙事性，影视剧则更胜一筹，因为它用镜头呈现出来的基本上都是在叙事，而小说在进入正题时会有一些背景的交代、场景的铺垫描写等，为主线提供补充和辅助作用。

与影视剧相比，文学是一种发展更为久远的叙事形式，因此形成了较为完善的叙事理论。一方面，当小说作为影视剧的蓝本历史时，前者为后者提供了丰富的改编题材和拍摄灵感；另一方面，小说以其成熟的叙事理论指导着影视剧理论的发展。基本上，影视剧的脉络也是遵循"序幕—发展—冲突—高潮—结局"的结构（万宇翔，2022: 147），使得情节有起伏。因此，小说和影视剧的脉络与手法可以说是双向互动、相辅相成的。

3. 《三体》的影视化改编

由于文字和视频是两种不同的媒介，信息传达的方式也会有所差异。《三体》电视剧对于原著的情节基本上没有太多的改动，反而把部分原著中描述较少但起着不可忽视作用的角色进行了详细的展现，使得整个故事线更加完整，同时采用了不同的技术手段和效果处理方式，让作品传达出的氛围和情感得到了升华。

3.1 情节的改编

对《三体》的第一次电视剧改编，导演秉持着严谨的态度，充分尊重原著的发展脉络。小说作为一种文字性的信息媒介，其场景具有一定的跳跃性，部分细节可能未必会交代清楚。而《三体》电视剧在遵循原著情节的基础上，进行了一定的顺序调整，使得前后衔接更连贯。例如叶文洁的往事和《三体》游戏的场景在原著中是穿插出现的，会让读者顿时难以在两个时空切换，而且这两个场景彼此之间的跳跃性较强，但关联性并非太大。而电视剧中把两个场景分开展现，尤其是《三体》游戏中的虚拟场景，呈现出恰如其分的效果，可以说是把想象变成现实了，同时又厘清了各自的故事线，从而让观众非常容易接受和理解了。

叶文洁的父亲叶哲泰是一条暗线，父亲之前的学生杨卫宁是看在他老师的面子上才给了叶文洁一个赎罪的机会，她才能来到红岸基地。究其原因，笔者认为可能是这部分情节可以点到为止，对整个故事所起的也只是补充作用，是叶文洁往事的一小部分。由此可见，电视剧版《三体》注重情节的详略得当，这是深深吸引和打动观众的原因所在，也正是它的精彩之处。

3.2 人物形象的改编

对影视剧来说，在人物塑造方面有着更高的要求，因为一个形象呈现在观众眼前是瞬时的，会顿时使观众形成一个总体的印象。而要通过文字描述来展现人物的气质，需要导演对于形象的构建以及角色的选取与契合度有一定的掌控能力，才能创作出符合观众期待的作品。

原著中描写潘寒这个人物的笔墨较少，他只是出现在《三体》游戏网友聚会的现场，而且也没有过多交代他的身份和用意。作为地球三体组织降临派的领导者，他还是地球环保组织的成员，而且也是串起《三体》游戏和科学边界的重要人物，这些都是电视剧版进行的补充和延伸，而原著中并没有展开过多的描述。此外，为了更鲜明地呈现这个人物的形象，还增加了慕星这个媒体记者的角色,她负责传播和报道有关三体的信息,让潘寒的这条故事线更加完整了。虽然潘寒惨死在三体组织聚会的现场,但他无疑为剧情的发展起到了推波助澜的作用。

另一个鲜活的人物形象是警官史强的助手徐冰冰:她行事果断,逻辑缜密,调查有理有据,被史强称为"以一抵十"的得力助手。而她在剧中也是一身英姿飒爽,给人雷厉风行的感觉。原著中对她的描写虽然是只言片语,可在剧中成为不可忽视的一员,没有她的协助,史强和汪淼就难以在短时间内获取有用信息,也很难开展他们的调查工作。

在阅读原著的时候,笔者一直在脑海里构建叶文洁的形象:一位历经沧桑,与三体人有过交涉的革命女性,抑或是德高望重、知识渊博的天体物理学教授,究竟是什么样的呢?她是一位具有多重性格的人物,作为读者很难从字里行间描绘其具体的形象。而荧幕中的叶文洁第一次登场就给笔者留下了深刻的印象,而且这种印象是相当具有震慑力的:无论是外貌神态,还是内在气质,都满足了笔者的期待,也就不难理解为什么能捕获观众的眼球。

3.3 情感表达与氛围的改变

表达情感是传达作品主题的重要一环,而这也离不开氛围的营造,从而需要采取一定的技术手段。如果氛围感营造得有代入感,会非常容易打动观众,引发人们的关注。而恰恰这又是一种无形的东西,要求剧组人员掌握相应的技巧,配合原著的情节加以处理。

最典型的就是剧中《三体》游戏的场景,CG(computer graphics,计算机绘图)特效的使用为剧中的视觉效果增添了不少特色。在以往的电视剧中,几乎没有在真人台词对话的剧情中穿插 CG 特效的,CG 特效在《三体》电视剧中的使用也算是一种全新的尝试,而且在剧情中的导入也达到了良好的效果,无论是游戏中的秦始皇、墨子、冯·诺依曼等人物的形象,还是原著中场景的还原,都在很大程度上满足了观众的预期。

原著中的古筝行动也是比较难以呈现的情节,这无疑是一个庞大的工程,光凭读者的想象也能够预料到这需要耗费巨大的精力。但剧组采取了真实场景和 CG 特效相结合的方式,让一个跟"审判日"号差不多的船体在水面上航行,在释放"古筝"和切割船体时运用 CG 特效。更让人觉得有诚意的是,剧中的船在切割之后的状态是一堆堆用挤压机碾压出来的钢,这在特效行业里被称作"刚体的动力学模型",而最后呈现出来的效果也确实令笔者震撼不已。

叶文洁的情感线对于塑造这个形象也具有重要作用。她对于红岸基地政委雷志成的隐忍,对于丈夫杨卫宁的决绝,以及将两人陷害后的云淡风轻,都需要恰如其分的氛围营造去刻画人物的内心。剧中采用较为悲壮的配乐和辽阔的视角,描述叶文洁站在红岸之巅内心的百感交集,那一幕的壮烈感留在笔者的脑海中挥之不去,而且耐人寻味:究竟是怎样强大的内心,才使得她能对所经历的一切都泰然自若?

另外,汪淼所看到的宇宙闪烁还有最后出现的三体人形象都经过技术手段在屏幕上呈现出来了,原著中只是一幅幅仅凭想象才能在脑海中浮现出的画面,在屏幕面前却变成了实实在在的情节,所以说影视科技真是一种神奇的东西,倘若运用得当,会引发观众产生强烈的共鸣。

3.4 《三体》改编的必要性

《三体》电视剧的改编无疑是小说影视化一次较为成功的尝试。在此之前，笔者抱着怀疑的态度，认为要把《三体》这样一个复杂的故事讲述清楚，并且还要拍摄成影视剧，实在是强人所难。但对于像《三体》这样的作品来说，影视化也是其合理的归宿，因为原著中的场景如果只是停留在文字层面，难免会让人觉得不够过瘾了。

影视剧是呈现科幻小说情节的绝佳方式，不仅可以使用影视技术造成视觉冲击，把原著字里行间的表达栩栩如生地展现在屏幕上，也可以满足读者对小说中场景的想象，使其更容易把握故事的发展脉络，获取更为完整的情节和异乎寻常的体验。《三体》电视剧通过把小说中抽象的人物形象具体化，把硬核的物理知识通俗化，把穿插的故事线生动化，实现了向观众传达原著情感的目的。

影视剧能够呈现出小说中的庞大叙事脉络。作为一部有着庞大叙事脉络的科幻小说，《三体》的框架构建必须足够坚实，才能使故事稳定发展，其影视化的改编也遵循了这条原则，为后篇《黑暗森林》和《死神永生》打下了良好的根基。虽然第一部交代的都是故事的背景和缘起，但在整个故事线中也是重要的一环，正所谓环环相扣，有了先前的铺垫，才会使整个故事达到前呼后应的效果，也能承接起交叉的不同情节，保证叙事的完整性。

4. 结语：影视剧创作的文学立场

面对种类繁多的影视剧，观众有了多样选择。影视文化在造成巨大冲击的同时，也带来了许多商业效益（王静，2018：118）。因此，从事影视行业的人员争相寻求更多、更好的剧本，而小说成为他们大多数时候的首选。但为了迎合市场的商业性需求，在将小说改编成影视剧的过程中，丧失作品原来风格的现象可谓屡见不鲜，有些甚至是滥竽充数。

同时，作家也经常面临创作的瓶颈，好的故事往往需要时间的沉淀。这就使得市场上出现原创剧本供求不平衡的状况。因此，个别创作者也会为了能尽快将自己的作品拍摄成影视剧，开始向影视剧本的创作倾斜，但改编后的效果也经常是不尽如人意。

由此可见，为了打造高质量的影视剧改编，需要影视从业者和创作者的双向努力。对于创作者来说，要坚守自己的文学立场，保持充分的创作热情，而并非为了迎合作品被改编成影视剧而创作，否则就降低了作品本身的文学价值，只看到眼前的商业利益，而未考虑长足的发展。如当下众多的网络写手，只追求更新的速度和数量，忽视了作品本身的质量，其作品会随着时间的流逝逐渐湮没在岁月的尘埃中。文学诞生于影视剧之前，千百年来它赋予读者的精神意义是影视剧所无法替代的，创作者应当明白文学的价值与意义并不一定是要通过改编成影视剧才能实现的；相反，小说本身就具有文学价值，它融入了创作者的灵感与心血，也是作者对现实或是内心世界的写照。

对于影视人员来说，并不能一味地追求经济利益。因为受众的品位是难以调和的，如果拍摄出来的作品他们不买账，那么创作这些影视剧的人员总有一天也会丧失在影视市场中的一席之地。所以他们应不断创作出精良的作品，在对小说内容充分把握的同时，呈现方式也需要符合受众的期待。《三体》就是一个不错的例子，制作团队从剧本开发到拍摄完成花费了四年多的时间，其中多次邀请原著作者刘慈欣坐镇指导。因此，影视从业者需要借助相应的科技手段，掌握影视剧呈现的技巧，既不破坏原作品的意境与文学性，又要采取恰如其分的处理方式，在综合考虑多种因素，尤其是细节的前提下，逐步打磨剧本，才能创作出优质、受观众喜爱的作品。

参考文献

[1] 黄书泉，2003. 论小说的影视改编[J]. 安徽大学学报（2）：67-74.

[2] 刘慈欣，2008. 三体[M]. 重庆：重庆出版社.

[3] 万宇翔，2022. 《本杰明·巴顿奇事》电影改编研究[J]. 戏剧之家（29）：146-149.

[4] 王静，2018. 《别让我走》：从小说到电影的转换[J]. 电影文学（24）：118-120.

浅析莫迪亚诺《青春咖啡馆》中的创伤书写

汪鑫波

1. 引言

帕特里克·莫迪亚诺是法国当代最伟大的作家之一，迄今为止已出版三十多部作品，斩获十余项文学大奖。2014 年，莫迪亚诺荣获诺贝尔文学奖，诺奖评委会称"他运用追忆的艺术，写出人类最不可捉摸的命运，并揭示了德占时期法国社会的众生相"。莫迪亚诺的早期作品（如《星形广场》《夜巡》《环形大道》）均以德占时期为背景，聚焦法国犹太人的身份问题，而在 20 世纪 70 年代中期以后，他的作品（如《一度青春》《往事如烟》《时光》《青春咖啡馆》等）主题逐渐转向对人类困境的探索和思考，他更多地书写个体生命在历史长河中的渺小性和荒诞性，有时甚至会走向虚无。《青春咖啡馆》便是他创作后期的代表作品之一，被法国《读书》杂志誉为"镶嵌在莫迪亚诺无与伦比的丰碑式全部作品上的一颗璀璨夺目的宝石。"（金龙格，2010：278）该书的中文版译者金龙格写道："小说以一种既写实又神秘的笔调，交织谱出青春岁月的青涩、惶惑、焦虑、寂寞、孤独与莫名愁绪，描写了以一个弱女子从不断探寻生命真谛到最终放弃生命追寻的悲剧命运……全书充满一种挥之不去的忧伤情调。"（金龙格，2010：287）小说以 20 世纪 60 年代的法国巴黎为故事背景，描述了一群 18 到 25 岁左右的年轻人聚集在孔代咖啡馆中享受着艺术与文学的庇护，他们从不考虑未来，过着放荡不羁、今朝有酒今朝醉的生活。在咖啡馆的常客中有一位光彩夺目的女子，她总是坐在最里端的位置，很少与人交谈，甚至别人连她真正的名字都无从得知。故事围绕这位年轻女子的失踪展开，通过四个叙述者的讲述，将她的一生经历娓娓道来。

国内外文学评论界对于莫迪亚诺的关注始于 20 世纪 80 年代后期，相较于国内，国外的莫迪亚诺相关研究较为成熟和丰富。2000 年以前，国外学者的研究主要集中在主题学和创作手法两个方面，其中比较重要的著作有科林·尼特贝克和佩内洛普·休斯顿合著的《帕特里克·莫迪亚诺：身份的迷失》（*Patrick Modiano: Pièces d'identité*，1986），这是第一部关于莫迪亚诺及其小说的研究专著，对莫迪亚诺系列小说的主题和写作手法进行了探究。此外，朱尔斯·贝德纳（Jules Bedner）主编的论文集《帕特里克·莫迪亚诺》（Patrick Modiano，1993）对莫迪亚诺小说的模糊性和小说中反复出现的特征进行了总结研究。而 2000 年以后，国外学者开始结合后现代理论、视觉艺术理论等展开对莫迪亚诺小说的研究，并对作品中的地理要素、女性形象等方面产生了浓厚的兴趣。如安·L. 墨菲（Ann L. Murphy）在《帕特里克·莫迪亚诺〈暗店街〉中的迷宫形象》（"The Figure of the Labyrinth in Patrick Modiano's *Rue des Boutiques Obscures*"，2003）一文中，从序列、符号、代码等角度对文本加以解读，指出后现代性与莫迪亚诺的联系及对其写作的影响。米歇尔·特兰瑟姆在《摄影和后记忆：想象莫迪亚诺的〈多拉·布吕代〉和〈暗店街〉的过去》（"Photography and Postmemory: Imagining the Past in Modiano's *Dora Bruder* and *Missing Person*"，2017）一文中认为莫迪亚诺通过想象的后记忆重建来再现他的角色缺失的过去,阐明了摄影对恢复记忆的重要意义及其与一代人想象中的创伤的关系。

国内莫迪亚诺的研究起步较晚,20世纪90年代左右还处在早期译介阶段,研究程度尚浅,但在其2014年获得诺贝尔文学奖后迎来一波研究热潮。国内学者的研究主要集中在主题和叙事特征两大方面,厦门大学的冯寿农和武汉大学的周婷可称为国内对莫迪亚诺及其小说研究的代表人物。1997年,冯寿农出版了著作《帕特里克·莫迪亚诺小说世界里的身份问题》,并发表了《荒诞与现实——兼评莫迪亚诺的小说》(袁文卓、徐梅,2015)、《论莫迪阿诺小说世界中的全息结构》(1989)、《莫迪亚诺的结构主义诗学——评他的抗战文学"占领三部曲"》(2008)等多篇论文,此外还以第二作者身份发表了《寻根与遗忘——试论莫迪亚诺<暗店街>的文学主题》(2015)和《试论莫迪亚诺"既视式"的记忆艺术》(2017),对莫迪亚诺的小说叙事策略及主题均进行了较为深度的研究;而周婷在《法国研究》上发表了多篇与莫迪亚诺研究相关文章,对莫迪亚诺小说中的寓言、人物的失语与沉默、蝴蝶意象的应用等进行了具体的阐释,她的《论莫迪亚诺小说中的神秘机制》(2012)是目前中国知网唯一可考的莫迪亚诺研究的相关博士论文,现已作为专著出版。

关于莫迪亚诺小说中的创伤书写,国内外均有学者展开研究。20世纪的人类历史充满着灾难性的事件,人们在20世纪经历了两次世界大战、种族大屠杀、核爆炸、恐怖袭击等毁灭性的苦难,这些经历给人们留下了无法言说却又不可磨灭的创伤。莫迪亚诺于1945年出生在法国巴黎,那时二战刚刚结束,战争留下的痕迹还未彻底消除,而法国犹太人在德占时期遭遇的种族大屠杀也依然历历在目,战争的记忆、犹太人的历史以及不幸的童年经历(父母缺席、兄弟早逝)共同构成了莫迪亚诺的独特创伤经验。近年来,有关历史书写、大屠杀书写的研究不在少数,像莫迪亚诺一样书写人类历史和种族大屠杀、揭示人类困境与命运的作家得到了越来越多的关注。莫迪亚诺本人的创伤经验为学者从创伤书写的角度研究其作品提供了有力的支撑。国外研究方面,有研究者从莫迪亚诺的《多拉·布吕代》(1997)开始,借助"后记忆""多向记忆"等理论对三代大屠杀作家的大屠杀书写进行分析,也有学者从空间的角度而非创伤理论的角度考察莫迪亚诺小说中的创伤书写。国内研究方面,既考察了莫迪亚诺小说中的大屠杀创伤书写,如刘曦、王大智在《空白的伤口:论莫迪亚诺小说中的大屠杀创伤书写》(2020)一文中从作品本身的空白特质出发,从叙事空白、空间空白、记忆空白三个维度解读莫迪亚诺笔下空白的伤口,从而阐释莫迪亚诺创伤叙事的伦理使命;又对莫迪亚诺小说中的主题进行总体把握,进而探讨作者的创伤经验,如孟天娇在《论莫迪亚诺小说中的逃离情结》(2016)一文中认为莫迪亚诺有一种逃离情结,而"情结起源于创伤",从而分析出该情结是在莫迪亚诺的个人成长经历、犹太人的文化传统和法国社会思潮的共同作用下产生的。杨晓青在《论帕特里克·莫迪亚诺小说中的身份主题》(2016)一文中提出莫迪亚诺小说中的主人公经常出现"父亲缺失"的现象归因于莫迪亚诺童年时期父亲的严厉专制造成的心灵创伤,对莫氏作品中的身份缺失和利用失忆逃避创伤的方式进行了系统的考查。

综上所述,目前已经有不少研究者关注到莫迪亚诺本人的创伤经验及对其小说创作的影响,从后现代理论视角或小说主题对其作品中的创伤现象进行阐释,但鲜少从小说的具体文本出发深度挖掘小说中的创伤书写。身份和记忆是贯穿莫迪亚诺小说创作的主题,而隐藏在主题背后的是一种追寻,对身份的追寻、对自我的追寻、对逝去的时光的追寻……这种追寻的过程或许也正是作者尝试正视创伤、表征创伤,从而疗治创伤的过程,因此展开对莫迪亚诺作品中创伤书写的研究,有助于我们更好地了解作者的创作思想以及他对历史、对人类困境的独特思考。目前，国内有关《青春咖啡馆》的研究主要是借助国际情景主义以及后现代主义理论进行阐释，而本文以《青春咖啡馆》为例，从文本出发探寻作者自身的创伤经验，从而梳理作品中呈现的创伤书写及创伤疗治的方式。

2.《青春咖啡馆》中的创伤书写及疗伤策略

《青春咖啡馆》的故事发生在 20 世纪 60 年代初的巴黎，作者在开篇引用了居伊·德波的一段话："À la moitié du chemin de la vraie vie, nous étions environnés d'une sombre mélancolie, qu'ont exprimée tant de mots railleurs et tristes, dans le café de la jeunesse perdue."（德波，2006：3）金龙格将其译为"在真实生活之旅的中途，我们被一缕绵长的愁绪包围，在挥霍青春的咖啡馆里，愁绪从那么多戏谑的和伤感的话语中流露出来。"（莫迪亚诺，2010）这段话为全文奠定了一种感情基调，也点明这部作品题目的来源。居伊·德波是情境主义国际运动的代表人物之一，情境主义国际是 20 世纪 50 年代至 70 年代席卷欧洲大陆的一次重要社会文化革命思潮。在二战以后，科技快速发展，人们的物质生活展现出空前的丰富，商业和消费开始占据人们的日常生活，随之而来的却是精神上的迷茫和贫乏，情境主义国际运动应运而生，呼吁人们用创造生活取代"被动生活"，旨在"改造社会和日常生活……战胜被动，才有可能恢复现有的存在，并通过积极的'情境'创造和技术利用来提高人类生活。"（德波，2006：37）居伊·德波在其著作《景观社会》一书中提出"在现代生产条件无处不在的社会，生活本身展现为景观的庞大堆聚，直接存在的一切全都转化为一个表象"（德波，2006：3），剥削阶级通过对工作和自由时间的商品化和异化，即刻意营造景观，宣传现代化的生活方式而获得对被剥削阶级的统治权，分散人们的注意力，掐灭人的创造性与革命性，从而掩盖剥削和压迫的强制性。德波（2006）认为在景观社会里，人们因对景观的迷恋而丧失自己对本真生活的渴望和要求，而资本家则依靠控制景观的生成和变换来操纵整个社会生活。人最终从占有的主体变成了被动的客体，实际上人被物质所占有，因此形成了经济上的富裕和精神上的贫乏之间的鲜明对比。《青春咖啡馆》中故事的发生背景正是情境主义国际运动最活跃的时期，因此作者在开篇引用这段话无可厚非，且事实上故事中的年轻人正是按照情境主义国际的规则生活着，他们无拘无束，放荡不羁，四处漂泊，居无定所，时而会聚集在巴黎塞纳河左岸的孔代咖啡馆里谈论着艺术和文学，却从不去关心和谈论未来，在咖啡馆的墙上，"永远也别工作"的标语十分醒目。本文试图从小说文本所呈现的创伤书写来探寻背后隐藏的莫迪亚诺的创伤经验。

逃离是受创主体在创伤压力下的常见反应。在《青春咖啡馆》中，主人公露姬一生都在不断地逃离，小说用四位叙述者共同讲述露姬在逃离中寻找幸福但最终无果走向死亡的悲剧故事，这四位叙述者分别是巴黎高等矿业大学的大学生、受露姬丈夫委托寻找露姬的私家侦探、露姬本人和露姬的情人罗兰。在大学生的叙述里，他对露姬的最初印象是"她到孔代这里，是来避难的，仿佛她想躲避什么东西，想从一个危险中逃脱"（莫迪亚诺，2010：3），在私家侦探的描述中，"……未成年流浪……从那以后，愈发不可收拾，再也没有人能把她拦住，在茫茫黑夜里向西漫游……结婚之后再次出逃，但这一次却是朝左岸逃，就好像过河之后，她就摆脱了迫在眉睫的危险，并得到了保护。"（莫迪亚诺，2010：53）在露姬自述的篇章里，她甚至这样说道："只有在逃跑的时候，我才真的是我自己。我仅有的那些美好的回忆都跟逃跑或者离家出走连在一起。但是，生活总会重占上风。"（莫迪亚诺，2010：82）显然，露姬的一次次的"逃离"以失败告终,但不断出逃的露姬形象与莫迪亚诺的童年记忆是密切相关的。

创伤书写源自对创伤经验的一种再现,进行创伤书写的创作者可以通过写作过程来唤醒内心深处沉睡的创伤记忆。在莫迪亚诺2014年诺贝尔文学奖的获奖演说中,他这样说道:"童年生活的几个片段是我日后作品的胚胎。小时候我常常远离父母,被托付给他们的朋友照看,但我对这些照看我的人一无所知……过了很久之后,我的童年才让我觉得像一个谜,令我困惑不解……仿佛写作和想象可以帮助我揭开这些谜团,窥探这些秘密。"(黄荭,2015:64)小说的主人公露姬也有着同样的命运,她并不知道自己的父亲是谁,从小和母亲一起生活,但母亲为了维持生计不得不选择夜晚在红磨坊工作,因此露姬的童年中母亲的角色基本上是缺位的,不幸福的童年会导致极大的孤独感和不安全感。莫迪亚诺也说道:"约莫九岁、十岁的光景,有时候我会独自出去溜达,虽然怕迷路,但我依然越走越远,直到塞纳河右岸陌生的街区……刚进入青春期,我就努力克服自己的恐惧,开始在夜里游荡,坐地铁去更遥远的街区。"(莫迪亚诺,2015:64)露姬亦是如此,在母亲去工作的夜晚,她便会一人偷偷跑出去在街上"流浪",还因此两次被抓到警察局询问。

遗忘或记忆空白是莫迪亚诺小说中人物创伤经验的表征之一,人物因为遗忘而丢失身份,从而丧失生命的基点。在露姬叙述的部分,她有过数次遗忘的表现。

"我记不起来了。更确切地说,某些细节回想起来的时候已经乱成一团了。五年来,我再也不愿意去回想所有这一切。只要出租车爬上那条街,只要再见到那些熠熠闪烁的招牌——"夜行者"、皮埃罗……我已经记不起拉罗什福柯街的那家酒吧叫什么名字了……有时出现的是记忆的黑洞。之后,又有一些细节陡地浮现在脑海里,这些细节非常清晰,清晰得都没有什么意义了……一些细节把另外一些细节给掩盖了,那些细节更难回忆起来。"(莫迪亚诺,2010:70,73)

因为遗忘所造成的记忆空白,回忆变成了一个个断裂的、非连续的片段,所以莫迪亚诺总是不断地想要去解开这些谜团。

"有些人的童年是合乎逻辑的,容易理解的。而我的童年是被割裂的,是一个个我难以拼接的凌乱片段。我的童年回忆缺少逻辑性,因为有太多的游离,太多我搞不清为什么的地点和人的变化。所有这一切都让我觉得迷惑。"(艾克、郑立敏,2015:168)

"我感觉在今天,记忆远不如它自身那么确定,要不停地抵抗失忆和忘却。因为透过这层覆盖一切的遗忘,我们只能捕捉到一些过去的碎片、断裂的痕迹,飞逝的、不可捉摸的人类命运。不过,这或许就是小说家的使命,在遗忘的白纸上,重现几个模糊的字迹,就像那些迷失在大海中漂浮着的冰川。"(黄荭,2015:67)

面对创伤,莫迪亚诺在小说中提到了两种疗治创伤的尝试。第一种尝试是建立"固定点",试图保存记忆、抵抗失忆。在小说中,这个概念是由孔代咖啡馆的常客保罗提出的,他试图建立一本花名册,记下三年以来光顾咖啡馆的所有客人的名字以及他们每次进店的日期和确切的时刻,甚至想要把"在某些时刻围着一盏灯转悠的那些飞蛾铭记下来,以免被人遗忘。"(莫迪亚诺,2010:9)他坚信"必须在大都市的漩涡中心寻找一些固定点。"(莫迪亚诺,2010:9)保罗在出国之前将花名册交给了大学生,而大学生则发出了这样的质疑:"要找到一个人一生的线索,他真的觉得一个名字和一个地址就足够了吗?"(莫迪亚诺,2010:12)保罗能做的,只不过是将别人的影子固定几秒钟罢了。在熙来攘往、川流不息的人潮中,尽管最后这些人和记忆都会销声匿迹,但我们仍然希望可以时不时记住一副面孔,哪怕可以固定的记忆只有短短几秒钟。我们无法阻挡汹涌的人潮将我们卷走、让我们失去控制，但或许当我们试图去与他人建立关系、编织一张关系网时，那些随机性的相聚会变得更加固定一些。如果说人的一生都活在这样一种漂浮的状态里，那么当孤独的人们相遇时，或许以为可以抓住彼此，将彼此连接在一起，以留下星星点点的回忆，来抵抗这种处在浩荡人潮中的茫然和无措，甚至与别人偶然间的邂逅与交流，都会被视为自己茫茫人生中的一根救命稻草。露姬与母亲之间充满障碍与失语的苍白交流让她早已习惯缄默不语，在她第一次被带到警局时，她敏感地察觉到警察之间以"你"（tu）相称，警察最开始询问她时对她以"您"（vous）称呼，在提出送她回家的时候使用的是"你"，在最后和她告别时又使用了"您"。这样一个简单的人称变化却在露姬的心中激起了波澜，她在被以"你"相称时产生了一种特别的感觉，或许是一种"被亲近"的温暖。然而，最后的"您"又让她回到现实，在警察走后，她写道："我感到一种恐惧……我感觉从今以后要独自一人面对人生，无依无靠，没有人来帮我。无论是我母亲，还是其他人。"而在她第二次被带到警局时，她意外地收获了警察的"关心"，尽管这种关心只是警察例行的询问，但依然让露姬感受到前所未有的温暖，她逐渐放下戒备与警察交谈起来，并且在说完后感到如释重负。

"倘若所有那一切都白纸黑字地写了下来，那也就意味着都结束了，就像人死了会在他的坟墓上刻上名字和日期一样……我从来都没有机会和任何人说话。所有这些话语从我这里脱口而出时，那是何等的解脱啊……我的一段人生结束了，这段人生是命运强加到我头上的。"（莫迪亚诺，2010：65）

小说中莫迪亚诺进行创伤疗治的第二个尝试便是"逃逸线"，小说中的人物在其精神与感受、所处的地理空间及日常行为等各方面尝试逃离，甚至渴望一直保持逃离状态，从而在对日常生活的抗拒中接近自由的"逃逸线"。"逃逸线"是法国哲学家德勒兹经常使用的概念，在其著作《千座高原》（*A Thousand Plateaus*，1987）中，他详细区分了三种类型的"线"：坚硬线、柔软线和逃逸线。坚硬线指质量线，透过二元对立所建构僵化的常态，比方说人在坚硬线的控制下，就会循规蹈矩地完成人生的一个个阶段，从小学到大学，到拿工资生活，到退休；柔软线指分子线，搅乱了线性和常态，没有目的和意向；逃逸线完全脱离质量线，由破裂到断裂，主体则在难以控制的流变多样中成为碎片，这也是人们的解放之线，只有在这条线上人们才会感受到自由，感受到人生，但也是最危险之线，因为它们最真实。小说中露姬的死亡就是彻底追求"逃逸线"的结果，她认为只有在逃跑时才能真正找到自己。由于缺乏母亲的陪伴，露姬的成长过程是孤独的，青春期时的逃跑或许正是对这种孤独的逃离。成年以后，露姬与相识两个月的男人快速结婚，或许以为这样就可以结束自己长期以来的孤独状态，却发现自己的丈夫对自己的内心和自己想要的生活一无所知，孤独并没有消失，反而变本加厉，于是她又逃走了，在丈夫的家里她甚至几乎没有留下任何痕迹。她有了情人，并且成为孔代咖啡馆的常客，但其他人对她的过去甚至对她的名字都一无所知，露姬这个名字其实是咖啡馆的人给她的命名，但却能够让她感到放松，或许这种没有任何羁绊的交往才能使她感到安心。此外露姬还遇到过一个名叫亚娜特的女孩，并开始和她一起吸食一种被称作"雪"的白色粉末，吸食过后露姬说道："那东西让我产生一种神清气爽和轻松自如的感觉，我坚信在大街上侵袭我的恐惧和迷茫的感觉可能永远也不会在我身上再现。"（莫迪亚诺，2010：79）显然，这种短暂的快感让露姬以为自己可以摆脱长期困扰自己的恐惧和痛苦，然而她又一次失败了。在书店邂逅的陌生人向她发出的询问"您找到您的幸福了吗？"（莫迪亚诺，2010：81）让她感到短暂的沉醉与快乐，因此她与康特尔酒吧的那些人断绝了往来，并且她发现每当她与什么人断绝往来的时候，她便可以再一次体会到这种沉醉。如果将最初的逃离视作对创伤的应激反应，那么在不断的逃离中，露姬已经在不知不觉中展开了对于真正的自由，即"逃逸线"的无限追求，在不断追求、无限接近"逃逸线"的过程中，露姬感受到了自由，感受到了真实，感受到了解脱，可惜最终，也正是这危险的"逃逸线"让露姬放弃了自己的生命。在小说最后，露姬仿佛给自己"打气"说道："Ça y est. Laisse-toi aller."（译作：都准备好了，你尽管去吧）（2010：132），随后从窗子上一跃而下，结束了自己的生命。或许这就是她对"逃逸线"最后一次也是最极致的一次追求，也为读者留下了一种挥之不去的悲伤和哀愁情绪。"那么，您找到您的幸福了吗？"这句话或许不只是对露姬的提问，也是留给所有读者的思考：我们作为个体在历史长河中是如此的渺小和微不足道，人生寻寻觅觅，危机和恐慌时时袭来，在时代大潮中的我们总是身不由己，我们该如何去把握自己的人生？我们是否应该同时又如何继续对身份的确认和对生命的追寻？

3. 结语

在《青春咖啡馆》中，我们既看到了小说主人公的创伤表征，从而挖掘出蕴藏在文本中的莫迪亚诺本人的创伤经验，同时也发现了莫迪亚诺对创伤的治疗尝试。莫迪亚诺在诺贝尔文学奖获奖演说中称自己是"战争的孩子。"（黄荭，2015：59）的确，个人的童年创伤、犹太人民族的历史创伤、法国的国家战争创伤以及现代人的荒诞困境共同构成了莫迪亚诺的独特创伤经验。记忆和追寻是贯穿莫迪亚诺三十余部作品的主题，而在这主题背后隐藏的正是他对于创伤的书写。面对创伤，莫迪亚诺提出的两种疗治创伤的尝试分别为抵抗遗忘的固定点和忘却逃离的"逃逸线"，但最终是否真的可以使创伤得到疗治，他并没有给出明确的答案。但可以肯定的是，莫迪亚诺从未放弃对人类困境的反思和对疗治创伤的不断尝试，他将自己的创伤经验隐藏到文字的背后，在此过程中他的痛苦得到疏解，读者也可以产生共鸣和思考，这或许就是莫迪亚诺的作品的意义所在，正如加缪在《西西弗神话》（2012）中所说："重要的不是治愈，而是带着病痛活下去。"

参考文献

[1] BEDNER J, 1993. Patrick Modiano: etudes reunies par[M]. Amsterdam: Editions Rodopi.

[2] DELEUZE G, GUATTARI F, 1987. A thousand plateaus: capitalism and schizophrenia[M]. Minneapolis: University of Minnesota Press.

[3] HUESTON P, NETTELBECK C, 1986. Patrick Modiano: pièces d'identité[M]. Paris: Lettres Modernes.

[4] MODIANO P, 2007. Dans le café de la jeunesse perdue[M]. Paris: Gallimard.

[5] MURPHY A L, 2003. The figure of the labyrinth in Patrick Modiano's "Rue des Boutiques Obscures"[J]. The French Review, 77(2): 340-350.

[6] TRANTHAM M, 2017. Photography and postmemory: imagining the past in Modiano's *Dora Bruder and Missing Person*[J]. Logos, 10:60.

[7] 艾克，郑立敏，2015. 唯写作最真实——莫迪亚诺访谈录[J]. 当代外国文学，36(1)：166-169.

[8] 德波，2006. 景观社会[M].王昭凤，译. 南京：南京大学出版社.

[9] 冯寿农，1989. 论莫迪阿诺小说世界中的全息结构[J]. 外国文学评论（4）：58-65.

[10] 冯寿农，2008. 莫迪亚诺的解构主义诗学——评他的抗战文学"占领三部曲"[J]. 国外文学（3）：109-115.

[11] 黄荭，2015. 莫迪亚诺获奖演说[J]. 世界文学（2）：55-67.

[12] 加缪，2012. 西西弗神话[M]. 杜小真，译. 北京：人民文学出版社.
[13] 金龙格，2010. 镶嵌在丰碑作品上的璀璨宝石[J]. 世界文学（4）：278-288.
[14] 刘曦，王大智，2020. "空白"的伤口：论莫迪亚诺小说中的大屠杀创伤书写[J]. 当代外国文学，41(1)：89-97.
[15] 孟天娇，2016. 论莫迪亚诺小说中的"逃离"情结[D]. 西安：陕西师范大学.
[16] 莫迪亚诺，2010. 青春咖啡馆[M]. 金龙格，译. 北京：人民文学出版社.
[17] 翁冰莹，冯寿农，2015. 寻根与遗忘——试论莫迪亚诺《暗店街》的文学主题[J]. 当代外国文学，36(2)：125-131.
[18] 翁冰莹，冯寿农，2017. 试论莫迪亚诺"既视"式的记忆艺术[J]. 外国文学研究，39(1)：70-79.
[19] 晓照，2015. 2014年诺贝尔文学奖得主帕特里克·莫迪亚诺专辑[J]. 世界文学（2）：5-8.
[20] 杨晓青，2016. 论帕特里克·莫迪亚诺小说中的"身份"主题[D]. 银川：宁夏大学.
[21] 袁文卓，徐梅，2015. 国内帕特里克·莫迪亚诺研究综述[J]. 伊犁师范学院学报(社会科学版)，34(1)：107-110.
[22] 周婷，2012. 论莫迪亚诺小说中的神秘机制[D]. 武汉：武汉大学.

《最后的礼物》中的家庭创伤书写

郭真巧

1. 引言

"创伤"一词源自希腊语。作为一个纯粹的医学术语,"创伤"的本义是指由外力造成的身体伤害。"创伤"既可以指小伤口,也可以指致命伤。19世纪70年代,首先被解释为精神病理学。在此基础上,皮埃尔·珍妮特和西格蒙德·弗洛伊德对癔症的心理发病机制的研究逐渐将"创伤"引入精神分析,以解释特定的异常心理状态,并逐渐将其扩展到现代创伤理论。现代文学创伤理论建立在创伤心理分析的基础上,进一步探讨了文学作品中所体现的创伤症状。它包括创伤人物的特征、创伤语言的修辞特征和创伤叙事的特征。虽然心理意义上的创伤通常指创伤事件,但文学创伤理论更多地关注创伤的后果,而不是创伤事件本身。凯·埃里克森认为,这种转变是合理的,因为人们对创伤的反应更多地揭示了创伤的本质,而不是创伤性事件是什么(Janet, 1991)。

《最后的礼物》是诺贝尔奖文学奖获奖作家古尔纳的代表作,其研究目前处于起步阶段,但随着诺贝尔奖文学奖的颁发,古尔纳作品研究不断升温,目前学者们的研究多集中于古尔纳的《天堂》《海边》《离别的记忆》,对于《最后的礼物》这一作品的研究数量并不多,且多聚焦于小说中的记忆、身份、沉默,多立足宏大话语,往往以后殖民理论解析文本。事实上,与其说《最后的礼物》是后殖民时代的产物,不如说它是现代家庭的个人创伤记忆。整部小说充满着对创伤的回忆与复原。基于此,本文将立足细小叙事,探讨文本中家庭创伤记忆的表征、疗治以及创伤叙事,以期阐明家庭创伤记忆的文学书写意义及其对当今世界流散、边缘群体的启示价值。

父亲阿巴斯抛妻弃子,逃离非洲,自此他的过去变成创伤,无法揭露亦无法言说;母亲玛丽亚姆逃离寄养家庭再到对他人隐瞒自己的过往,创伤主题贯穿整个人生;女儿汉娜生在英国却不被社会所认可,种族的创伤使她陷入身份认同困境。面对创伤,阿巴斯、玛利亚姆与汉娜通过重述自己的人生过往、重建与他人的关系及重构自我身份,走向了创伤疗治和自我救赎之路。

2. 创伤表征:沉默与身份认同危机

首先是小说中的核心人物阿巴斯。不同于妻子,阿巴斯的沉默既是主观选择的,又是客观强加的。阿巴斯曾谈过他游历的国家,做过的各种糟糕的工作,"但从来没有提到过他的家庭,甚至不提他来自哪里。"(古尔纳,2022:43)当然,阿巴斯也并不是对过往的所有事情都闭口不谈,而是有选择地进行讲述。其实,读者可以从小说中的细节处窥探阿巴斯的些许内心世界,比如他喜欢阅读有关大海、历史、流浪和旅行的故事:"在那些日子里,在他开始好转之后,他又开始看《奥德赛》了。"(古尔纳,2022:29)他是一位典型的异邦流散者,"是跨越国界（或具有国界性质且具有不同文化的地区）的流散。"（朱振武等，2019）他流散的因由则与他过往的创伤经历息息相关。疲累的童年、暴虐的父亲、抛妻弃子的遭遇使他受到创伤，变得无法言说。"创伤过后，受害者旋即可能彻底忘记了这一事件。即便是创伤记忆又返回到人们脑海当中，它们通常也是非语言的，即受害者可能无法用言语来描述它们。"（赵雪梅，2019）"无法用言语来描述它们"指的是创伤的不可言说性，这种不可言说性就是阿巴斯始终沉默的原因之一。非常不幸的是，当他在新的土地上安居多年后，妻子、儿女的陪伴使得创伤对他的影响逐渐减弱，阿巴斯终于愿意向家人敞开心扉时，疾病剥夺了他开口的能力，他被迫沉默着，与自己内心深处的痛苦记忆交缠斗争，他被迫成了被叙述的对象。阿巴斯的沉默揭示了阿巴斯以及以阿巴斯为代表的移民面临着的身份认知障碍。他们盘踞游离在回忆与家园之中，无法与新的社会构建和谐统一的关系。阿巴斯的沉默是移民创伤的最真实体现，是呈现移民经历的最好方式。

　　心理学研究表明，创伤受害者的年龄越小，在创伤面前就越无助。玛丽亚姆出生时就遭受了命运的考验——出生几天的玛丽亚姆就被生母抛弃，之后多次辗转于寄养家庭的生活给她留下了难以愈合的心理创伤。玛利亚姆的童年生活残酷且动荡，年幼的她像一个物品被不同家庭接纳而后又抛弃，寒冷、黑暗、贫穷是她关于童年的记忆。"一无是处"是她给自己贴上的标签，她从未在社会中找到一丝丝安全感和归属感。作家对其出生的描写耐人寻味，"她这般戏剧性地来到世上"（古尔纳，2022：13），仿佛她的到来是一件本不该发生的事。而生母丢弃她时留下的字条也只是简单地写着"她叫玛丽亚姆，他们不让我留下她"（古尔纳，2022：13）这样的字眼。出生时就饱受苦难，到了成长时期，玛丽亚姆更是命运多舛，在她最需要和渴望家庭的温暖时，却一次又一次被迫辗转于寄养家庭，遭受着不同程度的忽视与虐待。贫穷与不受重视是之前寄养家庭留给她的共通记忆。童年时期的玛丽亚姆无论怎样努力，都无法改变苦难的命运。卑微的出身与残酷的童年使玛丽亚姆"像一件物品被不同的家庭接纳又丢弃"（古尔纳，2022：7）。这样的创伤经历使她选择将她的故事说与孩子们听，而将自己最为恐惧的、屈辱的那一部分深深埋在心底。内心深处的那一部分记忆饱含创伤，这是玛利亚姆在面对新的和谐家庭生活时选择沉默的原因。往日经历的创伤盘踞于玛丽亚姆的脑海和记忆中，即使成家后的生活安稳幸福，她也无法主动向家人提起她试图"抹去"的过往。也就是说，玛丽亚姆隐瞒过去本质上是为了逃避往昔的糟糕经历，使困扰她的难言之隐龟缩到内心深处。"受伤者潜意识中对创伤相关的刺激物持续性地回避，现实中的症状为主动回避与创伤经验相关的事物、人物、情景、语言等。"（古尔纳，2022：14）玛丽亚姆沉默的原因与她过往的痛苦经历息息相关。回忆过往时，玛丽亚姆"一想到费鲁兹和维贾伊，她就浑身一哆嗦，回回都是……然后轻轻地把这段记忆推开"（古尔纳，2022：13）。同时，玛丽亚姆有着一种强烈的疏离感，"也经常通过回避、分散注意力或其他的摆脱方法试图逃避痛苦的回忆、思想和感受"（古尔纳，2022：15）。

　　二代移民汉娜作为在文化夹缝中生存的代表，她选择了"伪装"的生存法则。她不断借用"欧洲身份"来掩饰自己的"非洲身份"，执意叫自己为安娜，强迫自己融入她并不欣赏的文化群体之中。小说中的汉娜一直是一个"双面人"，在家庭中，她的非洲身份无处隐藏，而在社会中，她的名字叫"汉娜"，是一名在英国土生土长的教师。而这种双重身份并没有给汉娜带来安全感与归属感，汉娜的非洲身份与欧洲身份相互拉扯，这种拉扯在第二章"搬家"中尤为激烈：一方面，在搬家时，她享受作为"白人家属"的优越地位与便利条件，带着优越感给搬家工人发号施令，洋洋得意，自命不凡，此时"欧洲身份"占据上风；另一方面，在搬家后，午夜梦回之时，象征着非洲身份的破旧阴森的老宅、古怪而又强烈的负罪感萦绕着她，此时的"非洲身份"又让她无法忽视。双重身份的拉扯实则是她在文化裂缝下摇摆、困惑、迷失自己的体现。父母的沉默和自己不明的身世使汉娜在自己从小生活的地方缺失安全感，自己的黑色皮肤与英国社会格格不入。尽管汉娜交到了白人男友尼克，可尼克的叔叔迪格比认为汉娜不"英国"，尽管汉娜就出生并生活在英国。尼克妹妹的男友迪格比也不断追问汉娜是哪里人，以及汉娜成为英国人之前是哪里人，甚至打听汉娜的父亲从何而来。安东尼咧嘴笑道："你要把我们的黑人弄哭了。"（古尔纳，2022：118）歧视意味浓厚的"黑人"一词令汉娜非常震惊："汉娜惊讶地看着他，看着他那张咧着嘴笑着、皮肤厚实、肌肉结实的脸，还有他眼神中的嘲弄。"（古尔纳，2022：118）人们日常交谈中的玩笑，温文尔雅背后的复杂眼神，不经意地一瞥，下意识的一个动作，都能够释放出种族主义的气息。"种族主义是指凭借肤色、血缘等似是而非的种族特征肆意剥夺一部分社会成员的权利，并为建立一种所谓'优等种族'统治'劣等种族'的秩序体系提供合法性依据的社会思潮，是人类发展史上产生的最丑恶的观念之一。"（王义桅，2018：22）对非洲而言，在后殖民时代，尽管直接的殖民统治已经结束，但是种族主义的话语仍旧以各种变种存在于英国社会。正是这样的话语给予汉娜以深深的恐惧和创伤，陷入了身份认同的危机中。汉娜的创伤经历不仅仅代表着流散二代、移民二代在异邦文化中的境遇，更反映出广大流散者、社会边缘女性在社会中挣扎求生的困难。古尔纳从"一家之言"与"一人之成长经历"出发，揭示出社会中的流散者、混乱者、失声者遭遇的共同创伤经历。

3. 创伤疗治：流散群体的和解之道

探析家庭创伤的表征与根源并非出于追忆往昔的兴趣，而是辨认受创者内在世界、治疗创伤的必要过程。随着创伤研究的不断发展，人们不再把创伤看作不治之症，而是积极寻求治愈创伤的手段。目前的主流观点是，创伤治疗需要受创者直面创伤，而"最有效的方式是通过记忆、叙述和与他人交流。""通过讲故事、叙述创伤经历才能去除受创者过去的伤痛，并且帮助受创者继续生存下去。"（Foster，2000：4）讲述行为，一方面能让讲述者（也就是受创者）的负面情感得到宣泄，在心理上感到被他人理解；另一方面，通过倾听者对他人受创事件的客观分析、公正评价，讲述者可能改变自己以往的消极观念，转而以积极行动应对创伤事件。而家庭受创者的自述是贯穿本作的创伤治疗手段。

《最后的礼物》中，父母阿巴斯和玛利亚姆家庭创伤的本质在于过去经历的恐惧，而二代移民汉娜和贾马尔的创伤在于对自我身份认同的缺失。重拾过去、向后代讲述自己的经历便是父母试图消除这种恐惧的方式；倾听父母话语、拥抱自我身份、回到非洲寻根则成为二代移民汉娜与贾马尔的治愈良方。

疾病使阿巴斯从主动沉默转向了无法发声的状态。他于病榻上不断回想过去，陷入低沉的自我反思中。长时间的缄默和恢复缓慢的身体状态让阿巴斯叙述的冲动日益增长。"在黎明前的那几个小时里，当世界在他周围寂静无声时，他躺在床上，感觉到身体的内部正在腐烂。他用手抚摸着支撑着一切的骨骼，想着有一天它很快就会坍塌在他体内融化的腐烂中。"（古尔纳，2022：126）最终在黑暗里，阿巴斯艰难地开口和玛利亚姆述说了故乡和逃离的婚姻。长久以来，阿巴斯第一次将个人经验转变为语言叙述，在药物、疾病的混乱之中，他用冷静的语言展示了隐藏已久的个人记忆，同样在这种叙述中回顾了在异国文化中被挤压和侵犯的个人身份，与自己达成了无奈的和解。

阿巴斯的回忆与自述强烈地刺激了妻子玛利亚姆。在不断地纠结和反复中，玛利亚姆决定按照"将苦难常态化"的个人准则，向子女述说了自己在寄养家庭中被打压和猥亵的时日。玛利亚姆认为，面对苦难，语言和信息的交换"可以把她的震惊降到更为普通的程度，把所发生的事情纳入熟悉的剧情"。"她听取她朋友们的讲述，她们之间把悲剧变成了可以容忍的事情。她们把所描述的不幸归咎于医生、命运甚至是不幸本身。"（古尔纳，2022：12）玛利亚姆对创伤的叙述"可以建立叙事、自我和身份之间的联系，并有助于受创者在社会环境中形成对自我和身份的认识。"（曾艳钰，2014：10）这意味着玛利亚姆在内心中选择不再与过去的苦痛做无意义的斗争。

玛丽亚姆向家人讲述自己的过往，这是她走向创伤自愈的第一步。"讲述"对创伤受害者来说，是实现创伤治愈、重获新生力量的重要保证，因为"通过讲故事、叙述创伤经历才能去除受创者过去的伤痛，并且帮助受创者继续生存下去"，长时间的缄默和阿巴斯对过往的自述使得玛丽亚姆也主动向家人述说自己经历的苦难。通过"讲述"，玛丽亚姆向子女坦承自己年幼时在寄养家庭中受到的歧视和不公。当成功跨越沟通的壁垒之后，家人之间的有效交流也使得玛丽亚姆从创伤阴影中走出来，因为她意识到"一个人把这些事情憋在心里，任由它们毒害你的生活——这么做是多么的可悲。"（古尔纳，2022：13）玛丽亚姆采用叙述的方法讲述过往，可以"将自己遭受的打击弱化成更加司空见惯的东西，将刚刚发生的变故置入熟悉的剧情背景之中"。事实上，玛丽亚姆的叙述意味着她"在内心中选择不再与过去的痛苦做无意义的斗争"。因此，只有受创者自己直面过去的创伤，挣脱囿于创伤的桎梏，把痛苦的经历讲述出来，受创者才能脱离创伤、走向治愈之路。正是如此，当远离创伤事件发生的时间和空间时，母亲不再一味回避，开始主动向下一代的家庭成员传递自己昔日的家庭记忆。

在父母的坦承下，汉娜、贾马尔开始接受自己的身份。在与自己的家庭产生隔阂，又在白人家庭中遭受指责，经历了两头空的尴尬境地之后，汉娜一边审视着自己曾经视之为标杆的英国文化，一边回望曾被自己刻意忽视和摒弃的非洲文化，以及她不得不面对的移民经历和身份问题后，决意放弃幻想和伪装，摆脱对过往的抵触，构建全新的自我身份。故事就以汉娜和贾马尔讨论是否动身去桑给巴尔结尾。尽管汉娜对于回归故乡一事仍充满了不安，她也逐渐认识和接受了自身身份的复杂性和流动性。也许总有一天，他们能够踏上那片也属于自己的故土，去看看父亲口中那棵熟悉的大树，汉娜也能自信地构建非裔英国人这一独特的混杂身份，正如她心目中所期望的一般，"能够大大方方地说，这就是我"。

我们可以直观地感受到阿巴斯鼓起勇气留下的"最后的礼物"的巨大力量，父母的讲述弥补了女儿身份认同的裂痕，鼓励了其他人勇敢面对伤痛，修复了家庭成员的关系，使家人更紧密地联系在一起。这也是作者尝试传达的信息：虽然流散者们身处他乡，但家庭的温暖、血缘的纽带永远是救赎和依靠；流散者虽活在异地，却也不必压抑自己，追求刻意的融入。坦承自己的复杂身世，直面自己的真实身份，脱下面具，拥抱自我的阿巴斯寄托着作者对社会边缘群体、对流散群体追寻自我价值，寻找个人幸福的强烈期盼。

4. 创伤叙事：时间与梦境

《最后的礼物》基于叙述者的记忆，记忆片段的交织和组合在小说中创造了一种独特的时间穿梭感。笔者认为，小说中对时间颠倒和梦境的叙事是典型的创伤叙事手法。通过塑造时间上的无序与颠倒，模糊现实世界与过去、梦境、幻想世界的界限，小说呈现了创伤心理学的独特症状，即创伤经历不可控地反复和闪回。

汉娜的梦境是创伤的典型表现。典型的创伤经历本质上是反复的，受到创伤的人会通过梦境或类似梦境的形式重新体验创伤，这些梦境是强制性的，不受个人意志控制。汉娜在搬家后又做起了一个关于一幢阴森老宅的梦。这幢房子其实是汉娜内心深处的非洲身份的象征，是她拼命要压抑、掩饰的东西。作者在描述梦中的老宅时写道："她住在房屋的一边，另一边早已年久失修，破败不堪""顶梁塌陷，近乎朽烂""疲惫的色彩"。（古尔纳，2022：90）破烂的房屋实则是汉娜内心潜意识对非洲身份的看法。在她的理解中，非洲身份使她困扰，让她以及全家人疲惫不堪、饱受创伤，更让她在这片土地上永远自卑，无法过上她所渴望的生活。"废弃的那半边空房子看上去像个谷仓，空空荡荡"（古尔纳，2022：91），则是因为汉娜在成长过程中一次又一次隐藏自己的非洲身份，将真实的自己压抑到内心深处，在通过伪装结交到白人男友后，她内心的非洲身份被更深地隐匿起来。

然而汉娜并非一个完全虚荣、全无自我意识的伪装者，在她潜意识中，她是被谴责的、愧疚的、负罪的。"这种残败带着恶意，带着警觉，带着指责""挥之不去的犯错感""她有一种心里发毛的感觉"。（古尔纳，2022：91）梦境在搬入新家后出现，表明汉娜潜意识中的非洲身份从未湮灭，且又开始抗争。"流散者在本土文化与异域文化空间的张力下流离、徘徊、焦灼、无望，既有对新世界的向往，又有对故乡的留恋"。（朱振武、袁俊卿，2019：155）虽然汉娜不是一代移民，但她的身上流淌着黑色的基因，他的父亲来自遥远的非洲大陆，她在探索社会时不可避免地会对非洲产生一定的认同，这种认同体现在汉娜的潜意识——梦境中。在体会到被服务的优越感后，汉娜愈发渴望融入白人的社会，为此她需要更努力地伪装自己，需要将非洲身份压抑到内心更深的地方，所以她才会在梦境中感到强烈的愧疚。在梦境中的汉娜与现实中的汉娜一样，以撒谎、伪装的手段来获取别人的认可。"哪怕是在梦里面，她也知道她在对人家撒谎……她知道他们也没法让这栋房子摆脱那种充满恶意的衰朽……她有责任料理此事，可她却失职了。"（古尔纳，2022：91）潜意识中的汉娜似乎明白，谎言背后是更大的谎言，谎言永远不可能成为现实，不管她多努力地靠近、融入白人群体，最终都是一张由谎言织成的、不堪一击的网。梦境中的破败老宅是汉娜内心对非洲身份归属的渴望，是潜意识中对非洲身份的认同。在汉娜的梦境中，汉娜从未见过自己的男友，"尼克从来没有在梦境中完全现身。"这表明，汉娜的真实非洲身份依然被白人所鄙夷，不管她多努力地融入，依旧无法靠非洲身份来博得别人的好感与尊重，这也是众多移民采取"伪装隐藏"的生存法则的原因。身份危机在一次次梦境中不断加深，梦境重复的过程也是对创伤反复体验的过程。

小说中另一个值得注意的叙事现象是大量使用插叙。在整部小说中，叙述者阿巴斯、玛利亚姆都大量使用插叙来介绍故事背景或事件背景。整部小说以阿巴斯卒中开始，在阿巴斯与玛利亚姆的回忆中不断将故事版图拓充完整。阿巴斯总是在病榻上不断回想过去，总是陷入低沉的自我反思中。"在黎明前的那几个小时里，当世界在他周围寂静无声时，他躺在床上，感觉到身体的内部正在腐烂。他用手抚摸着支撑着一切的骨骼，想着有一天它很快就会坍塌在他体内融化的腐烂中。"（古尔纳，2022：126）"就在黎明破晓前的那几个钟头，他拖着被摧垮的病体躺在那里，无力反抗，身上打着冷战，因为虚弱，也因为痛苦——一想起十八岁那年他意外迎娶的那个年轻女子，这痛苦便袭上心来……"（古尔纳，2022：140）除了阿巴斯以外，整部小说还交织着玛利亚姆与汉娜的回忆碎片。这些回忆碎片并非来自自主自发的回忆，而是创伤体验。兰格认为，受到创伤的人对世界的感知是分裂的，创伤的世界与现实的世界平行存在，受创者的叙事世界是共识的而非历时的，这意味着他永远无法与当下共存。（Langer, 1993）主人公不受控制的闪回记忆就是创伤最好的表现。

5. 结语

在《最后的礼物》中，阿巴斯一家不仅仅代表着移民及二代移民在异邦文化中的境遇，还反映出广大流散者、社会边缘群体在社会中挣扎求生的困难。古尔纳以"一家之言"出发，揭示出社会中的流散者、混乱者、失声者遭遇的共同困境。通过文字聚焦在阿巴斯一家身上，我们可以直观地感受到自我身份迷失、边缘化的处境给流散边缘群体留下巨大创伤。但古尔纳显然不止于此，古尔纳描绘创伤，也描绘愈合：父亲阿巴斯留下最后的礼物，弥补了女儿身份认同的裂痕，鼓励了妻子勇敢面对伤痛，修复了家庭成员的关系，增强了家庭的精神纽带。这也是作者尝试传达的信息：虽然流散者们身处他乡，家庭的温暖、血缘的纽带永远是救赎和依靠；流散者虽活在异地，却也不必压抑自己，追求刻意的融入。坦然承认自己的复杂身世，直面自己的真实身份，脱下面具，留下救赎的父亲阿巴斯、勇敢揭开伤疤的母亲玛利亚姆、拥抱自我的女儿汉娜寄托着作者对边缘女性、对流散群体追寻自我价值，寻找个人幸福的强烈期盼。阿巴斯留下的最后的礼物，是阿巴斯留给家庭的疗愈之所，更是古尔纳留给全世界流散群体的治愈良方。

参考文献

[1] FOSTER D A, 2000. Trauma and memory[J]. Contemporary Literature, 41(4): 740-747.
[2] LANGER L L, 1993. Holocaust testimonies: the ruins of memory[M]. New Haven: Yale University Press.
[3] 董美银，王佳英，2014.《时时刻刻》中理查德的创伤解析[J]. 边疆经济与文化（2）：123-124.
[4] 古尔纳，2022. 最后的礼物[M]. 宋佥，译. 上海：上海译文出版社.
[5] 韩晓燕，田晓丽，2016. 制度、文化与日常确证 外来移民及其子女的情景性身份认同[J]. 清华大学学报（哲学社会科学版），31(6)：175-182，195.
[6] 籍晓红，王婷婷，2020.《无声告白》中的童年创伤与复原[J]. 中国轻工教育（5）：91-96.
[7] 李蔓莉，2018. 移民二代歧视感知与社会融入研究[J]. 青年探索（4）：100-112.
[8] 王义桅，2018. 欧美种族主义何去何从[J]. 人民论坛（5）：22-24.
[9] 曾艳钰，2014. 后"9·11"美国小说创伤叙事的功能及政治指向[J]. 当代外国文学，35(2)：5-13.
[10] 赵冬梅，2011. 心理创伤理论与研究[M]. 广州：暨南大学出版社.
[11] 赵雪梅，2019. 文学创伤理论评述——历史、现状与反思[J]. 文艺理论研究，39(1)：201-211.
[12] 朱振武，袁俊卿，2019. 流散文学的时代表征及其世界意义——以非洲英语文学为例[J]. 中国社会科学（7）：135-158，207.

库切的《福》：空白的背后

蒋茜茜

1. 引言

约翰·库切，通常被称为 J. M. Coetzee，是南非最著名的当代作家之一。库切自处女作《黄昏之地》发表以来，创作了许多世界闻名的小说，《福》是其中最著名、最常被讨论的小说之一。自 1986 年出版以来，《福》同时受到评论家的赞扬和批评。《福》是一部包含多重解读的作品，这可能是受到库切英国文学教授生涯的影响。《福》似乎形成了一个后现代主义框架，后殖民主义、解构主义、元叙事、后殖民女权主义等各种后现代主义理论都可以放进去。这一特点显然促使了评论家对文本进行多角度的分析，比如姜小卫的《沉默与言说：库切小说〈福〉与后殖民批判》一文，就是典型的从斯皮瓦克的后殖民理性批判出发研究《福》中后殖民主义的文本。Nushrat Azam 的《对库切的后殖民小说〈福〉中的"声音"和"他者"的女性主义批判》则明显是从后殖民女性主义来研究《福》的文章。《福》的研究者们似乎可以从自己感兴趣的任意一个角度切入并进行研究，并且毫无违和感。这本小说包罗当代文学批评热点的特征让我们有理由怀疑身为文学教授的库切是否故意这样做，以迎合评论界的潮流，因为小说中确实存在一些无法得到普遍认可的情节。例如为什么这部小说实际上没有一个完整的故事，为什么小说中寥寥可数的几个主要人物几乎没有激情可言，为什么这本小说没有直接表现出政治因素，等等。就这些问题而言，笔者在此认为，库切在这部小说中可能是故意留出了一些空白，以达到他的艺术目的——反欧洲中心主义和话语权。本文拟从历史、情感以及政治等三个角度来审视《福》中的空白，并探讨这些空白是以何种形式达到了库切反抗欧洲中心主义与话语权力的目的的。

2. 历史的空白

《福》的互文对应文本是 18 世纪初英国现实主义作家丹尼尔·笛福所写的《鲁滨孙漂流记》。众所周知，《鲁滨孙漂流记》不仅是英国现实主义的开端之作，还是一部反映欧洲早期殖民实践的作品。尽管小说的主体部分是描述鲁滨孙在荒岛上的冒险和劳动，但小说在一开头就向读者介绍了他的家庭、他姓氏的来源、他其他的航海冒险。后来流落荒岛，鲁滨孙还坚持写日记，这一切仿佛是在向我们真实地展现他的人生。换言之，笛福笔下的克鲁索是一个有完整的历史的人，人们基本可以通过作为"前景"的小说去还原作为"背景"的历史（陈榕，2006）。然而，在《福》中，这种还原完全是不可能成功的，因为库切在该小说中描写的人物均缺乏"历史"，读者只能偶尔在小说中找到与人物过去相关的一两个微小片段。在库切的小说《福》中，四个主要人物之一的克鲁索"没有写日记"（库切，2007），也没有做任何记录。更重要的是，他本人所讲的关于他自己的历史"有多个版本，各个版本之间如此不一致"（库切，2007），这让苏珊·巴顿认为克鲁索"不再知道什么是真相，什么是想象"（库切，2007）。从这一点来看，库切笔下的克鲁索（Crusoe）与丹尼尔·笛福笔下认真记日记的克鲁索（Crusoe）完全不同。笛福笔下的克鲁索（Crusoe）关注时间的线性流变，而库切笔下的克鲁索（Crusoe）却对此漠不关心，他唯一在意的是他的梯田，这也是为什么他濒死之际听到苏珊说"会在梯田上种植作物，让它开花结果"流泪的原因（库切，2007）。也许就像斯皮瓦克曾经写过的那样，"与其说《福》是关于历史和劳动的时间，不如说它是关于空间和位移"（Spivak，1990）。因为克鲁索（Crusoe）确实说过"我会留下我的梯田和墙……这些就足够了……"（库切，2007）。Catherine Gallagher 等新历史主义者十分关注细节，强调将"理论和方法的总结建立在绵密的具体细节组成的网络之上"（Gallagher、Greenblatt，2000），然而库切在《福》中所给出的微小片段非但无法展现其细节网络、使读者勾勒出人物的具体经历或者故事，反而留下了巨大的空白。

笛福笔下的克鲁索通过他的日记将自己塑造成为了殖民主义历史的开拓者，然而库切笔下的克鲁索却由于某种不知名的原因（可能是缺少笔墨）而放弃，或者说无法记录自己的历史。在欧洲经典作品中，克鲁索被这些历史塑造为一个勇敢、独立、智慧的人物，成为个人主义和"资产者"（Watt，2001）的典型。移民殖民作家库切塑造的克鲁索则与之相反，他似乎没有其欧洲同名前辈身上的创造力和生产力，他的梯田光秃秃的，没有种植，更不可能有产出和成就可言。不仅如此，他对他自己的历史或故事叙述无能为力，以至于读者既无法获知他的过去，又无法了解他的真实性情，只能对他有相对浅薄的认识：他是一个年老、固执、热爱梯田的人。库切的克鲁索并未构成典型也无法展现其背后的历史，反而呈现出空白，不禁让人怀疑，谁才能代表真实的克鲁索呢？库切并没有就此在小说中作出回应，他的目的显然不在于描述真实的克鲁索，而恰恰在于埋下怀疑经典权威的种子。读者由此获得了选择相信与不相信、认可与不认可对克鲁索形象描绘的真实性的自由。

库切故意构建的历史空白一方面激发了读者探索完整故事、挖掘隐藏信息，另一方面瓦解了处于中心的欧洲经典中克鲁索形象的权威性以及传统史诗故事的固定结构。与中心经典权威形象的瓦解同时展现在我们面前的是对欧洲中心主义的强烈反抗。也就是说，小说中的历史空白促使读者打破旧有观念、摆脱对经典形象的盲目信任，转而研究这种形象塑造背后的复杂的权力动机，引起对欧洲中心主义的审视，促进对边缘文化的关注和认同。

3. 情感的空白

《福》对情感的描绘方式十分与众不同，比起在其中看到传统的亲密关系，我们似乎更多地感受到了隔阂与疏离。或许这是由于库切本人并未将关注点放在这种亲密关系上，就如蒋晖在《苏珊·巴顿与写不出来的非洲小说》中所写到的，"库切的小说缺乏引发读者共鸣的强烈的情感要素，对人、对大地、对爱情、对友谊，库切都拒绝投入感情的赞颂"（2016）。这样奇特的情感描写使得小说的主要人物之间的关系变得异常复杂，尤其是在涉及小说中不断游走的核心角色苏珊·巴顿时。她与克鲁索、星期五以及福先生相互之间无论在身体上有多么紧密的联系，在情感上却始终存在一片空白，彼此无法真正接近，更遑论相互安慰。或许我们能找到一点苏珊竭力跨越这种情感空白、与其他人建立真正的情感联系的努力，但她最终也未能成功。就比如她坦诚道"如果我确信我要在岛上度过余生，我会再次向他献身，或者恳求他，或者做任何必要的事情来怀孕和生孩子"（库切，2007），或许对她而言孩子是完全的内在情感的化身,但在小说中她由始至终都未曾真正拥有一个孩子——她声称的女儿也被拐走了。由此可见在这疏离、孤独的世界上,情感空白是普遍存在的,接下来笔者将通过小说中更多的细节来探讨情感空白是如何在库切的主题中发挥作用的。

尽管库切习惯于选择女性作为其作品的主人公,《福》的主人公苏珊·巴顿仍是其众多作品的主人公中十分特殊的一位:社会规约性在她身上远远小于其他的女性主人公。在未得到主人福先生的同意时就擅自住到他的家里,不光如此,她还随意拿走福先生家里的东西变卖换钱。重要的是,苏珊并不认为这种行为值得给予特别关注,仿佛这种"非法"行为就是她的天生的生存方式,而文明世界的法律她却有意无意地忽略了。值得一提的是,苏珊在荒岛上却主动与克鲁索讨论过荒岛上是否有法律。在文明世界中忽视法律,在荒岛上关注法律,苏珊身上存在的这种矛盾相向的状态在一定程度上展现了其对西方文明社会的规约的反抗。这种反抗在她与克鲁索和福先生的两性亲密行为里形成的情感空白中展现得更为突出。

总而言之,通过苏珊·巴顿与克鲁索、福先生、星期五的不成功的情感交互所形成的种种情感空白,不仅展现了在后现代社会描写中人与人之间疏离的普遍性,还通过这些情感空白形成了一个以苏珊·巴顿为中心的格局,而克鲁索、福先生、星期五则被置换到边缘,这无疑构成了小说反抗与欧洲中心主义一起压迫女性的父权中心主义的局面。

4. 政治的空白

正如在本文开头就提到的那样,库切的《福》既备受赞誉,又受到许多批评。这些批评往往有同一个根源,即《福》背离了南非在 20 世纪 80 年代的政治需求,就如哈里特·吉尔伯特在 1986 年 12 月 9 日的《新政治家》中所批评的那样:"在索韦托燃烧的时候,玩这种后现代的游戏?"(Kannemeyer, 2014)很显然,《福》不能满足像吉尔伯特这样希望在小说中看到展现南非政治的真实画面的读者,对他们而言,小说最好还能有些针砭时弊的作用。但《福》是否真如吉尔伯特所批评的那样,仅仅是后现代的文学游戏,全然忽略南非的政治?或许我们能从库切的采访回答中找到答案:"《福》是对南非局势的回避,但只是从狭隘的时间角度对南非局势的回避。它不是对殖民主义或权力问题的回避。它也可以被视为谁在写作的问题?谁手握笔杆,谁就占据了权力的位置?"(Morphet, 1987)从这个回答中,我们可以了解,库切的《福》表面上的确不是在关注现实的政治,然而,在更深层次上他关注的是比现实政治更基础的权力问题,是谁来叙事,如何叙事的问题,亦即语言的问题。正如摩尔所言,"库切对语言的力量和局限性有敏锐认识,尤其是当语言影响到社会和政治现实时。"(Moore, 1990)在他看来只有了解这些问题,才能实现真正的政治解放。简单来说,读者所感知到的政治空白是库切有目的地建构起来的。

笔者之所以在这里说政治空白是库切有目的的建构,是因为尽管无法在文中找到直接的政治相关内容,但在阅读的过程中,读者却能够反复感受到小说中的政治隐喻,以至于生出想要在小说之外继续探查以佐证相关政治隐喻的想法。在某种程度上,克鲁索、苏珊还有星期五在岛上的生活,可以被视为整个南非政治状况的缩影。克鲁索代表南非统治阶级的阿非利卡人,正如小说中,苏珊认为"他(克鲁索)有着国王般的形体,是岛上真正的国王"(库切, 2007)。阿非利卡人统治着南非,而克鲁索统治着小岛,岛上的一切都属于他。他开垦梯田却不种植,表明他只想占有土地而非利用土地,在这一点上与种族隔离时期的阿非利卡人的土地政策相同。苏珊代表着当时的自由主义白人,他们主张个人权利、经济自由和平等机会，并反对种族歧视和政府干预。在小说中主要体现为苏珊认为应当把语言教给星期五（黑人），这样他或他们就能"了解他的意思"并且"表达自己的意见"（库切，2007）。星期五则代表着黑人群体，尽管克鲁索和苏珊是"文明世界"的代表，但为三人提供生活必须物质的是他，即最辛苦劳作的是星期五，最受压迫的也是他。星期五的生活状态代表着南非黑人在种族隔离时期的状况。

从以上的例子可以看出，库切建构的政治空白，非但没有压缩文本的政治性，反而形成了一种展现政治性的特殊手法。这种相对抽象的隐喻手法为读者提供了自由的思考空间，使他们能够超越具体的政治背景，思考更广泛的权力结构。更简单地说，库切利用了这种政治空白，使小说表面的中心聚焦在话语权力和叙事方式上。读者在充分理解并反思话语权力和叙事方式之后，就能够去探讨和思考更广泛的政治议题，并以此促使全人类追求真正的政治解放。这或许才是库切认为《福》从长远来看并没有从南非退出的原因：他真正关注的是世界范围内的政治，南非当然包含在内。库切及其作品由此也获得了世界性。

5. 结论

尽管库切的《福》因为缺乏传统经典中的故事情节而略显单调，但《福》中所包含的内容其实极其丰富，正如斯蒂芬·沃特森所写到的，"他（库切）的作品的坚实核心存在于其他地方，在作品本身之外，存在于一些被抹去、隐含、几乎没有提及的东西中。"（Huggan et al. 1996）《福》中被"抹去、隐含"的内容十分丰富，本文关注到了这一特征，从文本的历史、情感、政治空白三个方面入手进行考察。这些空白首先激发读者对完整信息的探索和对隐藏信息的挖掘；其次瓦解了欧洲中心主义、父权中心主义的权威，引起对边缘人物和文化的认同；最后引发了读者对叙事方式的反思，促使读者审视背后的权力动机。本文并非一篇从某个理论出发的写作，与之相反，本文是从各种理论研究中的未尽之处出发，对小说进行的整体考查，以在小说中寻找到一些隐藏但具有普遍重要性的内容。

参考文献

[1] GALLAGHER C, GREENBLATT S, 2000. Practicing new historicism[M]. Chicago: University of Chicago Press.

[2] HUGGAN G, WASTON S, 1996. Critical perspectives on J.M. Coetzee[M]. London: Palgrave Macmillan.

[3] KANNEMEYER J C, 2014. J.M. Coetzee: a life in writing[M].Melbourne: Scribe Publications Pty Ltd.

[4] MOORE J R, 1990. J.M. Coetzee and Foe [J]. The Sewanee review, 98(1): 152-159.

[5] MORPHET T, 1987. Two interviews with J.M. Coetzee, 1983 and 1987[J]. TriQuarterly, 69: 454.

[6] SPIVAK G C, 1990. Theory in the margin: Coetzee's Foe, reading Defoe's Crusoe/Roxana[J]. English in Africa, 17(2): 1-23.

[7] 缺 WASTON 1996 文献，补充

[8] WATT I P, 2001. The rise of the novel: studies in Defoe, Richardson and Fielding[M]. Oakland: University of California Press.

[9] 陈榕，2006. 新历史主义[M]//赵一凡，张中载，李德恩. 西方文论关键词. 北京：外语教学与研究出版社：670-681.

[10] 库切，2007. 福[M]. 王敬慧，译. 杭州：浙江文艺出版社.

《最后的礼物》的创伤书写与身份重构

刘铮儒

1. 引言

阿卜杜勒拉扎克·古尔纳是坦桑尼亚裔英国作家。2021 年，古尔纳因"毫不妥协并充满同理心地深入探索着殖民主义的影响，关切着那些夹杂在文化和地缘裂隙间的难民的命运"被授予诺贝尔奖文学奖。古尔纳的代表作包括《朝圣者之路》(*Pilgrims Way*)、《天堂》(*Paradise*)、《海边》(*By the Sea*)等。《最后的礼物》是古尔纳创作的第八部小说，讲述了移民阿巴斯一家在英国的艰难生活。阿巴斯四十多年前离开了他的故乡桑给巴尔，从此过上了流浪的生活。他最终与玛丽亚姆结婚，并育有一子一女。他对过去生活的一切都保持沉默。汉娜和贾马尔是阿巴斯的孩子，他们都在文化认同的危机中不断挣扎着。父亲对过去的沉默让他们自觉被围困在永恒的黑暗中。经历了卒中后的阿巴斯最终决定将自己的人生故事记录下来，作为给家人的最后的礼物。孩子们重新认识了他们的父亲和他的家乡，而玛丽亚姆从这份录音中汲取力量，踏上了寻根之路。故事以作为二代移民的汉娜决心远赴桑给巴尔结束。小说呈现了两代流散者在复杂的文化环境中的心灵危机以及面临自我身份困境的困惑、挣扎与选择。古尔纳在其作品中深度刻画了阿巴斯一家作为流散者在英国的生活经历和流散记忆，这些回忆与经历给阿巴斯、玛利亚姆和汉娜留下了难以磨灭的创伤。

国际上对古尔纳的研究始于 20 世纪 90 年代，对《最后的礼物》的研究，大多集中在亲缘关系和叙事研究两方面。国内对古尔纳作品的研究尚处于起步阶段，关于古尔纳和《最后的礼物》的研究大多集中在流散文学的书写、后殖民批评以及流散者的身份问题。创伤与疗救作为文学创作中的重要主题，在《最后的礼物》中贯穿始终。本文以创伤理论为基础，分析小说中三位主要人物阿巴斯、玛利亚姆和汉娜的创伤及其成因，进而揭示人物如何通过身份重构进行创伤疗治，体现出古尔纳对流散群体之困境的人文关怀和对其寻找心灵出路的指引。

"创伤"一词起初用于病理学，之后发展到临床医学及心理学，随着研究的深化，逐渐被扩展到文学、哲学以及社会学等领域。弗洛伊德认为，创伤患者的苦痛根植于记忆，这可以看作创伤是记忆再现的最早论述。他将创伤从病理学意义上的身体创伤转入精神分析理论中的心理创伤，把创伤的形成与受抑制的意识联系起来，并指出："一种经验如果在一个很短暂的时期内，使人的内心受到最高度的刺激，以致其不能用正常的方法适应，从而使内心有效能力的分配受到永久的扰乱，我们便称这种经验为创伤的"（弗洛伊德，1987：45）。凯西·克鲁斯在前人研究成果的基础上，在《未认领的经历：创伤、叙事和历史》一书中，第一次正式确立了创伤理论的概念："在突然的或灾难性的事件面前，一种压倒性的经验，对这些反应通常是延迟的，以幻觉和其他侵入的现象而重复出现的无法控制的表现"（克鲁斯，2016：96）。朱迪斯·赫尔曼对心理创伤进行了如下定义："心理创伤的痛苦源于无力感，在受到创伤当时，受创者笼罩在无法抵抗的力量下而感到无助"（赫尔曼，2015：135）。他认为，受到创伤的人可以从社会中找到归属感，他们可以通过与外部社会建立正常的接触和交流而从创伤经历中恢复过来。

2. 创伤记忆

朱迪斯·赫尔曼在《创伤与复原》中说："尽管时过境迁，受创者还是会不断在脑海中重现创伤事件，仿佛发生在此时此刻"（赫尔曼，2015：26）。阿巴斯的创伤记忆缘起于不幸的童年。他的父亲奥斯曼是个暴力、苛刻的人，常常责骂、殴打阿巴斯，甚至阻止阿巴斯继续上学。直到阿巴斯晚年卧床不起时，回忆中的父亲仍然是一个负面形象："他的名字叫奥斯曼，是一个严厉刻薄的男人，以自己的强势为荣，说话总是带吼"（古尔纳，2022：40）。作为父亲的奥斯曼并没有履行他相应的责任，作为儿子的阿巴斯缺乏来自父亲的爱护与关注。阿巴斯本应该过着无忧无虑的童年生活，但因缺少来自家人的关爱，导致他对家庭没有归属感，这也成了他极少谈论童年经历的原因之一。童年经历是造成阿巴斯内心创伤的首要原因。

"儿子"这一身份给予阿巴斯的只有饱受折磨的回忆。在他 18 岁时，阿巴斯娶了富有的穆斯林商人的女儿谢里法为妻。然而，婚后仅 6 个月，妻子就临近分娩。阿巴斯陷入了无尽的怀疑、恐慌，甚至绝望之中。他无法说服自己这个孩子是他的。于是，阿巴斯抛弃了他的妻子，逃离了家乡，开始了他的流浪之旅。在此段婚姻关系中，阿巴斯几乎没有享受过放松与愉悦。他搬进谢里法家的大房子，同妻子的父亲、姑姑、两个兄弟以及他们的妻子和孩子住在一起。在这个新的家庭中，阿巴斯没有获得归属感，他和妻子之间社会地位的差异只换来了其他家庭成员的蔑视和嘲笑。"他曾经对自己的未来所怀有的一切幸福与满足感都离他而去了。每天早上醒来，他脑子里的第一个想法就是，他又得忍受他们的轻蔑了。这个想法让他的心中充满了深切的痛苦。"（古尔纳，2022：94）作为丈夫，阿巴斯并没有得到妻子及其家人的尊重，在这个表面和谐的新家庭里，他被当作仆人一样对待。丈夫的身份只给阿巴斯带来了丧失尊严的痛苦，而非幸福感与责任感。这严重破坏了他内心的安全感和秩序感。这段不堪回首的记忆成了阿巴斯内心深处的秘密。"创伤记忆的形成既需要主体参与冲突性事件，又需要主体在事后对事件进行回顾辨认，确证创伤的存在"。（袁丹，2023：49）阿巴斯内心的羞耻阻止他向妻子和孩子们吐露真相，创伤的记忆在他内心反复回放了三十年，无法找到倾诉和解脱的出口。

阿巴斯的妻子玛利亚姆面临的创伤记忆起源于她的出身。玛利亚姆自出生起身份就是不确定的。"她是被人在埃克塞特医院的急诊室门外发现的，一个弃婴……那是一个钩针编织的米色襁褓，上面别着一个棕色的信封，像是一个送货地址，或是一份标签。"（古尔纳，2022：57）没有人知道她的父母姓甚名谁，在血缘身份上，玛利亚姆失去了自己的归宿。"身份就是一个个体所有的关于他这种人是其所是的意识"。（钱超英，2006：85）玛利亚姆对于自己最基本的血缘身份一无所知，这种对自我身份的不确认成了伴随她一生的创伤。童年的玛利亚姆辗转于寄养家庭中，不但没有获得一丝来自家庭的关爱，反而被冷漠甚至暴力对待。"他们的房子也很冷，但除此之外屋里还有臭气……有时候她会挨打。"（古尔纳，2022：21）在被第三个寄养家庭抛弃后，年幼的玛利亚姆便产生了自己一无是处的想法，直到她来到了最后一个寄养家庭，被维贾伊和费鲁兹夫妇收养。在这个家庭中，玛利亚姆终于获得了短暂的幸福，但好景不长，表哥迪内希开始对她进行语言和身体上的骚扰。玛利亚姆无计可施，只能每晚出门躲避表哥的伤害与威胁，却被养父母责怪自己不够听话懂事。在鼓起勇气向养父母坦白事情的真相后，玛利亚姆反倒被费鲁兹打了一巴掌。家庭的纽带在此时出现了最大的切口，本就在身体和精神上备受创伤的玛利亚姆非但没有得到家庭的信任和帮助，反倒被言语污蔑和暴力相待。绝望的玛利亚姆选择亲手割断这层关系，她决心出逃，彻底离开这个让她蒙受羞辱、遭遇不公的家庭。

首先，玛利亚姆的创伤来源于无法知晓和确认自身身份的无助。其次，在不同的寄养家庭辗转五次的童年经历使玛利亚姆丧失了来自家庭的关怀。在最后一个寄养家庭里承受的欺压和侮辱更迫使她走上绝望的流浪之路。创伤记忆使玛利亚姆成了边缘人一般的存在，而她被迫选择默默把苦难内化于心，这无形间加剧了她内心的创伤。

3. 创伤症状

赫尔曼认为心理创伤痛苦形成最根本的因素是对人生的无力感，在受到创伤后，受创者在无法抵抗的力量下感受到无助和绝望，导致其对社会的安全感逐渐消失，最终反映在精神层面，理性逐渐弱化。（Foster，2000：57）阿巴斯试图通过沉默与过往彻底割裂。阿巴斯对妻子极力隐瞒，担心玛利亚姆发现他的婚史，他也拒绝让孩子们知道太多有关桑给巴尔的往事。妻子玛丽亚姆不了解他，他的孩子们无法理解他，甚至开始与他疏远。阿巴斯患上了沉默症，正如玛利亚姆所言："他一直生活在耻辱之中，无法向任何人谈及此事"。（古尔纳，2022：194）

阿巴斯最严重的创伤症结在于他的移民身份。他一直处于一种漂泊不定的流亡状态，正如萨义德所解释的那样，"流亡就是无休止地东奔西走，一直未能安定下来，而且也使其他人不能安定，无法回到更早、更稳定的安适自在的状态，而且更可悲的是，永远也无法安全抵达、无法与新的家园或境遇融为一体"。（萨义德，2003：34）尽管在英国生活了数十年，阿巴斯对英国文化和社会仍然感到格格不入，一直到去世都是一个边缘人一般的存在，他也从未完全被这个陌生的国度真正接纳过。小说中的第一章就展示了阿巴斯对这个英国社会的无所适从："他知道自己身上出了点不同寻常的事情——那是一种越来越强的无助感，让他不由自主地呻吟起来，他身上的血肉一面发热，一面萎缩，取而代之的是一种陌生的空虚感"。（古尔纳，2022：7）"他没穿够衣服。他身边的其他人都穿着厚重的羊毛外套，戴着手套，围着围巾，仿佛他们凭着实践经验，早就知道这天到底有多冷，而他，尽管在这里生活了这么多年，却还是不知道"。（古尔纳，2022：8）孤独、无助、无法言说，这些都是阿巴斯饱受创伤的表征。他独自承受着"水土和文化、精神适应的痛苦，体验着文化归属的焦虑，承受着迷失自我的风险，感受着孤独、迷茫、彷徨的情绪，陷入没有中心、被抛出主流社会、行走在边缘的境地"。（朱振武等，2022：48）阿巴斯内心怀着强烈的不安全感和疏离感，而未能履行好丈夫和父亲的责任以及面对家人百般隐瞒所带来的痛苦和罪恶感，在精神上和身体上对他进行着双重折磨。

玛利亚姆的创伤症状则体现在她对于阿巴斯的坦白表现出的痛苦和迷茫。身为妻子的玛利亚姆对丈夫的过去不甚了解，她既不了解阿巴斯的故乡桑给巴尔，又对阿巴斯内心最深的秘密——抛弃曾经的妻子——一无所知。直到阿巴斯卒中后，玛利亚姆才在阿巴斯逐渐敞开自我的讲述中得知这个秘密，对于他的袒露，玛利亚姆的内心迎来了矛盾的拷问。她一边责问阿巴斯，"你其实并没有真的和我结婚"；一边又陷入遭遇欺骗的心痛中："她的脑海中生成了一幅画面，那是一对母子的身影，走在一片陌生的土地上，不过就是一个女人和一个孩子的黑影或是剪影，沿着一条小道前行。她不确定为什么这幅画面会给她带来如此大的痛苦"。（古尔纳，2022：135）除此之外，因为担心被孩子们误解，玛利亚姆也对自己曾遭受的不公正的侵害闭口不谈，在家庭关系中拒绝谈论创伤，这反而造成了更大的创伤隐患与伦理危机。

家庭中的女儿汉娜遭遇的创伤则归结于家庭创伤的代际传递。汉娜出生并成长在英国，父亲阿巴斯拒绝谈论太多他的母国坦桑尼亚的事，母亲玛利亚姆对自己的过去的创伤也闭口不言，导致汉娜对遥远的故乡和父母的过去几乎处于一无所知的状态。"在异国，家庭是帮助流散二代构建个人身份的基本途径"。（朱振武等，2022：49）汉娜没能在构建自己的原生身份时获得来自一代移民的帮助，自然对自己的身份陷入了迷茫。一方面，汉娜不能接纳自己的移民身份，为自己的肤色和出身产生自卑感，甚至对于父母的移民身份也充满了不理解。汉娜称自己的家庭为"缺陷家庭"（古尔纳，2022：33），她不理解为什么父母要对自己曾经的故事和经历保持缄默，觉得整个家中都弥漫着异样的气息，与父母和家庭产生了强烈的疏离感。另一方面，对自己原生身份的不确认、对移民身份的自卑感又导致汉娜产生了强烈的不安全感，她急于拥抱新的社会身份，因此用尽方法融入英国文化社会中。

然而自己的移民出身和父母未知的过去一直是压在汉娜心中的一块巨石。在她尽力融入白人男友尼克的家庭时，汉娜的身份屡屡受到质疑和歧视。这个看似包容的白人家庭传递给汉娜的只有高高在上的审视甚至恶意。当他们用高傲且理所当然的态度谈论非洲时，汉娜只能保持沉默；当他们问起汉娜的家乡时，汉娜别无可谈，只能承认自己不知道。这些人的态度先是意外，继而转变为替汉娜感到悲哀："我深感震惊。你是说你不知道，还是说你不想知道？听到你如此漠不关心地谈论你的家乡，我感到悲哀"。（古尔纳，2022：79）汉娜不能进行自我身份认同的痛苦却成了白人口中的笑谈。汉娜经受来自家庭的创伤，被迫遭遇白人审视的痛苦，她陷入深深的自我拉扯中。

4. 创伤疗治

阿巴斯的创伤修复是通过坦言内心深处的秘密完成的。"通过讲故事、叙述创伤经历才能去除受害者过去的伤痛，并且帮助受害者继续生存下去"（尚必武，2011：85），向他人叙述内心受到的伤害，是受创者走出心灵创伤的重要手段之一。阿巴斯因卒中而卧于病榻，他不断回忆过去，内心反复承受煎熬，终于决定将自己的过去讲述给妻子玛利亚姆听。"他越想越兴奋，就等着她能抽出身来聆听，只是因为吐字费劲才灰心沮丧。"（古尔纳，2022：99）在这种坦诚的回顾中，阿巴斯终于重新审视了自己的移民身份，与过去的自我达成了最终的和解。

自我身份的重构是玛利亚姆治愈创伤的路径。她最终选择向孩子们吐露自己被伤害过的事实。这意味着玛利亚姆在内心中选择不再与过去的苦痛做无意义的斗争。"苦难的吐露促使她拔去了记忆中的锐刺，得以重构个人身份认同"。（朱振武等，2022：49）作为母亲的玛利亚姆不再一味回避，选择承担责任，主动向下一代家庭成员传递曾经的创伤回忆。而在故事的最后，玛利亚姆决定重拾"女儿"这一身份，在子女的陪伴下回到三十年未归的曾经的家庭。更为重要的是，玛利亚姆开始去难民中心做志愿者，重新开始自己的社会生活。在此之前，玛利亚姆的社会身份一直是"移民""流散者"，而"重构个人身份认同"的选择给予了玛利亚姆这个饱受创伤、不被认可的社会边缘女性重新探寻自己的身份、实现自我价值的机会。在与家庭和社会的重新互动中，玛利亚姆的旧日创伤被治愈，个人身份也得到了确立。

在作为二代移民的汉娜想要融入英国社会的梦想因男友及其家庭的对待彻底破灭后，她明白自己的身份只能换来屈辱的对待。"当移民在移入社会里受到歧视的时候，因为感受到威胁与排挤，反而会加强对原有种族身份的认同"。（韩晓燕等，2016：176）汉娜终于认识到，一味地拒绝承认自己的非洲身份只是一种不能正视自我的逃避行为。原本对父亲的重婚罪和母亲被伤害的经历耿耿于怀的汉娜在听完父亲留下的"最后的礼物"后，也彻底释怀了。"记忆是人类建构并确立自我身份的重要手段"（尚必武，2011：87），正视家庭的创伤记忆让汉娜知晓了父母的难言之隐和自我的身份之源。她最终理解沉默的父母，陪伴母亲回到曾经的养父母家，踏上寻根之旅。汉娜在家庭关系和婚恋关系中受过创伤，在白人社会中被边缘化，在陷入身份危机时一味逃离原有的文化和传统，最终完成了自己的身份重构，接纳自己作为流散者后代的身份，并对自己的原生身份进行积极探索。

5. 结语

在《最后的礼物》中，古尔纳致力于深入探究流散者及其后代作为"边缘人"的创伤、沉默与困境。阿巴斯、玛利亚姆和汉娜都遭遇了不同程度的内心创伤。阿巴斯是流浪半生的人，童年在家庭中被苛待，抛弃妻子来到异国他乡，备受创伤的同时保持沉默的态度度过了后半生。不论是作为儿子、丈夫、父亲还是移民，他始终都陷于自我身份的困境中，直到死前把秘密说出，阿巴斯的心结才得以解开。玛利亚姆的一生都伴随着创伤，从出生的身份不明到在寄养家庭间屡次辗转，她对自己的身份始终持不认同态度。被寄养家庭伤害至深的玛利亚姆出走后仍然遭遇身份危机，直到她作出选择，直面创伤，并对自己的身份进行再探寻。身为流散者后代的汉娜由于没有从父母处获得原生身份的确定，一开始选择背弃自己的文化传统，却也遭受了白人社会的鄙夷。汉娜最终选择重新审视自己的选择，得以重构自己的文化身份，也走上了重拾自我的希望之路。在古尔纳的安排下，小说中的主要人物最终都正视自己过去的创伤，走向了自我和解和接纳，进行身份重构，寻找自我救赎，实现了创伤的治愈。这不仅体现了古尔纳对流散者命运的关怀，也为面临身份困境的流散者提供了一条引导之路。

参考文献

[1] CARUTH C, 2016. Unclaimed experience: trauma, narrative, and history[M]. Baltimore: The Johns Hopkins University Press.
[2] FOSTER D A, 2000. Trauma and memory[J]. Contemporary Literature, 41(4): 740-747
[3] 弗洛伊德，1987 精神分析引论新编[M]. 高觉敷，译. 北京：商务印书馆.
[4] 弗洛伊德，2004. 弗洛伊德文集：第四集[M]. 杨韶刚，译. 长春：长春出版社.
[5] 古尔纳，2022. 最后的礼物[M]. 宋佥，译. 上海：上海译文出版社.
[6] 韩晓燕，田晓丽，2016. 制度、文化与日常确证——外来移民及其子女的情景性身份认同[J]. 清华大学学报(哲学社会科学版)，31(6)：175-182，195.
[7] 赫尔曼，2015. 创伤与复原[M]. 施宏达，陈文琪，译. 北京：机械工业出版社.

[8] 钱超英，2006. 流散文学与身份研究——兼论海外华人华文文学阐释空间的拓展[J]. 中国比较文学（2）：77-89.
[9] 萨义德，2003. 文化与帝国主义[M]. 李琨，译. 北京：生活·读书·新知三联书店.
[10] 尚必武，2011. 创伤·记忆·叙述疗法——评莫里森新作《慈悲》[J]. 国外文学，31(3)：84-93.
[11] 袁丹，2023. 创伤理论视域下《喜福会》的家庭记忆书写研究[J]. 东莞理工学院学报，30(2)：48-53，78.
[12] 朱振武，游铭悦，2022. 身份认同与共同体意识——最新诺奖作家古尔纳《最后的礼物》的创作旨归[J]. 山东外语教学，43(2)：71-82.

现实空间与心理空间的叙事比较研究
——以《在城崎》为例

张佳琪

1. 志贺直哉与心境小说

志贺直哉是活跃于大正到昭和时期的日本小说家，并作为白桦派的代表作家蜚声日本文坛，被誉为"小说之神"。他的文章偏向写实，用简洁的语言表现了强烈的自我意识，也是私小说、心境小说的代表作家，可谓"一语天然万古新，豪华落尽见真淳"。其作品多反映了和父亲的不和等真实经历以及调和的过程，饱含从生活中汲取的雨露所凝结的思想。最具代表性的作品是以在城崎温泉的疗养经历为原型的短篇小说《在城崎》，和描写直面人生危机并与之抗争的主人公的生活写照的唯一一篇长篇小说《暗夜行路》。他被很多作家崇拜，同时给芥川龙之介、小林多喜二等作家的创作带来了巨大影响。芥川龙之介在《文艺的，更加文艺的》（1927）中说，志贺直哉的小说是"不像小说的小说"，是一种无情节的、散文化的小说。

《在城崎》是志贺直哉于 1917 年发表于《白桦》上的短篇小说。主人公"我"被山手线电车撞飞后背受伤，为了养伤，前往城崎温泉待了一段时间，在那里偶然目击了蜜蜂、老鼠和蝾螈的生死场景。目睹了动物死亡的"我"，开始思考生存和死亡的意义，察觉到生与死并非对立的两极，自己与死亡之距也并非如此遥远。

"这也是一部真实的小说。老鼠的死、蜜蜂的死、蝾螈的死，都是那时几天亲眼看见的事。从那以后所感受到的，我想是可以坦率而诚实地写出来的。所谓心境小说，也不是由从容而产生的心境。"（志贺直哉，1974）文学的土壤是生活，志贺直哉的才思也是源于生活经历的所见所闻，但在其中又融入了思想的流动、精神的升华所构成的心境调和。著名评论家伊藤整分析，心境小说与破灭型的私小说不同，是以完善自我为目的的调和性文学（伊藤整，1945）。所以志贺直哉用意识勾勒补全城崎温泉的全貌，在一桩桩看似细微的邂逅中，穿行于现实与心境之间，成为"小说之神"。

2. 空间之于文学的意义

空间本身最早作为一个物理范畴被人们熟知，不管是东方的宗教文化，还是西方的苏格拉底等哲学家的思辨文化，对于传统空间的定义都认为人与空间存在着紧密的相关性，同时空间是人的认知对象。近代经由弗兰克、海德格尔、列斐伏尔等哲学家对于空间问题的探究和发展，空间不再是人们一直所漠视的和生息无关的客观的物理或地理空间，而是蕴含着社会关系与社会生产的空间形式。空间被看成某种意识形态的产物，反过来又表现、生产、强化这种意识形态，并且是意识形态转化为实际的关键，因而空间对于生活于其间的人来说具有决定意义（余新明，2008）。列斐伏尔在《空间的生产》这本著作中将空间分为三种形式：

空间实践、空间表征、表征空间。空间的物质特性在空间实践这一形式中被充分展现，而精神层面的想象空间则在空间表征中被无限放大，它们共同构成了文学艺术中的表征空间。

对文学研究而言，空间理论的价值比起提供在方法论上的新突破，更在于认识论层面的极富颠覆性的尝试，从而也构建了空间在文学批评知识体系和文学表征中的重要地位。由于空间不仅具有物理属性，而且具有哲学和社会学属性，文学批评理论中逐渐有了从空间角度切入的具体方法和实践，这一变革也使得空间、地方和文学的动态关系在文学研究宇宙中闪烁出新的光芒。1998 年，克朗在他的著作《文化地理学》中就文学空间理论提出自己的阐释，文学对于地理学的意义，在于显示社会如何为空间所建构，建构这一地理空间的社会意义的正是文学的主体性。文学与空间理论的关系不是前者再现后者，文学不可能置身空间之外而只能投身空间中（克朗，1998）。通过对克朗在文学与地理学交叉学科视域下的文学地理景观（空间）的研究，在一定程度上亦可为时下文学研究领域的跨学科研究策略提供些许启发（孟浩，2017）。

3. 空间叙事学与超现实空间理论

后经典叙事学发端于 20 世纪 80 年代，戴维·赫尔曼的《复数的后经典叙事学》（1999）宛如一把钥匙一般开启了这一研究领域的大门。解构主义、女性主义、后结构主义、精神分析等叙事学批评理论乘着新兴的文学作品和流派如雨后春笋一般层出不穷，在当时已经成熟的叙事学理论土壤中仿佛掀起了一场颠覆式的文学革命，在一定程度上对经典叙事学造成了冲击，将文学的历史车轮推入后经典叙事学阶段。叙事作品对"空间"的存在有了更加主动的认知，而且不只是停留在物理空间层面，还注重社会空间和心理空间的认知（赵红红等，2017）。

梳理我国的空间叙事学先行研究历史，大致可分为四个阶段。20 世纪 80 年代属于发展初期，主要进行关于叙事学理论著作的翻译和引进工作；20 世纪 90 年代进入发展中期，有学者不甘于对国外已有理论的探索，而是以此为基础构建本土化叙事理论，如叶世祥的《鲁迅小说的空间形式》、董小英的《叙述学》等研究成果相继登场。张世君的《〈红楼梦〉空间叙事的分节》，用空间叙事学理论别开生面，开辟对于我国古典文学新的研究道路。2000 年后进入逐渐成熟的开拓阶段，经过多位学者的铢积寸累，空间叙事学的研究逐渐积累起来。学者申丹在《叙事学研究在中国与西方》（2005）一文中回顾了国内外叙事研究的发展历程，梳理了经典叙事学与后经典叙事学的关系，对西方文化语境下的叙事学与本土叙事进行了详细的比较和分析。2008 年后，空间叙事学进入快速发展时期，程锡麟对于西方空间叙事理论的框架和内容做了至纤至悉的论述；龙迪勇则指出："无论是'经典叙事学'，还是'后经典叙事学'偏重的都是时间维度，而有意无意地忽视了空间维度上的研究，现在随着各种问题的凸显和各种研究条件的成熟，叙事学已经到了该重视空间维度研究的时候了。"（龙迪勇，2011）

龙迪勇作为国内研究空间叙事学的大家，将空间叙事理论做了更加条分缕析的阐述，《空间叙事研究》对小说文本故事空间和形式空间的研究填补了学术界的空白，从理论上论证了小说这种时间性媒介如何表现空间，使本来司空见惯的小说文本再次得到更明晰有力的阐释（云燕，2015）。

超现实空间叙事在当代小说叙事中扮演着重要角色，是当代小说叙事空间化的标志之一（陈宸，2022）。超现实空间已经突破了传统因果、时间顺序等串联的叙事结构的桎梏，并且承担着叙事的重要作用。超现实空间又称虚拟空间，较为常见的有梦境空间、心理意识空间等。梦境是一个人埋藏于内心最真实的感受，被秩序规范、关系等级等人类社会客观因素所制约的潜意识则通常可以通过梦境这一按钮开启，心理意识空间是内心世界的产物，在叙事学研究中，超现实空间理论为其浇灌了新的养料。在超现实空间的小说中，虚拟空间与现实空间并不是泾渭分明的，二者可以共存不悖。美国心理学家威廉·詹姆斯提出"意识流"这一概念，即人的意识宛如潺潺流水、粼粼流光、永不停歇，超越时空的界限，不断与感知到的外界事物相连。作者为如实展现意识的流动，需放弃正常的时空顺序与因果关系，转而根据心理意识时空进行叙事。于是时间颠倒、空间重叠就成为该类作品的常见情形，其所要叙述的事件从时间顺序中解放出来，文本自然而然呈现出一种叙事的空间化倾向。

4.《在城崎》的空间叙事特点

《在城崎》作为一部时间和空间共存的作品，相较于时间维度，空间维度在其中承担了举足轻重的作用，本文从小说中设定的"城崎温泉城の崎温泉""部屋""川"等物理空间和作者自己的心理空间等多维空间进行文本分析，考察空间叙事维度下反映的作者对于自然生灵以及生死的反思。

在志贺直哉的小说中，我们总能看到他对客观外在物的声、光、色、影、形在顷刻间引发人的意识流动的精妙描写。他根据天马行空的意识流动，使不同的心理时空被自然地穿插起来。《在城崎》的故事主线极其简单，并且没有明显的因果关系，围绕三个场景以及三种动物的生死给"我"带来的心境的变化而展开，但志贺直哉通过构筑人物不断变换的心理意识空间把简单的叙事构思得非常丰满，通过超现实空间的引入，进一步深化了叙事的抒情效果以及对于死亡的超脱这一主旨。

首先，第一点是由城崎温泉所代表的现实空间。"我"选择城崎温泉作为车祸后疗养的居所，其中各种实体化的风景组合所勾勒出的画卷充满了细节感与真实感，同时其又具有封闭性，把这个空间和外界真实世界相隔离，渲染清冷寂静的氛围以烘托"我"的心境。

例如：

"ある午前、自分は円山川、それからそれの流れ出る日本海などの見える東山公園へ行くつもりで宿を出た。「一の湯」の前から小川は往来の真中をゆるやかに流れ、円山川へ入る。或所迄来ると橋だの岸だのに人が立って何か川の中の物を見ながら騒いでいた。それは大きな鼠を川へなげ込んだのを見ているのだ。"

"我"打算前往圆山川以及东山公园时，从"一之汤"温泉前方出发，与一条轻柔地缓缓流淌着的小溪同道，随后便望见被鱼钎刺穿头颈的不断挣扎的老鼠以及拿石头不断投掷老鼠的围观取笑的人群，温泉与河流的交汇处也是故事情节的核心之处，空间随着"我"步伐的移动而随之流转，到达众目睽睽之下老鼠濒死挣扎的画面，这种鲜明的对比引发了作者对死亡的思考，如若缺少紧扣现实空间的指引，那么这样散文化的小说也仅仅是散而无韵，一个浸润着柔软的清泉的宁静和谐的现实空间就这样被在垂死中求救的老鼠刺破，强烈的空间冲突也推动了叙事的戏剧性进一步深入。

再如：

"或夕方、町から小川に沿うて一人段々上へ歩いていった。山陰線の隧道の前で線路を越すと道幅が狭くなって路も急になる、流れも同様に急になって、人家も全く見えなくなった。あの見える所までという風に角を一つ一つ先へ先へと歩いて行った。物が総て青白く、空気の肌ざわりも冷々として、物静かさが却って何となく自分をそわそわとさせた。"

随后物理空间又转向一个新的场景，仿佛镜头一般慢慢推移，穿过一个个拐角后"我"的视野和"我"的身处之境带领读者到另一个空间，开启一场新的叙事，溪流由缓至急，周围渐渐一片空虚，万物都变得苍白清冷，没有任何绚烂的景色，只有"青白く"这一抹淡淡的颜色，宛如青烟似的淡薄而不真实，奠定了城崎温泉这幅画的主色调，同时感情基调也浸入读者心底。随着空间的变换，为我接下来和蝾螈的相遇以及思考做了铺垫。通过场景空间营造不断变换的氛围感，无须传统叙事的铺陈，而"我"的心境已在这种寂冷之中悄然发生了变化。

现实的物理空间是心理空间的基础，城崎温泉作为短篇小说中空间描写的一个出发点，超越了地理名词的意义，用各种空间标识物作为素材，融入声音、颜色以及温度等多种感官进行分析，宛如一幅画卷一样徐徐展开

第二点是由作者心理反映出的虚拟空间，却与中国叙事者善于书写的包含传奇仙境、鬼神幻觉的虚幻空间有所不同，志贺直哉的此作品中的虚拟空间分析主要集中在主人公的幻想与回忆中。

例如：

"淋しい考えだった。然しそれには静かないい気持がある。自分はよく怪我の事を考えた。一つ間違えば、今頃は青山の土の下に仰向けになって寝ている所だったなど思う。青い冷たい堅い顔をして、顔の傷も背中の傷も其儘で。祖父や母の死骸が傍にある。それももうお互いに何の交渉もなく、——こんな事が想い浮ぶ。"

全文叙事中并无描绘"我"当时受伤却没有丧命的细节，而是用一种寂寞而又宁静的心境作为回忆大门的钥匙引领读者进入到"我"徘徊生与死的边缘的时刻，至此某种空间的凝固性悄然丧失，从物理的空间中的景观转移到自己的心境，运用意识描绘自己孤寂淡漠的状态，幻想出当时若是不小心就可能丧命从而和自己的祖父和母亲埋葬在一起的虚拟空间，这个虚拟空间虽然是存在于"我"脑海中的一个假设，但也混杂着现实世界带给我的心理暗示，超越现实空间的桎梏给予了叙事更深层次的内涵。求生的本能不管是人还是动物，在死亡袭来时会驱使自己不懈抗争，人在濒死之际才能最深地理解生的意义，才最深地发现生的渴求，即使死亡是定数的归宿。

再如：

"で、又それが今来たらどうかと思って見て、猶且、余り変わらない自分であろうと思うと「あるがまま」で、気分で希う所が、そう実際に直ぐは影響はしないものに相違ない、しかも両方が本当で、影響した場合は、それでよく、しない場合でも、それでいいのだと思った。"

连续的心理描写为读者创造了一个完整的心境空间，在现实景物的描绘之后，则毫不掩饰地抒发了"我"对此景的感受和心境。"我不愿看到老鼠将死的样子""注定的命运是死，老鼠却在拼命逃脱"。细腻的心理空间也具有浓厚的抒情色彩，没有复杂的故事的情节，甚至连老鼠的死亡也没有任何因果与背景，所用语言也并非从大处落墨，笔法汹涌澎湃，而是从小处着眼，从一点显示全貌，描写玲珑剔透、细致亲切，并呈现出复杂多元的心理意识空间，给读者创造一个细微却又引人入胜的真实世界，文章自然地联系到"我"的受伤，以及受伤

后自己所采取的行动，这正与追求活命的老鼠并无两样，以此伸展到"我"对生与死的深入思考，是叙事散文化以及空间的抒情特征升华的泉眼。

第三点是现实空间与心理意识流空间交相辉映。

志贺直哉利用叙事写景，把文学的力量注入妙不可言同时又真实可信的描写中去倾诉内心的情感。在作品中又巧妙地处理景物现实空间与心理意识空间二者的关系，勾画空间中的真实的笔触，与隐藏于简化之下的深处的独具的心理空间存在相辅相成互为表里，交相辉映的关系。

例如：

"自分は「范の犯罪」という短編小説をその少し前に書いた。それは范の気持を主にし、仕舞に殺されて墓の下にいる、その静かさを自分は書きたいと思った。"

通过蜜蜂的死亡这一现实事件，联想到另一个虚拟的意识流空间——自己创作的小说《范的犯罪》里的世界。姓范的华人由于妻子婚前曾与自己的朋友有染而燃起嫉妒之火，加之自身的心理压抑，最终将妻子杀害。"我"在小说中详细的刻画了范的心路历程，而在此文中蜂之死的现实空间不仅仅是一幅生命逝去的风俗画，还是触发虚拟空间的装置，把叙事视角流畅地转换到超现实空间，这一高超的叙事技巧进一步增强小说对于心境的剖析与艺术性。

再如：

"遠く町外れの灯が見え出した。死だはちはどうなったか。その後の雨でもう土の下したに入ってしまったろう。あのねずみはどうしたろう。海へ流されて、今ごろはその水ぶくれのした体をごみといっしょに海岸へでも打ち上げられていることだろう。"

"我"踏上了回归旅馆的归程，看到了远处的灯火，物理空间营造了一种平静孤独的氛围，而"我"的内心却突破时空限制，重新飘到了蜂之死、鼠之死的空间，只保留这一份清冷的意蕴围绕着"我"，变成了打开对于生死的思考的钥匙，使文章逐步进入心境中最深刻的感悟"生与死并非对立的两极，对于我而言好像并无差别"。

志贺直哉经由个人与三种动物的时光，向内窥见自由的自我，并由此超脱物理空间，向着纷繁多彩的心理空间遨游——这个空间是他对自我与外界关系的理解的象征，也是最终改变心境，超脱生死于物外与自己和解的过程。

5. 结语

从空间叙事的角度来看，作为"小说之神"的志贺直哉完美地诠释了内容层面以及形式层面的空间的叙事技巧和魅力。内容层面既有封闭的现实空间，又有想象和回忆的虚拟空间，形式层面上打破了时间的序列性，用时空交错和现实与心理空间交错等技巧，使文本呈现丰富的空间形式。《在城崎》所描绘的不仅是当下时态，而是过去、现在、未来交织在一起，而且回忆、意识流的虚幻世界与现实世界交织一起，从双重空间的交叠中为读者打开了探索心境的道路。

志贺直哉描绘的是景物，而挖掘、流露的却是情感与心境。他把这无形的情绪穿过现实空间、心理与意识空间的透视，使之呈现于读者面前，从空间叙事的角度入手，亦可以更好地去参悟志贺直哉对生的欣喜与对生的渴求、对死的寂寞与对死的静观。

参考文献

[1] CRANG M, 1998. Culture geography [M]. London: Routledge.
[2] 列斐伏尔，2022. 空间的生产[M]. 刘怀玉等，译. 北京：商务印书馆.
[3] 陈宸，2022. 论当代小说中的超现实空间叙事[J]. 文化学刊（10）：84-87.
[4] 龙迪勇，2011. 空间在叙事学研究中的重要性[J]. 江西社会科学，31(8)：43-53.
[5] 孟浩，2017. 迈克·克朗文学空间理论研究[J]. 大学教育（6）：87-88.
[6] 余新明，2008. 小说叙事研究的新视野——空间叙事[J]. 沈阳大学学报（2）：79-82.
[7] 云燕，2015. 叙事的空间与空间的叙事——读龙迪勇《空间叙事研究》[J]. 江西社会科学，35(1)：251-255.
[8] 赵红红，唐源琦，2021. 当代"空间叙事"理论研究的演进概述——叙事学下空间的认知转变与实践[J]. 广西社会科学（3）：74-81.
[9] 志賀直哉，1974. 志賀直哉全集第八卷[M]. 東京：岩波書店.

朦胧诗中的模糊修辞——以舒婷的诗为例

张文俊

1. 引言

自扎德(Lofti A. Zadeh)发表论文《Fussy Sets》(模糊集)并提出了著名的模糊理论(Fuzzy Theory)以来,科学思想方法迎来了划时代的变革,模糊数学、模糊逻辑学、模糊语言学、模糊心理学等学科应运而生。模糊修辞学是介于模糊语言学与修辞学之间的交叉学科,吕季明(1988)认为模糊修辞"具有多学科性,即边缘科学的性质"。"模糊修辞学基本上是一种应用科学",目的是把模糊语言学的研究成果应用于实践,利用模糊词语和模糊结构的特点和规律达到准确描述事物和表达模糊观念的目的。

在模糊修辞学正式问世之前,模糊语言学已取得大量研究成果。模糊语言学以模糊语言为研究对象,集中探讨模糊语言的成因、模糊度与交际功能等。模糊修辞学与其不同,不以静态的语言因素的模糊性为研究对象,而是研究语言在运用过程中产生的模糊现象,即模糊言语。模糊修辞学不是去探讨自然语言本身的模糊性质,而是去研究在语言活动中模糊手段的表现形式,及如何利用模糊语言现象来提高表达水平(吴家珍,1988)。

人类语言本质上是精确的,也是模糊的,二者构成了语言的矛盾统一性。在一些不愿精确、不必精确或不能精确的言语环境中,如果一味采用定量、定性的词句来表达,往往难以满足交际的需要,还会使语言枯燥乏味、令人窒息,影响交际目的的实现(夏云,2001);相反,如果用模糊的方式来表达,往往能达到更好的效果。

除了上述语用功能外,模糊语言还具有审美功能。模糊修辞所传递的美学信息是极其丰富的,它所产生的多种美学效应能使人获得内蕴丰富、意味绵长的美学享受(陈意德,2001)。

诗歌,作为文学作品的最高艺术形式之一,具有极高的美学价值,通常比其他任何文学样式都更需要模糊修辞(陈位祥,1993)。诗歌的本质是模糊的,诗歌的模糊修辞现象是最普遍的,诗歌的魅力主要通过模糊修辞来体现,模糊是诗歌语言及其表达的特点(陈位祥,1993)。模糊修辞的各种修辞手段创造的含蓄美、朦胧美、色彩美、和谐美等极大地提高了语言的交际功能,模糊修辞的美学效应可以和其他任何修辞格相媲美(陈意德,2001)。

盛行于 20 世纪 70、80 年代的朦胧诗常因其晦涩、怪僻而遭人诟病。人们读过之后常不知其所云,读了又似乎没读。造成朦胧诗作这种"朦胧感"的其中一个原因就是模糊修辞的使用。因此,本文拟就朦胧诗派代表人物之一舒婷,对其诗作中的模糊修辞使用进行分析,以期揭开朦胧诗的神秘面纱。

2. 舒婷及其诗作简介

舒婷(原名龚佩瑜),1952 年出生于福建厦门石码镇,是朦胧诗派的代表作家之一,著有诗集《双桅船》(1982)、《会唱歌的鸢尾花》(1986)、《始祖鸟》(1992)、《舒婷的诗》（1994）、《一种演奏风格》（2009）等，散文集《心烟》（1988）、《硬骨凌霄》（1994）、《真水无香》（2007）、《自在人生浅淡写》（2015）等，曾获全国中青年优秀诗歌作品奖（1980）、第一届全国新诗优秀诗集奖（1983）、庄重文文学奖（1993）、新诗百年杰出贡献奖（2017）等。

舒婷曾在 20 世纪 80 年代初受到一般读者的欢迎，她在抒情方式上更接近中国诗歌沉郁、忧伤、节制的抒情传统。她早期的诗常以梦的破碎表现在动荡岁月中成长的一代人"渴望有所贡献，对真理隐隐约约的追求，对人生模模糊糊的关切"与"不被社会接受，不被人们理解"的矛盾与苦闷，表现个人面对历史与现实的痛苦与无奈。

本文选取的舒婷的三十六首诗作来源于杨克、陈亮主编的《朦胧诗选》（杨克等，2009：75-142）。

3. 模糊修辞在舒婷诗中体现

模糊修辞在诗歌中主要体现在模糊词语、意象的模糊组合、模糊的韵律手段等（陈位祥，1993），上述表达方式在所选的舒婷的诗中均能找到例证。

3.1 模糊词语

模糊词语包括在程度、范围、方位、地域、时间、动作、趋势、颜色、数量、心理等方面有伸缩性的模糊词。

3.1.1 以表程度和范围的词构成模糊修辞

表程度和范围的副词大多数都可以在诗歌中起到模糊修辞的作用，比如通过修饰其他词语一起构成模糊概念的最、很、极、更、非常、多么、那么、这样、十分等；还有本身具有模糊性的微、刚刚、将、大概、几乎等。具体例子如下：

"在我微颤的手心里放下一粒珠贝

……

它是这样伟大

……

它是这样渺小"

——《珠贝》

"心也许很小很小

世界却很大很大"

——《童话诗人》

在所选取的三十六首诗作中，并非每一篇都出现了表示程度或范围的词，可见舒婷的感情抒发并不主要以程度词得到强化。此外，这些词的分布具有很大的不均衡性，"很"出现的频率最高，单是在《童话诗人——给G.C》中就出现了 8 次，《会唱歌的鸢尾花》中出现 4 次，每次都是以"很……很……"的结构连续出现 2 次。"这样"共出现 6 次，其后常加双音节词，如"这样渺小""这样伟大"。程度副词的使用可以给读者无限的解释空间，比如"心"到底小到什么程度才算"很小"，"这样安慰你"究竟是以怎样的姿态安慰别人？每个人对"大""小"等词的感知都是不同的，这些问题也都是无解的。

3.1.2 以情态词构成模糊修辞

情态词本身表示的就是一种不确定性，是介于是、否两极之间的连续统一体。情态词可以用来表频率（usuality）、概率（possibility）、倾向（inclination）、义务（obligation）。

（1）以表频率的词构成模糊修辞

频率词包括总是、常常、从未、一再、每天、多少次、不再等，具体例子如下：

"我<u>常</u>悲哀的仰望你的照片"

——《啊，母亲》

"也许我们的心事
<u>总是</u>没有读者"

——《也许》

"我那<u>无数次</u>
流出来又咽进去的泪水啊"

——《会唱歌的鸢尾花》

频率词的使用可以产生一种动态感。倘若诗人交代了具体次数，那么事件就已完成了，读者很难成为参与者融入进去。使用频率词恰能创造一种"某事正在进行"的感觉，读者能够置身其中，从而激发更多的情感共鸣。例如，若把"我那无数次流出来又咽进去的泪水啊"中的无数次改成一百次，读者能感受到的是"曾经绝望过"，哭了一百次以后也许就不哭了，而"无数次"能让读者产生"正在绝望"且"仍会绝望"的感觉，读来更加痛心疾首。

（2）以表概率的词构成模糊修辞

对某事发生概率的推测完全是个人主观臆测的结果，每个人的臆测结果都不尽相同。"也许""或许""说不准"等词常用来表示某事发生的可能性。具体例子如下：

"<u>也许</u>藏有一个重洋
但流出来，只是两颗泪珠"

——《思念》

"<u>或许</u>只要伸出手去
金苹果就会落下"

——《还乡》

舒婷主要使用"或许"一词来表达不确定的揣测，《也许》一诗全篇都是"也许"。"也许"既表达了多种情况的可能，又抒发了自己为理想而奋斗的决心和信念。这样写，避免了直白，增加了诗味，诗歌显得含蓄蕴藉。

（3）以表倾向的词构成模糊修辞

倾向反映的是是否想从事某事的主观意图，包括愿意、宁可、想要等。具体例子如下：

"<u>愿</u>我化为白色的小鸟"

——《海滨晨曲》

"我就是土壤
<u>想</u>这样提醒你"

——《赠》

倾向情态词的使用充满了浪漫主义色彩，往往表示与现实相反的情况。"我"永远不可能化身白色的小鸟，土壤也永远不可能提醒别人。

（4）以表义务的词构成模糊修辞

义务表达的是一种客观上的"不得不"，这类词包括应该、应当、必须等。具体例子如下：

> "是的，生命<u>不应当</u>随意挥霍"
>
> ——《人心的法则》
>
> "我<u>必须</u>是你近旁的一株木棉，
> 作为树的形象和你站在一起。"
>
> ——《致橡树》

这类词传达了一种强烈的情感倾向，使"我"的形象宛如一位烈士般决绝。但是舒婷在诗中此类词语使用得并不多，她的豪迈之气是并非借助义务情态词直接表达的。

3.1.3 以颜色词构成模糊修辞

所有颜色词都是模糊的。颜色在光谱上是连续不断的，可是任何一种语言标志颜色的词都是有限的。这些词把连续的光谱分割成若干界限不清的片段，所以颜色词的语义便是模糊的。颜色的不同不仅仅区别于相邻的颜色之间，还区别于同一颜色之间的深浅程度。具体例子如下：

> "我要<u>葱绿</u>地每天走进你的诗行
> 又<u>绯红</u>地每晚回到你的身旁
> ……
> "我的<u>黄</u>皮肤光亮透明
> 我的<u>黑</u>头发丰洁茂盛
> ……
> "不要哭泣了<u>红</u>花草
> ……
> "虽然再没有人
> 扬起<u>浅色</u>衣裙
> 穿过蝉声如雨的小巷
> 来敲你的<u>彩色</u>玻璃窗"
>
> ——《会唱歌的鸢尾花》
>
> "我的
> <u>黑沉沉</u>、<u>血汪汪</u>、<u>白花花</u>的土地啊"
>
> ——《土地情诗》

所选舒婷诗中出现的颜色词主要有白（6次）、黑（5次，除去黑夜）、绿（3次）、蓝（2次）、红（6次）、金（1次），具体的颜色词有琥珀色（1次），表示一类颜色的词有浅色（1次）与彩色（1次）。同一颜色又以雪白、苍白、洁白、白花花、白、幽蓝、蓝色、黑沉沉、黑色的、黑、鲜红、绯红、猩红、葱绿等具体色彩呈现。

可见，舒婷诗中的颜色词并不丰富，很多诗里未提及任何颜色，只能依靠读者自己想象画面。绚丽多彩并非她诗歌的特色。她最钟爱的颜色是黑与白，给人一种黑白影片的感觉。可就是这黑白底色中偶尔出现的红、绿、蓝等颜色更能抓住读者眼球，使意象更加实景化，给读者留下深刻印象。

3.1.4 以全称量词、统指代词构成模糊修辞

全称量词如都、全部等在语义上也是模糊的。作为读者，我们并不知道具体数目。汉语

中的部分全称量词可作统指代词使用，如一切、全部，故将具有全称量化义的兼类词于此处一并讨论。具体例子如下：

"让<u>所有</u>粘住的翅膀，
<u>都</u>颤抖着飞开去吧。"
……
"<u>凡</u>亮起来的
人们<u>都</u>把它叫做星"

——《黄昏剪辑》

"使春天的彩虹
在<u>所有</u>眸子里黯然失色
……
"汲取一生<u>全部</u>诚实与勇气"

——《人心的法则》

舒婷对"都"字情有独钟，三十六首诗作中共出现28次。"一切"出现22次，"全部"出现1次，"所有"出现4次。其中，在《这也是一切》中，全诗"一切"与"都"交错使用，分别出现18次与17次。黄瓒辉（2013）认为"都"在量化事件时具有左向约束的特点，表明"都"在量化事件时，表示的仍然是"无一例外"，即一个事件的集合中的每个成员都无一例外地具有某种性质（无一例外地能与另一个集合中的一个成员对应起来），而现实生活中多多少少总会有例外的发生。例如，人们总是把凡亮起来的叫作星吗？台灯、路灯、荧光棒该如何解释？

此外，全称词的使用可以看作夸张的修辞手法，在下文讨论夸张辞格时将不再赘述。

3.1.5 以人称指示词构成模糊修辞

指示词天生具有模糊特征，必须在语境中才能知道具体所指为何。常见的指示词有人称指示词、篇章指示词、空间指示词、时间指示词。由于时间、空间指示词的丰富多样性，将在下一小节单独论述，本小节仅讨论人称指示词。具体例子如下：

"一早<u>我</u>就奔向你啊，大海
把<u>我</u>的心紧紧贴上<u>你</u>胸膛的风波"

——《海滨晨曲》

"<u>它</u>是这样伟大
<u>它</u>的花纹，<u>它</u>的色彩"

——《珠贝》

"<u>她</u>是<u>他</u>的小阴谋家"

——《自画像》

"但山峰绝非有意
继续掠夺<u>我们</u>的青春
<u>他们</u>的拖延毕竟有限"

——《小窗之歌》

从人称来看，舒婷诗里出现频率最高的是第一人称"我"（共227次），其次是第二人称"你"（共170次）。第一人称的使用便于直抒胸臆，可以直接表达强烈的情感。第二人称以对话式的语体将读者带入诗中，情感交流更为顺畅。舒婷诗中"我"和"你"常连用，给人一种视角转换感,而且常用"我们"来并指"你"与"我"。

有些人称指示词能联系语境找到指称对象,比如"你"在《海滨晨曲》中指大海,在《啊,母亲》中指"我的"母亲。有些人称指示词能联系创作背景找到指称对象,如"你"在《童话诗人》中指顾城。有些人称指示词则找不到具体指称对象,留给人们无限遐想,比如《自画像》中的"她"与"他"可以指称任何恋爱中的情人。

3.1.6 以表时间的词构成模糊修辞

时间是一个外延很难划定的模糊概念(伍铁平,1980),对时间的定义往往采用循环论证,比如夏季是介于春秋之间的季节,秋季是介于夏冬之间的季节。时间本身是一个连续体,相邻的时段不能被划分出分明的界限,而诗歌却要对时间进行切分,这就会使得表时间范畴的词语具有模糊性。舒婷诗歌中的时间包括四季、日夜等。具体例子如下:

"和鸽子一起来找我吧
在<u>早晨</u>来找我"

——《会唱歌的鸢尾花》

"四月的<u>黄昏</u>里
流曳着一组组绿色的旋律"

——《四月的黄昏》

"<u>傍晚</u>的海岸<u>夜</u>一样冷静
<u>冷夜</u>的山岩死一般严峻"

——《致大海》

舒婷诗里出现最多的季节是春天,表达了舒婷对美好未来的希冀。然而,"夜"的大量使用(16 次)还是流露出舒婷对那个特殊时代的不满,作为亲历者,她的生活仿佛无时无刻不处于黑暗中,因此映射到她的诗作中。与"夜"搭配出现的词有"梦""夜""月""灯",可见,舒婷诗里的"夜"并非伸手不见五指的漆黑之夜,她的"夜"是绚丽的,是充满希望的,她相信黑夜过后便是黎明。

3.1.7 以语气词构成模糊修辞

语气词的使用有助于情感的抒发,可是语气词的精确意义是无法确定的。舒婷诗中出现的语气词有啊、吧、呵,具体例子如下:

"<u>啊</u>,在心的远景里
在灵魂的深处"

——《思念》

"生怕记忆也一样退色<u>呵</u>
我怎敢轻易打开它的画屏"

——《啊,母亲》

"祈求回答,她一言不发,
需要沉默时她却笑<u>呀</u>闹<u>呀</u>"

——《自画像》

舒婷使用最多的语气词是"啊"(33 次),语法上主要表达诗人对话语内容、命题内容的态度的强化,表现为加强陈述句话语的肯定或否定语气;语用上帮助传递并凸显说话人的某种情感或情绪（何鸣，2019）。"啊"既出现在句首，也出现在句中与句末，语用意义有轻微差别。

3.1.8 以叠词构成模糊修辞

叠词指相同的词、词素或音节重叠使用构成的词。重叠之前的形式称为"基式"，重叠之后的形式称为"叠式"（李宇明，1996）。王独清认为，用叠词"是一种表人感情激动时心脏振动的艺术，并是一种刺激读者，使读者神经发生振动的艺术"（邹问轩，1963：25）。汉语叠词包括 AA、ABB、AABB、ABAB 等各种构式，具有丰厚的美学阐释。舒婷诗中出现最多的是双字叠词。具体例子如下：

"凤凰树又<u>轻轻</u>摇曳
铃声把<u>碎碎</u>的花香抛在悸动的长街"
——《路遇》

"我拽着你的胳膊在堤坡上胡逛
绕过<u>一棵一棵</u>桂花树"
——《无题》

"落叶积深的台阶
都像<u>一页页</u>掀不动的记忆"
——《旧宅》

叠词的使用具有增强语势、加强修辞的效果。它使文字产生一种韵味的变化，变得更有节奏，从而表达更丰富的情意，呈现出一种艺术效果，给人以美的享受；能使描写对象更加形象，增加语言感染力。比如凤凰树"轻轻"摇曳，使读者心情舒缓；长街上的"碎碎"花香仿佛能从诗句中飘向读者的嗅觉。倘若用精确的语言表述凤凰树每分钟摆动的频率、花香在空气中的分子密度，那么这些感觉将全部消失，该诗将很难走进读者内心。

3.1.9 以普通词巧妙组合构成模糊修辞

普通词语在诗句中能够通过不符合常理的巧妙组合，于不协调中形成言语表面语义的不确定，构成模糊修辞，从而唤起读者的联想力。具体例子如下：

"它目睹了<u>血腥的光荣</u>
它记载了<u>伟大的罪孽</u>"
——《珠贝》

"四月的黄昏里
流曳着一组组<u>绿色的旋律</u>"
——《四月的黄昏》

"在<u>脆薄的寂静</u>里
做<u>半明半昧</u>的梦"
——《往事二三》

由这种词语变异引起的模糊修辞在舒婷诗中十分常见，足以可见诗人天马行空般的想象力。旋律怎能是绿色的呢？寂静又如何脆而薄呢？孤立地看，各个意象之间甚至毫不相关，但一旦被串成一个有机整体，组合成诗篇，便呈现出诗的完整画面，读者凭借联想和想象，可以捉摸到诗人贯穿意象的情丝，去填补意象之间的空白（陈位祥，1993）。

3.2 模糊语句

利用句子及其组合形式来构成模糊修辞十分常见。模糊语句产生于诗句对日常语法规则和搭配方式的变异。制造模糊语句常常通过减少语句成分，比如主语、谓语、宾语等，给人一种不确定感、模糊感来实现。除此以外，还可以通过名词用作动词、形容词用作动词以及虚词活用等词类活用方式，或宾语前置、主谓倒置等改变语义结构等，构建一种新的表达方式，达到模糊修辞目的（李玥，2009）。具体例子如下：

"<u>（省略主语）</u>天生不爱倾诉苦难

并非苦难已经永远绝迹"

——《惠安女子》

"就这样

<u>（省略主语）</u>握着手坐在黑暗里"

——《会唱歌的鸢尾花》

如将省略成分补全，则应该是"惠安女子天生不爱倾诉苦难""我们握着手坐在黑暗里"。通过比较可以发现，如果补全，整首诗将失去句子的节奏以及韵律的美感，繁冗以及拖沓，无法产生原作悠远、含蓄的美感。

4. 模糊辞格在舒婷的诗中的运用

具有模糊性的辞格叫作模糊辞格。吴家珍（1999）对汉语六十种辞格进行初步分析后发现，与模糊修辞密切关联的约占五分之四。辞格的模糊性主要表现在两个方面：一是指辞格内部的模糊性，即某一辞格在表意方面所呈现出的模糊性，二是指辞格之间的模糊性，即某一辞格与另一辞格在类属边界方面的不明晰性、亦此亦彼性，非此非彼性，也就是中介过渡性。模糊辞格在修辞上往往具有形象生动、凝练含蓄和新颖别致的显著特点。本文主要研究的是辞格内部的模糊性。在诗歌中，模糊辞格通常有比喻、拟人、夸张、排比等。

4.1 比喻

比喻一般是由本体、喻体和喻词三部分构成，根据本体、喻体和喻词这三部分的异同和隐现情况，比喻可以分为明喻、隐喻和借喻三类。比喻往往是用具体、熟悉的事物描绘抽象、陌生的事物，使人易于理解，可以使语言凝练、含蓄，增强语言的形象性和生动性，启发读者联想，给人留下深刻而鲜明的印象。

比喻成功与否的关键在于相似点。太相似则没有新奇感，流于平庸；太不相似，则彻底失去比喻的目的（李玥，2009）。舒婷诗中的比喻主要追求新颖，具体例子如下：

"但愿灯<u>像</u>今夜一样亮着吧"

——《赠别》

"蓓蕾<u>一般</u>默默地等待

夕阳<u>一般</u>遥遥地注目"

——《思念》

"阳光，蛇<u>一样</u>
在阴冷的墙根游动"

——《旧宅》

舒婷诗中明喻所占比例很大，尤以"像"字作喻词的明喻句居多。本体通常不省略，读者能明确知道把什么比作什么。本体、喻体间相似性不大，十分新奇，比如阳光的移动比作蛇的游动，台阶比作掀不动的记忆，都能使读者耳目一新，带来奇妙的阅读体验。

4.2 比拟

比拟是根据想象把物当成人来写，或把人当成物来写，或把甲事物当成乙事物来写的修辞方式（李玥，2009）。诗歌中一般是拟人，赋予景观、事物等以人的特性、情感。一般来说，物没有人的情感，自然就没有人的特性，但是通过比拟修辞，将人与物相连，赋予物以人的情感和动作，物给人造成模糊感，从而起到模糊词格的作用。具体例子如下：

"星星一定<u>疲倦</u>了"

——《流水线》

"<u>风</u>将<u>邀请</u>饥渴的<u>林木舞蹈</u>"

——《旧宅》

"黑色的<u>墙耸</u>动着<u>逼近</u>
<u>发出</u>渴血的，阴沉沉的<u>威胁</u>"

——《礁石与路标》

"月<u>色</u>还在<u>嬉笑</u>着奔下那边的石阶吗"

——《还乡》

太阳、月亮、星星等自然景象在舒婷诗中获得人的动作与情感。星星可以疲倦，阳光可以嫉妒，月亮可以笑着奔向石阶，星星可以笑着从草丛中钻出……利用比拟制造模糊感，使词格具有模糊性，人格化的物比原物更生动、更可爱、更具亲和力，虽然其形象只存在于读者想象之中，但是由于形象生动，贴近读者熟悉的事物，代入感更强，更能引发读者的情感共鸣。

4.3 夸张

夸张也是常用的模糊修辞格，读者一旦知道使用夸张格就不会将其当作客观现实来看待，因为夸张显然是模糊的。经过夸张后，原来的事物在受众的意想中发生变化，无论是夸大还是缩小，通常都会对原来事物的性状或功能有所强化。夸张修辞所表达的话语既生动、委婉、含蓄，又风趣、幽默，具有艺术渲染力和感染力。夸张可以直接增强显性的态度意义，更重要的是通过激发、启示等多种方式间接引发隐性的态度意义（布占廷，2010）。舒婷诗中夸张手法使用的具体例子如下。

"今夜的风中似乎<u>充满</u>了和声"

——《还乡》

"啊，浪花<u>无边无际</u>"

——《惠安女子》

"无论时代的交响怎样立刻卷去我的回应
你<u>仍</u>能认出我那<u>独一无二</u>的声音"

——《会唱歌的鸢尾花》

夸张辞格本身就具有的模糊性在现实中都不能被实现,所以关于诗歌的理解只能在想象中进行,无法清晰表现出来。声音的传播速度、范围都有其阈值,再大的声音都不可能"充满"整个夜晚;声波传播时间太短或受到干扰,则可别度下降,不一定"仍然"被认出。同样,太阳不可能遍布每一寸土地,总有一部分位于黑暗之中。梦与海浪也有边界,想象力有多大,梦就有多大;海浪再大也不能超过大海的边界。

4.4 排比

汉语中的排比被定义为"将三个或三个以上结构相似、语气一致、意义相关的词组、句子、段落排列起来,用以增强语势、加深感情"。不过也有学者认为两项也可构成排比,因此接下来的讨论里二项排比也考虑在内。具体例子如下:

"你有你的铜枝铁干,
　　像刀、像剑
　也像戟;
　……
"我们分担寒潮、风雷、霹雳;
　我们共享雾霭、流岚、虹霓。"

——《致橡树》

"我来了,你却意外地娴静温柔
　你微笑,你低语
　你平息了一切"

——《海滨晨曲》

"美丽的梦留下美丽的忧伤"

——《神女峰》

舒婷诗中的排比句式十分丰富多彩。有名词的排比,如"寒潮、风雷、霹雳";有动词的排比,如"绝不犹豫、绝不后退、绝不发抖";有简单句式的排比,如"呵,母亲"每小节都会出现一次;还有排比句式的互相嵌套,如"呵,母亲"中嵌套着"不是……不是……是……"这一结构。排比句式的使用使舒婷的诗歌更加朗朗上口、铿锵有力,这种声音上的磅礴气势可以看作她对那个特殊时代的反抗。

5. 结语

本文从模糊修辞学的视角出发,对朦胧派代表诗人之一舒婷的三十六首诗作进行了赏析,就其模糊修辞使用特征进行简要描述。作为一名敏感的女性诗人,舒婷善于在诗歌中使用模糊修辞来表现她特有的温情、浪漫和理想主义色彩。模糊修辞的使用给她的诗歌蒙上了一层朦胧的色彩,给人以独特的审美感受。

在对舒婷的诗歌中的模糊修辞使用的细致描绘上,本文有以下三个发现。

(1)舒婷善于用表程度和范围的词,表频率、概率、倾向的情态词,全称量词、统指代词、人称代词、表时间的词、语气词、双字叠词、词语巧妙组合构成模糊修辞,不善于用颜色词,但这并不影响我们对其诗歌中五彩斑斓画面的想象。

(2)舒婷善于用模糊语句,对句子各成分进行非常规处理,从而给人一种不确定感、模糊感,达到模糊修辞的目的。

（3）舒婷善于用比喻、比拟、夸张、排比等修辞格，使诗歌产生强烈的整体美感效应。

诗歌之美在于其音之美、形之美、义之美，然而囿于时间、精力等原因，本文未能从韵律角度及诗形方面对舒婷的诗歌进行分析。此外，本文仅对舒婷部分代表作进行了分析，未能对整个朦胧派诗人的写作风格进行分析。并且，在对上述模糊词语、模糊词格分类方面，尚有重复、不明确之处，希望后续研究可在此基础上完善。

参考文献

[1] 布占廷，2010. 夸张修辞的态度意义研究[J]. 当代修辞学（4）：53-59.
[2] 陈位祥，1993. 诗歌与模糊修辞[J]. 暨南学报（哲学社会科学）（2）：135-144.
[3] 陈意德，2001. 论模糊修辞及其美学效应[J]. 外语与外语教学（5）：28-30.
[4] 陈意德，2001. 论模糊修辞及其语用功能[J]. 天津外国语学院学报（2）：27-30.
[5] 陈意德，2001. 论语言的模糊性与模糊修辞[J]. 湘潭大学社会科学学报（1）：146-148.
[6] 陈永敬，2008. 排比的构成特征及排比项数限制的心理机制[D]. 武汉：华中师范大学.
[7] 陈治安，文旭，1996. 模糊语言学研究的回顾与展望[J]. 外国语（上海外国语大学学报）（5）：29-34.
[8] 韩庆玲，1998. 模糊修辞学研究综述[J]. 修辞学习（2）：8-10.
[9] 何鸣，2019. 现代汉语语气词"啊"的意义和功能研究——语法-语用互动视角[D]. 长春：东北师范大学.
[10] 黄瓒辉，2013. "都"和"总"事件量化功能的异同[J]. 中国语文（3）：251-264，288.
[11] 李宇明，1996. 论词语重叠的意义[J]. 世界汉语教学（1）：11-20.
[12] 李玥，2009. 广告语中的模糊修辞[D]. 天津：天津大学.
[13] 刘云平，2010. 广告中的模糊修辞[D]. 上海：上海交通大学.
[14] 吕季明，1988. 模糊修辞基本理论概述[J]. 当代修辞学（4）：42-44.
[15] 任利华，2005. 模糊修辞及其语用功能[D]. 西安：西安电子科技大学.
[16] 王宏，2003. 模糊语言及其语用功能[J]. 外语教学，2003(2): 9-12.
[17] 王希杰，1983. 模糊理论和修辞[J]. 新疆大学学报（哲学社会科学版）（3）：107-113.
[18] 吴家珍，1988. 谈独语句式的连用——连用形式与修辞功能[J]. 当代修辞学（1）：22-23，34.
[19] 吴家珍，1994. 当代汉语模糊修辞探寻[J]. 国际关系学院学报（4）：41-48.
[20] 吴家珍，1999. 再谈汉语模糊修辞[J]. 修辞学习（3）：15-17.
[21] 吴世雄，陈维振，2000. 中国模糊语言学的理论研究述评[J]. 福建师范大学学报（哲学社会科学版）（2）：76-81.
[22] 吴世雄，陈维振，2001. 中国模糊语言学:回顾与前瞻[J]. 外语教学与研究（1）：7-14，79.
[23] 伍铁平，1979. 模糊语言初探[J]. 外国语（上海外国语学院学报）（4）：39-44.
[24] 伍铁平，1980. 模糊语言再探[J]. 外国语（上海外国语学院学报）（5）：46-52.
[25] 伍铁平，1997. 模糊语言学综论[J]. 西南师范大学学报（哲学社会科学版）（6）：88-90.
[26] 夏云，2001. 模糊修辞与诗歌的表现力[J]. 福建外语（2）：61-65.
[27] 杨克，陈亮，2009. 朦胧诗选[M]. 北京：中国青年出版社.
[28] 张飞，2008. 文学语言的模糊修辞研究[D]. 昆明：云南师范大学.
[29] 邹问轩，1979. 诗话[M]. 哈尔滨：黑龙江人民出版社.

对话复调：《承诺》中的众声喧哗

张雨婷

1. 引言

2021 年，在三次提名布克奖后，达蒙·加尔格特凭借新作《承诺》获得殊荣，成为继纳丁·戈迪默和库切之后第三位获布克奖的南非作家。作为南非结束种族隔离和进入政治现代化的见证者，加尔格特与许多南非作家一样，密切关注南非的社会变革。他的早期作品常被解读为南非后种族隔离时代的政治寓言。

然而，随着历史进程步入 21 世纪，加尔格特不仅对社会转型有所思考，还对人与他者关系等根本性的人类问题进行了深入探索，这展现了他对当代南非社会的多元关怀（郑梦怀，2009）。《承诺》一书便是他对南非社会最新的观察与诠释。故事围绕着种族隔离的结束展开，记录了白人家庭斯沃特中四位家人的死亡。斯沃特承诺将其土地上的房屋所有权交给他们的黑人女仆莎乐美，以回报她对他们的忠诚。然而，未能遵守承诺的家庭成员相继离去，只留下了最小的孩子阿莫尔来履行承诺。

笔者发现，《承诺》在叙事上具有复调特征。"复调"作为一种音乐概念，由苏联著名文艺学家巴赫金在《陀思妥耶夫斯基诗学》中首次引入小说理论。复调反对小说话语的一元独白，推崇不同声音主体间的交互，以形成一种"众声喧哗"的氛围。除了挖掘史料价值，解读政治寓言外，加尔格特在《承诺》中还留下了更具文学性的趣味。他实验性地将戏剧、电影和史诗的创作手法相结合，构建了具有独特活力的小说世界，创造出了巴赫金诗学视界下多音齐鸣的复调效果。与此同时，他对叙事声音的特殊处理也为喧哗的众声注入了新的活力，使《承诺》的叙事与复调理论形成了有趣的对话。

2. 众声汇聚：多视角与内聚焦

《承诺》的戏剧生命力来源于非实体的或非中心人物的多样化视角。葬礼前，蕾切尔的鬼魂在房子里游荡。她亲吻了安东，做了她最喜欢的事情，看到了自己的身体，终于确认了自己的离去。鬼魂是西方戏剧中的一个重要形象。鬼魂最原始的悲剧色彩往往体现在对死亡与生前不能圆满的遗憾（王珏，2009）。由于疾病带来的死亡，蕾切尔的故事主要由他人讲述。借助鬼魂的视角，加尔格特带回了逝者的声音，还留下了意味深长的讽刺："你怎么知道她是鬼魂呢？许多活着的人也面目模糊、漂泊无依，这不是逝去的人独有的弱点"（加尔格特，2022：66）。此外，加尔格特还创造了一个奇怪的流浪汉，他有着感知来自其他次元精怪的能力。在西方文学作品中，流浪者叙事尤其善于利用见证性叙述者在观察或理解事物方面的能力缺陷来营造作品的讽刺效果（斯科尔斯等，2015：275）。加尔格特笔下的流浪汉同样有此意味。在自私、丑陋、精神崩溃的人身上，他看到的是巨大的精怪，而在阿莫尔身上，他看到的是柔和的蓝色火焰，这也间接表明了主人公阿莫尔的独特性。在《承诺》里，无论好坏，无论阴阳，无论主次，人物的声音均被展现了出来，这不仅丰富了故事情节，还颠覆了叙事的权威，更凸显了人物的内在价值和复杂性，使故事中的多元声音翻滚涌动。

与戏剧性的出场人物同时存在的，是加尔格特在叙事中采用的电影技法。电影之所以是一种叙事形式而非戏剧形式，乃是因为它没有直接、不带叙述地对故事加以呈现。相反，它总是借助于一个受到操控的视角，即摄影机镜头（斯科尔斯等，2015：292）。加尔格特在故事中所使用的并非全知全能的视角，而是一种自由间接叙事风格。镜头聚焦到人物内心，在展现其意识流动、切换的同时，故事情节也随之改变。加尔格特也曾表示，他的叙述手法受电影摄像启发，跳跃的视点"摆脱了传统的限制"，使他能够"自由驾驭人物内心跌跌撞撞、有待听取的不和谐音"（Galgut，2021）。

比起跨越 32 年的宏观时间线，故事本身停留的时间也如电影镜头般异常短暂。《承诺》每一部分的故事都聚焦在了葬礼前后几天，当新的章节开始时，人物和情境总是突然切入，没有任何前情回顾。这种运镜方式，让一个家族的悠久历史通过四次"快闪瞬间"展现出来。加尔格特在获奖后的采访中曾谈到，他最关心的是"时间的流逝和过去的时间"，因为在这种情况下，他能够表达在那个时刻整体精神碎屑的一部分（范德弗里斯等，2023）。在《承诺》转瞬即逝的镜头捕捉之外，加尔格特创造了一种时间的缝隙，给读者留下了广阔的想象空间。当读者从不同角度想象流逝的时间时，文本之外的声音也随之拥有了多样化的可能性。

对话是复调小说的核心。在复调小说中，"一切莫不都归结于对话，归结于对话式的对立，这是一切的中心。一切都是手段，对话才是目的"（巴赫金，1998：340）。在《承诺》中，加尔格特向内探求人物，巧妙地运用意识流手法，让微观对话在人物心中展开。这些对话承载着不同的声音，使得人物的内在冲突与思考得以表现。

阿莫尔内心的对话与选择为故事创造了一个有力量的结局。"想再多也没用。要么现在就行动起来，要么把该死的骨灰带走。将安东放进你的随身行李中？让安东的骨灰罐蹲在你房间的角落里？不，绝对不行。早就受够他了。把他撒向风中吧"（加尔格特，2022：424）。安东和阿莫尔这对兄妹的关系在整个故事中都被描绘得模糊不清。他们都有着异于其他家人对社会、对生命的感知，但安东沉迷于反复无常的决定，这最终让他走向了精神崩溃。阿莫尔撒骨灰的决定首先是对哥哥遗愿的遵从，意味着死亡带来的兄妹关系的最终和解。更重要的是，于阿莫尔而言，骨灰的散去暗示了她与过去关系的彻底决断，不仅是与斯沃特家族的历史，还是与家族所代表的阿非利卡人的历史。这段独白展现了阿莫尔对人生和历史的深刻思考，使得故事的余音绕梁不散。

3. 喧哗之中：作者的在场

在谈到复调小说中的多声部时，巴赫金说："有着众多的各自独立而不相融合的声音和意识，由具有充分价值的不同声音组成真正的复调——这确实是陀思妥耶夫斯基长篇小说的基本特点"（巴赫金，1998：4）。尽管《承诺》的故事中充斥着多种声音，但它们并不是完全独立的。加尔格特在《承诺》中对叙述者声音的独特处理使之成为对经典复调叙事的创造性反叛。

韦勒克等人提到，叙事方法的主要问题在于作者和他的作品之间的关系。戏剧的作者隐藏在背后，而史诗的作者讲述故事，并加入自己的评论，贯彻自己的风格（韦勒克等，2010：218）。以詹姆斯学派为代表的现代文学魔术师们则发明了一个伟大的把戏，叫作作者的消失。在亨利·詹姆斯看来，最戏剧性的讲故事方式是叙述者隐匿于一个被称为"中心意识"的人物身上。然而，在《承诺》中，叙述者的声音并未被隐藏。相反，加尔格特发现，让读者更多地意识到有人在讲故事或许大有裨益（范德弗里斯等，2023）。叙述者介入的声音有时是讽刺、客观的，而在另一些时刻，叙述者则会悄无声息地滑入人物，与他们的视角融合在一起。

当道貌岸然的巴蒂牧师上厕所时，叙述者突然插话道："从来没有哪个小说人物做过他此刻正在做的事情，就是掰开他的两瓣屁股，以便更痛快地释放痛苦。这法子可以让你确信，你并非虚构人物"（加尔格特，2022：162）。叙述者在此的声音既幽默又讽刺，因为书中人物在否认其虚构性的同时，读者将发现他们确实是在读一本小说。这种打趣的提醒形成了一个环形回声空间，让叙述者、人物、读者参与到了对话之中（范德弗里斯等，2023），颇具一种由史诗的混合叙述模式发展出的浪漫嘲讽式特点。

人称的转换是叙述者加入喧哗众声的重要标志，指向不明的自由间接风格见证了叙述者与人物的声音的融合。1995 年橄榄球世界杯决赛是南非长期分裂的族群在国际体育赛事中的首次凝聚，当斯沃特一家聚集在电视机前观看时，众人皆因自己是曼德拉新南非时代的一员而感到自豪，此时一个未知的声音响起："很难不为我们美丽的祖国流下热泪。我们都很棒，跟这一刻一样棒"（加尔格特，2022：145）。在这个瞬间，叙述者的声音似乎与一个群体合为一体。代词"我们"不仅指涉斯沃特家族，更代表在民族情绪高涨时刻的所有南非人。叙述者借"我们"之口，展现了新南非成立之初的蓬勃希望，创造了一个超越种族主义的"狂欢时刻"。

此外，加尔格特还运用元小说的技巧，借安东之口，对《承诺》进行了精彩的反思。故事里的安东一直在写一部小说，其自杀后，手稿才被阿莫尔发现。安东的小说有着这样的结构："这个男人将走过不同的人生阶段（每两个相邻的阶段大约间隔十年），不断成长，继而彻底走向成熟，经历希望、挫败、回归、成熟四个阶段，会随着季节的变化而变化。"（加尔格特，2022：209）在此刻，读者会发现，安东小说的四个部分（春天、夏天、秋天、冬天）正好对应了四场葬礼的时间。不同的是，安东这本虚构性小说的主人公亚伦会拥有胜利的夏天，而真正的安东则将在夏天死去，作者在这一嵌套叙述中藏了巨大的隐喻。尽管这本书尚未完成，但在空白处的插话里，作者借安东之口向读者发问，引导读者思考悬而未决的问题：这是一部家族传奇，还是一部农场小说？这是喜剧，还是悲剧？安东的小说与《承诺》的故事形成了镶嵌式对话。两种文本共存的对话不仅使得小说结构由扁平走向立体，还使文本阐释的可能性由单一走向多元，形成了独有的叙述张力。

4. 喧哗背后：对话与沉默

加尔格特的叙事创新在无意中与巴赫金的复调理论形成了一场伟大的对话。巴赫金认为，复调的实质恰恰在于：不同声音在这里仍保持各自的独立，作为独立的声音结合在一个统一体中，这已是比单声结构高出一层的统一体（巴赫金，1998：27）。在复调小说中，由于小说作者赋予了他们自由思考的空间，每一个人物都将成为一个具有独立意识的思维主体，他们可以和其他小说人物进行平等交流对话，并且这些对话都受其自身意识的支配。但在《承诺》中，加尔格特巧妙地让原本隐匿的叙述者声音适当地参与到了本就多元的众声之中，让其与它们一起，组成了一曲乐音更加喧哗，氛围更加丰富的复调音乐。

从本质上讲，《承诺》讲述的是斯沃特家族的故事。加尔格特在采访中也曾表明，他写作的初心实际上是洞察这个家庭的变迁（Gevisser，2021）。《承诺》将家庭和国家命运交织起来，让历史时刻更加凸显，实际上是加尔格特独特的构思所结出的意外果实。《承诺》的释读与故事中的声音具有同样的多元性和未完成性，这一点激励着读者进一步思考加尔格特创新复调叙事的原因。

在叙述者的幽默声音中，加尔格特探寻着文学的活力与乐趣。"尽管故事本身很沉重，故事的主题——衰落、死亡也很沉重，但我认为叙事声音可以是很轻松的，正是在这种叙事声音里，我找到了乐趣"（Gevisser，2021）。顽皮的声音为文本带来了生命力，反讽的视角让加尔格特建立起了与沉重话题的距离，叙事者的加入成为了喧嚣悲剧舞台的喜剧性调剂。在这个未知叙事声音打开的空间里，加尔格特可以自由评论角色——"你在急需帮助之时却遭人抛弃，阿尔文，你的救星在哪里？请记住，只有正直的人才会受到考验！"（加尔格特，2022：96）也可以评论讲故事的方式——"他为什么要模糊我们的视线，他是怎么把我们的时间浪费在他那些故事上的？"（加尔格特，2022：296）此类刻意留下的，与读者、与人物互动的问题，又何尝不是作家在喧哗众声中表达自我的一种复调尝试呢？

在叙述者的冷静声音中，加尔格特也提醒着读者文学的建构本质。当阿莫尔前往莎乐美家履行承诺时，叙述者作出了略显滑稽的假设："还不想去那里，等她拿到文件再说。虽说她还得等上一阵子才会拿到，但我们可以假设她拿到了，假设律师今早拟好了一份文件，给了她，于是那份文件就在你眼前，她手里正拿着它"（加尔格特，2022：410）。《承诺》中有很多这样的时刻。加尔格特用叙述者客观的声音提醒着读者，他们正在阅读一篇小说。这种技巧非但没有使整个故事变得毫无意义，反而迫使读者思考：这个故事是如何建构的？叙事声音如果有能力进入特定的人物或选择特定的角度，那么整个故事中是否存在着未被充分表达的声音？在叙述者的积极带动下，读者不仅仅是内容的接收者，也成为了故事的潜在参与者。

喧嚣之中，沉默和缺席依旧在场。尽管《承诺》的故事名义上围绕着黑人女仆莎乐美展开，但她的声音却被完全掩盖了。在一部如此乐于探究人物声音，甚至是非实质、非中心人物内心的小说中，这种隐藏是别有用心的。它反映了斯沃特家族对莎乐美的忽视及莎乐美身份的边缘化，即使是阿莫尔，也对这位老仆人了解甚少。但，从为数不多的勾勒中，读者可以窥见的是：莎乐美对斯沃特家族是心怀好感的，她会为去世的人祈祷，也会在阿莫尔归还房屋时，为了不伤害她的感情，选择慷慨接受，尽管她有充分的理由像卢卡斯一样愤怒。在加尔格特看来，莎乐美的失声不仅仅是真实世界里南非的问题，还是一个文学问题，激励读者在一部喧闹的复调小说中寻找通往唯一沉默的答案（范德弗里斯等，2023）。

5. 结语

与故事所涉及的时空不同，《承诺》是加尔格特站在种族隔离结束近 30 年的时间点上，对南非进行的实验性回望。他将宏大的历史分割成了碎片，让四场葬礼成为了横截面，聚焦人物内心，使得历史之外的人类生存体验得以浓缩表达。一种和谐而不同的叙述者声音，为基调悲伤的故事注入了活力，为喧哗吵闹的众声增添了厚度。

值得注意的是，作为一名白人作家，在历史和家庭的叙述中夹杂着多种声音时，加尔格特并未意图为南非指明前进的道路，尽管这通常被视为一些作家的责任与使命。他所创造的，更像是一种特殊的困境。故事中，阿莫尔虽然放弃了继承，但她送出的房屋却依旧是"金杯毒酒"。归还土地建立的并不是一种亲密的关系，而是一种"奇怪而简单的融合"（加尔格特，2022：419）。在加尔格特眼中，这样的选择仅仅代表着他所构想的一种本能：放弃你所拥有的，因为这是正确的做法（Gevisser，2021）。南非历史留下的裂痕或许尚无法弥合，但加尔格特仍然在困境中摸索着一丝亮光。在那一刻，一切喧哗趋于宁静，叙述者的声音进入了阿莫尔，一段纳入历史音调和生命感悟的乐句缓缓流出："爱已不在，只剩善意，或许比爱更为强烈"（加尔格特，2022：194）。

参考文献

[1] GALGUT D. Damo Galgut Q&A[EB/OL]. (2021-11-15)[2023-05-04]. http://thebookerprizes.com/damon-galgut-qa.

[2] GEVISSER M. Most of the stories have been told by now, it's just the ways of telling that are new-Damon Galgut talks with Mark Gevisser about his new novel, the Promise[EB/OL]. (2021-06-18)[2023-05-06]. http://johannesburgreviewofbooks.com/2021/06/18/most-of-the-stories-have-been-told-by-now-its-just-the-ways-of-telling-that-are-new-damon-galgut-talks-with-mark-gevisser-about-his-new-novel-the-promise/.

[3] 巴赫金，1998. 巴赫金全集[M]. 晓河等，译. 石家庄：河北教育出版社.

[4] 范德弗里斯，王敬慧，胡笑然，2023.《诺言》的创作与叙述者的声音——访谈布克奖得主达蒙·加尔古特[J]. 上海交通大学学报(哲学社会科学版)，31(4)：1-9.

[5] 加尔格特，2022. 承诺[M]. 黄建树，译. 桂林：广西师范大学出版社.

[6] 林星宇，2022. 新南非的未竟承诺——评 2021 年布克奖获奖作品《承诺》[J]. 外国文学动态研究（4）：46-56.

[7] 斯科尔斯，费伦，凯洛格，2015. 叙事的本质[M]. 于雷，译. 南京：南京大学出版社.

[8] 王珏，2009. 简论西方戏剧中鬼魂形象的演变[J]. 戏剧文学（11）：71-74.

[9] 韦勒克，沃伦，2010. 文学理论[M]. 刘向愚，译. 北京：文化艺术出版社.

[10] 郑梦怀，2022. 见证变革·理解道德·剖析人际——达蒙·加格特小说创作的三重维度[J]. 外国语文研究，8（6）：66-73.

狄金森自然诗歌中的道家意蕴

尹 慧

19 世纪美国女诗人艾米莉·狄金森生前籍籍无名，在其逝世后，她的 1000 多首诗歌得以整理发表。最初，她的诗歌按照不同主题分类，其中含有大量以自然为主题的诗歌，蕴含着诗人对生命、万物和自然的看法与理解。在人类文明历史长河中，自然一直是文人墨客欣然提笔于纸上的话题，而后随着工业文明发展，环境逐步显露变化并发出警告，人们也开始思考人与自然的关系。回首发现，中国古籍中早已有对人与自然相处之道的阐述。本文以《道德经》中提供的自然观为基础，分析狄金森以自然为主题的诗歌中体现的人与自然关系，试图找出东西方文明在人与自然问题上的相同立场。

1. 生态危机与生态伦理

自迈入 21 世纪以来，人类居住的环境，和未涉足的自然区域都面临着前所未有的挑战。对木材的需求致使森林遭受过度的砍伐，快速发展伴随着大量工业废水流向地表水体，人造化工制品对大气的污染导致臭氧层破坏，多种生物种族的快速灭绝等问题接踵而至。气候变化造成的全球变暖导致海平面的不断上升，其已经威胁到生活在沿海城市的一些居民。气候变化还会导致一些传染性疾病的产生，以及对一些人们的心理健康也会造成威胁。

人类想要活下去，想要后代的延续就离不开自然界的馈赠，自然环境是人类赖以生存的物质基础。人类就这样依靠着它在地球上生活着，发展并不断进步。直至 20 世纪中期，人们开始意识到自然的破坏与资源的耗竭已经成为一个亟待思考与解决的问题。尤其是贪欲争夺引发的两次世界大战对自然造成的破坏是不可逆的。"以道佐人主者，不以兵强天下，其事好还。师之所处，荆棘生焉。大军过后，必有凶年。"（《道德经》第三十章）《道德经》中早已言明，军队所到之处，一定会有所破坏。百姓的安全、性命得不到任何保障，四处是伤残的肉体，鲜血浸染进土地。对环境的破坏更甚，农耕田地中的作物被士兵踏为平地。生态环境的严重破坏紧紧跟随着人类渴望的物质丰富而发生。财富分配不均造成的贫富悬殊，少数人掌控着大部分的财富与资源，大多数人为机器所控制和奴役，精神生活进而空虚，道德几近沦丧等社会问题也随之凸显，缠绕在人们心中（罗美云等，2016）。

面对逃不开、躲不掉的环境问题，人类会祈祷上苍以求平息其怒气，后伴随科学兴起，又发明治理环境的技术，然而问题依然没有得到解决。人类认为自己就是天地间的主宰、人定胜天，自然环境与自然资源也是为人类服务的。但不论制定出多少强制执行的法规，不论投入多少人力、物力、财力，环境问题都没有得到彻底的解决，甚至没有得到有效的改善。人们开始反思，人类在开发利用自然环境而养活自己的过程中，"没有去善待自然环境，人类漠视和否认自然环境的权力"（Des Jardins，2002：2）。人类开始思考自然环境所处的地位，开始从人类自我中心论转向非人类中心伦理，思考其他动物和植物的道德身份。阿尔伯特·施韦哲提出了"敬畏生命"理论，他寻求重建自然与伦理之间的联系。保罗·泰勒在《尊重自然》中从哲学方面论证了生物中心伦理并给出了人类敬畏自然的理由。他提出人在尊敬自然时，其行为和品德就是好的和道德的，并从"生命的目的中心"对其进行论证（泰勒，1986：80）。而在中国，早在成书于春秋时期的《道德经》中，就清晰地提及并论证了自然与人类的关系，人类应如何与自然相处。

2.《道德经》中的自然哲学

"有物混成，先天地生。寂兮寥兮，独立不改，周行而不殆，可以为天下母。吾不知其名，字之曰道，强为之名曰大。"（《道德经》第二十五章）《道德经》说明了"道"是什么，老子知"道"的存在，却不知其形态。老子强调了"道"并非一种虚无缥缈构想出来的精神产物，而是一种真实的物质存在。不可道也不可名，只能强行为其取名为"道"。它牵引着天、地、人三者数年来按其自然状态正常地运转，不强行使其偏离，无为而无不为。"人法地，地法天，天法道，道法自然"（《道德经》第二十五章）则阐明了"道""天""地""人"四者间的关系。人不违背地的法则，方可获得安宁；地遵循天道运行，厚可载万物；天不违背道的法则，生育滋养万物。道的本性即为自然，不可违背（王弼，2011：66）。

《道德经》中蕴含着深刻的自然哲学，可将道家自然观总结为同源自然、顺应自然、崇尚自然、回归自然四个方面（朱叶，2019）。同源自然即整个世界是一个有机的整体，都由同一种物质衍生而来，这种本源性即为道。"道生一，一生二，二生三，三生万物。万物负阴而抱阳，冲气以为和。"《道德经》第四十二章道出了万物是如何化生的。万物万形，都可归为一，可理解为自然生态界的万物中有一共同之物，使得万物能自然生长，生机勃然。道生一，则意味着无中生有；二则为阴阳，即事物内部本质，使得万物自身能从内部进行调节至和谐的状态，而后显现为外部的欣欣向荣。"无名天地之始，有名万物之母"（《道德经》第一章），揭示了有与无的关系。"无"则是没有具体形象，不可名状，即为"道"，道的生成则有了天地。"有"指可识可见有形象的具体事物，天下万物生于有，有生于无。等到化生成具体事物，有其自身形状之后，又得到道的生长养育。

同时，同源性还暗含着一种万物平等的思想，如都由一母所生，则无贵贱之分。因此，都由道化生而来的万物，也应是平等的，我们都应尊重生命。在破坏甚至过度使用自然资源前，我们除了从为保护自身利益的功利主义出发进行反思，更需要考虑我们对其他生命的道德责任，生命的存在本身即为一种善，善则为存在提供了一种价值和意义。"昔之得一者，天得一以清，地得一以宁，神得一以灵，谷得一以盈。万物得一以生，侯王得一以为天下贞。"（《道德经》第三十九章）一即为道，于天、地、神、谷、万物、侯王而言，因其各自内含的"道"都达到了最适宜的状态，"清、宁、灵、盈、生、贞"都是各自怡然之资，无高低贵贱之分。"天地不仁，以万物为刍狗。圣人不仁，以百姓为刍狗。"（《道德经》第五章）天地无为，不偏爱，亦不打压，任万物各自生长，自相治理。然无为非不为，"天地不为兽生刍，而兽食刍；不为人生狗，而人食狗。"（王弼，2011：15）故万物间形成食物链，并非是食他者或能制作工具，驭他者则高一级，这是天地顺应自然，万物自相治理的结果。"天道无亲，常与善人"（《道德经》第七十九章），也说明了天道是平等对待世间万物的，不亲近某一物，不疏离某一方。只是出于公平，会多帮助善人（罗美云，2016），可谓"天之道，其犹张弓欤？高者抑之，下者举之；有余者损之，不足者补之。天之道，损有余而补不足。"（《道德经》第七十七章）借此以维持生态界的动态平衡。

顺应自然，即随"道"而行，不可妄作。因胡乱作为而陷入凶险之境的案例比比皆是，20世纪七十年代，密西西比河出现的"氧亏现象"，因为使用过多的化肥养料致使河沿岸的土地营养过剩，随着河水上涨，这些营养物质流入河中，海藻植物大量繁殖，抵挡了阳光的照射，河水中溶解氧也不足以维持海中大量生物的需求，进而导致大量水中生物无法存活。这影响了当地渔民的生活，更是破坏了当地生态的平衡。《道德经》中早已给出了对破坏万物本性行为的警示，"知常曰明。不知常，妄作，凶。"（《道德经》第十六章）"常"不偏不彰，不瞰不昧，不温不凉，过则破坏平衡。人类时常会有欲使苗长，欲使叶繁的破坏生物内部气韵的想法，对于这种欲望，老子给出警示，我们要去除那些极端的、奢靡的以及过度的欲望。欲常使人沉迷，招致祸害。知道满足才可长久，适可而止才不会遇到危险。"道常无为而无不为，侯王若能守之，万物将自化"。（《道德经》第三十七章）无为思想贯穿了整个《道德经》，无为即顺应自然，无不为则万物由之以始以成。顺应万物本性，万物自会有所成。

崇尚自然，即崇尚生命。"名与身孰亲？身与货孰多？得与亡孰病？"（《道德经》第四十四章）强调了生命的可贵。好名贪货总归是有损生命的。从人类自身利益出发，崇尚生命，热爱万物，注重身心的和谐，也可避免沦为机器的奴隶。

回归自然，世间万物最终将回到最原始的状态。"夫物芸芸，各复归其根。归根曰静，是谓复命。"（《道德经》第十六章）归根则静，"静"是长久之道。"绳绳不可名，复归于无物，是谓无状之状、无物之像。"（《道德经》第十四章）"无物"即为"道"，有物形成于其中，只是不可见形，听之不闻。芸芸众生，终归于道。

3. 狄金森诗歌中的自然观

狄金森几乎没有离开过她所居住的小镇，一生栖居在父亲的房子里，花园里的小世界，自然中的大环境都是她冥想并汇成诗歌的对象。例如，对不同鸟类的特征的观察和描写，表现了一个热爱自然的人的敏锐的眼睛与耳朵。通过鸟类来表达她对神学的思考，谴责他人对自然的破坏等。除了对大自然的直接热爱，狄金森还钟爱酒，酒让她沉醉。于她而言，酒是大自然的产物，通过酒她与大自然对话，沉浸在大自然中，也能让她像蜜蜂一般沉醉在花蜜中。狄金森的1775首诗歌中，描写自然的诗歌或借用大自然中的一花一草，一蜂一蝶表达自己体悟的诗歌不在少数。透过其中一些诗歌也可窥见狄金森对于自然的思考与《道德经》中的自然观有契合之处。

一首《捕捉不到的色调，最美》写出了狄金森对大自然的认知，描写了自然的一种不可捉摸性。恰似《道德经》中对"道"的理解。永恒不变的"道"不是可以谈论言说得出的，它没有可定的内涵和有限的外延让我们能用语言来为之命名。

"我捕捉不到的色调，最美
那光彩何其邈远
就算我能在巴扎上展示
一个基尼只许看一眼"（狄金森，2014：627）

不可捕捉的色调，不可触之的排列，不可捉摸的姿态都在彰显着自然带给狄金森的体悟，视之不见，听之不闻，博之不得。"主宰"二字表明诗人似乎掌握了自然的奥秘，可又转瞬即逝，就好似一阵微风掠过，它不在乎你留住了几缕，须臾间已从指缝溜走。独留诗人怅惘，好似被戏弄一番，纵然如此，诗人的心中仍是对大自然的崇敬，她知晓这捕捉不到且捉摸不透的色调是最美的。诗人还是试图揭开大自然的秘密，这种神秘像一辆战车在狄金森的心中突突地往前冲，搅动着诗人的心，诱发出一种渴望与急切。

狄金森的一首"奉蜜蜂"，选用了自然界中的一些常见的生物来亵渎神明，戏仿耶稣告诫门徒为万民施礼时所用的话语，在表达对教会的反抗的同时，还唱出了自然在其心中崇高的地位。

"代表蜜蜂
代表蝴蝶
也代表微风，阿门！"（狄金森，2014：18）

诗人开篇便列举了大自然中的有生命之物，黄龙胆、枫树、即将开败的花儿、歌雀、老蜂构成一幅夏天颜色绚丽的风景画。编织、游行、致辞等词将诗歌中提到的动植物拟人化，显示这些有灵性的动植物在诗人眼中与能做出此种行为的人类无二无别，她能倾听大自然的声音，大自然也有与人类同样的世界。"代表蜜蜂，代表蝴蝶，也代表微风，阿门！"也表达了诗人对自然的崇敬。她用三个大自然中常见的事物替换了教会的三位一体，在那个基督教，牧师占据着极其重要的地位的时代，狄金森代替了牧师的职位，为大自然布道，足以见大自然在其心中的地位以及大自然的权威性（Vendler，2021：33）。同样，大自然也让她能倾听蜜蜂扇动翅膀的嗡嗡声，欣赏蝴蝶翩翩舞姿，感受夏日微风轻拂过浸润触感，使其思如泉涌，两者相互成就。而在另一首诗"清晨比往日更柔顺"（狄金森，2014：12）中，诗人欣然接受大自然的更替，跟随夏日离去的脚步，去迎接色彩饱满的秋日。诗歌描绘了诗人清晨散步时的场景，眼前清晰可见的毛栗和浆果，远处一片枫叶红以及落叶覆盖了的原野。而诗人为了跟上这秋日的步伐，也配上了一个小饰品。小小的一个动作，却表现出了狄金森顺应自然的变化，而非妄图留住夏日的玫瑰。玫瑰出了城，却换来了更沉淀厚重的色彩。其中蕴含的思想也与道家的平衡思想不谋而合，有所失亦有所得。一处失了的色彩，总会在其他地方显现，损有余而补不足。

在一首《群山换上的新装》（狄金森，2014：140）中，一张纯白的画布上，诗人逐一描绘着色。重重山峦换上的是何样的新装还未可知，紫光溢满村庄，草色也更加幽深，朱红色的印记，多种色调的混合再伴随着乱撞的苍蝇的出现，让我们猜测或许是夏天到了，跟随画笔的流动，我们看到了一只昂首阔步的公鸡，弥尔顿的《欢乐颂》中高啼的雄鸡携带着大自然的明媚走进了狄金森的诗里。再看到处处点缀着的鲜花，让我们感叹，这是春天的颜色。狄金森谜一样的话语带领着我们领略了大自然的神奇，让我们融入这种奇妙之中。一一罗列的生命，玄妙莫测的变化，狄金森那敬畏和醒觉的意识给她的自然风光带入一种幸福感。由远处的风光移步到眼前的光景，"告诉我们春天唤醒了大自然的壮丽，也唤醒了家庭生活的欢笑。这种幸福在一种花儿处处皆可期许的富足中达到顶峰"（Vendler，2021：40）。生活在这样的地方，诗人已满足，赏山间明月，嗅青草芳香，乘大树荫凉，见素抱朴，少私寡欲。然这宁静的画面中忽地混入了斧头的尖唱，一纸水墨画被划破。斧子一边尖叫着，一边砍伐树林。诗人在此处称其为不和谐的声音，表达了对世人破坏自然的批判。之后，狄金森运用尼哥底母的典故，把春天的奥秘同重生的奥秘结合（Vendler，2021：41）。春天，万物复苏，这其中暗含了循环的思想。新年伊始，花儿回到了最开始的状态，而在之前它还经历了幻化为无的过程。这是天地间万物遵循的规律，盈满则亏，复归其根，汇于无物。

"青铜，烈焰
北方，今晚
它的形成，如此妥帖
对自己胸有成竹，
对于惊慌，如此疏远
对宇宙或者对我
表现出君王的冷漠
以严威的色彩"（狄金森，2014：290）

一首《青铜，烈焰》（狄金森，2014：290）描写了北方的极光出现时带给人的震撼，以此来表达了对大自然的崇敬。"妥帖"是大自然的光景带给狄金森的感受。妥帖给人和谐之感，自如却也丝毫不紊乱，未被外界干扰，按照其自身本质的状态自在为。在另一首诗歌中，诗人也明确表述"自然就是和谐"，但想要用我们浅薄的学识去描绘自然，参透自然的奥秘又是何其无力。"像君王一般如此冷漠"，让她感受到自然的疏远，她似蝼蚁，似刍狗，不只是诗人，世间的万物也都如此。此处可看，天的运行是最接近于道的，效法道之无为而任万物自化。然人道却不是如此，她浸染了自然的威严，却试图用这借来的光芒去蔑视草梗，轻视氧气。这是狄金森用对自己的嘲讽，来夸赞自然的壮丽奇观，与其相比，自己不过如马戏团的表演一般令人发笑，她也终将埋藏于草丛间，自然中的瑰丽景色却会长久延续，天地所以能长且久者，以其不自生。

狄金森所作的大量诗歌中，死亡是一个重要的主题。将死神的到来看作一位绅士的等待，通过对一朵霜花的慢慢凝结来感知死亡的过程，苍蝇嗡嗡声让她感知到灵魂渐离时的形态，这些都充满了狄金森对现世的思考和对生命本质的理解。（汪玉枝，2017）

在《按安卧在雪花石膏寝室》（狄金森，2014：216）中，埋藏的肉体安卧在白玉般的石壁中，然在上方的城堡中，微风依旧轻拂，蜜蜂仍在不停地嗡鸣，鸟儿似乎也在应和歌唱。这幅充满生机，和谐的自然界的画面，与下面毫无知觉，了无声息的肉体形成了巨大反差，他不再能触及到清晨洒下的第一缕阳光，也见不到正午时炽热的火光。纵然这里躺的曾经是有思想、睿智的魂灵，终将归于天地之间，等待新的生命萌芽。其中蕴含着人不论做任何努力都不能阻挡最终会归于一的自然秩序，唯有尊道自化。

在试图认识自然这方面，从《道德经》和狄金森的部分诗歌中可以看出两者对自然的崇敬，万物同源平等，又都将复归于无物。中西方在应对环境问题时，也提出了不同的理论。彼得·辛格主张根据动物是否具有像人类一样的忍受和享乐的能力赋予这些动物道德责任；汤姆·里根则从判定动物是否是"生命的主体"出发，论证一些动物应有的权利。还有学者从以生物而非仅仅人类为中心的伦理出发探讨生命的固有价值。面对21世纪自然对人类无休止的索取作出的回应，遭到严重破坏的生态环境以及仍在产生的不可忽视的人为影响，我们在遵循自然无为思想的同时，还应做出行动来修复已经遭到破坏的自然。尊重自然，顺应自然，保护自然，结合中国优秀的传统文化中蕴含的自然哲学思想，打造人与自然生命共同体。

参考文献

[1] DES JARDINS J R, 1993. Environmental ethics: an introduction to environmental philosophy[M]. Belmont: Wadsworth Publishing Company.

[2] TAYLOR P W, 2011. Respect for nature: a theory of environmental ethics[M]. Princeton: Princeton University Press.

[3] VENDLER H, 2010. Dickinson: selected poems and commentaries[M]. Cambridge: Harvard University Press.

[4] 狄金森，2014. 狄金森全集[M]. 蒲隆，译. 上海：上海译文出版社.

[5] 罗美云，梁晓阳，2016. 论《道德经》的生态伦理思想[J]. 学术交流（3）：22-26.

[6] 王弼，2011. 老子道德经注[M]. 北京：中华书局.

[7] 徐莹，2021. 在道法自然与辩证自然之间——基于《道德经》《自然辩证法》文本的考察[J]. 山东社会科学（7）：67-74.

[8] 张俊芳，赵晓娜，2012. 生态视镜中《道德经》的思想镜诠[J]. 北方论丛（4）：122-125.

[9] 朱叶，王小平，2019.《道德经》的自然观与《黄帝内经》中医理论体系的构建[J]. 中医杂志，60(18)：1535-1538.

Analysis of the Translation Methods and Motives of *Public Law of Nations* from the Perspective of Skopos Theory

任佳琦

1. Introduction

International law mainly refers to legal regulations between countries, covering binding principles, regulations and systems, which adjust the relations and behaviour among nations during worldwide interactions. With better relations between countries in contemporary times, more emphasis is supposed to be laid on the research of international law. Since it serves as the criterion of dealing with cooperation, problems and conflicts among nations, it is self-evident that we should pay more attention to the research of its evolution and practice, from which we can benefit a lot.

After the association between China and the West in Ming Dynasty and Qing Dynasty, what so call "international law" commenced its journey in China. It is well-acknowledged that our earliest contact with international law began with Martino Martini (Wei Kuangguo), a Jesuit missionary's translation of the Latin masterpiece, *On Laws and God as Legislator*, written by Francisco Suarez, a Spanish scholar in 1648. Nevertheless, the translating task was suspended on account of Martino Martini (Wei Kuangguo)'s returning home. After that, at the end of the 1680s, China signed an international treaty with Russia, which served as the product of western international law, known as *the Treaty of Nerchinsk*. It was the first treaty in modern times between China and foreign countries. Before the Treaty of Nerchinsk, we were never involved with treaty relations, and western international law was not widely put into use, either (Zeng, 2008). Besides, in 1839, on the eve of the first Opium War, Lin Zexu, serving as the imperial envoy, received instructions given by Daoguang Emperor to ban the opium smuggling in Guangzhou. In order to obtain more information of foreigners, he assigned the task to his subordinates to collect works of western international law. Afterwards, Peter Parker, an American doctor, and Yuan Dehui, one of Lin's staff, were both invited to translate several chapters of Swiss publicist, E.De Vattel's masterpiece, *Law of Nations*, into Chinese, which were later included in Wei Yuan's records and maps of the world. However, due to the fiasco in the Opium War and Lin Zexu's deposition, the introduction of western international law was also suspended. Lastly, in the 1860s, an English customs office worker Robert Mart (He De) had translated items about legateship in Henry Wheaton's *Elements of International Law* to encourage the late Qing government to send representatives abroad. After 20 years, under the support of an American envoy, Anson Burlingame (Pu Anchen), as well as the Ministry of Foreign Affairs in the late Qing Dynasty, the American missionary, William Alexander Martin (Ding Weiliang) presented the complete translating task of *Elements of International Law*, naming it *Public Law of Nations*, which set the foundation of the western international law's introduction into China (He, 2001).

However, in the long course of translation history, especially from the Opium War to the May 4th Movement, scholars always gave priority to the research on great translators like Yan Fu, but overlooked the influence on the translation upsurge made by missionaries from the West. Besides, as for the research emphasis on missionaries, more attention has been paid to general topics, such as history, education, religion and press, and few scholars have discussed the contribution to translation made by missionaries. Most importantly, the emergence of *Public Law of Nations* represents the official introduction of modern international law into China.

It is William Alexander Martin (Ding Weiliang), one of the most renowned American Protestant missionaries, who arrived in China in the late Qing Dynasty, that accomplished the stunning feat, the Chinese version of Henry Wheaton's *Elements of International Law*, *Public Law of Nations*. He set out to work on the task in 1962 in Shanghai. The next year, the Ministry of Foreign Affairs in the late Qing Dynasty mandated four Chinese Christians to assist his translation, and the mission was accomplished in the mid of April in 1864. After the modification and revisions of Chinese officials, the finished translating work, *Public Law of Nations* was published in 1865, prefaced by the Prime Minister of the Ministry of Foreign Affairs in the late Qing Dynasty, printed 300 copies, and assigned to every province and treaty ports. The legal masterpiece consisted of 4 volumes, 12 chapters, and 231 sections (He, 2001).

Apart from that, in every translating practice, the motive serves as an element of vital importance. It strongly inspires the translator's efforts, especially under the specific cultural and social condition in the late Qing Dynasty, and that's the reason why research of the translation made by William Alexander Martin (Ding Weiliang), a missionary, is much more complex. As a consequence, it is of enormous significance for our comprehension of *Elements of International Law*'s translation, *Public Law of Nations*, to figure out the translation methods and motives of the translator.

What's more, Skopos theory is regarded as the classic translation theory, thriving in Germany in 1970s. After its three phases of development, Skopos theory's influence had been expanded and more research attention was paid to this theory. It exerts enormous emphasis on the function of the translation, which destabilizes the conventional concept of original text-based translation, and attaches significant importance to the Skopos of translation. Consequently, in order to dig into the motives and intentions of William Alexander Martin (Ding Weiliang), Skopos theory naturally becomes the best choice.

Currently, scholars tend to discuss the first comprehensive international law in the late Qing dynasty, *Public Law of Nations*, in their papers from the following angles. Lai Junnan (2011) expatiates the reason why Ding Weiliang translated international law into "万国公法" or "公法". Li

Fupeng (2019) further talks about legal terms' translation shift from "律例" to "公法". Some researchers not only analyze translation methods of "万国公法", but also lay emphasis on the significance of their introduction into China in the late Qing Dynasty. Zeng Tao (2008) narrates the earlier confrontation of international law between China and the West, as well as the practice of western international law in *the Treaty of Nerchinsk*. He Qinhua (2001) cites the translation of some legal and professional terms to display the significance of the introduction of international law into China for people's transition of legal cognition in the late Qing Dynasty. Jiang Zhigang (2018) adopts the theoretical model of the spread of international regulations involved with translation practice among different cultural backgrounds, which displays the formulation process of China's concept of sovereignty in modern times. Gao Liping (2012) especially narrates the translation methods and motives of three representative figures from the U.S., Young John Allen (Lin Lezhi), William Alexander Martin (Ding Weiliang) and John Glasgow Kerr (Jia Yuehan), in which we can perceive that the author speaks highly of missionaries' function in the translation field of the late Qing Dynasty. Other scholars including Fu Deyuan (2008) and Zhang Yongxin (2005), attach great importance to the source text's edition of *Public Law of Nations*, used by Ding Weiliang, and particularly the former writer, and give detailed evidences from different perspectives.

To conclude, precedent theses have discussed *Public Law of Nations* on the basis of legal terms' translation its motives, introductory history, the significance of its introduction into China in the late Qing Dynasty, and the exact edition of the source text adopted by the translator. However, this thesis will take the analysis of the translation methods and motives of *Public Law of Nations* as the object of study, which enormously increases the originality and creativity of the dissertation.

2. Skopos Theory

Skopos theory consists of the Skopos rule, the coherence rule, and the fidelity rule, among which the Skopos rule is of the utmost importance. Based on Skopos theory, the translation process is determined by the Skopos of translation, and translation should be acceptable in both culture and situation where it is applied to and can be comprehended by the readers. Moreover, translation should be faithful to the original text as well, while the degree and form of fidelity depend on the Skopos of translation and the translator's understanding.

2.1 The Skopos Rule

Skopos theory serves as the paramount rule of the three principles, which means that translation is determined by its Skopos. As for Vermeer (1987), every text possesses its own specific function, and the text and translation should serve for the function. Therefore, it can be explained that "translate/interpret/speak/write in a way that enables your text/translation to function in the situation in which it is used and with the people who want to use it and precisely in the way the want it to function" (Nord, 1997). Skopos theory can be summarized as that "the prime principle determining any translation process is the purpose of the overall translation action" (Nord, 1997). Besides, Skopos theory highly stresses the Skopos of the target text, which means "the communicative function the target text is intended to achieve for a target-culture audience in their social-cultural situation" (Bian, 2006).

2.2 The Coherence Rule

The Coherence Rule is the same as the Intratextual Coherence Rule. In light of this principle, the translation of a text must be readable and acceptable, which facilitates the reader to better comprehend the content as well as makes sense in the actual usage of the target language.

Vermeer supposes that any text is "an offer of information from which each receiver selects the items they find interesting and important" (Nord, 1997), and the target text is "an offer of information formulated by someone else in the source culture and language" (Nord, 1997). As a consequence of the dissimilarity in the cultural background and utterance convention of different readers, the Coherence Rule points out that "a translation should be acceptable in a sense that it is coherent with the receivers' situation" (Reiss & Vermeer, 1984).

2.3 The Fidelity Rule

The Fidelity Rule is the same as the Intertextual Coherence Rule. According to this rule, there is a correlation between the source text and the target text, and more specifically, the source text provides information for the target text. And this kind of correlation "depended on the translation purpose and the translator's interpretation of the source text" (Nord, 1997). Thus, the Skopos of translation and interpretation of the translator are two key elements, which means the Fidelity Rule is not the utmost imitation of the source text, but the fidelity of the core relation between the source text and the target text out of the Skopos. The Fidelity Rule, however, under some circumstances, will be out of action owing to the restriction of the Skopos Rule and the Coherence Rule. As an illustration, when there is enormous disparity between the Skopos and the forms, translators will make adjustments to the language in the translating process so as to serve target-language's Skopos.

3. Analysis of the Translation Methods of *Public Law of Nations*

In this section, the writer will exemplify specific translation methods adopted by Ding Weiliang during the process of translating *Elements of International Law*, containing methods of free translation, amplification and transliteration.

3.1 Free Translation

As for the translation of the title of Henry Wheaton's *Elements of International Law*, Ding Weiliang did not literal-translate it into "国际法原理" or "国际法要素", but free-translated it into "万国公法", elaborating that he translated "international" into "万国" instead of "国际", and combined the meaning of "elements" and "law" together as "公法". First of all, as for the translation of "international" at present, translators will possibly adopt "国际". In the late Qing Dynasty however, individuals were more familiar with the concept, "万国". For instance, another American missionary, Young John Allen (Lin Lezhi) created a serial journal, called *International Gazette*, which in Chinese is " 《万国公报》 ". Thus, it is self-evident that "万国" was far more common than

"国际" at that time. In addition, the distinctive usage of "公" and the meaning of character "公" includes meanings in the translation also deserves our attention. From the angle of modern translation, it's obvious that there is no words carrying the meaning of "公" in the title "Elements of International Law", and the meaning of the character "公" includes meanings like "justice", "equity" or "public". Yet after some careful consideration, it can be realized that on the one hand, "公" represents that the legal work can be widely-used all over the world, with the meaning of "public"; on the other hand, as a legal text, *Public Law of Nations* is supposed to be just and equal, which carries the same point as "公" in Chinese. To summarize, Ding Weiliang successfully killed two birds with one stone by the translation practice of "公" in the title, and that's also the reason why the concept "公法" lasted a very long time until the outset of the 20th century.

Furthermore, when demonstrating the legislative power of the Union, Henry Wheaton cited America as an example, saying that "The legislative power of the Union is vested in a Congress, consisting of a Senate, the members of which are chosen by the local legislatures of the several States, and a House of Representatives, elected by the people in each State." (Wheaton, 1964). "Senate", as we know, means "参议院", while Ding Weiliang translated it into "上房", and by analogy, translated "Houses of Representatives", which means "众议院", into "下房". It can be assumed that Ding Weiliang's translation has some correlation with our ordinary usage, "上院" and "下院" in daily life. "上" firstly denotes that members in the Senate are selected by the local legislatures of every State, and secondly denotes that they are aristocrats from the upper class, whereas "下" implies that members in the House of Representatives are selected by the masses of every State, and they are farmers or businessmen from the under class. Apart from that, rather than translating "Senate" and "House of Representatives" into "参议院" and "众议院", Ding Weiliang substituted "房" for "院" due to people's lack of a clear concept of "院" in the late Qing Dynasty, and "房" abstracts "院" as what these two parties do: members aggregating together in a room for a meeting or other affairs. Similarly, Ding Weiliang translated "Congress" (国会) into "总会", carrying the meaning of "aggregation", similar to the supreme authority of the government in the late Qing Dynasty; what is more, he translated "Union" (联邦) into "合邦", expressing the idea of "unity" and "getting together". And for the same effect of expression, he also translated "Germanic Confederation" (德国邦联) into "日耳曼系众邦会盟".

In addition, when it comes to the binding power of international law, Henry Wheaton narrated in his work that "…the law which prevails between nations being deficient in those external sanctions by which the laws of civil society are enforced among individuals; and the performance of the duties…being compelled by moral sanctions only, by fear on the part of nations of provoking general hostility" (Wheaton, 1964). By contrast, Ding Weiliang, to some extent, conformed to the meaning of the original text, but he utilized "内情" to take place of "moral sanctions", expressing the viewpoint that the binding power of international law was much less than internal law in every country, so it's up to countries themselves to abide by international law with their moral awareness. "内情" literally means "internal conditions" in modern English, without carrying a particle of meaning of "morality", which gave rise to difficulties for Chinese to understand it. Generally speaking, in the late Qing Dynasty, as for expressions with the meaning of "morality", "天理", "情

理" or "天道" are more reasonable words to be put into practice. From the author's perspective, Ding Weiliang's intention of free-translating "moral sanctions" into "内情" was to make a comparison between "external sanctions" (外部制裁) and "moral sanctions" (道德制裁). And "内" conveys the idea of "internal" and "mental" in Chinese, which are related to the two aims of Ding Weiliang's intention: firstly, helping with Chinese people's understanding by comparisons between "外" and "内", and secondly, delivering the meaning of "mental" in correlation with "moral" in the source text.

Moreover, Ding Weiliang translated "natural law" (自然法) into "性法", which sounds weird in our modern thinking pattern. Nevertheless, the translation, as far as I am concerned, is an advisable decision. For one thing, in traditional Chinese cognition, "性" signifies human nature, in other words, people's origin. Considerable Chinese classics had discussed this concept. Taking Xuncius' doctrine of evil human nature as an example, he upholds the idea that nature is endowed by heaven, in western culture, by God, and it cannot be acquired by learning or engaging in some specific work. Consequently, it's a marvellous idea to use "性法" to translate "natural law". For another, Henry Wheaton wrote in his work: "There is no legislative or judicial authority, recognized by all nations, which determines the law that regulates the reciprocal relations of States. The origin of this law must be sought in the principles of justice, applicable to those relations." (Wheaton, 1964) Simply speaking, natural law derives from conventions made with individual nations as well as the common obedience. Besides, as for Grotius, he asserted that "there is a law audible in the voice of conscience, enjoining some actions, and forbidding others, according to their respective suitableness or repugnance to the reasonable and social nature of man" (Wheaton, 1964). In brief, law, from deeper perspective, can restrict people's actions in terms of their own conscience and human nature instead of powerful enforcement, which means the phrase, "性法", is able to convey the idea of "natural law" from both Chinese and western perspectives.

Lastly, there are also other legal terms created by Ding Weiliang in conformity to Chinese people's thinking habits. To set an example, in *Elements of International Law*, Henry Wheaton narrates that "in treating of the question as to the competent judicature in cases affecting ambassadors, he says, 'The ancient jurisconsults assert, that…'" (Wheaton, 1964). Ding Weiliang translated "jurisconsult" (法学家) into "法师" in *Public Law of Nations*. As for normal comprehension, "法学家" refers to someone who has a knowledge of Buddhism and is capable of guiding men to practice Buddhism or Taoism. While, "法师" here serves as the free-translating outcome in order to convey the thought of "masters who are proficient in law with higher social status", helping with people's understanding in the late Qing Dynasty.

3.2 Amplification

Ding Weiliang pointed out his principle of translating Henry Wheaton's legal text in chapter "凡例" in *Public Law of Nations*, narrating that his strict goal to translate the text succinctly and concisely to the greatest extent, without adding any subjective thought to the translation, yet some lengthy expressions were abridged despite its inclusion of all provisions in the source text. Nevertheless, many evidences have been figured out that the translator also added extra information to his translation. For example, there is recordation that when England and America were having conferences in the U.S., the American negotiator had written off to the British plenipotentiary on the 8th August, 1842, but the name of the American negotiator was not clarified in the source text, only with interpretation of "Mr. Webster" in annotations. However, in Ding Weiliang's translation, he clarified the American negotiator's name, "畏卜思达", the transliteration of "Mr. Webster", in the text so as to be more complete and intelligible for people's comprehension. Besides, when Ding Weiliang demonstrated the treaty of the right of foreign vessels to navigate on the interior waters of Turkey, which connects the Black Sea with the Mediterranean, he clarified the five countries taking part in the treaty-making in 1841, including Britain, France, the Ottoman Porte, Prussia and Russia. Compared with the source text, Henry Wheaton only kept a record of "the treaty concluded at London the 13th July, 1841, between the five great European powers and the Ottoman Porte" (Wheaton, 1964), which can be deduced that Ding Weiliang tried to imbue Chinese people with global awareness through clearly citing more specific information of other countries.

Apart from that, the original writer described in *Elements of International Law* that "the term international law has been since proposed by Mr. Bentham as well adapted to express in our language, in a more significant manner that branch of jurisprudence" (Wheaton, 1964). It is clear that Wheaton did not specify who Mr. Bentham was in the text, whereas Ding Weiliang translated "Mr. Bentham" as "英国公师本唐", adding specific information about his nationality as well as profession to make it clearer for people to know about the identity of Mr. Bentham. By analogy, the original legal work wrote: "The theory of these ordinances is well explained by an eminent English civilian of our own times. 'When', says Sir William Grant…" (Wheaton, 1964) The author did not clarify the identity of Sir William Grant, either, but Ding Weiliang still translated it with more details into "英国公师戈兰得" for the same intention as mentioned above.

3.3　Transliteration

Considering that Chinese ministers might lack the necessary knowledge of foreign languages, Ding Weiliang craftily took transliteration into account during the process of translation. To begin with, when he encountered the leaders' names of foreign countries, in order to avert confusions, he transliterated "president" into "伯里玺天德". Ostensibly, that is the pure outcome of transliteration, and instead of assisting Chinese people's comprehension, it may make it more obscure. Yet after proper study, we can discover that "伯里玺天德" contains the meaning of "wielding imperial jade seal and possessing virtues", the same as the Chinese Emperor.

Similar to the translating method at present, in light of the translation of people's names in *Elements of International Law*, Ding Weiliang also made use of transliteration to retain the original pronunciation of the source language. Instances are as follows. "Hugo Grotius" was transliterated into "虎哥", "Cumberland" into "根不兰", "Hobbes" into "霍毕寺", "Pudendorf" into "布番多", "Bynkershoek" into "宾客舍", "Huberus" into "胡北路", "Wolf" into "俄拉费", "Vattel" into "发得耳", "Heffter" into "海付达", "Bentham" into "本唐", "Savigny" into "赛宾尼", "Madison" into "马的逊", "Grant" into "戈兰得", etc.

On top of that, there are also practices of transliterations about names of places in *Public Law of*

Nations, also to keep the original pronunciation in the source text so as to avoid more subjective modifications which may result in misunderstanding. For instance, "Cracow/Krakow" was translated into "戈拉告", "Paris" into "巴勒", "Wallachia/Walachia" into "袜拉儿", "Servia/Serbia" into "塞尔维", "Sardinia" into "萨尔的尼", "Polizza" into "波里萨", "Sweden" into "瑞威敦", "Norway" into "挪那瓦", "Ireland" into "阿尔兰", "Warsaw" into "瓦锁", "Utrecht" into "乌达拉", "Dunkirk" into "顿及耳客", "Huningen" into "虎凝", "Basle" into "巴细耳", "Verona" into "非罗那", etc.

All in all, Ding Weiliang conformed to Skopos theory by virtue of the three translation methods. To begin with, he spent massive efforts searching for appropriate Chinese characters with relevant meanings to cater to Chinese people's thinking pattern, which accorded with the Skopos rule to encourage more people to know more about international law. In addition, concerning the differences between Chinese and English, Ding Weiliang endeavored to adopt more idiomatic usages in Chinese during the process of translation, which also abided by the coherence rule to make the translation more acceptable in the target culture. What's more, owing to Chinese people's lack of knowledge about western legal system, some specific translations may not fully deliver the true meaning of the source text, but due to the fact that the restriction of the Skopos Rule, Coherence Rule and the Fidelity Rule may be out of action under some circumstances, Ding Weiliang still generally complied with Skopos theory in his translation.

4. Analysis of the Translation Motives of *Public Law of Nations*

In this section, the writer will elaborate the translating motives of Ding Weiliang from two aspects: the external motives and internal motives.

4.1 External Motives

There are two main factors that contribute to the translation of *Elements of International Law* from the outside.

On the one hand, the translator, Ding Weiliang himself purports to make the international law more accessible for Chinese so as to help with the diplomacy. On his arrival in Ningpo, Zhejiang Province, China, Ding Weiliang had been to the north of China twice as the translator to take part in negotiations between China and America with the American envoy, which can be regarded as one of his initial motives to translate *Elements of International Law*. After these experiences, he gradually realized that what accounted for the government of the late Qing Dynasty's frustrations in foreign affairs all the time should be seen as the lack of the vitally important weapon, international law, as a hedge against foreign powers. When Ding Weiliang noticed that the ruler of China, the Emperor, was capable of laying down the law randomly without conferring with others, he became aware of that China was a typical country ruled by the Emperor instead of by the law. And that is the reason why every time the Foreign Affairs in the late Qing Dynasty could not put forward potent arguments in order to fight for a fairer outcome against foreign countries. Even sometimes, the negotiation should have ended with something beneficial to China, but as a result of Chinese people's lack of international-law knowledge, we still got the short end of the stick. Especially after the second

Opium War, Ding Weiliang started to be conscious of the urgency to introduce the western legal system into China. As a consequence, he took advantage of his job in the American Presbyterian Mission Press to embark on the translation of Henry Wheaton's *Elements of International Law*, and 6 months later, the first draft of *Public Law of Nations* came out. Moreover, in chapter "凡例", he clearly pointed out that Henry Wheaton's work would be useful and instructive for both China and foreign countries. Furthermore, he narrated in his memoir, *A Cycle of Cathay*, that to some extent, China lagged behind in legal information, just like her deficiency in other sciences. She should be grateful for the introduction of knowledge in these fields from the outside (Ding, 2004). This shows Ding Weiliang's motive to accelerate Chinese people's process of getting exposed to international law for a more effective diplomacy with self-esteem.

On the other hand, the Ministry of Foreign Affairs in the late Qing Dynasty also showed great zeal for the translation of legal masterpieces as references in diplomacy. In the preface written by Dong Xun, an officer in the government of the late Qing Dynasty, attached to *Public Law of Nations*, similar emphasis was laid on the external motives of international law's introduction, saying that there are a great number of countries outside, but without laws, how could one be a country? And that's the reason for Ding Weiliang's translating *Elements of International Law*. In addition, it is written in "筹办夷务始末" that when the Ministry of Foreign Affairs browsed through the first draft of *Public Law of Nations*, it was supposed that there were some clues to be followed, but its essence of being a book consisting of foreign legal items, which were dissimilar to Chinese legal systems, should also be paid enough attention to. From this perspective, in spite of their suspicion of *Public Law of Nations*, the Ministry of Foreign Affairs in the late Qing Dynasty still reached a consensus to introduce the legal work into China in terms of its assistance to China's diplomacy.

4.2 Internal Motives

After the discussion in the previous section about external motives of the translation, the internal motives of Ding Weiliang himself will be illuminated in this section.

To begin with, one of the most vital motives of Ding Weiliang's translation was to create a better condition for his future life and career in China. In his memoir, *A Cycle of Cathay*, Ding Weiliang described that after his vocation in the U.S., he came back to China and spent some time translating Henry Wheaton's *Elements of International Law*, asserting that this work would affect the relation between China and America as well as affect his own life in the future. More importantly, in the memorial from Ministry of Foreign Affairs in the late Qing Dynasty in August, 1864, it was reported that Ding Weiliang had pleaded with officers many times to print and publish *Public Law of Nations*, and officers saw through his motives in two angles: one of them was to boast about the western legal system, and the other was to emulate the success of the Italian Christian missionary, Matteo Ricci and to establish a reputation in China.

On the other side of the coin, as a missionary, Ding Weiliang's essential target was regarded as the propagation of Christian gospel, and the publication of *Public Law of Nations* would further facilitate his missionary career as well as the advancement of Christianity in China. When he was editing the report for *New York Times*, America, he specified his motive that people had realized that missionaries became an independent power all around the world. Politicians had been certain about the significance of missionaries for propagation. Through their work, the western ideology would definitely make an impact on China. On top of that, he also explained his motive for translating *Elements of International Law* in his letter to missionary, Walter Lowrie of the Presbyterian Church in Ningpo, China, saying that he engaged in this task not for others' assignments, but for its function to inspire the atheistic government to acknowledge the God and his eternal justice. More importantly, it might also impart some knowledge about Christianity (Liu, 2000). Besides, facing with the suspicion from American Presbyterian Church about his translation for six months, with no relation to missionary activities, Ding Weiliang was convinced that the importance of this task for the late Qing Dynasty could be comparable to the translation of the Bible, which would certainly make positive impact on missionary activities in China (Covell, 1978).

5. Conclusion

To summarize, as for the translation methods, Ding Weiliang successfully adopted free translation method, amplification method and transliteration method to meet his purpose. With free translation, he catered to the Chinese thinking pattern for a better comprehension of the legal work; with amplification, he clarified much information in the source text to help Chinese readers to cultivate certain global awareness; with transliteration, he presented leaders' names as well as places' names of foreign countries to avoid possible confusions for Chinese people's lack of knowledge about other countries in the late Qing Dynasty. These practices of translation methods in *Public Law of Nations* published in 1864 even set an example for the future translating tasks on account of its precision and originality. As for the translation motives, for one thing, the external motive for Ding Weiliang's translation serves as the need of a western legal system to better settle down international affairs with foreign countries; for another, the internal motive for his translation should be his future expectation to achieve some remarkable successes in China, as well as his fundamental reason coming to China, more clearly to say, to diffuse the Christian gospel and raise the Christian awareness of Chinese people, which is always regarded as the basic task as a missionary.

Nevertheless, there are still limitations of this thesis and there should have been more comparisons between the source text and the translation text in the analysis to prove the writer's conclusions; but on the positive side, since there are few dissertations analyzing *Public Law of Nations* from the perspective of Skopos theory, the originality of this thesis as well as the writer's courage to break the ice still deserves to be encouraged and commended.

Bibliography

[1] COVELL R R, 1978. W. A. P. Martin: Pioneer of Progress in China[M]. Washington: Christian University Press.
[2] NORD C, 1997. Translating as a Purposeful Activity[M]. Manchester: St. Jerome Pubishing.
[3] REISS K, VERMEER H J, 1984. Groundwork for a General Theory of Translation[J]. Tubingen: Niemeyer, 101.
[4] REISS K, 2000. Translation Criticism—The Potentials and Limitations: Categories and Criteria for Translation Quality[M]. Manchester: St. Jerome Publishing.
[5] VERMEER H J, 1987. What Does it Mean to Translate?[J]. India Journal of Applied Linguistics, 13(2): 25-33.

[6] WHEATON H, 1964. Elements of International Law[M]. New York: Oceana Publications Inc.
[7] 卞建华, 2006. 关于翻译目的论相关问题的讨论——与克里斯蒂安•诺德教授的四次网上交流（英文）[J]. 中国翻译, 27(1): 44-46.
[8] 丁韪良, 2004. 花甲忆记[M]. 沈弘, 译. 桂林：广西师范大学出版社.
[9] 傅德元, 2008. 丁韪良《万国公法》翻译蓝本及意图新探[J]. 安徽史学(1)：45-53.
[10] 高黎平, 2012. 传教士翻译与晚清文化社会现代性[D]. 上海：上海外国语大学.
[11] 何勤华, 2001. 《万国公法》与清末国际法[J]. 法学研究(5)：137-148.
[12] 惠顿, 2003. 万国公法[M]. 丁韪良, 译. 北京：中国政法大学出版社.
[13] 江治刚, 2018. 主权规范传播与中国近代主权观的形成——基于国际规范传播的翻译实践视角[J]. 外交评论（外交学院学报）(2)：34-64.
[14] 赖骏楠, 2011. 《万国公法》译词研究——兼论 19 世纪中日两国继受西方国际法理念上的差异[J]. 法律科学（西北政法大学学报）(2)：3-12.
[15] 李富鹏, 2019. 改造"律例"——晚清法律翻译的语言、观念与知识范式的近代转化[J]. 政法论坛(6)：87-99.
[16] 刘禾, 2000. 普遍性的历史建构——《万国公法》与 19 世纪国际法的传播[M]. 陈燕谷, 译. 石家庄：河北教育出版社.
[17] 曾涛, 2008. 近代中国与国际法的遭逢[J]. 中国政法大学学报(5)：103-111+159.
[18] 张用心, 2005. 《万国公法》的几个问题[J]. 北京大学学报（哲学社会科学版）(3)：76-84.

新媒体环境下中国特色词汇的英译技巧探析
——以中国日报网"新闻热词"栏目为例

黄晴宇

1. 引言

随着中国国力的日益增强，对外交流传播日益频繁，中国特色词汇的翻译问题备受关注，其准确性会影响国际社会对中国政治、经济、文化等方面的正确理解。在当前新媒体传播技术不断发展的背景下，选择恰当的翻译策略，尽可能实现词汇翻译的准确性和宣传的时效性，为我国对外传递中国声音、弘扬中国文化提供助力。

本文选取的词来自中国日报网"新闻热词"栏目，其中的"热词"是中国特色词汇的核心凝练，是新时期治国理政思想理念的鲜活呈现，具有较强的政治属性。

中国特色词主要是指在中国特色发展过程当中形成的一些词语，大部分是一些新词，描述新事物、新概念和新表达而创造出来的一种特定的词语。具体而言，广义的中国特色词汇是指能植根于中国的，中国特色的各民族的词汇。狭义的中国特色词汇，指反映中国特色、中国国情、文化、思维的汉语词汇（张洁等，2017）。中国特色词汇衍生于中国文化，在一定程度上反映了某个阶段民众广泛关注的社会现象或问题，是一个国家丰富文化内涵的重要载体，要使国外读者了解中国文化，应通过词汇载体来传播内涵。对此，深入探究蕴含我国传统文化的中国特色词汇，能够帮助翻译人员更加深刻地认知特色词汇的特点，明确其翻译原则，对于跨文化交际和中国文化走出去具有重要意义。

近年来，中国特色词汇的英译问题引起诸多学者的关注。总体看来，大部分学者，如王祥兵（2002）、朱天文（2003）、贾卉（2008）、范勇（2010），着重探讨西方主流媒体如何处理中国特色词汇，通过外刊对汉字词语的翻译进行考察，探讨意识形态在汉字词语翻译中的作用。吴磊（2009）等学者则从新闻传播学的角度研究中国特色新词翻译，对中国特色新词的英译现状进行了梳理，并讨论了其翻译策略。也有个别学者关注中国特色新词的专题研究，如张健在《报刊新词英译纵横》（2001）中对报刊新词的产生、特点、内容进行了详尽的论述，对报刊新词的英译提出了对策和方法；陈德彰在《热词新语翻译谭》（2011）中探讨近来涌现出的众多汉语新词的英译问题，涉及多个领域，包括社会热点问及网络流行语等，从词汇角度探讨汉英语言的异同；以及杨全红的《汉英词语翻译探微》（2020）系统地介绍了汉语新词英译的特点、标准、对策以及易犯错误。此外，随着新媒体迅猛发展，李中强（2012），张瑞玲、陈正华（2015），吕晓敏（2021）等学者转而开始分析新媒体背景下新闻热词的翻译技巧和策略。然而，基于新媒体环境，以特定网站特定时间段为研究对象，具体探讨中国特色词汇翻译原则和方法的研究仍然较少。

2. 中国日报网"新闻热词"栏目下中国特色词汇的主要特征及主要原则

《中国日报》于 1981 年创刊，是新中国成立以来创立的面向海内外发行的第一份全国性英文日报，中国日报网是《中国日报》的旗下网站，创办于 1995 年，是国际社会了解中国的重要媒体，是世界了解中国和研究中国的权威性读物。作为备受海内外人士普遍关注的英文媒体，《中国日报》一直致力于通过官方话语传播我国的新闻思想及新闻动态，而旗下中国日报网的英语点津"新闻热词"栏目，会对某一时期各热门领域使用频率较高的重点词语进行总结，精选高频双语特色词汇，让读者了解各个领域、各个地区正在发生的事情，起到信息传播的作用。同时，该栏目也会提供了大量汉语流行词汇的英文翻译，以帮助广大英语爱好者找到表达新事物、新观点的准确英文用语，是英语爱好者了解国内外新闻时事的重要媒介，也为外国读者提供了解国内新闻的有效途径。

2.1 中国特色词汇的主要特征

（1）涵盖领域广泛

特色词汇不仅仅牵扯到政治事件本身，还涉及社会、经济制度、文化、军事等方面的内容。一方面，中国日报网中的特色词汇覆盖面大，类型庞杂，涉及政治、经济、科技、社会、文化和生活等各领域的内容。政治类词汇，例如"小康社会""命运共同体""中华民族伟大复兴"等；经济类词汇，例如"绿色债券""结构性货币"等；科技类词汇，如"天问一号火星探测器""嫦娥五号"等；社会类词汇，例如"希望工程""绿色奥运"等；文化类词汇，例如"高考状元""素质教育"等；生活类词汇，例如"剪彩""贺岁片""月光族"等，涵盖了中国国情的方方面面，展示了动态的中国形象。另一方面，随着电视、网络、报纸等媒体在日常生活中的普及，特色词汇的形成更为生活化、口语化，且产生数量多，传播速度迅速，更新频率频繁，覆盖的受众群体也越发广泛。

（2）时代特色鲜明

中国特色词汇具有突出的时代性，通过不同的语言表现出特定的社会、经济、政治和文化的具体内容。随着社会的飞速发展，很多新词，如政治口号、网络语言、不经常使用的老话会被引入到现有的语言体系，随之产生许多具有时代标签的词汇，中国日报网中特色词汇的变化贴切地反映当时的社会情况，是社会各个方面的缩影。如从 21 世纪初期的"科学发展观""义务教育""践行社会主义荣辱观""小康社会"到现在的"一带一路""人类命运共同体""中国式现代化"等，这些词无不透露出强烈的时代气息。

（3）传统文化性突出

中国特色词汇反映中国和中国人民的独特事件和思想，带有浓厚的中国传统文化的底蕴。一些词汇还表现了中国文化历史背景和特殊的中国人的生活方式。中国日报网中的特色词汇存在独特文化性，可作为我国思维模式与民族文化的一种反映。如孝悌、无为、逍遥等词汇嵌入文化内涵，体现了中国人传统的观念行为；如老字号、吊脚楼等特色词汇，是沿袭特定历史环境中所遗留下来的语言文化产物，不但彰显了我国民族特征，而且对我国历史文化起到了一定的承载作用。

2.2 中国特色词汇的主要翻译原则

由于新媒体环境下不同网站具备不同特点，在翻译中国特色词汇时，也需要具体翻译原则进行指导，因此，笔者以中国日报网"新闻热词"栏目为对象，具体总结了中国特色词汇英译应遵循的三个主要原则。

（1）忠实词汇本意

在翻译标准方面，我国与西方国家的翻译学者都提出了各自的主张。其中，严复先生提倡"信、达、雅"的原则，张培基先生坚持"忠实通顺"的原则；美国著名翻译家奈达则提出重视"作用对等"。这些观念之间即使侧重方向有所不同，但都明确要求译文要忠实于源语言，最大程度地保持源语言的风格。这为广大翻译人员提供了应遵循的方针，翻译人员要想将中国特色词汇所蕴藏的文化内涵充分展现出来，就要依据自身的情感进行控制，并维持原文语意。在此基础上，按照自己的理解，用恰当的句式将其传递给目的语受众，让其深刻体会我国传统民族文化的深厚内涵，感受东方特色文化的魅力，激发受众的阅读意愿。因此，要想给出最准确、最恰当的翻译，绝不能断章取义、词不达意，一定要忠实于词汇本意。《中国日报》对中国特色词汇的翻译主要涉及中国特色的政治制度、组织机构和传统文化等方面。对此，《中国日报》基本上都采用直译法：如将"民族复兴"译为"national rejuvenation"，"文化软实力"译为"cultural soft power"等，既生动形象，又简洁直观。直译法能较好地保持原作的语言特点和民族文化风格，传播中国文化；或采用音译法，将"功夫"翻译为"kongfu"，将"豆腐"翻译成"toufu"，将"叩头"翻译成"kowtow"等，不仅保留了中国文化的特色，还能引起目的语读者的关注，并与语言交流的语境相适应。

（2）符合文体特点

新闻文体不同于散文、小说等的文体，有其自身的特殊性。朱亚星（2015）总结道："其语言有生动形象、标新立异、简洁明了、诙谐风趣等特点，为了吸引读者的阅读兴趣、迎合大众求奇求新的心理，也为了加强宣传效果，在用词方面往往使用一些时髦词、俚语、典故等来表现。"译者在翻译这些中国特色词汇时，应考虑新闻词汇的灵活性和通俗性，借助一些修辞手法将原文所使用的夸张、讽刺等感染力极强的表现手法体现出来，尽量使目的语达到与原文等同的效果。《中国日报》采用的策略是达意为主，直译为辅，例如"One should keep expenditure within the limits of income"（量入为出），"know your enemy and know yourself and you can fight a hundred battles without danger"（知己知彼，百战不殆）。这些翻译大多采用的是英语中常见的短小精悍的词语，对汉语原文进行了明确且标准的处理，方便英语读者理解。

（3）服务新闻读者

黄友义（2004）谈外宣翻译时，提到需要翻译工作者熟知"外宣三贴近"原则，即贴近中国发展的实际，贴近国外受众对中国信息的需求，贴近国外受众的思维习惯的原则。对此，翻译人员以服务新闻读者为目标，针对不同的受众群体，在源语言文本中展开系统化的深入探究，从中找到并明确最佳翻译方法，这样既能准确表达源语言的真正内涵，又能传递我国民族特色文化信息，实现翻译前后文本的对等，有效推动我国民族特色文化的传承（陈桂峰，2018）。

例如，中国日报网在翻译"落汤鸡"一词时，采用替换法，将"落汤鸡"译为"a drowned rat"。替换法是用西方读者所熟悉的形象来代替汉语中的比喻形象，使译文达到与原文相同或相近的表达效果，并在一定程度上弥补因不能保留原形象所造成的损失（陈三东，2005）。老鼠在西方文化中寓意为否定之形象，公鸡比喻骄傲，如果直译为"a drowned cock"，不会有"狼狈"之义，故转换形象，将"落汤鸡"译为"a drowned rat"，既考虑了语言的民族特色和语言结构，又反映了译语的文化背景和表达习惯，能使目的语读者更好地理解习语。在翻译"低头族"一词时，通过移译将其译为"phubber"。移译指借用目的语中相对应或基本对应的词语转移（杨全红，2003）。为了描述人们对智能手机过度迷恋的现象，澳大利亚的 Macquarie Dictionary（麦考瑞词典）杜撰出一个新的英语词汇：phub。此词为合成词，由 phone（手机）和 snub（冷落）构成，合在一起的 phub 意为"专注手机而冷落（身边的人）"。而"低头玩手机的人"，也就是我们常说的"低头族"，就可以说成 phubber。因此，中国日报借用英语文化中已有的词来转译汉语中富有文化内涵的热词，贴近国外受众的思维习惯的原则。尽管两种不同文化的差异是存在的，但也是有共性的，这决定了移译的可能性，在一定程度上弥补了文化空缺。

3. 中国日报网"新闻热词"栏目下中国特色词汇英译的翻译方法

"中国特色词汇是根植于我国民族情感与民族信仰之中的，对我国民族的思维模式及生活态度有着良好体现"（李静涵，2017）。作为构成句子的最小单位，中国特色词汇负有社会文化内涵，而为了在翻译中尽可能地忠实于原文，保持特有的语言风格，基于词汇的主要特征及主要原则，中国日报网会采取直译、直译加注、音译、音译加注等主要翻译策略。笔者将2023 年 1—6 月所搜集到的 210 个词汇按照不同的翻译方法进行分布研究，发现主要分为四类，见表 1。

表 1 中国日报网特色词英译方法分布

类型	直译	音译	直译+注释	音译+注释	其他
数量	146	23	16	11	14
比例	69.52%	10.95%	7.61%	5.23%	6.66%

3.1 直译法和直译加注法

所谓的直译法，顾名思义，就是依照中文特色词汇单字的顺序，并依照其表面的意义进行翻译。它要求译文既要保持汉语原文的内容，又保持原文的形式，尤其要保持原文的比喻、形象和民族地方色彩等（齐骥，2015）。在对中国特色词汇进行直译时，要忠实于原文内容，忠实于原文形式，并且注重目的语的流畅性。

例 1：文化自信

译文：cultural confidence

习近平在庆祝中国共产党成立 95 周年大会上的讲话中提到："文化自信是一个民族、一个国家以及一个政党对自身文化价值的充分肯定和积极践行，并对其文化的生命力持有的坚定信心。"文化，特别是思想文化，是一个国家、一个民族的灵魂，中华优秀传统文化孕育了中华民族宝贵的精神品格，可以为治国理政提供有益的启示，也可以为道德建设提供有益的启示。中国日报网站直接将"文化自信"直译为"cultural confidence"。通过直译法，忠实于单词的语义，译文的形式接近原文，既体现了原作者的思维过程，又力求保留原作者的语言特点和独特的表达方式，让外国读者更容易理解"文化自信"的含义，以及中国强调"文化自信"的意义。

诚然，为了保留汉语的文化意象，多采用直译的翻译手法，但考虑到完全直译可能会给英语读者的理解造成一定的阅读障碍，利用直译加注法，对直译的词汇进行补充说明，可更好地完成这类词汇的翻译。中国特色词汇采用直译加注的方式并不鲜见，通常是以直译法再现源语文化专有项的民族特色，辅之以注释法消除跨文化理解上的鸿沟（张洁等，2017）。该方法不仅保留了原文语言的表达效果和民族色彩，也能保证英文读者能够充分理解原词和相应的文化特点。一些政治类的数字缩略语和概念类的词汇主要是以直译加注的形式进行翻译。

例 2：两个不动摇

译文：two unswervinglys（We will unswervingly consolidate and develop the public sector of the economy, and at the same time unswervingly encourage, support and guide the development of the non-public sector of the economy.）

2012 年，党的十八大报告明确"两个毫不动摇"——毫不动摇巩固和发展公有制经济，毫不动摇鼓励、支持、引导非公有制经济发展。这一中国特色词汇承载了丰富的文化信息，具有一定的隐含意义，由于中西的文化差异，单纯直译无法让目的语读者产生对应的联想，这时为了避免误解，采用直译加注释的翻译方法，既传播了中国文化，又可以使目的语读者正确领会词汇的内涵。

3.2 音译法和音译加注法

音译法是指将中国民俗文化当中的一些特殊词汇通过汉语拼音表达的方式直接与英语对应起来。这种方法在专业技术引进、人名、地名、商标的翻译当中都极为常见。即在翻译中国特色词汇的过程中，根据中文的读音选择读音尽可能相同的英文字母组合在一起。

例 3：天问一号

译文：Tianwen-1

中国国家航天局在 2020 年"中国航天日"线上启动仪式上宣布，中国行星探测任务正文命名为"天问系列"，第一个火星任务被命名为"天问一号"，后续的行星任务将依次编号。据中国国家航天局总工程师葛晓春介绍，"天问"一词源于中国伟大诗人屈原的长诗《天问》，这是屈原对天空、星星、自然现象、神话和人类世界的追问，反映了他对传统观念的追问和追求真理的精神。"天问"一词充满了鲜明的中国文化色彩，中国日报网采用了音译的方法，将"天问"译为"Tianwen"，可以尽可能表达源语文化背景，表达了中华民族对真理追求的坚韧与执着，体现了对自然和宇宙空间探索的文化传承。

例 4：蓉宝

译文：Rongbao

2023 年成都第 31 届世界大学生夏季运动会吉祥物"蓉宝"的英文采用了音译法来处理，"蓉宝"耳朵、眼睛、尾巴似火焰形态，将憨态可掬的熊猫形象与热情的火焰元素融为一体，体现了成都人的热情奔放，传递出令世界难以忘怀的"成都温度"。"蓉宝"承担着推广我国文化的重任，它的形象具有中国传统的艺术表现形式。无法用现有的词汇来进行准确的翻译，采用音译的方法译为"Rongbao"，可以保证译名的一致性，又可以减少歧义，同时充分保留了中国特色，能够使目的语读者将其与大运会吉祥物联系在一起。

汉语拼音音译保留了中国传统特色，又顺应了英语交际的环境，但是由于汉英两种发音系统不同，要在音译中语音完全相同是不可能的，这时会采用音译加注释的翻译方法，先用汉语拼音转换某词语，再以文内作注或文外加注的方法将该词语中特有的文化内涵表述出来，达到文化信息传递的目的。音译加注在保留源语读音和文化特色的基础上，将该词语包含的特有内涵表述出来，使读者感受到原汁原味的中国文化。

例5：碰瓷

译文：Pengci（deliberately crashing a car to claim compensation）

"碰瓷"原指一些不法分子在古董行业贩卖古董时，往往别有用心地把易碎的瓷器放在路中间，等着路人不小心把它打碎，借机进行敲诈。如今泛指一些敲诈勒索行为。日常生活中，"碰瓷"现象仍大量存在，尤其是在开车时。"碰瓷"是一个具有中国语言特征的词，是中国北京话，于是，中国日报网通过音译翻译，然而，许多外国读者不了解这种方言的具体含义，因此在括号中专门解释了"碰倒瓷器"的含义，意思是"故意撞车索赔"。

这类词汇大部分都是承载着中国特有的背景和历史，在西方的熟知度和普及率并不高，采用音译加注释的方法进行翻译，可以让目的语读者了解更多的中国文化，而不仅仅是词汇本身的读音。此译法可以营造出一种浓厚的异域情调，在引起西方读者"注目"的同时，也能照顾理解需要，填补文化认知空白。

4. 结语

中国特色词汇是中国文化的重要表现之一，是构建中国话语体系最根本的部分，研究其翻译策略对推动我国文化"走出去"以及构建我国对外话语体系有的重要意义。

本文基于中国特色词汇的主要特征和原则，以中国日报网"新闻热词"栏目为研究对象，具体探讨新媒体环境下中国特色词汇的主要翻译方法，总结归纳出中国日报网中国特色词汇的英译方法主要为：直译法、直译加注释、音译法、音译加注释等。这些翻译方法，不仅保留了中国文化的特色和文化身份，而且还原了中国文化的真正内涵，向全世界对外传递中国声音、弘扬中国文化、更好地实现"连接中外，沟通世界"，有助于新媒体的对外宣传工作。

参考文献

[1] 曹明伦，2005. 谈英语报刊新闻的基本特点及其翻译[J]. 中国翻译（6）：87-88.

[2] 陈德彰，2011. 热词新语翻译谭[M]. 北京：中国对外翻译出版公司.

[3] 陈桂峰，2018.文化传播视角下中国特色词翻译方法[J].黑河学院学报，9(12)：144-145.

[4] 陈三东，2005.英语比喻性词语的文化内涵及其翻译[J].伊犁教育学院学报（1）：80-84.

[5] 陈顺意，2019.《中国日报》的文化特色词译介[J]. 中国科技翻译，32(3)：56-59.

[6] 范勇，2011.美国主流媒体表达中国文化特色词汇的显异策略：基于对2009年《纽约时报》涉华报道的实证研究[J].上海翻译（1）：65-69.

[7] 何东，2016. 新闻热词翻译对英语新闻传播效果的影响[J]. 新闻战线（8）：77-78.

[8] 贾卉，2008.意识形态与美国《新闻周刊》涉华词语的翻译[J].上海翻译（2）：27-31.

[9] 李静涵，2017.翻译伦理观下的中国特色词汇翻译[J].文教资料(31)：32-33.

[10] 李中强，2016. 新媒体背景下的汉语新闻英译研究：以《中国日报》手机报为例[D]. 厦门：厦门大学出版社.

[11] 刘彩莉，崇宁，华芳，2019. 新闻热词的信息传播功能——以《中国日报》一周热词榜为例[J]. 新闻知识（2）：28-30.

[12] 刘静，2019.《中国日报》(China Daily)时政新闻报道中常用语的特点及翻译策略[J]. 新闻传播（10）：20-21.

[13] 吕晓敏，2021. 新媒体背景下对外传播中中国特色词汇的翻译策略——以手机《中国日报》为例[J].中国广播电视学刊（1）：79-81.

[14] 齐骥，2015.从归化异化看《习近平谈治国理政》的中国特色词汇英译[D].北京：北京外国语大学.

[15] 汪东萍，2020.《政府工作报告》中国特色词汇的文化对应与英译策略研究[J]. 学术研究（12）：34-40.

[16] 王祥兵，2002.论《时代》周刊中国报道文章对汉语文化词语的翻译[J].上海科技翻译（2）：19-22.

[17] 吴磊，2009. 传播学视阈下的新闻翻译研究[J]. 新闻界（3）：112-113.

[18] 杨全红，2003．汉英词语翻译探微[M]. 上海：汉语大词典出版社.

[19] 赵娇，2021. 基于纽马克翻译理论的中国新闻热词英译研究——以中国日报网"一周热词榜"为例[D]. 成都：西华大学.

[20] 赵石楠，2014. 从功能对等角度浅析外宣翻译策略——以中国特色词汇翻译为例[D]. 天津：天津理工大学.

[21] 张洁，刘静，朱荔芳，2017. 中国特色词汇英文翻译方法及策略研究[J]. 中国海洋大学学报（社会科学版）（3）：112-117.

[22] 张瑞玲，陈正华，2015.新媒体背景下的新闻热词英译策略探析[J].合肥工业大学学报(社会科学版)，29(4)：116-121.

[23] 朱天文，2003.美国新闻期刊中汉英翻译采用的策略和方法[J].上海科技翻译（3）：33-35.

[24] 朱亚星，2015."中国日报网"中新闻时髦词的英译[D].长沙：湖南师范大学.

科幻翻译的文学性——以 *Philia, Eros, Storge, Agápe, Pragma* 的汉译为例

陈 霞

1. 引言

20 世纪初,苏联形式主义提出"文学性"这一概念,将文学学科单独划分出来,文学性归于文学领域研究;英美新批评主义从语义学出发,重视文学作品本身的特性,强调从内部分析文本,重新审视文本本身的价值;结构主义从文本结构出发,研究文本语言的运行机制和系统及文本基于这个系统和机制所产生的价值和意义;解构主义明晰了文学与其他学科之间的区别,将文本逻辑一一打碎,使得文学性不再是研究的重点。从这一系列的研究我们不难看出,文学性一直处于文学研究的核心,也是学者长久以来关注的焦点问题。

科幻小说是一种类型文学,兼具科学、幻想,要求高度逻辑自洽。根据小说中科学和文学不同侧重,可以进一步将其分为"软科幻"和"硬科幻"两种类别。作为一种具有创造性的特殊文类,怎样理解科幻小说的文学性?在翻译中如何体现其文学性?本文以加西亚的短篇小说 *Philia, Eros, Storge, Agápe, Pragma* 汉译为例,从科幻小说翻译出发,探讨科幻小说文学性的呈现及其在翻译中的表达,以丰富对科幻小说文学性的研究。

2. 何为文学性和翻译的文学性

苏联形式主义最早开始对"文学性"这一理念进行研究。托多罗夫指出:"文学科学的对象不是文学,而是'文学性',也就是使一部作品成为文学作品的东西"(托多罗夫,1989)。"文学性"理念一经提出,便成为学者讨论的热点问题。雅格布森认为,文学性只存在于文学领域,跳出文学领域再谈文学性毫无意义,要实现真正意义上的文学研究,就要将文学学科单独划分出来,避免文学研究被纳入社会学领域,而文学性便是文学研究的核心。此外,不同于以往文学研究从文本外部意义出发,形式主义立足于语言学,从语言内部结构着手,从内部寻找规律,分析语言形式,强调文学的"诗性功能",推动文学成为"科学的学科",促使文学研究科学化。

随着苏联形式主义不断发展,文学性研究在西方文论中的影响不断扩大。英美新批评主义强调文学作品本身的特性,从内部分析文本,抛开作家身份背景,社会、历史、文化等外部因素影响,重新审视文本本身的价值,也增强的文学研究科学性。兰色姆提出"构架-肌质"论,要求从剖析文本内部结构,从内部分析文本意义。韦勒克同样强调这种"本体论批评",不过还提出文学与美学的关系。他指出:"我们必须正视'文学性'的问题,它是美学的中心问题,是文学和艺术的本质"(韦勒克,2015:270)。英美新批评主义追求文本审美功能,要求文学要通过美学来实现其审美价值,与其他学科领域区别开来。

如果说英美"新批评"主义从语义学的角度探究文学本质，那么结构主义则从功能主义出发，强调语言结构的功能意义，认为"决定作品能成为文学作品的根本原因是在于结构，而不在于语言内涵和意义"（刘浔，邓千流，2010：83）。文学性这一诗学研究的目标是要提出一套关于文学话语的结构和功能的理论（赖大仁，2021：32）。结构主义从语言内部结构出发，并不简简单单阐释个别具体文本的内部结构，而是研究文本语言下的运行机制和系统及文学文本基于这个系统和机制产生的价值和意义。

后现代文论进一步扩大文学性适用范围，以解构主义为指导，打破仅限于文本的探索。伊格尔顿认为，"文学性"是语言的某些特殊用法，但这种用法是既可以在"文学"作品中发现，也可以在"文学"作品之外的很多地方找到（伊格尔顿，2007：5）。与形式主义不同，解构主义不仅将文学性放在文学领域探讨，同样也探究文学之外的文学，强调"去中心化"，颠覆文学性的中心地位。而西方文论开始后理论转向的时代，对于文学性的探讨又趋向于回归文学本身，突出特点是要求回归文学研究，把文学性理解为文学本质特性而不只是文本特性，以此对文学和文学性作出新的阐释。

无论是苏联的形式主义，还是英美批评主义、结构主义，以及后现代文论等对文学性的探讨。我们不难看出，虽然每个理论流派强调文学性的侧重点不同，但始终都没有跳出语言学模式，没有摆脱语言学的影响，讨论关注的重点一直是从文学的语言形式出发，文学性也主要从语言学、修辞学、符号学等方面进行探讨，但语言本身成为研究对象，排除其他领域，纯粹讨论文学本身，是否固步自封，陷入绝对化和片面化的困境？将文学独立出来进行研究固然有其科学性，但文学本身涉及政治、经济、社会、历史等诸多领域，同时也依托读者认知反应产生意义，仅从语言学领域探讨文学性，必然缺失研究的客观性，那这种失去客观性的科学性，还科学吗？

对于国外文学性研究的困境，一些国内学者也提出了不同的观点。童庆炳认为审美是区别文学与非文学的根本特征。"气息""氛围""情调""韵律"和"色泽"就是文学性在作品中的具体的有力的表现（童庆炳，2009：53）。孟繁华将文学性归结为情感性，认为文学区别于上述学科最重要的标识，就在于文学是诉诸人的情感、处理人的内宇宙的一个领域，强调文学的情感功能（孟繁华，2023：1-2）。还有学者从"文学性"的动态性出发，对文学性进行探讨，以及坚持"文学性"是语言机制等观点。

文学性问题一直以来都备受关注，何为文学性这一点也困扰无数学者。目前，国内外对于文学性的研究，大多集中在语言形式和审美情感两大板块，无论从哪个维度把握，我们都要坚持研究的客观性、科学性。综合以上文学性相关的研究，我们可以大致总结出，文学性是一种文学属性概念，抽象的关系概念。它不是一种文学手段，而是塑造文学的过程，是一种机制和系统，是一种文学能力。文学性具有诗性功能，可以使语言文学化，是使文学成为文学的东西。文学性强调审美性和情感性，而实现文学性的途径则可以通过改变文本形式和结构来实现。

3. 科幻小说的文学性呈现

20世纪以来，随着自然科学的不断发展，前沿技术，尖端科技不断更迭，人们对于科学技术的畅想也不断深入，科幻小说迎来了繁荣发展的春天，有关科幻小说的研究也层出不穷。

何为科幻小说？美国的科幻杂志编辑雨果·根斯巴克曾这样定义科幻小说："'科幻小说'

（scientifiction）是迷人的浪漫故事，融合了科学事实和预言性的想象"。苏恩文认为，"科幻小说是这样一种文学类型，它的必要和充分条件是陌生化与认知的出场，以及二者之间的相互作用，它的主要的形式策略是用一种拟换作者的经验环境的富有想象力的框架结构"（苏恩文，2011：8）。

无论是根斯巴克对于科幻小说的界定，还是苏恩文对科幻小说的总结，我们不难看出科幻小说的最大特点，就是它神秘又陌生的科学内容和浪漫迷人、天马行空的幻想。而这样一种具有创造性的特殊文类，它的文学性又该如何把握呢？

科幻小说处于科技文与通俗小说之间，这就决定了科幻小说必然具有两种文类的特性：科学性和文学性（一般文学性）。当然，这也决定了科幻小说的文学性也必然不同于一般小说的文学性。从科幻小说的这两方面特性来说，科幻小说文学性应当包含两个方面：科学性和一般文学的文学性。

科学性。科幻小说主题多为宇宙探索、人工智能、思想实验、机器人大战、外星人入侵等，多数文本中还包含大量科学术语、程序指令，给读者认知带来一定的困难，使读者与平时熟悉的认知环境相脱离。换句话说，也就是读者的已知经验被推翻。这样的内容注定了读者在阅读科幻小说时，认知会受到一定阻碍。那么需要对这一部分进行修改，使其符合读者的认知期待吗？答案是否定的。就其科学性来说，科幻小说不同寻常的主题，独特的叙述方式，以及新奇的内容本身就极具创造性，魅力十足，能激发出读者极大的阅读兴趣，所以这也就注定了科幻小说的文学性不同于一般文学小说，其独有的科学性也应当属于科幻小说的文学性。

文学性。科幻小说不同于一般文学小说，但究其文类，科幻小说仍然属于小说文体，仍然具有小说文体的特征、结构和功能，我们同样应当从小说文体出发来把握科幻小说的文学性。科幻小说陌生的内容和形式使得读者在阅读这些"陌生"材料时的阅读期待被打破，给读者认知造成一定的负担，如果文本还缺乏一般文学的文学性，科幻小说便很容易滑入枯燥无味的科技文领域。为避免这一情况，在处理科幻小说时，就要与纯粹的科技文区分开来，必须保留一般小说的文学性。从以上形式主义、英美批评主义、结构主义、解构主义等流派及国内学者对文学性的研究可以看出，一般小说的文学性强调语言审美性和情感性，从文本的结构和语言表达、叙事结构、修辞等方面进行考量，保留小说文本的通俗易读的特征，使文本具有可读性。

4. 文学与科学的共荣：翻译实践中的科幻文学

4.1 实现文学性的途径

科幻小说独特的文学性要求我们在翻译时不仅要满足一般文学作品的审美要求，还要照顾科幻文学独有的科学特性。既要满足读者对小说文本的阅读期待，又要在科学内容上保持陌生化。由这两点出发，接受美学理论与科幻文本的翻译要求非常契合。

接受美学是由姚斯提出的一个文理概念。"期待视野"是接受美学理论最核心的观点，强调读者将以往的经验和知识与文本相结合。"期待视野"的重构，是向前代读者的"期待视野"变过去，提出那时曾经提出过的问题，以明白那时的读者是如何理解这部作品的（王锺陵，2012：177）。它强调读者将"前经验"和知识与文本相结合。读者阅读新文本时，"前经验"

被强化、修改或者纠正，又进一步形成我们的已有知识。文本与前经验重合越多，读者期待视野就越被满足，作出的认知努力就越少。

期待美学的另一重要概念"召唤结构"由沃尔夫冈·伊瑟尔提出。伊瑟尔强调文本是一个不确定的"召唤结构"，这个结构中包含否定和空白两大概念。"空白使本文中各部分之间的联系处于开放状态，并以此激发读者去协调各部分之间的关系——换句话说，它们激发着读者在本文内发挥基本的作用，而各种类别的否定则召唤熟悉的明确成分，这只是为了排除这些成分"（伊瑟尔，1991：216）。空白给予读者想象的空间，是读者想象的前提。"否定"打破读者原有的期待视野，帮助读者修改意识中熟悉的"已知"，从而来构建新的意义。在伊瑟尔看来，文学作品是有交流的功能。这就要求我们在阅读时，文本意义无法完全满足读者的期待。这里就要求文本内容和形式上要"陌生化"。

接受美学理论强调读者"期待视野"的满足，用读者熟悉的文本内容和形式，减轻读者认知负担，完美契合科幻小说翻译中一般文学性的要求。另外，接受美学召唤结构中的"陌生化"，又使得文本内容不再老生常谈，给读者带来新鲜感，引起读者阅读兴趣。

4.2 文学性的再现

本文将以 *Philia, Eros, Storge, Agápe, Pragma* 汉译为例，结合接受美学理论所强调的"陌生化"和"期待视野"两个概念，从科幻小说科学性和一般文学性两个方面来具体阐释科幻小说特有的"文学性"。

（1）科学性的保留——正式化指令

根据 Searle 言外行为分类的标准，指令性言外行为是指说话者在一定的语境中通过话语试图使听话者（在不同程度上）做某事的行为。指令语包括请求、邀请、命令、建议、劝告、禁止、吩咐、告诫等（骆京景，庞继贤，2010：86）。在许多科技文本中，经常会看到这些指令用语，但部分指令的使用并不正式，举例如下。

①原文：Recalibrating. <u>Mission not paramount?</u>

译文一：重新校准中。<u>任务不优先？</u>

译文二：重新校准中。<u>任务优先，是否否认？</u>

译文三：重新校准中。<u>是否解除任务优先？</u>

分析：根据原文内容来看，此处是机甲根据操控者要求发出的确认指令，译文一很容易发现"<u>not</u>"这个词并非标准的指令用语，翻译成"不"并不符合指令用语客观庄重的表达特点，对此译者修正为译文二的"是否否认"。译文二相对于译文一来说，更加符合指令用语的表达，但这里同样存在一个问题，搭配不当。在计算机语言中，并不常用否认来搭配某项操作，更常见的搭配为"解除"。因此，此处做最后一版修改，改为"重新校准中。是否解除任务优先？"，更符合科技文本语言特点，保留文本的科学性。

②原文：He dropped to his knees, sliding across to their kitchen garden, and grabbed the pitchfork he'd left there. He was ready to throw when it said, "No." Then, "Wait."

译文一：他突然跪了下来，滑向菜园，抓起之前留在那里的干草叉，准备向无人机扔去。此时，无人机却给出指令："不""暂停"。

译文二：他突然跪了下来，滑向菜园，抓起之前留在那里的干草叉，准备向无人机扔去。此时，无人机却给出指令："禁止射击""暂停攻击"。

分析：可以看到两个指令"No."和"Wait."如果这里直接译为"不""等等"就非常口

语化，机器人发出指令一般为事先设定的程序，并不会以正常人类口吻进行表述，所以此处将其修改为"禁止射击""暂停攻击"，使语言表达更加正式。

③原文：

"Recalibrating…Countermeasures disabled. Malfunction addressed. Shell warning. Shell warning. Cease and desist."

Explain.

"Containment failure. Shell failure imminent. Final option engaged."

Explain.

"Survival paramount. Cease and desist. Disengage recode."

译文一：

"重新校准中……对抗措施失效。故障已处理。机身警告。机身警告。停止。"

解释原因。

"安全壳破损。机身即将损毁。启动最终方案。"

解释原因。

"生存优先。停止。解除重新编码。"

译文二：

"重新校准中……对抗措施失效。故障已处理。机身警告。机身警告。停止。"

原因报告。

"安全壳破损。机身即将损毁。启动最终方案。"

原因报告。

"生存优先。停止。解除重新编码。"

分析：同样，此处可以看到日常用词"Explain"，如果直译为"解释"，很明显不符合机器人语言特点。机器人对状况进行说明解释，我们在科技文本中通常处理为"报告"，此处修改为"原因报告"更加符合科技语言特点。

（2）科学术语"约定俗称"

Words	Draft	Target Translation
suit	智能套装	宇航服
deadlock	僵局	死锁
star chart	星状图	星图
interstellar communications	星际通讯	星际通讯
shield	护盾	防护罩
visual sensor	视觉传感器	视觉传感器
landing beacon	着陆信标	着陆信标
heat-shapes	热成像	热成像
stasis cocoon	静态防护层	静态防护层
smartfleet	智能舰队	智能舰队
pulsing light	脉冲光	脉冲光
bipedal shell	双足攻壳	双足机甲
hololibrary	全息图书馆	全息库

"专业科技术语词汇反映客观现实，没有感情色彩，一般只用于科学领域文章，有着严格的定义且往往是单义词，语义界限非常明确"（温雪梅、邱飞燕，2010）。本文中有着大量的专业科技术语，且部分术语语义模糊，在处理时也相对棘手。专业术语翻译方式多种多样，有直译、音译、意译、形译、创造新词等，以及约定俗成的翻译法。在科技英语翻译中，我们需要根据具体的科技语境和特定的专业类别给出正确的术语。在通常情况下，根据术语的特征，会有一些预定俗称的方法和译名（温雪梅、邱飞燕，2010）。本文中涉及术语众多，无法用某种单一译法涵盖，且文本本身属于小说文本，部分科技术语需要根据上下文语境才能确定，使用约定俗成法对小说文本中的科技术语进行翻译更为恰当。例如：

①原文：The suit brought up a star chart, then adjusted the zoom as she focused on the blinking cursor over a planet, all the way down to a meandering river and a town not far from it.

译文一：身上的智能套装自动打开了一张星图，调整了变焦。伊娃将光标聚焦在一颗行星上，顺着往下调，定位到一条蜿蜒的河流和附近的一个城镇。

译文二：身上的宇航服自动打开了一张星图，调整了变焦。伊娃将光标聚焦在一颗行星上，顺着往下调，定位到一条蜿蜒的河流和附近的一个城镇。

分析："suit"这个词在我们生活中非常常见，通常我们会处理为"套装""西服"等。但如果用于科学领域，它便成为了一个科技术语。译文一将"suit"处理为"智能套装"，是因为考虑到这句话主语是"suit"，却发出了"brought up a star chart"的动作，所以这里译者认为这里的"suit"应该为一种不需要人手动操作便可以自行打开星图的"智能套装"，但随后译者联系上下文发现，主人公是驾驶飞船在太空航行，这里的"套装"应该是太空特有的，有一定自动功能的"宇航服"。

②原文："If she's in control," Sibling-Rachel pointed out. "She's in deadlock."

译文一："如果她能控制的话，"瑞秋点明，"她应该是遇到了麻烦。"

译文二："如果她能控制的话，"瑞秋点明，"她应该陷入了'死锁'。"

分析："Deadlock"也是一个较为常见的词语，通常可以翻译为"僵局""困境""死锁"等，此处"She's in Deadlock"一般译法会处理为"她陷入了困境或遇到麻烦"，但联系前文"If she's in control,"我们便很容易发现逻辑出现了问题，那么这里只有可能"Deadlock"并非我们常用的"困境"这一含义，而是一个专有术语"死锁"。经查证，"死锁"为计算机系统中一种阻塞的现象，且这里的"she"应当是一个有计算机程序的机甲，所以根据上下文情况，译者将其处理为"死锁"。

（3）文学性的增添——俗语运用

《辞海》给俗语下的定义是"俗语也叫俗话、俗言，流行于民间的通俗语句，带有一定的方言性，指谚语、俚语、惯用语及口头上常用的成语等。"俗语贴近生活，具有生动、活泼、非正式、不稳定等特点。随着时代不断发展，新事物、新观念不断涌现，俗语也逐渐被大众接纳为正式的标准用语，电影、杂志、小说也常常见到它的身影。在本文中译者也使用了大量中文俗语来进行翻译。例如：

①原文：She could see the ripple effect of her vote sweep the entire chamber, like stalks of grass before a great wind.

译文一：就像狂风吹倒草茎，这张反对票带来的连锁反应席卷了整个大厅。

译文二：一石激起千层浪，这张反对票带来的连锁反应席卷了整个大厅。

分析：此处主要描述主人公就是否进行战争一事而投出一张出人意料的反对票，这张票震动全场。这里原文将这种连锁反应比喻成"风吹草低"这样一种画面，但这样的比喻在中文中是无法接受的，而中文对等的比喻"一石激起千层浪"，也是用于比喻连锁反应，此处使用中文俗语进行替换，更能贴合中文读者的表达习惯，增强文本文学性。

②原文：<u>Thankfulness inundated her.</u> I'm okay. You're not.

译文一：<u>她心里无比感激。</u>"我没什么问题，但你的情况好像不太好。"

译文二："<u>谢天谢地</u>。我没什么问题，但你的情况好像不太好。"

分析：此处是女主人公看到"姐姐"安全归来时，无比感激的心理状态。译文一采用直译的方式，意思也实现了完整传达，却不够简洁，而且这里我们很明显可以看到人称的转换，从第三人称"her"转为了第一人称"I"。前后文全部属于对话内容，没有必要进行视角转换而增加读者阅读负担。因此译文二处理为俗语"谢天谢地"，非常简洁地传达出主人公内心的感激之情，且将视角统一为第一人称，更加符合读者认知习惯。

③原文："<u>I prefer to be present. The future will take care of itself.</u> Whenever we're together, that's how it will be. Now. About your question …" She drew his head down to hers and there was no more talking for some time.

译文一："<u>我宁愿活在当下。一切都会好的。</u>我们会一直在一起，就是这样。现在。你的问题……"她扳过迪伊的头，靠到她头上，好一会儿没有再说话。

译文二："<u>我宁愿活在当下。船到桥头自然直</u>。我们会一直在一起，就是这样。现在。你的问题……"她扳过迪伊的头，靠到她头上，好一会儿没有再说话。

分析：此处采用意译翻译方式将"I prefer to be present. The future will take care of itself."译为"我宁愿活在当下。一切都会好的。"意义表达完整，却不够生动，而中文对应的俗语"船到桥头自然直"，不但可以正确传达原文意义，还使得语言更为灵动活泼，大大提高了文本的可读性。

（4）语境重构

语境重构即指英文中的"recontextualization"，主要起到协调知识生产和知识再现的作用。叙事是小说的重要组成部分，但由于中外语言表达和认知习惯差异，我们在阅读外语文本时，往往感觉生涩拗口，不得不对文本内容进行一定的调整以适应自己的阅读习惯，这时我们便会对叙事内容进行语境重构。Van Leeuwen 和 Wodak 提出四种常见的改造转换法：要素删减、要素重组、要素替代，以及要素添加用于语境重构（Van Leeuwen、Wodak：1999）。本文根据具体要求，选择性地采用了这四种方式对文本进行加工处理，使得文本更加符合中文读者阅读习惯。例如：

①原文：Dee brought her food, <u>water to wash</u>, and fresh clothes.<u> He apologized for not having an entertainment node and shared his hololibrary instead.</u> He spent a lot of time outside, or moving around in the kitchen, doing chores. He was an excellent cook who scaled and gutted fish out in the yard with glittering flashes of his nimble knife. He was fond of ground provisions, which she usually shunned at home but enjoyed here <u>becausehe often roasted them over an open flame.</u>

译文一：迪伊给她带来了食物、<u>洗漱用水</u>和干净的衣物。<u>他的生活一向寡淡无味，没有什么娱乐活动，为此他感到抱歉，所以给伊娃分享了自己的全息库。</u>一般情况下，迪伊不是在外面干活，就是围着厨房打转，做做家务。就做饭来说，迪伊可谓是一把好手。他用那把灵巧便携，闪闪发光的小刀，在院子里刮除鱼鳞，清理内脏。他喜欢吃<u>明火烤制</u>的红薯，伊娃向来是不吃的，但在迪伊这里，却也吃得津津有味。

译文二：迪伊给她带来了食物、水和干净的衣物。他的生活一向寡淡无味，没有什么娱乐活动，不过为了能给伊娃找点乐趣，他分享了自己的全息库。一般情况下，迪伊不是在外面干活，就是围着厨房打转，做做家务。就做饭来说，迪伊可谓一把好手。在洒满阳光的院子里，他操起他那把灵巧便携，闪闪发光的小刀，杀鱼刮鳞，清理内脏。迪伊喜欢吃烤红薯，伊娃向来是不吃的，但在迪伊这里，却也吃得津津有味。

分析：译文一可以很明显看出，直译原文内容，基本上也可以传达出原文语义，但读起来拗口，不通顺，且缺乏美感和张力，于是译者再次进行了修改。

第一，省译。将"洗漱用水"省译为"水"，将"because he often roasted them over an open flame"删去，"明火烤制的红薯"省译为"烤红薯"。后文并没有对"洗漱"和"明火烤制"再加以强调，省译为"水""烤红薯"也并不破坏原文本意，且省去后句段读起来更加朗朗上口，所以进行省译处理。

第二，省译。"apologized"是英文中比较常见的表达，此处想表达为"为自己无法给伊娃找些乐子而感到不好意思"，但是在中文中这个词义却相对较重，所以此处省去"apologized"，转而使用连词"不过"来衔接迪伊为自己歉疚而作出的行动，顺理成章，"apologized"含义也蕴含在了迪伊的行动中。

第三，替换。"with glittering flashes of his nimble knife"中的"with"译文一中直译为"用"，语义上并无差别，但是鉴于后文都是"scaled and gutted"这样的动词搭配，所以此处替换为动作强度更大的动词"操起……小刀"，更加贴合中文读者的审美习惯。

第四，语义重组。"in the yard with glittering flashes of his nimble knife"，这里我们不禁会想象这样一幅画面，在院子里，迪伊拿在手里的刀闪闪发光，但是读者不禁发问，刀无法自己发光，那这里为什么是闪闪发光呢？很明显，院子里有阳光，阳光下的小刀反光，所以才会有"glittering flashes"，所以此处根据中文读者习惯，将语义进行重组，"在洒满阳光的院子里"就为下文"闪闪发光的小刀"做好了铺垫。

②原文：The room had two white chairs that faced each other and nothing else. It was square, black, and windowless, but illumination made the walls sparkle with the light of stars. Eva sat in one of the chairs, waiting.

译文一：房间里除了两把相对放置的白色椅子外，什么也没有。这个房间四四方方，屋内一片漆黑，没有窗户，但灯饰映在墙壁上闪烁着点点星光。伊娃坐在其中一把椅子上等待。

译文二：一间没有窗户的房间，四四方方，屋内漆黑一片，除了两把相对放置的白色椅子和灯饰映在墙上的点点星光外，什么也没有。伊娃坐在椅子上静静等待着。

分析：此处是文中对一处房间的描述，译文一采用直译的方式，我们可以看出"房间里除了……""这个房间……"两个主语一致，全部翻译显得叙述冗长多余，毫无美感。所以我们将省译一个主语，将修饰房间的形容词重组成几个短句。"一间没有窗户的房间，四四方方，屋内漆黑一片"，剩余部分根据逻辑"房间里有……"进行重组，这样句型就被整合成了"一个什么样的房间+房间里有什么"这样的结构，符合中文叙述习惯，最后将省译"其中一把椅子上"，使得内容更加简洁。另外，此处增加一个副词"静静地"来修饰"等待"，使得语句更为通顺，读起来朗朗上口。

从以上四个部分可以看到，接受美学理论所强调的"陌生化"和"期待视野"的满足使得科幻小说翻译中的科学性和文学性得以保留。前两个部分（正式化指令和科学术语"约定俗称"）合理规范地译好指令用语和科技术语，使得文本科学化、正式化，生出"陌生感"，使读者实现认知的更新，保留了文本的科学性。在后两个部分（"俗语运用"和"语境重构"）中，使用目标语读者耳熟能详的俗语，调整文本结构符合读者表达习惯，对文本难度进行一定的调和，增强科幻小说的一般文学性。

5. 结语

一直以来，文学界对于何为文学性一直争论颇多。无论是苏联形式主义从语言学方面介入，英美新批评主义从语义学出发，结构主义从功能主义着手，还是解构主义的文学"去中心化"，以及部分学者从审美、情感性、阅读体验等方向对文学性进行探讨，我们都必须明白，不管从哪个方向出发，文学性并非一成不变的。"任何文学史形成的文学性都是依据于时代的，不同的时代观念造就不同的文学性观念，我们应该根据时代变化和周边情况的变化，而改变文学性的应用范围"（王峰，2016：126）。以往对文学性的探讨大多集中于传统文学文本细腻的表达，但随着时代的进步，新时代的文本必定也具有独特的文学性。科幻小说作为时代的产物，是小说领域的一种特殊文类，生来便具有科学性和文学性两种特性，也正是科幻小说的这两种特性，才共同构成了科幻小说特有的"文学性"，而接受美学理论"陌生化"和"期待视野"两大概念，既保留了科幻小说中陌生的书写材料，又满足读者的认知期待，调和文本难度，增强可读性，完美契合科幻小说这两种特性。在科技飞速发展的今天，新事物层出不穷，我们应当以发展的眼光，以接受美学的概念为指导，重塑科幻小说的文学性。

参考文献

[1] VAN LEEUWEN T, WODAK R, 1999. Legitimizing immigration control: a discourse-historical analysis[J]. Discourse Studies, 1(1): 83-118 .

[2] 赖大仁，2021. "文学性"问题百年回眸：理论转向与观念嬗变[J]. 文艺研究（9）：32-43.

[3] 刘浔，邓千流，2010. 西方"文学性"研究的回顾及其启示[J]. 外国文学（33）：82-83，92.

[4] 骆京景，庞继贤，2010. 学术论文中指令语分布特点及其话语策略分析[J]. 甘肃联合大学学报(社会科学版)，26(5)：85-89.

[5] 孟繁华，2023. 文学性意味着什么——从阅读经验看文学性[J]. 文艺争鸣（1）：1-3.

[6] 童庆炳，2009. 谈谈文学性[J]. 语文建设（3）：55-59.

[7] 托多罗夫，1989. 俄苏形式主义文论选[M]. 北京：中国社会科学出版社.

[8] 苏恩文，2011. 科幻小说变形记：科幻小说的诗学和文学类型史[M]. 丁素萍，李靖民，李静滢，译. 合肥：安徽文艺出版社.

[9] 王峰，2016. 科幻小说何须在意"文学性"[J]. 探索与争鸣（9）：124-127.

[10] 王鍾陵，2012. 论姚斯的接受美学理论[J]. 江苏社会科学（3）：174-182.

[11] 韦勒克，2015. 批评的诸种概念[M]. 罗钢，王馨钵，杨德友，译. 上海：上海人民出版社.

[12] 温雪梅，邱飞燕，2010. 科技术语翻译之"约定俗称"与创新[J]. 中国科技翻译，23(3)：13-15，19.

[13] 伊格尔顿，2007. 二十世纪西方文学理论[M]. 伍晓明，译. 北京：北京大学出版社.

[14] 伊瑟尔，1991. 阅读行为[M]. 金惠敏等，译. 长沙：湖南文艺出版社.

林语堂译创《武则天正传》研究

余 琴

1. 译创与《武则天正传》

1.1 译创

译创是在翻译基础上的一种再创作,用目标语对原语文本加以改编,以自然流畅的方式传递原文信息(黄德先,2013:29)。译创兼具翻译和创作的特点,可以采取改编、重述和改写等多种写作方式,十分灵活,其既适用于翻译,又适用于跨文化写作,甚至实际创作,应用范围十分广泛。接下来作者将从译创的定义、发展和意义分别进行阐释,从而对该研究理论进行一定的基础理解。

关于"译创",学界有这样的共识。首先,大家都认为翻译就是译创,是一种再创造,并将这种理念应用于自己的翻译实践之中。其次,都从交流和解释的视角看待翻译过程,因此更加看重译者对原材料的重新加工和对目的语读者的考虑。最后,都强调译创不只是涉及语言,它的本质是保留和转换文化传统,翻译成为一种跨文化的创造活动。译创理论体现一种文化翻译观,即"创作是一种文化翻译,翻译是一种文化创造的活动"(Salvador,2005:190)。所谓"译创",指的是"以创作为主,其中隐含和夹杂着大量翻译的创作现象。这种形式既不是严格意义上的创作,又与传统意义上的翻译不同,可以说是创作与翻译的'杂糅',是介于翻译与创作之间的一种状态"(冯智强,2012:31)。

译创这一概念最先是由印度诗人兼翻译家普鲁肖塔玛·拉尔和巴西诗人兼翻译家阿洛多·德·坎波斯分别于 1957 年和 1969 年提出,二者都用了"transcreation"这一术语,来表达一种翻译和创作并存的写作方式。拉尔认为,面对丰富多样的原材料,译者必须进行编辑、调和和改变,他的工作在许多方面都变成了译创(Lal,1964:5)。而德·坎波斯在 1969 年也提出"译创"这一术语,用来指反对形式/内容二分法,转而关注文本诗学形式的一种翻译实践,旨在实现诗歌的不可译性,不仅翻译意义,还翻译形式(Nobrega、Milton,2009:259)。他指出,翻译不是合成或解决矛盾的行为,而是译创,一种激进的实践(Gentzler,2007:90)。1999 年,他在牛津大学举办的一次研讨会上,发表的"The Ex-Centric's Viewpoint: Tradition, Transcreation, Transculturation"一文中,将译创定位于通过巴西的巴洛克混合主义而形成的传统和通过任意同化世界文化遗产而形成的文化融合之间(Jackson,2010:143)。坎波斯将翻译作为跨文本的写作手段,将译创由一个诗歌翻译理论发展为一个普遍翻译理论和文学理论。随后,该理论在各个领域都得到了认可和发展,使之进一步拓展成为一个多语言的、符际的、跨学科的文化理论。

而国内一些学者最初在介绍印度和巴西的后殖民翻译理论时对这一术语也有所提及,但是采用不同的说法。比如"翻译创造"(蒋骁华,2002)、"超越性创造"(谢天振,2008)以及"译创"(詹成,2011)等。后来的学者使用"译创"这一说法的较多,进一步介绍了译创在文学翻译和非文学翻译领域里的应用。直到在林语堂的作品中，我们仍可以看到他的创作和翻译之间界限模糊，相互交织杂糅，从而形成了"译中有创，创中带译"的独特创译一体风格。而这种创作特色也开启了中国文化对外传播的"林语堂模式"。

译创的目标就是把原文中的意图、风格、音调、信息的情感特征传递给目标读者，激发他们的兴趣，让他们采取行动。这个术语也招致一些批评，因为它被认为是允许过度偏离原文，鼓励自由翻译，甚至抛弃原作。可是传统的翻译观却认为翻译是原作的一种可怜复制，如今翻译被看作一种创作行为，在另一种语言里生产出一个新的原作。

在全球化和多元化的时代，译创作为一种新的研究思路和灵活的写作方式，对翻译研究和文化研究都有着重要的现实意义。它使我们重新思考原作和译作、源语语言文化和目的语语言文化之间的关系。同时，译创也为文化传播和文化杂合提供一种有效的手段，既可以使源语文化向外输出，又可以将世界文学和本民族优秀传统文化进行融合交流。

1.2 《武则天正传》

在林语堂的小说中，《武则天正传》的副题为《唐邠王回忆录》，其中涉及的文献极多，林语堂声称所有的史实都来自《新唐书》《旧唐书》。除此之外，骆宾王的《讨武曌檄》作为所有长篇中唯一一篇全文翻译收录的文章，也是研究林语堂先生翻译思想和策略的理想样本。

该书作为一本历史传记类读物，主要讲述公元 690 年，武则天作为女性登上中国最高政治舞台的那段真实故事。小说内容以武则天的孙子邠王对整个历史脉络和事件进行回忆为叙述框架，从唐太宗病逝前几日写起，一直写到武则天垂暮的老年。林语堂创作的《武则天正传》没有跨过男性视阈，字里行间都是批判性言语。不仅在正文中讲述她为谋得权力而一步步地精心策划、残暴无情，而且在小说的附录中列出她一生所谋害人的名单。

从古至今，从官方到民间，关于武则天成为中国历史上唯一以女性之躯挤进封建政治权力格局最高层的叙述层出不穷。在不同版本的文学叙述下，她已经不只是一个单纯客观的历史人物，还是充满虚构与想象的文学载体，负载着叙述者对于现实的关注和对未来的想象。

2. 翻译案例探析

纵观近年对于林语堂英文作品的翻译研究成果，虽然视角多样，但是仍然存在一定空白。大多数研究者都是将其英文作品分为创作文本和翻译文本两个部分来分析，而对林语堂的那些将翻译和创作杂合在一起的作品，却没有得到翻译学者的足够重视。很大程度上是因为学界一直将其当成原创作品来看待，并不会从翻译研究的角度去分析，但是一接触到这些作品，我们又会不可避免地谈到翻译现象这一事实。由此，当引入"译创"这一理论后，便能够对此类英文作品产生一个比较清晰的认识。以林语堂的《武则天正传》为研究内容，以译创手段为研究手段，本节将从该作品标题、叙述角度、文化负载、人物形象四个方面角度的翻译来探究林语堂先生在译创《武则天正传》过程中的创作手段及其创作效果。

2.1 作品题目的翻译

译创作为一种跨文化活动，它不仅是语言之间的转换过程，还传播着国家之间不同的文化。而人物的名称同样折射的是源于社会特有的价值观、宗教信仰、社会习俗、意识形态等富有民族特色的文化元素。但是，原文文本中蕴含着某种信息的文化负载词在译入语环境中通常不被人熟知。为了有效地传递原文语义，译者往往选择归化策略（王传英等，2011：109）。

再回看林语堂将《武则天正传》译为"Lady Wu"这一标题时，就不难发现，林语堂也认同此类观点。即武则天的魅力来自人们发现她很难融入任何既定的社会框架。她作为一个女人，是一个"异类"，也很难将她与其他著名女性相提并论。虽然林语堂很乐意将武则天描述为一位杰出的女性，但他不愿意将其与伊丽莎白一世等其他女性统治者相提并论，他认为武则天是这一类人的对立面。她是情妇、篡位者、皇后……她是女皇帝。然而，她打破了更多的先例，造成了比历史上任何男性阴谋家更多的混乱。正是因为武则天不局限于任何单一身份的框架下，林语堂并没有借"empress""queen""loyal"一类用词来介绍她，而是将其回置于一位女子的形象，她首先是自己，其次才是母亲或者妻子。通过这一标题的翻译，我们可以看到在那时的林语堂已经拥有极具张力的女性主义意识。同时，在这一思想指导下的翻译，也将人物的个性凸显，作品中主人公的人格魅力提升，为西方读者对中国故事的接受和理解打下一定基础。

此外，溯及原文，可以看到的是，林语堂将该作品题目译写成"Lady Wu"，但是在文中也出现其他的称呼来表示武则天的身份。当她还是初次进入宫廷之时，译为"Wu Meiniang"；当她坐在唐高宗的身旁时，又冠以"empress"的头衔……最后，"Lady"一词的选择，在英文中是对贵族女性的称呼，并且，它可以让西方读者联想到莎士比亚名著中的"Lady Macbeth"，一个为权力而双手沾满鲜血的女人，与武则天有着很多相似之处（单原，2014：129）。可见，在跨文化交流语境的视域下，林语堂不但强调中西文化的"和而不同"，而且更加注重不同文化之间的共性与会通，没有过分强调中国文化的特殊性，从而使得中国文化在西方逐渐得到认同，进而得以融入世界文化的发展潮流。

2.2 叙述角度的翻译

"一个人怎样写自己的祖母呢，如果祖母是一个娼妓怎么办？"文中这个与众不同的开篇，可以让读者感受到整部传记小说的感情基调。在《武则天正传》中，林语堂没有采用中国传统传记的纪传体或者编年体体例，而是借鉴西方现代传记专注于某个主题的所谓传记小说的表现方式。正如他在原作序言中写道，至于叙述的口吻，我决定用武后的孙子邠王守礼的看法为观点，借以产生直接的真实感。这样一个叙述主体的选择，收获的不仅是"真实"，而且还使传记叙述聚焦的方式发生了根本变革（郭洪雷，2009：47）。

传统跨文化中的中国叙事里，作家都以古代历史、人物、故事为依托，以此更好地传达中国传统文化和价值观念。而这种以中国为代表的东方文明主题，和以资本主义为依托的西方文明产生了强烈的对比冲突。林语堂在《武则天正传》中带来的特别之处首先在于叙述视角的新颖。这样的叙述角度，将叙事主体人物化，以回忆录的方式写传记，将史书中的武周故事转化为邠王守礼亲历其境，是他在宫廷生活中的"耳濡目染"和人生经历，保证叙述的流畅，为作品赢得了真正的修辞效果，使读者对于唐太宗至武则天去世这段近百年历史，王室内部为掌控国家权力的宫廷斗争产生更加深刻的认识。

2.3 文化负载词句的翻译

林语堂始终以一种文化多元主义的眼光来看待中外文化，各国文化都不是目标和归宿，都是作为世界文化中的"一元"，各有优势与不足。他既反对国粹派，又不赞成崇洋媚外，因此，他对中西文化的论述是"求同存异"，既发现中西文化的相通之处，又寻求二者之间的差异。

武则天所处的唐代，是一个官职体系日趋完善复杂的时代，也是一个文化欣欣向荣的时代。面对复杂的唐代官职体系，林语堂又是如何让西方读者能够很快接受并理解的呢？面对官职名称，他在文中是这样描述——The top of the government was divided into three departments: ①the imperial secretariat, was closest to the emperor; ②the chancellery, headed by the lord chancellor and two vice-chancellors, who were to assist and advise the emperor in matters of government policy; and ③ the cabinet, which had charge of the ministries（林语堂，2009：47）。林语堂将"门下省"翻译成"the imperial secretariat"，生动地传达了门下省在唐代的官职体系中是国家制定和传达政令的部门；又将尚书省译为"the cabinet"，后者属于西方国家的政权划分，但是尚书省在中国也是政府的政令执行部门，两者实际权力都是一样的（高路，2013：184）。

其次，对于官职品级，他这样写道：In the square, spreading below her and bending on their knees, there were officials and representatives of the conquered races and princes all in their formal gowns. Those were the officials and princes with gold and jade belts above the third rank in front wearing purple…the sixth and seventh ranks green in two shades, with silver belts, etc（林语堂，2009：53）。林语堂通过对文武百官和诸番夷的使节的不同穿戴进行描述，以此来体现出不同等级的官员，这样使目的语读者更容易接受和理解。对官员的服饰颜色和特征都作出详尽的描述与翻译，以及对官员的玉带都描写得淋漓尽致，可以让外国读者领悟到唐代服饰因官职不同也各有千秋，进而体会中国古代严谨的官职体系制度，由此对中国的官僚和服饰文化进一步深入了解和研究。

当然，除此之外，还可以在该作品中看到一些中国特有文化表达的体现，就像他把"好事不出门，坏事传千里"写成"Wise counsel spreads slowly, but wicked gossip travels fast."其中好事译成"wise counsel"，"坏事"则是"wicked gossip"，将"wise"和"wicked"相对，而没有从中国人的传统思维出发去写成"bad and good"来区分好坏之别。而古语"牝鸡司晨"则写成"Hens cry cock-a-doodle-do"。将整个成语进行了解释，本义是"母鸡报晓"，但在旧时指妇女窃权乱政，林语堂在这里并未明确译出，只是采用形象隐晦的译法体现出来，可见，翻译作为对外传播文化的有效手段，无疑要尽力保留圆滑的原有风味和特色。在作品中，还有一处出自诗经的名句"赫赫宗周，褒姒灭之"，林将其译为"A splendid house like the Jou was destroyed by Powse"，译文中保留"褒姒"这一人称名词，且未作多余解释，目的也无可置疑。在对外叙述中国故事的时候，人名是承载整个故事脉络的主线，即使是不重要的角色，但也是中国传统文化的一部分。保留，也是文化自信的体现。这一译法也让感兴趣的西方读者不得不去自行查阅到底何为"Powse"，从了解文化出处到理解其在历史背景下的真正含义，这无疑也是完成一次文化交流传播的表现。

2.4 人物形象的翻译

作为主要为西方读者写作的林语堂，在他生命的最后三十年里，林语堂对武则天的研究完全具有时代特征。他曾自述"写这本《武则天正传》，是对智能犯罪做一项研究"（周启来、孙良好，2010：34）。在他的笔下，将武则天作为一名智能罪犯来研究，她从作为先帝才人到病逝上阳宫的一生中，林语堂又将她如何谋划或授意构陷和杀戮，进而推翻李唐王朝的一生写得淋漓尽致，给予极端人性以一种最低层次的控诉和一种最高强度的鞭挞，体现出作者对于人性、人生等基本生存问题的现代化考量。在林语堂的作品开篇第一章，就将武则天描述为"a woman most feline, predatory, cruel, with a love for pomp, ceremony and splendor, who would stop at nothing—including murder—to attain what she desired"。他笔下的这个女人，"贪婪、残忍，喜欢浮华，仪式和辉煌，为了达到她想要的目标，会不择手段，包括谋杀。"因为林语堂想把武则天"当作一个结合了犯罪与高智商的独特人物，其野心达到了真正的疯子程度"，但其手段残酷，精确并且非常理智的。此外，武则天因其性行为而成为一个不同寻常的创作对象。在林的作品中，他评论了她享受男性后宫的非凡活力："At sixty-nine she grew a new wisdom tooth and at seventy-six, probably as a result of Yije's aphrodisiacs, she grew a new set of eyebrows. Nobody would have been surprised if she grew a pair of whiskers."。换句话说，武则天的性能力和永不满足的欲望，成为男性作家撰写传记中痴迷于她那兽性和恶魔本性的核心。她生命的矛盾结局使后来的大多数传记作家加强自我对中国社会女性的解释。而林语堂就是一个典型的例子。在评价武则天的成就时，他再次强调了这个"邪恶的女人"在生命结束时不知怎么接受自己的从属地位的形象："So ended the extravagant life of the most notorious queen of all China's history. And the evil which she did lived after her."。

在体现人物形象方面，林语堂有其叙述能力的独到之处，但在他的译创中同样存在一些不足之处。比如，他在文中写道：They have certain ambitions, hopes and desires to seek their place in life and live in comfort and security, and they have no other means except through the men that interest them. "Interest"一词对于女性读者而言过于刺眼。前句中讲述女性是如何充满志向，抱有希望，或是寻求安身立命之处的渴望，这些都是人类对美好的共同向往和奋斗目标。但在后句中加上"Interest"一词，便把这些人类共同追求的基本生活条件，仅仅因为主体是女性，便只能通过"取悦吸引"男性这唯一手段才能达到。不管是置于武则天所处的封建时代语境下来描述当时的中国女性，还是对于阅读本书的西方语境下的女性读者而言，都以极强的大男子主义口吻，对这位在封建时期反抗挣扎的中国女人进行不可反驳的控诉。站在中国男性的视角上对整段历史进行叙述，与西方的女性主义和解放思想产生冲突，这不是单例。比如文中提到：男性皇帝三宫六院就是天经地义，但武则天有"废妃"的思想，却违背传统。林语堂认为，唐高宗可以为所欲为，而武则天就应该墨守成规；男尊女卑的陈旧意识，对李世民以"政治作为"衡量，而武则天却以"传统道德"加之束缚。显然，林语堂并未从客观中立的观点对武则天进行分析，使得整部作品的叙述既站在皇权意识的制高点，又有着极强的男权话语。

由此，不难看出，即使是学贯中西文化的林语堂，在创译的过程中也难免会有偏颇，更何况他以一位男性作家的身份对在中国传统历史上唯一一位有着政治背景的女性作出个性化的叙述和评价，使得整个作品承载着作者自我的现实欲望与忧虑。这也从侧面中体现出"译创"手段在思想表达上的实现若是过于活跃，则整个叙述故事难免带有主观意志。如何把握好"译创"的度，或者说创译与创作的分界如何衡量判断，这也是值得进一步探讨的话题。

3. 结论

《武则天正传》是林语堂先生译介的中国历史上辉煌的李唐王朝中曾经"疯狂与荒谬"并存的一段历史。该作品在当时不仅旨在为西方读者提供一扇了解中国古代政治和宫廷的大门，还倾注了林语堂本人对历史人物命运跌宕的情怀，以及对生命的赞叹和人生的思考。相比于林语堂的其他英文传记作品，《武则天正传》算不上是一部成功之作，但也有一些可圈可点之处。通过"译创"的手段，将目标语读者的兴趣和情感引入到中国这一段风云变幻的历史中。从林语堂的作品中，我们可以看到他所持有的是世界文化多元的立场。站在世界文化的背景下，林语堂肯定了文化的多元形态，承认不同的文化会互补与会通，从而摆脱了"非此即彼"的简单思维，能够用客观全面的视野来看待中国文化和世界文化。

创造性写作与翻译从未被看作是两件不同的事情，它允许对原文的极端改变，所以"译创"的文本必须流畅，更重要的是目标读者能够完全理解。对于翻译而言，通常用忠实、准确来描述翻译质量。对译创而言，应该考虑更多地沿着创造性、原创、大胆等思路。作为英语学习者，应该以语言学研究为基石，以文化传播为主体，以东西文化融合为目标，不断地进行身份与角色的转换，以林语堂先生的"两脚踏东西文化，一心评宇宙文章"为志，在新时代的教育背景下，打破单一的学科人才教育模式，培养复合型翻译人才。当然，译者在译创的时候难免会有主观色彩，林语堂也是如此。对此，也应该以辩证的态度来思考和借鉴，从而实现跨文化交流中"美美与共，天下大同"的终极文化理想。对于林语堂作品的研究，不仅对当下中国文化外译具有积极的启迪作用，还对于加快中国文化"走出去"具有重要的现实意义。

参考文献

[1] GENTZLER E, 2007. Translation and identity in the Americas: new directions in translation theory[M]. London: Routledge.
[2] JACKSON K D, 2010. Transcreation: the Brazilian concrete poets and translation[J]. The Translator as Mediator of Culture: 141-160.
[3] LAL P, 1964. Great Sanskrit plays in modern translation[M]. New York: New Directions.
[4] LIN Y T, 2009. Famous Chinese stories: retold by Lin Yutang[M]. Wlico:Mumbai.
[5] NOBREGA T M., MILTON J, 2009. The role of Harold and Augusto de Campos in bringing translation to the fore of literary activity in Brazil[J]. Agents of Translation(81): 257- 277.
[6] SALVADOR D S, 2005. Translational passages: Indian fiction in English as transcreation?[J]. Less Translated Languages: 189-205.
[7] 单原, 2014. 译"境"胜于译义——以林语堂《武则天传》中的文化外译为例[J]. 名作欣赏（30）：128-129，170.
[8] 冯智强, 2012. "译可译,非常译"——跨文化传播视阈下林语堂编译活动的当代价值研究[J]. 外语教学理论实践（3）：30-35.
[9] 高路, 2013. 目的论下看《武则天传》中官职翻译[J]. 芒种（10）：183-184.
[10] 郭洪雷, 2009. 简论林语堂的跨语际传记写作[J]. 浙江师范大学学报(社会科学版), 34(2)：45-49.
[11] 黄德先，殷艳, 2013. 译创：一种普遍的实践[J]. 上海翻译（1）：29-33.
[12] 蒋骁华, 2002. 印度的翻译：从文化输出到文化抗衡[J]. 中国翻译（2）：75-77.
[13] 林语堂, 2009. 武则天传[M]. 北京：外语教学与研究出版社.
[14] 王传英，赵琳, 2011. 依托影视字幕翻译开展案例教学.[J]. 外国语文, 27(4)：109-113.
[15] 谢天振, 2008. 当代国外翻译理论导读[M]. 天津：南开大学出版社.
[16] 詹成, 2011. 改译策略在儿童文学翻译中的运用[J]. 语文学刊（9）：61-63，76.
[17] 周启来，孙良好, 2010. 林语堂笔下的武则天形象[J]. 温州大学学报（社会科学版），23(1)：34-38.

关联翻译理论下"曰"字英译策略探讨
——基于《虬髯客传》四个英译本的分析

李佳怡　汤朝菊

1. 《虬髯客传》简介及其译本选取

《虬髯客传》是传奇类文学体裁，以隋末唐初政治格局为宏大叙事背景，讲述传奇人物的传奇故事，主要描写隋末有志图王的侠客人物"虬髯客"在"真命天子"李世民面前折服并出海自立的故事，曲折反映了广大人民厌恶战争，期待天下太平安定的美好愿望。全文以红拂女和李靖的爱情故事为线索，成功刻画了"风尘三侠"——李靖、红拂女、虬髯客的人物形象。虬髯客：豪爽大方、不吝钱财、嫉恶如仇、具有领袖气质的英雄侠客。李靖：有"礼"、有"才"、有"胆识"，是性格沉稳、内秀，考虑周全的"布衣之士"。红拂女：美丽且有勇有谋、干脆爽朗的乱世女侠。

该传奇故事有很多版本，作者也是众说纷纭，载于各文献的《虬髯客传》的汉语源文本可能因版本不同而有差异，《虬髯客传》的译本也较多，其中以英译本最多。研究唐传奇《虬髯客传》的相关文献很多，其中关于译本分析的文献也有从各种理论视角来进行讨论的，比如根据目的论来进行文化负载词的译本讨论等（汤朝菊、吕由、李琴，2022）。其他文献也用从各种不同的理论视角来进行分析。

本文选取四个英译本进行言语动词"曰"字的对比分析：（1）周劲松译本，简称"周本"（周劲松，2016）；（2）Wang Jing 译本，简称"Wang 本"（Wang，2010）；（3）杨宪益、戴乃迭译本，简称"合译本"（杨宪益、戴乃迭，2009）；（4）Birch 译本，简称"Birch 本"（Birch，2000）。因为这几个译本是基于大致相同的《虬髯客传》原文翻译。各译本的详细情况见表1。

表1 《虬髯客传》简介及其译本概况

中文标题	文献载体	英译本标题	译者	出版社及出版年
《虬髯客传》	《翻译基础十二讲》	未译	周劲松	电子科技大学出版社，2016
《虬髯客传》	《唐代传奇选》	The Man with Curly Beard	杨宪益 戴乃迭	外文出版社，2009
《虬髯客传》	Tang Dynasty Tales: a Guided Reader	Qiuran Ke Zhuan (The Tale of the Curly-Bearded Guest)	Wang Jing	World Scientific，2010
《虬髯客传》	Classical Chinese Literature: An Anthology of Translations, from Antiquity to the Tang Dynasty	The Curly-Bearded Hero	Birch C	Columbia University Press, 2000

2. 关联翻译理论及其应用

Dan Sperber 与 Deirdre Wilson 所提出的关联理论是以会话含义理论和交际理论为基础发展而来的。在此基础上，发展了关联翻译理论。关联翻译理论强调言语交际行为是一种明示推理行为。

首先，翻译是译者和目的语受众之间的交流，对于目的语受众而言，译者就是沟通者（Gutt，1991）。翻译过程主要涉及三个主体——作者、译者、译文读者，三者在语内和语际翻译过程中进行了两次"明示—推理"过程。在翻译过程中，译者不仅要准确把握原文本作者的明示意义，还要分析原文本作者的风格、语气和背景来推断原文本作者的隐含目的。同时，译者还要考虑目标语，即译文读者的语言和文化习惯，使译文读者用最少的努力获得核心信息，找到最佳关联，即原文本作者的目的和译文读者的要求在认知语境上与原文相似。

其次，关联翻译理论比较适合对话语境，强调认知语境在翻译中的作用。认知语境主要包含：（1）物理环境信息，主要包括话语对话发生场景的信息。（2）记忆信息，包括以前对话内容，文化信息和知识储备等（谢卫霞，2018）。译者应将语言视为对一个动作的连续反应过程，不应割裂开来。语言的表达必然是由一个事物或行为引发的，要考虑语言表达当前或之后的结果影响。因此，认知语境对于译者把握言语之下的驱动因素和表达方式十分重要。关联翻译理论认为语境效果和加工努力是心理过程的抽象维度。越接近实现最佳语境效果，理解语篇所花费的加工努力越少，关联性就越强（国夏，2019）。

由于"曰"字是对话提示词且与会话翻译息息相关，对会话内容有着很强的语用功能。因此，从关联翻译理论入手，探究"曰"字会话背后隐藏的意思，并将其传递给语言接受者，最终达成双方理解上的一致，有助于探索古汉语动词"曰"字的翻译技巧。

3. "曰"字的翻译策略及其例句分析

古汉语中的"曰"字常常用作动词，表示"说、称、说道"等含义，具有多种语篇功能，涉及本文的主要有三种功能。（1）表述功能：表示"说过""说道"等含义。从关联理论的角度，可以将"曰"字看作表述动作的表示，它可以表达说话人对于所述事实或观点的认可、承认或推定。通过"曰"字的使用，说话人将所述内容视为可信、有说服力或具有权威性，从而加强话语的信服力。（2）陈述功能：在古汉语中，"曰"也可以用于陈述事实，表达观点等。从关联理论的角度，陈述意味着对事实、观点、想法等的描述和展示。使用"曰"字陈述时，既可以用来描述自己的观点和看法，又可以引述他人的观点和见解。在语言交际中，陈述功能是信息传递的核心，也是语言交际的基本要素。（3）指示功能：有时，"曰"也可以用于指示或强调某个事物或观点。从关联理论的角度，指示是一种指向某一对象的语言行为。使用"曰"字的指示，可以用来指向某一概念、观点或事实等，加强话语的说服力和表达力。这些功能既可以单独使用，也可以组合使用，以实现更加准确、生动、丰富的语言表达。

根据关联翻译理论，古汉语"曰"字在《虬髯客传》中，其语篇功能比较多样，本文归于三个大类。（1）"曰"衔接大信息单元，（2）"曰"衔接小信息单元，（3）"曰"衔接等量信息单元。其中，大信息单元需要增加相应的"增量"翻译处理策略，小信息单元也相应需要"缩量"或省略翻译处理策略，等量信息单元主要采取直译或省译策略。

3.1 "曰"衔接大信息单元

古汉语的"曰"在很多语境下是与大信息单元相连接的,当"曰"字所在的句子信息密集,含量较大时,一般采取"放大处理",即增译法。此时,可以根据具体的语篇功能,通过增加相应场景后,用短语、副词或者使用多个语言点共同描绘等技巧来丰富信息的表达,以增加"曰"字的内涵。

（1）增加情景

增加情景主要是指对话发生在某个场景之后,为了更好将对话融入背景,可以加入相应的场景信息,通过有关联的信息词汇、时态、语态或语篇手段来链接,形成一个较大的信息单元,以便更好地连接场景与对话。比如:

例1:【原文】公既去,而执拂者临轩,指吏曰:"问去者处士第几？住何处？"

【周本】Seeing him off, the whisk holder drew close to the window and <u>urged the errand boy</u>: "Hurry up to ask the man just left who he is? Where he stays?"

【合译本】When he was leaving, she <u>said to the officer at the door</u>, "Ask him his name and where he lives."

【Wang 本】After Li Jing had left, the singing girl with the red whisk stood by the window, pointed (at his back), <u>and asked an official</u>, "What is the rank of the gentleman who is leaving? Where does he live?"

【Birch 本】When Li had taken his leave this girl followed him into the anteroom and pointed him out to an attendant, whom <u>she asked to ascertain</u> Li's position, family situation and address.

例 1 中,原文本表现红拂女的机警和过人的胆识,她从自己的认知中判断来访者非一般人,必定是有才有识之士,因此迫切想结交,而原文"指吏曰:'问去者处士第几？住何处？'"反映了她急切想知道客人的相关信息,为后续故事埋下伏笔。但是如果把原文"曰"简单翻译为"说话"的直陈功能,就失去了很多信息量,尤其是古汉语的高浓缩语义文本,在翻译为他语文本的时候,需要进行策略处理。

从上述的四个译本中,可以看出,各个译本都翻译出了"曰"字的直接语义,周本用"urged",合译本用"said to",Wang 本用"asked",Birch 本用"asked to"。但是对于其间接或者隐含的语用涵义,各个译本却处理不同。

就大信息单元而论,在时态上,用于描述客人离开的状态时,虽然周本和合译本语法表达技巧不一样,但是都使用了进行时态,周本"Seeing him off",合译本"When he was leaving",而 Wang 本和 Birch 本都使用了完成时态。在语境和语义关联上,周本和合译本通过增加进行时态语境表达了红拂女的急切心情,而且周本在此基础上增加了"hurry up"的信息。

从场景信息增量来看,周本的一系列动词及时态的使用无疑具象化了场景人物的情态:"Seeing him off"→"drew close to the window"→"urged the errand boy"→"hurry up to ask",把红拂女爱才惜才及迫切结交来访者的心情最大限度地表达出来了。合译本虽然也用了进行时态,相比之下,其他增量信息几乎没有,而且还有一处对原文理解造成歧义的翻译"she said to the officer at the door"。Wang 本和 Birch 本更加忠实与原文本的语义关联"公既去",所以使用了完成时态,从关联理论来看,更符合场景的真实,读者较少通过努力推理就能明白其涵义。除了类似于周本的系列动词连用:"After Li Jing had left"→"stood by the window"→"pointed [at his back]"→"and asked an official",Wang 本还增加了"the singing girl",更加明确红拂女的身份，而且在"曰"字的具体内容部分，Wang 本准确译出了原文本"处士第几"（What is the rank of the gentleman）。同理，Birch 本使用了"Li's position"。在词汇选择上，Wang 本的"gentleman"一词选用也蕴含了红拂女的修养，不是一般的"the singing girl"，这一点其他译本都没有做到。

Birch 本在对原文本"处士第几"的处理上还增加了"family situation"的信息，更加减少了读者推理的努力程度。对于原文本"执拂者临轩"的翻译，Birch 本处理得很好"this girl followed him into the anteroom and pointed him out to an attendant"，从关联翻译来看，达到了最大关联，而且对红拂女身份的界定还采用了"this girl"的模糊语义，表明了译者对其人格的尊重。

从关联翻译理论角度，增译情景有助于更好衔接上下文，使逻辑更加合理，画面切换更加自然，读者可以用较少的推理努力去理解原文的隐含意义。

（2）增加心态及动作的语义内容

译者作为语言桥梁，在翻译时应该尽力顺应原作者、人物的心理世界。心态主要涉及交际者的性格、情感、信念、意图等心理因素（沈克琳，2013）；动作主要涉及交际者的潜在目的及心意表现。在透彻理解原文本内容的基础上，译者增加人物对话心态和动作的语义内容，可以更加凸显人物对话时的语气、表情、意图、愿望等状态，体现出说话的方式或者目的，丰满了人物性格，使对话更加活灵活现。从关联翻译理论角度，这样的增译可以减少译者的理解努力，更容易理解原文本的核心语义。

例2：【原文】公曰："杨司空权重京师，如何？"曰："尸居余气，不足畏也……"

【周本】Lijing spoke out his worries: "How about Premier Yang? He's almighty all over the capital area, after all." The girl assured him: "There's no need to be afraid of a walking skeleton …"

【合译本】"But Councillor Yang has great power in the capital; how can it be done？" said Li. "Never mind him — he's an old imbecile," she replied. "Many maids have left, knowing that he will fall …"

【Wang 本】Li Jing said, "Minister Yang has absolute power in the capital. What to do about that？" She said, "He lives like a corpse with only one breath left and is not to be feared …"

【Birch 本】"But what can I do," Li Jing asked, "when Councilor Yang has such power now in the capital？" "There is little to fear from him. He is the corpse in which a little breath remains …"

例 2 是红拂女与李靖的对话，深入探讨文章内容可以感知李靖的提问体现了其担忧，而红拂女的解答主要是为了安抚李靖。由于此处包含了人物说话的心理，因此如果将"曰"简要概括为说话功能，恐失内涵。关于例2中一问一答的两个"曰"，四位译者的处理均有不同。周本译为"spoke out his worries""assured"。合译本译为"said""replied"。Wang 本两处均译为"said"。Birch 本第一个"曰"译为"asked"，第二个则省略。从关联翻译理论的角度，周本的译文显然进行了人物心理活动的增量翻译，这样能更好体现出人物在对话时的心态，有利于突出塑造人物的性格。其余译本在"曰"的翻译上尊重原文本字面意义，进行了直译。但它们在再对话的具体内容上也不同程度地体现了人物的心理活动和动作意图。从关联翻译理论来说，都减少了读者的推理难度。

（3）增加社交世界必要信息

社交世界包括社交场合、社会环境、规范交际者言语（陈首为，2014）。英译对话时，需要将原文本中一些潜在的社交规则增添出来，考虑交际者所处的社会环境、社会文化制度对话语的影响。因此，为了使得古文对话中的内容更具有合理性，有时需要在"曰"字的内涵中，增加有关社交仪式感的内容表达。

例3：【原文】公前揖曰："公为帝室重臣，须以收罗豪杰为心，不宜踞见宾客。"

【周本】Seeing this, Lijing bowed and came up with the words as the following: "Your Honor, as the backbone of the empire, is supposed to be the model in canvassing for talents instead of distancing them by such a reception."

【合译本】Li approached and said with a bow, "As chief councilor to the imperial house, Your Highness should be thinking of how to rally good men, and should not receive visitors sitting."

【Wang本】Li Jing stepped forward, bowed to him, and said, "You, sir, are a mighty minister of the imperial court, with heavy responsibilities. You ought occupy yourself with thoughts of congregating and collecting extraordinary people. It is inappropriate to receive guests while reclining on a couch."

【Birch本】But Li Jing came forward, bowed and said, "Your Highness is supreme in the service of our imperial house. Your first concern should be to win the respect of men of heroic mettle, and this you are hindering by remaining seated to receive those who seek audience."

例3中，原文想展现的是李靖的有勇有谋，并甘于有理有据地在杨素面前献策，同时为后续故事埋下了伏笔，此处如果按照"曰"的原文信息等量翻译，则会使得对话不符合逻辑。因此，增量一些必要的社会潜规则在此处显得十分重要。

对于"曰"的字面处理，四个译本均展现了其陈述功能。周本译为："came up with the words as the following"，其余三个译本则均译为："said"。对于"曰"字的处理则体现在说话时的社交潜规则动作，以及说话时社交信息增量。除周译本外，其他几个译本都使用了连动结构，是几个动作环环相扣，增加了动作的接续性，其中Wang本译得最好，"Li Jing stepped forward, bowed to him, and said"系列动作的并列展示，表明了李靖的精明睿智和真心诚意。从关联理论来看，该种译法更加清晰交代了说话的社交环境，使得对话更加符合逻辑，减少了读者的阅读疑惑，读者可以用较少的推理努力去理解原文的隐含意义。

3.2 "曰"衔接小信息单元

《虬髯客传》中有的"曰"衔接的是小信息单元，此时，翻译时主要采取"缩小处理"，可以使用省译等策略，减少冗余信息。

例4：【原文】问其姓，曰："张。"问其伯仲之次。曰："最长。"

【周本】Lijing felt a bit relaxed and the talk was soon geared into a pleasant chatting, by which, not only was the girl known to be surnamed Zhang and the eldest daughter in her family …

【合译本】Asked her name, she told Li it was Zhang, and that she was the eldest in her family.

【Wang本】Li Jing asked for her family name. She answered, "It is Zhang." He also asked her rank in the family and she replied, "I am the eldest."

【Birch本】Li Jing asked her surname and her position in her family, and she replied that she was the eldest child of the Zhang family.

例4中，原文是李靖了解红拂女的家庭情况的一些快问快答，节奏较快，且信息内容同属一类，信息含量也较少，因此，此处的"曰"的表述功能显得较弱。

从上述译本中可以看出，除了Wang本以外，其余三个译本皆采用了信息的缩小处理。其中周本采用的策略是提炼对话关键信息并将其形式改为第三人称叙述句，将"曰"字后的信息进行了压缩处理。但是在之前增译了场景切换的信息，进行了画面的自然切换。Wang 本则较为忠实于原文，依然将"曰"字提示说话的功能直译出来，译为"asked""answered"和"asked""replied"，突出"曰"字表述功能中的回答作用。但是这样译会显得太过于死板，信息量有冗余。Birch 本也尽量进行了间接引语的转换，即减量处理。

从关联理论来看，对于"曰"字衔接小信息单位的句子，使用"缩小处理"，有助于读者快速抓住对话内容的核心简短信息，减少推理步骤，缩短推理进程，以达到最佳关联。

3.3 "曰"衔接等量信息单元

《虬髯客传》中的"曰"字有时衔接的是等量信息，此时，翻译时可具体分为以下两种情况。

无大量连续性对话时，可以采取直译"曰"字的翻译策略，可译为 said、explained、spoke、queried、answered、questioned 等。如果该句话中包含多重含义，可以将句子分为两段。

例 5：【原文】曰："靖之友刘文静者与之狎，因文静见之可也。兄欲何为？"

【周本】"My friend Liu Wenjing keeps an intimate relationship with him because Liu thinks highly of him," Lijing <u>queried</u>, "Why should you ask for a visit like that?"

【合译本】"I have a friend named Liu Wenjing who knows him well," <u>said</u> Li, "We can arrange an interview through Liu. But why do you want to see him?"

【Wang 本】Li Jing <u>said</u>, "My friend Liu Wenjing knows him intimately. It is possible to see him through Wenjing; however, my elder brother, what do you want to do?"

【Birch 本】"I have a friend named Liu Wenjing, who knows him well," <u>answered</u> Li Jing, "I can arrange an introduction through him. But what is it you want of him?"

例 5 中，原文此处出现在虬髯客与李靖的一问一答中，没有更多大量的连续性问题，而李靖回答的内容也是信息含量适中，未有更多暗含的物理环境信息或记忆信息，因此在此处对"曰"字的英译策略处理主要体现在传达其陈述功能。

在以上四个译本中，有关"曰"的译法，周本为"queried"，Birch 本为"answered"，合译本和 Wang 本均为"said"。其中，周本和 Birch 本主要体现了陈述功能中的回答作用，而合译本和 Wang 本则只概要地展现了说话的提示词这一作用。总的来说，四个译本的翻译都体现了"曰"字的直译法。

此外，在句意分层上，由于原文句子包含两层含义，周本、合译本以及 Birch 本都将句子使用逗号加后引号断开，再插入"曰"字的英译表达，再进行下一个意群的翻译处理。Wang 本尽管未在形式上作出如此明显的断隔处理，但也在句中使用了分号断开了两个意群。

从关联理论来看，在"曰"字衔接等量信息单元时，通过直译的方法来表达其陈述功能，有助于读者直接了解原文的等量信息。此时，译者不需要作出额外的翻译处理，以免弄巧成拙。同时，有意识地对"曰"字后的多层意群作断隔处理，有助于读者更好更快地把握译文信息，减少梳理理解时间以缩短读者的推理过程，达成"最佳关联"。

有大量连续性对话时，可以采用省译"曰"字的策略，直接使用标点符号引出说话内容。

例 6：【原文】曰："年几？"曰："近二十。"曰："今何为？"

【周本】"How old is he?" "Nearly 20." "How about him for the moment?"

【合译本】"How old is he?" "Only twenty." "What is he now?"

【Wang 本】The guest said, "How old is he?" Li said, "He is almost twenty years old." The guest said, "What is he doing now?"

【Birch 本】"How old is he?" "Nineteen only." "And what is his position at present?"

例 6 中，此段发生在虬髯客与李靖的交谈中，主要内容是虬髯客询问李靖有关李世民的情况，特点是对话密集，信息含量适中。该种情况"曰"字出现频率极高，主要是对话提示作用，并无其他隐含之意，因此，对于"曰"字的处理则值得深究。

以上四个译本中，周本、合译本以及 Birch 本都采用了"曰"字的省略译法，直接使用引号引出说话内容，以避免重复，保障对话的流畅。Wang 本直接全部译出了"曰"，且都使用同一个"said"，这样显得比较生硬，不仅内容单调，而且信息冗余，也打断了对话的流畅性，失去人物间对话的生动感。

从关联理论来看，在上述情况下直接采用引号代替其指示作用，不仅有利于行文的流畅，也有利于读者减少阅读障碍，缩短推理时间，直接理解原文含义。

4. 总结

"曰"字作为衔接说话者和说话内容的衔接手段，在中国古汉语中出现的频率极高。想要准确翻译出"曰"字的内涵，需要从不同的翻译视角进行策略处理。

根据关联翻译理论，可以讨论译者的不同处理方法，从与原文的最大关联和读者的最少推理努力，可以看出译文的翻译效果。译者需要以明示推理原则、最佳关联性原则和认知语境为指导，全面考虑对话的画面感、信息度，深入挖掘原文的言下之意，并让原文和译文保持最大的等值，使得原作的语言特色、风貌在译作中得到尽可能完整的展现。

就唐传奇《虬髯客传》所选的四个译本中，译者对古汉语"曰"字的不同翻译处理，可以归纳为几种情况。当"曰"字所出句段信息含量大时，可以采取"放大处理"，增译对话情景，心态及动作以及社交世界的必要信息。当"曰"字所在句段信息含量较小时，可以采取"缩小处理"，将对话改为第三人称或叙述句。当"曰"字所在句段信息含量适中时，且无连续对话时；可直译"曰"字，有连续对话时，可省译"曰"字，直接用标点符号引出说话内容。因此，译者应该根据原文信息含量，选择合适的翻译策略，使得原文的语言特色、人物性格都尽可能地展现。同时，译者要注意灵活使用各种"曰"字的翻译技巧，避免阅读译文时让读者感到味同嚼蜡，丧失画面感。

参考文献

[1] DU G T, 2000. The Curly-Bearded Hero[M].Birch C,trans.//MINFORD J, LAU J S M. Classical Chinese literature : an anthology of translations, from Antiquity to Tang Dynasty. New York：Columbia University Press: 1057-1064.

[2] DU G T, 2010. The Tale of the Curly-Bearded Guest[M].Wang J,trans.//NIENHAUSER W. Tang Dynasty tales: a guided reader. Singapore: World Scientific: 189-206.

[3] GUTT E A, 1991. Translation and relevance: cognition and context[M].Oxford: Blackwell.

[4] 陈首为，2014. 从言语行为理论看对话翻译[J]. 南风（6）：46.

[5] 杜光庭，2004. The Man with the Curly Beard [M].杨宪益，戴乃迭，译.//沈既济. 唐代传奇选. 北京：外文出版社.

[6] 国夏, 2019. 《金瓶梅》人物对话英译研究[D].上海：华东师范大学.
[7] 沈克琳, 2013. 顺应论关照下的小说对话翻译[J]. 太原城市职业技术学院学报（11）：180-181.
[8] 汤朝菊, 吕由, 李琴, 2022. 传奇小说中的文化负载词英译目的论——基于《虬髯客传》五个英译本的分析[J]. 西南科技大学学报(哲学社会科学版), 39(1)：37-44, 82.
[9] 谢卫霞, 2018. 关联理论指导下的小说对话翻译——以小说 The North Water 的选择为例[D]. 上海：上海交通大学.
[10] 周劲松. 虬髯客传[M]//周劲松. 翻译基础十二讲. 成都：电子科技大学出版社, 2016:136-145.

女性主义翻译研究视角下《三体》日译本研究

周小萱

1. 引言

自刘慈欣科幻小说《三体》英译本 *The Three-Body Problem* 于 2015 年斩获"雨果奖"(Hugo Award) 以来，引发各界广泛关注，中国科幻小说《三体》的海外译介之旅随之开启。其中，由早川书房出版，大森望主导翻译的《三体》日译本"三体"于 2019 年出版并引起轰动，紧接其后推出了两部续作。根据早川书房的统计数据，《三体》系列在日本的纸质和电子书籍销售量高达 65 万册，引发了现象级文学事件（卢冬丽，2022）。《三体》在日本的译介大获成功。这为中国科幻作品的外译、翻译学研究提供了绝佳案例。

《三体》日译本采用了汉日直接翻译和英日间接翻译交叠的翻译手法（卢冬丽、邵宝，2021），对其的研究既不能脱离刘慈欣原语文本，又不能忽略刘宇昆的英译本。为适应英语读者，英译者刘宇昆在翻译中对原语文本进行了调整。其中关于女性描写的修改，引起了女性主义翻译研究者们的广泛关注。而日译本针对这些修改是如何处理的？折射出译者怎样的性别意识？对于中国科幻作品的海外译介有什么启发？本文将从女性主义翻译的角度出发，对《三体》日译本进行具体分析与探讨。

2. 翻译研究之于女性主义

在 20 世纪六七十年代的西方妇女解放运动浪潮中，女性主义作为一种社会文化批评话语，逐渐占据人们的视野。性别也被区分为"文化性别"(gender) 和"生理性别"(sex)。与主张文化性别归属于个人本质，很大程度上由生理性别所决定的文化女性主义不同，80 年代的后结构主义的性别理论认为文化性别并非由生理性别决定，而是在话语中构建的。唤醒人们的性别意识，成为女权运动的首要任务之一（孟令子，2016）。

福柯关于权力和话语关系的阐述中提到：话语可能是权力的结果，也可能是权力实现的手段；话语可以传播权力，同时也可以揭露、反抗、消解权力（福柯，2002）。女性主义者希望通过解构传统的男性中心主义话语，构建更加平等的男女关系，翻译研究是其实践的天然场所。17 世纪法国修辞学家梅内将翻译比作"不忠的美人"，这一譬喻影响深远，也揭示了长久以来西方译论中翻译在文学系统中，有着女性在社会体系中类似的、低等的、附属的地位。受到文化女性主义的影响，女性主义翻译研究强调女性译者的主体性和生产性，张扬"叛逆"，在重读与重写中完成女性主义话语对文本的操控（谢天振，2008）。

而后结构主义理论的性别概念下，女性主义翻译研究不再局限于女性译者"性别政治"的战场，更加注重话语对性别的"操演行为"。拓宽视野后的女性主义翻译研究注意到性别是"相对的、局部的，受制于多重历史文化因素而不断变化的"（孟令子，2016），进而对译者在翻译过程中无意识和有意识的性别体现更加关注。除了女性译者对译本有意识的性别操控，男性译者有意识或无意识的考量也纳入了研究范畴（李红玉，2008）。同时，译者作为身处某个特定社会历史文化中的个体，无论男女，其性别意识往往具有一定的本土化特点（陈瑛，2013）。

3.《三体》及其日译本

《三体》自 2006 年 5 月连载于《科幻世界》杂志，在国内荣获各大奖项，单行本销量也达到了科幻文学的巅峰。由美籍华裔科幻作家兼翻译家刘宇昆翻译的《三体》英译本 *The Three-Body Problem* 斩获第 73 届"雨果奖"最佳长篇小说奖，更使其当之无愧地成为了世界科幻文学冉冉升起的新星。

《三体》作为一部在世界取得广泛影响力的科幻小说，其女性角色塑造也有可圈可点之处。与传统男性中心主义作品中附属性质的女性形象不同，《三体》中的女性角色大多以冷静睿智的科学家形象出现，对情节推动起着重大作用。《三体》第八章 "寂静的春天"借女性角色叶文洁提出人类之于其他物种暴行的反思——"反对对生命做等级划分"（刘钊，2013），更是与生态女性主义不谋而合。但在女性主义视角看来，刘慈欣在《三体》中展现的性别观念并非"完美无缺"。在"豆瓣"的读者书评中，不乏质疑《三体》性别意识落后的批评。女性主义发展日新月异，任何性别意识模型都不能做到放之四海而皆准。个体的性别意识往往受到其所处的历史文化环境和个人认知水平的影响，这就要求译者在译介过程中发挥主体性，使文本适应于目标语受众。

在针对刘宇昆《三体》英译本的翻译研究中，女性主义翻译研究者们指出了刘宇昆针对原语文本的改动，并采用弗洛图总结的女性主义翻译策略对刘宇昆英译本的翻译手法进行归纳与分析。这些研究肯定了刘宇昆作为译者的主体性，对其在译本中践行的女性主义翻译观展开了探讨和分析（阙春花、吴亚芝，2019）。

《三体》日译本与英译本一样，由当地知名的专业科幻文学出版社负责，"它们在准确把握科幻读者的阅读审美、译者选择、翻译批评方面拥有很大的话语权"（卢冬丽，2022）。日译本主笔人大森望在《三体》日译本后记中详细地说明了日译本翻译的过程：《三体》首先由光吉樱和湾仔共同完成汉-日的翻译，再由科幻文学翻译家大森望将日译本与刘宇昆英译本进行对比，进行逐行的修改与重写。日译本的最终呈现结果，有八成以上为大森望的译文。大森望在后记中提到，自己的工作是将"翻译小说翻译为科幻小说"，以带给日本读者最接近完美的阅读体验。因此，日译本在女性描写方面的处理在体现译者个人性别意识的同时，一定程度上也反应了日本本土化的性别因素。

4. 译例分析

现有的针对《三体》英译本的女性主义翻译研究大多使用弗洛图总结的三种女性主义翻译策略——补充、加注与前言、"劫持"（谢天振，2008）。其中"劫持"在女性主义翻译研究范畴中，指译者将原语文本中那些不符合女性主义思想观点的内容进行改写，是译者对原语文本重新编码的最直观体现。

由于"劫持"语段是译者对原语文本重新编码、彰显自身性别观念的最直观体现，现有的关于《三体》英译本的女性主义翻译研究都聚焦于刘宇昆对于《三体》原语文本的改写。同理，为了揭示日译本潜在的性别观念，本文也从女性主义翻译研究的视角出发，聚焦"劫持"语段，把《三体》日译本与英译本、原语文本进行对比。发现日译本对于英译本中的"劫持"语段主要采用了"采纳英译本"和"还原原语文本"两种截然不同的处理方法。

4.1 采纳译本

例1

"她父亲留下了一堆唱片，她听来听去，最后选择了一张巴赫的反复听，那是最不可能令孩子，特别是**女孩子**入迷的音乐了。"（刘慈欣，2008）

"Her father left behind some records. She listened to all of them and finally picked something by Bach as her favorite, listening to it over and over. That was the kind of music that shouldn't have mesmerized **a kid**."（Liu，2016）

"あの子の父親はコードをたくさん残してくれたけど、あの子はそれをぜんぶ聞いていたあとで、最後にバッハをお気に入り選んで、何度も何度も繰り返し聴いていた。**子供**にとりこにするような音楽じゃなかった。"（劉慈欣，2019）

如上文所述，《三体》塑造了许多科学家女性，她们往往冷静睿智，拥有异于常人的聪慧和天赋。此处的描述对象杨冬是一名年轻有为的物理学家，刘慈欣通过设置幼年杨冬反复听巴赫的情节，显示其自幼便展露出对理性美与抽象美的感受力。但此处作者有意或无意凸显性别的表达，难免将读者引向"女孩子不能欣赏巴赫""相比男孩，女孩更难对理性和抽象的美产生兴趣"的刻板印象联想。故日译本和英译本在此处删去性别词，将"女孩子"改写为"孩子"，以免文本"陷入二元对立的性别意识中"（何高大、陈水平，2006）。

例2

"我生性冷淡，对女性，我比周围这些和尚更不感兴趣，但她很特殊，她那**最没女人味的女人味**吸引了我，反正我也是个闲人，就立刻答应了她。"（刘慈欣，2008）

"I'm naturally a cold person. I had less interest in women than the monks around me. This woman **who didn't adhere to conventional ideas about femininity was different**, though. She attracted me. Since I had nothing to do anyway, I agreed right away."（Liu，2016）

"ぼくは生まれつき冷たい人間で、まわりの坊さん連中とくらべても、女性に対する関心が薄かった。でも、玉菲は特別だった。**伝統的な女性らしさという概念にこだわらない**ところに惹かれた。どのみち、ほかにやることもなかったから、ぼくはすぐさま彼女の提案を受け入れた。"（劉慈欣，2019）

此处是男性科学家汪淼对"科学边界"成员，日籍华裔物理学家申玉菲的描述。"最没女人味的女人味"这一表达，体现了角色汪淼的性别意识，刻画了在男性中心主义传统下对女性进行"审视和评价"的男性形象。在女性主义文化批评中，基于拉康和福柯的"凝视理论"（赵一凡、张中载、李德恩，2006），批判男性中心主义的艺术呈现通过"审视"对女性完成规训的行为。而"女人味"一词充满了男性中心主义社会对女性的刻板印象与规训。日译本和英译本将该词解构为"传统的女性特质"，消除了规训意味，使文本更易为女性主义者接受。

例3

"'我们的要求很简单：让统帅走，然后咱们一起玩什么都行。'女孩接着说，**样子有些娇嗔**。"（刘慈欣，2008）

"'Our demand is simple: Let the commander go,' the young woman said. 'Then we can play whatever game you want' **Her tone suggested that she wasn't afraid of Shi Qiang and the soldiers at all**."（Liu，2014）

"「われわれの要求はシンプルです」少女は**史強や兵士を恐れるようすもなく、おだやかに言っ**た。「総帥を解放してください。そのあとは、なんでもあなたたちの求めるゲームにつきあいましょう」"（劉慈欣，2019）

例 4

"士兵们枪上电筒的光柱集中在那个拿核弹的女孩儿身上，这个**艳丽的死亡之花**手捧着一千五百吨 TNT，灿烂地笑着，仿佛是在舞台聚光灯下迎接着掌声和赞美。"（刘慈欣，2008）

"The flashlights attached to the soldiers' guns focused on **the young woman** holding the nuclear bomb. While she held the destructive power of 1.5 kilotons of TNT in her hands, she smiled brightly, as though enjoying applause and praise on a spotlit stage."（Liu，2016）

"兵士たちの銃に装着されているライトの光が、核爆弾を持つ**少女**に集中した。TNT火薬に換算して一・五キロトンの破壊力を手にした少女は、スポットライトに照らされて舞台に立、拍手喝采を浴びているかのように華やかな笑みを浮かべた。"（劉慈欣，2019）

例 5

"'站住。'核弹女孩向大史抛了个媚眼**警告**道。"（刘慈欣，2008）

"'Stop,' the young woman **warned** Da Shi."（Liu，2016）

"「止まれ」少女が**警告**した。"（劉慈欣，2019）

例 6

"少女**袅袅婷婷**地向潘寒走去。"（刘慈欣，2008）

"She walked toward Pan Han **casually**."（Liu，2016）

"**気軽**な足どりで潘寒のほうに歩み寄っていった。"（劉慈欣，2019）

淡化和删除女性化描写是日译本和英译本女性主义翻译的重要手法之一（阙春花，2019），例 3、例 4、例 5、例 6 四处均为对于叶文洁女护卫的描写，意在表现三体叛军为了"信仰"不惧生死的癫狂状态。原语文本中，作者多次强调女护卫年轻美丽，举止轻佻，这样的描写似乎意在塑造"蛇蝎美人"的意象——这种表现手法常见于好莱坞主流电影的恶女叙事：女性角色的美丽并非剧情进展的推手，而是一种面向男性和观众的展示。而揭露拥有致命吸引力的女性的邪恶本质，对她们进行惩罚，也是完成男性凝视的同时控制男性焦虑的一种手段（赵一凡、张中载、李德恩，2006）。对于这种电影中将女性物化的惯常叙事，以劳拉·马尔维为首的电影批评家运用凝视理论开辟了精神分析女性主义电影批评的传统（赵一凡、张中载、李德恩，2006）。为避免这种饱受女性主义者批判的男性凝视描写，日译本和英译本都对原语文本的内涵进行了进一步的解读和去女性化修改：如例 3 女孩展现出的"娇嗔"并非迎合男性凝视，而是表现其对"敌人"的"毫无畏惧"。

例 6 的译法与例 3 类似，日译本和英译本都对"袅袅婷婷"一词进行了"去女性化"翻译，用"気軽な足どりで""casually"保留了原文中女孩与潘寒对峙时淡然的状态，又淡化了"恶女叙事"可能给读者带来的不适感。

例 4 中"艳丽的死亡之花"属于饱含性别隐喻的表达，和例 6"抛了个媚眼"一样在英日译本中都被直接删除，削弱表达中的女性色彩，避免男性凝视，使文本的性别意识更加中立。

例 7

"以她不可能具有的力量和极其精巧的受力角度。"（刘慈欣，2008）

"by applying her **unexpected strength** at just the right angle."（Liu，2016）

"思いがけない力と正確な手さばきで。"（劉慈欣，2019）

从女性主义视角来看，"以她不可能具有的力量"这样的表达，存在贬低女性生理特点的嫌疑，此处日译本参考英译本"unexpected strength"将这种绝对化的表达改写为更为温和的"思いがけない力"。

4.2 还原原语文本

对于英译本的"劫持"改写，日译本并非机械地全部采纳。在另外一些语段，日译本将英译本中改写的内容又还原了原语文本的表达。

例 8

"'是的，'**女作家**点头赞同，'从文学角度看，《三体》也是卓越的，那二百零三轮文明的兴衰，真是一首首精美的史诗。'"（刘慈欣，2008）

"'Yes,' **the author** agreed, and nodded. 'like the literary elements of *Three Body*. The rises and falls of two hundred and three civilizations evoke the qualities of epics in a new form.'"（Liu，2016）

"「ええ」**女流作家**が相槌を打った。「あたしは文学的な面に惹かれる。文明 203 の興亡は、新しいかたちのすばらしい叙事詩だった」"（劉慈欣，2019）

例 9

"正像那位**联合国女官员**所说，他是个魔鬼！"（刘慈欣，2008）

"Like that **UN official** said, he is a demon!"（Liu，2016）

"あの**国連の女性担当官**が言ったように、あいつは悪魔だ！"（劉慈欣，2019）

在女性主义者倡导的更加平等的性别意识语境中，避免对于性别不必要的强调，并认识到强调性别是一种偏见和歧视。例 8、例 9 为关于性别词汇的翻译，在英译本中，删除多余的性别词汇是避免二元对立的性别意识的方法。"女作家""女官员"给人以"这些职业本来大多数为男性"的隐含意义。而日译本将原语文本中的性别再次还原，沿袭了日语的使用习惯，也体现出日译本与英译本在性别意识上存在的差异。

例 10

"沉默再次降临。两三分钟后，叶文洁护卫中的一员，一名**苗条美丽的少女**动人地笑了笑，那笑容是那么醒目，将很多人的目光引向了她。"（刘慈欣，2008）

"A few moments later, one of the bodyguards near Ye, **a young woman, smiled**."（Liu，2016）

"またも沈黙が降りた。ややあって、文潔のそばにいた護衛のひとり、**スレンダーで美しい少女**が**魅惑的**な笑みを浮かべたかと思うと…"（劉慈欣，2019）

例 11

她已经用一条看上去**如春藤般柔软的玉臂**夹住了潘寒的脖颈……（刘慈欣，2008）

Before anyone could react, she wrapped **one of her slender arms** around Pan's neck…（Liu，2016）

少女は**春の藤のように細くたおやかな腕**を潘寒の首に巻きつけ…（劉慈欣，2019）

例 10、例 11 与例 3、例 4、例 5、例 6、例 7 相同，也是针对叶文洁护卫女孩的描写，如前文所述，英译本为避免饱受女性主义者批判的"男性凝视"和"恶女叙事"，对于该角色的女性化外貌、神态、动作描写都进行了"去女性化"的删减和改写。此处也不例外，英译本删去了"苗条美丽"和"动人地"等饱含女性色彩的形容。将"如春藤般柔软的玉臂"去除比喻修辞，翻译为"one of her slender arms"，达到了去男性凝视的效果。

此处日译本并未采纳英译本的译法，而是选择了贴近原语文本的表达，把"苗条美丽"翻译为"スレンダーで美しい"、"动人地笑了笑"翻译为"魅惑的な笑み"，"如春藤般柔软的玉臂"翻译为"春の藤のように細くたおやかな腕"，将饱含女性色彩的描写还原到了日语译文中。

据上述译例分析，日译本明显借鉴了英译本中的"劫持"语段，但并非全单照收。"采纳英译本"和"还原原语文本"两种处理手法的混用体现了日译本独特的性别观念。相对英译本，日译本呈现出一种更为折中的性别意识，这与女性主义在日本的传入和发展情况不谋而合。"女性主义"这一概念最早作为西方思想传入日本并发展至今，已经不能单纯地被视作西方的舶来品。在不断的发展中，日本女性主义呈现出与当地固有文化背景和社会情况紧密相关的本土化特点（陈晨，2022）。关于日本女性主义的本土化，日本的女性学和性别研究学者上野千鹤子提出过"文化相对主义"的视角，并认为这样的视角既能窥见日本女性主义发展的特点和可能性，也揭示了其局限性和问题（上野千鹤子，2006）。

在"还原原语文本"的译例中，可以看出，英日两个译本对于职业性别歧视的敏感度有所区别。如针对"女作家"和"联合国女官员"的翻译，日本并未采用删去性别词的译法，这与日本社会中女性的职场处境息息相关。尽管越来越多的双职工家庭在日本出现，但在长期"男主外，女主内"的日式传统家庭观念的影响下，女性的职业发展依然存在一定的阻碍。另外，"女流作家"这一词汇来源于日本平安时代盛极一时的女性写作。这些由日本女性作家所书写的日记、物语等文学作品影响深远，给日本本土文学留下了深刻的烙印。尽管女性主义主张不必要的性别强调是对女性的歧视，但在日本人的文化记忆中，"女流作家"一词一贯以中性的，甚至隐含褒扬色彩的形式出现。

而针对饱含女性色彩的描写，日译本也呈现出比英译本更加"宽容"的特点，针对《三体》中的女性化描写，特别是例3、例4、例5、例6、例7、例10、例11中关于"护卫少女"的女性化外貌和神态描写，英译本选择了"能删尽删"的翻译策略，以避免一切可能让读者感到"男性凝视"的描写。而日译本对于这类描写采取了"部分删除，部分还原"的处理方式。从日本读者反馈层面来看，日本主流读书评论网站"読書メーター"中关于女性角色的讨论多关注小说情节，鲜有针对作品性别意识的不满评价。

总的来说，《三体》日译本所折射出的性别意识与日本的女性主义本土化发展密不可分。译者大森望在《三体》的日译过程中，发挥主体性地对文本进行了本土化的女性主义翻译实践。这给中国作品的海外译介启发：翻译应灵活结合目标语地区的女性主义本土化发展，最大程度地适应于当地读者。

5. 结论

本文从女性主义翻译研究的视角出发，对比《三体》日译本、英译本和原语文本，聚焦日译本对英译本"劫持"语段的处理，发现日译本主要采取了"采纳英译本"和"还原原语文本"两种处理手法，并据此分析了两译本之间存在性别意识的差异。两个译本分别在目标语国家取得巨大成功，一方面是女性主义在全世界发展的体现，另一方面也印证了"翻译中的性别意识往往具有一定的本土化特点"这一观点。这为本国作品的海外译介提供了宝贵参考，成功的译介应考虑到时代变化中的目标语本土化的性别意识并与之相适应。

参考文献

[1] LIU C X, 2016. The Three-Body Problem[M]. Liu K, trans. New York: Tor Books.

[2] 刘慈欣, 2019. 三体[M]. 大森望, 译. 东京：早川书房.

[3] 上野千鹤子, 2006. 日本型フェミニズムの可能性. 女という快乐[M]. 东京：劲草书房.

[4] 陈晨, 2022. 20 世纪 80 年代中日"妇女学/性别研究"本土化的比较考察——以李小江与上野千鹤子的理论实践为线索[J]. 日本文论（2）：143-161, 207-208.

[5] 陈瑛, 2013. 译者性别身份与译作人物形象再建——以《洛丽塔》两个中译本为例[J]. 外国语言文学, 30(2): 113-116, 131.

[6] 福柯, 2002. 性经验史[M]. 佘碧平, 译. 上海：上海人民出版社.

[7] 何高大, 陈水平, 2006. 雌雄同体:女性主义译者的理想[J]. 四川外语学院学报（3）：110-114.

[8] 李红玉, 2008. 译者的性别意识与翻译实践——谈性别视角下的《紫色》四译本[J]. 中国比较文学（2）：19-28.

[9] 刘慈欣, 2008. 三体[M]. 重庆：重庆出版社.

[10] 刘钊, 2013. 浅析《三体》中的生态女性主义认知[J]. 吉林广播电视大学学报（3）：97-98.

[11] 卢冬丽, 2022.《三体》系列在日本的复合性译介生成[J]. 外语教学与研究, 54(5)：783-792, 801.

[12] 卢冬丽, 邵宝, 2021.《三体》在日本的生态适应——英日间接翻译与汉日直接翻译的交叠[J]. 中国翻译, 42(6)：95-102.

[13] 孟令子, 2016. 从女性主义翻译到性别与翻译[J]. 中国翻译, 37(5)：23-31, 128.

[14] 阙春花, 吴亚芝, 2019. 从女性主义视角看《三体 3：死神永生》英译的"劫持"现象[J]. 外国语言文, 36(6)：621-632.

[15] 谢天振, 2008. 当代国外翻译理论导读[M]. 天津：南开大学出版社.

[16] 赵一凡, 张中载, 李德恩, 2006. 西方文论关键词[M]. 北京：外语教学与研究出版社.

生态翻译学视域下《雷雨》王佐良英译本赏析

唐 杰

1. 引言

《雷雨》是剧作家曹禺于 1934 年创作完成的一部话剧名著，其情节跌宕起伏，人物栩栩如生，享有崇高的艺术地位。剧本讲述了民国时期一个封建专制家庭的悲剧故事，并从中揭示出更深层次的时代及社会问题。1958 年，王佐良与巴恩斯（Barnes）将此剧合译为英文。此时正值新中国成立初期，翻译潮流多是对内译介国外革命文献与进步文学，王佐良对《雷雨》这一长篇戏剧的汉译英可谓别树一帜。《雷雨》王佐良英译本（以下简称"王译本"）以其地道而生动的表达再现了原作的魅力，一经推出，便广获赞誉，成为戏剧翻译的典范之作。王译本的现实意义不仅在于推动优秀的中国文学作品"走出去"，还在于呼应新旧社会变革与时代更迭中新中国意欲发出的新声。王红娟（2013）认为，王佐良英译这部既抨击黑暗又向往美好生活的《雷雨》，符合他本人的理想信念与对外宣传的需要，也对新中国以后的文学翻译方向起着重要的指引作用。

戏剧之翻译实非易事。英国著名翻译理论家苏珊·巴斯内特（Susan Bassnett）曾说，"戏剧翻译除了涉及书面文本由源语向目的语转换的语间翻译，还要考虑语言之外的所有因素"（Bassnett, 2014：87）。也就是说，戏剧翻译不仅需考虑译文的通顺达意，实现可读性，还需考虑其舞台演出效果，实现可表演性，此实乃于两难中求全。王佐良所译《雷雨》，理解透彻，译笔传神，实现了可读性与可表演性的融合统一，具有重要的鉴赏研究价值。本文拟运用生态翻译学的"多维转换程度"为理论工具，从语言维、文化维、交际维分析王译中的亮点与所长。

2. 生态翻译学视域下的译文评价与测定

生态翻译学肇始于 21 世纪之初，由胡庚申教授创立，从翻译适应选择论的基础上发展而来。其立足于自然生态与翻译生态的同构性和相似性，从生态整体主义理念综观翻译，以"适应与选择"为理论基石。其中，"适应"指译者对翻译生态环境的适应，即对语言交际、文化、社会，以及作者、读者、委托者等互联互动整体的适应；"选择"指译者以翻译生态环境的身份实施对译文的选择（胡庚申，2013：86）。基于此，生态翻译学认为翻译即"以译者为主导、以文本为依托、以跨文化信息转换为宗旨，是译者适应翻译生态环境而对文本进行移植的选择活动"（胡庚申，2013：148）。

生态翻译学视域下对译文的评价与测定，以"整合适应选择度"为衡量标准，其下辖三个参考指标：多维转换程度、读者反馈、译者素质。所谓多维转换程度，是指译者对原文生态与译文生态的多维度适应，具体体现在翻译中语言维、文化维、交际维的转换。读者反馈，顾名思义，即包括普通读者、专家读者、出版者等在内的多方对译文的评价与意见。译者素质则指影响译者适应具体翻译任务的基本素养，包括个人的能力、成绩、信誉等。三个指标之中，多维转换程度居于首要地位，是译者是否从多个维度适应翻译生态环境的重要准绳。要实现多个维度的适应性选择转换意味着，译者既需勉力降低对原文生态的破坏程度，又需尽量保持译文生态的整体性，而原文生态与译文生态主要体现在语言生态、文化生态、交际生态等方面（胡庚申，2013：240）。同时，生态翻译学倡导译者在翻译实践中遵从"多维度适应与适应性选择"的翻译原则，其具体的翻译方法则落实在"三维转换"，即"相对地集中于语言维、文化维和交际维的适应性选择转换"（胡庚申，2011：8）。由此可见，"三维转换"既是生态翻译学中翻译方法的简括，也是生态翻译学中对译文进行评价与测定的核心要点所在。

3. 《雷雨》王译本中的适应性选择转换

曹禺出身于官僚家庭，在其成长过程中见识到诸多腐败、专制的高级恶棍，他痛恨旧社会腐朽的制度，同情底层人民艰苦的遭遇，因而在1934年以"不劳动者不得食"为主导思想创作了《雷雨》（王育生，1979）。可以说，《雷雨》当时所处及其所构建的社会生态均压抑而黑暗，曹禺的创作目的便在于对之进行深刻地揭露剖析。翻译《雷雨》时，王佐良需适应原文的生态环境，也需适应当时的社会主义意识形态、文化外宣环境等因素综合而成的翻译生态环境，对译文作出适应性选择转换，使处在资本主义社会的英美读者既能读懂剧本故事情节，又能理解中国封建旧社会的黑暗与败亡之必然，同时更新对于业已新生了的中国的看法。

王译中的适应性选择转换可从语言、文化、交际三个维度进行分析，这"三维"长期以来是翻译研究中关注的焦点，也是译者在具体的翻译实践活动中，有所侧重地做出适应性选择转换的支点。由此"三维"对王译本进行分析，一方面契合于生态翻译学所强调的相互关联、相互作用的整体观思想，能以较具全局性的视角对译本进行品鉴；另一方面，借助其分明的框架体系，能更具条理地看待并理解具体译文之形成，实现对译文所长的更清晰把握。

3.1 语言维

语言维的适应性选择转换，即译者在翻译过程中对语言形式的适应性选择转换。这种语言维的适应性选择转换是在不同方面、不同层次上进行的（胡庚申，2011：8）。在戏剧翻译中，译者既要忠实地传达原文的意思，又需关注其语言形式与风格特征，如口语化、音乐性等，从而在语言表达上对应作出恰当的适应性选择。

例1

贵：你看，你看，你又急了，急什么？我不跟你要钱。喂，我说，我说的是——（低声）他——不是也不断地塞给你钱花么？

四：（惊讶）他？谁呀？

贵：（索性说出来）大少爷。

Lu: There you go again! Getting worked up over nothing! Don't worry. I'm not after your money. No, what I mean is—(*lowering his voice*) he—hasn't he been giving you money?

Feng (taken aback): He? Who?

Lu (bluntly): Master Ping.

此例中，原文句子口语化特征明显，用词简单且多重复，句式均短促而细碎。对于句首"你"字的三次重复，王译并未照搬，而是采用了精简的倒装句式"There you go again!"。一来，此句式作为英文中的习语，具有极高的大众性与日常性，能迅速地拉近表演者与观众的距离；二来，此句式之惯用情景常暗含说话者对某一经常性行为的不满情绪，便于观众把握台词语气态势与人物关系特点。此外，另一习语"get worked up over nothing"的应用也十分出彩。原文此处为问句，王译则为陈述句，其中省略了"you are"，使句子更为简短明快，同时使习语所表达的"无缘无故生气"的含义也更为突出，再加上感叹号的使用，更加贴切地再现了原文所含的恼怒语气。同理，"be after something"也是英文中地道的说法，能够在符合口语表达简洁性、易懂性的同时，忠实地传达出源语"要钱"的含义与情态。在处理最后的问句时，王译还原了原文的语言形式，采用了否定疑问句，彰显出鲁贵此时的反问语气。可见，在翻译中王佐良并不刻板地拘泥于原文句式，而是以满足对话意义传达、人物神态再现为要，进行灵活的适应性选择转换。

例 2

贵：（无聊地唱）"花开花谢年年有，人过了个青春不再来……"

Lu (singing dispiritedly):

Every springtime brings the flowers

Which died in last year's autumn rain;

The springtime of this life of ours,

Once past, can never come back again ...

戏剧语言之天职在于服务舞台表演，故应当朗朗上口，具有一定的节奏感，给予观众以听觉享受。对此，老舍（2000：48）曾指出："话剧中的对话是要拿到舞台上，通过演员的口，送到听众的耳中去的。由口到耳，必涉及语言的音乐性"。此处原文句子的音乐性并不十分鲜明，仅主要体现于"花开花谢"这一 ABAC 式四字语，赵永新（1997：44）认为 ABAC 式四字语具有音节美，富有感情色彩。原文句尾虽然并无押韵，但王佐良却凭借其高超的翻译技巧与艺术创造力，使译文形成隔行交互押韵，即第一行中"flowers"对应第三行中"ours"，第二行中"rain"对应第四行中"again"。译文如此处理，既符合王佐良所推崇的"以诗译诗"之理念，又体现出其在音韵节奏上，所主动进行的适应性选择转换。带有尾韵的王译各行简短明快，较之原文具有更强的节奏感与韵律感，唱词的音乐性与表现力也因此得到增强，更为悦耳动听。

3.2 文化维

文化维的适应性选择转换，即译者在翻译过程中关注双语文化内涵的传递与阐释（胡庚申，2011：8）。这一维度的适应性选择转换，需要译者从两种文化系统的整体角度出发，关注二者之间的内容与性质差异，避免仅基于译入语文化的需要而对原文进行曲解。《雷雨》原文中存在不少带有中国传统文化色彩的文化负载词，如何在翻译中恰当地传递其内涵，便于异语文化背景的观众接收与理解，十分考验译者功底。

例 3

贵：——哼，她要是跟我装蒜，现在老爷在家，咱们就是个麻烦。

Lu：——Humph! If she tries to come the old acid with me, she'll find herself in an awkward situation, especially with the master at home now!

"装蒜"意指某人装腔作势。据杨琳（2016：41-42）考究，"装蒜"最早写作"装酸"。"酸"含有酸腐之意，用以讽刺装模作样、矫揉造作之人。后人因不知"酸"有装模作样的意思，故因声找字，写成自以为是的字。"装蒜"是中国人日常生活中经常使用的词，具有广泛的接受性，王译此处巧妙地运用了俚语"come the old acid with someone"与之对应。其一，巧妙之一在于，该俚语意为：表现得令人不快或咄咄逼人；以讽刺或刻薄的方式说话，与"装蒜"之含义十分吻合。其二在于，"acid"一词与"酸"同义，由此也与"装蒜"一词之源起"装酸"形成对应。此虽不一定为译者之本意，但亦成奇妙巧合。王译在关照观众理解效果的同时，再现了该词的含义与情态，使其文化内涵能够得以恰当传达。

例 4

繁：（揩眼泪，哀痛地）我忍了多少年了，我在这个死地方，监狱似的周公馆，陪着一个阎王十八年了，我的心并没有死。

(*Wiping her eyes, in an anguished voice.*) After all these eighteen years of misery in this soul-destroying place, this "residence of the Zhou family" that's more like a prison, married to a hateful tyrant—after all these years my spirit is still not dead.

对于翻译中的文化差异，王佐良（1989：18-19）曾有如此评论，"翻译里最大的困难是两种文化的不同。在一种文化里头有一些不言而喻的东西，在另外一种文化里头却要费很大力气加以解释"。此处，原文中的阎王便是中国传统文化中不言而喻的形象。阎王是传说中阴曹地府的最高统治者，能够审判死者，掌管往生轮回，常用以比喻凶恶、严厉之人。王佐良将之译为"hateful tyrant"，直截了当地刻画出阎王所喻指的周朴园严酷冷漠的封建专制主宰形象。如此，虽在一定程度上有损于原文的文化生态，但鉴于戏剧文本需用以表演，具有即时性且无注文外加注，因而采取阐释其实际含义的方式进行翻译，应为合理之举。王译是在包含观众、原文、译文等诸要素在内的整体翻译生态环境下，基于综合考虑而作出的文化维的适应性选择转换，有助于优化演出的直接效果。

例 5

贵：我是一辈子犯小人，不走运。

Lu: All my life I've just had one patch of bad luck after another, and every time it's been because some miserable nobody has put a spoke in my wheel.

此例中，鲁贵正抱怨自己失去工作，将之怪罪于鲁侍萍。"犯小人"是中国传统测字算命中的一种说法，意为招惹"小人"而受到陷害或运势不佳，与"不走运"含义相同。对于"小人"的理解，王鑫磊（2007：32-34）认为其最初的含义是"社会地位较低的平民"，而及至《论语》，孔子将作为"君子"对立面的"小人"拓展出一种宽泛的贬义，成为"道德水平低下的人"和"见识短浅的人"的通称。此处，王佐良将之译为"some miserable nobody"，应是对以上两种含义的综合。原因在于"小人"既是鲁贵的咒骂之语，"miserable"可体现出其愠怒及谴责语气；同时，"小人"又意指鲁侍萍，一个地位低下的女佣，"nobody"一词是对其低微身份的描述。此外，对于"犯"字的含义，王译的把握与传达也非常到位。"犯"指因招惹"小人"，而受到落井下石、挑拨离间一类的迫害。而"put a spoke in one's wheel"本意为给某人的车轮横插一根辐条，实则指破坏某人的计划或阻挠某人的行动。此译在较为准确地传达原文的文化内涵的同时，也再现了原文的形象性与生动性，体现出对译入语文化的适应性选择转换，能够克服中英两种文化差异带来的障碍，便于观众理解与欣赏戏剧表演。

3.3 交际维

交际维的适应性选择转换，即译者在翻译过程中关注双语交际意图的适应性选择转换（胡庚申，2011：8）。译者需在转换语言信息与传递文化内涵之外，侧重于交际层面的适应性选择转换，关注原文本身的交际意图是否再现于译文之中。《雷雨》作为戏剧文本，其交际的重要方面在于通过舞台表演向观众传递出原文的交际意图。这就要求译者注重译文动作性的实现，以便向观众展现人物的形体动作及心理活动，并下功夫提升观众接受度，达成更好的戏剧共鸣效果。

例 6

朴：去，跪下，劝你的母亲。

朴：（高声）跪下！

朴：叫你跪下！

Zhou: Go on! Down on your knees and persuade her!

Zhou (shouting): Down on your knees!

Zhou: Down on your knees, I said!

戏剧语言的动作性是其不同于小说、散文等文学体裁语言的一个重要特征。孟伟根（2012：65）认为，动作是戏剧塑造人物、表现现实生活的重要手段，戏剧必须以动作抓住观众，进而形成与观众的交流。此例中，周朴园正愤怒而专横地要求周萍跪下以逼劝繁漪喝药。对于三处重复的"跪下"，王佐良没有保持原有语言结构，将之对应译为"Kneel down"，而是译为"Down on your knees"。在发音上，以"down"为开头较之"kneel"更具爆发力；形式上，"Down on your knees"省略了动词，仅依靠副词与介词——"down on"——就简洁地传递出语言动态，这两点均有利于演员情绪的释放与面部动作呈现，使观众更直观地感受戏剧冲突并理解人物特点。此外，"I said!"语言脆落，易于表现，展示出周朴园愤怒的语气，以及其作为一家之主，对周萍与繁漪所具有的强烈压迫力。王译对动作性的再现与突显，能够更好地向观众传递原文的交际意图，亦即，使人物语言于观众而言具有说服力，能够饱满地塑造人物性格，并清楚地体现人物相互关系。

例 7

大：（抽出手枪）我——我打死你这老东西！

贵：（站起，喊）枪，枪，枪！（僵立不动。）

Hai (drawing his pistol): I'll—I'll kill you for that, you old swine!

Lu (leaping to his fees and shouting): Help! Help! He'll shoot me! (He stands petrified with fear.)

言为心声，戏剧语言动作性的其中一个层面，即体现在揭示人物心理的动作上。此处，鲁大海因鲁贵斥责母亲的言论而被激怒，拔出手枪装作要打死鲁贵。鲁贵恐惧万分，一时间竟语无伦次，只顾得连喊三声"枪"。王佐良并未简单地将之对应译为"Gun"，而是基于对鲁贵心理活动的把握，及适应目标观众的需要进行选择转换，以"Help"一词更为直观地向观众传递出他内心的极度恐惧，与寻求帮助及祈求宽恕的意图；同时，也更为生动形象地刻画了鲁贵欺软怕硬、贪生怕死的个性特点。

例 8

大：（忍着）妈，他这样子我实在看不下去。妈，我走了。

鲁：胡说。就要下雨，你上哪儿去？

Hai (keeping his temper): I'm not staying here any longer if he's going to be like this, Mother. I'm going.

Ma: Don't be silly. It'll come on to rain any minute. Where would you go, anyway?

大：（狞笑）没有什么，周家逼得我没有路走，这就是一条路。

鲁：胡说，交给我。

Hai (smiling grimly): It's nothing, really. If the Zhous drive me to the wall, this will be one way out.

Ma: Nonsense. Give it to me.

戏剧是包括演出者和观众等所有参与者在内的活动，是一个完整的交流系统。戏剧符号只有被戏剧观众所接受才能产生其意义和价值（孟伟根，2012：144）。此例中，第一处"胡说"是鲁大海因忍受不了鲁贵的蛮横无理，而要冒雨离家时，其母给予的劝慰；第二处"胡说"则出自鲁大海私藏手枪，其母发现后的斥责。王佐良在处理这两处相同的表达时，采取了不同的译法，以贴近原文实际的交际意图。"Don't be silly"既显示出母亲对于孩子冒雨离开的担心，又在表面怪责的话语下，隐含着母亲内心深处的爱护之情，将鲁侍萍疼爱孩子的温柔慈母形象塑造得更为立体。而"Nonsense"则再现了原文的斥责口吻，揭示出鲁侍萍害怕儿子大海会因枪取祸的心理动态，具体而生动地再现了其忧惧不安的语气、神态。王译的灵活处理建立在对观众接受度的充分考量之上，使得译文更具有戏剧表演张力，也使得演员与观众的直接交流更具有感染力。

4. 结语

生态翻译学认为翻译即适应选择，在多维度的选择性适应与适应性选择的翻译原则之下，其又集中体现为语言维、文化维、交际维的适应性选择转换。通过本文具体译例的分析可知，《雷雨》王译本在戏剧语言的口语化及音乐性、文化负载词内涵的传递，以及从语言动作性及观众接受度等方面再现原文交际意图，做到了灵活恰当的适应与选择。当然，王译本中成功的适应性选择转换还远不止于此。实际上，正是因为王译本从不同维度，整体上地适应了特定的翻译生态环境，具有较高的多维转换程度，才能在英语世界取得成功，成为经久不衰的戏剧译本。

参考文献

[1] BASSNETT S, 2014. Ways through the labyrinth: strategies and methods for translating theatre texts[M]// Hermans T.The manipulation of literature: studies in literary translation. New York: Routledge: 87-102.

[2] 胡庚申，2011. 生态翻译学的研究焦点与理论视角[J]. 中国翻译，32(2): 5-9, 95.

[3] 胡庚申，2013. 生态翻译学建构与诠释[M]. 北京：商务印书馆.

[4] 老舍，2004. 出口成章[M]. 上海：复旦大学出版社.

[5] 孟伟根，2012. 戏剧翻译研究[M]. 杭州：浙江大学出版社.

[6] 王红娟，2013. 王佐良对新中国英语翻译事业的贡献[J]. 兰台世界（16）：108-109.

[7] 王鑫磊，2007. 先秦典籍中"小人"一词词义变化及原因——关于儒家思想对先秦时期"小人"词义影响的思考[J].河北学刊（1）：32-36.

[8] 王育生，1979. 曹禺谈《雷雨》[J]. 人民戏剧（3）：40-47.

[9] 王佐良，1989. 翻译：思考与试笔[M]. 北京：外语教学与研究出版社.

[10] 杨琳，2016. "装蒜""一屁股债"考源[J]. 文化学刊（4）：41-43.

[11] 赵永新，1997. 析 ABAC 式四字语[J]. 语言教学与研究（3）：140-147.

《虬髯客传》英译本中的叙事重构
——基于蒙娜·贝克叙事理论

谭鑫玥

1. 引言

《虬髯客传》作为中国古典小说，具有浓厚的中国传统文化价值，不仅在语言风格上沿袭了六朝志怪小说的传统，多用四字句，句法较整齐，与骈文接近，同时文中也有大量的文化负载词，如官名、地名、度量衡等，这对译者来说无疑是一大挑战。《虬髯客传》同时也是一篇唐传奇小说，具有个性鲜明的人物、曲折离奇的故事情节以及丰富的背景环境描写。因此，如何还原《虬髯客传》小说的故事性和叙事性，将小说原有的传奇色彩表现得淋漓尽致，这是译者的另一大挑战。本文所选英译本为电子科技大学外国语学院周劲松教授版本，周教授所译版本不仅展现出了古典小说的传统文化价值，还充分考虑了原文本的叙事性，重构了文本的叙事，将整个故事呈现得具有逻辑性，也更加贴切目标读者的阅读感受。本文将从蒙娜·贝克叙事理论角度出发，深入剖析周教授译本中叙事性的灵活转换，为古典小说翻译中的叙事角度带来更多启示。

2. 《虬髯客传》叙事分析

《虬髯客传》叙事风格技巧高超，首先对于人物的描述和塑造，叙事镜头不断推进，人物出场顺序是以层次渐进、"一山还比一山高"的模式构成（林保淳，2020）。小说首先从隋炀帝开始铺垫，用较小的篇幅提及杨素，接下来才是李靖的出场，展现他的侃侃而谈和智慧，而后是有胆有谋、镇定自若的红拂女出场，在他们为爱私奔后，诡异神秘的虬髯客骑着跛驴潇洒而至，最后才是气度非凡的真命天子李世民登场。小说环环相扣，叙事结构随人物增加逐渐完整，直至最后一人出场，整个故事情节才清晰明了，且每个人物联系都更加紧密，这样的叙事手法层次分明，引人入胜。

其次，《虬髯客传》叙述视角多样化，小说开篇交代故事背景运用了非聚焦型视角，从上帝视角对杨素进行了介绍。后文随着人物出场，小说出现了大量的对话描写，叙述视角加入内聚焦性视角，从不同的人物语言去展现各自的人物形象。同时多重内聚焦视角也有所应用，比如在红拂女眼中的李靖是"阅天下之人多矣，无如公者"，而在虬髯客的话中，李靖又增添了"贫士也"这一形象。此外小说中还有外聚焦型视角，比如从外貌对红拂女的描写，"观其肌肤、仪状、言词、气性，真天人也"。小说就在这样的多视角穿插中不断丰富，各个人物的言行举止、性格风度也描摹得丝丝入扣。

最后，《虬髯客传》语言风格简洁，甚至有多处省略，但人物表现和情节的丰富性极强，这都源自一些单一字词的深刻含义，简单的字也将小说的叙事效果发挥到最佳，比如"独目工"中的"独",不仅能够表现红拂女对李靖的迷恋,也能从侧面刻画出李靖的出众。

3. 蒙娜·贝克叙事理论

蒙娜·贝克《翻译与冲突:叙事性阐释》一书中将叙事理论与翻译领域相结合,提出了叙事翻译理论(罗婕,2018)。蒙娜·贝克提出,翻译的本质就是"再叙事",因此在翻译过程中,译者往往会使用相应策略去强化、弱化或更改原文文本中的某些叙事内容,从而对文本内容进行重构(段佳慈,2016)。

蒙娜·贝克叙事翻译理论框架共包括四个方面,即时空建构、选择性采用建构、标签建构和参与者定位建构(Baker, 2006)。这四个方面的提出基于叙事的四大特性,首先,叙事具有时空性,叙事要素通常按照叙事背景进行一定的排列组合,所呈现的顺序在叙事中都有意义。其次,叙事具有选择性,叙事要素在不同情节或主题的需要下,难免会出现被强调或被省略的情况。同时,叙事具有关联性,叙事分为不同部分,这些部分并非独立,而是相互关联构成叙事整体。最后,叙事具有因果性,任何一个叙事都试图引导读者接受叙事中的因果关系,由此来引导读者作出相应的回应(黄婷等,2016)。因此,译者在翻译过程中,需要充分考虑叙事因素,采取不同策略对叙事进行重新建构,从而达到叙事最佳效果。

4. 《虬髯客传》英译本中的叙事重构

4.1 时空建构

时空建构是指译者选择某一叙事文本,并将其置于一种特定的时空框架内,并以此来突出强调叙事(张美芳、钱宏,2007)。译者可以将原文叙事从原来所处的时空嫁接到另一个时空或社会背景中,以符合译者自身的翻译目的或目的读者的阅读习惯与文化背景。《虬髯客传》背景设立于隋末唐初之际,译者通过有意强调或弱化原文本中的时空背景,达到不影响读者理解并使原文叙事更加流畅的效果。

例1

原文:隋炀帝之幸江都也,命司空杨素守西京。

译文:It was some time in the last few years of the Sui Dynasty. Whilst Emperor Yangdi was on his inspection tour to the city of Jiangdu (presently Yangzhou), Premier Yangsu was in charge of the garrison at the city of Xijing (presently Xi'an) at His Majesty's requests.

分析:作为小说的开头,译者并没有直接开始对原文进行翻译,而是增添了"It was some time in the last few years of the Sui Dynasty"一句,对小说的叙事背景进行了定位,完整交代了故事的背景是在隋、唐之际,不仅使得故事不显突兀,增强了叙事的流畅性,同时强调了文本中的时空背景,更能让读者感受到其中的时代感,可读性增强,更加引人入胜,达到了叙事效果。

译文中出现文内注的地方一共有三处,开篇第一句话占两处,即 Jiangdu (presently Yangzhou), Xijing (presently Xi'an),另一处为"贞观十年",其译文为"In the tenth year during the region of Li Shiming (636)"。原文本中所提到的不论是地名还是年号名,都是中国古代的特殊命名法,因此译者为了符合读者的时代背景和阅读习惯,选择了文内注的方式,采用最简洁的处理方式,不仅为读者排除了阅读障碍,同时也没有影响叙事的流畅性。

例 2

原文：其夜五更初。

译文：Deep in the darkness at about 4 o'clock that night.

分析："五更"同样属于传统中国文化词汇，"更"在古代指的是夜间计时的单位，一夜分为五更，五更指寅时，即第二天三点—五点，而现代计时方法通常为 12 小时计时制或 24 小时计时制，译者直接将其译为"4 o'clock"，充分考虑了现代读者的阅读感受，并且在时间前还加上修饰性短语"deep in the darkness"，使叙事更加丰富完整，更能展现出叙事是在天黑的凌晨中，更具故事性和画面感。

4.2 选择性采用文本内容

选择性采用则是译者通过对原文本内容进行删减或增加，以达到抑制、强调或阐释原文本中隐含的叙事或某些更高层面的叙事（张美芳、钱宏，2007）。译者在翻译《虬髯客传》的过程中，根据叙事情节进行了多处的增译或删减，选择性地进行强调或弱化，从而让叙事更加层次分明，尤其是对于主要人物形象的刻画，更加鲜明生动，叙事重点更加突出。

例 3

原文：张氏以发长委地，立梳床前。

译文：Zhang was standing in front of the bed combing, the hair falling down to the earth like a cascade.

分析：本句出自红拂女梳头场景，译者在忠实原文的基础上，对红拂女"发长"增添了新的描绘："the hair falling down to the earth like a cascade." 女性的头发常常就是美的象征，后续出场的虬髯客也被红拂女的长发吸引，因此有"看张梳头"的场景，这说明原话意在展现红拂女的娇媚，与前文的"佳丽人""真天人"是相呼应的，因此译者对红拂女的描写清楚叙述出了该意味，将叙事的画面感烘托了出来，也能够激发读者的想象空间。

例 4

原文：公怒甚，未决，犹刷马。

译文：Lijing showed no signs of action towards this but kept grooming the horses, while in his heart, the flame of anger was burning aloud and on the very point of breaking out.

分析：本句最能刻画李靖的人物性格，当虬髯客都已经进屋看红拂女梳头时，而李靖还在外面刷马，"未决"真的是因为他的懦弱吗？作为"风尘三侠"之一的人物，当然不是这样。译者将此句放大化处理，原句的八个汉字，译成之后 32 个单词，将李靖内心的"未决"展开，处理为"while in his heart, the flame of anger was burning aloud and on the very point of breaking out"，充分表现了李靖有勇有谋，同时也沉得住气，绝不鲁莽行事的性格，也让读者深刻感受到李靖内心世界的变化，这是原句所隐含的叙事，译者直接将其挑明，让故事对李靖人物性格的刻画更加生动，也让文本阐释更加清晰。

例 5

原文：脱衣去帽，乃十八九佳丽人也。素面画衣而拜。公惊答拜。

译文：Overcoat off and hat down, a girl of amazing beauty of about 18 years old was standing before his eyes and greeted him with a deep bow. Taken by the surprise, Lijing bowed back all in a fluster. The girl wearing no cosmetics on the face but really luxurious clothes on the body explained.

分析：本句整体上从李靖的视角出发，向读者展现了李靖眼中红拂女进屋后的形象，一是完成了对人物外貌的刻画，二是明确表达出两位人物关系，译者加上"standing before his eyes"就让叙事的逻辑关系更加清晰明了。同时在翻译中，译者将"素面画衣而拜"一句进行了拆解，将红拂女的"拜"和李靖所发出的动作"公惊答拜"进行了结合，而"素面画衣"则放在了"拜"之后，事实上这是符合叙事逻辑的，也会让整个动作更加流畅，红拂女一进屋就开始脱衣去帽，再拜李靖，而李靖看到此景也应该是立马作出了回拜，等整个过程都完成后，李靖才能对红拂女的外貌进行更细一步的观察，所以译者所作出的选择性建构让这个叙事更加具有连动的画面感，也更加符合情理。

4.3 标签建构

标签建构主要是指用特定的单词、短语和术语去描述叙事文本中的人物、地点、事件等要素，以此为读者提供一个理解框架，引导并制约读者对叙事的反应，从而达到重新叙事的目的，通常是针对个别词汇进行修改（张美芳，钱宏，2007）。译者在《虬髯客传》中通过对特定人名或称谓的转变，实现了叙事解读，明示了叙事中的人物身份和特征，也将人物关系和情感烘托了出来。

例 6 红拂女第一次见到李靖

原文：问去者处士第几？住何处？

译文：Hurry up to ask the man just left who he is? Where he stays?

例 7 红拂女第二次见到李靖，夜奔李靖住所

原文：妾侍杨司空久，阅天下之人多矣，无如公者。

译文：I have been in service of Premier Yang too long and seen people to many here, but I can find no one your superior.

例 8 红拂女和李靖私奔后

原文：张氏遥呼："李郎且来见三兄！"

译文：Miss Zhang called gladly to the outdoor: "Li, my lord, come up to meet brother Third."

例 9 虬髯客和李靖的对话

原文：观李郎之行，贫士也。

译文：Brother Li, it seems by your appearance you are not that rich.

分析：例6、例7和例8分别是红拂女和李靖相识到相恋的变化过程，红拂女初次见到李靖时，对李靖的称呼直接是"the man"，显示两人关系陌生，当红拂女夜奔李靖住所，对他的称呼是"your superior"，一方面展现出红拂女对李靖的崇拜之情，另一方面表现出两人关系在此刻还处于彼此客气的状态，同时这样的描述也侧面表现出李靖确实有过人之处，以及红拂女眼光的独到，是一个有思想的女性形象。然而在例3中，红拂女对李靖的称呼已经变成了"Li, my lord"，这也就表明此时两人关系的更进一步，能够直接以姓氏相称，同时my lord也能表现出古时女子对丈夫的尊敬，这样的层层递进，也是剧情走向的线索，让故事的叙事在各个方面都符合逻辑。

例8和例9形成一组鲜明的对比，译者并没有同时将两个"李郎"都译为表层意思的"Lijing"，而是根据人物关系有不同的译法，一个是"Li, my lord"，另一个是"Brother Li"，直白地向读者展现出了说话者之间的人物关系，"brother"这样的叫法也体现出虬髯客和李靖

之间关系的逐渐亲密，从刚见面的"公怒甚"到该情节两人关系的缓和，这些称谓的变化都能体现故事情节的曲折变化。

例 10 李靖初见红拂女

原文：佳丽人

译文：A girl of amazing beauty

例 11 李靖细看红拂女

原文：真天人也

译文：really a stunner

例 12 虬髯客看红拂女

原文：异人

译文：extraordinary girl

小说中对于红拂女的外貌形象描写有多处，本文一共选取了三处对红拂女外貌描写的总结性词汇。例 10 和例 11 都是李靖视角下的红拂女，出现于同一个场景之中。例 1 是红拂女初进屋，李靖对其大致观察后的描述，而例 11 是李靖"观其肌肤仪状、言词、气性"后发出的感叹，因此译者在翻译时用词也进行了轻重之分。在译"佳丽人"时用的是"amazing beauty"，在译"天人"时则选用了"stunner"，与"stunner"相比，"amazing beauty"的程度更轻。虽然两者都能表现红拂女惊为天人的美，用词却是循序渐进的，不仅避免了用词的单调性，还符合叙事的逻辑，即从进门初看到细致观察，红拂女在李靖视角中呈现着变化。例 3 "extraordinary girl"是从虬髯客视角出发，在和红拂女进行交流后，虬髯客不仅被红拂女的外貌所吸引，也感叹她的胆识，所以译者选用"extraordinary"这个词不仅仅是停留于表面，还让人物叙事特征更加明显。

4.4 参与者再定位

参与者再定位是指在翻译过程中，参与者之间的关系，参与者与读者或听者的关系均可以被重新定位，这种重新定位主要是通过语言手段对时空、方言、语域、别称等进行操控（张美芳，钱宏，2007）。《虬髯客传》中大部分的故事情节是在人物之间的对话中展开的，译者通过巧妙的语言手段将故事中的参与者进行了重新定位，让小说叙事逻辑更加完整，叙事线索更加清晰，读者在阅读时也更加有画面感。

例 13

原文：妓诵而去。

译文：She murmured the feedback to her heart and stepped off quietly.

分析：原文对小吏向红拂女的转述环节进行了省略，缺少画面衔接感，这需要读者想象进行缺失画面的弥补。但译者直接采用"feedback"这个词，巧妙地将小吏的传话作用展示给了读者，且原句没有被破坏，让小吏自然而然地参与在故事其中，更加明显地定位了红拂女和小吏在这一环节的关系，不仅让叙事画面更加流畅，还让叙事参与者更加清晰。

例 14

原文：公问谁？曰："妾，杨家之红拂妓也。"

译文："Who is that?" he asked. "It's me, the courtesan holding the red whisk at Yangsu's house."

分析：该场景出现在红拂女夜奔李靖住所，李靖在屋内询问来者何人，译者在翻译时灵活增译了"It's me"，红拂女站在屋外，对话双方彼此陌生，译者的处理不仅能展现双方对话的松弛感，拉近红拂女和李靖之间的关系，同时也让读者仿佛身临其境，让读者和角色之间的参与感更加强烈。此外，"It's me"的译法也是英语对话中常见的，靠近了目标读者的阅读习惯，使得叙事更加完整，充满情感。

例 15 曰

原文中出现了大量的对话，而基本上都是由"曰"字带出疑问和回答，《虬髯客传》英译本中译者对"曰"进行了灵活处理，如在红拂女和李靖坦诚对话的片段中。

原文：公曰："杨司空权重京师，如何？"曰："尸居余气，不足畏也。"

译文：Lijing spoke out his worries: "How about Premier Yang? He's almighty all over the capital area, after all." The girl assured him: "There's no need to be afraid of a walking skeleton."

分析：原文中李靖和红拂女在讨论司空杨素，译者分别将两个"曰"译为"spoke out his worries"和"assured"，这样的译法将李靖和红拂女的情感直白表露出来，李靖此时作为一个布衣平民，对于位高权重的杨素自然内心有害怕担忧，因此译者直接用"spoke out his worries"发问，然而红拂女在杨素身边侍奉已久，知道杨素本性，并且为了回答李靖的担忧，译者用了"assured"这个词，表现出红拂女一方面对李靖的保证，同时也能展现她对自己计谋的自信。译者这样的翻译不仅对故事中参与的角色进行了重新定位，表现角色间情感的纠结，也让读者能够参与到更加完整的叙事之中，用两个"曰"烘托出了更深刻的意义。

原文：问其姓，曰："张。"问其伯仲之次。曰："最长。"

译文：Lijing felt a bit relaxed and the talk was soon geared into a pleasant chatting, by which, not only was the girl known to be surnamed Zhang and the eldest daughter in her family.

分析：红拂女和李靖在进行了主要信息的问答后，二人开始了较为次要信息的谈论，李靖问红拂女的姓和家中排行，这样的对话与前文相比信息含量比较轻，因此译者直接将其译为陈述句，不仅对李靖的心情转变有所补充暗示"a bit relaxed"，同时也用"geared into a pleasant chatting"引出所叙述话题。译者所作出的改变巧妙避免了"曰"的重复出现，也让叙事的信息有层次、轻重之分，红拂女和李靖在这一对话中的参与感没有那么强烈，只涵盖相关的基础信息。

5. 结语

周劲松的《虬髯客传》英译版本充分考虑了一个故事的叙事性，从蒙娜·贝克叙事理论来看，译者采用了时空建构、文本内容选择性采用、标签建构和参与者再定位四个角度，对《虬髯客传》中的叙事进行了重构，不仅让叙事画面和情节更加完整、具有逻辑性，还让小说中的各个人物特征和性格叙事更加鲜明直接，灵活的叙事转换让整个故事更有丰富的层次感。周劲松的翻译版本也为古典小说的翻译带来更多启示，即关注原文本的叙事，还原故事的连贯性和结构性，这也为推动中国文化走出去，建立自身文化机制作出了良好范例。

参考文献

[1] BAKER M, 2006. Translation and conflict: a narrative account[M]. London: Routledge.

[2] 段佳慈，2016. 蒙娜·贝克"叙事理论"对国内翻译研究的启示[J]. 译苑新谭（8）：128-134.
[3] 黄婷，黄勤，2016. 莫娜·贝克的叙事理论在翻译中的应用[J]. 翻译论坛（4）：15-18.
[4] 林保淳，2020.《虬髯客传》新读[J]. 太原学院学报（社会科学版），21（6）：100-103.
[5] 罗婕，2018. 从《翻译与冲突:叙事性阐释》看蒙娜·贝克的翻译研究转向[J]. 戏剧之家（10）：246.
[6] 张美芳，钱宏，2007.《翻译与冲突——叙述性阐释》评介[J]. 外语教学与研究（4）：317-320.
[7] 周劲松，2016. 翻译基础十二讲[M]. 成都：电子科技大学出版社.

译者主体性视角下《道德经》两个英译本对比研究：以第五章与第四十二章为例

黄雅琪

1. 引言

《道德经》又名《老子》，为春秋时李耳所著，是一部意义深刻、发人深思的哲学著作。而对于翻译富含中华文化思想的古籍，译者主体性对于译文的影响尤为明显。在任何翻译活动中，译者作为原文与译文两种语言文本的媒介与桥梁，需结合自身知识理解原文内容，基于特定的翻译目的，采取一定的翻译策略与方法，进而将源语转化为目标语。本文选取中国学者吴经熊（John C. H. Wu，1899—1986）和英国汉学家阿瑟·韦利（Arthur Waley，1888—1966）的英译本为对照译本，对《道德经》第五章及第四十二章在结合自身思考的基础上进行翻译比较研究。研究完成后，译者将探讨比较两译本的异同，试寻求两译本与原文差异之处的翻译解决办法，并总结鉴赏两译本。

2. 译本介绍

本文所选取的译本有四个特点：（1）译者分别为中国译者和国外汉学家；（2）译作发行时间不存在过大时间差，属于同一时代，思想方面不存有本质性差异；（3）两本译作均有良好的销售记录①；（4）二者的翻译风格差异较为明显。

首先，二者翻译风格的差异，体现在对《道德经》的认识层面。吴经熊认为《道德经》中传递表达的道家文化与以基督教为代表的西方文化有相似之处。他倾向于在注释中选择性地突出两种文化的相似性与同源性，使用通俗易懂的语言以及简单的句式来阐释翻译《道德经》。韦利则认为《道德经》中代表与传达的中华文化有特殊之处及独一无二性，倾向于使用准确、正式的语言来展现《道德经》中提及内容的"真实面貌"。

其次，为翻译目的方面。吴经熊翻译《道德经》的目的是向西方读者介绍宣传中华文化，希望通过构建中西相似的文化语境，对外宣传中国文学文化，终极目的在于实现中华民族伟大复兴。基于此，他十分注重目的语读者的反映与可接受度。他倾向于使用简洁明了的句式与语言，传递中国古籍中所蕴含的丰富哲理，达到向西方世界传播中华文化的最大效果。虽

---

① 韦利译本是英语世界比较通行的版本。1934 年，由 Allen and Unwin 公司在伦敦首次出版，自第一版出版之后，收到了极好的社会反响，多次再版，对老子思想在西方传播产生极大影响。此外，吴经熊译本也获得了西方读者的认可。其译文于 1939 年首次刊登在英文期刊《天下月刊》（*T'ien-hisa Monthly*）上，随后 1951 年，出版《老子〈道德经〉新译》（*Lao Tzu, "Tao Teh Ching ," A New Translation*），该译本前后共计 12 次再版。1989 年，Shambhala Publication, Inc.获得了该译本版权，在波士顿和伦敦同时出版，随后不断再版。

然吴经熊在语言形式上迎合了西方读者的口味，突出强调《道德经》与其他西方典籍的相似性，但他也绝没有放弃突出《道德经》作为中国古籍的独特性，而是注重运用注释这一副文本的作用，将民族文化与西方文化联系在一起。阿瑟·韦利认为《道德经》翻译需要侧重老子哲学思想的阐述与传达。他认为，翻译分为两种，一种是"文学翻译"（literary translation），另一种是"文字翻译"（philological translation）（Arthur Waley, 1934）。在他看来，《道德经》翻译属于文字翻译范畴，并试图通过这种方式来挖掘老子创作《道德经》时的真实意图。韦利指出，《道德经》最重要的作用在于其内容能够发人深思。因此，韦利翻译时更注重文字翻译的准确性，尽可能地面面俱到，不追求文学之美，句式较为复杂。

最后，在翻译策略方面。吴经熊提倡意译，对于《道德经》中部分表达，他认为采用意译的方式更能体现原文内涵。他倾向于使用西方读者熟悉的基督教知识来翻译、解释《道德经》，也会结合西方的相关知识来解释文中的专有名词，以彰显中西文明的相似性，促进西方读者对译本的接受与理解。但他也没有选择以完全归化的方式来翻译《道德经》，而是选择以充分性与接受性兼顾的方式来进行译介。阿瑟·韦利并没有遵循什么特定的翻译策略，但在译本序言中他曾提及，有一种翻译为"历史性"（historical）翻译，另一种与之对应的为"文本式"（scriptural）翻译（Arthur Waley, 1934）。并且，他还在长达 84 页的导读当中详细阐述、补充了许多关于《道德经》的知识，如撰写时的历史背景、所用文学方法、作者介绍等，每个章节后也会附上释义或作出评论（杨玉英，2019）。他翻译《道德经》时采用的翻译策略更加偏向于"历史性"翻译，忠实于原文，注重传达《道德经》思想层面的内涵，不会因为追求文字之美而牺牲内容。

基于此，本文对比研究所选用的译本极具代表性与典型性，有利于探讨学习合适的翻译处理方法，对于归纳与总结如何翻译富有中华文化内涵的古籍具有一定参考与借鉴价值。

3. 译本比较

本章节中，作者将以贾德永的《老子译注》为今译版本，比较吴经熊、阿瑟·韦利两位译者在原文理解上与老子的写作意图是否存有不同之处。本章节将会对比研究译文文化层面与语言层面，即词汇句法层面的翻译选择，试分析两位译者如何发挥译者主体性，分别以何种翻译目的选择相应的翻译策略与技巧，试探讨赏析两译本间的异同。

3.1 第五章

原文：<u>天地不仁</u>，以万物为刍狗；<u>圣人不仁</u>，以百姓为刍狗。天地之间，其犹橐籥乎？虚而不屈，动而愈出。<u>多言数穷，不如守中</u>。

英译（吴经熊）：<u>HEAVEN-and-Earth is not sentimental</u>;

It treats all things as straw-dogs.

<u>The Sage is not sentimental</u>;

He treats all his people as straw-dogs.

Between Heaven and Earth,

There seems to be a Bellows:

It is empty, and yet it is inexhaustible;

The more it works, the more comes out of it.

No amount of words can fathom it:

Better look for it within you.

英译（阿瑟·韦利）： Heaven and Earth are ruthless;

To them the Ten Thousand things are but as straw dogs.

The Sage too is ruthless;

To him the people are but as straw dogs.

Yet Heaven and Earth and all that lies between

Is like a bellows

In that it is empty, but gives a supply that never fails.

Work it, and more comes out.

Whereas the force of words is soon spent.

Far better is it to keep what is in the heart.

今译：天地无所偏爱，把万物当成祭祀用的刍狗看待；圣人无所偏爱，把百姓当成祭祀用的刍狗看待。天地之间，不正是像个风箱吗？空虚却不会穷竭，发动起来就生生不息。政令繁多反而会加速败亡，不如持守虚静（贾德永，2013）。

本章中，老子论述了道的客观性，并警示为政者应当向道学习，持守虚静。他告诉世人，天地是纯粹的自然与客观，万事万物都在客观规律作用下发生。天地没有目的，没有意志，任由万物自生自灭（孙以楷，2013）。

在文化层面，"圣人不仁"中的"圣人"应当理解为"依道而行"之人（骆飚，2022），两位译者都将其翻译为"the sage"。老子在《道德经》第25章中曾提到："人法地，地法天，天法道，道法自然。"这里的"人"指的是行自然无为之道者。作者认为先秦各家学派都有理想中的圣人形象与标准，若单纯泛译为"the sage"，则无法突出《道德经》中独一无二的圣人形象，无法阐释《道德经》中所要表达体现的圣人标准。但若意译此词，又将牺牲句子的形式之美。因此，作者认为可以通过副文本的方式将"圣人"的内在涵义在译本当中额外阐明。

在词汇层面，"天地不仁"中的"不仁"一词，骆飚（2022）在其释本中表示，"不仁"意为天地任由万物自然生长，不会插手干预这一自然规律。由此可见，"不仁"不应理解为"不仁不义"，应当理解为天地无所偏爱。因此，此处韦利翻译的"ruthless"显得不甚完美，他将"不仁"理解为了"冷酷""无情"之意，并不能算合理的翻译；相比而言，吴经熊翻译的"not sentimental"在某种程度上，表达出了"道"客观理性的性质特点。在他看来，天地是理性的，没有情感就不会有所偏爱。

在句法层面，两位译者都注意到了原文互相对应的句子形式，也尽量在译文中体现这点。但相较而言，吴经熊除了"all things""all his people"在字符数量方面没有完全对照之外，其他都做到了一一对应。并且，其译文不仅做到了如原文般两个译文小句之间的对照，还在"不仁"这一处做到了译文与原文的对照，处理得十分巧妙。他将"不"翻译成"not"，将"仁"翻译成"sentimental"。从译文不难看出，他理解到了老子在第五章中想要传达的"道之客观性"，且他并没有采用"正说反译"这一翻译技巧，将"不仁"用"rational"直接替代，而是在译文中也保持了两个字符，与原文相对应；而韦利除了如吴经熊一样，在"万物""百姓"之处没有做到对齐之外，他还在"圣人不仁"之处的译文加了一个"too"。

作者认为，此处两个译者对于并列排比的不同翻译处理，根源在于二者的文化背景不同。

吴经熊作为中国本土译者，他了解中国语言之中并列排比的成分并不一定需要关联词来表达，因此在译文当中也并没有特意强调"万物不仁"与"圣人不仁"的并列排比关系。韦利十分注重内容的传达与贴合，他注意到两小句之间分号的存在，并且西方世界十分注重句子的逻辑结构，注重逻辑词的使用。因此作为西方人的他，认为此处有必要将并列排比关系突出强调，并将这种思考结果转化为了译文中的"too"。此外，笔者认为"天地不仁"与"圣人不仁"应当存在递进的逻辑关系，天地指的是"自然""道"，而圣人指的是有道者、守道者。此处的"too"似在逻辑层面更能将圣人与天地连接起来，让两者体现出某种隐形联系。从这个层面理解，韦利的处理也十分精妙。"too"的增添虽在某种程度上略微破坏了句子的形式之美，但也表现出韦利在处理《道德经》英译过程中的严谨与思考，值得译者们参考学习。

"多言数穷，不如守中。"为老子给为政者的警示之言，告诫他们为政要效法自然，切忌"多言"，重要的是守住根本，不如不言、无为，从而获得延续（孙以楷，2013）。吴经熊译本将这句译为"No amount of words can fathom it: ..." "fathom" 意为捉摸、探索，根据下文内容，此处"it"所指应为"道"。吴经熊将此句理解为"再多的话都不能捉摸透道，不如在自己的内心寻找它。"韦利则将本句理解为"言语的力量很快就会耗尽，不如保留自己心中的想法。"相较而言，吴经熊译本对这句话的理解与原文想要表达的意思有所出入，而韦利译本的后半部分则较为贴合原文意思，不如无为，不"多言"，选择守中，保留自己内心的想法。

3.2 第四十二章

原文：<u>道生一，一生二，二生三，三生万物</u>。万物负阴而抱阳，冲气以为和。人之所恶，唯孤、寡、不榖，而王公以自名也。故物，或损之而益，或益之而损。<u>人之所教，我亦教人。</u>"强梁者不得其死！"吾将以为教父。

英译（吴经熊）：<u>TAO gave birth to One,</u>
<u>One gave birth to Two,</u>
<u>Two gave birth to Three,</u>
<u>Three gave birth to all the myriad things.</u>

All the myriad things carry the Yin on their backs and hold the Yang in their embrace,
Deriving their vital harmony from the proper blending of the two vital breaths.

What is more loathed by men than to be "helpless" "little" and "worthless"?
And yet these are the very names the princes and barons call themselves.

Truly, one may gain by losing;
And one may lose by gaining.

<u>What another has taught let me repeat:</u>
<u>"A man of violence will come to a violent end."</u>
Whoever said this can be my teacher and my father.

英译（阿瑟·韦利）： Tao gave birth to the One;
The One gave birth successively to two things,
Three things, up to ten thousand.
These ten thousand creatures cannot turn their backs to the shade
Without having the sun on their bellies,
And it is on this blending of the breaths that their harmony depends.

To be orphaned, needy, ill-provided is what men most hate;
Yet princes and dukes style themselves so.

Truly, "things are often increased by seeking to diminish them
And diminished by seeking to increase them."
The maxims that others use in their teaching I too will use in mine.
Show me a man of violence that came to a good end,
And I will take him for my teacher.

今译：道产生作为统一体的原始混沌之气，统一体又分裂为阴和阳两个对立面，这两个对立面又产生了和气，新生的和气产生了万物。万物背阴而向阳，阴阳两气互相激荡而生成新的和气。人们所憎恶的是孤独、无助、不善，王公贵族却用来自称。所以一切事物，有时减损它，却反而得到增加；有时增加它，却反而受到减损。别人怎样教导我们的，我也用来去教导别人。强狠霸道的人绝对没有好下场，我把它当作教育人的总纲（贾德永，2013）。

本章节老子首先阐述道之下，天地万物产生的过程，接着又借此告诫为政者要循道而为，要"守弱"。本章中首次出现"阴阳"这一概念，与"有无""难易"等概念般，表示对立的立场（骆飚，2022）。

在文化层面，两位译者都将"道"音译为"TAO"或"Tao"。"道"作为《道德经》核心概念，内容复杂深刻，很难以某个词或字来代替表达其多重含义。此处将"道"进行音译，作者认为两位译者都有自身的考量。作为中国译者，吴经熊的翻译目的是向西方世界宣传中华文化。通过将"道"音译为"TAO"，很好地保留了《道德经》中"道"这一概念的神秘感，传达出了"道"的捉摸不透与难窥本质。音译策略能够很好地将道家思想中的"道"之理念留存于西方读者心中，有利于引导西方读者通过下文对"道"的概念化阐释，进一步在心中领悟"道"。作为汉学家的阿瑟·韦利，在其译本的开篇第一章"道可道，非常道"，便先将"道"译成了"the Way"。其译本中，"道"的翻译并不统一。"道"一词在中文当中有多重意思，在《道德经》当中也有着丰富内涵，而"way"在英语中也拥有不同语境下的含义，可引申为"方法""习惯"等。作为西方人的韦利选用"the Way"来翻译"道"，在某种程度上也可以说是忠实于原文的考量。但在第十五章之后，其译本中音译的"Tao"开始频繁出现，标志着韦利在深入翻译《道德经》之后体会到，单纯用"the Way"来代表"道"并不足以涵盖道的深刻内涵。并且，音译也有利于保留汉语的语言特色，让读者更加接近中华文化，为"道"这一概念蒙上神秘面纱，有利于促进目标语读者体验原文所传递的极具鲜明特色的中华文化。

此外，两位译者在译本中都将"一"翻译成"One"，虽这也不足以概括"一"的丰富内涵，但作者仍较为赞同此处理方式。中国道教的"一"文化历史源远流长，并一直为人所推崇，"一"并非只有一种含义，而且是集具体概念与抽象概念于一体的文化名词（吴琼，2015）。若译者凭借个人理解，贸然将"一"翻译为某一特定的名词或表达，不仅某种程度上不尊重原文和源语言文化，还会影响目标语读者对该词汇概念的理解与思考。两位译者在寻求合适译词未果之后，用"One"来对应原文的"一"的处理办法秉持了极大的严谨态度。

在词汇层面，此句末尾的"万物"，吴经熊译为"all the myriad things"；韦利译为"ten thousand"。作者认为此处译词，吴经熊译本更为恰当。虽然韦利此处忠实于原文内容，但此处将"万物"直译为"ten thousand"仍有失妥当。此处他相当于用了可穷尽的数字来代表了"万物"所指的无穷尽，某种程度上反而未忠实于原文。

在句法层面，吴经熊译本表现出了原文的节奏感与对照性，进行了较为工整的排比；而韦利译本通过添加定冠词 the 来表示"一"的特指，而"二"与"三"并没有与"一"的译文相对照，而是译为"two things""three things"。韦利不仅漏译了"二生三"，每一句的"生"还采用了不同的表达方式，虽然表达更为多样，但无法体现原文的形式之美。

在词汇层面，"教父"并非"老师与父亲"的意思。"教父"指"教人的基本准则"，"父"意为"规矩、准则"（许渊冲，2006）。两位译者都未能准确理解句子当中"教父"之含义，都将这个词理解为"把某个人当作自己的老师或者父亲"。通过阅读上下译文可以发现，他们将"以"理解为了"某个人"，故将"教父"具象化理解为"老师或父亲"是有迹可循的。

吴经熊译本中，将此句划分在同一节中，从译文不难看出，他将"人之所教，我亦教人。'强梁者不得其死！'"连在一句之中，并使用冒号进行连接。他理解为，他人教授给我的就是"强梁者不得其死！"这一道理，而我亦会如此传授于他人。因此，无论谁能够告诉我这个道理，他都是我的老师或者父亲。这个译文错译原因在于，对原文的句意划分产生了歧义。而从韦利译本最后一句的"show me"可以看出，这句话的主语也是人，因此自然而然地也将原文中的"以""教父"与人联系到了一起。但此句话的正确理解应当将"人之所教，我亦教人"理解为一个意群，将剩下部分理解为另一意群。由此可见，正确划分意群，分别理解，能更好地减少歧义。

4. 结语

吴经熊与阿瑟·韦利在第五章和第四十二章的翻译处理各有千秋。从二者的译文中不难看出，译词的不同选择，或同一句子的不同译法均体现出了译者自身的考量，即译者主体性。吴经熊倾向于选择凸显原文含义与中华文化内涵的译词，使用简洁明了的句式与语言，达到传播中华文化的最大效果，注重目的语读者的反映与可接受度，选择以充分性与接受性兼顾的方式来译介《道德经》，力争保留句子美感。阿瑟·韦利注重凸显原文的历史意义，侧重传达老子的哲思，挖掘其创作《道德经》的真实意图，倾向使用正式的语言，注重准确性，句式较为复杂，不因追求文字之美而牺牲内容。

作者认为，在典籍翻译领域，译者应充分发挥自身主体性，将原文理解与译文处理依托于自身的研究与思考，选择最恰当的方式进行翻译。翻译与做学问并不是割裂开的两个独立体，而是统一体。做好典籍翻译，译者需深入研究相关典籍，研究作者遣词造句之意图，深入理解其传递出的哲思明理等。调查研究的过程有助于提升译者对原文的理解，从而形成自己的独到见解。有助于使译文贴合原文内容，尽量做到忠实于原文，正确传达其哲思。而在此基础之上发挥译者主体性，又能使得译文具有内涵与深意，让译文新颖，使读者眼前一亮，提升译文的文学性与可读性，促进文化、哲思的传播。

参考文献

[1] LAO TZU, 1951. Tao Teh Ching[M]. WU J X, trans. New York: St. John's University Press.
[2] LAO TZU, 1934. The way and its power[M]. Waley A, trans. London: Allen and Unwin.
[3] 贾德永，2013. 老子译注[M]. 上海：上海三联书店.
[4] 骆飚，2022. 道非道——《老子》研读[M]. 杭州：浙江大学出版社.
[5] 孙以楷，2013. 《老子》今读[M]. 合肥：安徽大学出版社.
[6] 吴琼，2015. Arthur Waley《道德经》译本研究[D]. 石家庄：河北大学.
[7] 许渊冲，2006. 道德经与神仙画[M]. 北京：五洲传播出版社.
[8] 杨玉英，2019. 《道德经》在英语世界的传播与接受研究[M]. 北京：学苑出版社.
[9] 赵颖，2016. 吴经熊《道德经》译介的转喻视角分析[J]. 上海翻译（3）：56-61，94.

"深化"和"浅化"之论在古文翻译中的运用
——以周译《虬髯客传》为例

肖雨杨

1. 引言

中国文学中的经典译作在全球范围内传播并得到认可。唐传奇,作为中国古典小说逐渐成熟的标志,扮演着文化输出的主要角色。其中,《虬髯客传》作为唐传奇中的巅峰之作,以隋末乱世和英雄辈出为背景,生动地刻画了红拂女、李靖以及虬髯客三位引人入胜的角色。要在不同文化环境中成功传播这些经典作品,必须深刻理解译入语文化的需求和期待,文学作品才能得以广泛传播。因此,以"中国文化走出去"为目标的翻译工作,应该根据具体情境随事而制,以精湛的艺术表达讲述中国故事,突出作品的故事性以吸引读者(任丽萍,2021)。

《虬髯客传》不仅是一部小说,还融合了诗歌和史记的语言特点,风格上也有与骈文相近的一面。它的叙述简洁,文辞古雅,文化内涵丰富,是一种介于诗歌和小说之间的体裁。因此,本文将以许渊冲的"三化"理论为出发点,基于电子科技大学副教授周劲松的《虬髯客传》译本(以下简称"周译"),采用"深化"和"浅化"的方法,深入分析周译如何体现《虬髯客传》的故事性、传奇性和文学性。

2. 许渊冲"三化"理论之"深化"与"浅化"

许渊冲,中国著名翻译家,因其将中国古典诗词翻译成英法韵文的杰出表现而被誉为独一无二的专家。他的翻译理论中的"三化"概念受到了钱锺书的启发。钱锺书曾言:"文学作品的最高翻译境界是'化',把作品从一国文字转变成另一国文字,既能不因语言习惯的差异而露出生硬牵强的痕迹,又能完全保存原有的风味,那算得入于化境。""化境"历程十分艰辛,但凭借许渊冲的再创作,通过"加词、减词、分译、合译、正说、反说、深化、等化、浅化",是可以进入"化境"的(许钧,1996),就应该入于"化境"。仔细分析一下,"化"又可以分为三种:"深化、等化、浅化。"在"等化"中,当源语和目标语在表层和深层含义上一致时,可采用"等化"方法,主要用于句子结构调整和主动、被动转换等情境。本文分析的焦点不在"等化"技巧上,故不再详述。

许渊冲(1984)在《翻译的艺术》中说道:"直译专门词语不能传达原文的'意美'时,需要变'浅化'或'深化'的方法"。这一观点不仅适用于诗词翻译,还适用于小说、散文等各种文学体裁的翻译。通过"深化",译者将抽象概念具体化,通过增加适当的词汇来清晰地表达,以保留原文的文化色彩和深层含义。当直译难以传达原文的"意美"时,"深化"能够使读者更好地理解译文,深化原文中省略的信息,传递出作者的意图。与此相反,"浅化"是将抽象概念转化为更通用的概念,特别适用于涉及文化背景的翻译内容。在一些情况下,直译无法实现表层和深层含义的一致性，需要采取"浅化"方法，以不影响整体翻译效果为前提，舍弃一部分特定文化意义，侧重保持古文的故事性和文学性（姜丹丹，2012）。例如，在处理典故等内容时，若直译需要读者查阅注释才能理解，将会破坏读者的阅读连贯体验。

许渊冲（2003）在其出版的《文学与翻译》一书中说道，"所谓'深化'，包括特殊化、具体化、加词、一分为二等译法；所谓'浅化'，包括一般化、抽象化、减词、合而为一等译法。"至于要对文本作深化还是浅化的处理，则要看具体语境。"比如，在回答许钧有关'三化'无常、不免失度的质疑时，许渊冲这样回答：许钧认为'化无定法''深浅无常'，难以掌握。我却认为只要自问译文是否使自己'知之、好之、乐之'就能掌握。所谓'知之'，就是知道原作说了什么；所谓'好之'，就是喜欢译文怎么说法；所谓'乐之'，就是'说什么'和'怎么说'使你感到乐趣。"（祝一舒，2021）

我们可以看出，许渊冲的"三化"方法强调了对读者感受的考虑，即要让一部译作有读者，让读者喜欢，产生共鸣。在唐传奇古文的翻译中，因为中国历史文化的元素和价值观与西方世界的距离较远，如何克服唐传奇小说给英语读者带来的神秘感和陌生感，值得深入讨论。唐传奇小说的魅力之源，在于故事的趣味性和传奇性，想要得到传播，其译介目的在于讲故事，关注可读性，在翻译中必须要考虑英语国家的文化传统、大众读者的心理期待和阅读习惯。

3. 《虬髯客传》周译版本中"深化"手法的运用

所谓"深化"，是透过原文的表层形式，探究其深层内容，包括：抽象词具体化；一般名词特殊化，必要时可以运用典故；加词；一分为二；等等。这一翻译技巧使译文神韵更加深刻（闫敏，2022）。

3.1 构建故事要素——加词法

原文 1：隋炀帝之幸江都也，命司空杨素守西京。

译文 1：It was some time in the last few years of the Sui Dynasty. Whilst Emperor Yangdi was on his inspection tour to the city of Jiangdu (presently Yangzhou), Premier Yangsu was in charge of the garrison at the city of Xijing (presently Xi'an) at His Majesty's request.

解析：原文 1 描述了隋炀帝巡幸江都并命令杨素守卫西京的情节，同时引入了主要人物杨素。但由于唐传奇是一种早期的小说形式，"小说文体的发生，源于叙事……历史叙事的形式原则，给唐代小说提供了一个形式外壳……也正是在这个意义上，我们将把唐前小说作为'前小说'而不是正式写就的文学小说来看待，唐初至建中以前是从'前小说'到唐代小说文体发生之间的过渡期"（韩云波，2001）。可以见得，唐传奇小说的叙事手法简单，故事叙事框架尚未完全成熟。

因此，周译在文章开头采用了深化翻译的加词法，增译"It was some time in the last few years of the Sui Dynasty"，这一表述来构建时空背景，契合了西方小说的叙事方式，也符合西方读者的阅读习惯，以吸引读者的兴趣，同时为故事的提供时空框架。

原文 2：公方刷马，忽有一人，中形，赤髯如虬，乘蹇驴而来。

译文 2：Out of the door, Lijing was about to groom their horses, before he found a man of middle height characterized by a beard of fiery bristles coming up on the back of a lame donkey.

解析：原文 2 描述了在二人奔赴太原的途中，在灵石旅馆休息时，公方刷马的场景，此时突然出现了一个中等身材、有着赤髯如虬胡须的人，他骑在一匹跛腿的驴子上，慢行而来。前文叙述了红拂女在屋内梳头的情景，接着情节切换到了李靖刷马的场景，涉及到了空间场景的转换。在有关唐传奇叙事视角及小说场景空间构建的文章中，刘天振（2001）曾指出，唐人传奇建构文本的最重要谋略之一就是作者们善于通过极富灵性的视角操作，制造变幻多姿的叙事模式，使文本叙事风貌在话语结构及时空等诸方面焕发出独具小说审美魅力的奇幻色彩。周译本通过增译"Out of the door"，将场景转换显化出来，巧妙地实现了自然过渡和切换，为读者呈现出画面的空间感，使叙事逻辑更为严谨，使故事情节更加完整，也保留了原著的传奇色彩。这种空间和场景的转换，还暗含了中国文化中男主外、女主内的传统观念，该翻译能够巧妙地实现这种文化传递。

3.2 塑造人物形象——具体化

原文 3：一日，卫公李靖以布衣上谒，献奇策。

译文 3：One day, Lord Lijing, then a commoner, asked to present a roll of well-wrought schemes for the country's re-thriving.

解析：在原文 3 中，描述了卫公李靖一天以布衣身份前来上谒，呈献出一卷精心制作的国家振兴方案。这一情节是李靖首次出现在故事中，他当时还是一个普通的平民，却提出了有关国家兴衰的重要建议。根据原文中的"卫公"以及历史背景，可以了解到李靖是隋朝末年至唐朝初年的历史人物，取得了卓越的成就，是唐朝的开国功臣之一和著名的军事家，后来被封为卫国公，因此人物形象非常重要。周译本将"献奇策"具体化为"a roll of well-wrought schemes for the country's re-thriving"，增强了读者对场景的感知和理解。首先，他将"策"翻译为"a roll of"（一卷），这样的处理在后文提到杨素"收其策而退"时更为合理，也增强了读者的沉浸感，生动地展现了李靖布衣上谒，智慧勇敢的形象。其次，使用了"well-wrought"（深思熟虑的）这一词汇，强调了方案的精心制定，暗示了李靖的高明和谋略，这样的选择充分展示了李靖作为历史人物的特质。

原文 4：公不自意获之，愈喜愈惧，瞬息万虑不安，而窥户者无停屦。

译文 4：The more he was exhilarated, the greater his tenseness, which drew him all of a sudden into a sea of worries and forced him to tiptoe to the window to keep an eye on watch from time to time.

解析：在原文 4 中，描写了李靖与红拂女会面后的复杂心情。他在红拂女的胆识和义气下感到愈加高兴，但这种喜悦也伴随着担忧和不安。他开始担心二人的未来，同时也为自己的感情而担忧，这种情感冲突和复杂性在文中得到了生动的描写。周译本通过选用"exhilarated"来表达李靖的高兴情感，强调了他因为红拂女而兴奋的状态，增强了这种情感的强度。然后，原文中使用了"tenseness"来表达李靖的紧张和担忧，强调了他的忧虑和不安。这种对比的运用突出了李靖复杂的心理状态，使人物形象更加立体和丰富。

此外，作者又用"瞬"和"万"突出李靖的复杂心情，译文中的"a sea of worries"使用了夸张的手法，使译文充分体现了一种文学性，表现李靖的欣喜和牵挂，使他陷入一片忧愁之海，描写生动形象；"tiptoe"和"keep an eye on"这两个短语形象地描绘了李靖的动作，以幽默的方式呈现了李靖窥视窗外的场景，增强了人物形象的立体感。

原文 5：食竟，余肉乱切送驴前食之，甚速。

译文 5：After the meal, the remains were roughly chopped to feed the donkey, and the animal wolfed down what was given in a moment.

解析：原文 5 描述了虬髯客食毕后将余肉喂给驴的情景，这一场景凸显了唐传奇小说的生动性和传奇色彩。虬髯客骑着这头跛驴登场，然而后文揭示了他的富有和侠义心肠，他将自己的财富全部奉献给了李靖和红拂女，协助李世民统一天下。虬髯客的驴在文中吃肉，且食之"甚速"，这个情节强调了虬髯客的传奇性和神秘色彩。在周译本中，使用了"wolfed down"和"in a moment"来表达驴子吃肉的情节。"wolfed down"强调了驴子狼吞虎咽的方式，增强了场景的生动性。"in a moment"则突出了驴子吃得非常迅速，进一步强化了这一场景的传奇性和戏剧性。

3.3　增强译文画面感

（1）一分为二法

原文 6：素面华衣而拜，公惊答拜。

译文 6：Taken by the surprise, Lijing bowed back all in a fluster. The girl wearing no cosmetics on the face but really luxurious clothes on the body explained.

解析：原文 6 描述了红拂女夜晚突然出现在李靖面前，两人相互拜见的情景。在这一时刻，红拂女以素面华衣的形象向李靖行礼，而李靖也因为这突如其来的惊喜而心情愉悦。周译本的翻译强调了李靖的惊讶和慌乱，以及他回礼的动作。

在这个翻译中，周译本采用一分为二的译法。一分为二的翻译技巧既可以指一句中文，在翻译的过程中被拆译成了两个或两个以上的句子，又能指代原文中一个词语或一处表达，被重复翻译，处理为两个结构进行强调，起到放大表达效果的作用。这里"惊"字被翻译为"Taken by the surprise"和"all in a fluster"，不仅进行了增译，还通过音节的对称突出了李靖的意外和慌乱，生动地展现了李靖手忙脚乱、慌张地回礼的场景，放大了情感的表达，给读者带来了身临其境的感觉。

（2）具体化

原文 7：当公之骋辩也，一妓有殊色，执红拂，立于前，独目公。

译文 7：When Lijing was vehemently in his speech, his very gesture, however minute, failed no touch of the eyesight of the one among the beautiful girls who was holding a red whisk and standing ahead.

解析：这句话描述了当李靖在慷慨陈词时，一位美丽的女子手持红拂，站在前方。这一场景突显了红拂女对李靖的关注和欣赏，她受到了李靖才气的吸引，心生一见钟情之感。原文中的"骋辩"生动地描绘了李靖的雄辩之态，宛如疾驰的骏马。而"独目公"则简练而有力地表达了红拂女对李靖的专注，将其他人都置于次要位置。在翻译这一段时，需要注重传达原文的美感、文学性以及场景感，以确保读者能够身临其境。

周译本通过具体化的手法，使用恰当的副词、形容词和名词，构建和还原了原文带给读者的画面感。周译中运用了"vehemently"一词来描述辩论的激烈，将读者引入氛围中。而"独目公"则通过从李靖的角度来描述红拂女的视线，凸显了她的专注，增强了故事感。另外，"minute"通过形象的细腻描绘，深化了红拂女对李靖的一见钟情。这也才有了后文红拂女心怀激动，向小吏询问李靖住处的情节。若只单纯地表达为"红拂女一直看着正在讲话的李靖"，既无助于情节推动，又不符合后文所描述的二人的关系，未能将原作隐含的意思表达出来。最后，红拂女所持的扇子原本是由马尾制成的，尽管可以直译为"horse whisk"，但这种译法可能显得平淡。因此，采用"whisk"一词来保留原文中的美感和神秘感，更能符合原作的语境。

4.《虬髯客传》周译版本中"浅化"手法的运用

许渊冲先生（2005）说过，"浅化可以使人知之"。汉语中很多表达都蕴藏着典故和深意，这往往会使文化背景与我们差距较大的西方读者如堕云雾中。此时可用"浅化"策略，将原文意义用浅显易懂的词句表达出来，最大限度地消除目的语读者的文化障碍和阅读障碍。

4.1 处理文化词汇——一般化

原文 8：一日，卫公李靖以布衣上谒，献奇策。

译文 8：One day, Lord Lijing, then a commoner, asked to present a roll of well-wrought schemes for the country's rethriving …

解析：在先前的分析中，李靖的身份出现了一个叙述矛盾。原文中提到他是唐朝的"卫公"，被后人尊称为"李卫公"，但故事的背景设定在隋朝末年。此时，李靖还是一个普通的布衣平民。这个矛盾是由作者的叙述视角导致的。"第三人称全知视角是唐传奇中采用最为普遍的一种叙述方式……'叙述婉转、文辞华艳'的唐传奇，即使表面看来是完全采用史家笔法写成的作品，其叙述者形态和叙述层次都已发生了内在变化"（刘天振，2001）。

在翻译时，必须小心处理这种时间错位的情况。使用注释或者过多的外部解释可能会让读者感到困惑，因为西方读者通常具备现代小说的素养，对于中国古典小说的叙事方式可能不太熟悉。而且，注释过多也会打破故事的连贯性和流畅性。"这种在全知叙述大框架下，看似无意、实有意的局部限知叙述，隐喻着小说文本的叙述层次开始发生内在变化"（刘天振，2001），凸显了唐传奇委婉曲折，耐人寻味的意味，在翻译中要考虑到作者的用意。

周译本选择将"卫公"这个文化负载词翻译为"Lord"，将特殊名词做了一般化处理，化难为易，而没有翻译成"公爵"（Duke）。这个选择是合理的，因为它既保留了原文中对李靖尊贵地位的尊重，又避免了对李靖身份的混淆。使用"Lord"相当于对李靖的一种尊称，类似于"李靖先生"的古称，这有助于传达他在故事中的高贵地位，而不是特指他的社会地位。此外，通过增译"then a commoner"来强调李靖从前是一个普通人，以更好地表现他的身份转变。这种翻译方式能够帮助读者理解原文的重点和情感，保持了句子的流畅性和可读性，也解释了原文中的传奇色彩。

原文 9：公既去，而执拂者临轩，指吏曰："问去者处士第几？住何处？"

译文 9：Seeing him off, the whisk holder drew close to the window and urged the errand boy: "Hurry up to ask the man just left who he is? Where he stays?"

解析：这句话描写了红拂女在送别李靖后，急切地派遣小吏去询问李靖的身份和住处。在翻译这一句子时，需要处理涉及文化背景的特定术语"处士第几"。直译为"家中排行第几"虽然能传达原文的意思，但可能会显得不够自然，并且在后文没有回答的情况下可能令读者感到困惑。实际上，"处士第几"所表达的更多是礼仪上的一种询问，类似于询问对方的身份。因此，周译选择了对这一表达进行一般化处理，将其翻译为"他是谁"，这更贴近了英语读者的理解，同时也保持了叙述的流畅性。

4.2 实现情节连贯——合而为一

原文 10：问其姓，曰："张。"问其伯仲之次。曰："最长。"

译文 10：Lijing felt a bit relaxed and the talk was soon geared into a pleasant chatting, by which, not only was the girl known to be surnamed Zhang and the eldest daughter in her family.

这句话描述了李靖和红拂女的一问一答。此时，两人通过交流加深了彼此的了解，李靖逐渐放下了戒备，准备更好地接纳对方。通过这次对话，他不仅得知了红拂女的姓氏是张，还了解到她是家中的长女。

周译本通过"by which"直接接出红拂女的自述，摒弃原文的对话形式，将两个"曰"字省略，直接进行陈述，这种译法既保持了原文情节的完整性和流畅度，又让译文变得更加简洁明了。这也强调了"曰"字可以根据信息的强弱程度、话语内容的重要性和目的进行"浅化"。

5. 结论

《虬髯客传》作为一篇唐传奇，其情节丰富，人物饱满，语言流畅精练。周劲松的译本采用了"深化"和"浅化"的方法，以更好地传达故事性、传奇性和文学性。通过"深化"，他构建了故事要素，塑造了人物形象，并增强了译文的画面感。这些"深化"的翻译手段补偿了源语文本转换为目标文本中的缺失，使得西方读者更容易理解和欣赏这一古老文学作品，同时保留了原作的文化内涵和艺术魅力。通过"浅化"，他处理了文化词汇并推动了故事情节，省译了不用重点处理的元素，确保了译文的流畅性和可读性，使故事更紧凑、更引人入胜。

通过对译文的分析，可以发现古文翻译中故事性、传奇性、文学性的实现，需要合理使用增译和减译的手段。周译本在该策略的指导下完整保留了唐传奇的风采，他的译文为中国古典小说提供了策略和技巧，十分值得学习借鉴。

参考文献

[1] 黄淞，2006. 非文学翻译中汉译英的"三化"问题[J]. 重庆邮电大学学报（社会科学版）（4）：591-592.

[2] 韩云波，2001. 刘知几《史通》与"小说"观念的系统化——论唐传奇文体发生过程中小说与历史的关系[J]. 西南师范大学学报（人文社会科学版）（2）：94-100.

[3] 姜丹丹，2012. 诗歌翻译中"三化"理论的应用——以《江城子·悼亡妻》两种英译文为例[J]. 长江大学学报（社会科学版），35（4）：108-109.

[4] 刘天振，2001. 唐传奇叙事视角艺术及其叙事文体的独立[J]. 北方论丛（2）：90-94.

[5] 任丽萍，2021. 讲好中国故事与旅游译介——《徐霞客游记》译介为例[J]. 外语教学理论与实践（2）：108-115.

[6] 王娇，2020. "三化"理论在中国传统诗词翻译中的应用——以许渊冲《人月圆》英译本为例[J]. 汉字文化（10）：133-134.

[7] 许钧，1996. "化"与"讹"——读许渊冲译《红与黑》有感[J]. 外语与外语教学（3）：44-47.

[8] 许钧，2011. 文字·文学·文化：《红与黑》汉译研究[M]. 南京：译林出版社.

[9] 许渊冲，1984. 翻译的艺术[M]. 北京：中国对外翻译出版公司.

[10] 许渊冲，2003. 文学与翻译[M]. 北京：北京大学出版社.

[11] 闫敏，贾晓云，2022. "三化论"视角下许渊冲诗词"意美"的英译策略研究[J]. 上海理工大学学报（社会科学版），44（2）：136-140.

[12] 詹思雅，2019. 基本层次范畴理论视角下的"三化"——以中国古代文言小说英译为例[J]. 山西青年（12）：7-9.
[13] 周劲松，2016. 翻译基础十二讲[M]. 成都：电子科技大学出版社.
[14] 祝一舒，2021. 许渊冲翻译美的创造之路与"三化"论[J]. 西安外国语大学学报，29（4）：82-86.

意象图式下的《早发白帝城》及其英译本研究

张 瑶

1. 引言

认知语言学中有许多值得研究的问题，意象图式理论便是其中之一。据李福印的研究统计资料（李福印，2004），意象图式是近年来，认知语言学的研究中，备受关注的热门话题。《早发白帝城》是李白的代表诗歌之一，作于诗人被赦返回江陵的途中，表达了诗人的愉悦之情。之前的分析多停留在运用意象图式理论，从翻译的角度，来分析译者在翻译中国古典诗歌时如何更加准确而又能做到符合目标人群的用语习惯。但是，很少有人分析是什么导致了这种用语的差异性。本文旨在探讨李白诗歌《早发白帝城》及其英译本（许渊冲版本）的意象图式是如何表现出来的，并分析其用语特点和区别。

2. 文献回顾

2.1 关于意象图式的文献回顾

在 CNKI（中国知网）以"意象图式"为关键词进行搜索，从论文的主题分布情况来看，对"意象图式"这一理论的研究主要在理论本身、文本分析、介词分析、教学实践等领域。例如，李福印（2007）在其研究中，阐述了意象图式的定义、常见图式、主要特点和发展轨迹。刘丽华和李明君（2008）除了研究上述李福印所探究的内容，还探讨了意象图式在神经科学、心理学和语言文学领域的情况。陈晓湘和许银（2009）以介词 on、over、above 为例，研究了意象图式理论对多义介词习得的影响和作用，并最终发现，意象图式理论对多义介词教学的积极性作用。杨俊峰（2011）探讨了在翻译古典诗歌的意象时，意象图式理论有着怎样的作用。谭业升（2013）以两个《红楼梦》英译本中"社会脸"的表达为研究对象，建立语料库，探究了意象图式、涉身体验与创造性翻译认知过程的关联。

2.2 关于诗歌《早发白帝城》的文献回顾

对诗歌《早发白帝城》的研究集中在教学实践上，并利用不同理论对诗歌本身进行分析，以及分析诗歌英译本的三个角度。肖跃田（2008）以李白的诗歌《子夜吴歌》和《早发白帝城》及其英译为例，讨论了由数字模糊语义生成的文化意象的英译。涂艳华（2005）比较了《早发白帝城》的四篇译文，分析了运用直译和意译的方法来翻译诗歌时存在的问题，并指出了英汉语言在组织、音律和意境上的不同表现。杨虹（2002）探讨了《早发白帝城》一诗中"猿声"的新解。文献检索发现，运用意象图式理论分析《早发白帝城》的论文共有两篇。刘越（2014）以前后图式为理论基础，分析了诗歌。李彩霞和张琳瑜（2013）从路径图式角度出发，分析了原诗歌及其两个英译本。

2.3 总结

通过对"意象图式"和"早发白帝城"的文献回顾，我们可以发现，意象图式这一理论应用广泛，可以用于文本（小说、诗歌等）、词汇（介词、动词等）等方面。将意象图式和《早发白帝城》结合在一起进行研究的论文却仅有两篇，且这两篇论文都仅从一个意象图式的角度出发分析文本。因此，都在一定程度上没有完全分析出《早发白帝城》这一诗歌中所蕴含的所有的意象图式。因此，本文以《早发白帝城》原文本和许渊冲先生对其的英译本为研究对象，分析对比两个文本中体现的所有的意象图式，从而进一步分析古典诗歌在英译过程中存在的问题。

3. 理论部分

3.1 意象

不言而喻，意象在中国古诗词中占据了一个极其重要的地位。王泽龙曾说（2004：1），"意象有如情节之对于戏剧与小说，'是诗歌独特的叙事方式'，体现着诗歌生命的基本结构和功能单位"。由此可见，意象在诗歌中占据着至关重要的地位。诗人借用特定的意象，经过脑海中的二次加工，创作出独一无二的意境来描绘具体的人、景、物，抒发其在当时当地的思想情感。读者阅读诗歌，找寻其中意象，想象这些意象构造出来的意境，如同身临其境般体会诗人所经历的人事物，从而体会到诗人想要传递给他人的感悟。因而，意象，以其独特的方式，为读者和诗人之间，搭建起了一座沟通的桥梁。

3.2 意象图式

（1）定义

对意象图式理论研究的历史并不久远。1980年，Lakoff和Johnson在 *Metaphors We Live by*（《我们赖以生存的隐喻》）一书中，运用了"意象"（image）这一概念。随后，两人于1987年都在各自的专著中，阐释了"意象图式"这一理论。1987年，Johnson在其专著《心中之身》（*The Body in the Mind*）一书中，将意象图式定义为"意象图式是感知互动及感觉运动活动中的不断再现的动态结构，这种结构给我们的经验以连贯和结构。"李福印（2007）总结了另外两位学者对意象图式的定义。1995年，Gibbs和Colston在其研究中，认为，"通常来说，意象图式是空间关系和空间运动的动态模型表征"。此外，在2004年，Oakley提出了自己对意象图式的定义："简单而言，意象图式是对感性经验的压缩性再描写，其目的就在于将空间结构映射到概念结构当中去。"由此我们可以看出，意象图式是一种将外部空间关系进行高度抽象处理的过程。通过运用意象图式，经过大脑的抽象化、概念化处理，我们可以将具体的外部世界，转化、归纳为具有相似认知特征的、高度凝练的再现，最终实现一个从具体到抽象、从个性到共性的过程。

意象是具体的，意象图式是抽象的，中国古典诗歌可以抽象为意象图式，再经由意象图式转化为具体的英文诗歌，从而实现了"具体—抽象—具体"的思维转变。意象图式在其中充当着中介的作用。

（2）特性

许多学者对意象图式的特性进行了描述，在此列举一些文献引用次数较多的学者的观点，并对其进行总结。Lakoff 和 Johnson 两人一致认为，意象图式具有体验性、想象性、抽象性和动态性等特征（王寅，2017）。李福印（2007）认为，意象图式的特性有五点：可以高度抽象为简图，是一种语域，具有正负特性，有静态和动态两种本质，运用意象图式的过程中注意焦点会发生变化。刘丽华和李明君（2008）总结出了意象图式的九个特征，分别是：前概念性、不同程度的图示化、与客观世界的互动、结构的逻辑、类比的表征、内部的复杂结构、多重感觉的综合、可转换、可成群出现。总的来说，意象图式是一种运用人体的身体感知，对外部世界中具体事物的发展变化进行高度概括凝练，从而形成的一种抽象的、具有代表性的表征。

（3）分类

意象图式有很多种分类。我们现在常用的意象图式，是由 Johnson 于 1987 年，在其著作《心中之身》中提出的。Johnson（1987：126）在其著作中提到了最具有代表性的 27 种意象图式。而在《语言学教程》中，胡壮麟（2006：117-118）向我们列举并定义了九种意象图式，分别是：中心-边缘图式、容器图式、循环图式、力图式、连接图式、部分-整体图式、路径图式、标量图式、垂直图式。

中心-边缘图式涉及到从中心到边缘的距离范围。例如，"自私的人"这一说法，就是将"自我"当成中心，将"他人"当作边缘。

容器图式、闭合或不闭合的容器。例如"国内、国外"这种说法，就是将自己的国家看作一个闭合的容器，以边境为闭合分界线。

中心-边缘图式和容器图式的区别就在于，前者倾向于二维空间，强调"距离"；后者倾向于从三维空间看待事物，强调"立体"。

循环图式涉及不断发生的事件或系列事件，其结构包括：起点，不受阻碍的事件进程，回到起点，在其上有一个从高峰到低谷的结构。例如，年复一年、日复一日。

力图式涉及因果互动关系，包括：力的起始和目标、方向和密度、起点和目标的运行轨迹、因果率。例如：反作用力、引力。

连接图式由两个或两个以上的生理或隐喻连接起来的实体组成。例如：情侣之间，就是通过一系列因素将男女双方连接在一起。

部分-整体图式涉及生理或隐喻的部分与整体的关系。例如：家庭与社会、某个身体部位和身体。

路径图式是指从一点到另一点的生理或隐喻的移动，由起点、终点和系列中间各点组成。例如，长跑过程中，设定一段一段的目标来激励自己。

标量图式涉及生理或隐喻的数量的增加或减少，其组成部分有：封闭或开放的数量级数、数量级数的位置、一个或多个平均数、数量的刻度。例如：我们生活中在菜市中买东西时的斤两。

最后一个是垂直模式，这涉及了"上""下"关系。例如：升国旗、太阳东升西落。

4. 运用意象图式分析文本

4.1 用意象图式分析《早发白帝城》原文

在分析《早发白帝城》这首诗歌之前，我们需要了解一下这首诗歌的写作背景（李永祥，

2014：116）：李白因为受到永王事件的牵连，被流放到夜郎（今贵州省桐梓县一带）。经历了一年的路程之后，在唐肃宗乾元二年（759）春天到达白帝城。就在将要折入夜郎时，传来肃宗的大赦令，李白本人也在赦免名单之中。惊喜之余，诗人随即乘舟归东陵，并在途中写了这首诗歌。

原文如下：

早发白帝城

李　白

朝辞白帝彩云间，千里江陵一日还。
两岸猿声啼不住，轻舟已过万重山。

第一句"朝辞……一日还。"隐含了三个意象图式，分别是路径图式、中心-边缘图式和容器图式。

路径图式由"辞"字体现。"辞"意为"告辞、告别、离开"。"朝辞白帝"就是说在早上离开白帝城。"辞"就是暗示了位置移动的开始，因此，白帝城是移动的起点。"还"意思是"回到、到达"。再结合背景，就可以推断出，此处路径图式的终点是江陵。因此，这句话呈现出了一个"辞白帝城—还江陵"的路径图式。

中心-边缘图式涉及中心与边缘两个概念，强调一种二维空间上的距离。第一句的前半句中，"间"一字，意为"在……之间、在……中间"。白帝城位于夔州奉节县，与巫山相近。因此，这里说的彩云，指的就是巫山的云彩（晓茅，2017）。"白帝彩云间"呈现的是以白帝城为中心，以云彩为边缘的"白帝城-彩云"的中心-边缘图式。除此之外，"辞"和"还"这两个字也暗示了一个中心-边缘图式。"辞"意味着，诗人乘船远离白帝城，远离边缘之地；"还"意味着诗人离江陵越来越近，也是指离权力中心越来越近。因此，这个地方，表面上是描写了一个物理上的中心-边缘距离问题，但实际上隐含了一个以"权力为中心"的中心-边缘图式。

容器图式的重点在于要形成一个有或者没有边界的区域或容器，强调的是三维空间。白帝城高耸入云，由此被云彩包围。所以，我们可以将周围的云彩看作一个容器，被四周云彩包围的白帝城就是处容器之中的物体。

第二句"两岸猿声啼不住，轻舟已过万重山。"中，包含了中心-边缘图式、容器图式、路径图式和垂直图式。

中心-边缘图式体现在"两岸猿声啼不住"的"两岸"中，从这一次可以看出，岸边离诗人较远，处于一个边缘位置。这句话从诗人的角度出发，因而诗人处于中心位置。所以形成了一个"诗人-两岸"的中心-边缘图式。

容器图式体现在"轻舟已过万重山"这一句中，两岸的连绵起伏的、数不胜数的山峦是边界，包围在河流上的小舟，从而形成了另一个容器图式。

第二句诗歌中的路径图式比较隐晦。主要是由"过"这个字所体现的。"过"意思是"经过、走过、经由"，暗示了路径。"万重山"则是路径中一个个小点。结合上一句和背景，我们知道，这首诗歌就是在作者从白帝城返回江陵时所作。因此，这里的路径图式中的起点仍旧是白帝城，终点也仍旧是江陵。

垂直图式涉及"上""下"关系。诗人在船上，与周围的山峦相比，其地理位置更低，山峦则是地理位置相对较高的物体。诗人看向周围的山峦，其视线应是向上的。因此，这里形成了一个"轻舟—万重山"的垂直图式。

4.2 用意象图式分析《早发白帝城》英译本

本文选取了许渊冲先生的译本进行分析。

Leaving White Emperor Town at Dawn（许渊冲，2005：97）
(Translated by Xu Yuanchong)
Leaving at dawn the White Emperor crowned with cloud,
I've sailed a thousand li through canyons in a day.
With monkeys' sad adieus the riverbanks are loud;
My skiff has left ten thousand mountains far away.

在第一句话"Leaving at dawn the White Emperor crowned with cloud, I've sailed a thousand li through canyons in a day"中，一共包含了几种意象图式，分别是：路径图式、中心-边缘图式、容器图式。

路径图式体现在 leaving 一词。Leave 一词在韦氏高阶英汉双解词典中共有 11 种释义。这里的 leave 取其中"to go away from (a place)"的意思。中文意思是"离开"，对应了原文的"辞"。Leaving 后接状语 the White Emperor，表明路径的起点是 the White Emperor，结合背景知识，可以知道路径的终点是江陵。

Crowned with 体现了中心-边缘图式。Crown 一词在此处的意思是"to be on top of something/ to form a top of something"。With 一词取词典中"having a particular characteristic, possession, etc"的意思，即"拥有"。Cloud 围绕在一起，堆积在 the White Emperor 之上，形成一个以 the White Emperor 为中心，以 cloud 为边缘的中心-边缘图式。这里的 with 对应着原文本第一句的"间"（在……之间、在……中间）。

容器图式由 through 表现出来。Through 一词在这里，取词典中"from one side or end to the other"的意思，意为：从一端到另一端。通过这个意思，将 canyons 看作一个容器，诗人是一个运动的物体，此时此刻正在 canyons 所形成空间当中，从而形成一个容器图式。这里的"through"对应的是原文本中最后一句中的"过"（经过、走过、经由）。

第二句译文"With...far away"体现了容器图式和路径图式。

With 一词在这里的意思是"used to say that something fills something, covers something, etc."。With 在这里意为：以某物填充或覆盖。在这里，表达出来的意思就是猿声充满了两岸的山峦。以山峦为容器，猿声为填充物，塑造出一个容器图式。

Away 体现了路径图式。当它作为副词时，在词典中有 7 种释义，在此取其中"from this or that place: in or to another place or direction"的意思。从这一个定义中，可以清晰地感受到，skiff 作为移动的物体，朝着一个方向驶去。虽未提及起点和终点，但是结合全文，可以推断出起点是 the White Emperor，终点是江陵。在这里，"away"一词对应着原文本中的"还"（回到、到达）一字。

4.3 对比原文和英译本的意象图式

在《早发白帝城》原文本的意象图式分析中，可以发现，其意象图式主要由动词"辞""还""过"，名词"两岸"和"间"表现出来，以动词居多。

而在英译本中的意象图式，主要由动词"leaving"和介词"with""through"和"away"表现出来，以介词居多。

出现这一现象的原因就在于，英语介词在某些时候可以扮演动词的角色。无论是简单介词，还是边缘介词，又或是符合介词，都有相当一部分具有表示动作意义或状态的功能（李淑娥，1998）。这也就能很好地解释，为什么英译本中第一小句中的 with 对应着原文本第一句的"间"（在……之间、在……中间）；第二小句中的"through"对应的是原文本中最后一句中的"过"（经过、走过、经由）；第四小句中的"away"一词应着原文本中的"还"（回到、到达）一字。

原文本和英译本的意象图式都包括了路径图式、容器图式和中心-边缘图式，但是原文本中体现这些图式的用词更多，例如：译者在翻译原文第一句话时，省去了对"江陵"这一地点的翻译。通过对全文本的分析和对背景知识的了解，能够看出这两句话都表现出了"辞白帝城—还江陵"的路径图式，看似这样的处理并没有什么意义表达上的错误，但是，原文本中出现的"江陵"二字被删除，其存在感也就自然而然地减弱了，进一步来说，就是减弱了作者的返程的目的地。全诗想要表达诗人能够回到江陵这个政治权力中心的喜悦之情，但是在翻译的过程中，这一地点被删去，因此也就失去了原文中诗人距离权力中心越来越近的这一个隐含着的路径图式。所以，译本在传递思想时，就会使得传递给读者的思想情感较原文更加单薄。

除此之外，原文本第二句中出现的垂直图式，并没有在译本中得到体现。原文本中的垂直图式，主要是由"轻舟"和"万重山"这两个意象的对比所凸显出来的。译者在翻译的过程中，将"万重山"这一意象省略了，这就意味着将原文本中的"路径图式+垂直图式"变为了单纯的"路径图式"。省略原文本中的"万重山"意象，进而将原文本构造的意境简化。原文本的容器意境中，诗人置身于万重山之中，这一意境的构造会使得读者产生一种身临其境之感，从而更容易体会到诗人的情感。译文删去了这一意象之后，虽在表意上没有什么错误，但是在传情方面稍显逊色。

5. 结论

通过分析《早发白帝城》原文本及其对应英译本的意象图式，有三个发现。第一，原文本中表现出中心-边缘图式、容器图式、路径图式和垂直图式；而英译本只表现出了原文本的前三种意象图式。第二，原文本中用来构造意象图式的词汇数量远远多于英译本当中的词汇；第三，原文本中运用了名词、动词来构造意象图式，且以动词居多，英译本中则运用动词和介词，且以介词居多。笔者认为，出现这种情况的原因是介词具有充当动词的功能。

综上所述，我们可以看出，虽然在翻译的过程中，许渊冲先生很好阐释了原文本的表层意义，在表意方面达到很好的效果。但是在翻译过程中，却没有很好地传递文本的深层意象结构。这就造成了最终在传达诗人情感时，无法使得目标域读者更加真切地体会到原文本中诗人构造的意境以及想要传达的强烈情感。因此，在翻译的过程中，我们不仅需要保障字面上的词汇、语义对等，还需要保证其深层结构——意象图式能够一致。只有这样，才能在文化交流中更好地传递我国博大精深的古典诗学文化。

参考文献

[1] JOHNSON M, 1987. The body in the mind: the bodily basis of meaning, imagination, and reason[M]. Chicago: University of Chicago Press.
[2] LAKOFF G, JOHNSON M, 1980. Metaphors we live by[M]. Chicago: University of Chicago Press.
[3] 陈晓湘，许银，2009. 意象图式理论对多义介词 On、Over、Above 习得作用的实证研究[J]. 外语与外语教学（9）：18-23.
[4] 胡壮麟，2006. 语言学教程[M]. 北京：北京大学出版社.
[5] 李彩霞，张琳瑜，2013. 唐诗英译的意象图式视角——以《早发白帝城》的两个英译本为例[J]. 海外英语（21）：159-160，176.
[6] 李福印，2004. 当代国外认知语言学研究的热点——第八届国际认知语言学大会论文分析[J]. 外语研究（3）：1-3，9，80.
[7] 李福印，2007. 意象图式理论[J]. 四川外语学院学报（1）：80-85.
[8] 李淑娥，1998. 论英语介词的动词功能[J]. 长沙大学学报（3）：71-74，77.
[9] 李永祥，2014. 李白诗集[M]. 济南：济南出版社.
[10] 刘丽华，李明君，2008. 意象图式理论研究的进展与前沿[J]. 哈尔滨工业大学学报（社会科学版）（4）：110-117.
[11] 刘越，2014. 意象图式视角下李白诗歌分析——以《早发白帝城》为例[J]. 中小企业管理与科技（下旬刊）（2）：207-208.
[12] 梅里亚姆-韦伯斯特，2017. 韦氏高阶英汉双解词典[M]. 北京：中国大百科全书出版社.
[13] 谭业升，2013. 译者的意象图式与合成概念化——基于语料库方法的《红楼梦》"社会脸"翻译研究[J]. 外语与外语教学（3）：55-59.
[14] 涂艳华，2005. 浅议《早发白帝城》及其四篇译文[J]. 江南大学学报（人文社会科学版）（1）：87-89.
[15] 王寅，2017. 基于认知语言学的翻译过程新观[J]. 中国翻译，38（6）：5-10，17，129.
[16] 王泽龙，2004. 中国现代诗歌意象论[D]. 武汉：华中师范大学.
[17] 肖跃田，2008. 数字模糊语义及文化意象的解读与英译——以《子夜吴歌》《早发白帝城》及其英译为例[J]. 外语教学（4）：95-97.
[18] 晓茅，2017. 李白诗[M]. 武汉：崇文书局.
[19] 熊礼汇，2005. 李白诗选[M]. 北京：人民文学出版社.
[20] 杨虹，2002.《早发白帝城》中的"猿声"新解[J]. 学语文（2）：22.
[21] 杨俊峰，2011. 从古典诗歌中的意象翻译看意象图式理论的阐释空间[J]. 外语与外语教学（4）：66-70.